Special Edition

Using

Using

MICROSOFT®

Internet Explorer 4

que®

Special Edition

Using

Using

MICROSOFT®

Internet Explorer 4

que®

Eric Ladd & Jim O'Donnell

Special Edition Using Microsoft Internet Explorer 4

Contents at a Glance

Table of Contents

IV | Webcasting

V | Webmaster Section

22 HTML Primer   437

Credits

PRESIDENT
Roland Elgey

SENIOR VICE PRESIDENT/PUBLISHING
Don Fowley

PUBLISHER
Joseph B. Wikert

PUBLISHING DIRECTOR
Brad R. Koch

PUBLISHING MANAGER
Jim Minatel

MANAGER OF PUBLISHING OPERATIONS
Linda H. Buehler

GENERAL MANAGER
Joe Muldoon

MANAGING EDITOR
Thomas F. Hayes

DIRECTOR OF ACQUISITIONS
Cheryl D. Willoughby

ACQUISITIONS EDITORS
Jill Byus
Jane Brownlow

PRODUCT DIRECTORS
Robert L. Bogue
Mark Cierzniak

PRODUCTION EDITORS
Elizabeth Barrett
Kathryn J. Purdum

EDITOR
Kristin Ivanetich

PRODUCT MARKETING MANAGER
Kourtnaye Sturgeon

ASSISTANT PRODUCT MARKETING MANAGER
Gretchen Schlesinger

TECHNICAL EDITORS
Ron Ellenbecker
Will Kelly
Ryan Miller

ACQUISITIONS COORDINATORS
Michelle R. Newcomb
Virginia Stoller

SOFTWARE RELATIONS COORDINATOR
Susan D. Gallagher

EDITORIAL ASSISTANT
Jeff Chandler

BOOK DESIGNER
Ruth Harvey

COVER DESIGNER
Sandra Schroeder

PRODUCTION TEAM
Marcia Deboy
Christy M. Lemasters
Tony McDonald
Anjy Perry

INDEXER
Tim Tate

Composed in *Century Old Style* and *ITC Franklin Gothic* by Que Corporation.

I would like to dedicate this book today, August 25, 1997, to my father, James O'Donnell. Happy Birthday, Dad!

—Jim O'Donnell

In memory of my mother, Beth T. Ladd. You did good, Mom.

—Eric Ladd

About the Authors

Jim O'Donnell was born on October 17, 1963, in Pittsburgh, Pennsylvania (you may forward birthday greetings to **odonnj@rpi.edu**). After a number of unproductive years, he began his studies in electrical engineering at Rensselaer Polytechnic Institute. Jim liked RPI so much that he spent 11 years there getting three degrees, graduating for the third (and final) time in August, 1992. He can now be found plying his trade as an Aerospace Engineer in metropolitan Washington, DC (he's not supposed to say for whom). He's not a rocket scientist, but he's close.

Jim has been writing and technical editing for Macmillan Computer Publishing and Que Books since 1994, contributing to and editing over 30 books. In addition, he coauthored *Special Edition Using Microsoft Internet Explorer 3* and *Platinum Edition Using HTML 3.2, Java 1.1, and CGI*. When he isn't writing or researching for Que, or talking on IRC (Nick: JOD), Jim likes to run, play hockey, collect comic books and PEZ dispensers, and play the Best Board Game Ever... Cosmic Encounter. He can be found on the World Wide Web at **http://www.rpi.edu/ ~odonnj**.

Eric Ladd (erl1@access.digex.net) is an Internet/World Wide Web consultant living in Washington, DC. He currently works (by day) as a Project Manager for Advanced Technology Systems in Arlington, Virginia, where he leads a team of Internet developers that support the Federal Deposit Insurance Corporation (FDIC). By night, he toils endlessly for Macmillan Computer Publishing, coauthoring *Platinum Edition Using HTML 3.2, Java 1.1, and CGI*, *Special Edition Using Microsoft Internet Explorer 3*, and contributing to over half a dozen other titles.

Eric earned two degrees in mathematics from Rensselaer Polytechnic Institute in Troy, New York, where he also taught calculus, linear algebra, differential equations, and complex variables for six years.

Outside of work and writing, Eric enjoys hitting the gym, biking, country dancing, and being dragged around the city of Washington by his Boxer Zack.

Acknowledgments

Both Jim O'Donnell and Eric Ladd would like to thank the editors and staff at Que for their encouragement and support during this project. Special thanks in particular to Mark Cierzniak, Robert Bogue, Jill Byus, Katie Purdum, and especially Jane Brownlow, for their sound advice, unwavering patience, and continued support—especially when things got "challenging" near the end of the book.

Jim would like to thank his Mom and Dad. Those trips to the library when he was young instilled a love of books, both reading and writing, that continues to this day. He would also like to extend his thanks and fondest wishes to Tobin (it's *still* your fault!) and to all of his roommates and friends; especially Richard, who gets to put up with him when he is writing. Jim has two special thank yous. First, to Ryan, thanks for everything and I'm glad I know you. Second, to my co-author Eric, it's been a pleasure working with you the last year and a half, and an even greater pleasure being friends for the last ten or so years.

Eric would have gone stark-raving mad during this project if it weren't for the support of many terrific friends and co-workers including Bob Leidich, Tara Bridgman, Jeff Long, Helen Hobson, John Guzman ("YEAH!"), Anthony Smith, and Mark Abbott. Special thanks also go to Eric's father, Robert, and sister, Brenda, for their continued patience with his writing endeavors. Finally, Eric is deeply grateful to his co-author Jim for his good business sense, staunch support, and loyal friendship over the course of three finished books and a new one just beginning. Jim: I can't believe we're doing this to ourselves again!

We'd Like to Hear from You!

QUE Corporation has a long-standing reputation for high-quality books and products. To ensure your continued satisfaction, we also understand the importance of customer service and support.

Tech Support

If you need assistance with the information in this book or with a CD/disk accompanying the book, please access Macmillan Computer Publishing's online Knowledge Base at **http://www.superlibrary.com/general/support**. If you do not find the answer to your questions on our Web site, you may contact Macmillan Technical Support by phone at **317/581-3833** or via e-mail at **support@mcp.com**.

Also be sure to visit QUE's Web resource center for all the latest information, enhancements, errata, downloads, and more. It's located at **http://www.quecorp.com/**.

Orders, Catalogs, and Customer Service

To order other QUE or Macmillan Computer Publishing books, catalogs, or products, please contact our Customer Service Department at **800/428-5331** or fax us at **800/835-3202** (International Fax: 317/228-4400). Or visit our online bookstore at **http://www.mcp.com/**.

Comments and Suggestions

We want you to let us know what you like or dislike most about this book or other QUE products. Your comments will help us to continue publishing the best books available on computer topics in today's market.

Mark Cierzniak
Product Director
QUE Corporation
201 West 103rd Street, 4B
Indianapolis, Indiana 46290 USA
Fax: 317/581-4663
E-mail: mcierzniak@que.mcp.com

Please be sure to include the book's title and author as well as your name and phone or fax number. We will carefully review your comments and share them with the author. Please note that due to the high volume of mail we receive, we may not be able to reply to every message.

Thank you for choosing QUE!

Quick Start Section

Overview of Microsoft Internet Explorer 4.0

Version 4 of Microsoft's Internet Explorer Web browser represents a leap forward from Internet Explorer 3, including all of the same ease-of-use features and wide compatibility, plus more. In addition, Microsoft has made available a wide assortment of other applications to round out the Internet capabilites of the suite.

One of the most striking new features included with Internet Explorer 4 is its integration with the Windows 95 user interface. With this integration, it becomes possible to "activate" your desktop by putting Web pages and desktop components right on your desktop. Additionally, the Windows 95 Explorer becomes integrated with Internet Explorer, allowing you to use the same interface to look at your local files as used with the Internet. The integration of Web browser and operating system added with Internet Explorer 4 gives you a sneak preview of what you'll be able to do with Microsoft's upcoming Windows 98. Finally, the Start menu and taskbar are more Internet-Aware, allowing you access to the Internet even when the browser isn't running.

The other striking feature of this whole suite of programs is that they are completely free. ■

Find out about Internet Explorer 4

Microsoft has included all of the great features first seen in Internet Explorer 3 into the next generation of its Web browser, and has further enhanced it with many features to make it easier to use.

Integrate the Web right into your desktop

Internet Explorer 4 includes an option for Shell Integration that gives you the first taste of what Microsoft has planned for the future; full integration of the Internet and Web into its operating system.

Learn about the other applications included with the Internet Explorer 4 suite

The Internet Explorer 4 suite includes Outlook Express, an Internet Mail and News client, FrontPage Express, a streamlined version of Microsoft's FrontPage HTML editing program, and NetMeeting, an Internet conferencing program.

Internet Explorer 4

On first glance, the Internet Explorer 4 Web browser, shown in Figure 1.1, doesn't look very different from its predecessor, Internet Explorer 3. And, for good reason, as it still contains all of the features that made Internet Explorer 3 an award-winning browser, and resulted in Microsoft quickly eating into Netscape Navigator's share of the Web browser market.

FIG. 1.1

Internet Explorer 4 makes it easier to perform all of the tesks you need to do when browsing the Web.

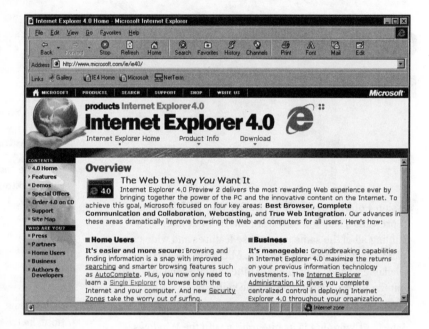

Some of the features that made Internet Explorer 3 the Web browser with the fastest growing slice of the market, and are still present in version 4, are:

- **Modularity**   Microsoft's Internet Explorer suite splits its Web browsing, authoring, mail, and news functions into different applications. This allows each individual application to be small and easier to download, and makes it easier for users to pick and choose which application they want for each function.

- **Speed and Memory Usage**   One result of the more modular nature of Internet Explorer is that, in general, the Web browser and other applications are faster and have a smaller memory footprint.

- **Support of Internet Standards**   Internet Explorer and its companion suite of applications supports a wide array or Internet standards for Web browsers, secure communications, content ratings, code signing, video and audio conferencing, and more.

- **Support for Established Technologies**   By including support for JavaScript (with the JScript scripting language), Navigator plug-ins, Java applets, and Netscape HTML extensions such as frames, Internet Explorer supports the widest array of technologies of any Web browser.

■ **Support for New Technologies**   In addition to supporting existing technologies, Internet Explorer includes support of Microsoft's ActiveX Technologies, including the scripting language Visual Basic Scripting Edition (VBScript), ActiveX Controls, ActiveX Documents, Cascading Style Sheets, and some of its own HTML extensions.

With Internet Explorer 4, Microsoft has taken a leap forward with its Web browser, and includes the following new features:

■ **Ease of Use Features**   Among its new ease-of-use features, Internet Explorer 4 has a new Search Panel to make Internet/Web searches easier, AutoComplete on the address line to make it easier to reenter URLs, and a simple click-and-drag method for reogranizing your Favorites any way you want.

■ **Increased Compatibility**   Internet Explorer 4 has increased its compatibility with other technologies, in particular having greater compatibility with version 1.1 of Netscape's JavaScript language.

■ **Greater Control Over Your Content and Browsing**   Internet Explorer 4, with its Smart Favorites, Subscriptions, Webcasting capabilities, and Offline Browsing, gives you more control over what information you see and when you see it.

■ **New Techologies**   With increased capabilities in their support of Cascading Style Sheets, and Microsoft's Dynamic HTML, Web authors have unprecedented control over the way their Web pages appear and how they interact with their users.

Configurability

Internet Explorer 4 allows you to configure it to your heart's content. You can control what type of multimedia and advanced content is displayed on your browser, how hypertext links appear, the color of your text and background, and how the toolbar appears. As shown in Figure 1.2, Internet Explorer even allows you to customize the Home button, as well as the buttons on its Links Bar. This enables you to make many of your favorite Web sites just a single mouse click away.

FIG. 1.2
Internet Explorer 4 can be customized to make it easier to find and go to your favorite Web sites.

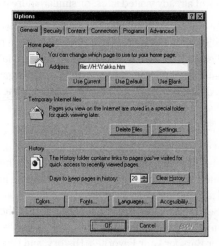

As you read earlier in this chapter, Internet Explorer ships with a suite of applications to cover most of your Internet needs. And while these programs are completely free, they are all top-notch performers. However, Internet Explorer allows you to use any application you desire for your Mail and News, and also allows you to set up any application to cover your other Internet needs (see Figure 1.3).

FIG. 1.3
You can configure Internet Explorer 4 to use your favorite Mail and News clients, or use Outlook Express, which comes as part of the Internet Explorer Suite.

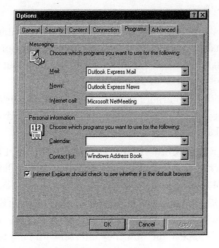

Ease of Use

Some of Internet Explorer's ease of use features are simple things that can make Web browsing a lot easier. The drop-down list on the Address Bar, for example, contains a history list of the Web sites you have visited, allowing you to quickly and simply jump back to one of them. The Address Bar also features AutoComplete; this feature automatically tries to complete the Web address you are entering, as you enter it, based on sites you have previously visited. This makes entering the addresses of already visited sites, or similar addresses, much easier.

Figure 1.4 shows the Favorites menu. With Internet Explorer 3, Microsoft introduced the ability to store Favorites (similar to Netscape Navigator bookmarks) in the same sort of folder/subfolder heirarchy as the files on your hard drive. However, within a folder, Favorites still were sorted alphabetically. Internet Explorer 4 allows you to easily organize the contents of a Favorites folder any way you'd like, by simply clicking and dragging the Favorite to a new location.

Anyone who has spent any time on the Web has gone through the process of using a Web search engine such as Yahoo or Alta Vista. Given the large number of possibilities these search engines usually return, the task of switching back and forth between the search results and each possible Web site became a tedious process. Through the simple innovation of the Internet Explorer 4 Search Explorer Bar, Microsoft has eliminated at least part of this problem. As shown in Figure 1.5, the Search Explorer Bar is a separate area of the browser, which is used to enter search parameters, and in which the search results are displayed. Internet Explorer 4 also features Explorer Bars for your Favorites, History, and Channels lists.

FIG. 1.4
With Internet Explorer 4, Microsoft has added a new level of ability to organize your favorite Web pages, and to automatically update them.

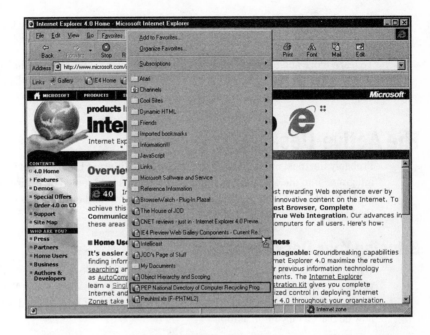

FIG. 1.5
Internet Explorer 4's new Search Explorer Bar makes it easier for you to use your favorite search engines on the Web.

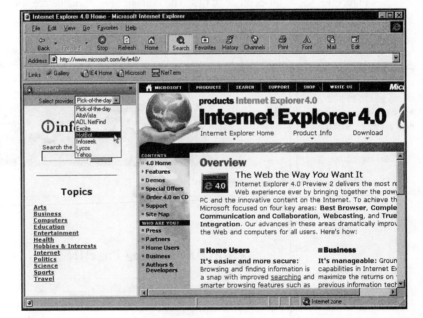

Now, when you want to check the results of your search, you can easily load each possibility in turn, without switching back and forth from one window to another.

To learn more about Internet Explorer 4, see Chapter 2, "What's New in Internet Explorer 4.0?", Chapter 3, "Quick Start: Internet Explorer 4," and Chapter 8, "In-Depth: Internet Explorer 4."

The Active Desktop

Probably the most unique and exciting feature of Internet Explorer 4 is how its capabilities are integrated into the operating system. Microsoft has long touted its desire to completely integrate Internet and Web capabilities into its application and operating system products. Internet Explorer 4 offers a first look at what this means.

Bringing Your Desktop to Life

What does Microsoft mean by an Active Desktop? A couple of things actually. The first is that you can now treat your desktop just as if it were within the window of a Web browser (Internet Explorer to be precise). This means that anything that can be displayed within a Web page can now be placed on your desktop!

Figure 1.6 shows an example of this. The familiar desktop icons are still there, along the left-hand side of the desktop, but the background is not just static artwork. There are such Web page objects as an embedded graphic and live hypertext links.

FIG. 1.6
The Active Desktop allows you to embed any Web browser object right on your desktop

Desktop component

Embedded graphic

Live hypertext link

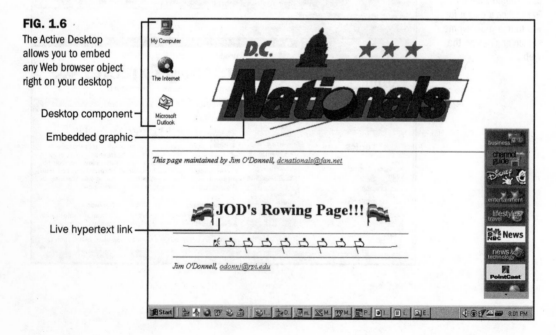

But more than that, there are several Internet components right on the desktop. The embedded Web page shows my rowing page right on the desktop. The Microsoft Channel Guide desktop component is shown along the left side of the desktop.

This leads into the second major feature of the Active Desktop. While the technology behind it might be complicated, the idea is simple. Through their Subscriptions ability, Web pages listed in your Favorites folders or displayed on the desktop can automatically update themselves over the Internet. Additionally, Microsoft's Webcasting technology allows you to set up your system to automatically receive content from the Web.

Shell Integration and the Unified Explorer

Internet Explorer 4's shell integration will also become apparent the first time you use the Windows 95 Explorer. As shown in Figure 1.7, the user interface for Explorer looks a lot more like that of Internet Explorer. In actuality, though they still appear a bit different from one another, the two applications are virtually the same under Internet Explorer 4.

FIG. 1.7
The Unified Explorer allows you to access your hard drive and the Internet with the same interface.

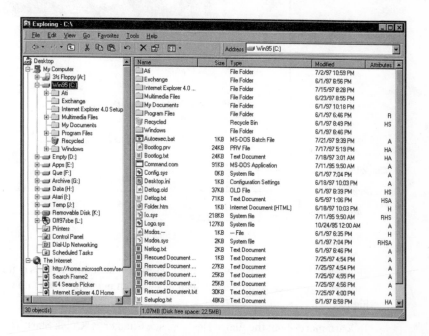

Shell Integration allows you to use the Windows 95 Explorer to look at the contents of your hard drive in a way similar to looking on the Web. Each of the files on your system becomes its own hypertext link, whose contents can be a single mouse click away. The Explorer interface also allows the same navigation interface as Internet Explorer, with Favorites and Back and Forward buttons to make it easier to move back and forth across your system.

Finally, the Explorer is now Internet-Aware. The Internet appears as just another entry under your Desktop, and the Explorer Find capabilities extend to Internet searches.

Internet-Aware Taskbar and Start Menu

The final examples of the integration of Internet Explorer 4's capabilities into the operating system are the Internet-Aware additions to the taskbar and the Start menu. Figure 1.8 shows what the taskbar can look like, if you want it to (it can, of course, also be configured to be much smaller). Not only does it have the familiar Start menu button, system tray, and taskbar, but you can also place the Address Bar and Links Bar from Internet Explorer 4 on it, giving you access to them all the time. In addition, it also features a Quick Launch Bar that gives you instant access to any of your applications, and a new button to surface or restore your desktop.

FIG. 1.8

You can put your Link and Address Bar right on your Windows 95 taskbar, allowing you instant access to the Internet.

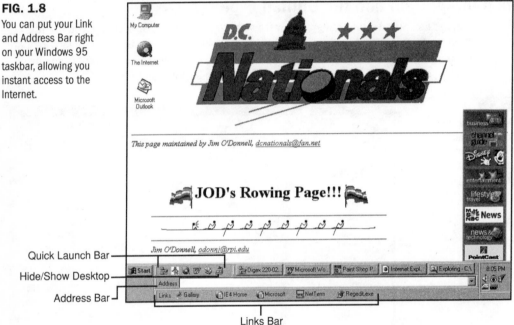

Finally, the Start menu is now also Internet-Aware, including entries in it for your Favorites, and giving you access to Internet Searches without needing to start up your browser (see Figure 1.9).

To learn more about the Active Desktop, see Chapter 4, "Quick Start: The Active Desktop," and Chapter 9, "In-Depth: The Active Desktop."

Outlook Express Mail and News

With Internet Explorer 3, Microsoft released its first Internet Mail and News Clients, a common program for accessing Internet Mail and UseNet news. With Internet Explorer 4, Microsoft has upgraded these two applications, and released it as Outlook Express (see Figure 1.10).

FIG. 1.9
The Internet-aware Start menu allows you to initiate Internet searches without calling up your browser.

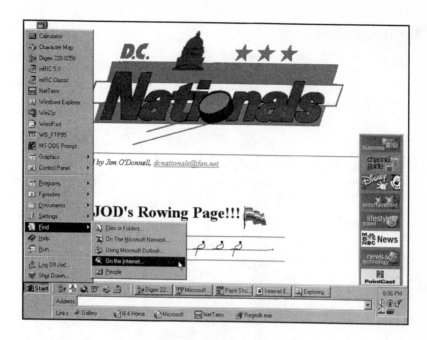

Outlook Express still gives you a common interface for accessing your Mail and News, has a number of features for organizing and filtering your Mail and News, and also allows you to use HTML to format your mail.

FIG. 1.10
Outlook Express gives you the same easy interface for Mail and News, and even supports HTML formatting.

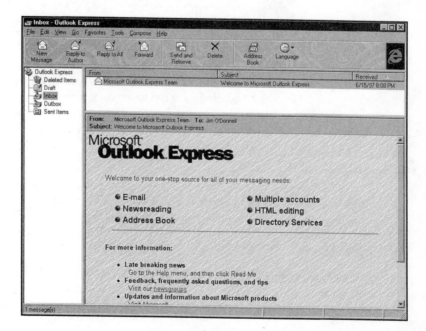

Internet Mail

One of the nicest new features of Outlook Express is that you can now configure it to read mail from multiple Internet Mail accounts, a feature that still isn't present in some commercial mail software (see Figure 1.11). It retains Internet News' ability to allow access to any number of News servers, as well.

FIG. 1.11

Unlike many other Mail clients, Outlook Express allows you to easily set up multiple Internet Mail accounts, as well as multiple News servers.

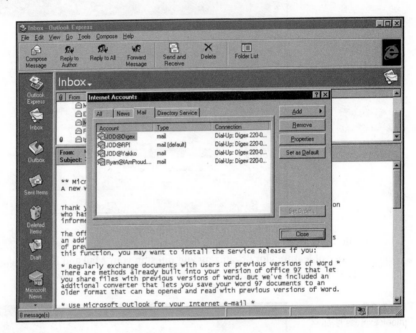

One nice feature of Outlook Express is its Inbox Assistant (see Figure 1.12). This allows you to set up filters that automatically process incoming mail, allowing you to place incoming mail into appropriate folders. More generally, you can move, copy, forward, reply to, or delete mail automatically based on who it is to, who it is from, or its subject. Tired of those unsolicited advertisements you keep getting from certain providers or addresses? Just delete them.

Accessing UseNet News

Part of the beauty of Outlook Express is that it allows you to interface with your news in exactly the same way as with your mail. Just as you can have multiple mail accounts, so too you can access and subscribe to newsgroups from multiple news servers (see Figure 1.13). You can filter and process news articles, and read, forward, and reply to them in the same way you do with mail.

One nice feature of Outlook Express is its ability to "thread" incoming articles according to subject (see Figure 1.14). This organizes articles by subject and puts replies together, and allows you to more easily follow individual conversations (or threads) with a newsgroup.

FIG. 1.12
Outlook Express's Inbox
Assistant allows you to
automatically process
your mail based on a
number of criteria.

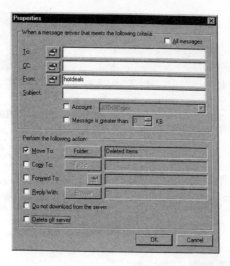

FIG. 1.13
Outlook Express
enables you to access,
view, and subscribe to
UseNet News from a
variety of sources.

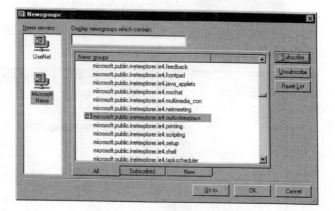

To learn more about Outlook Express, see Chapter 5, "Quick Start: Outlook Express Mail and News," and Chapter 10, "In-Depth: Outlook Express Mail and News."

FrontPage Express

FrontPage Express, the Web page editing program included with Internet Explorer 4, is based on its "older brother," FrontPage. It is a What You See Is What You Get Web page editor, that allows you to create and edit Web pages without dealing directly with HTML. You can start with a new page, open up any local Web page, or even load one directly from the Web (see Figure 1.15), and start editing.

FIG. 1.14

Incoming UseNet News articles are threaded to allow you to more easily follow a conversation.

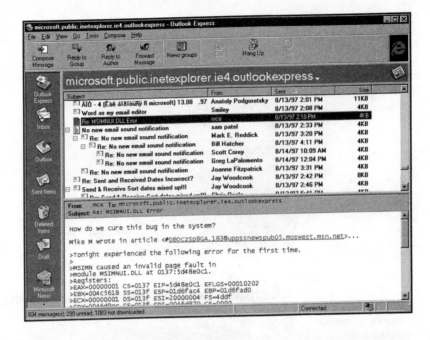

FIG. 1.15

FrontPage Express allows you to open files either from your local hard drive or from anywhere on the Web.

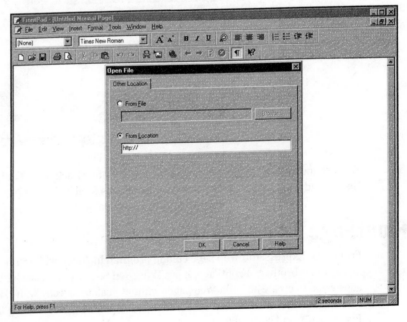

FrontPage Express strives to be a What You See Is What You Get editor, allowing you to create Web pages without knowing any HTML. Often, however, because of the idiosyncracies of Web browsers, FrontPage Express does an imperfect job of showing you what the resulting page will really look like (see the Que Internet and New Technologies page in Figure 1.16). Still, FrontPage Express is able to give you a pretty good rendition of what a Web page will look like. It's a great tool for those who don't know much HTML or are just getting started out with creating a page. And, with some of its tools, it can even be of use to more veteran Web authors.

FIG. 1.16
You can edit Web pages and HTML documents downloaded right from the Web by FrontPage Express and save them to your local system.

Figure 1.17 shows FrontPage Express's Insert menu, which gives you an idea of the sort of things that can be easily inserted into a Web page using FrontPage Express. In addition to standard HTML elements such as breaks, horizontal rules, and images, you can also insert such sophisticated objects as ActiveX Controls and WebBot Components. The dialog for inserting ActiveX Controls makes the process relatively painless, prompting you for the required information and allowing you access to the control's properties (see Figure 1.18).

One of the things FrontPage Express can do is work the special Web View mode of the new Internet Explorer 4 shell-integrated Explorer (see Figure 1.19). This mode allows you to customize the appearance of any folder on your hard drive, when viewed with Explorer.

FIG. 1.17
FrontPage Express gives you the ability to easily add any number of sophisticated objects and constructs into your Web pages.

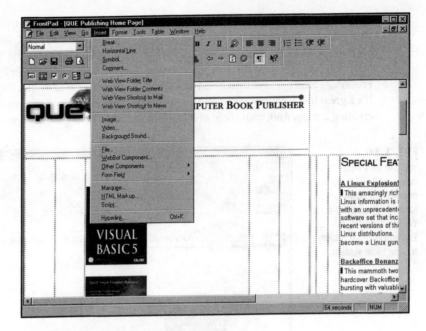

FIG. 1.18
Inserting ActiveX Controls into your Web pages is made easier with FrontPage Express's assistance.

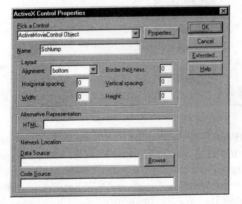

To learn more about FrontPage Express, see Chapter 6, "Quick Start: FrontPage Express," and Chapter 11, "In-Depth: FrontPage Express." You might also want to read Chapter 19, "Microsoft FrontPage and Image Composer," to find out what else is in the full version of FrontPage.

FIG. 1.19

FrontPage Express has special capabilities for working with the Web View option of Explorer.

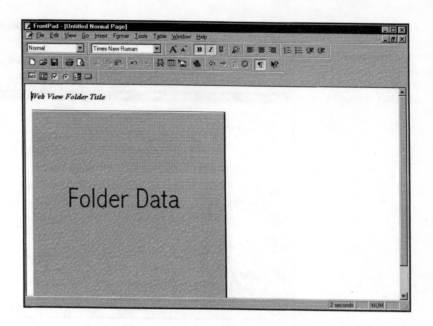

NetMeeting

The final major application included in the Internet Explorer 4 Suite is Microsoft NetMeeting. NetMeeting is Microsoft's application, free like the other applications discussed here, for Internet conferencing. Like their other Internet applications, NetMeeting conforms to established standards for audio and video transmission over the Internet, which will allow NetMeeting to work with any other such compatible applications.

Along with the NetMeeting application, Microsoft runs a user locator server and Web site, which can be used to find and establish connections with other NetMeeting users (see Figure 1.20). These connections can be established directly, in order to arrange set conferences with one or more people. The server allows users of NetMeeting to find others for other types of conferences. Once you find someone listed on the server Web page, by simply clicking on their hypertext link, you can attempt to establish a conference with them (see Figure 1.21).

NetMeeting has the following capabilities:

■ **Chat**   As shown in Figure 1.22, NetMeeting's chat abilities allow the members of the conference to converse with one another by sending text messages back and forth. If more than two people are in the conference, your outgoing messages will be sent to all of the other members of the conference.

FIG. 1.20
Using Microsoft's Internet Conferencing Server, you can easily find people to connect with using NetMeeting.

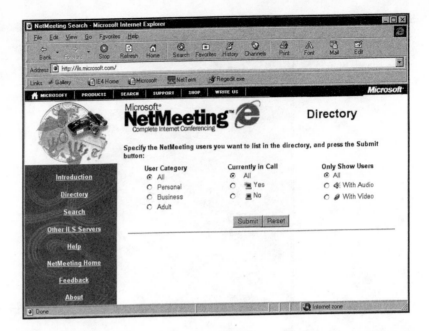

FIG. 1.21
The directory lists all of the people currently using NetMeeting and registered with it.

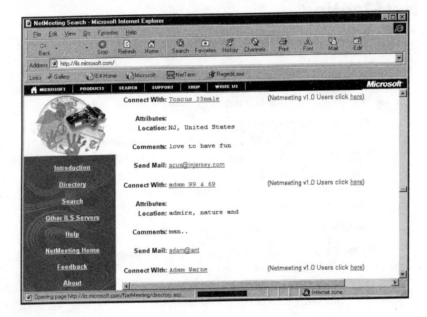

FIG. 1.22

Two-way text chat is just one of NetMeeting's many capabilities.

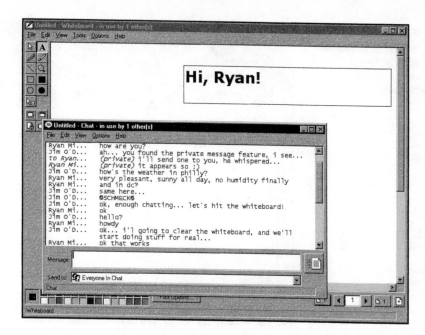

■ **Whiteboard**   The NetMeeting White Board is a Microsoft Paint-like application, but allows all members of the conference to use it and draw on it simultaneously. In addition to being able to use the standard drawing and text tools on the White Board, it can also be used as a clipboard for exchanging still images.

■ **Audio**   Similar to Internet Phone, and a number of other Internet audio applications, NetMeeting possesses audio connection abilities and allows two-way transmission of audio over the Internet. It also comes with a special Audio Tuning Wizard that allows you to tune your audio performance according to the speed of your Internet connection, the speed of your system, and the capabilities of your audio hardware.

■ **Video**   NetMeeting's video capabilities are especially exciting, coming, as they do, in a free application. As shown in Figure 1.23, you can establish a conference with someone, and transmit video back and forth to them, anywhere in the world. This works best with a dedicated, high-speed connection to the Internet, but can also be used relatively well through as slow a connection as with a 28.8K modem.

■ **Application Sharing**   The final capability of NetMeeting, one which makes true conferencing and shared work over the Internet possible, is application sharing. If you are conferencing with someone, you can actually start up any of your Windows 95 applications, and then "share" it with anyone in the conference. This allows them to take control of the application, and use it, while you look on. They don't even have to have the application on their own system. As you can imagine, this isn't the fastest way to run an application, but it is a good way for more than one person to do so when they are separated by any amount of distance.

FIG. 1.23

You can set up two-way video and audio conferencing with NetMeeting

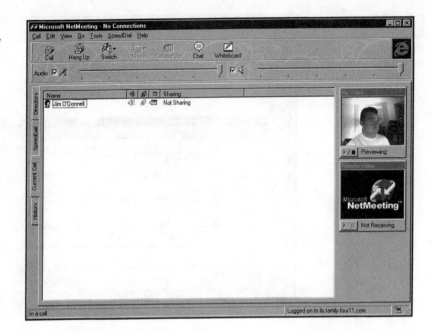

To learn more about NetMeeting, see Chapter 7, "Quick Start: NetMeeting," and Chapter 12, "In-Depth: NetMeeting." ●

CHAPTER 2

What's New in Internet Explorer 4.0?

The title of this chapter would be more aptly named "All of This is New in Internet Explorer 4?" because of so many new features included in this release of the browser. Microsoft has taken the basic shell of Internet Explorer 3 and left it intact while adding numerous enhancements to the browser's functionality. The following few pages will introduce you to some of the new features found within release 4, though all of them will be covered in more detail later in the book. For now, sit back, get comfortable, and enjoy the tour of Internet Explorer 4's new capabilities. ■

Let the browser work for you

Use Subscriptions to alert you when online content is updated.

Web pages come alive with Dynamic HTML

Learn how Dynamic HTML makes surfing Web pages more fun and broadens the scope of what's possible for content developers.

Tune in to premiun channels

As more and more sites configure themselves for Webcasting, you'll be able to tune them in using Internet Explorer.

Use advanced search techniques

With Internet Explorer's new Search Bar feature, you can locate what you are searching for while you view the list of search results.

Subscriptions

If you are like other Internet users, you most likely tire of visiting the same Web sites over again just to see whether there have been any recent updates to the content. With the introduction of Subscriptions, Internet Explorer 4 spares you from wasting your time (and online charges) downloading content that you've already seen. Once you've subscribed to a page, Internet Explorer 4 keeps track of the last time that you visited the page and lets you know when the content has been updated. You do not have to do any special modifications to Internet Explorer to enable Subscriptions; they are in place as soon as you install your new browser.

Subscribing to a Web site initiates a very interesting and complex process in which your computer sends out an intelligent "spider" to retrieve information at specific intervals, comparing the information to what the spider already knows has been collected before, and downloading any new content to your machine for you to view later. Once this content has been downloaded, you can take it anywhere. When you try to access the subscribed site, you can view it live online or run it off your hard drive if you are not connected to the Internet.

To add a Web site to your Subscriptions, simply click Favorites, Subscriptions, Subscribe. You will be asked for the Web site address and how often you want the site to be checked. Once you take care of these settings, you don't have to worry about any other details. Your Subscriptions are automatically updated at the interval you specify.

When one of your Subscriptions has been updated, you will notice a special red star called a gleam on the icon next to your subscribed item. This is an indicator that the page you've subscribed to has changed.

▶ **See** "Subscriptions" to find more on Subscriptions, **p. 391**

 T I P   You can also configure Internet Explorer to send you an e-mail message when a subscription is updated.

N O T E   Subscriptions are very easy to use if you're on a corporate LAN with 24-hour access to the Internet because you can set up Internet Explorer to do subscription updates automatically. If you log in to the Internet with a modem, you have to explicitly tell Internet Explorer to go out and update subscriptions. You can do this by choosing Favorites, Subscriptions, Update All. ■

You are probably saying to yourself, "This is great, but I still have to check my Subscriptions list to see what has been updated." Microsoft has gone to great lengths to make Subscriptions even easier than that. When one of your Subscriptions has been updated, the icon with the gleam on it will appear in your Taskbar, letting you know instantly that updated information is waiting for you at one of theWeb sites to which you've subscribed (see Figure 2.1).

FIG. 2.1
Subscriptions let you
know when content is
updated with a special
gleam on its icon.

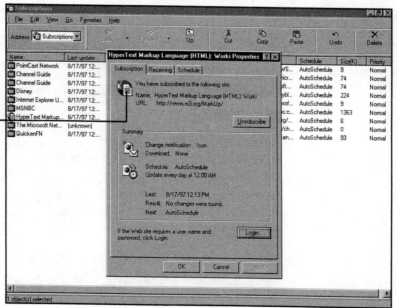

"Gleam" an icon indicating
a change to a site

Dynamic HTML

In the past, the most dynamic interactivity that a Web site could offer its viewers was created with a scripting language such as Perl, JavaScript, and VBScript, or other compiled applications like those created in Visual Basic or Java. Though all these interactive programming techniques are still widely implemented today, Internet Explorer 4 extends HTML functionality another way—through Dynamic HTML. Dynamic HTML is not HTML, but an extension of HTML that is contained within the markup code of an HTML page. Dynamic HTML enables the Web author to control completely all HTML tags within a Web page and to change elements by triggering events such as **OnLoad**, **OnExit**, and **MouseOver**.

Dynamic HTML has four key uses when used within Web pages:

- **HTML Object Model**   With this model, Dynamic HTML allows access to all HTML tag functions contained within a Web page. You can load these functions at runtime or when an event is triggered, as when you pass your mouse over a specific icon.

- **2D Positioning**   Using Cascading Style Sheets (CSS), Dynamic HTML extends physical positioning of elements within a Web page for exact placement. This ensures that each user will always see the same layout of a Web page, regardless of the type of display the user is looking at. To get an idea of what's possible with Dynamic HTML positioning, check out Microsoft's version of the once-popular computer game Asteroids at http://www.microsoft.com/ie/ie40/demos/asteroids.htm (see Figure 2.2).

FIG. 2.2
Dynamic HTML allows
the Web author total
control over how images
are displayed and
manipulated.

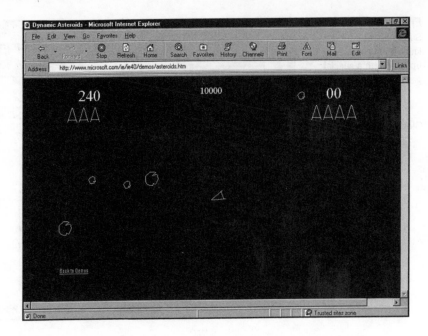

■ **Data Binding**   This feature allows you to manipulate embedded data sources or
   databases that are connected remotely in your Web pages. When you have a small
   amount of data that you wish to display within cells in a Web page, depending on various
   parameters, you can use data binding to quickly access and display the results. To see an
   example of data binding in action, point Internet Explorer to **http://www.microsoft.
   com/ie/ie40/demos/arcadia/default.htm**.

■ **Dynamic HTML Multimedia Controls**   Similar to ActiveX controls, these components can be used in any Web site that has a specific need for multimedia elements,
   such as volume controls and gauges. Lights, Camera, Action, located at **http://
   www.microsoft.com/ie/ie40/demos/count.htm**, is a good place to start playing
   with and researching Dynamic HTML multimedia controls.

Dynamic HTML is a very new technology. In fact, Internet Explorer 4 is the very first browser
to use Dynamic HTML elements, though other browsers are certain to follow. To learn more
about this new technology, visit the Dynamic HTML Web site at **http://www.microsoft.com/
ie/ie40/features/ie-dhtml.htm**. This site offers specific language documentation and a
plethora of ideas on how to incorporate Dynamic HTML into your own Web pages.

AutoComplete

One very interesting and very helpful feature of Internet Explorer 4 is AutoComplete. Simply
put, AutoComplete finishes typing the Uniform Resource Locator (URL) after you enter the
first few characters. When you began your adventure on the World Wide Web, you probably

entered a few long Web addresses by hand, a long and tedious process. Until the advent of AutoComplete, the only way to return to previously viewed sites without retyping the address was to save the address as a favorite. If you forgot to save a location as a favorite, you had to repeat the long process of keying in every character of the Web site address. Now, if you want to quickly return to a previously viewed site, you can simply type the first few characters of the Web site address in the Address Bar and let Internet Explorer search through its history file and intelligently complete the address for you. Once the address is complete, you can simply hit Enter to view the content.

Sometimes, you may have visited different parts of a large Web site and want to return quickly to a specific section. Though AutoComplete is intelligent enough to retain different site addresses that it visits, you must lend a helping hand when trying to access a specific address. For example, suppose you have visited Microsoft's Web sites on Front Page and Internet Explorer 4. Once you begin typing the address **http://www.microsoft.com/** into the Address bar, AutoComplete will complete the basic URL automatically. If you want to visit the Front Page site again, simply type a slash (/) after the basic address. As soon as you type the slash, "frontpage" automatically appears in the Address Bar because you have previously visited the Front Page Web site and it appears first in the list as a result of alphabetization. If you type the letter "I" in the highlighted section, "frontpage" will change to "/ie/ie40". If you hit Enter, you will be taken directly to the Internet Explorer 4 home page.

Another way to use AutoComplete is to right-click an address that Internet Explorer 4 is trying to complete, select Completions from the list, and choose the address to which you want to go. Once the address is selected, your Web browser will automatically load that site's content.

Search Bar

Have you ever tried to search for something in an online search engine, only to be confused by the long list of (possibly) relevant links that are returned? Chances are, you eventually find what you are looking for after repeatedly following hyperlinks on your topic and switching back to the search engine results and trying again. Searching for content is much more intelligent in Internet Explorer 4 than ever before, thanks to the addition of the Search Bar.

To begin searching, simply click the Search button on the Toolbar and a search interface will appear, as shown in Figure 2.3.

You'll notice that your Web browser is now split into two windows—one to to choose your search engine and to specify your search criteria, and one to display the pages that are returned as search result links. After you have typed in a term or phrase to search for and then click the Search button, the results will be displayed in the left side of your browser. When you click one of the links, the new page will appear in the right side of your browser. This is a really helpful feature when you need to explore Web sites to see how they fit your search criteria and then switch to another page by clicking a second link in the search results window. Once you've found the content that you're looking for, simply right-click anywhere within the body of the Web page that you wish to look and choose Open in New Window from the pop-up menu.

FIG. 2.3

Internet Explorer's new Search interface enables you to view Web pages and returned search results within one browser window.

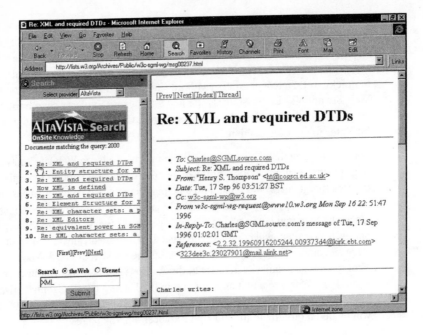

You have your choice of an impressive group of search engines to choose from when using the Search Bar. These include:

- AltaVista
- AOL NetFind
- Excite
- HotBot
- InfoSeek
- Lycos
- Yahoo!

When you select one of these search engines from the drop-down list in the Search Bar, the left side of the browser window will change to match the input interface for that search engine.

Drag-and-Drop Favorites

You can easily control the layout of your Favorites by dragging and dropping items within the Favorites list. Normally, Internet Explorer organizes your Favorites in alphabetical order, even in different folders. If you want your Favorites to appear in a different order, simply click the one that you want to move and drop it where you want it to stay. You can even move links between Favorites folders, so you can intuitively arrange all your saved favorites.

It is also possible to create a shortcut on your desktop to one of your items in the Favorites list. Simply select the item for which you want a shortcut and drag it to the desktop. A new icon is created for you, enabling you to double-click it and open the Web site to which it points at any time.

Offline Browsing

Though offline Web site viewers have been available for a few years now, Microsoft is the first company to incorporate offline reading within the Web browser itself. Offline reading is the ability to surf a series of Web pages, or an entire Web site, without being logged on to the Internet. Internet Explorer 4 enables you to download Web content while you sleep, work, or do anything even more productive away from the computer.

Allow your mind to ponder the capabilities of this type of automated Web site retrieval. One main advantage of reading offline is speed. Once you download an entire Web site to your Web browser, you don't have to wait seconds or minutes for graphics and other multimedia elements to appear. As you click a hyperlink, you are transported to the next page instantly, or at least as fast as your browser window can load it from the hard drive. A second advantage of offline reading is the fact that all of the elements that make up a Web site reside on your own hard disk, which means that you can use any of the Web page components in your own Web pages. It is not a bad idea to borrow ideas from other Web pages—just make sure that you have permission before using copyrighted graphics or other multimedia components. A third great use of offline reading is loading an entire Web site on a laptop computer for presentations. For example, your company may have an exceptional Web site that you would love to demonstrate in a presentation. Instead of reaching for the phone cord and dialing in at 28.8Kbps speed, simply download the entire site the night before your presentation and then amaze your audience with the speed and style of your site.

> **CAUTION**
>
> While you can download the content of an entire site to your hard drive, you may not be able to download some of the functionality. For example, you could download a form as part of your offline browsing, but you can't bring the CGI script that processes the form along with it.
>
> Also, when downloading a lot of content, make sure you have sufficient room on your hard drive to accommodate it.

Drag-and-Drop Quick Links

Veteran Internet Explorer users know that they can edit and change the Quick Link buttons located on the Toolbar to something a little more useful. The old way of doing this was to go to the Options window, select Navigation, and edit the button properties, but now Internet Explorer 4 offers a much faster and easier way to do it.

Part
I

Ch
2

If you come across a hyperlink for which you would like to make a Quick Link button, follow these steps:

1. Identify the hyperlink for which you wish to make a Quick Link.
2. Click the hyperlink and drag it to the Quick Link button that you want to replace. Voilá! The button has changed according to your wishes.

The only limitation that you will encounter is that only a maximum of five Quick Link buttons can be on the Toolbar at one time.

Much More Than Just a Browser

Everything you've read about in this chapter has focused on what's new and exciting with the Internet Explorer browser. But through it all, don't forget that Internet Explorer is not just a browser, it's a suite of Internet-related client software. Here are some of the other components of the Internet Explorer suite and what you can do with them:

- Use Outlook Express to send e-mail messages, including messages with HTML-based content
- Participate in UseNet news groups, also with Outlook Express
- Compose Web documents in support of a personal or corporate site with FrontPage Express
- Use Microsoft NetMeeting to collaborate with others on projects, and
- View high-end multimedia content with the NetShow Player.

All of these components come together to create a set of programs that can support every facet of your Internet experience. ●

CHAPTER 3

Quick Start: Internet Explorer 4

Two years ago, Microsoft's presence was barely felt in the Web browser market. The first two releases of their Internet Explorer browser lagged far behind the Netscape browser (later rechristened Netscape Navigator) in features and ease of use. But all that changed when Microsoft began to focus on the Internet—their Internet Explorer 3 browser was very highly regarded and has been steadily gaining market share from Netscape's offerings.

Now, with Internet Explorer 4, Microsoft continues the evolution of their Internet and Web-based products. Version 4 of their Web browser continues to evolve as a sophisticated, easy-to-use Web browser that supports most of the latest Web technologies. In addition, Internet Explorer 4 shows the first steps in Microsoft's strategy to fully integrate their Web browser into the operating system. ■

Install and set up Internet Explorer 4

This chapter will show you how to install and get Internet Explorer 4 running in just a few minutes.

Connect to the Internet

You can use your existing Internet service provider with Internet Explorer. If you're just getting started, Microsoft's Internet Connection Wizard will lead you step-by-step through the process of establishing your first connection.

Learn Internet Explorer's toolbar and menus

Internet Explorer uses the Windows 95 interface with which you are familiar to control its operations and configuration.

Find out about the basics of Web navigation

By design, navigating around the Web is just a matter of a few clicks of the mouse. Internet Explorer adds features to make it even easier to find and keep track of interesting information.

Installation and Set Up

Microsoft has eased the installation process for their Internet Explorer 4 suite of applications with the addition of the Active Setup Wizard. This Wizard runs on your local system and enables you to only download the software and components that you need—it can analyze your system, and then connect over the Internet to the Microsoft Web site to automatically download and install only what you need.

There are two ways to go about your initial installation of Internet Explorer 4. The first of these is to go to Microsoft's Internet Explorer 4 download Web page at **http://www.microsoft.com/ie/ie40/download/**. From here, you can download the Internet Explorer 4 Active Setup Wizard, a 400K application in the file **ie4setup.exe**. Once this has been downloaded onto your system, you can execute it and it will begin the process of downloading and installing Internet Explorer 4.

In addition to using the Active Setup Wizard, you can also download the entire distribution file for Internet Explorer 4. Depending on which distribution you pick—there is a *Minimal, Standard*, and *Full* installation—this download will be somewhere in the range of 14-22M. Once you have downloaded the distribution file to your local system, you can begin the installation by executing the file.

 TIP If you want to get up and running in a hurry, start with the Minimal or Standard installation. Once the Internet Explorer 4 Web browser is installed, you can easily download its other components when you need them.

The installation process using either the Active Setup Wizard or the downloaded installation file is very similar. The only difference is that the Active Setup Wizard will need to download the selected Internet Explorer 4 components from the Internet before it begins to install them. Once the installation has begun, you will see an alert box similar to that shown in Figure 3.1. After you click Next, you will be led the rest of the way through the installation process.

Most of the questions you will be asked throughout the installation process are pretty basic—you can stick with the defaults given for most of them. One of the more important questions you will be asked, shown in Figure 3.2, is whether or not you want to enable Internet Explorer 4's Web Integrated Desktop. This fundamentally changes some aspects of the way the Windows 95 Desktop, Explorer, Taskbar, and Start Menu operate. Since it can be enabled or disabled any time after the program has been installed, so you should go ahead and choose Yes.

Once you have finished going through all of the steps in the installation process, all you need to do is restart your machine and you will be ready to go!

Using an Established Internet Connection

If you have an established Internet connection, you don't need to do anything else to access the Internet and the Web with Internet Explorer, once you have installed it. Just start the program,

enter an URL (Uniform Resource Locator—this is usually a Web address in the form **http://
www.rpi.edu/~odonnj**), and you're off.

FIG. 3.1
Microsoft's Active Setup
Wizard leads you
through the download
and installation process
of the Internet Explorer
4 suite of applications.

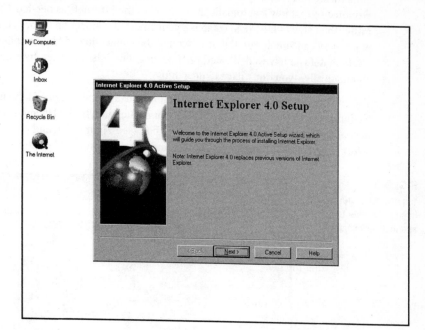

FIG. 3.2
Internet Explorer 4's
Web Integrated Desktop
brings Web functions to
your Windows 95
Desktop and Explorer.

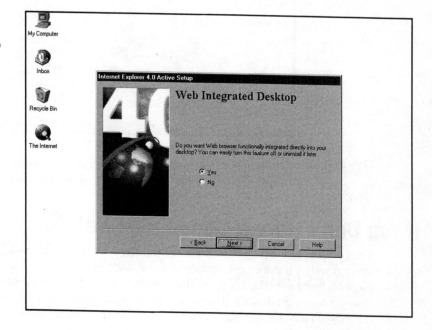

Even if you have an existing Dial-up Networking connection, however, there is a benefit to configuring Internet Explorer so that Internet Explorer knows about it. You can set up Internet Explorer so that it will automatically connect to the Internet "as needed." This means that rather than always having to establish your Internet connection before running Internet Explorer, you can simply run the browser and the connection will be established automatically. (Note that if you have a dedicated LAN connection to the Internet, Internet Explorer can use it automatically—you don't have to do a thing.)

You can configure Internet Explorer to automatically establish your Internet Explorer by selecting View, Options, and selecting the Connection tab. In the Dialing section, check the Connect to the Internet using a modem check box (see Figure 3.3), and click the Settings button to select which of your existing Internet connections you would like Internet Explorer to use.

FIG. 3.3

You can configure Internet Explorer to automatically connect.

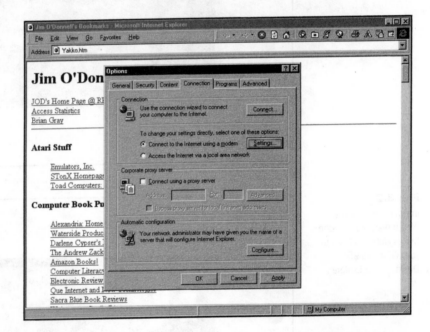

Now, the next time you start up Internet Explorer, the first time it needs to access something on the Internet, it will automatically start up your Dial-up Networking connection.

If You Don't Have a Connection Set Up

If you don't already have a connection to the Internet either through a corporate LAN or a local Internet service provider, establishing such a connection can seem a daunting task, particularly if you are doing it for the first time. The number of Internet service providers (ISPs) has exploded recently, particularly in metropolitan areas. Choosing which ISP to use and then configuring the Windows 95 Dial-up Networking to use it can be intimidating.

Microsoft has done its best with the release of Internet Explorer 4 to make this process as painless as possible. Included with the Internet Explorer suite of programs is the Internet Connection Wizard. The first time you run Internet Explorer 4 or any time you execute the Connection Wizard from the Start Menu, it will offer to lead you through the process of creating an Internet connection.

The Internet Connection Wizard leads you through the following steps.

1. Click Next at the first, introductory screen, to get the screen shown in Figure 3.4. If you are creating a new Internet connection, select the top radio button and click Next again.

FIG. 3.4

If you're starting from scratch, the Internet Connection Wizard and the Microsoft Internet Referral Server can hook you up with an Internet Service Provider in your area.

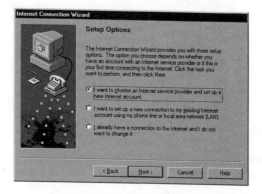

Part

I

Ch

3

2. Click Next after reading the next screen. Another informational screen appears that explains what the Connection Wizard will do.

3. At the next screen, you are prompted for your area code and the first three digits of your phone number. The Microsoft Internet Referral Server will use this information to find the recommended local ISPs. Enter the desired information.

   In the next step, the Connection Wizard will try to call up the Microsoft Internet Referral Server, so make sure your modem and phone line are available. When you have done this, click Next.

4. Now, the Wizard will call and connect to the Internet Referral Server. After the connection is established, the Wizard will pass your information to the Server and download the local ISPs that Microsoft recommends. For my area, for instance, I received the list shown in Figure 3.5.

5. From here, you can elect either to get more information about any or all of the ISPs shown or to sign up with one of them. To sign up with a provider, click the Sign Me Up hypertext link. (Though you might not realize it, the list of providers shown is actually a Web page viewed through Internet Explorer—the Internet Connection Wizard is able to create a special instance of the Web browser without borders or navigational controls to lead you through the rest of the sign up process.)

   Once you have selected an ISP, the specific one that you choose will lead you through the rest of the process of establishing your Internet connection.

FIG. 3.5

You can find out more information about the recommended ISPs or sign up on the spot.

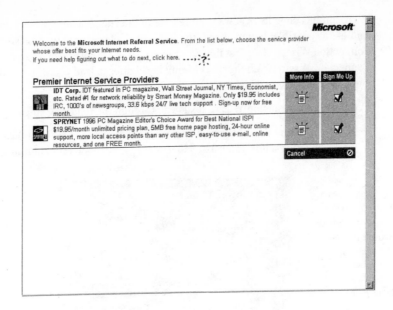

Once you have finished the process started by the Internet Connection Wizard, you should be all set for connecting to the Internet and the Web with Internet Explorer.

Internet Explorer Toolbar

Many of the operations, configuration options, and other capabilities of Internet Explorer 4 are accessible through the set of toolbars at the top of the browser window (see Figure 3.6). You can get any options that you cannot access on the toolbars through one of the menus—I will discuss these in the next section.

Internet Explorer has three "toolbars":

- **Standard Toolbar**   This toolbar contains the standard Web browser buttons. The operations of these buttons will be described more in the following sections.

- **Address Bar**   This bar shows the current URL that the Web browser is viewing. You can type new addresses directly in this bar, and it also has a drop-down list (accessed by clicking the down arrow on the right side of the bar) that gives you access to a history list of places you have visited.

- **Links Bar**   The links bar contains five Quick Links. By default, they take you to different Web pages on the Microsoft or Microsoft Network Web sites. You can change the sites to which these buttons link by using a special subdirectoy of the Favorites folder.

You can enable or disable these toolbars as a group, through the View, Toolbar menu selection. You can also individually enable them and even move them around. To enable or disable individual toolbars, right-click one of the toolbars. In the resulting pop-up menu, you can toggle any of the three toolbars on or off.

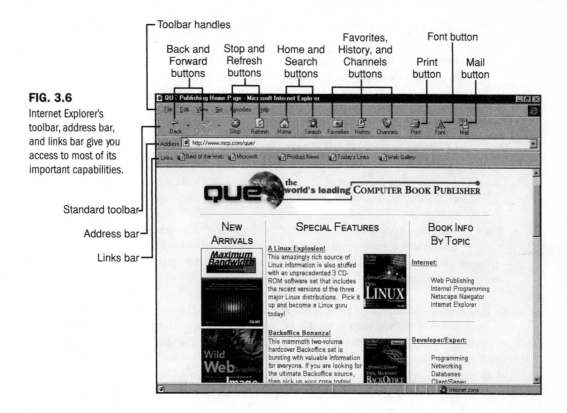

FIG. 3.6

Internet Explorer's toolbar, address bar, and links bar give you access to most of its important capabilities.

To move the toolbars around, use the mouse to click and drag the toolbar handles. If more than one toolbar is on the same line, you can slide them back and forth to reveal more of less of each one.

Internet Explorer Menus

The Internet Explorer menus give you access to all the necessary operations for configuring and using the Web browser. You also can conduct some functions accessible through the menus through the toolbars. Most menu functions also have keyboard shortcuts to make them easier to access.

Internet Explorer has six menus, each of which gives you access to a different group of options:

■ **File Menu**   The options under this menu enable you to open, save, and print Web pages and provides an interface between Internet Explorer and other applications such as Mail, News, Personal Information Managers, and Internet Conferencing. The "history" list of recently viewed files and Web sites is also shown under this menu.

■ **Edit Menu**   This menu gives you access to the standard Windows 95 Cut, Copy, Paste, and Select All options, as well as a Search option to find text on the currently displayed document.

- **View Menu**   Under this menu are options for stopping the current page load or refreshing it, changing the size of the font in which the current page is displayed, or viewing its HTML source.

    Perhaps the most important option under this menu is the Options selection, which gives you access to the configuration options present with Internet Explorer.

- **Go Menu**   This menu's selections are primarily for navigation, enabling you to go back and forward through your list of recently displayed Web pages, go to your Home or Search pages, or go to Microsoft's Best of the Web page.

    In addition to the navigation options, this menu also gives you access to your applications for Mail and News sending and receiving, such as Outlook Express; Personal Information Manager, such as Outlook; and Internet Conferencing, such as NetMeeting.

N O T E   Microsoft sometimes uses the terms Start Page and Home Page interchangeably. Either is used to refer to the Web page, either local or on the Internet, to which your Web browser opens automatically on start up. Both terms refer to the same thing, so don't get confused when one term or the other is used. ■

- **Favorites Menu**   This menu gives you access to your Favorites, Web sites and local documents that you want to be able to access (similar to Netscape Navigator bookmarks). I will describe the use of this menu (and the toolbar button that gives access to the same information) a little more in the Favorites section later in this chapter.

- **Help Menu**   Through this menu, you can access help information for Internet Explorer, either local help information downloaded and installed along with Internet Explorer or information on the Microsoft Web site.

Configuration Options

As I mentioned in the last section, through the View, Options menu selection, you can access the different configuration options available with Internet Explorer. The Options dialog has six tabs, each of which gives you access to a different group of configuration options.

General Options Tab

The General Options tab gives you access to various simple configuration options. Through these options, you can set your Home Page, decide where Internet Explorer stores its temporary files, and determine how long items in the History list are kept around. It's a good idea not to keep history entries along too long because they can begin to fill your hard drive.

> **CAUTION**
>
> Because of the way Windows 95 stores files, (each file takes up a minimum amount of space, depending on your hard drive and partition size) it is particularly important to keep an eye on how many entries are in your History folder.

Also, each entry in the History folder (along with each item in the Internet Explorer cache and Favorites folder) is a separate file. So, even an Internet address that might take up 20 or 30 bytes might be stored as an entry in your History folder and take up a lot more space.

If you do a lot of Web browsing, it's possible to create quite an extensive History folder. That's why it is important to set the number of days to keep these entries to a number no bigger than necessary.

Additionally, you can access other options by clicking the Colors, Fonts, Languages, or Accessibility buttons. The Colors button enables you to select your default Web browser colors. The Fonts button enables you to set the default proportional and fixed fonts used by the Web browser. If you have a foreign language version of Internet Explorer, you can use the Languages button to select from different display languages. Finally, the Accessibility button enables you to set some options to make your Web browser easier to use.

Security Options Tab

Flaws in the security of Microsoft Web browsers has been well-publicized. Microsoft very quickly fixed each of these security flaws and put extensive security features into the latest release of its browser.

The Security Options Tab gives you access to these features. The default security settings that come with Internet Explorer 4 should be sufficient for you to get started. There is an entire chapter on security later in this book, if you'd like to find out more.

▶ **See** "In-Depth: Security," **p. 297**

Content Options Tab

This tab gives you control over what content you will allow your Web browser to load, and is mainly of use if children will be using your Web browser. Internet Explorer uses the PICS content rating system; you can set up the Web browser through this option to screen out Web sites with particular types of content. It is also possible to screen out unrated Web sites (the vast majority of sites are currently unrated).

It is also through the Content tab that you maintain and access certificates, which are digital signatures belonging to individuals and corporations. These certificates enable you and Inter-net Explorer 4 to reliably verify the identity of software vendors from whom you download programs and other information.

The final set of options under this tab enable you to configure the Microsoft Wallet ActiveX Control, which you can use with compatible Web servers to set up secure payments of merchandise over the Internet.

Connection Options Tab

As you saw in the section on connecting to the Internet earlier in this chapter, you use the Connection Options tab to tell Internet Explorer what Dial-up Networking connection, if any,

Part

I

Ch

3

you use to connect to the Internet. In addition, this option tab is the one with which you can configure your browser to connect to the Internet through a proxy server (which is present on many corporate Web LANs).

Programs Options Tab

As shown in Figure 3.7, the options under this tab enable you to configure which applications Internet Explorer uses to access Internet Mail and News. Once you configure these applications, you can use the Mail toolbar button to launch the appropriate program.

FIG. 3.7

Internet Explorer enables you to decide what applications it uses for Mail and News, as well as which ones to use when accessing other types of files.

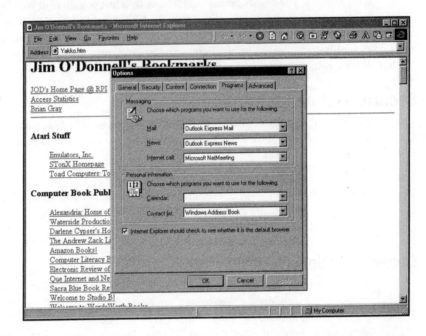

For other file types, the application that Internet Explorer uses is controlled by the Windows 95 Explorer File Types database. Unlike Netscape Navigator, which maintains its own list of plug-ins and helper applications to handle different types of files you may find on the Internet or on your local system, Internet Explorer uses the same database of file types that the underlying operating system uses.

Advanced Options Tab

A number of options under the Advanced Options Tab explain how to configure Internet Explorer to do a number of things. As with the Security Options Tab, most of the defaults for these options will be sufficient to get you started. I will discuss these options in greater depth later in this book.

▶ **See** "Advanced Options Tab," **p. 124**

Favorites

In Internet Explorer 3, Favorites were stored hierarchically and sorted alphabetically. In other words, it was possible to create folders and subfolders to organize Favorites, but it was not possible to arrange them within those folders other than alphabetically.

Internet Explorer 4 maintains this Favorites functionality but adds the capability to sort the entries within the folders any way you want. To do this, all you need to do is pop up the Favorites menu using the Favorites menu or display the Favorites Browser Bar by clicking the toolbar button. From either of these locations you can click and drag the entry you want to move, and release it where you'd like it to be (see Figure 3.8).

FIG. 3.8
A simple click-and-drag interface enables you to organize your Favorites any way you'd like.

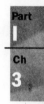

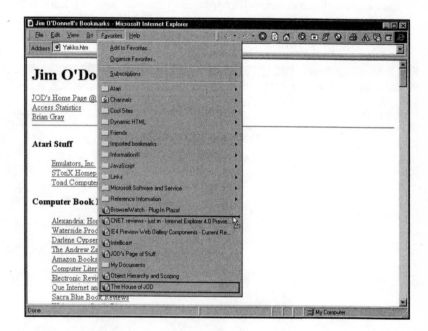

N O T E   Internet Explorer 4's Browser Bars are an exciting new feature of the Web browser that make frequent tasks much easier. There are four Browser Bars, enabled through the Search, Favorites, History, and Channels toolbar buttons. Each of them places a dedicated panel along the left side of the Web browser window for accessing its appropriate function. You can find out all about these new tools in Chapter 8, "In-Depth: Internet Explorer 4." ■

▶ **See** "Using Internet Explorer's Explorer Bars," **p. 114**

Using Text and Graphic Links to Maneuver the Web

Unless you have never used a Web browser before, you are familiar with the concept of the hypertext link within a Web page. The link consists of two things, the anchor and the link itself. The first part, the anchor, is the visible part—it is the text or graphics within the Web page or other HTML document that you can actually see.

The two most common types of anchors are text and graphical anchors. Given the graphical nature of the Web, you can expect many anchors to be graphics. Figure 3.9 shows a graphical anchor used for a hypertext link. (In this case, the graphic is used as an image map and will take you to different locations depending on where you click it.) Links with graphic anchors are sometimes shown with a border to indicate the presence of the link, but (as shown in Figure 3.9) not always. The sure way you can tell the presence of a hypertext link of any sort is that the mouse cursor will change to the pointing finger when you pass it over such a link.

FIG. 3.9

You can attach hypertext links, indicated in your browser by the pointing finger mouse cursor, to simple graphics or to imagemaps.

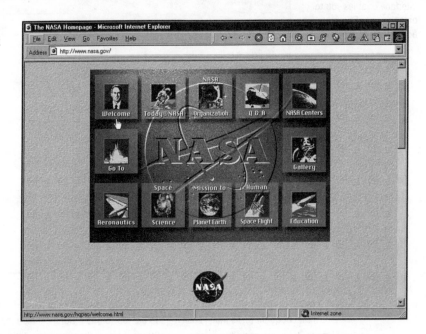

In addition to graphic anchors, you can use text anchors with hypertext links. Figure 3.10 shows such a link. Notice that, as with graphic anchors, the mouse cursor changes to indicate the presence of this type of link.

But what does a hypertext link do? Clicking it will take you to another Web page or another location within the current page, which involves the second part of a hypertext link, the link itself. When you press a hypertext link, the Web browser will go to the Web page or document indicated by the location in the link.

FIG. 3.10
A well-designed Web site will always include text links in addition to graphics to allow for nongraphical Web browsers.

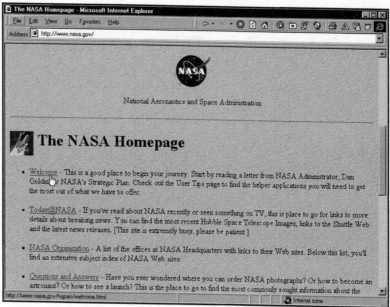

Many browsers, including Internet Explorer, will tell you where a hypertext link points when the mouse passes over it. Internet Explorer uses the status bar at the bottom of the Web browser window for this purpose. For instance, Figure 3.10 shows that the displayed hypertext link points to the Web page **welcome.html**.

N O T E You might have noticed that the toolbars in Figures 3.11 and 312 look a little different, and are much more compact than the ones shown in earlier figures. As mentioned earlier in this chapter, the toolbars and menu bar can be moved around and configured to make the Web browser look the way you want it to look. ■

▶ **See** "Using the Toolbars," **p. 112**

Using Navigation Buttons and Menus

One most common button you will use when Web browsing is the Back button, located on the toolbar (you can also access it with <u>G</u>o, <u>B</u>ack or by pressing Alt+Left Arrow). With this button, you can go back to the previous Web page. You can also use the Forward button (<u>G</u>o, <u>F</u>orward or Alt+Right Arrow) to move forward in the list of visited Web pages (this button becomes active once you have gone back one or more pages).

Part

I

Ch

3

Your Home Page, a Place to Start, and Search Engines to Find the Things You Want

As I mentioned previously, Internet Explorer enables you to select your Home Page. Internet Explorer automatically loads this page when it starts up or when you hit the Home toolbar button (Go, Home Page).

 TIP Use a locally-stored document as your Start Page. Then, when you start Internet Explorer, there won't be any delays for it to load a page off of the Internet. If you also use Netscape Navigator, then your Navigator bookmarks file might be a good file to use.

Other than random "surfing" from Web page to Web page via hypertext links, the most common way to find information on the Web is by using one of the many search engines that exist. These search engines enable you to enter keywords and will search for Web pages that match them. This is the most common way to search for Web pages on a topic of interest.

Internet Explorer has a Search button (Go, Search the Web) that you can use to access many Web search engines. With Internet Explorer 4, however, Microsoft has added a new capability to this, the Search Browser Bar.

As shown in Figure 3.11, when you click the Search button, the left panel of the browser window displays a search Web page. This page gives you access to some of the most popular Internet and Web search engines. You can select a search engine from the drop-down list, type your keyword(s) into the textbox and start your search.

FIG. 3.11
Internet Explorer 4 features a dedicated Search Browser Bar that enables you to access many of the most popular search engines.

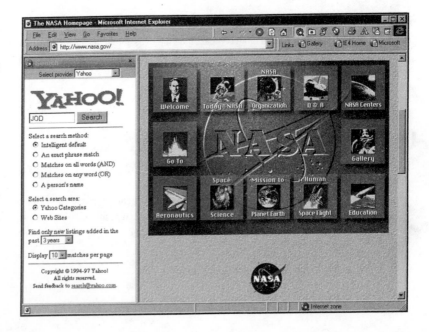

Now, unlike as in the past, the results of your search display along with the current page you are looking at (see Figure 3.12). This enables you to look at the pages that resulted from your search while still seeing the search results. In the past, it was necessary to jump back and forth between the search results page and the candidate pages of your search. The Search Browser Bar makes it a lot easier to find what you are looking for quickly.

FIG. 3.12

The dedicated Search Browser Bar remains active until you click the Search button again, enabling you to view the results of your search and the resulting Web pages simultaneously.

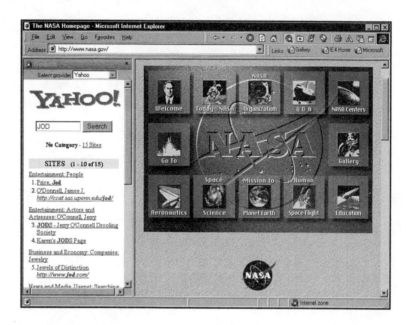

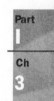

When you have found what you are looking for, you can click the Search button again to re-move the Search Browser Bar. Or, you can start a new search.

Favorites

The final way to navigate the Web is using the Favorites, which are stored within the Favorites menu or the Favorites Browser Bar accessed through the toolbar button. When you are look-ing at a Web page to which you'd like to be able to come back, you can select the Favorites, Add to Favorites option and select the subfolder in which to store the new Favorite entry.

Once you have stored a Favorite in the Favorites folder, all you have to do to return to it is select the Favorites button, find the desired Favorite within the hierarchy, and click it. Internet Explorer will then load it. ●

CHAPTER 4

Quick Start: The Active Desktop

Feature for feature, the Internet Explorer 4 Web browser compares very well with Navigator, the browser component of Netscape's Communicator suite of Internet and Web applications. Both companies tout the superiority of their product, and a case can be made for each. Which you prefer is largely subjective, because neither Web browser, taken by itself, is substantially more advanced than the other.

The most exciting feature of Microsoft's Internet Explorer suite of applications and technologies, which makes it stand out against its competition, is the Active Desktop. Through the Active Desktop technology, Microsoft has integrated its Web browser and access to the Internet and to the Web into parts of its operating system—offering a first taste of the future of Windows. Using it, you can embed live HTML documents and Web pages, Java applets, and anything else that can be viewed in a Web browser *right on your desktop*.

In addition, it offers you an Explorer with which you can use the same interface to view both the Web and your local system. You can even customize how individual folders on your hard drive appear when you view it. Finally, the Windows 95 Taskbar and Start Menu have Internet access built right into them, making the Internet just a mouse click away, no matter what you are doing. ■

Learn about the Internet Explorer Active Desktop

Perhaps the most exciting new feature of Internet Explorer 4 is its "Active Desktop," which turns your desktop into a Web browser where you can place Web pages, Java applets, and anything else from the Web right there.

Find out how to download and install desktop components

Desktop components are special applications meant to be placed on your Active Desktop. This section will show you where to find some of them and how to get them.

Use the integrated Explorer on your local system or on the Web

Internet Explorer 4 brings the same interface to your Windows 95 Explorer as with your Web browser, so you can use one way to access both the Web and your local system.

See how the Windows 95 Taskbar and Start Menu are made "Internet-aware"

Learn about the few, simple additions Microsoft has added to the standard Taskbar and Start Menu to allow you instant access to the Internet, no matter what you are doing.

The Active Desktop

After you've installed Internet Explorer 4 with Web Integration, you will be able to make your desktop come alive. Figure 4.1 shows you an example of what you can do.

FIG. 4.1
Internet Explorer 4's Active Desktop brings the Web right to your desktop, bringing it to life.

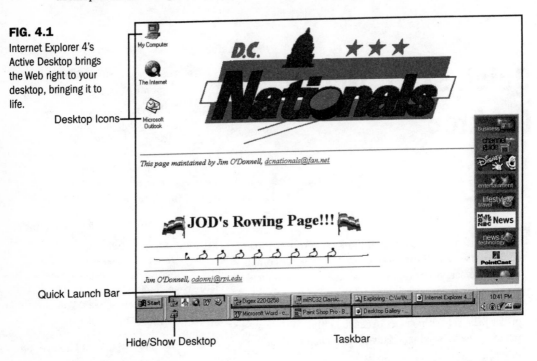

Anything that can be shown in a Web browser can exist in the Active Desktop! That means that you can place separate Web pages, Java applets, ActiveX Controls, graphics, and sounds all right on your desktop. In fact, not only can you do all of this, but Microsoft has devised desktop components, Web objects that are especially designed for the desktop. Downloading and installing items to include on your Active Desktop is easy, too.

The Active Desktop Icon Layer

Before the Active Desktop, your standard Windows 95 desktop was a simple thing. You had a background color or graphic with icons placed on top of it. The Active Desktop keeps this simple arrangement by dividing your desktop into two layers: the HTML layer and the Icon layer.

Figure 4.1 shows that, even on the Active Desktop, there is still a place for your traditional desktop icons. Anything you could put on your desktop before can still go there. Shortcuts to applications, your Recycle Bin and My Computer icons, Internet shortcuts, all of them can still be there. Think of the icon layer as a transparent layer on which your icons sit: They are still there, but you can see through them to what lies underneath.

The Active Desktop HTML Layer

The Active Desktop replaces the background color, pattern, or image with an HTML Layer. This is where the fun is with the Active Desktop. Any Web object or component that you could display in your Internet Explorer 4 Web browser can be embedded in the HTML Layer of the Active Desktop.

Not only can you place these elements on your desktop, but, as you will see later in this chapter and in the In-Depth chapter on the Active Desktop, you can move, resize, and set them up to automatically update themselves.

▶ **See** "Installing and Configuring Desktop Components" to find out all the details about configuring your Active Desktop, **p. 133**

Desktop Components

In addition to the ability to install any Web page, HTML document, Java applet, ActiveX Control, or other conventional Web objects onto your desktop, Microsoft has created what it calls Desktop Components that you can place on your Active Desktop. Technologically speaking, Desktop Components aren't really anything new; they use the same Web technologies embodied in the other types of Web objects I mentioned earlier. What is different, however, is the packaging.

Desktop Components are Web objects that are especially designed for you to place on your Active Desktop. This means that they are, for the most part, relatively small so that you can easily place them on your desktop. Also, their content tends to focus on news and information that you might want to see at a glance—news and sports information, stock tickers, time and weather information, and the like.

Downloading and Installing Components

Though there will doubtless be many sources of desktop components once the Active Desktop becomes more firmly established, a good place to start is at Microsoft's Desktop Component Gallery at **http://www.microsoft.com/ie/ie40/gallery/**.

At the Desktop Component Gallery, once you have found a component you would like to download onto your desktop, the process of doing so requires only a few mouse clicks.

Once the component is shown on the gallery Web page, to download it and install it on your Active Desktop, all you need to do is click the **Put it on my Desktop** hypertext link, and it'll be on its way to your system.

Part

I

Ch

4

FIG. 4.2

Just one mouse click is all you need to get this desktop component and install it on your desktop.

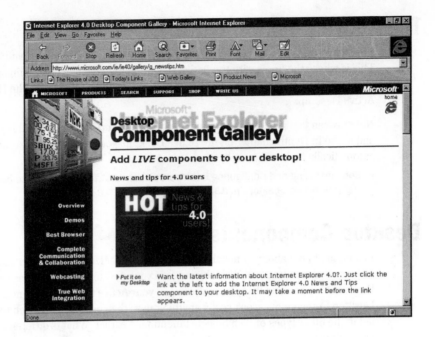

Component Configuration

Once you have downloaded the component to your system, you have a few options of how to configure it. Because many of these components are designed to deliver information right to your desktop, you can configure them to automatically update themselves according to any schedule you desire (see Figure 4.3).

You enter these schedules by using a new feature of Internet Explorer 4 called a subscription. In short, a subscription is a way of configuring a Web page so that it will automatically update and download to your system on some scheduled basis.

▶ **See** "Subscriptions" for more information on how to set up and use Internet Explorer 4 subscriptions, **p. 391**

Once you download, install, and configure the desktop component on your system, it'll look something like that shown in Figure 4.4. With the desktop component installed, you can be constantly updated with the latest information on the things you care about most.

Creating Your Desktop

With a host of desktop components to place on your desktop, plus *any page on the Web*, not to mention Java applets, ActiveX Controls, and anything else, you'll need a way to create a desktop suited to you, your work habits, and need for information. Fortunately, Internet Explorer 4's Active Desktop technology enables you to do this.

FIG. 4.3

You can enter subscriptions for your desktop components so that they regularly refresh themselves with new information.

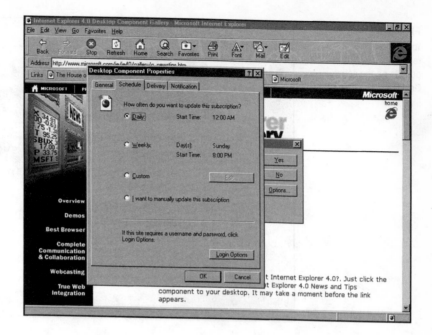

The first thing you really need to be able to do, of course, is see your desktop components. Normally, your desktop will be cluttered with windows and dialog boxes, the Taskbar, and Office Shortcut bar—the things on which you are actually working. Microsoft has added a quick way to bring your desktop to the surface, which enables you to see all your components and other information on it. Figure 4.1 showed the small Hide/Show Desktop button located in your Quick Launch bar. Clicking this button once brings the desktop to the top; clicking again restores your desktop to normal.

To arrange your desktop to your satisfaction, you also need to be able to move and resize the components and objects that are on your desktop. To do this, pass the mouse cursor over a desktop object, as shown in Figure 4.4.

When the mouse cursor is over any desktop object, a border will appear around it. You can use that border to drag the component anywhere on the desktop you'd like, or to resize it. You see the other configuration option of the Active Desktop when you look at the Display properties, by selecting the Display Control Panel option or by right-clicking the desktop and selecting Properties from the pop-up menu. This gives you the standard Display Properties dialog, but Internet Explorer 4 has added a new tab, the Web tab. Through this tab, you can enable and disable downloaded desktop components on your Active Desktop.

Another change made in the Display Properties dialog box by the Active Desktop is to the Background tab. Now, in addition to being able to set your wallpaper to a graphic image, you can also use an HTML document as your background.

FIG. 4.4
You can resize and
rearrange desktop
objects on the Active
Desktop any way you'd
like.

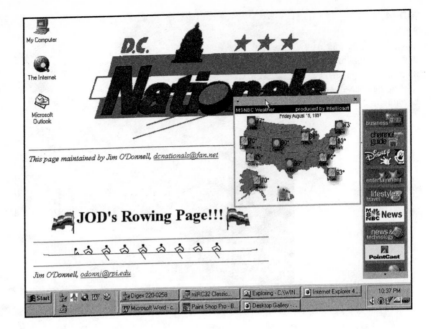

The Integrated Explorer

Another innovation of Internet Explorer 4 and its increasing integration into the Windows 95
operation system is the new Integrated Windows 95 Explorer (see Figure 4.5). The new Explorer interface is very similar to the Internet Explorer interface in that each has the same
navigation controls, for instance, and each has a Favorites menu that makes use of the same
Favorites folder on your system—you can specify either Web or local documents as your favorites!

TIP Use the new Explorer Back and Forward buttons to go back and forth between two directories on your
hard drive if you're working on files in both.

Notice the Internet entry in the Explorer. With the integrated Explorer, the Internet appears as
just another entry on your system.

Explorer WebView

Located under the View tab of the View, Options menu selection are the configuration options
of the new WebView Explorer mode (see Figure 4.6). With these options, you can select either

the new WebView or standard Windows appearance and control how the Explorer interprets mouse clicks.

FIG. 4.5
The new integrated Explorer enables you to browse through your hard drive or through the Web using the same interface.

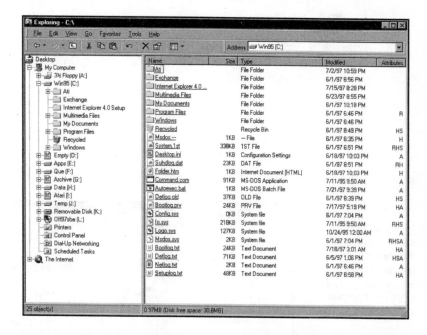

FIG. 4.6
You can select or disable WebView's appearance and interface options depending on whether you like them.

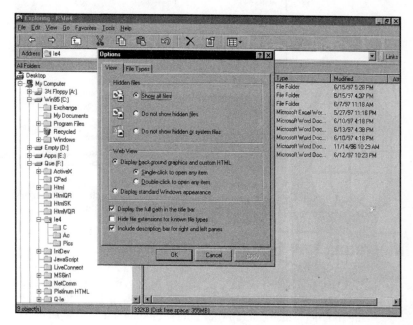

N O T E In the current release of Internet Explorer 4, the View, Options dialog shown in Figure 4.8 is only accessible through a single-pane Explorer window, such as you get when you double-click your My Computer icon. ■

By default, under the new Explorer WebView, all files on your hard drive are treated as hypertext links. Under the Single-click to open any item option, mouse operations are interpreted by the Explorer as follows:

■ If you pass the mouse over a file or directory, the cursor becomes a pointing finger, and the entry name is underlined (similar to a hypertext link).

■ If you hold the mouse over a file or directory, without clicking, for a few seconds, it is selected (see Figure 4.7).

■ Single-clicking the item opens or launches it, whether or not you selected it.

FIG. 4.7
By default, WebView enables you to interact with items on your hard drive just as hypertext links, requiring only a single mouse click to launch them.

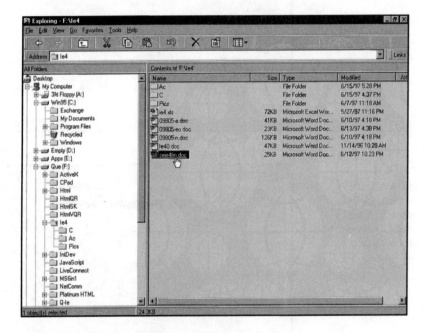

Selecting the Double-click to open any item option restores the normal Windows 95 behavior, requiring a single-click to select an item and a double-click to launch it.

Integrating Your System and the Web

Figure 4.8 shows another example of the integration of your local system and the Internet and Web that is achieved with the integrated Explorer under Internet Explorer 4. The Tools, Find menu option, familiar from the old Explorer, now includes "Internet-Aware" options such as On the Internet, which calls up your Internet Explorer 4 Search page, and People, with which you can find people on such Internet services as Four11.

FIG. 4.8
Internet Explorer 4 builds Internet capabilities right into familiar Explorer menu options.

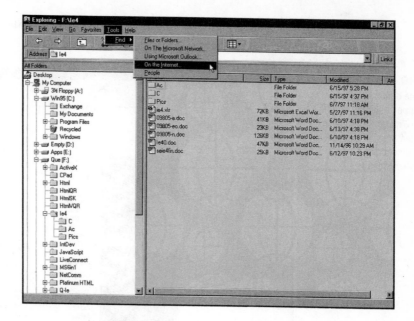

Customizing Explorer WebView

Another exciting capability of the new Explorer is the ability to customize the WebView of any folder on your hard drive. To do this, browse to the folder and select View, Customize This Folder, or right-click it and select Customize This Folder from the pop-up menu. You will then get the dialog box shown in Figure 4.9. By selecting Create or edit an HTML Document, you call your HTML editing program, and you can customize the appearance of that folder when it is viewed with WebView.

FIG. 4.9
You can create an HTML document from any folder on your hard drive and customize it with your Web page editing program.

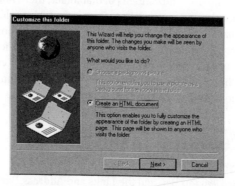

If you don't make any changes to the default WebView appearance of the folder, it will look something like that shown in Figure 4.10. When using this option, a file called Folder.htm is created within the folder that includes the HTML instructions necessary to create the WebView appearance of the folder. You can change the appearance of the folder within the

Part
I

Ch
4

Explorer WebView using any HTML authoring program. FrontPage Express has some special abilities to work with WebView files.

FIG. 4.10

The default WebView appearance for a folder in Explorer includes an area that will give you information about a selected file.

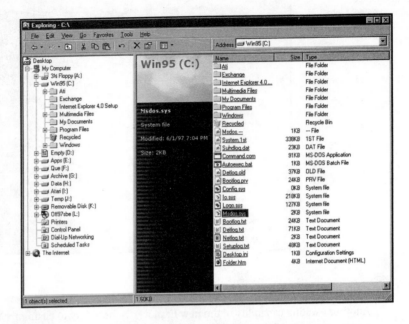

The other possibility for customizing the appearance of a folder shown in Figure 4.9 is to Choose a background picture. With this option, you can select a background image and font color to go with the WebView appearance of the folder. Figure 4.11 shows an example of this.

Why would you want to customize the appearance of a folder on your hard drive for WebView? If you are the only person who uses the contents of that folder, there might not be any reason to do so. If other people use that computer, however, or if the folder is located on a network for other people in your company, you might be able to use the view customization to your advantage. For instance, as shown in one example on the Microsoft site, if a folder contains files with the travel schedules of all of your employees, you could customize the view of the folder to include not only the files, but also hypertext links to the company of Internet resources for travel, lodging, or any other relevant information.

Using the Web Integrated Taskbar

In addition to the conventional Taskbar, Start Menu, and System Tray, Internet Explorer 4 adds the Quick Launch Bar, the Desktop Bar, and the Links and Address Bar from the Web browser. Additionally, the Hide/Show Desktop button on the Quick Launch Bar gives you quick access to the desktop. As in the Internet Explorer Web browser, you can enable and disable, as well as move around, these different toolbars to take up as little or as much space as you can spare (see Figure 4.12).

FIG. 4.11
When using background colors and images, make sure you select a text color that will give proper contrast.

FIG. 4.12
As with the Web browser, you can rearrange the different toolbars with respect to one another.

▶ **See** "Using the Internet Explorer 4 Taskbar" for information on how to add applications to the Quick Launch Bar, **p. 140**

Part

I

Ch

4

Access the Internet from the Start Menu

Finally, Internet Explorer gives your Start Menu access to the Internet, with the same Favorites menu and additional Find options as were included with the new Explorer, as shown in Figure 4.13.

FIG. 4.13

The new Start Menu also allows you quick and easy access to the Internet.

CHAPTER 5

Quick Start: Outlook Express Mail and News

One big problem with today's Internet software is that users generally accumulate one program for each task they want to accomplish. For example, if you send and receive e-mail, you must have some sort of dedicated e-mail client on your computer. Likewise, if you read UseNet newsgroups, you must have a program installed on your system that is dedicated to reading news. However, new Internet software solutions are being introduced that incoporate many of these Internet programs into one suite, such as with Microsoft Internet Explorer 4.0.

Outlook Express for Internet Explorer 4, which is a light version of Microsoft Outlook that was designed to be bundled with Internet Explorer, introduces a bundled solution for reading mail and news within the same program interface that is both a time saver and a help to your computer because less hard drive space is eaten up. You might think that Microsoft held back on features in Outlook Express to combine mail and news reading capabilities, but the exact opposite is true. Outlook Express is one of the most versatile, easy to use programs for Internet text communications today. And it's free. ■

Set up Outlook Express Mail for the first time

This chapter shows you how to get your Mail configuration just right—the first time.

Send and receive e-mail messages easily

You don't have to be an Internet expert to use e-mail effectively.

Create a new News profile with Outlook Express News

Configure Outlook Express News correctly and begin using it immediately.

Read and post newsgroup messages

Explore the world of UseNet newsgroups and become an expert in no time.

N O T E   It is not necessary to use Outlook Express as your e-mail and news software. If you are currently using other software such as Eudora and Free Agent to read your mail and news you may continue to do so. It is also not necessary for you to use Outlook Express in order to use Internet Explorer 4.0. ■

Up and Running with Outlook Express Mail

Outlook Express Mail is an easy to use, full-featured e-mail client with which you can organize mail messages into folders, create group lists, format messages with hyperlinks and images, and much more. It looks much like the Internet Explorer Web browser itself from the toolbar and menu functions. Those who have previously used Microsoft's Internet Mail will feel right at home with Outlook Express Mail and will love the new features that make it the best freeware e-mail client available today.

Though Outlook Express Mail is related to the Outlook personal information manager (PIM) that is available with Office 97, it does not offer quite as much functionality when it comes to previewing and organizing messages. Don't let this scare you, however. Because Outlook Express Mail is a scaled-down version of its big brother Outlook, the program will actually perform faster as a result of its smaller size.

Setting Up Outlook Express Mail

When you launch the Outlook Express Mail client from the start menu, you are immediately greeted with the Internet Connection Wizard, waiting for you to input your e-mail information so that you can begin to be productive. Once you enter your information, you can begin composing, sending, and receiving Internet mail. Configuring Outlook Express Mail is quick and easy. After answering only a few questions about your e-mail account, you will be up and running in no time.

You will need to get some information from your Internet Service Provider before you can complete the setup of Outlook Express Mail. Use the following helpful form to keep your e-mail information at a stone's throw.

E-mail Address _____ (for example, *joe@provider.com*)

E-mail Account Name _____ (for example, *joe*)

E-mail Account Password _____ (that is, your password)

SMTP Server Address _____ (for example, *mail.provider.com*)

POP3 Server Address _____ (for example, *mail.provider.com*)

Nowadays, it is uncommon to have a different address for the SMTP and POP3 servers. Because you may be working with a legacy access provider, Microsoft has kept the availability of both with this new release. With all of your information at hand, let's get going.

The first item of information that you are asked to provide when setting up an e-mail account is an Internet Mail Account Name. This name should be something unique, such as Joe's E-mail, especially if you are going to use Outlook Express Mail for multiple e-mail accounts. To enter your Internet Mail Account Name, follow these steps:

1. Type a unique name into the empty field for your profile name, as shown in Figure 5.1. This name should be something descriptive so that you know that you're working with the correct e-mail account.

FIG. 5.1

Your Internet Mail Account Name is used for the profile that you create when adding a new e-mail user.

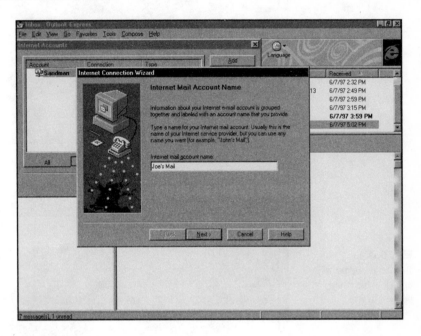

2. Click Next to continue.

   The next screen that appears in the Internet Connection Wizard is Internet Mail Display Name, as shown in Figure 5.2. This name will appear in the From field when a recipient receives a piece of e-mail from you. Follow these steps to configure your Internet Mail Display Name.

3. Type your name, or whatever you wish to appear, in the From field of all your recipient's e-mail articles within the empty text box labeled Internet Mail Display Name.

4. Click Next to advance to the next step.

   Next, you are asked to provide your complete e-mail address, not just the username, as shown in Figure 5.3. Make sure that you enter the domain name as well as your username in this box.

5. Select the empty text box and type your complete e-mail address. This should be formatted as *joe@provider.com*.

6. Click Next to advance to the next configuration screen.

Part

I

Ch

5

FIG. 5.2
The Internet Mail Display Name entry will appear as the sender's name in an e-mail message that you send.

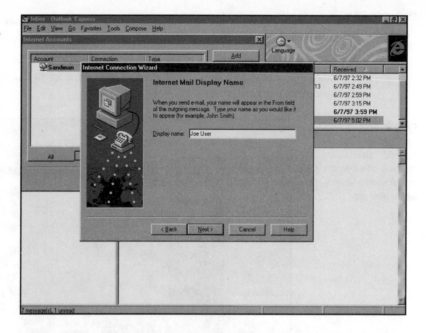

FIG. 5.3
The e-mail address will appear in the return address in your outbound e-mail.

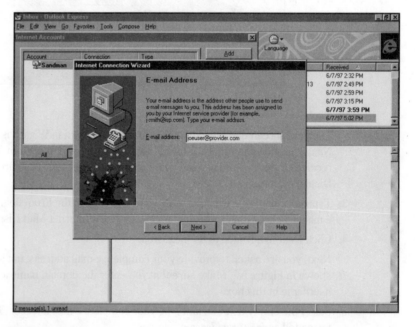

The next screen that appears, as shown in Figure 5.4, asks you to provide information about the e-mail servers that you check for your mail and the one through which you send your outgoing mail. Most of the time, your SMTP and POP3 servers will have the same address. Contact your Internet service provider if you have any questions about your e-mail servers. Follow the steps below to successfully set up your e-mail server information.

FIG. 5.4
The E-mail Server address is used when checking and sending e-mail.

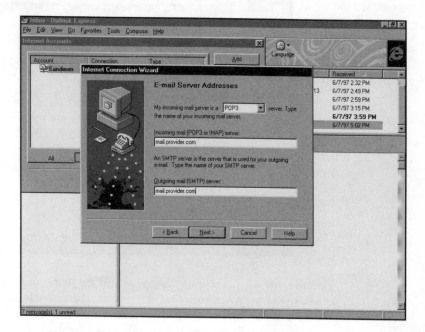

7. Select the type of incoming mail server that you use to check mail. Most users will select POP3, though IMAP is provided as a choice if you have that type of service.

   N O T E IMAP is a new e-mail protocol that is offered by some providers. The major advantage that it has over POP3 is that it enables you to review the subjects of your e-mail messages before you download them to your e-mail client. ■

8. Type the incoming mail server address into the empty Incoming Mail Server text box. Your address will most likely follow the format *mail.provider.com*.

9. Tab down to the next empty text box, labeled Outgoing Mail (SMTP) Server, and enter your outgoing mail server. Again, this address will follow the format **mail.provider.com**.

10. Click Next to continue setting up the program.

    You're almost finished setting up Outlook Express Mail now. The next step is to enter information about your Internet Mail Logon, as shown in Figure 5.5. This is most likely the same logon that you use to connect to the Internet. Follow these steps to successfully configure the logon settings.

Part
I

Ch
5

FIG. 5.5

Provide your username and password in the Internet Mail Logon so that your e-mail server can properly identify you.

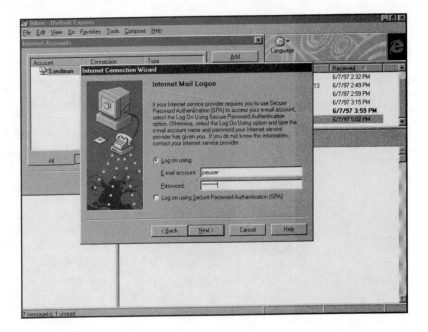

11. Select the type of logon process that you will use for your e-mail. You will see an option for Secure Password Authentication at this point. This option is one of the new ways that passwords can be digitally encoded and protected for transmission across the Web. Most providers have not implemented Secure Password Authentication yet, so you probably don't need to select this logon.

12. In the E-mail Account text box, enter in the name of your e-mail account. For example, if your e-mail address is *joe@provider.com*, you would enter "joe" in the text box.

13. Enter your password into the Password text box. As you type your password, you will not be able to see what you're typing. Remember, if you should make a mistake when typing your password, you can delete what you have typed or start over and save the new password.

14. Click Next to continue the set up process.

    The next screen that appears is Choose Connection Type, as shown in Figure 5.6. In this screen, you tell Outlook Express Mail how you are connected to the Internet. Follow these steps to complete this set-up screen.

15. Select the radio button next to the type of connection that you have to the Internet. If you are a dial-up user with a modem, simply choose Connect Using My Phone Line. If you have an ISDN connection or a dedicated service, choose Connect Using My Local Area Network.

16. Click Next to continue.

17. The last step to setting up Outlook Express Mail is to click the Finish button to complete the settings or to click the Back button to review your entries and make any changes. Once you have clicked the Finish button, the Internet Connection Wizard will close and Outlook Express Mail will be ready for you to use.

FIG. 5.6
You must state what kind of connection you have to the Internet before you can send and receive e-mail.

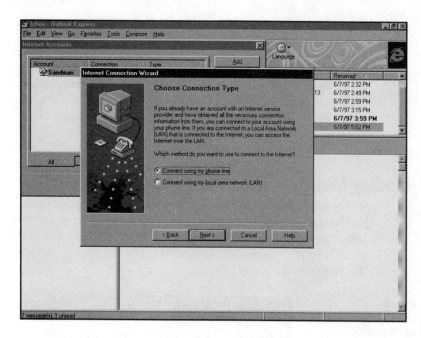

Getting Mail

When you begin using Outlook Express Mail at your primary mail client, you can check whether you have existing mail on your mail server. Before you can check or send your mail, however, you must make sure that your connection to the Internet is up. If you use a dial-up connection to the Internet through a modem, it is up to you whether you initiate the connection yourself or wait until Windows prompts you to connect when you try to talk to your mail server.

You can retrieve e-mail in several different ways, but all function exactly the same way. You can retrieve your mail from the toolbar or you can use a two-key combination on the keyboard. Follow these steps to check your server for e-mail:

To check for e-mail using the toolbar:

1. Click the Send and Retrieve button on the toolbar.

2. Type your password into the Logon screen that appears and click OK.

To check for e-mail using the keyboard:

1. Press CTRL+M to bring up the Logon screen.

2. Type your password into the Logon screen and click OK.

Part
I

Ch
5

After you have started the mail checking process by using any of the preceding techniques, Outlook Mail Express sends a request for new mail to your mail server along with your e-mail account information. If there is any mail on the server, the server will enable you to download the messages.

CAUTION

It may not be a good idea to choose Remember Password when you are prompted from the Logon window when you check your mail. Though this is a handy feature because you don't have to type your passowrd repeatedly, it can also be a privacy nightmare. When Outlook Express Mail has your password memorized, it will check for mail on the server without any intervention from you, which means that your coworkers or anyone else who has access to your computer can use your mail client to check for new mail or any mail you still might have residing in the mail client.

Reading Mail

After you have checked and received your mail, the next step is to read it. Outlook Express Mail handles e-mail in a unique fashion in comparison to other mail programs. Outlook Express is a three-paned Windows program in which you can switch between folders, browse mail articles, and read mail articles—all at one time. Figure 5.7 introduces the Outlook Express Mail interface.

FIG. 5.7
Outlook Express Mail sports an easy-to-use interface that is also easy to understand.

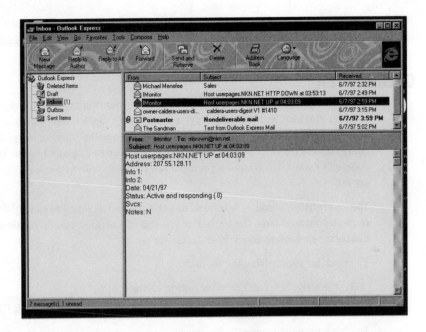

If you want to preview your mail, simply highlight the article in the e-mail list pane and the article text will appear in the preview window below it. If you want to see the entire body of the message at once instead of in the preview window, simply double-click the mail article that you wish to read. Double-clicking the mail article causes the contents to appear in a stand-alone window, as shown in Figure 5.8.

FIG. 5.8
You can read incoming e-mail within the preview pane or as a stand-alone message.

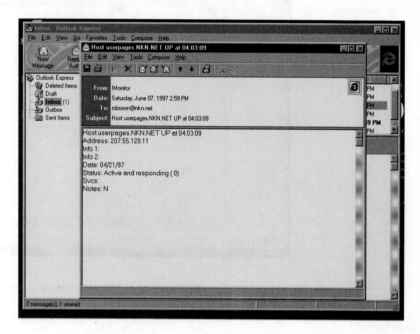

After you've finished reading your mail, simply choose File, Close to close the message. If you want to delete the mail article, you can right-click the article name and choose Delete. As a failsafe to keep you from deleting mail that you really need to keep, deleted mail is moved to the Deleted Items folder. With this folder, you can move the mail back into your Inbox or any other folder if you do not really want to delete it. To delete it for good, you must select the Deleted Items folder in the left window pane and choose to delete the e-mail again. Once you delete a piece of e-mail from the Deleted Items folder, you cannot recover it.

Part
I

Ch
5

Creating and Sending E-Mail

By now, you are starting to see the power of Outlook Express Mail and you're probably about ready to being composing and sending your own e-mail messages. You'll be happy to know that Outlook Express Mail provides a simple-to-use interface for composing mail, as well as replying to mail that you receive. The following steps will guide you to successfully composing and sending a piece of e-mail:

1. Click the New Message button on the toolbar. A blank, unaddressed e-mail window will appear, awaiting your content, as shown in Figure 5.9.

2. Type the recipient's e-mail address into the To field. This address must follow the format *username@provider.com*.

FIG. 5.9

An empty e-mail message in Outlook Express Mail holds many possibilities.

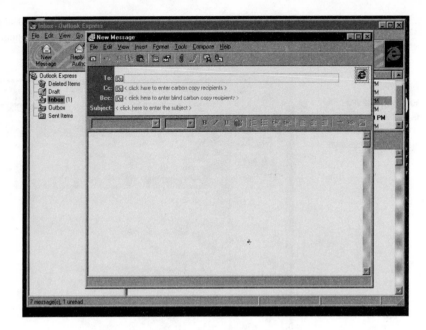

3. Type another recipient's address in the CC field if you want to send a copy of this message to another user. Entering an address in the BCC sends a blind carbon copy of the e-mail to a different recipient. The primary recipient will not know that you have sent a copy to another recipient.

4. Enter a subject in the Subject line. The subject can be a brief description of the body of the message or an off-the-wall statement to grab the reader's attention.

5. Type the body of your message in the body area. Notice the small formatting toolbar that appears above the body of your message. With this toolbar, you can adjust the font type, font size, formatting of the body; create hyperlinks; and include pictures. Note that not every e-mail client understands this type of formatting in e-mail. Your completed piece of e-mail might look like the one pictured in Figure 5.10.

6. Click the Send button on the toolbar when you are finished writing your message. A dialog box will appear when you click Send, alerting you that the e-mail message will be placed into the Outbox folder and will not be sent until you choose Send and Retrieve from the toolbar.

7. Click the Send and Retrieve button on the toolbar to send your e-mail message out to your mail server. Once your mail server has the message, it will send your mail to its recipient right away.

That's it! You now know how to check for, compose, and send mail.

▶ **See** "In Depth: Outlook Express Mail," **p. 155**

FIG. 5.10
Many different
formatting techniques
are available for
personalizing e-mail
messages.

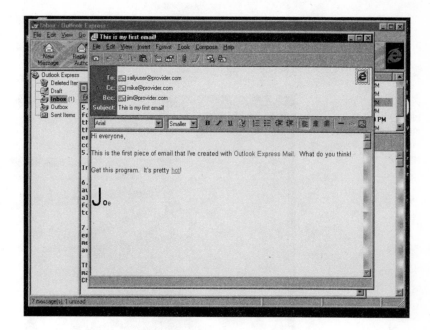

Up and Running with Outlook Express News

Many Internet users are now adept at the two basic functions of the Internet itself: viewing the World Wide Web and using e-mail. Most, however, do not know anything about UseNet newsgroups at all. UseNet newsgroups are a huge public forum on a wide range of topics (more than 24,000) that allow people to read and post articles on similar subjects. For example, more than 400 newsgroups are dedicated to Microsoft products. With the rising costs of phone-based technical support, this type of 24-hour service is invaluable.

Almost every Internet service provider today offers UseNet newsgroup access as part of its basic service at no charge. This is one service that you should definitely take advantage of, and Outlook Express News makes it all possible for even the Internet novice to begin using it immediately.

Setting Up Outlook Express News

Configuring Outlook Express News is much like setting up Outlook Express Mail, though the information that you provide is regarding your ISP's news servers instead of mail server information. You again use the Internet Connection Wizard to streamline the set up process. When you launch Outlook Express News for the first time, the Internet Connection Wizard will launch automatically and prompt you for information. Follow these steps to quickly get online with UseNet newsgroups:

Part

I

Ch

5

1. Enter a name for your news profile in the Internet News Account Name window, as shown in Figure 5.11. This name should be something like Joe's Mail or, if you're using multiple news servers, you can title it something like ISP News 1. Click Next to advance to the next set-up screen.

FIG. 5.11

Identify your news profile with a unique Internet News Account Name.

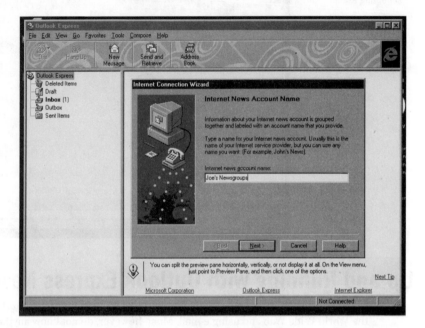

2. Enter your display name in the Internet News Display Name text box, as illustrated in Figure 5.12. This name will appear when you post a new news article or reply to an existing one. Click Next to continue.

3. Insert your e-mail address in the Internet News E-mail Address box. This e-mail address will appear in your posting, should someone wish to e-mail you directly. Click Next to advance.

4. Enter your news server name in the Internet News Server Name window, as shown in Figure 5.13. This is the server that you will use to read newsgroups. Your ISP can provide you with the server's address. If your server requires you to log in before reading news, select the My news server requires me to log on checkbox. Click Next to continue.

> **N O T E** If your news server requires you to enter a password, check that option and proceed to the next screen, which will prompt you for your password. To continue, click the Next button and proceed. ■

5. Click the radio button next to your connection type in the Choose Connection Type window, such as what is shown in Figure 5.14. Click Next to continue.

FIG. 5.12
The Internet News
Display Name appears
when you post an
article to the
newsgroups.

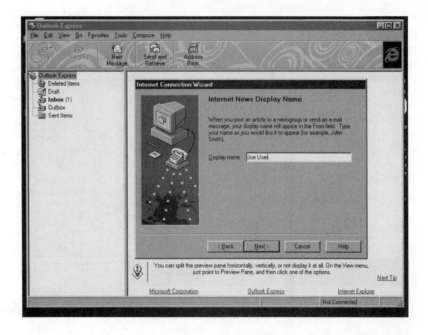

FIG. 5.13
You must supply an
Internet News Server
Name to access and
read newsgroups from
your host server.

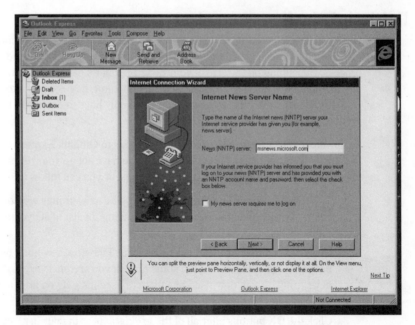

Part

I

Ch

5

6. Click Finish to complete the setup or choose Back to review your information. After you
   click the Finish button, your news settings are complete and you're well on your way to
   reading UseNet newsgroups.

FIG. 5.14

Outlook Express News must know how your computer connects to the Internet to function properly.

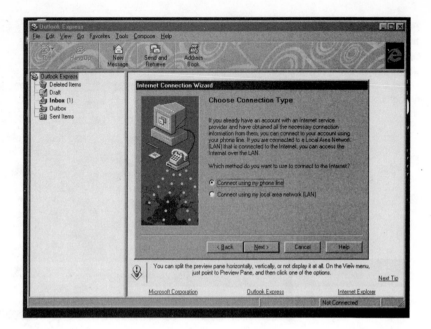

Retrieving the Newsgroup List

Once you have configured all of the program settings from the last section, you must download the entire list of newsgroup subjects from your news server. Be warned—this can be a lengthy process. Depending on the size of your news provider's newsgroup list, you could be downloading for 10 minutes or more. You will be happy to know, however, that you only have to download this list once. As you add new groups, you only have to download the list of the new groups, not the entire list.

To download the current active list of newsgroups to Outlook Express News you can do one of two things: You can follow the prompts after you have set up your news account information that will automatically download the newsgroups, or you can follow these steps:

1. Click Tools, Newsgroups from the menu. The newsgroups window will appear and your computer will immediately begin downloading the list of active groups, as shown in Figure 5.15.

2. Get a cup of coffee or tea. Read a magazine. Pick up a new book by QUE at your local bookstore. In other words, kill some time. If you are on a very fast connection, the newsgroup list will download in a matter of seconds. If you are on a 14.4Kbps modem, you could be waiting for 10 to 20 minutes.

3. Click the OK buttons after all of the groups appear in your list. You will know the process is complete when the Downloading Groups window disappears.

Now that you have downloaded the full newsgroup list to your machine, it is time to subscribe to a few groups and read the content.

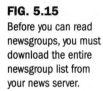

FIG. 5.15
Before you can read newsgroups, you must download the entire newsgroup list from your news server.

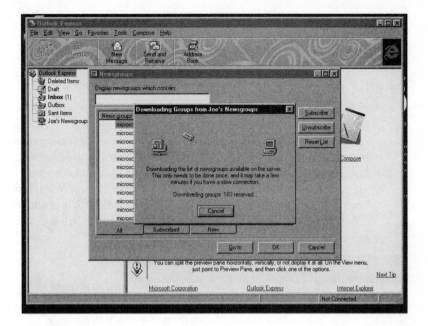

Subscribing to a Newsgroup

Let's be clear on one important point—subscribing to an Internet newsgroup does not cost any money. It is called subscribing because you essentially bookmark a newsgroup so that you don't have to search the entire group list when you want to read articles about a subject in which you are interested. There is also no limit to the number of newsgroups to which you can subscribe. Because thousands of groups are available for reading, you may find yourself subscribing to 10, 20, or more.

You're probably thinking to yourself, "Great. Here are all of these topics and I now have to read through the entire list to find what I'm looking for." Luckily, the developers of Outlook Express News anticipated this thinking and incorporated a handy search tool within the news list interface.

To subscribe to a newsgroup, follow these steps:

1. Type a topic in the Display newsgroups text box. Try to keep your search targets to single words, such as "birds," "www," and "pictures." A list of like newsgroup topics will replace the global list. Some newsgroup titles are very long, and, as a result, you may need to resize the width of the newsgroups list pane to read them clearly.

2. Highlight the group to which you want to subscribe and click the Subscribe button. Follow this step until you are satisfied with all of your subscriptions.

3. Click OK when you are finished subscribing to newsgroups.

   To check out the list of groups to which you are subscribed, simply click the Subscribed tab in the Newsgroups window.

Any time that you wish to subscribe to additional groups, unsubscribe from any groups, or check for new groups, simply launch the Newsgroups window and use the different tabbed sections.

Reading and Posting News Articles

Reading and posting new articles in Outlook Express News is much like working with e-mail in Outlook Express Mail. The three-pane interface, in which you read, send, and organize news articles, is used again. The left pane enables you to switch between newsgroup topics. As soon as you click a group, Outlook Express News will attempt to download any new article headers from the group. Unlike e-mail, the body of a message is not downloaded until you select the message header in the upper-left corner of Outlook Express News. Like Outlook Express Mail, double-clicking the news article header will launch the article in a stand-alone window. If you only highlight the article header, the body of the message will appear in the preview pane below the article list.

To reply to an existing article, follow these steps.

1. Highlight the article header to which you want to respond.

2. Click the Reply to Group button on the toolbar. A new article window will appear with the original author's comments separated by the ">" character.

3. Enter your comments into the body of the message and click the Post Message button to complete your post. Unlike with Outlook Express Mail, newsgroup articles that you post will immediately be sent to your news server.

Perhaps you've looked through all of the article headers in a newsgroups but still haven't found any information in which you are interested. Well, nothing is stopping you from creating a new newsgroup thread. To post a new article, follow these steps:

1. Click the New Message button on the toolbar. A blank article will appear, waiting for your input.

2. Compose the text of your article. When finished, click the Post Message button to send your article to the news server.

    If you are posting an article where you are requesting a response, keep in mind that it can take many hours, if not days, for your message to propagate across the Internet. Most users have found that they will see a reply to their postings within 24 hours, however.

    ▶ **See** "In Depth: Outlook Express Mail," **p. 155**

CHAPTER 6

Quick Start: FrontPage Express and the Internet Publishing Wizard

Software makers aren't just producing browsers anymore—they're producing entire suites of Internet-related software. Browsers now come bundled with e-mail and news clients, collaborative conferencing components, and increasing support for multimedia content. They're also shipping with tools that enable users to compose their own Web documents. In the case of the Internet Explorer suite, the document authoring component is called FrontPage Express.

For the most part, FrontPage Express is the editor portion of Microsoft's FrontPage 97. FrontPage is a high-end tool intended for use by Webmasters who have to maintain a large site or by developers who are writing active content. FrontPage Express is more of a tool "for the rest of us" and is ideal for small, personal sites made of just a few pages.

Setting up FrontPage Express

With the Internet Explorer suite installed, it's a simple matter to get up and running with FrontPage Express.

Using FrontPage Express to create a simple document

You use FrontPage Express just as you would a word processing program. Once you've created your document, FrontPage Express writes the HTML code that reproduces the document on a browser screen.

Enhancing your document

FrontPage Express can do a lot more than just the basic stuff. It features support for images, forms, tables, and Internet Explorer-specific extensions to HTML.

Publishing your document

Microsoft's Internet Publishing Wizard makes converting and uploading your finished document a snap.

TIP   For more details on using FrontPage, consult Que's *Special Edition Using FrontPage 97*.

This chapter gets you started with Microsoft FrontPage Express by introducing you to the program's authoring interface and features. You'll learn how to put together a simple document using FrontPage Express and how to publish the document on the Web using the Internet Publishing Wizard. ▓

Screen Layout and Features

To fire up FrontPage Express, choose the FrontPage Express icon under the Internet Explorer Suite program group. When the program starts, you'll see the screen shown in Figure 6.1. The editing window is initially blank, enabling you to get started on a new document right away.

FIG. 6.1

FrontPage Express looks much like a word processing program when you first start it.

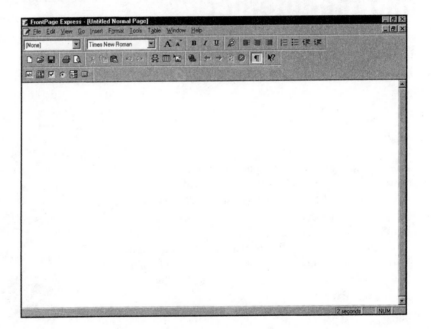

You can configure a few things in the FrontPage Express interface to your preferences before you begin to compose a document. The View menu lets you toggle the following items on or off:

▓ **Standard Toolbar**   The Standard Toolbar plays host to buttons that handle the common file operations (New, Open, Save), printing, cutting, copying, pasting, and undo/redo. You can also insert tables, images, hyperlinks, and Web Bots with Standard Toolbar buttons.

- **Format Toolbar**   The upper toolbar is called the Format Toolbar. Here you can find drop-down lists of fonts and HTML styles along with buttons that control font size, color, effects, and alignment.

- **Forms Toolbar**   It's easy to place the popular graphical user interface (GUI) controls found on HTML forms with buttons on the Forms Toolbar. Here you'll find buttons for text boxes, radio buttons, check boxes, multiline text windows, drop-down lists, and action buttons.

- **Status Bar**   The Status bar provides messages to you while you're creating your documents. For example, as you move your mouse pointer over a toolbar button, a description of that button's function shows up in the Status Bar. Another neat Status Bar feature shows approximately how long it will take for your document to download using a 28.8Kbps connection.

- **Format Marks**   Format marks refer to things like paragraph and line breaks. You can choose to have these displayed with this View menu option.

You can also choose which font and character set you want to use when composing your documents. By choosing Tools, Font Options, you call up the dialog box shown in Figure 6.2. The default selection is for a U.S./Western European language, which means the ISO-8859-1 character set is to be used.

FIG. 6.2
You can choose a separate character set when writing in languages other than English.

With these options set, you're ready to start using FrontPage Express to create HTML documents.

FrontPage Express makes just about any authoring task simple, but for starters, the focus will be on the very basic tasks. The balance of the chapter takes a look at the following document-authoring activities:

- Starting a new document
- Editing an existing document, including those that you download from the Web
- Adding and formatting text
- Inserting images and hyperlinks
- Publishing your finished document

Part

I

Ch

6

Starting a New Document

When you first start FrontPage Express, you have a blank slate on which to create your document, so technically, you're ready to go just by starting the program. But FrontPage Express has some other useful features that can help you put up certain kinds of pages almost effortlessly.

By choosing File, New, you call up the dialog box shown in Figure 6.3. In the dialog box, you can select one of six different document templates or wizards, which include the following:

- Normal page
- Confirmation form
- Form Page Wizard
- New Web view folder
- Personal Home Page Wizard
- Survey form

FIG. 6.3
FrontPage Express's templates and wizards make creating certain kinds of pages a simple matter.

Starting with a Blank Page

Choosing the Normal Page option just gives you the same blank slate you see when you start the program. If the type of page you need to create does not mesh well with the other templates or wizards available, choose the Normal Page option.

 If there's a certain type of page you create frequently, you can create your own template for it and save it as a template file (.htt extension). This template will then be available for you to use later when you call up the New Page dialog box. You can store templates wherever you'd like, but in the interest of keeping your templates organized, you should store them in a common FrontPage Express working folder.

Creating a Confirmation Form

The Confirmation Form template assists you in creating a page that acknowledges input from an HTML form. If you select this option, you'll see the page shown in Figure 6.4. Note that the page has several bracketed items that would be filled in with the information the user entered into the form. You are by no means forced into using the structure put forward on the Confirmation Form template. Indeed, you are free to do whatever customization you need to make it fit your needs.

FIG. 6.4
Confirming a user's form input is an important courtesy. FrontPage Express has confirmation support built right in.

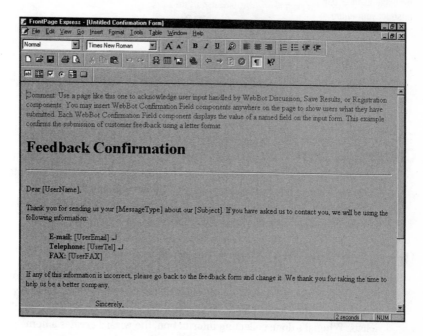

NOTE The comment at the top of the Confirmation Page template points out that the template is best used in conjunction with WebBot Discussion, Save Results, or Registration components. Web Bots are preprogrammed functions that FrontPage Express lets you drop into your documents just as you would an image or a horizontal line. ■

▶ **See** "Using WebBots," **p. 196**

The Form Page Wizard

The FrontPage Express Form Page Wizard walks you through a series of dialog boxes that ask you what kind of information you want to gather on your form (see Figure 6.5). The wizard keeps a list of all the questions and, once you have composed them all, will write them out on the page in one of a number of different formats. On the surface, it just looks like FrontPage Express is setting up several form fields with prompting text in front of them, but it's important to realize that FrontPage Express is also composing the "behind-the-scenes" parts of the form as well. These parts include matters like making sure the right code is in place to produce the desired form control and giving each piece of form input its own unique name.

TIP Always instruct the Form Page Wizard to set up the form fields in an HTML table. Doing so makes all the fields line up nicely and produces a much more attractive form.

FIG. 6.5
By polling you for the type of information you need to collect, FrontPage Express can construct your entire form page.

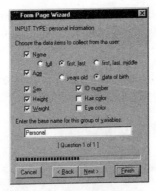

Creating a New Web View Folder

FrontPage Express gives you a "Web View" of contents on your computer's hard drive by using the New Web View Folder template. In addition to listing files and folders, you can customize the look and feel of each folder and set up links to other Windows shell components and Internet mail and newsgroups.

Using the Personal Home Page Wizard

The Personal Home Page Wizard "interviews" you over a series of dialog boxes and then builds for you a personal home page based on the information it gathered. You can even specify the presentation format for most sections, choosing from bulleted, numbered, or definition lists. When it's done collecting information, the wizard creates a home page shell that you can fill in with other personal information (see Figure 6.6).

N O T E The Employee Information section of the Home Page Wizard is useful if you're doing a page for a corporate intranet, but you may not find it valuable for a personal page you're publishing through your Internet service provider. ■

Creating a Survey

The final template is for creating a Survey Form. Choosing the template puts a prepared survey in the FrontPage Express window. The survey is in three parts and has the traditional Submit and Clear buttons at the bottom. You're free to delete any parts that you don't need and edit any remaining parts to include the questions that you want to ask. Like the Confirmation Form, the Survey Form is also intended to work with Web Bots, particularly when it comes to how the survey results are saved.

Editing an Existing Document

If you already have some documents you've worked on and you need to go back and make edits, you won't have much use for the options you'd get by selecting File, New. Rather, you're more likely to choose File, Open to reveal the dialog box shown in Figure 6.7. This dialog box offers two options. The first is to open a file that lives on your computer. To do this, simply click the Browse button and navigate your way to the file you want to edit.

FIG. 6.6
FrontPage Express will set up an entire home page for you based on what you type into a few dialog boxes.

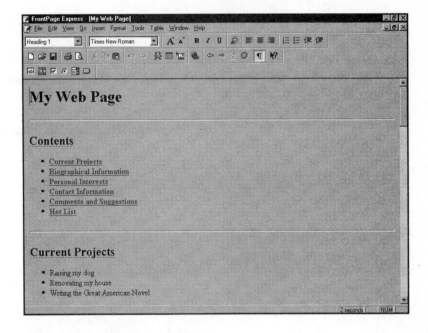

FIG. 6.7
With FrontPage Express, you can edit a Web document on your hard drive, or you can pull a document off the Internet and edit it.

Part
I
Ch
6

Your other option is to give FrontPage Express the URL of a document on the Web so the program can download and display the file for editing. To do this, click the From Location radio button and type in the URL of the document you want to edit. FrontPage Express will make an HTTP request for the document and load it into editing window (see Figure 6.8).

This feature is useful if you have a document that you've already published to your server that needs a quick change. With the FrontPage Express download feature, you can transfer the document to your machine, make the update, and republish it—all with the same program!

FIG. 6.8

You can download any published file on the Web and edit it in FrontPage Express.

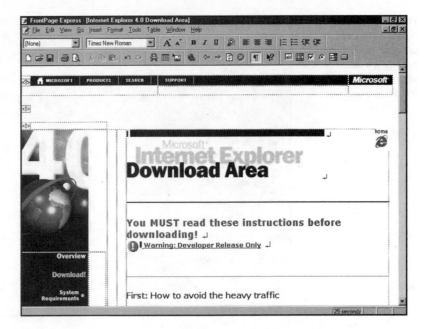

One other way you can work with an existing document is to pull it into FrontPage Express using the Insert, File command. If you choose this menu option, you'll be presented with a standard dialog box in which you can navigate to the file you want to import. FrontPage Express can read in HTML, plain text, Microsoft Word, WordPerfect, and Microsoft Excel files.

With a new document started or an existing document read into FrontPage Express, you're ready to start using the program's editing features. The rest of the chapter focuses on how you can use FrontPage Express to create or modify content.

Composing a Text Document

What makes FrontPage Express so easy to use is that it works much like your favorite word processing program. You can type text right into the FrontPage Express window or import it from another file. Once there, you can format the text with any one of dozens of styles to make it look just the way you want it to look on the Web. FrontPage Express takes it from there and writes out the HTML code that a browser would need to reproduce the page you created on a user's screen.

The Format Toolbar

You can do most of the common formatting tasks by using a list of buttons on the Format Toolbar. The styles drop-down list at the left edge of the Format Toolbar gives you quick access to all six heading styles; bulleted, numbered, menu, and directory list styles; the address style; and the term and definition components of the definition list style. To use any of these styles, simply highlight the text to be formatted by dragging your mouse pointer over it and then select the desired style from the list.

 TIP You can format a bulleted or numbered list even more quickly by using the appropriate button near the end of the Format Toolbar.

With the font drop-down list, which is next to the styles drop-down list, you can change the typeface in which the on-screen text is rendered. The default is Times New Roman, but you can choose from any of the fonts that are installed on your computer. You apply new fonts in the same way that you apply new styles—just highlight the text you want to format and choose the font you want from the list.

CAUTION

Changing document fonts can be tricky because you can't possibly know what fonts every potential reader of your page has at his or her disposal. When you use fonts other than Times New Roman, try to use those that are commonly found on most computers, such as Arial, Courier, Helvetica, Garamond, or Century Schoolbook. This increases the likelihood that your readers will be able to see and appreciate the font effects you're creating.

Following the fonts drop-down list on the Format Toolbar are buttons with which you can increase and decrease the font size. You can use these buttons to create effects like small caps, in which each letter in a word is capitalized and the first letter of the word is in a larger size. To change the size of text that's already on the screen, you can highlight text and click the appropriate button. You can also click either of the buttons to change text size as you type.

Next on the Format Toolbar are the familiar B, I, and U buttons. These apply bold, italic, and underlined formatting, respectively. The underline style is now part of standard HTML, but using a lot of it can be confusing to users who are accustomed to seeing underlined text and thinking that it is a hyperlink.

With the Text Color button, you can change the color of the document text from its default black to any other color you wish. When you highlight the text you want to paint and click the Text Color button, you'll see the Color dialog box shown in Figure 6.9. You can choose from one of the basic colors available or you can add your own custom colors to the palette. To define your own colors, click the Define Custom Colors button to expand the dialog box to include a color spectrum box. You select a color in the spectrum by moving the cross hatch around over it. When you've found the color you want, click the Add to Custom Colors button at the bottom right of the dialog box.

Part

I

Ch

6

FIG. 6.9

Coloring text is as easy as selecting a color from FrontPage Express's basic palette (or you can define your own set of colors).

The next three buttons on the Format Toolbar should also look familiar to anyone who has used a word processor. These buttons apply left-justified, centered, or right-justified alignments to text. Because they control a block type of format rather than a character-level type of format, you will most likely be highlighting large chunks (lists or entire paragraphs) of text when you use them.

N O T E   In spite of the <CENTER> tag becoming part of standard HTML, FrontPage Express does center alignment via the <P ALIGN="CENTER"> tag. ▨

The final set of buttons on the Format Toolbar apply bulleted or numbered list styles or increase or decrease the indentation level.

Formatting with Menu Commands

The formatting options available to you from the Format Toolbar are those most commonly used, but they don't offer you a great deal of flexibility. For example, the numbered list button just creates a standard numbered list. But what if you want to use Roman numerals instead of Arabic numerals? The numbered list button does not give you the option to change the numbering scheme, so you'd have to either renumber the list items by hand or dig a little deeper into FrontPage Express to find support for different numbering. Fortunately, FrontPage Express is much more than what you see in the toolbars. This section takes a look at the FrontPage Express menus that are most helpful with text formatting tasks.

Under the Insert menu, you'll find a couple of interesting options to help you. Choose Insert, Break to insert a line break into your document. You can break to the next available line or you can break all the way to the first line that has a clear left or right margin.

Horizontal lines are a great way to break up long passages of text. To add a line to your Web document, place the cursor where you want the line to go and choose Insert, Horizontal Line. The line will appear below the cursor and run across the width of the screen.

Choose Insert, Symbol to call up the dialog box you see in Figure 6.10. From this dialog box, you can select a special character to insert into your document. Many of these characters are those with diacritical marks that must be represented by special HTML codes called entities.

Being able to choose a special character from a dialog box is much simpler than trying to remember the entity for each of character!

FIG. 6.10

The Symbol dialog box is a welcome feature for authors coding in languages other than English.

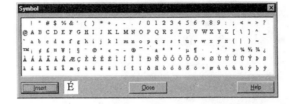

Comments are notes or instructions to other HTML authors who are reviewing or editing your documents. Comments appear in the HTML source code but are not rendered by a browser. To place a comment into one of your documents, select Insert, Comment and type in the comment text into the dialog box. FrontPage Express displays comments in color and with the word "Comment:" in front of them.

The other helpful menu is, of course, the Format menu. Choose Format, Font to call up the dialog box you see in Figure 6.11. On the Font tab of this dialog box, you can set a whole host of different font attributes including face, size, color, and effects. The Special Styles tab (see Figure 6.12) is home to a number of styles supported by HTML. Many of these styles are called logical styles because they denote what the text means rather than say how the text should look. You can also apply the blinking style from this tab, and you can set up superscripts and subscripts by using the Vertical Position option.

FIG. 6.11

With the Font tab of the Font dialog box, you can change several typographical attributes simultaneously.

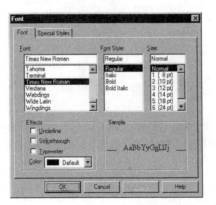

Part

I

Ch

6

Select Format, Paragraph to open a dialog box from which you can select a standard paragraph style or one of six heading styles. You can simultaneously choose the alignment you want to apply as well by using the drop-down list near the bottom of the dialog box. The Extended button enables you to add your own attributes to the HTML tags that control the paragraph format that you are applying.

FIG. 6.12

The Special Styles tab provides support for other useful HTML style instructions that don't have a home elsewhere.

If you don't like the standard bulleted and numbered list styles, you can choose the Format, Bullets and Numbering option to gain access to different types of bulleted and numbered lists. Figure 6.13 shows the Numbered tab of the List Properties dialog box in which you can choose numbers, upper- or lowercase letters, or upper- or lowercase Roman numerals for your numbering scheme. You can even choose to start numbering at a value other than 1.

FIG. 6.13

You can choose variations on bulleted and numbered lists in the List Properties dialog box.

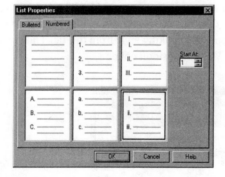

What you've learned in the past few sections is more than enough to get you started with simple text markup with FrontPage Express. One other tip to keep in mind as you format text is to use FrontPage Express's context-sensitive right-click menus. For example, if you highlight a piece of text and right-click your mouse on it, you'll see a menu pop up next to the text that gives you quick access to font and paragraph properties. The same holds true for right-clicking lists and horizontal lines as well.

Adding Graphics and Links

Lots of text gets boring pretty quickly, so you'll need to be able to do more with FrontPage Express than just format text if you want your pages to be engaging. One very popular way to add variety to Web documents is to place images on them, and FrontPage Express makes it very simple to do this.

To put a graphic on a page, click the Insert Image button on the Standard Toolbar or choose Insert, Image. Either technique will call up a dialog box with which you can browse for the image file on a local drive or download the image from another server on the Web. Once you tell FrontPage Express where to get the image, it retrieves it and places it at the cursor position on the page (see Figure 6.14).

CAUTION

Be careful about downloading graphics from the Web to use on your pages. You should secure permission from the owner of the graphic first so that you don't risk copyright infringements.

FIG. 6.14

FrontPage Express drops images right onto the page you're composing.

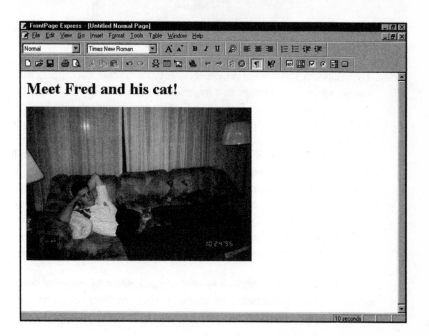

Once the image is in place, you can alter how the image is presented by right-clicking it and selecting the Image Properties option from the pop-up menu that appears. This menu takes you to the Image Properties dialog box you see in Figure 6.15. For a regular image, the General and Appearance tabs will be most useful to you. On the General tab, you can change the image source file and specify a low-resolution version of the image or text alternative for the image. If you're going to use the image as a hyperlink anchor, you can even set up the URL of the linked document on the General tab. You can adjust border size, the amount of space around the image, and alignment properties from the Appearances tab.

N O T E Use the Video tab to set up an Audio Video Interleave (AVI) video clip. Internet Explorer has inline support to display AVI video. ■

Part

I

Ch

6

FIG. 6.15
You can modify an image's presentation by adjusting the settings in the Image Properties dialog box.

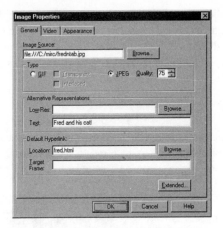

Hyperlinks in a document provide connections to other documents with related content. You can set up text or an image as a hyperlink anchor so that when users click the anchor, their browsers load the linked document. Setting up a hyperlink with FrontPage Express is easy to do, thanks to the Create or Edit Hyperlink button on the Standard toolbar. To make text into a hyperlink anchor, simply highlight the text and click the toolbar button. What you see next is the dialog box shown in Figure 6.16. Depending on where you want to link, you select one of the tabs in the dialog box. The Open Files tab shows a list of files you have open in FrontPage Express at the time and is useful if you're working on several related pages simultaneously. If you're linking to a document on another server, choose the World Wide Web tab and enter the URL of the document in the field you see there. If you're linking to a page you haven't created yet, choose the New Page tab and give the new page a title and a file name. FrontPage Express will create the new page and keep it open so you can finish it later.

N O T E   To set up an image as a hyperlink anchor, highlight the image and then click the Create or Edit Hyperlink button. The options you see in the dialog box are the same as those for setting up text as a hyperlink anchor. ■

FIG. 6.16
With FrontPage Express, you can link to other open FrontPage Express files, documents on the Web, and files that you haven't even created yet!

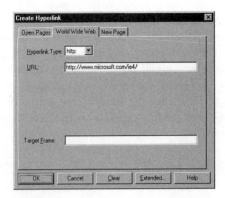

Saving and Publishing with the Web Publishing Wizard

As you work on a document, you should periodically save your work so that you don't lose it to a computer crash or a power outage. To do this, choose File, Save As to reveal the Save As dialog box. The first thing you're asked for is a title for your document and a publishing location. Because you're probably not ready to publish the whole document when you save it the first time, click the As File button instead and navigate to the folder where you want to save your work. As you continue to develop the page, choose File, Save regularly to record your changes to the file.

Once your document is ready to go out on the Web, you'll want to avail yourself of FrontPage Express's publishing capabilities. To do this, choose File, Save As and specify the URL under which you want to save the document. FrontPage Express will then ask whether you want to save the document and any of its dependencies to the current FrontPage Web.

After you confirm the save operation, FrontPage Express will launch the Microsoft Web Publishing Wizard (see Figure 6.17). The wizard will walk you through all of the steps necessary including:

- Choosing which Web server you want to publish on and giving it a name with which you can reference it
- Selecting your service provider
- Verifying your connection information
- Logging you on to the remote server and transferring the file

NOTE When choosing a service provider, you'll find that the Wizard provides a list of ISPs that Microsoft has a partnership arrangement with, but you can configure your own ISP by choosing the Other Internet Provider option. You can choose a dial-up Internet connection or, if you're in a corporate setting, a LAN connection. ■

Part
I

Ch
6

FIG. 6.17
The Microsoft Web Publishing Wizard takes the hassle out of up-loading finished Web documents to a remote server.

Quick Start:
NetMeeting

Until the release of personal Internet conferencing tools, such as Microsoft NetMeeting, just about the only way to communicate with other Internet users in real-time was through Internet Relay Chat (IRC). While IRC remained a viable solution for instant Internet communication for years, text-based communication can only take you so far. Using IRC for collaboration and file sharing did work, but it was complicated and, not very effective. NetMeeting takes real-time Internet communication to a whole new level by combining three different ways of communicating with advanced collaboration features, such as application sharing and Whiteboarding. Best of all, NetMeeting is a free application that you can download at your convenience from Microsoft's Web site on the Internet. ■

Download and install NetMeeting

Find out how to download NetMeeting from Microsoft's Web site and install it on your system.

Use the power of the Internet Locator Service (ILS)

Always know who you're connecting to an ILS directory, which allows you to make available your personal information to other NetMeeting users, while also being able to see their own.

Communicate with others in a variety of ways

NetMeeting allows you to exchange information in real-time with others through text, audio, and video.

Extend your computer's reach

Application sharing, whiteboarding, and file transfer enable you to work with others as though you were next to them.

Up and Running with NetMeeting

Before you can begin installing and using NetMeeting, you need to meet a few system requirements before anything else can happen. Though the requirements are not anything exotic, you will need to meet them to use NetMeeting to its fullest potential. You will need:

- 486DX/2 66 MHz or better computer
- 16M or more of system RAM
- 8M free space on your hard disk
- Sound card (full-duplex is best) and speakers

Video conferencing is possible in the current release of NetMeeting, if you have a video camera to take advantage of it. The Connectix QuickCam is the perfect low-cost choice for you, if you want to try out video conferencing on the Internet. The QuickCam does not require special hardware, such as a video capture card, has a relatively low cost, and is supported by Windows NT 4.0. The black and white unit sells for about $100 and the color model starts at $200. Either model is a great choice for use in conjunction with NetMeeting.

Downloading NetMeeting from the NetMeeting Web Site

You can freely download NetMeeting from the Internet, barring any connection charges. To download the most current version of the software, point your Web browser to the NetMeeting home page at **http://www.microsoft.com/netmeeting**. You can find any product updates, new releases, and documentation at this site, so make sure you check back, periodically.

N O T E The full installation of Internet Explorer 4 includes Microsoft NetMeeting, and it is also possible to download it from the Internet Explorer 4 component download Web page. How to do this will be shown in Chapter 12, "In-Depth: NetMeeting." In this chapter, you'll find out how to download the program separately from the NetMeeting Web site.

▶ **See** "Installing NetMeeting with the Active Setup Wizard" to find out how to automatically download and install NetMeeting with Internet Explorer 4's Active Setup Wizard, **p. 202**

Once you reach the NetMeeting home page, just look for the download hypertext link, and you will be led through the steps needed to download the self-executing archive containing the latest NetMeeting installation. You should download this file to a directory on your hard drive.

NetMeeting Installation and Setup

After you have completely downloaded NetMeeting to your machine, you can install it. Locate the folder into which you downloaded the NetMeeting self-executing archive and execute it. The installation routine will initialize and prompt you for information. The installation process is very straightforward—unless you want to install NetMeeting in a directory other than the default, you can accept the defaults at all the prompts.

After the installation is complete, a new entry will appear in your Start menu titled Microsoft NetMeeting. Simply select the program icon to begin setting up NetMeeting for use on your computer.

When you launch NetMeeting for the first time, you are led through an initial configuration process. After some informational screens, you will be asked if you'd like to log on to an Internet Locator Service (ILS) directory server (see Figure 7.1). ILS servers allow you to list yourself as running NetMeeting and currently connected to the Internet, and are a great way to make it easier for people to find you online. They also allow you to see who else is currently online.

FIG. 7.1
Choose an existing ILS to begin quickly communicating with NetMeeting.

Next, you are presented with a form to fill out that will become your user profile when listed on a directory server. Remember that other users will see this information, so be careful about the information that you supply. After filling out the form, click Next to continue and you will be asked to choose how you wish to categorize your information: for business use, for personal use, or for adult-only use.

The final initial configuration setting you will be asked to perform is to configure your audio using NetMeeting's Audio Tuning Wizard. At the next screen, you will be prompted to read a short passage aloud so that NetMeeting can successfully test and capture your microphone settings, as shown in Figure 7.2. When you are ready, click the Start Recording button and read the small snippet of text until the test is over. The test only lasts for nine seconds, so you will not be reading very long. Click Next once you have completed the test.

Part
I

Ch
7

FIG. 7.2
NetMeeting must test
your computer's audio
abilities before you can
talk online.

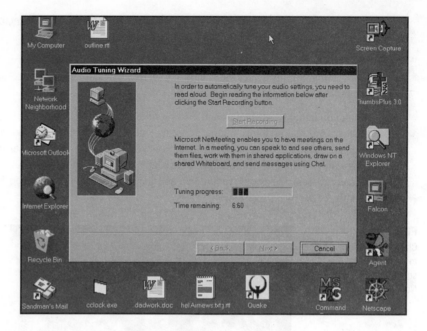

The Basics of Using NetMeeting

When NetMeeting is first launched, there are enough new icons and buttons to thoroughly confuse and puzzle you. Let's take a minute to outline some of the basic functions of the NetMeeting interface, as shown in Figure 7.3.

NetMeetings main toolbar gives you the following buttons:

- **Call** Places an outgoing call to a selected user or from a manually entered address
- **Hang Up** Ends an online conversation by hanging up your end of the line
- **Stop** Ends a connection with the Internet locator service
- **Refresh** Requests a new list of users from the Internet locator service
- **Properties** Enables you to find out more information on a user, that user's connection, and that user's hardware
- **Speed Dial** Connects to an address specified in your Address Book
- **Send Mail** Sends a piece of e-mail to a selected NetMeeting user

In addition to the toolbar buttons, NetMeeting also uses a tabbed interface running down the left side of the screen to allow you to select what is currently displayed in the main window.

FIG. 7.3

NetMeeting's interface puts a wide array of options at your fingertips.

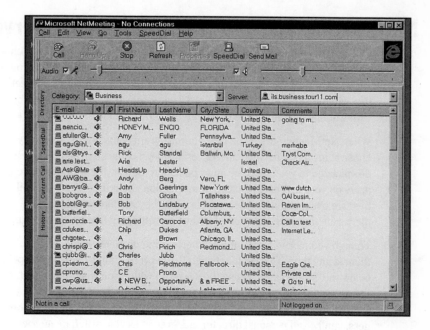

The options there are:

- **Directory**   Enables you to view the users registered in the Internet locator service
- **Speed Dial**   Quickly calls another NetMeeting user who has an entry in this area
- **Current Call**   Provides an area for whiteboarding, text chat, and file transfer for your current conversation
- **History**   Enables you to review past conversations and quickly connect to users with whom you have spoken before

You can adjust your microphone and speaker output with the audio settings below the toolbar. The user window supplies current information depending on the window tab that you have selected.

Most of the functions beneath the various windows mirror the functions of the toolbar and tabs. The Tools menu is very important, however, because it enables you to adjust your audio and video settings and launch the file transfer, application sharing, and whiteboarding sections of the program. You will also set sharing rights and control other NetMeeting options here.

If you need help at any time, simply select the Help menu and choose Help Topics. You may find it useful to switch to the Index portion of the help screen and type in the subject on which you are looking for help. The Contents tab is not as well defined as other Microsoft application help files, though the program functions are probably simple enough for you to figure out on your own.

Part

I

Ch

7

NetMeeting and the Internet Locator Service

One task that you had to perform when setting up NetMeeting was to choose a default Internet Locator Service (ILS) server to log on to when using the program. If you think for a moment about the size of the Internet and the number of users who use NetMeeting, you will realize that without some kind of centralized locator server, you would never be able to find anyone with whom to communicate unless you called someone directly.

When NetMeeting first launches, your program connects automatically to the ILS that you chose at installation. Once the server has been connected, an updated list of logged in users is downloaded to your machine and updated in the viewing window. Once the information appears on your screen, you can get information about users, such as their real names, whether they are using audio or video, and in what they are interested. This information comes from the profile that each user completed when setting up his or her program.

Though you picked a default ILS when setting up NetMeeting, you can switch between all of them at any time. To switch between ILS servers, simply click the drop-down server menu below the Toolbar and choose the server to which you wish to connect. Most choices that you are presented with are Microsoft's own servers for NetMeeting users, though there are others, such as specialized servers hosted by Four11 (**http://www.four11.com**), that include business, family, and personal directories. As soon as you switch to another ILS, your computer will begin receiving the current list of users and all of their information.

N O T E   If you are using NetMeeting on your company's intranet, you may want to think about running your own ILS for your company. This can be a great time-saver when trying to connect to coworkers because an organized directory can help keep a list of active users current. To download your own copy of the ILS server software, point your browser to **http://backoffice. microsoft.com/download/locator.asp**. ▨

Making a Call

You can making a call within NetMeeting in two basic ways—choosing a name from the ILS list or placing a direct call to a specific user.

To call a NetMeeting user who is registered in the ILS server that you are on, simply double-click that user's name. When the initial request goes out, NetMeeting looks to the ILS server to which you are connected to verify that the party that you are calling is currently still connected and not in another meeting. If the desired party is available to speak, a request is sent to it asking whether it will accept a call from you. That party has the choice of accepting or rejecting the call. Don't feel bad if you are rejected. Many new NetMeeting users don't know to label their descriptive information to tell you that they are waiting for a particular connection.

Sometimes, a user who you try to call is already in a NetMeeting conversation. If you send a request to a user already in a conversation, both members of that conversation are asked whether you can join. If both users agree, you become part of a three-way party line in which everyone can hear and see what the other users are saying and doing.

The second way to call a NetMeeting user is to "dial" him or her directly. If you click the call button, you will be prompted with the New Call window, as shown in Figure 7.4.

FIG. 7.4
If you know the desired end user's name, simply enter it in the New Call window and dial.

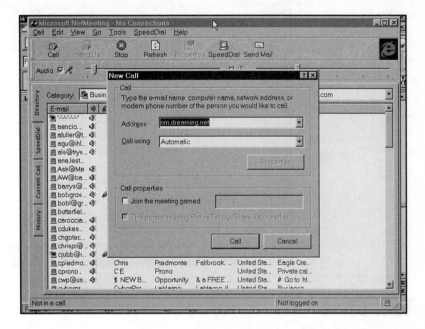

You must enter some kind of address into the New Call window before you can make the call. This address can be an e-mail address, a network address or name, or the phone number of a user's modem. It is also possible to call another directory server, though it is easier to simply connect to the ILS server and select your user from the list. Once you send out the call request, the same process applies for connections on the receiving end. The user can accept or reject your call.

Once your call is accepted or you accept an incoming call, the members of the call will be listed in the Current Call window tab, as shown in Figure 7.5. Their names, audio and video capabilities, and sharing information will all be listed.

Audio Chat

To initiate an audio chat, simply start talking. As long as the user on the receiving end has a sound card, speakers, and a microphone, you should be able to hear each other just fine. If the sound quality is not up to par, you might ask the user to whom you are connected either to raise or to lower the level of his or her microphone settings. Also remember that you are having this conversation over the Internet and low connection speeds will have a great effect on the quality of your conversation.

Part
I

Ch
7

FIG. 7.5
All the members of
your NetMeeting
gathering will appear
in the Current Call
window when you
are connected.

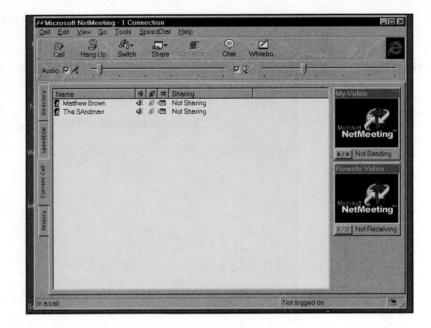

Text Chat

Not all NetMeeting users have audio equipment for vocal conversations. If this happens to you, fret not—you can use text-based chat to communicate your ideas. To begin the chat program, click Tools, Chat. A new chat window will appear on your computer as well as your partner's computer. It will look much like the chat window depicted in Figure 7.6.

Using Chat is simple. Type your comments in the Message line and hit Enter to send them to the other person in your conversation. Whatever you type will appear with your name at the left, and whatever your partner types will appear with his or her name to the left of the message.

Once your text-based chat is over, simply close the Chat window and continue with your next call in NetMeeting. When you close down Chat, remember to tell the other party that you are ending the conversation. Otherwise, that user could be in Chat by him- or herself for a very long time!

Video Conferencing

Video conferencing is more of an automatic function rather than an option. If NetMeeting detects that you have a camera connected to your PC, it will automatically begin transmitting video to your connected party. Your party has total control over whether video (or audio) will be displayed at all, which makes sense because many NetMeeting users are on 28.8 Kbps modem connections and don't have enough Internet bandwidth to handle constantly downloading that much information.

FIG. 7.6
A chat program enables
you to talk to users
without microphones.

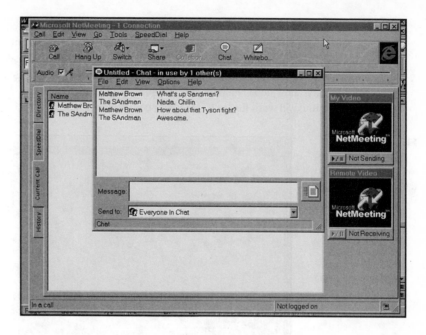

When you use video in a NetMeeting conversation, the video window(s) will appear on the right side of your NetMeeting screen, out of the way of Chat, whiteboarding, and application sharing. A NetMeeting conversation using video is pictured in Figure 7.7.

FIG. 7.7
Adding video to your
NetMeeting conversa-
tions allows for a more
visual meeting over the
Internet.

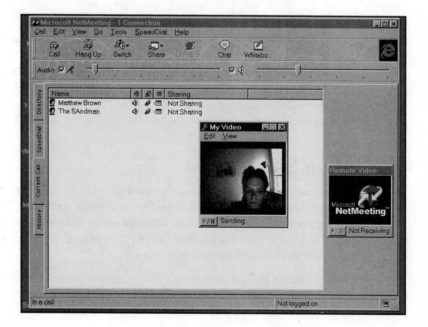

Part
I

Ch
7

If your video does not appear as clearly as you wish it to be, you can adjust the default settings for your equipment. To change your video settings, choose Options from the Tools menu and choose Video, as shown in Figure 7.8. Here you can change when you send and receive video information, how large the video window appears, whether you want faster video or better video quality, and video camera properties such as brightness and hue. Most of the time, your default setting will work fine in NetMeeting conversations as is.

FIG. 7.8
If you're having trouble with your camera, adjust the settings in the Video Options window.

Less than 5 percent of NetMeeting users have a video camera attached to their PCs, so don't be discouraged if you can't find any fellow video users. The number of cameras attached to PCs is growing every day, and someday soon everyone will be able to see you at your best (or worst) in front of your computer.

Application Sharing

One of the most exciting ways that you can allow others to see what you are working on at your local PC is through application sharing. When you share an application, the other members of your conference can actually see exactly what you see as you work in the application. If you choose to collaborate with that application as well, the remote user can control the program as though it was on his or her own machine.

Once you configure application sharing, you can easily share any running application on your hard drive. You must have an application running on your system before you can share it. To share an application, click the Share button on the Toolbar and select the application that you want others to see. Until you click the Collaboration button, end users will not be able to control your application. This is very good if you want to demonstrate how a program works without intervention from other users. If you do want to allow others to control your application, simply click the Collaboration button on the Toolbar. The other members of your discussion will then be able to fully control every aspect of that program. Figure 7.9 demonstrates sharing Windows Explorer with a NetMeeting client.

FIG. 7.9
You can share any application that is running on your computer with any NetMeeting user.

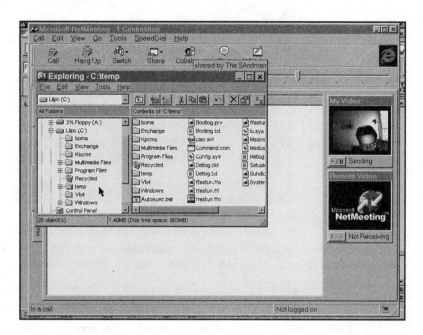

CAUTION
When you share an application and click the Collaboration button, the end user has complete control over the application that you are sharing. They can, in essence, perform any function in your application that you can normally achieve locally on your computer. Think about this the next time you decide to share your disk formatting utility with someone!

Whiteboarding

Whiteboarding enables two or more users to work on an electronic sketchpad simultaneously. This is a great tool for brainstorming remotely or simply creating basic artwork. When you start the Whiteboarding program by choosing Tools, Whiteboard, a blank whiteboard program appears on your screen, as well as on the remote user's screen. The Whiteboard application looks and acts much like Windows Paint, with tools such as pens, squares, rectangles, and a large color palate from which to choose. The basic Whiteboard application is pictured in Figure 7.10.

Part
I

Ch
7

FIG. 7.10
Whiteboarding enables
two remote users to
share the same
drawing board.

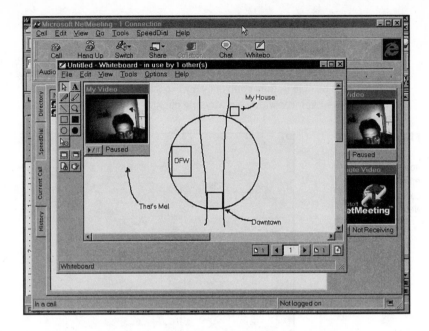

Once you load the whiteboard application, you can begin collaborating right away. Remember that audio chat is still active, so you can talk while you work. There are many uses for whiteboarding; the following list presents just a few ideas:

- **Brainstorming** List your ideas on the same document at the same time
- **Maps** Walk your friends through exactly how to get to a specific location
- **Graffiti Wall** Have everyone in your NetMeeting chat express him- or herself with art
- **Illustrating Ideas** Show others exactly what you mean on all their screens
- **Sharing/Whiteboarding** Share an application and make notes at the same time

File Transfer

The last of NetMeeting's major function is the File Transfer application. Suppose you were connected to another NetMeeting user and you wanted to send a file that you were working on to him or her. One way that you could do it would be to attach the file to an e-mail document and hope that your recipient received it before your conversation ended. You could also start up a separate file transfer process using an FTP application, but this might adversely affect the quality of your conferencing connection through NetMeeting. With NetMeeting, however, you can also initiate its own File Transfer application and send the desired file immediately.

To use File Transfer to move a file between NetMeeting users, follow these steps:

1. Click Tools, File Transfer, Send File. The standard Windows file window will appear, enabling you to select the file that you wish to send.

2. Select a file to send and click Send. The file will be sent immediately.

When a user receives a file that you send, he or she is prompted by a window asking him or her if he or she wants to open the file, close the file (for saving), or delete the file. This enables the end recipient absolute control over files he or she receives. ●

In-Depth Section

CHAPTER 8

In-Depth: Internet Explorer 4

Microsoft has been a player in the Web browser arena for a short time—their first serious entry, Internet Explorer 3, was released more than a year ago. In spite of this brief history in Web and Internet software, however, their latest Web browser release, Internet Explorer 4, represents the latest and greatest of technologies and capabilities for looking at information on the World Wide Web. Internet Explorer supports more technologies and more Internet standards than any other Web browser on the market today.

Though Internet Explorer is very easy to use, and you can start browsing the Web as soon as you install it and establish an Internet connection, there are also many ways to configure the browser. You can set up your own links and buttons to go to your favorite sites, download Web sites and view them offline, and configure many other options so that the browser works the way *you* want it to work. ■

Learn how to install and update Internet Explorer

Microsoft has included an Active Setup Wizard to ease the process of initially installing Internet Explorer, as well as updating its components with new versions when they become available.

See how Internet Explorer implements standard Web features

Internet Explorer supports all the features you have come to expect when using the Web: text, graphics, multimedia content, and other advanced Web technologies.

Take an in-depth look at how to use Internet Explorer

Internet Explorer comes configured so that, once you are connected to the Internet, you can use it right "out of the box." But, it also includes many features and options that you can use to configure it to work exactly as you want.

Get started with Internet Explorer's advanced features

Internet Explorer 4 supports a number of new and advanced features, such as Smart Favorites, Channels, and Security Zones. You can start learning about these features in this chapter, and they will be covered in greater depth in their own chapters.

Installing the Internet Explorer 4 Suite

In Chapter 3, "Quick Start: Internet Explorer 4," you learned how to install the Internet Explorer suite of applications from the self-executing archive file that you can download, either from Microsoft or from a number of other sources on the Internet. That is certainly the quickest way to get Internet Explorer up and running on your system. Because of the speed with which Web applications tend to change these days (Internet Explorer 3 went through three releases in the first year it came out), however, it is likely that you will eventually want to download either the Internet Explorer 4 Web browser or one of its components from the Web.

Fortunately, Microsoft has begun a new system for making this process a lot easier, through their Active Setup Wizard. Now, instead of completely downloading a 14-2M archive file even to begin the installation process, you can download a 500K or so application that will run the Active Setup Wizard.

The purpose of the Active Setup Wizard is to analyze your system and automatically determine what Internet Explorer components have newer versions than those you have installed on your system. To do this, you only need to download the Wizard itself, establish your Internet connection, and execute the Wizard.

Obviously, you will eventually need to download from the Internet or the Web all the software that you need to have installed—installing the complete Internet Explorer 4 suite of applications can take quite a long time over a dial-up connection. By creating and enabling you to use the Active Setup Wizard, however, Microsoft has made it easier for you to only download the applications that you need, saving you time and making your time on the Web more efficient.

The steps in using the Active Desktop Wizard follow:

1. Once you have downloaded the Wizard, establish your Internet connection and execute the Wizard.

2. The Wizard will start and guide you through the process of downloading the Internet Explorer 4 suite and installing it, either in full or in part (see Figure 8.1).

FIG. 8.1
Microsoft's Active Setup Wizard enables you to download and install components of the Internet Explorer 4 suite automatically.

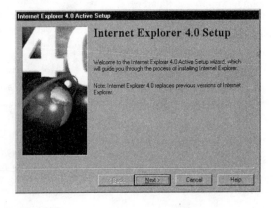

3. The Active Setup Wizard will ask you a series of questions regarding the options you wish to include in your download. If you don't have any version of Internet Explorer on your system, you will be given the option of downloading the following installations of the suite:

- **Minimum**   This installation includes a minimum set of applications you need to use the Internet Explorer 4 Web browser.

- **Standard**   The standard installation adds a few other components to the minimum set, most notably the Outlook Express Mail and News client.

- **Full**   The full installation contains all the components of the Internet Explorer 4 suite.

TIP If your initial installation is over the Web (not from the CD-ROM installation), choose the Minimal or Standard installation. Doing so will get you up and running as soon as possible, and you can always add components later.

4. If this is not your first installation, the Active Setup Wizard will analyze your system and then check the Microsoft Web site to see whether there are any new versions of the Internet Explorer 4 components that are more recent than those installed on your machine. You will have the option of downloading just those new components or of downloading and installing all the components (see Figure 8.2).

FIG. 8.2

You can save connection time on the Internet by downloading only the software components that you need.

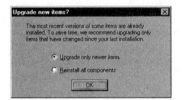

By being able to download and install components that are already on your machine, you can recover those components if any of the files necessary to run them become corrupted.

5. After the download procedure has finished, you will need to reboot your machine to complete the installation.

Getting Connected

In addition to Internet Explorer, you only need one more thing to get started on the Web: an Internet connection. If you already have a connection to the Internet, either through an Internet Service Provider (ISP) or a permanent connection to the Internet (such as through a corporate local area network, or LAN), there is nothing else you need to do.

If you need to establish your first Internet connection, it gets a little more complicated. The number and quality of ISPs available to you will depend very strongly on where you live—it varies greatly, depending on the part of the country or the world in which you live. If you are not familiar with what ISPs are available in your area, a few good resources might be the Yellow Pages, the business or computer section of your local newspaper, or good old-fashioned word-of-mouth from friends or colleagues in your area who already have ISPs.

As shown in Chapter 3, "Quick Start: Internet Explorer 4," though, there is another alternative—using Microsoft's Internet Connection Wizard to lead you through the process of finding and setting up an account with a local or national provider of Internet service. This wizard will connect you to a referral service run by Microsoft, using your modem and a toll-free number, and will suggest a number of recommended ISPs in your area. If you would like to find out more information about this process, see that chapter, or Appendix A, "Getting Online."

▶ **See** "If You Don't Have a Connection Set Up," **p. 32**

▶ **See** "Types of Services," **p. 620**

Features of the Internet Explorer 4 Browser

The best way to experience all the capabilities of the Internet Explorer 4 Web browser is to use it. Plenty of demos are on the Microsoft Web site and throughout the Web and the Internet that showcase the capabilities of this browser. Also, throughout this book, you will get an up-close and personal look at the different things that you can do with the browser.

What follows is an overview of the many different features of the browser, highlighting its support of many standard aspects of HTML, as well as new technologies. Many of these capabilities are discussed in their own chapters elsewhere in this book—this will be noted, where appropriate. The other features will be discussed more fully later in this chapter.

■ **HTML 3.2 and 4.0**   Internet Explorer 4 fully supports the current HTML standard, HTML 3.2, as well as the proposed standard, HTML 4.0.

You can read more about Internet Explorer's HTML support in the chapters that are part of this book's Webmaster section.

■ **Multimedia content**   As with Internet Explorer 3, this version of Microsoft's Web browser includes full support for many kinds of multimedia. In addition to the standard support for text and GIF and JPEG graphics, Internet Explorer 4 supports XPM, BMP, and PNG graphics, as well as inline AVI animations. In addition, it directly supports AU, WAV, and MID sound files. Through its support for ActiveX Controls, such as Microsoft's own ActiveMovie Control, Internet Explorer 4 can also be used to view a much wider range of multimedia content, such as QuickTime and MPEG movies, and sound in many other formats.

■ **Configurability**   Through its menus and options dialog boxes, Internet Explorer 4 enables you to configure it to work the way you'd like it to. You have full control over the

browser's security arrangements, default colors and fonts, toolbar and menu arrangements, and many other things. It even enables you to use a client-side style sheet to
format incoming text exactly as you want it.

■ **Ease of Use**   Internet Explorer 4 includes a number of new features, different than its
predecessor and competing Web browsers, that make using it much easier. These
features include Explorer Bars, which divide the Web browser window into two sections,
enabling you to manipulate the browser while immediately seeing the results. Another
very handy feature is Autocomplete, which will try to automatically complete URLs and
local document filenames when you begin to type them into the Address Bar.

■ **Offline Browsing**   Virtually all Web browsers download HTML documents and their
accompanying images, sounds, and other pieces into a cache on your local hard drive
during the course of viewing and presenting them to you. Often, however, it is hard to
determine what documents are in your own cache. Internet Explorer 4's offline browsing
features make it very easy for you to browse through files that you have in your cache,
allowing you to work through the Web browser without an active connection to the Web.

■ **Companion applications**   Similar to the Netscape Communicator package, the various
installations of Internet Explorer 4 are bundled with different combinations of companion applications to complement the capabilities of the Web browser and one another. As
with Communicator, it is possible to use these applications together and to call one from
another. Internet Explorer also enables you to specify other applications to perform
these functions, thus not requiring you to use their programs.

Some of the applications that might be bundled with Internet Explorer 4, depending on
what installation you have, follow (each of these applications is described with chapters
in the Quick Start and In-Depth sections of this book):

- **Outlook Express Mail and News**   This application is Microsoft's latest Internet
  Mail and News client, allowing you to access multiple Mail and News accounts.

- **NetMeeting**   NetMeeting is Microsoft's free application for Internet
  conferencing. It supports Internet standard methods for audio and video
  conferencing and also allows multiperson chat and shared whiteboard.

  One most impressive feature of NetMeeting is its capability of sharing applications
  across the Internet, even if the person with whom you are conferencing doesn't
  have the application. For instance, if you are in a conference with someone on the
  other side of the world, you can start Microsoft Excel on your machine and
  configure NetMeeting to share that application. Then, the other person can take
  control of the application and actually work with it from his or her location.

- **FrontPage Express**   FrontPage Express (formerly known as FrontPad) is a
  subset of the FrontPage application. FrontPage Express gives you the ability to
  create and edit Web pages and HTML documents without requiring you to know
  any HTML.

■ **Advanced technologies**   One of the most impressive features of Internet Explorer 4 is the many different technologies that is supports. Not only does it support existing technologies, such as Netscape's JavaScript and Plug-Ins, Sun's Java, and Internet standards (current or proposed) like Cascading Style Sheets and Dynamic HTML, it also adds support for Microsoft's own Visual Basic scripting language and ActiveX Controls. The full list of advanced technologies supported by Internet Explorer 4, which I will discuss in the last half of the Webmaster section of this book, follows:

- **Scripting Languages**   Internet Explorer 4 supports Microsoft's own Visual Basic Scripting Edition (VBScript), and JScript, which is its implementation of Netscape's JavaScript language.

- **Java Applets, Navigator Plug-Ins, and ActiveX Controls**   By including support for Java applets, Netscape Navigator plug-ins, and ActiveX Controls, Internet Explorer 4 is able to correctly view and fully render more Web pages than any other browser available today. In fact, the Java Virtual Machine that Microsoft has developed for Internet Explorer allows the browser to execute Java applets faster than any other browser, as well.

- **Cascading Style Sheets**   Before the advent of cascading style sheets, Web authors only had limited control over how their pages were rendered on their user's Web browser. The client browsers had a lot of control and leeway over how pages could be presented. That all changes with cascading style sheets.

   With cascading style sheets, you can specify exactly how your Web pages will be rendered on compatible browsers (and, because Netscape Navigator 4 also supports this standard, there are many compatible browsers). This specification includes controlling fonts and font sizes, colors, and precise positioning of Web page elements with respect to one another.

- **Dynamic HTML**   Dynamic HTML is the term used to indicate that all contents of a Web page, when viewed by a compatible browser, can be changed dynamically. Before Dynamic HTML, only a subset of Web page elements could be dynamically changed—Java applets, for instance, and HTML forms. With Dynamic HTML and a compatible browser, you can change anything on a Web page dynamically in response to user actions, such as mouse movement or mouse button clicks, or any of a number of other inputs. This capability increases the amount of interactivity possible without requiring further communication with a Web server.

■ **Operating system and application integration**   The single most striking feature of Internet Explorer 4 is the integration of its Web and Internet features into the Windows 95 operating system and other applications. This integration makes using your local system more like browsing the Web. It also makes many of your Web capabilities, such as initiating searches or accessing your Favorites, accessible from the Explorer, the Taskbar, and the Start Menu.

This integration is discussed in greater depth in the Quick Start and In-Depth chapters on the Active Desktop and Web Integration.

■ **Security** Microsoft has gotten a lot of bad press because of security problems that have been discovered in its products. Microsoft is obviously trying to tread a fine line between providing maximum capability to its customers while also being as safe as possible. To that end, Internet Explorer 4 supports a number of features to address the security problem, including code signing, personal and site certificates, and security zones.

You can find out all about the security features of Internet Explorer 4 by reading Chapter 16, "In-Depth: Security."

Navigating the World Wide Web

As you would expect, Internet Explorer supports all the standard ways of navigating around the World Wide Web and throws in some advanced features of its own. In general, the ways of navigating on the Web fall into two categories—either through the document you are viewing or through your Web browser. Internet Explorer 4 supports all the methods that are used to include hypertext links in Web pages; predominantly, links that use text and graphics anchors (see Figure 8.3), but also including server- and client-side imagemaps, scripts, Java applets, and server-based methods.

FIG. 8.3
Text and graphics are the most common anchors that Web authors can include in their Web pages; Internet Explorer 4 supports these and the less common anchors as well.

The navigational aids that Internet Explorer 4 supports that you can set up include the following:

■ **Navigation Buttons, Keys, and Menus** Internet Explorer 4 has toolbar buttons, shortcut keys, and menu options for performing simple navigational tasks. The functions that are generally used most often are Back and Forward, which load documents that you visited before and after the current document.

- **Search Engines**   Another very common tool used to navigate on the Web is one of the many Web search engines. Internet Explorer 4 provides special support for these search engines through their Search Explorer Bar, which I will describe later in this chapter.

- **Favorites**   Microsoft's Favorites are analogous to Netscape's Bookmarks—they are a way for you to remember the URL of Web sites that you think you might want to see again. Again, Internet Explorer 4 adds capabilities beyond what were present in Internet Explorer 3, giving you greater ability to sort the Favorites and, through Smart Favorites and Subscriptions, automatically giving you ways to keep track of site changes.

Using the Toolbars

When you first load and execute Internet Explorer 4, if you are familiar with previous versions of Internet Explorer or even with Netscape Navigator, nothing about the Web browser will immediately leap out at you. The most prominent feature of the Web browser, its toolbars and menu, look quite similar to previous versions and other browsers.

As shown in Figure 8.4, however, there are at least a few differences. Internet Explorer 4 supports three distinct toolbars: the Standard Toolbar, Address Bar, and Links Bar.

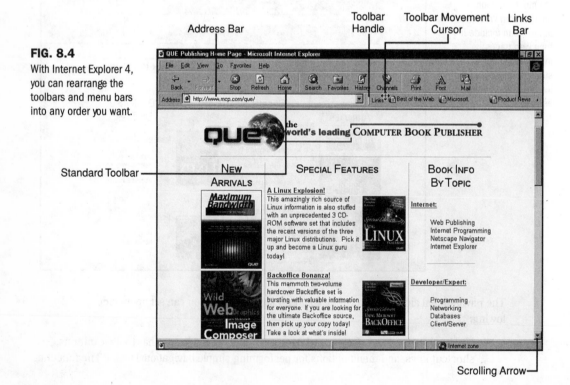

FIG. 8.4
With Internet Explorer 4, you can rearrange the toolbars and menu bars into any order you want.

In Figure 8.4 you will notice the handles included on each toolbar. By clicking the handle on any given toolbar and dragging the toolbar around, you can rearrange the order of the toolbars. Additionally, you can stack multiple toolbars on one line. In this case, the handles also enable you to slide the toolbars back and forth, revealing more or less of each. Whenever the contents of a toolbar are not fully visible, a scrolling arrow appears; clicking the arrow scrolls the contents of the toolbar in that direction to reveal the hidden elements.

Standard Toolbar

Internet Explorer's Standard Toolbar has three distinct sets of buttons that the user controls that you probably will use the most when running the Web browser. These three categories of buttons follow:

- **Navigational** The five navigational buttons enable you to go back and forth through viewed Web pages, stop the current page from loading, refresh the current page, or load your Home Page (also referred to by Microsoft occasionally as your Start Page).

 If the download of the current Web page has stalled, you can sometimes successfully load it by hitting the Stop followed by the Refresh button.

- **Explorer Bar** These four buttons give you access to the four Internet Explorer Explorer Bars, which are described a little later in this chapter.
- **Miscellaneous** The last set of buttons on the Standard Toolbar controls some miscellaneous functions, such as printing the current Web page, changing its base font size, or calling your Mail or News client program.

Address Bar

Internet Explorer's File, Open menu option is one way in which you can enter an URL or local filename to be loaded into the Web browser window. You can also do this by typing **Ctrl+O**. A more common way of entering the location of a desired document is by entering it into the Address Bar.

The Address Bar actually serves two purposes. First, the Address Bar will always display the URL or filename of the document currently loaded into the Web browser. You can also use it to enter new location information. The Address Bar of Internet Explorer 4 can interpret either URLs or file names. For instance, to view my Home Page as it exists on the Web, you would enter

```
http://www.rpi.edu/~odonnj
```

into your Web browser. If I want to view the local copy of my Web page, I can enter the following into the Address Bar:

```
F:\Home Page\index.html
```

Microsoft has also added a few features to the Address Bar to make the process of going to Web pages a little easier, particularly when it's a page that you have viewed at some point previously.

Drop-Down List   Instead of entering an URL into the Address Bar, you can click the down arrow button at its right. Doing so gives you access to a drop-down list that will show you one of two things. If the document you are currently viewing is on the Internet, the drop-down list will include the URLs of recently viewed Web pages. To go back to one of those pages, simply select it from the drop-down list.

If you are viewing a local document, accessing the drop-down list will instead reveal a Windows Explorer-like list of the hard drive directory structure. Using this interface, you can browse to and load any document on your local system.

Autocomplete   Another very useful feature of the new Address Bar is called Autocomplete. Whenever you enter an URL into the Address Bar, Internet Explorer will attempt to automatically complete the URL based on its list of previously viewed pages. For instance, if you have visited a number of Web pages and want to go to the Microsoft Web site, you can click the mouse in the Address Bar and start typing the URL of Microsoft's Home Page. Assuming you have visited it sometime in the past, once you get to the point of having typed `http://www.m`, with perhaps a few more letters—enough to uniquely identify the URL from others you have visited—the rest of the URL will automatically appear.

If you are entering a filename from your local system, Autocomplete also works. Because the complete contents of your local system are known to Internet Explorer, however, it will attempt to automatically complete the filename of any document on your local system, whether you have viewed it previously or not.

Links Bar

With the Links Bar, you can set up a number of buttons that give you instant access to a small number of Web pages. By default, Internet Explorer 4 comes configured so that these buttons take you to places within the Microsoft or Microsoft Network Web sites. You can add and remove buttons, however, and so customize where the buttons will send you.

Some common uses for establishing buttons on the Links Bar are buttons to give you an easy way to get to any frequently accessed Web site. A Web site that you consult to get the weather or whatever news, the Home Page of a friend or of a particular company, or even a local document might interest you. You can set up buttons on the Links Bar to cause any of these sites to immediately load into the Web browser window. You add and remove buttons through a special folder in the Favorites hierarchy; how to do this will be discussed in the Favorites Explorer Bar section later in this chapter.

Using Internet Explorer's Explorer Bars

With Internet Explorer 4, Microsoft has added a useful new feature to its browser that it is calling Explorer Bars. Explorer Bars give you easier access to some of Internet Explorer's features and make some common tasks a lot easier.

What exactly is a Explorer Bar? An Explorer Bar is Microsoft's term for a dedicated panel on which you can toggle that is used to give you access to one of a number of different features. When the Explorer Bar is enabled, it occupies a panel on the left of the browser window as the bulk of the window, to the right of it, continues to display the current Web page. By being able to view these two items simultaneously, it is easier to find the content you want on the Web.

Web Searches with the Search Explorer Bar

Clicking the Search toolbar button toggles the Search Explorer Bar, shown in Figure 8.5. This button will load Microsoft's "All-in-One" search page into the Explorer Bar, giving you access to a number of the most popular search engines on the Web. You can simply enter the keywords for which you want to search, select the desired search engine, and click the Search button.

> **CAUTION**
>
> Most Web search engines enable you to enter either "simple" or "advanced" queries. The simple queries tend to look the same for each search engine, with a few differences, but the advanced queries can look significantly different for each.
>
> The type of query available from Microsoft's all-in-one search page for each of the listed search engines is generally a simple one. If you need to use more advanced capabilities of any of the search engines, you need to go directly to their Web site using the main browser window (as opposed to using the Search Explorer Bar).

FIG. 8.5
Microsoft's "All-in-One" search engine page gives you convenient access to many of the most popular search engines.

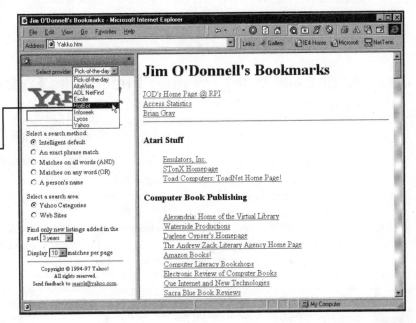

Search Engine drop-down list

After you conduct your first search using the Explorer Bar, you begin to see how convenient it is. Using a conventional browser and search engine, a typical session in which you search for something might consist of the following steps:

1. Browse to the Web search engine that you would like to use (many browsers have a Search toolbar button that either goes to a specific search engine or that you can configure to go to your preferred one).

2. Enter your search parameters into the search engine input form and start the search.

3. The search engine will then show you a page showing the results of your search in your Web browser window. Quite often, only the first results page of several (or many) will be shown.

4. You can then try to find your desired page. Click one of the hypertext links on the search engine results page, and that page will load into your Web browser window.

5. If the loaded page is what you need to find, you're done! If not, press the Back button to return to the results page.

6. Repeat steps 4 and 5, going back and forth from the search engine results page(s), until you find what you want.

Until now, this is how the search process has always proceeded. Having no alternative, you might not even have realized that there might be a better way. Internet Explorer 4's Search Explorer Bar just might be that better way.

If you repeat the preceding process using the Search Explorer Bar, there is one important difference. As long as the Explorer Bar is displayed, there is no need to jump back and forth between a search results page and the Web pages shown. As shown in Figure 8.6, with both of these present, the search results and the Web browser, you can go through the results and easily call them up until you find the information you want.

Manipulating and Using Favorites Through the Explorer Bar

Similar to the Search Explorer Bar, the Favorites Explorer Bar displays your current favorites in a panel along the right side of the Web browser window. The Favorites Explorer Bar displays the hierarchy of all of your favorites, and gives you the following abilities:

- Select a Favorite to load and display into your Web browser window.

- Organize your Favorites. You can do this in the Favorites Explorer Bar by clicking and dragging a Favorite and moving it into the desired position.

N O T E   It is through organizing your Favorites—either through this Explorer Bar, the Favorites menu, or through the Explorer—that you can configure the Links Bar of Internet Explorer 4. To do this, drag Favorites into the Links folder in the Favorites hierarchy. ■

T I P   When setting up Favorites to be displayed as buttons on the Links Bar, give them short but descriptive names to increase the number of buttons that you can display.

FIG. 8.6

When the search engine results and Web browsing window are both present, it is a lot easier to go through the results.

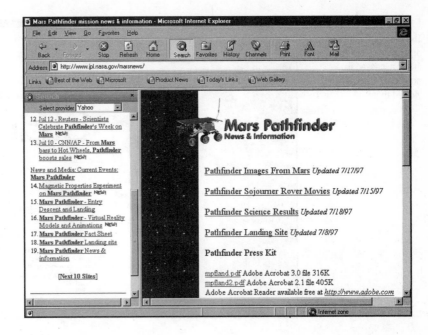

■ Operate on the Favorites, doing things like renaming them or changing their URLs. To do this, right-click the URL and select one of the options from the pop-up menu; for example, Rename or Properties.

■ Create Subscriptions to items on your Favorites list.

You can read a little more on Favorites later in this chapter, and for a complete treatment, consult Chapter 14, "In-Depth: Smart Favorites."

An Organized History with the History Explorer Bar

Just about every Web browser maintains a history list of Web pages and other documents that you have viewed, and many times copies of the pages themselves are stored locally on your system. In previous versions of Internet Explorer, you were able to access a History window that displayed all the complete history of Web pages you had viewed over during the previous number of days (and you could configure the number of days).

In Internet Explorer 4, the new History Explorer Bar gives you a more manageable way of approaching your History list. As shown in Figure 8.7, Internet Explorer 4 organizes your history of accessed Web pages within the Explorer Bar in the order in which you looked at them. The pages viewed within the last week are organized by day and those previous to that are shown by week.

FIG. 8.7
The History Explorer Bar organizes your history list of accessed files according to when you viewed them.

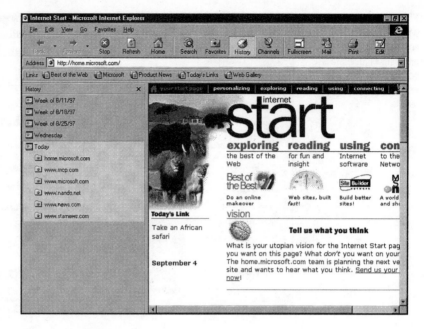

Surfing the Channels Explorer Bar

The final Explorer Bar included in Internet Explorer 4 is the one dedicated to showing you some of the channels that are available to you through the Web browser. In short, a channel is a Web site that is specially set up to be *pushed* onto your computer through an Internet connection, allowing you to set your computer to automatically receive content from across the Web.

You can find out much more about this exciting new technology in Chapter 21, "Premium Channels," later in this book.

Internet Explorer Menus

As I mentioned earlier in this chapter, Internet Explorer 4, once installed, is ready to go and is ready to allow you to start browsing the Web. It does include a large number of menus that allow you to access its features, however, and that allow you to configure it for optimal use.

The Internet Explorer Web browser includes six menus: File, Edit, View, Go, Favorites, and Help. These six menus support the following categories of functions:

■ **File**   The File menu supports such standard Windows 95 functions as the ability to open and close documents, print them, and exit the application. An option in this menu also allows you to work offline.

- ■ **Edit** The entries in the Edit menu are pretty standard, consisting primarily of the normal Cut, Copy, Paste, Select All, and Find options, which function as you would expect in a Windows 95 application. (Note that the find option is used to look for text on the current Web page, not to perform an Internet or Web search.)

- ■ **View** This is the main menu for configuring the appearance of the Web browser and setting its many options.

- ■ **Go** Options in this menu enable you to navigate through the list of Web pages you have viewed during the current session, as well as jump directly to various pages on the Microsoft Web site. Additionally, you can go through this menu to call some of the other applications in the Internet Explorer suite, such as Outlook Express Mail or News, or NetMeeting.

- ■ **Favorites** The Favorites menu gives you the same capabilities that you had through the Favorites Explorer Bar, discussed earlier in this chapter. You can use, rename, and move Favorites, as well as set up subscriptions to them. In addition, this menu, through the Add to Favorites option, provides you with the main way for you to add items to the Favorites.

- ■ **Help** Through this menu, you have access to the online help for Internet Explorer 4, including both local documents placed on your system when you first installed the application and documents located on the Web.

In the rest of this section, you can read about some of the configuration and operation options that you can access through the Internet Explorer menus. The options are also covered in Chapter 13, "In-Depth: Preferences," later in this book.

File

An addition to the File menu in Internet Explorer 4 that wasn't present in previous versions of the browser is the File, Work Offline selection. With this selection, you can view any Web pages that are on your local system, those either in your normal directories or that have been downloaded into your browser's cache. You might not notice any difference between working offline and normal operation, unless you move the mouse over a hypertext link for a Web page that is not on your local system or in your cache. As the mouse cursor changes into the familiar pointing finger, it shows an additional symbol to indicate that you can't follow that link while offline (see Figure 8.8).

If you attempt to follow such a link, Internet Explorer will display the alert box shown in Figure 8.9 and give you the option of either going online to follow the link or continuing to work offline (and ignoring the link).

View

The most important option under this menu is the View, Internet Options menu. When accessing pages on the local drive, the menu will be Folder Options. Selecting this option gives you the tabbed dialog box shown in Figure 8.10. It is through the tabs on this configuration dialog box that you can control most of the features of Internet Explorer 4.

FIG. 8.8
When working offline, you will only be able to view documents that are in your cache or on your local system.

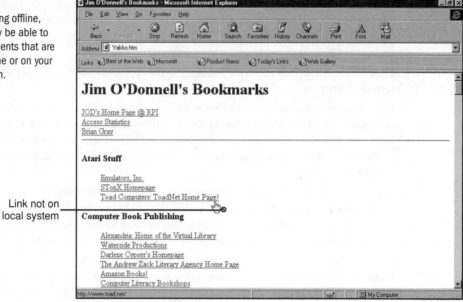

Link not on local system

FIG. 8.9
Internet Explorer's offline working ability enables you to review Web pages you downloaded off the Web without requiring additional connection time.

FIG. 8.10
All the options for controlling how Internet Explorer works are located in this dialog box.

General Options Tab With the options on this tab, you can control some basic Internet Explorer options, such as selecting your Home Page and controlling your temporary files and history list. You can also control the default colors, fonts, font sizes, and language that Internet Explorer uses.

You can access one extremely powerful, and potentially very useful, feature for people who might be vision impaired by clicking the Accessibility button. This button displays the dialog box shown in Figure 8.11.

FIG. 8.11
The ability to specify a client-side style sheet gives you almost total control over how viewed Web pages will be rendered in your Web browser.

There are two sections to this dialog box. The upper formatting section enables you to toggle whether Web-author-specified colors, fonts, and font sizes are used or ignored. The lower section enables you to select a client-side style sheet to be used to format incoming text. You can use this user style sheet to change aspects of how viewed Web pages are rendered.

User style sheets become particularly useful, though, as a way of making Web pages more accessible to people with some sort of vision impairment. For instance, if your vision is not very good, you might want the text of incoming Web pages to be displayed in large font. To do this, you could specify a user style sheet similar to that shown in Listing 8.1, which sets the font and font size of various types of text (for example, normal paragraph text, text appearing in tables, and so on).

Listing 8.1 big.css You Can Use Client-Side Style Sheets to Customize Your Display

```
<STYLE TYPE="TEXT/CSS">
<!-- Hide from incompatible browsers...
   H1  {font-weight: bold;
        font: 36pt verdana;}
   P   {font: 24pt verdana;}
   TD  {font: 24pt verdana;}
   TH  {font-weight: bold;
        font: 24pt verdana;}
   TT  {font: 24pt courier;}
<!-- -->
</STYLE>
```

Figure 8.12 shows a Web page viewed without this user style sheet enabled. By setting the style sheet to that shown in Listing 8.1, you would get the rendering shown in Figure 8.13, which is a great deal more readable.

▶ **See** "Style Sheet Tips and Tricks," **p. 536**

FIG. 8.12

Web pages that are perfectly readable to some people might not have large or clear enough type for people with visual impairments.

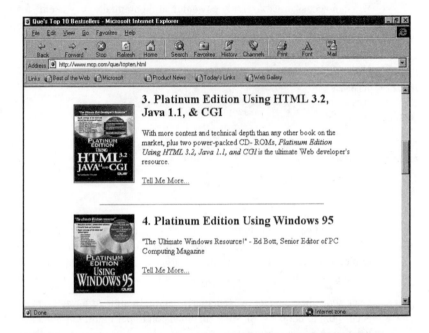

FIG. 8.13

You can use user style sheets to greatly increase the readability of many Web pages.

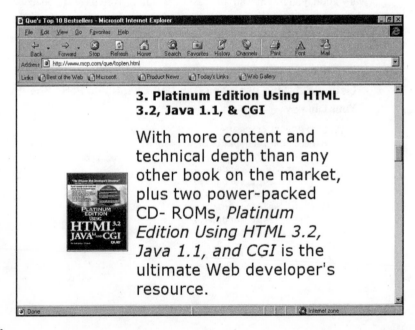

Security Options Tab   With Internet Explorer 4, Microsoft introduced the concept of the Security Zone. This concept, implemented through the Security Options tab, enables you to create different "zones" and to configure each zone with a certain level of security. You can then assign Web pages, Web sites, and domains into these zones. So, you might create a relatively low security zone and only put those Web sites in it that are within your corporate intranet or are otherwise known to you. Unknown sites should be put in a high security zone (see Figure 8.14).

▶ **See** "Configuring Internet Explorer Security Zones," **p. 298**

FIG. 8.14

Security zones make the process of securing your Web browsing environment from hostile programs and hackers much easier.

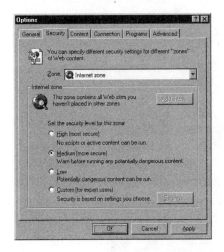

Content Options Tab   The options on this tab give you control over what types of content you will allow your Web browser to load. This option is particularly important if children will be using your Web browser. Through this tab, you can also maintain and access certificates, which are digital signatures belonging to individuals and corporations. Internet Explorer uses certificates to confirm the identity of the providers of content and applications over the Web and the Internet.

Also through this tab, you can set up profile, address, and credit card information within Microsoft's Profile and Wallet Controls. The concept behind these components is that you can enter this information once, be it your personal information or the data needed to conduct a credit card transaction, and then have it accessible to all compatible Web servers (see Figure 8.15).

Connection Options Tab   With the Connection Options tab, you can tell Internet Explorer 4 how you connect to the Internet. Though this information isn't strictly necessary—you can always establish your Internet connection using Windows 95 Dial-up Networking and then execute the Web browser—it does enable Internet Explorer to automatically create an Internet connection if it needs content on the Web and no connection exists (see Figure 8.16).

FIG. 8.15

By using the Microsoft Wallet, you can conduct secure credit card transactions over the Web.

FIG. 8.16

By configuring your connect information into Internet Explorer, you enable it to automatically connect to the Web.

Programs Options Tab   The selections on this tab enable you to configure which applications Internet Explorer 4 will use for Internet Mail and Internet News, Internet Conferencing, as well as the programs for its calendar and address book. By default, these selections will be configured to use the other applications in the Internet Explorer suite of applications, but you can configure them to use any appropriate application.

Advanced Options Tab   The final configuration tab contains a varied collection of options that allow you some control of many other aspects of Internet Explorer's operation. The general categories of options follow. Most of the default values for these options don't need to be changed—options that you might want to change are also noted in the following list:

- **Browsing**   These options control some aspects of Web browsing and the Internet Explorer user interface. A few examples are options to toggle Autocomplete and smooth scrolling of the browser window.

- **Multimedia**   With these options, you can enable or disable the display of any of several categories of multimedia content in Internet Explorer 4. You might want to disable one or more types of content if you are operating over a slow connection to the Internet.

- **Security**   These options concern security and which of the supported security protocols you would like to enable. You won't need to change any of these options during routine operation of Internet Explorer.

- **Java VM**   You can control a few things having to do with Microsoft's Java Virtual Machine, but you probably won't need to change these options.

- **Printing**   These options give you some added control over what is printed when you print a Web page.

- **Searching**   These options enable or disable the ability of Internet Explorer to try to "fill in" incomplete URLs with common domain names.

- **Toolbar**   If you like to minimize the amount of area your toolbars take, you can use this option to decrease the size of the toolbar icons used.

- **HTTP 1.1 settings**   These options are related to the HTTP protocol used to transmit information over the Web, and you probably won't need to change them.

Other Menus

You can use the options included in the other menus to perform the following functions:

- **Edit**   This menu contains the Windows standard Cut, Copy, Paste, and Search options (for searching for text in the current page, not for conducting Internet or Web searches).

- **Go**   The options in this menu give you access to Internet Explorer's navigational controls (usually accessed through the toolbar buttons). You can also call the applications you have set up for mail, news, conferencing, or your address book.

- **Favorites**   This menu gives you access to the same capabilities as the Favorites Explorer Bar, with the exception that it is through the Favorites, Add Favorites option that you can add the current Web page to your Favorites.

- **Help**   This menu gives you access to help information on Internet Explorer 4, both local help files and information on the Internet.

Part
II

Ch
8

ve

Find out how to configure Internet Explorer's Active Desktop

The Active Desktop enables you to bring your desktop alive with Web objects and dynamically changing content. You can find out how to set up your desktop here.

Learn how to configure the new Taskbar toolbars

Microsoft has added the capability to configure multiple toolbars through the Windows 95 Taskbar. See how to add, move, and rename toolbar buttons, as well as how to create new toolbars.

Internet Explorer 4 integrates with the Windows Explorer

With this release of Internet Explorer 4, the line between Internet Explorer and the Windows 95 Explorer is blurred. See how the Explorer interface can be made more "Web" like.

See how the Start Menu has become "Internet-aware"

Microsoft has added features to the Windows 95 Start Menu to enable you to access the Internet at any time, without launching Internet Explorer or any other application first.

d a Web
that have an
des support
ologies and
robably want
pressively, all

the Internet
the program
s the Active
egrated into
Active Desk-
nment—
receive a
ion adds
ght to your

Can't Reinstalling
Do on Network
TCP/IP
Also Dial-up-adapter
Click Prop.
" Bindings
✓ Check mark next to TCP/IP?

Introducing the Active Desktop

Though the specifics will vary a little bit with the specific release of Internet Explorer 4 that you have, Figure 9.1 shows what you might see after you install the suite for the first time. You can't see it by looking at this picture, but when you actually see it on the computer, you'll immediately see that this isn't your regular, static background. As well as the addition of the Quick Launch Toolbar (which I will discuss a little later in this chapter), this desktop shows movement!

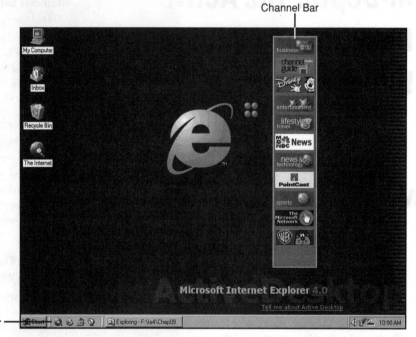

FIG. 9.1
The Internet Explorer 4 Active Desktop enables you to make your desktop a dynamic environment.

Channel Bar

Quick Launch Toolbar

Rather than being a static background image, the background of this introductory Active Desktop setup is an actual HTML document. This first becomes clear when you see the phrase "Microsoft Internet Explorer 4.0" scroll across the desktop screen—it's implemented using Microsoft's <MARQUEE> HTML tag. And because this is an actual Web page displayed as the background of your desktop, it can include anything that you can display with Internet Explorer 4. In this example, as shown in Figure 9.2, the background includes two hypertext links. The 4.0 link, if you are connected to the Internet, will load information about Internet Explorer 4 from Microsoft's Web site. The Tell me about Active Desktop link will bring up locally stored information.

N O T E When on the Active Desktop, you will see the symbol shown in Figure 9.2 to indicate a nonlocal hypertext link, if you are not currently connected to the Internet. ■

FIG. 9.2
The Active Desktop enables you to use HTML pages as your background so you can click hypertext links right from the desktop.

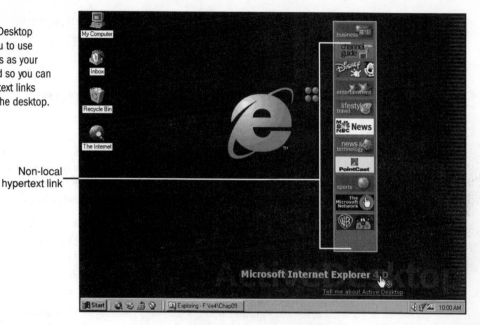

Non-local hypertext link

The other element displayed in this example is a desktop component called the Channel Bar, which gives you access to a list of channels available with which you can push content to the Internet Explorer Active Desktop. For more information on Channels, see Chapter 21, "Premium Channels."

The Active Desktop Icon Layer

As you might be able to tell from Figures 9.1 and 9.2, the Active Desktop consists of two layers: the HTML layer and the icon layer. In a sense, this isn't too big a change from the desktop before Internet Explorer 4. Then, the desktop consisted of a background layer over which icons were placed.

The HTML layer is where all the action occurs on the Active Desktop. But the icon layer is still necessary for you to access objects that you place on the desktop. The icon layer hasn't really changed from the standard Windows 95 desktop. It's like a piece of glass laid over the background behind it—you can place icons on it, but you can otherwise still see through it.

The Active Desktop HTML Layer

The big change with the Active Desktop is that the desktop background layer is no longer restricted to colors, patterns, or graphics. As you will see a little later in this chapter, this layer can now also be an HTML document (thus the name HTML layer). And, because the engine that drives the display of the HTML layer of the Active Desktop is Internet Explorer 4, *anything* that can be displayed in the Web browser can also appear on your desktop.

Even once the Active Desktop is installed, it remains possible to return to your conventional Windows 95 desktop. You can do this in two ways, both through the Display Control Panel. I will discuss these ways in the next section and later in the chapter.

Setting and Configuring Your Active Desktop Background

Much of the configuration of the Active Desktop is done through the Display Properties Control Panel dialog box. You can bring up this dialog box in a number of ways—the two most common ways are to select Start, Settings, Control Panel, and select the Display item from there, or, a slightly easier way, to right-click anywhere on the desktop and select Properties from the pop-up menu.

Choose settings for the Active Desktop in two of the tabs of the Display Properties dialog box. You select the background from the Background tab. Add, remove, and configure desktop components, which will be discussed in their own section later in this chapter, through the Web tab.

As shown in Figure 9.3, the Background settings tab is very similar to what it was before the Active Desktop. The difference now is that the Wallpaper entry is no longer limited to bitmap graphics (BMP) files. Wallpaper can also be an HTML document. When you installed Internet Explorer 4, a number of sample HTML documents that were included, meant to be used as Active Desktop backgrounds, were also installed in the Web subdirectory of your Windows directory.

 TIP   Both the Background and Web tabs of the Display Properties dialog boxes have Active Desktop "panic buttons;" you can check the Disable all web-related content on my desktop entry in either dialog box to turn off all aspects of the Active Desktop.

FIG. 9.3
You can use any HTML document as the Active Desktop background, but it's good to use those especially designed for that purpose.

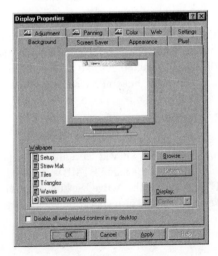

Figure 9.4 shows the results of configuring the Active Desktop background to use one of those included with the Internet Explorer 4 installation. In this document, the "Sports" banner across the top is just there for display, and the large gray area is meant to hold the Channel Bar buttons.

FIG. 9.4
The Active Desktop background can include the same elements as desktop components; here, the Channel Bar buttons are displayed in each.

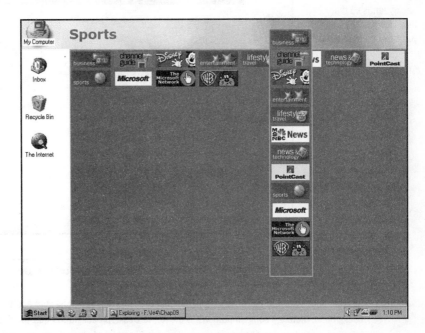

Part
II

Ch
9

A point that needs to be stressed here is that there is nothing special about the files used as Active Desktop backgrounds; they are simply HTML documents. You can edit and customize them just as with any other Web pages. For instance, if you don't like that the Active Desktop background shown in Figure 9.4 has an area for displaying Channel Bar buttons much bigger than it needs to be, you can edit the HTML file and fix it.

Looking at the HTML document for that background reveals that the gray region is created using an ActiveX Control; you can adjust its size by changing its parameters. Listing 9.1 shows the HTML code used to implement the Channel Bar ActiveX Control embedded in the page; the only change necessary was to decrease the height parameter from 100 percent to 16 percent. Figure 9.5 shows the Active Desktop that results. Note that for this figure, the Channel Bar desktop component was also turned off because the Channel Bar buttons are a part of this desktop background. You'll find out how to turn off desktop components in the next section.

Listing 9.1   The Active Desktop Can Display Embedded ActiveX Controls

```
<OBJECT id=0 name="DeskMovrW" resizeable="XY"
    style="width: 100%; height: 16%"
    classid="clsid:131A6951-7F78-11D0-A979-00C04FD705A2">
</OBJECT>
```

FIG. 9.5

As with any HTML document, you can edit those meant to be used as Active Desktop backgrounds so that they look just the way you'd like them to look.

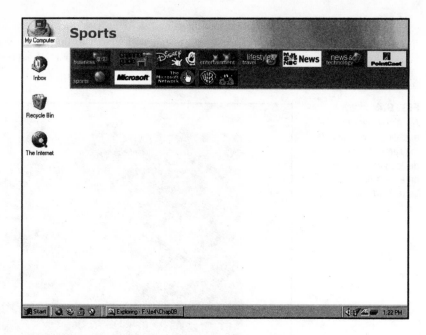

How Do I Design HTML Documents to Be Used as Active Desktop Backgrounds?

As mentioned earlier in this chapter, you can use any HTML document as your Active Desktop background. There are some limitations to the Active Desktop background that you should keep in mind when creating desktop backgrounds, however. Foremost of these limitations is that the Active Desktop background can't have a scrollbar; you need to make sure that the Web pages you use as your background will fit into whatever resolution screen you use.

Listing 9.2 shows HTML code fragment that does a good job of helping to make sure your Web pages fit onto the Active Desktop background. The two most important lines are the <BODY> and <TABLE> tags. The attributes in the <BODY> tag make sure that the contents of the page will occupy the whole screen and won't scroll. The <TABLE> tag enforces the same thing. The combination of the two allows the page to occupy the whole screen in a resolution-independent way.

One other restriction to keep in mind when designing HTML documents for the Active Desktop is to remember the icon layer. On top of your nice, painstakingly designed HTML desktop background is going to be a bunch of icons. You can use the HTML framework shown in Listing 9.2 to make room for the icons by changing the margins of the <BODY> tag. For instance, if your icons line the left side of your desktop, you could try setting LEFTMARGIN=50 or so.

Listing 9.2 HTML Framework Meant for Active Desktop Backgrounds

```
<HTML>
<HEAD></HEAD>
<BODY TOPMARGIN=0 LEFTMARGIN=0 RIGHTMARGIN=0 BOTTOMMARGIN=0 SCROLL=NO>
```

```
<TABLE WIDTH=100% HEIGHT=100% CELLPADDING=0 CELLSPACING=0>

<!-- Insert HTML code for the Active Desktop here -->

</TABLE>
</BODY>
</HTML>
```

Part
II

Ch
9

N O T E The HTML file you use as your Active Desktop background must be located on your local
system. ▪

Installing and Configuring Desktop Components

Earlier in this chapter, when I described the Active Desktop as having two layers, the familiar icon layer over an HTML layer, I was actually a little off the mark. It is probably more accurate to think of the Active Desktop as having three layers: *two* HTML layers underlying the layer for desktop icons.

Why two HTML layers? Because there are two distinct ways of placing HTML content onto your Active Desktop. The first way is through the Active Desktop background, as described in the previous section. In addition to this layer, you can also place any number of desktop components on the desktop. Practically speaking, these desktop components are placed above the background layer.

N O T E For the Active Desktop, a desktop component is just a name for any HTML document that is
placed on the desktop. A number of desktop components, created by Microsoft and others,
were especially designed to be placed on the desktop. Any HTML document can be placed there,
however, with the Active Desktop. ▪

Figure 9.6 shows the Web tab of the Display Properties dialog box. With this tab, you can configure and add desktop components to the Active Desktop. The Items on the Active Desktop list shows the components that have been configured for display on your desktop. Those components that are currently displayed are indicated by a check in the box beside their names. A silhouette of the profile of each displayed component on the Active Desktop is also shown.

Adding New Desktop Components

If you want to add a new desktop component, click the New button on the Web tab. You should see an alert box similar to that shown in Figure 9.7. This alert box gives you two alternatives. By answering Yes, you can be connected to Microsoft's Desktop Components Gallery, which will give you the opportunity to download and install components onto your desktop that were especially designed for the Active Desktop. If you answer No, you will be able to add any arbitrary Web object to the desktop. We will look at the specially designed desktop components first, before looking at arbitrary Web objects in the next section.

FIG. 9.6

The Web tab shows the currently displayed desktop components, along with an indication of which parts of the display they cover.

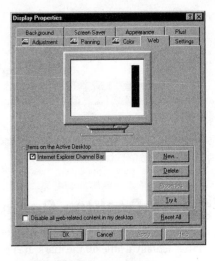

FIG. 9.7

You can either install premade desktop components onto your Active Desktop or create and install components of your own.

Microsoft's Active Desktop Gallery, shown in Figure 9.8, contains a collection of premade desktop components ready for you to download directly onto your Active Desktop. Most of these desktop components contain advanced Web technologies embedded in them; for instance, ActiveX Controls or Java applets. To begin the download process, simply click the hypertext link of the component that you would like to see.

By going through Microsoft's Active Desktop Gallery, you will find that the process of downloading and installing these desktop components is simplicity itself. Once you have clicked the hypertext link from the Gallery Web page, you will see a page similar to that shown in Figure 9.9. You'll see a preview of the desktop component that you want to download within the Web browser. If you decide that you do want to download it, you can click the Add to my Desktop (or similar) button to begin the download and install process.

Many desktop components in Microsoft's gallery require periodic updates to maintain their usefulness. For instance, the c|net NEWS.COM desktop component needs to connect to the Internet to update its headlines. The MSNBC Weather Map component would need to update its information every few hours. At the extreme end, the MSN Investor Ticker would require much more frequent updates to remain useful.

To schedule these updates, enter an Internet Explorer 4 Subscription for each desktop component. A Subscription configures Internet Explorer 4 to periodically check whether the document to which a given URL points has changed; if it has, the new information is automatically downloaded. Figure 9.10 shows the Subscribe dialog box that you get when downloading a desktop component. With this dialog box, you can decide when this component should be updated.

FIG. 9.8
Microsoft maintains a Desktop Component Gallery, which is a good place to start either setting up your Active Desktop or learning how to create your own components.

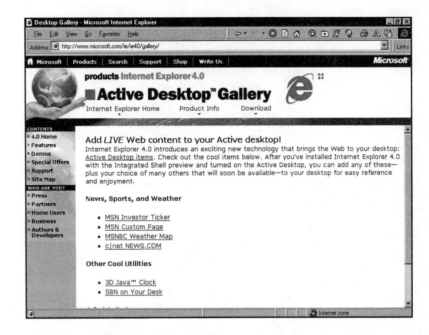

FIG. 9.9
Each page in the Desktop Components Gallery shows a preview of the component within the Web page and has a link to download it.

FIG. 9.10

You can configure desktop components to update their information according to a fixed schedule.

NOTE In general, modem users should usually manually update their subscriptions rather than scheduling them. Corporate users with permanent Internet connections have more freedom when scheduling updates. ▦

Once you have downloaded the chosen desktop component and entered its subscription, place it on your Active Desktop (see Figure 9.11). Once it's there, you still have the ability to do a number of things to configure it, which I will discuss in the next section.

FIG. 9.11

Newly installed desktop components placed on your Active Desktop will begin to function immediately.

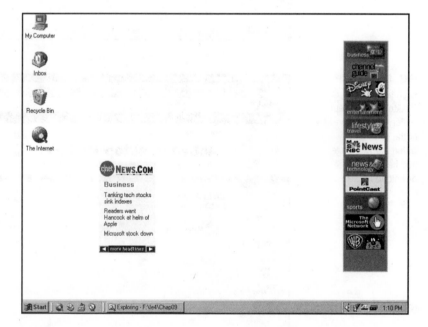

Configuring Desktop Components

Once you have placed a desktop component on your desktop, you still can configure it in a number of ways. The first things you might want to do to it are physical: moving or resizing the component. To do this, you must place the mouse cursor over the desktop component and hold it there for a few seconds. After this brief pause, the desktop component border will appear around it, enabling you to operate on the component (see Figure 9.12).

Part

II

Ch

9

FIG. 9.12
Once the desktop component border appears, you can easily configure its size or appearance.

Popup menu arrow

Desktop component border

Close button

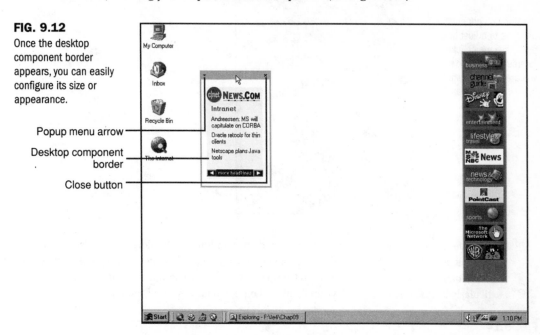

Through the desktop component border and using the mouse cursor, you can perform the following actions on the component:

- **Resize**   Move the mouse cursor to the edge of any border to resize the desktop component.
- **Move**   Click-and-drag with the mouse cursor on the bar at the top border of the component to move it around your desktop.
- **Configure the component**   Click the pop-up menu arrow on the border and select the Properties selection.
- **Configure the Active Desktop**   Click the pop-up menu arrow and select the Customize My Desktop selection to open the Display Properties dialog box.
- **Close the component**   You can close the desktop component by clicking either the close button or the pop-up menu arrow and selecting Close.

If you elect to configure the desktop component, as previously described, you will be given the configuration dialog box shown in Figure 9.13. With the Subscription tab, you can unsubscribe and view its current status. The Receiving tab of the desktop component properties dialog box controls how you are informed if the site in question has been updated and gives you control over whether the new information will be automatically downloaded. Finally, you can change the schedule under which the subscription operates through the Scheduling tab.

FIG. 9.13

You can configure desktop components at any time to adjust how often they are checked for updates and how you are informed when there is new information.

As I mentioned earlier, anything that you can display in Internet Explorer 4 you also can include in a desktop component. Figure 9.14 shows the Java clock applet desktop component downloaded from Microsoft's Desktop Components Gallery. Though the clock itself isn't particularly useful, it shows that Java applets can function on the Active Desktop.

FIG. 9.14

Java applets function as well on the Active Desktop as they do within the Internet Explorer 4 Web browser.

Java clock applet —

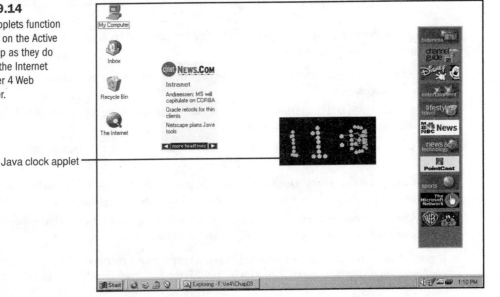

Installing Web Pages from the Internet

In addition to the items on the Microsoft Desktop Components Gallery, you can install any HTML document on your Active Desktop. To install a Web page from the Internet, all you need to do is enter its URL into the New Active Desktop Item dialog box, as shown in Figure 9.15. You will be given the chance to schedule it for updates through a subscription, just as with the regular desktop components. Once you place the component on your desktop, you can resize it and move it until you are satisfied with its appearance (see Figure 9.16).

Part
II

Ch
9

FIG. 9.15
You can place any HTML page on the Internet as a component on your Active Desktop.

FIG. 9.16
All the hypertext links in this Web page work, even when it is being used as a desktop component.

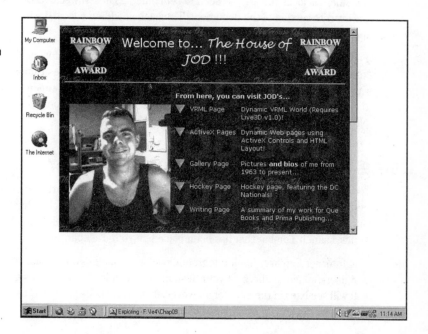

N O T E Note that, unlike HTML documents used as Active Desktop backgrounds, desktop components can use both horizontal and vertical scroll bars. ■

Putting Local Web Pages on Your Desktop

The process of placing a local Web page or HTML document on your Active Desktop is identical to that of placing an Internet document, with one minor and one more important difference. The minor difference is that instead of entering the URL of the file, you enter the local path and file name (see Figure 9.17).

FIG. 9.17

You can place local HTML documents on the Active Desktop by entering their path and file names.

The more important difference reflects the nature of the document in question. Because the document is local, there is no need to schedule updates; the Active Desktop will always reflect the current version of the document. Thus, when adding a local document to your Active Desktop, you skip the step of configuring the subscription.

Figure 9.18 shows a local HTML document placed on the desktop along with the Internet document already there. This figure does reflect one current restriction of the Active Desktop. Currently, there is no way to change the layering of multiple components on the desktop. If they overlap, the component you placed on the desktop last is on top, just as sheets of paper placed on a real desktop will be stacked first to last.

Using the Internet Explorer 4 Taskbar

As shown in Figure 9.1 at the beginning of this chapter, there are two obvious changes to your system once you install Internet Explorer 4 when you also enable integration of the browser into the shell. The first change is the presence of the Active Desktop. The second change is the Quick Launch Toolbar that has been placed on your Taskbar.

The Internet Explorer Shell Integration package enables you to place a number of predefined and user-defined toolbars on your desktop. By default, they appear as a part of the Taskbar. As you will see later in the chapter, however, they can also be "torn off" to be free-floating toolbars and can be docked on other sides of the display.

FIG. 9.18
Overlapping desktop components are stacked first to last on your Active Desktop.

Part
II
Ch
9

The easiest way to access the toolbar control is to right-click the Taskbar and select from the Toolbars submenu of the resulting pop-up menu from the following choices:

- **Address** Places an Address Bar on your Taskbar identical to the Internet Explorer 4 Address Bar

- **Links** Places a Links Bar on your Taskbar identical to the Internet Explorer 4 Links Bar

- **Desktop** Places a toolbar on your Taskbar that has one button for each icon on your desktop

- **Quick Launch** Includes buttons to quickly launch applications or documents from your system

- **New Toolbar** Enables you to create a new toolbar out of any existing folder on your system

As with the toolbars in Internet Explorer 4, you can rearrange and resize all the enabled toolbars on the Windows 95 Taskbar by clicking and dragging their handles and moving them around. Also, you can increase or decrease the total area taken by the Taskbar itself by resizing it. Figure 9.19 shows an example of the Taskbar after all the predefined toolbars are enabled and then rearranged.

FIG. 9.19
The new toolbars give you access to applications and the Web without first having to start the Internet Explorer Web browser.

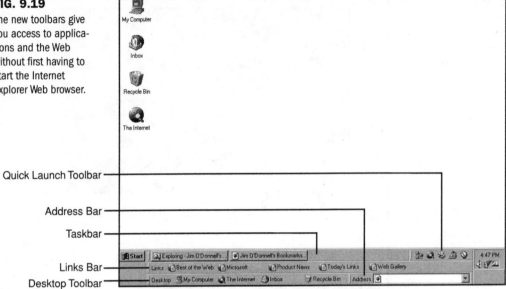

Quick Launch Toolbar

Address Bar

Taskbar

Links Bar

Desktop Toolbar

Configuring the Taskbar Toolbars

You can configure any of the toolbars that you have currently displayed on the Taskbar by right-clicking them and selecting one of the configuration options from the pop-up menu. The relevant selections follow:

- **View**   Enables you to choose between Large and Small icons for the toolbar
- **Show Text**   Determines whether a text label is displayed after each icon in the toolbar
- **Refresh**   Refreshes the contents of the toolbar

 You may have noticed in the normal operation of Windows 95 that the operating system sometimes gets "confused" about what icons it is displaying. If you notice a missing or incorrect icon in one of your toolbars, refreshing it will usually fix the problem.

- **Show Title**   Determines whether a text title is displayed for the toolbar

Note that because the Address Bar does not display icons, only the Show Title option is active for it. For all other toolbars, all the options are present.

Figure 9.20 shows the same toolbars as shown in Figure 9.19, with the following changes:

- The titles were disabled for all toolbars.
- The text labels were disabled for the Desktop Toolbar.
- The toolbars were rearranged to give more room for the Taskbar and for the Address Bar.

Now, obviously, toolbar arrangement will be a very subjective thing, and the setup you want will depend on how you work at your computer and how big your display is. With Internet Explorer 4, however, you have the ability to configure it any way you want.

FIG. 9.20
You can use the capability to disable text and titles to allow your toolbars to use space more efficiently.

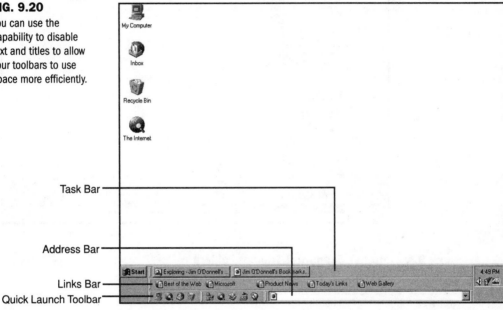

Task Bar

Address Bar

Links Bar

Quick Launch Toolbar

TROUBLESHOOTING

Why are some of the text labels on the Links Bar so wide when they don't need to be? When rendering the Links Bar, either in the Internet Explorer 4 Web browser or when placed in a toolbar, the width of the text label for each button is set to the same value. So, if there is even just one particularly wide text label, all the buttons will end up spaced far apart.

The best way to fix this problem is to shorten the names of the links in the Links Bar. There are several ways to do this—one way is depicted in Figure 9.21. Because the Links Bar buttons come from the Links subdirectory of the Favorites directory (which, in turn, is a subdirectory of your Windows directory), you can browse and rename each link to give it a short yet descriptive name. Once you have done this, you will need to disable and re-enable the Links Bar to see the changes. As shown in Figure 9.21, by doing this, you can use less space on the Links Bar and thus include more buttons (before it is necessary to scroll the toolbar).

Adding and Moving Toolbar Buttons

Because of the nature of toolbar buttons, it is easy to add, copy, delete, and move them around because each toolbar is really only a representation of a folder on your system. Table 9.1 shows the four predefined toolbars and the default location of the corresponding folder for each.

FIG. 9.21
Using short names for Links Bar buttons makes it possible to fit more of them on the screen at once.

Table 9.1   Internet Explorer 4 Toolbar Folders

Toolbar	Folder Location
Address	N/A
Links	C:\Windows\Favorites\Links
Desktop	C:\Windows\Desktop
Quick Launch	C:\Windows\ApplicationData\Microsoft\Internet Explorer\Quick Launch

So, any document, application, or shortcut that you drag into any of the preceding folders will be displayed as an icon with (optionally) a text label in the appropriate toolbar.

It is not necessary, however, to directly work with those subdirectories to add, delete, or move buttons. As demonstrated in Figure 9.22, you can move buttons around by clicking and dragging them from one place to another. And because a toolbar button is like any other object that you can move around on your system under Windows 95, not only can you move the button, but by holding down the Ctrl key while dragging it, you can create a copy of the button as well. In Figure 9.22, the icon for Outlook Express is being copied from the Quick Launch onto the Desktop Toolbar. Figure 9.23 shows the result of this operation—not only is the icon now in the Desktop Toolbar, it is also now displayed on the desktop.

The only change to a toolbar button that you can't directly make with the button itself is to rename it. To do this, you need to access the appropriate folder through the Windows Explorer or through another means.

FIG. 9.22
You can pick up and move around toolbar buttons as easily as files, folders, and shortcuts on your hard drive.

Click-and-drag
toolbar button

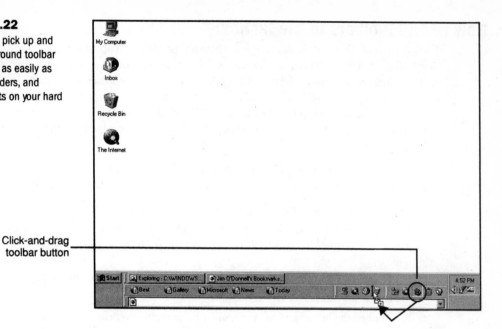

FIG. 9.23
The Desktop Toolbar is simply another representation of the contents of your desktop; changes to one are automatically reflected in the other.

Desktop icons

Desktop Toolbar

How to Add Toolbars to the Taskbar

The selection of the Taskbar pop-up menu I haven't spoken much about yet is the Toolbars, New Toolbar selection. With this selection, you can make *any* folder on your hard drive into a toolbar, which means that all the contents of that folder will be represented by icons in a toolbar. This toolbar would be a good place to keep frequently used applications or documents and can also be used to keep Internet shortcuts. Clicking shortcuts will launch Internet Explorer 4 and load applications or documents right off the Web (provided you have established an Internet connection).

Figure 9.24 shows an example of including a new toolbar on the Taskbar. In this case, I went through the following steps to display the Microsoft Office toolbar shown in the figure:

1. Right-clicked the Taskbar and select Toolbars, New Toolbar.

2. In the New Toolbar dialog box, browsed to **C:\Windows\Start Menu\Programs\Microsoft Office** and clicked OK to create the Microsoft Office toolbar.

3. Right-clicked the new Microsoft Office toolbar and unchecked the Show Text selection to turn off the text labels on the buttons.

4. Rearranged the buttons within the toolbar by dragging them into the positions that I wanted.

5. Positioned the new toolbar with respect to the other in its desired position.

FIG. 9.24

You can draw new toolbars from anywhere on your hard drive to make often-used applications and documents instantly accessible.

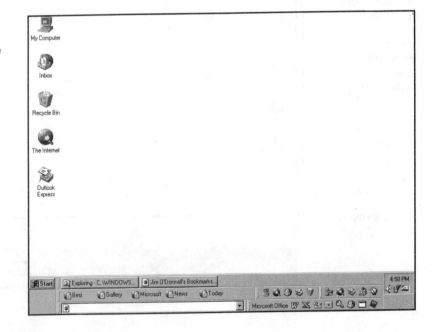

TIP A good source of folders to be made into toolbars are the folders in the **C:\Windows\Start Menu** directory because they are already meant to be used in the Start Menu to launch applications and documents.

Choosing Toolbar Icons

The last few options you have to consider when setting up your toolbars under Internet Explorer 4 are the size of the icons to use and the final placement of the toolbar itself—it is not necessary to leave the toolbar as part of the Taskbar. To change the icon size, right-click the appropriate toolbar and select <u>V</u>iew, Lar<u>g</u>e or S<u>m</u>all. Figure 9.25 shows the Quick Launch Toolbar with large icons.

FIG. 9.25

It is sometimes easier to determine what application or document corresponds to a toolbar button when it is represented by a large icon.

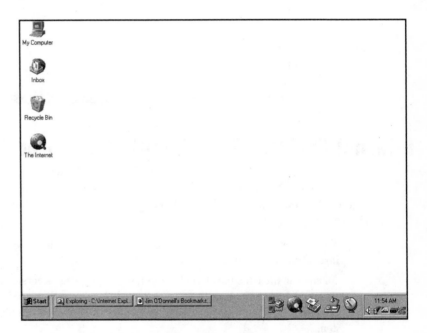

 TIP Large icons are sometimes useful when you have disabled text labels for a toolbar.

Finally, you can "tear off" and place any toolbar on the Taskbar anywhere on your desktop. To do this, grab the toolbar handle and drag it off the Taskbar. When you have the toolbar over the desktop, release the mouse button, and a free-floating toolbar is created. You can resize this toolbar and configure the buttons in it just as with a toolbar on the Taskbar. Figure 9.26 shows the Microsoft Office toolbar after it has been torn off, placed on the desktop, and configured to use large icons and no text labels.

FIG. 9.26
You can create free-floating toolbars with Internet Explorer 4 as well as those attached to the Taskbar.

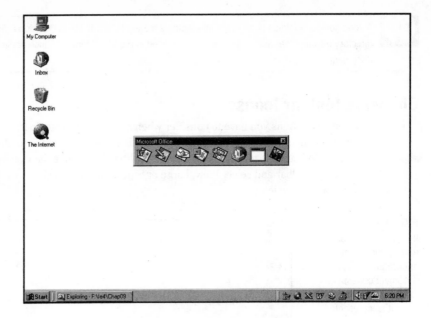

Internet Explorer 4's Integrated Explorer

With Internet Explorer 4 and its Web Integration, the line between the Internet Explorer 4 Web browser and the Windows 95 Explorer for browsing through your hard drive has disappeared. Figure 9.27 shows Explorer being used to view a Web page from the Internet. Note some of the signs of Web Integration.

- The Address Bar, which would display the full path and file name of a local document, instead shows the URL of the Web page being viewed.

- An entry in the left pane of the Explorer, which in previous versions of the Explorer only showed items on the local system (or items in local area networks), is labeled "The Internet." Whenever you view a Web page, its URL is placed in a hierarchy under this item.

- The Integrated Explorer's "smart" toolbar has changed from local to Web mode; it is now identical to the Standard Toolbar from the Internet Explorer 4 Web browser.

- The right pane, currently being used to display the Web page being viewed, can be divided further to show an Explorer Bar. Figure 9.28 shows the Favorites Explorer Bar.

The Integrated Explorer Smart Toolbar

You can use the Web Integrated Explorer in one of two modes: local mode, to browse through your local system, or Web mode, to surf the Web. It has a smart toolbar that automatically changes to reflect the current mode.

FIG. 9.27

Just as Internet Explorer has been capable of viewing files and browsing through folders on your local system, the Web Integrated Explorer can now view Web pages.

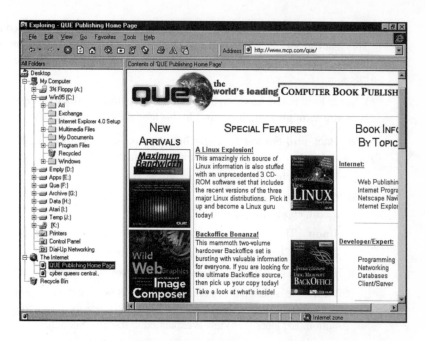

FIG. 9.28

When in "Web mode," the Explorer gives you access to everything you can do from the Internet Explorer 4 Web browser.

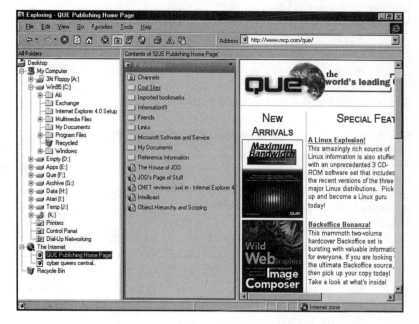

When in Web mode, the toolbar is identical to the Standard Toolbar used by Internet Explorer. This mode gives you access to the basic navigational features; the Browser or Explorer Bars for accessing searches, favorites, your history list, or channels; and a few miscellaneous features.

When in local mode, however, the toolbar reverts to something more appropriate for local browsing through your hard drive. In this mode, the toolbar has the following buttons:

- **Back and Forward**   These buttons give you a Web-browser-like ability to move back and forth through the list of folders you have visited on your system.
- **Up**   This button moves you up one level in the current hierarchy.
- **Cut, Copy, and Paste**   These three buttons give you access to the standard Windows 95 cut, copy, and paste functions.
- **Undo**   This button enables you to undo the last change you made through the Explorer.
- **Delete**   Click this button to delete the current selection and move it to the Recycle Bin.
- **Properties**   This button gives you access to the properties of the current selection.
- **Views**   In addition to enabling you to select the standard Explorer views (large or small icons, list, or details), you can access the WebView for the current folder through this button. Explorer WebView is explained in the next section.

Using Explorer's Internet Search Capabilities

Another addition to the Explorer menus that brings you closer to the Internet is the new additions to the Tools, Find menu. In addition to searching for files and folders on your local system, you can now use the Tools, Find, On the Internet selection to begin a Web search. Another very useful new capability initiated by selecting Tools, Find, People brings up the dialog box shown in Figure 9.29.

FIG. 9.29

Explorer now enables you to initiate Internet searches for people using any of a number of Internet and Web directory services.

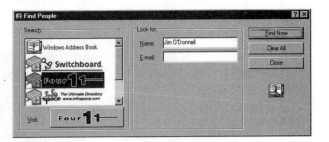

After you enter the name and/or e-mail address of the person you are hoping to find and select an Internet directory service, that service will be queried. The results of the query will be displayed in a scrolling list, and you will be able to browse through that list to see whether the desired person has been found. Once this is done, you can import that person's information into your Address Book (see Figure 9.30).

FIG. 9.30
By interfacing with Internet directory services, the Explorer offers you an easy way to try to find people.

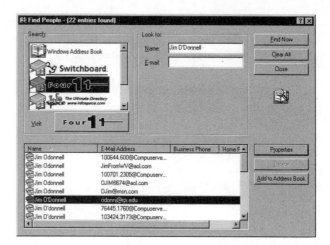

Using Explorer WebView

The Explorer WebView covers two different aspects of how the Explorer looks and behaves. First, it is possible to customize how certain folders *look* when viewed in WebView mode (how this is done is discussed in the next section). When a folder has been customized in this way, or for some folders that have predefined WebView appearances, you can toggle Web mode on and off to change from an HTML versus Explorer type appearance.

The other aspect that you can control is how folders and files behave, either in WebView or in the normal Explorer mode. This option, accessed through the General tab of the View, Options menu selection, determines whether files and folders behave in Web Style, in which simply placing the cursor over an item selects it and only a single-click is needed to launch it, and Classic Style, in which a single-click selects and a double-click opens. Figure 9.31 shows the dialog box in which these two modes are selected, and Figure 9.32 shows an example of the Explorer in WebView with Web Style links.

> **CAUTION**
> You might need to select View, Options from the single-pane Explorer (which you can display, among other ways, by opening the My Computer icon) to be able to select Web or Classic Style. For some reason, this option is not always available when you are in the two-pane Explorer.

Customizing How Folders Look in Explorer WebView

As I mentioned earlier in this chapter, some folders have predefined views when in WebView mode. Figure 9.32 shows the My Computer WebView. The Control Panel also has a predefined WebView appearance. For all other folders, you need to customize a WebView appearance. To do this for the folder currently displayed in Explorer, select View, Customize this Folder to get the dialog box shown in Figure 9.33. Through this dialog box, you can either create and/or edit the HTML document used for the folder's custom appearance, or simply attach a background picture to the current folder (or remove customization entirely).

FIG. 9.31
Web Style links make the way you browse through your local system similar to the way you browse the Web.

FIG. 9.32
When you pass the mouse cursor over a file or folder, the cursor changes to the familiar hand pointer because the file or folder acts as a hypertext link.

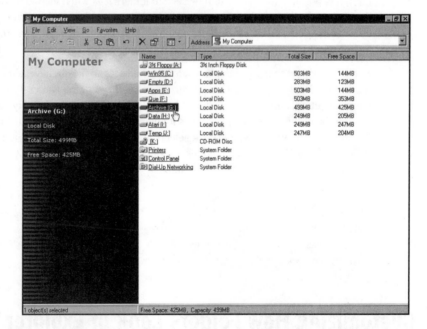

Figure 9.34 shows an example of attaching a background picture to a folder. In this case, I have attached an appropriate graphic to one of the folders on my hard drive. Figure 9.35 shows the default appearance of a folder when an HTML document is created to display the current folder.

FIG. 9.33

With WebView
Customization, you can
make the appearance
of each folder different.

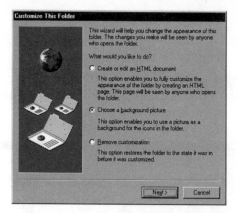

FIG. 9.34

Folder-specific
background images can
highlight the contents
of a folder.

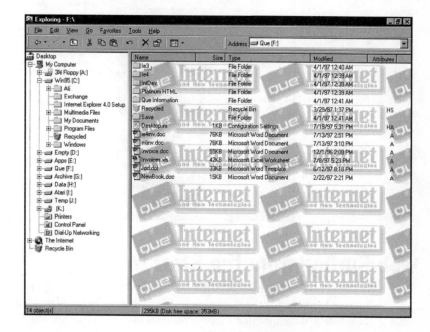

N O T E The WebView HTML document is stored within the current directory as a hidden file with the name `Folder.htm`. You can load that HTML file into your favorite editor and customize the appearance of that folder when it is viewed in WebView. You can add anything to the file that you can add to any other HTML document: images, Java applets, scripting, other hypertext links. The only lines in the file about which you need to be careful should look something like the following:

```
<!--webbot bot="HTMLMarkup" startspan
   u-src="file:///C:\PROGRA~1\MICROS~2\Data\FoldData.gif" -->
   <object id="FileList" border=0
           classid="clsid:1820FED0-473E-11D0-A96C-00C04FD705A2"
```

continues

continued

```
                style="position: absolute; left: 30%; top: 0;
                                width: 70%; height: 100%">
    </object>
<!--webbot bot="HTMLMarkup" endspan -->
```

This is the ActiveX Control used to display the contents of the folder. You can adjust the `style` attribute of the control but should probably not alter it otherwise. ■

FIG. 9.35
The full HTML WebView of a folder adds functionality and gives you further capabilities to customize its appearance.

Web Surfing from the Start Menu

The last changes that have been made to the desktop and the underlying operation system by Internet Explorer 4 Web Integration are a few changes to the Start Menu. The first change is the addition of the Find and Favorites options to the Start Menu. The Find submenu gives you the same ability to initiate Internet searches or to look for people on the Internet, as was shown with the Find menu in the Integrated Explorer. The Favorites menu enables you to launch Internet Explorer 4 to load a Web page listed in your Favorites menu without first executing the Web browser.

The second change to the Start Menu is the additional ability to arrange the entries on it in the same way that you can move toolbar buttons around. It is now possible to move elements of the Start Menu by clicking and dragging them around from one position to another. ●

CHAPTER 10

In Depth: Outlook Express Mail

The Outlook Express interface is one of the easiest to use for interacting with others through e-mail and Internet newsgroups. Ease of use does not make the program the best in its class, however. Outlook Express contains a wealth of options that enable you to reroute messages, customize your own settings, enable multiple accounts within one interface, and much more. Outlook Express actually puts the power into your hands in terms of what you want your program to do and how it will behave when you give it a specific task. Once you're finished with this chapter, you'll rule the world of text-based Internet communications. ■

Reroute incoming e-mail

Use the Inbox Assistant to forward messages and organize them into custom folders.

Address e-mail with the click of a button

Use the Address Book to keep track of all your e-mail contacts and organize them into groups.

Create multiple news server profiles

Learn how to subscribe to multiple news servers to find the most updated UseNet articles.

Block unwanted UseNet messages

Create newsgroup filters to keep out-of-place articles out of your subscribed newsgroups.

Using Outlook Express Mail

In Chapter 5, "Quick Start: Outlook Express Mail and News," you learned the basics of installing the program, setting up an e-mail account, composing an e-mail message, and the semantics of sending and receiving e-mail.

Now that the basics are out of the way, it is time for you to explore the rich options that Outlook Express Mail offers. Though many e-mail clients are just as feature rich as Outlook Express Mail, not many can hold a candle to its ease of use and simple (yet advanced) configuration options. The next few sections will cover such topics as enabling multiple account handling in Outlook Express, creating entries in the Address Book for your popular e-mail addresses, sending and receiving file attachments, security highlights, and mail routing options.

By the time you are finished with this section, you will have mastered the ins and outs of Outlook Express Mail and will have an ability that many Internet users cannot boast—complete control over your incoming and outgoing e-mail.

Creating Multiple E-Mail Accounts

Today, it's not uncommon for an individual to have more than one e-mail account. Generally, if your office is connected to the Internet, you will have one account that is provided by your company and, often, one account from a local Internet Service Provider that you use to access the Internet from home. Many users have become accustomed to installing a different e-mail client for each mailbox that they own because most e-mail programs can handle only one account at a time. With Outlook Express Mail, however, you can enter any number of e-mail accounts, then set up custom folders for each mailbox so that the contents of the mailbox are not confused. There is virtually no limit to the number of mailboxes that you can add to Outlook Express, making it possible to have an account for yourself, your spouse, and your kids, without loading multiple programs.

To install additional e-mail accounts, follow these steps:

1. In Outlook Express Mail, click Tools, Accounts. The Internet Accounts window will appear, showing you a list of installed mail and news accounts.

2. Click the Mail tab at the bottom of the Internet Accounts window to switch to a mail-only view.

3. Select the Add button and choose Mail. The familiar Internet Connection Wizard will appear and begin prompting you for information about your new account.

4. Enter your account name, mail server address, and password when prompted. Click Finish when your settings are complete. Your new account profile will appear in the Internet Accounts window as soon as you are finished, as shown in Figure 10.1.

FIG. 10.1

Outlook Express Mail enables you to create multiple e-mail profiles and has the capability to check multiple addresses for new mail.

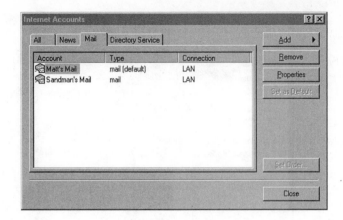

After you have created additional accounts, the default account (the account to which Outlook Express will open when started) will be marked with the word default. To switch to another e-mail account, simply select Tools, Accounts and highlight the mail account that you want to make default. After it is selected, simply click Set as Default and click Close. The next time you check for new e-mail with Outlook Express Mail, it will check all your accounts as long as you know the account passwords. For the time being, all your incoming mail will go to the same inbox. The next section describes how to use the Inbox Assistant to reroute incoming mail to specific folders.

Using the Inbox Assistant to Automate Your Mail

Now that you have the ability to check multiple e-mail accounts with one program, you will need to set up custom folders for the different incoming mail accounts and add special routing handlers with the Inbox Assistant. Creating a top-level folder for each of your incoming mail accounts is a wise decision. As long as you route your incoming mail properly, all of your mail will be separated and will never be confused with someone else's mail. To create a new folder for an additional mail account, follow these steps:

1. Click File, Folder, New Folder. The Create Folder window will appear as shown in Figure 10.2.
2. Select the existing folder under which you want your new folder to appear. If you want your new folder to be on the top level, simply highlight Outlook Express.
3. Type a new folder name. This name will appear as your new folder's title in the folders list. It is a good idea to make this title a specific one so that mailboxes are not confused.
4. Click OK to create the new folder.

Now that you have set up the new account folder, you will use the Inbox Assistant to route incoming e-mail to a specific location.

FIG. 10.2

By creating new mail folders, you can organize your mail by category or user.

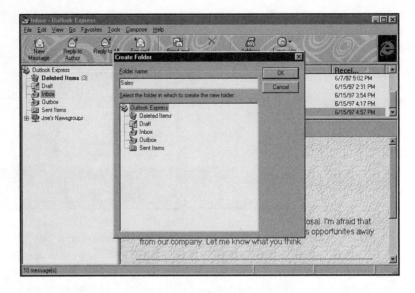

Rerouting E-Mail to a Different Folder   There are two main purposes for rerouting incoming e-mail messages. The first purpose is to separate mail from multiple incoming accounts into separate folders. This sorting is helpful for families and those with multiple e-mail accounts intended for the same user. The second use is for checking a single e-mail account with multiple recipients. This use is most often seen in a small office environment in which the entire location shares one e-mail address and special messages in the subject line single out the intended recipient. An example of this is if you had a global e-mail address for your company and different departments responded to a specific type of mail, such as information requests, sales information, placed orders, and general business.

The best way to organize something like this would be to have separate folders for each group and to request your mail senders to place a special line in the subject field of their messages such as "Sales," "Order," and "General." Once you have created folders for each of the different types of e-mail, you can begin using the Inbox Assistant to reroute the mail.

In certain situations, an ISP may host mail for an entire domain name and place all the messages into one global mailbox. Using the Inbox Assistant and custom rules, you can separate the incoming messages by intended recipients and organize them into separate folders. This is a key way to minimize online charges and to extend the reach of e-mail communications to everyone in your company.

To start the Inbox Assistant, click Tools, Inbox Assistant. It will look like the window pictured in Figure 10.3.

FIG. 10.3

Inbox Assistant enables you to pick your own rules to deal with incoming e-mail.

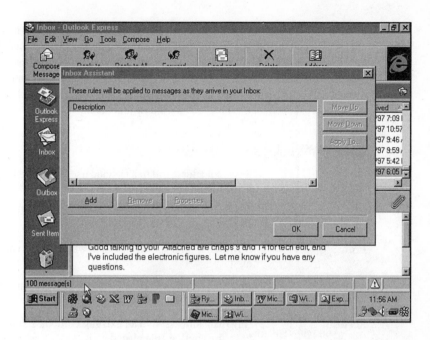

Part
II

Ch
10

The Inbox Assistant enables you to assign rules to incoming mail. With these rules, you can place e-mail messages directly into specified folders once received, respond automatically to incoming messages, and redirect incoming messages to another Internet mail account. Click Add in the Internet Assistant to begin making rules for your incoming mail. Figure 10.4 shows the Properties screen of the Inbox Assistant, where you will create rules for incoming mail.

FIG. 10.4

The Inbox Assistant enables you to reroute incoming e-mail within Outlook Express Mail or back out on the Internet to an external e-mail address.

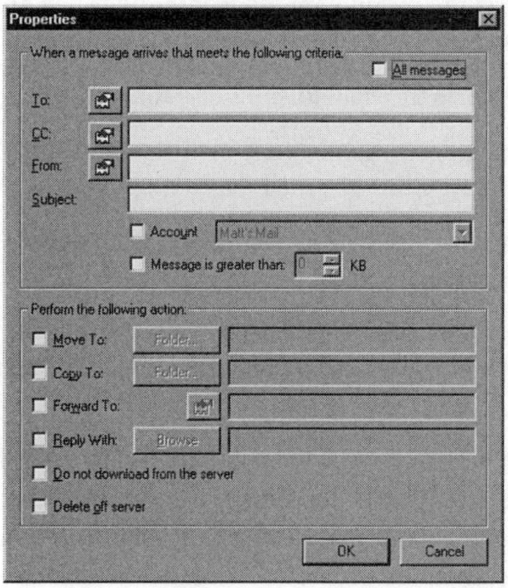

The Inbox Assistant Properties screen works on an "if-then" type of logic. For example, *if* you want every incoming piece of e-mail that has a subject line of "Sales," *then* you would enter in a specific folder location in Outlook Express Mail to hold it. The properties screen is broken down into two distinct sections: the top half looks for a mail identifier, and the second half instructs Outlook Express what to do with mail that meets the specified criteria. Table 10.1 provides a breakdown of the Properties window functions.

Table 10.1 Inbox Assistant Properties	
To	Any mail addressed to a specific user will have the routing rule placed on it
CC	Any mail carbon copied to a specific user will have the routing rule placed on it
From	Any mail from a specific location will have the routing rule placed on it
Subject	Any mail that has a specific subject line will have the routing rule placed on it
Account	Any mail addressed to an existing Outlook Express Mail account will have the routing rule placed on it
Message is Greater Than	Any message that is greater than a user-specified file size will have the routing rule placed on it
Outlook Express Mail performs the following actions (Routing Rule):	
Move to	Moves routed mail into a specific folder the user specifies
Copy to	Places the original message into the Inbox and places a copy of the message in a specified folder
Forward to	Forwards the mail to another e-mail user
Reply with	Automatically sends the e-mail sender a reply from an already-prepared piece of e-mail (auto-responder)
Do Not Download for from Server	Leaves a copy of the message on your e-mail server (only available IMAP mail servers)
Delete off Server	Deletes incoming messages from the mail server when an account is checked (only available for IMAP mail servers)

If you want all your incoming messages to be handled the same way, simply place a check in the box labeled All Messages at the top of the Properties screen. When this box is checked, all your incoming mail will be handled and routed with the same rules you set in the Properties screen. Figure 10.5 shows a completed properties screen in which incoming mail for Sales is routed to the Sales folder, and an automatic thank you greeting is sent back to the original message sender.

FIG. 10.5

Inbox Assistant rules enable you to reroute incoming e-mail anywhere you wish.

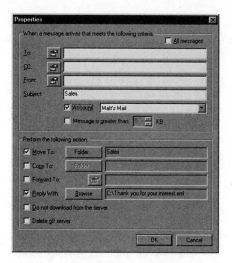

The ability to set up powerful rules for incoming mail was unheard of just a couple years ago. Using the Internet Assistant, you can ensure that all of your incoming mail is being rerouted to the right folder and recipient with only a few clicks of the mouse in the Properties window. Experimenting with the different rules is a great way to become accustomed to how the Inbox Assistant functions and how it can globally handle all your mail.

N O T E The process of rerouting e-mail to secondary recipients only happens when you check your mail within your copy of Outlook Express. Because the Inbox Assistant rules are set up locally on your system, an incoming message that follows criteria set up with rules in your e-mail program will reside on your local mail server until you check your mail. Once you have checked your mail, all rules are enforced within the Inbox Assistant, and messages will be forwarded. ■

Automating Forwarding Mail to Another User Though forwarding incoming e-mail messages is a simple task in Outlook Express Mail, many users do not use it to its full potential. Suppose you are going out of town on vacation but would like to check your e-mail at your relative's house. To do this, simply add a new rule in the Inbox Assistant to forward all your mail to a specific e-mail address. It's best to check with the intended recipient before you do this, however, to make sure that he or she doesn't mind a few extra e-mail messages for a few days.

You can also use mail forwarding to reroute unsolicited e-mail messages or spam, as it's called in Internet lingo. The majority of spam comes from only a few Internet domains. Though you will not be able to control all the unsolicited e-mail you receive, you can easily reroute those messages that come from the same server to your mail administrator so that he or she can attempt to do something about the problem. If you know the address from which the unsolicited e-mail is coming, simply generate a new rule in the Inbox Assistant to forward all incoming mail from that account to your mail administrator. Generally, it's safe to assume that an address such as **mail@domain.com** will go to the e-mail administrator's mailbox.

N O T E The spam problem on the Internet is getting out of hand and, unfortunately, there's not much that an end user can do about it at this time. By forwarding unsolicited e-mail to your mail administrator, your Internet Service Provider may be able to block further incoming messages from known spam mailboxes.

One precaution that you can take is to be careful to whom you give your e-mail address and to use a modified e-mail address when making posts on Internet newsgroups. Many people put an asterisk in their e-mail address when posting in UseNet newsgroups to confuse robots that do nothing but collect e-mail addresses for later spamming. ▨

Using the Address Book

If you use e-mail frequently, you probably tire of repeatedly typing e-mail recipients into your e-mail messages if they are addresses that you use often. Microsoft has anticipated this frustration and created the Address Book as a way for you to keep a directory of e-mail recipients handy and only a mouse click away. To start organizing your e-mail contacts, click the Address Book icon on the toolbar. When the address book appears, it will look much like the window shown in Figure 10.6.

FIG. 10.6
The Address Book stores not only e-mail addresses but information about the e-mail users as well.

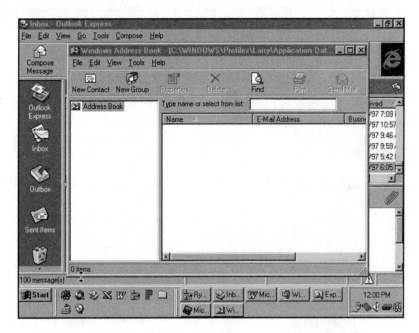

When the Address Book first appears, it is empty and waiting for you to add entries. Address Book entries are organized into two distinct categories, Contacts and Groups. Contacts are individuals and Groups are a collection of individuals who will all receive e-mail if you select them. Once you have set up Contacts and Groups, you can simply click the Address Book icon next to the To and CC fields to select your recipients from the Address Book.

Creating Contacts with More Than Just E-mail Information   The Contacts section of the Address Book contains not only a user's name and e-mail address but fields for personal and business information, notes about the user, and security information if the user has a digital security certificate. To create a Contact, follow these steps.

1. Click New Contact from the toolbar. The Properties screen will appear, waiting for you to input information about the e-mail user.

2. Enter the First Name, Last Name, and Nickname if the contact has one. You are not required to fill out all the fields.

3. Enter an e-mail address for the user. Click Add to add it to the e-mail addresses list.

4. You can continue to enter information under the Home, Business, and Notes tabs if you wish. These screens are optional.

5. Click OK to complete your new entry to the Address Book. Your completed Address Book entry will look much like that in Figure 10.7.

FIG. 10.7

Once you make an entry in the Address Book, you will never have to type a user's e-mail address again.

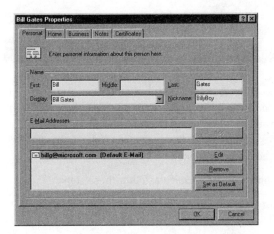

After you have made a few entries into the Address Book, you are now ready to access the Address Book when composing a piece of e-mail. To pull Address Book users when composing e-mail, follow these steps:

1. Click the New Message button in Outlook Express Mail to compose a new message.

2. Click the Address Book icon next to the To field and select your message's recipient(s), as shown in Figure 10.8.

3. Once you have selected the recipients for the To, CC, and BCC fields, click OK to resume composing your message.

Once you have closed the Select Recipients window, your message will be addressed to all those whom you selected from your Address Book list. Simply compose the rest of your message as you normally would, and click the Send icon when you are finished. All the recipients listed in your message will receive your message as though you entered each of their e-mail addresses separately.

Part
II

Ch
10

FIG. 10.8

The Address Book simplifies the composition of e-mail messages by enabling you to choose recipients from an organized list.

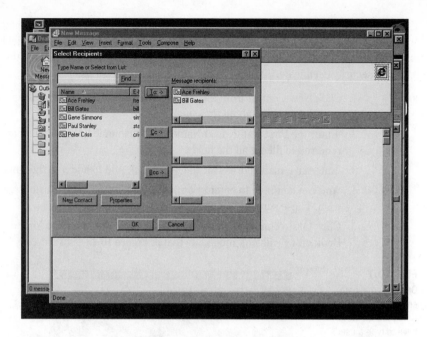

Group Addresses to Make Your Own Distribution Lists You might find that you send messages to groups of individuals more often than a single e-mail user. If this is true, you'll find it helpful to set up Groups in the Address Book for the users whom you e-mail collectively. Once you set up a Group, you will be able to e-mail a handful of users at once simply by clicking the Group name from the Address Book.

To create a new Group of e-mail recipients, follow these steps:

1. Click the Address Book icon on the toolbar. The Address Book window will appear with the current list of Address Book entries displayed in alphabetical order by first name.

2. Click the New Group icon on the toolbar of the Address Book. The Properties window will appear.

3. Enter a name for the new Group in the Group Name field.

4. Click the Select Members button. The Select Group Members window will appear. Double-click each member's name that you want to appear in the new Group. Click OK when you're finished.

5. Enter any comments or other information in the Notes field. This entry is optional. Click OK when you're finished.

Your new entry will appear in the Address Book, as shown in Figure 10.9.

Once you add your new Group to the Address Book, you can select the group when composing a new piece of e-mail just as you did when you selected individual Address Book entries. Compose the rest of your e-mail message and rest assured that all your intended recipients will receive the message. Is that a timesaver or what?

FIG. 10.9
With Groups, you can e-mail multiple accounts with only a couple clicks of the mouse.

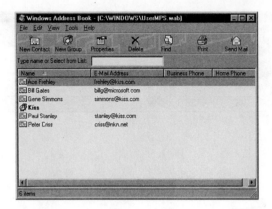

Mail Composition Options

So now you can send an e-mail message, set filters for your incoming e-mail, and use the Address Book effectively. But there's much more that you can do with Outlook Express Mail. It is now easier than ever to send files (intact!) across the Internet without needing external decoding programs, using special formatting techniques when composing e-mail, and automatically including outside text from a file on your hard drive into the contents of your e-mail message. Let's explore the composition options at your fingertips when using Outlook Express Mail.

Sending Files as Attachments   Have you ever sent an overnight package that contained only a floppy disk full of information? If so, you most likely spent $10 or more sending information that you could have sent as an e-mail attachment virtually for free, barring any connection charges to your ISP.

The process of sending a file attachment used to be an intimidating task. The only way to send a file through e-mail used to be to run a file through a UUENCODE program, paste the contents of the file attachment into your message, and hope that the user on the receiving end of the message had a UUDECODE program to use the file once he or she received it. Now the process is much easier, however, because Outlook Express Mail, along with most other e-mail packages, uses MIME (Multipurpose Internet Mail Extension) to encode and decode file attachments. In fact, the process is so easy now, it will become second nature to you in no time.

To send an attachment through e-mail, follow these steps:

1. Click the New Message icon to begin composing a fresh message.
2. Click Insert, File Attachment. The standard Windows file system dialog box will appear. Browse your file system and locate the file you want to attach to your message. Click OK once you have selected the file.
3. Finish composing the body of your e-mail message. You'll notice the attached file appears as the bottom of your e-mail message, as shown in Figure 10.10.
4. Click the Send button when you are ready to send your message.

Part
II
Ch
10

FIG. 10.10

When it comes to electronic documents, sending file attachments via e-mail is an easy way to save on shipping costs.

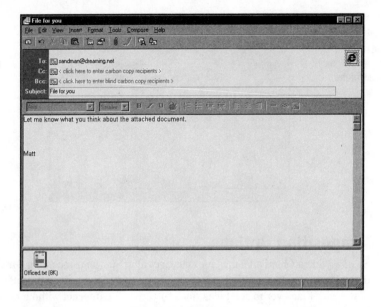

There is no limit to the number of files that you can attach to one e-mail message. It is good manners to separate your files into groups when sending many files at once, however. This way, your e-mail recipient will not be downloading one message for an hour. In fact, many large e-mail messages can crash even the most advanced e-mail servers, so be careful how much you send at one time.

If you receive a file attached to a piece of e-mail, simply open your mail message and double-click the attachment icon. The corresponding program file should launch with your attachment displayed in the active window. If you wish, you can save the attachment to your hard drive by right-clicking the icon and choosing Save As. At this point, you must choose a location to which to save the file on your hard drive and click OK to save the file for later use.

NOTE Limitations of Online Services: Some online services, such as America Online, limit file attachments to one per message. It is good practice to send each file attachment in a separate message or to Zip the individual files together into one larger file using a utility such as WinZip (**http://www.winzip.com**). ■

Sending Text from a File in a Message   Suppose you have a text-based document on your hard drive and want to include its contents into an e-mail message that you're composing. Instead of retyping the contents into your message, or even cutting and pasting in the information, you can simply use Outlook Express Mail's Insert Text from File feature to include the contents automatically. At the time of this writing, you can include only two types of text in an e-mail message—a simple text file (.txt) or an HTML file (.htm or .html).

To include text from a file in your e-mail message, follow these steps:

1. Click New Message from the toolbar to open an empty message.
2. Enter the recipient's name and the subject line of your message.
3. Click Insert, Text from File. The Windows file system dialog box will appear, prompting you for the location of the text file that you wish to include.
4. Locate the text file for inclusion and click Open. The contents of the text file will be placed in the body of your message wherever the cursor is resting.
5. Click Send to mail the message.

If you choose an HTML file for inclusion, Outlook Express Mail will read the HTML syntax and reproduce its layout within the mail message. Images, sounds, and other multimedia Web elements will not be included, however.

Using Background Images in Your Messages   If you want your e-mail messages to stand out over all others, you might try altering the background color of the mail message or include your own custom background image. Be warned, however, that only users of Outlook Express Mail or Microsoft Outlook will be able to see your custom e-mail message. With that said, let's change the way your e-mail message is displayed.

To add color to the background of your message, follow these steps:

1. Create a new mail message by clicking New Message on the toolbar.
2. Click Format, Background, Color. The Windows color palate will appear.
3. Click the color of your choice, as shown in Figure 10.11. The background color of your image will change to the color that you selected.

Part
II

Ch
10

FIG. 10.11
You can change the background of your e-mail messages to reflect a solid color to liven things up a bit.

To add a background image to your message, follow these steps:

1. Create a new mail message by clicking New Message on the toolbar.

2. Click Format, Background, Picture. The Background Image dialog box will appear.

3. Enter in the absolute URL to a picture file that you want as your background in the format http://www.*server*.com/*imagename*.gif. Click OK to make the change. Figure 10.12 shows an e-mail message with a custom background image displayed.

FIG. 10.12

You can include background images in your e-mail messages to give personality to your mail.

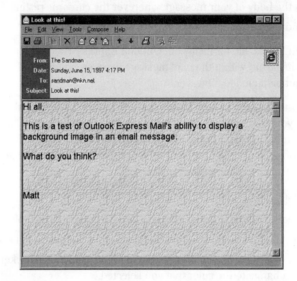

Formatting Text (HTML versus Rich Text)   With Outlook Express Mail, you can format all of the text in your message as though it were an HTML page. Many of today's mail clients, such as Netscape Mail and Eudora Pro, can read HTML formatted e-mail messages, though many older clients cannot. It is okay to use HTML formatting as your default when composing e-mail messages, though some recipients may not be able to see the added formatting capabilities. You'll find that using HTML for formatting your messages can really jazz up the look of your outgoing e-mail, however, and add functionality to the body of your message.

To switch between Rich Text formatting and HTML, follow these steps:

1. Open an empty e-mail message by clicking New Message on the toolbar.

2. Click Format, then choose between Rich Text and HTML, as shown in Figure 10.13.

When the default setting is HTML, you will have a special toolbar above the body of your message, as shown in Figure 10.14.

The HTML Formatting Toolbar functions are listed in Table 10.2.

FIG. 10.13

Sometimes you may want to revert to Rich Text formatting when e-mailing older e-mail programs.

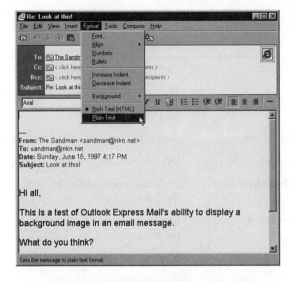

FIG. 10.14

The HTML formatting toolbar enables you to edit e-mail messages much like in a word processor.

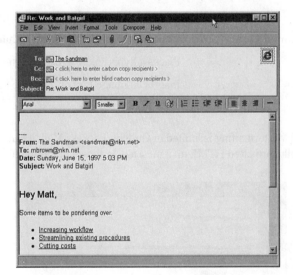

Table 10.2   HTML Formatting Toolbar Functions

Name	Function
Font Name	Enables you to choose the displayed font
Font Size	Adjusts the display size of the text
Bold	Places text in bold letters

continues

Table 10.2   Continued

Name	Function
Italic	Places text in italic formatting
Underline	Places an underline under selected text
Font Color	Changes the color of text
Formatting Numbers	Organizes items in a numbered list
Formatting Bullets	Organizes items in a bulleted list
Decrease Indentation	Decreases indentation between a paragraph of text and the left margin
Increase Indentation	Increases indentation between a paragraph of text and the left margin
Align Left	Aligns text flush with the left margin
Align Center	Centers all selected text
Align Right	Aligns text flush with the right margin
Insert Horizontal Line	Places a horizontal line break within your message
Set Link	Places a hyperlink to a text selection
Insert Image	Inserts an image (.gif or .jpg) into the body of your message

Though the HTML formatting is limited in Outlook Express Mail, it can still be useful. An example of a fully formatted HTML mail message is shown in Figure 10.15.

FIG. 10.15
Formatting messages with HTML make for a cross-platform messaging solution.

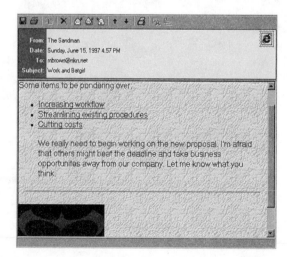

Advanced Mail Options

Outlook Express Mail has many program options that the end user can configure. These options give you total control over how to send messages, how to set reading options, how to use signatures, and how to set security features. To access the program options, click Tools, Mail Options. The four-tabbed options screen will open, enabling you to change any of the default settings.

Send Options   With the Send tab under Mail Options, as shown in Figure 10.16, you can control how and in what format mail is sent.

FIG. 10.16

Modifying the Send options gives you complete control over outbound e-mail messages.

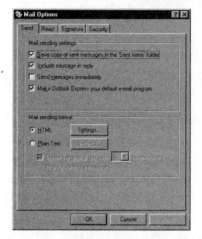

The mail sending options enable you to control what happens to mail as it is sent from Outlook Express. You should always check the first check box to ensure that you always retain a copy of sent messages in your Sent Items folder. This copy is most helpful should a recipient not receive a message and ask you to send it again.

The second check box controls whether the contents of a replied-to e-mail message are copied in the body of the e-mail. This copied message is a good idea so the recipient knows exactly what you're talking about in your message.

The third check box controls whether messages are sent out immediately after composing them. If you leave this unchecked, outgoing mail will not be sent until you click the Send and Retrieve button on the toolbar.

The fourth check box makes Outlook Express your default mail program. It is a good idea to keep this checked if you want Outlook Express and Internet Explorer to work hand-in-hand when dealing with e-mail links.

The Mail Sending Format option is a place where you can globally set the formatting capabilities a document can contain. By enabling HTML, you can format your messages with hyperlinks and pictures. Choosing Plain Text will limit the formatting ability of your document but ensure that all recipients can read the e-mail message.

Read Options　The Read tab, as shown in Figure 10.17, presents you with settings that control how often Outlook Express checks for mail, how you are alerted of new mail, and whether messages should be deleted when you exit the program.

FIG. 10.17

The Read options enable you to customize how read e-mail messages are handled within Outlook Express Mail.

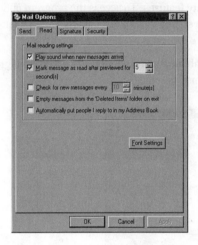

The first check box, when checked, will play a sound when new e-mail arrives. If you enable this, you will hear a bell when new mail arrives and will not have to check your mailbox for new messages quite so often because you will have an audible confirmation.

The second check box will mark your e-mail message as read after selecting it for a user-specified number of seconds. Even though a piece of e-mail might be marked as read, it is not moved from the Inbox until you move it.

The third check box controls how often Outlook Express Mail automatically checks the server for new mail. Having Outlook Express Mail check for new e-mail is a great way to keep your dial-up Internet connection active while you work on other things.

The fourth check box enables Outlook Express to delete anything in your Deleted Items folder when you exit the program. Though this feature can conserve disk space use, all messages that you delete are not recoverable, so think twice before enabling this feature.

The last check box will automatically create an entry in the Address Book for anyone to whom you send mail. This feature can be handy if you don't want to type out recipients' addresses every time you compose a piece of e-mail.

The Font Settings button enables you to change the default font size, font name, and fixed-pitch font. Most of the time, the default settings are fine, but feel free to experiment with your own custom settings.

Signature Options　The Signature tab, shown in Figure 10.18, enables you to create a signature file (or tagline) for inclusion in outbound mail. A signature can be something as simple as your name and e-mail address or as elaborate as a quote or short passage from your favorite book.

FIG. 10.18
The Signature tab enables you to create and use a tagline as an identifier at the bottom of your e-mail messages.

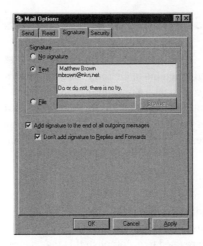

You can choose either No Signature, a Text signature that will come directly from the text box in this window, or a signature from a file located on your hard drive. To enable a Text signature, simply type in how you want your signature to appear and click Apply. If you want your signature file accessible to other programs on your hard drive, create a text file with your signature in it. After doing so, enter the path of your signature file into the File text box and click Apply. The two text boxes at the bottom of the Signature tab control exactly when Outlook Express Mail will use the signature file.

Security Options   The Security Options tab, as shown in Figure 10.19, controls digital signatures and encryption options.

FIG. 10.19
You can use a digital ID certificate for secure e-mail identification.

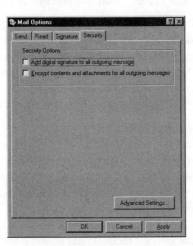

Now that security on the Internet is a big concern, Microsoft has made it possible for you to use personal digital security certificates when sending e-mail so that a recipient is assured that the mail he or she receives is really coming from your mailbox. If you are interested in acquiring a digital signature, point Internet Explorer to **http://digitalid.verisign.com/**.

Part
II

Ch
10

Outlook News Express: An Overview of UseNet Newsgroups

Before you dive into the advanced functions of Outlook Express News and into the sometimes complex world of UseNet newsgroups, take a few minutes to learn about the origin of UseNet, what people use UseNet newsgroups for, and a short list of rules that will ensure a smooth ride in the world of newsgroups. Soon you'll learn how simple UseNet is, how to find answers and provide solutions, and read interesting and insightful opinions on topics that relate to you.

History

In 1979, two graduate students from Duke University were searching for a way to exchange text-based messages. A third student, from the University of North Carolina, decided to give a helping hand to the other students and created the first Internet-based news transport system. A variety of UNIX shell scripts were used to accomplish this task. Once all the coding was completed, the first UseNet network was complete, using only two servers at remote locations. In 1980, a third server was added to the fold, again from Duke University, expanding the news network to new horizons. As word of mouth spread about the new information at hand, the public began to demand a tool that they could use to "read the news." The news interface was rewritten in late 1980 in the programming language called C, which allowed for a faster, more streamlined news client called A News.

Though A News was a monument in UseNet history, it simply wasn't very good. The program had a hard time handling large news threads and huge message bodies. It was soon to be re-written and called, naturally enough, B News. B News made its debut in 1982 after students at the University of California at Berkeley spent nearly two years getting their code up to par.

UseNet news articles used UUCP (UNIX to UNIX Copy Protocol) for the transport of mes-sages until 1986. UUCP was too slow and required too much overhead for messages to travel in a timely fashion between participating servers. A new transport software package became available called NNTP (Network News Transport Protocol) that allowed UseNet news articles to use TCP/IP and the Internet as its messaging system between servers. This software re-lease led to many participants of the UseNet system because many universities were already on the Internet.

From 1986, UseNet simply grew to epic proportions. All of a sudden, a remotely connected machine (via the Internet) did not have to run UseNet server software to read newsgroups. One of the first command-line newsreaders, TIN (Threaded Internet Netnews) is still widely used today on UNIX systems. As the GUI interface of the Macintosh and Windows systems became popular, new newsreaders were created, enabling millions of UseNet readers to scan articles, post opinions, and lend a helping hand to other Internet and computer users. UseNet news is still one of the most popular Internet technologies available today, which is a little ironic because UseNet was one of the first Internet applications created back in the 1980s.

Uses of Newsgroups

People access UseNet newsgroups for a variety of purposes, just as family members read the Sunday newspaper for a variety of reasons. Some use it for research, some read articles for entertainment, and others simply look to writers' opinions on informative topics. There is simply no single reason that users use UseNet. UseNet news articles are posted, updated, replied to, and read 24 hours a day. As one user posts a new article, thousands of servers across the world replicate the article into their existing news article base, enabling all Internet users to read the original posting shortly after it is composed.

Many corporate networks that have Internet connectivity are using UseNet newsgroups for IS support and advice. Suppose a new obstacle appears as you are planning a new node on your massive network and no one in your organization has come into contact with the problem before. The company could find a costly consultant to handle the network problem, do hours of research on the Internet and traditional networking books, or it could simply start by asking for advice on its problem in a targeted UseNet Newsgroup. The latter solution is the quickest and most cost effective. Because messages on UseNet are updated every second, the chances of finding a solution for your network problem are much greater than asking someone, or a group of individuals, about their like experiences. This is not to say that you should use UseNet news articles only for specific network problems. You can ask virtually any question about any topic and public replies can quickly help you move up to speed with your problem. This is the magic of UseNet.

UseNet newsgroups provide a wealth of information for all types of computer users, from the novice new user to the seasoned network veteran. At this time, only about three to five percent of all Internet newsgroups are related to the computer field. Because currently more than 24,000 public newsgroups are available, what are all of the other topics about? Many UseNet topics are about specific interests ranging from dolphin pictures to water-cooled Volkswagen cars to the rock group KISS. With topics ranging from nature to automotive mechanics, something is available on UseNet for everyone of all age groups.

Let's take a moment to examine the UseNet newsgroup hierarchy of topics. Though there are many different general headings, such as comp (computers) and rec (recreation), some are not so easy to figure out for the first-time UseNet user. Table 10.3 breaks down the hierarchy with a description of the types of groups that are found within.

Table 10.3 The UseNet News Hierarchy

comp.*	Computer topics, hardware, software, and so on
news.*	General UseNet topics
rec.*	Recreational topics: games, arts, music and TV, etc.
sci.*	Science, engineering, some social science
soc.*	Social issues
talk.*	Debate on a variety of topics

continues

Part
II

Ch
10

Table 10.3 Continued	
misc.*	Groups not fitting into one of the other hierarchies
alt.*	Where most of the "uncensored" Internet discussions take place. Many weird, non-mainstream, and otherwise bizarre groups call this hierarchy their home
bionet.*	Groups targeted toward biologists
bit.*	Bitnet mailing lists collected into newsgroup format
biz.*	Open to business and commercial traffic not appropriate in other groups
gnu.*	Groups for the Free Software Foundation's GNU project

If this is your first time using UseNet newsgroups, you should start by subscribing to **news.newusers.questions**. In this group, you can ask any question you want about UseNet and get answers from a variety of other users at different skill levels.

Newsgroup Etiquette

Before you start posting on any of the UseNet newsgroups, there are a few unwritten, yet understood, posting rules. Most of these rules should be common sense, especially with all of the hype surrounding the Internet today.

- **Don't Type in All Uppercase**   Typing in all uppercase characters makes it look as though you are shouting. It's also very hard on the eyes to read an article that looks like one long stream of text.

- **Look Before You Leap**   Spend a few days reading posts in newsgroups to which you've subscribed before you attempt to post an original article. Make sure that your post is in the correct group before you send your article. Read the FAQ (Frequently Asked Questions), if there is one, to learn more about the group and posting practices.

- **Do Not Flame**   Just because you disagree with someone's opinion does not give you the right to post a violent response to the original post. If someone flames one of your posts and you feel you have to reply, do so by e-mail or by taking the newsgroup thread to **alt.flame** or another designated flaming group.

- **Do Not Troll**   Trolling is the act of posting an article to a newsgroup solely to upset the readers of the group. Doing this is completely unnecessary and will likely result in your e-mail account becoming flooded by angry UseNet users.

- **Watch Your Cross-Posting**   If you feel that one of your UseNet articles is fit to be posted in multiple like newsgroups, do so with caution. Make absolutely sure that the point of your message is clear and relevant to the title of the group. Many UseNet users detest cross-posting, especially when an article does not fit into a group.

Remember that UseNet access is not a right, but a privilege. As long as you do not abuse your privilege, you will find that posting and reading posts in UseNet newsgroups is one of the most enriching forms of communication available to all Internet users.

Creating Multiple News Profiles

Adding additional news server profiles in Outlook Express News is quick and easy. All your news and mail accounts are held in one central location called Accounts, found in the Tools menu. To add a secondary news server, follow these steps:

1. Click Tools, Accounts to open the Internet Accounts window, as shown in Figure 10.20.
2. Click the Add button and choose News from the pop-up menu. The familiar Internet Connection Wizard appears and prompts you for information about you and your connection to the server.
3. Enter your real name and click Next.
4. Enter your e-mail address and click Next.
5. Enter the Internet address of the news server to which you want to connect. If the server requires you to log on using a username and password, place a check in the appropriate check box. Click Next to continue.
6. Enter in a friendly name for this particular news service that will distinguish it from all others. Click Next to continue.
7. Choose which type of connection you have to the Internet. Click Next. Click Finish on the last screen to complete the new server entry.

FIG. 10.20

Using multiple UseNet news providers enables you to have access to the most up-to-date news postings available.

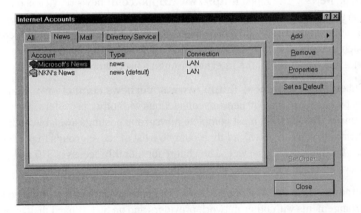

Once you've completed the preceding steps, an additional icon will appear in the Outlook Express left toolbar. To access any of your news services, simply click the icon and the newsgroups to which you are subscribed will appear in the upper-right window pane. Double-click the newsgroup subject to retrieve all of the articles that you have not read.

Free News Servers

Many free news servers are available for public access on the Internet today. Adding one of these groups to your current Outlook Express News profile is just as easy as I demonstrated in the previous section. Many of the free news servers in the following list are temporary, trial, or preview-based systems. Some may not be accessible at the time of this book's publishing. For a complete list of free active news servers, point Internet Explorer to NewzBot! at **http:// www.jammed.com/~newzbot/**. NewzBot! monitors free news servers with an automated Internet robot that calculates transmission speeds, number of groups available, and whether you are able to post to a particular server.

Commercial News Servers

After browsing your company or ISP's UseNet news service, you may find that it lacks many groups or portions of large articles about which you've seen other people posting. The only way to ensure that you receive the most articles possible is to subscribe to a news system that is dedicated to providing the most complete UseNet news access available. Most commercial UseNet news providers charge a monthly fee for full access, priced generally between $10 to $20 and allow you to sign up online. The key to a commercial UseNet news server is multiple incoming news feeds. The majority of Internet Service Providers have one main connection to the Internet and maybe a back-up connection to a secondary provider. With this type of setup, the typical ISP has only two incoming news feeds. Commercial news providers can have 10, 15, even 20 incoming news feeds from all across the Internet, however, providing not only the most complete list of postings, but the fastest as well. Three of the best commercial UseNet news servers are Zippo, Supernews, and Airnews.

Zippo News   The Zippo (**http://www.zippo.com**) news service is one of the oldest commercial news servers still in existence. Zippo offers thousands of newsgroups that you can read through a unique Web interface called Direct Read News or through dedicated newsreaders such as Outlook Express News. The monthly charge is $10 and you can access the interface with any computer on the Internet through a username and password check.

Supernews   Supernews (**http://www.supernews.com**) offers a unique UseNet service in that it has more than 30 peering connections with other providers. These connections allow for some of the quickest, most complete newsgroup postings available on the Internet. As you visit their site, you can download their complete list of active groups to peruse before you agree to pay for this monthly service. The charge for monthly access is $10 and you can access the service from any computer with Internet access.

Airnews   Internet America's Airnews (**http://www.airnews.net**) also boasts many peering arrangements with other network providers and an 80 GB hard disk array that keeps articles for two weeks, which ensures that you will not miss any posts if you go out of town. Airnews also hosts the Clarinet news feed, which contains up-to-date news articles from the Associated Press, Routers News Wire, and much more. The monthly charge is $10 and you can access the service through any newsreader.

Binary File Attachments

Some UseNet newsgroups contain file attachments much like e-mail messages. These attachments are known as binary files. The actual file is encoded using one of two techniques, MIME and UUENCODE. MIME (Multipurpose Internet Mail Extension) has recently become the standard for transferring files over the Internet through e-mail and news messages. MIME transfers the message intact, as though you were moving a file between two computers on your LAN. UUENCODE had been the standard way of attaching files to messages, though the process was at times tedious and complex. To make sense of the UUENCODED files that your e-mail or news program received, you had to have a UUDECODE program or a reader that could automatically complete the decoding process. Stick with MIME compliant e-mail and newsreaders and you'll be on the right track.

There are many UseNet newsgroups where binary files are posted. Most of the time, you'll see binary attachments in the alt.* hierarchy. Many of these are general pictures such as scenic views, animals, and pictures of family members. Most of the binary pictures posted in these groups are not for general viewing, however.

CAUTION

There are obscene, pornographic, and downright grotesque pictures posted in some of these groups all the time. Use caution when looking into such groups and make sure that you are available for supervision when a child is viewing newsgroup content.

Downloading Binary Files

Outlook Express News couldn't have made downloading binary files any easier. Outlook Express looks at a binary file attachment as a simple file and presents it as such. If the binary is a picture, the picture will appear in the lower pane of Outlook Express. Both pictures and software programs will display a paper clip icon in the body of the message to let you know when you have encountered a binary file and both will allow you to save it to your hard drive.

To see binary decoding in action, temporarily subscribe to a binary group such as **alt. binary.pictures.animals**. In this group, people post pictures of their favorite animals and occasionally post fishing trip pictures. A tip-off of a binary file is the content description. You will generally see a brief description and a file type, such as **duck.jpg 1/1**, which would mean that the binary attachment is some type of duck and is in the JPEG format. It also lets you know that the file is a complete post (1/1). Once you have found an article for which you want to retrieve the binary attachment, simply click the message header once to retrieve the body. Once you have downloaded the content, your binary file will open in Outlook Express News, as shown in Figure 10.21.

If you want to save the binary file to your hard drive, simply click the paper clip and click the pop-up menu that lists the file name. You will be presented with the familiar "What would you like to do with this?" menu and can choose to open the file or save it to your hard drive. It's important to remember that the binary attachment is not saved onto your hard drive until you tell your computer to do so.

FIG. 10.21

Outlook Express News automatically decodes binary attachments and displays them immediately. Note the paper clip icon in the right side of the message body.

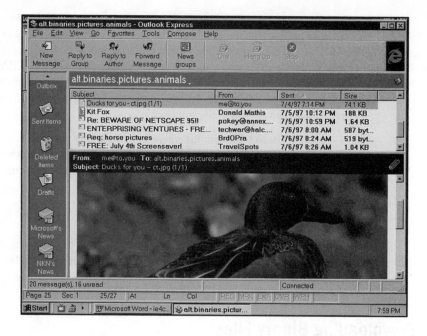

Posting Binary Files

You've seen all the binary files on the animals newsgroup and now you're jealous because you want to post a picture of your favorite duck. Be happy knowing that Outlook Express News can help you easily post whatever file you want as an article attachment. Make sure that the content you are posting relates to the function of the newsgroup to which you are posting.

To add a binary attachment to a UseNet newsgroup article, follow these steps:

1. Create a news newsgroup article by clicking New Message on the toolbar. An empty message will appear, enabling you to type in a Subject and compose the body of your message.

2. Click Insert, File Attachment. The Insert Attachment window will open, enabling you to browse your file system for the file that you wish to attach.

3. Highlight the file that you want to attach and click the Attach button. An icon for the attachment will be placed at the bottom of your article, letting you know that it's ready to be posted, as shown in Figure 10.22.

4. Click the Post Message button on the toolbar to send the message to the desired newsgroup.

That's it. Now you can post binary files to your heart's content and share your wonderful pictures and other files with other UseNet users around the world.

FIG. 10.22
Outlook Express News shows you what files are attached to your messages as soon as they are attached.

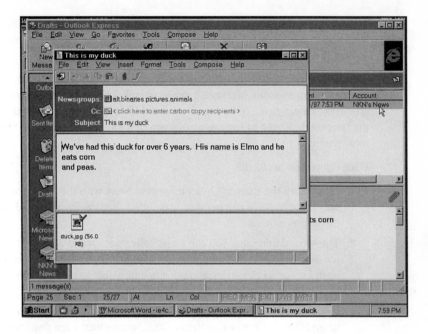

Using the Newsgroup Filters

Remember the Inbox Assistant that you used earlier in this chapter to reroute e-mail messages to appropriate folders and recipients? Well, there is something similar to the Inbox Assistant in Outlook Express News called Newsgroup Filters. This can be used to control UseNet news articles that you do not wish to read or take control of blocking certain posters that are known for their off-topic articles. The function of the Newsgroup Filters in Outlook Express News is close to the Inbox Assistant in Outlook Express Mail.

Spam

The biggest reason for controlling incoming UseNet messages with the filters is spam. Spam, as it relates to the Internet, is not the tasty treat from Hormel. Spam is flooding the Internet with many copies of the same message, in an attempt to force the message on people who would not otherwise choose to receive it. Most spam is commercial advertising, often for dubious products, get-rich-quick schemes, or quasi-legal services. Spam costs the sender very little to send—the recipient or the carriers, rather than the sender, pay for most of the costs.

There are two main types of spam, and they have different effects on Internet users. Cancelable UseNet spam is a single message sent to 20 or more UseNet newsgroups. (Through long experience, UseNet users have found that any message posted to so many newsgroups is often not relevant to most or all of them.) UseNet spam is aimed at "lurkers," people who read newsgroups but rarely or never post and give their address away. UseNet spam robs users

Part
II

Ch
10

of the utility of the newsgroups by overwhelming them with a barrage of advertising or other irrelevant posts. Furthermore, UseNet spam subverts the ability of system administrators and owners to manage the topics they accept on their systems.

As your experience on UseNet newsgroups grows, you will unfortunately see more and more content known as spam. Message headers to look for that almost always denote spam content are "Make money fast," "Free Pics Here," and "Read Me!" There are now even companies on the Internet dedicated to spamming newsgroups with content that just doesn't make sense for most groups.

What can you do to stop it?

- First, block the spam in Outlook Express News with the Newsgroup Filters. This is the only thing that you can personally do other than get involved with anti-spam groups on the Internet.

- The second thing that you can do is notify your system administrator of the spam messages. The system administrator of your ISP can take steps to stop the spam from an upstream network carrier, though it is impossible to block all of it.

- The third thing that you can do to block spam is to hold on to your e-mail address as though it were gold. Do not post on UseNet with your real e-mail address or give it out when filling out any online forms. Often, online forms are designed to become a part of big lists of e-mail addresses for mass-marketing. These lists often sell for thousands of dollars and are responsible for the junk e-mail that almost every Internet user receives.

Blocking Unwanted Messages

To block unwanted UseNet article postings, you're going to ultimately need the e-mail address of the person who is posting the content that you do not want to receive. You can also block messages by entering literal statements to block such as "Make money fast" or "Free." Blocking these two would remove any articles pertaining to making money fast or any messages containing the word "free" in the subject line. To block messages using the Newgroup Filters, follow these steps:

1. Click Tools, Newsgroup Filters. The Group Filters window will appear.

2. Click Add to make a new filter. The Properties window will open, enabling you to choose the content you are going to filter.

3. Choose which server or newsgroup for which you want to set the filter. You also have the option of creating a global filter for all of your subscribed newsgroups.

4. Enter the e-mail address of the poster that you wish to filter out, or type in a subject title in the Subject field, as shown in Figure 10.23. You can do both, if you want.

5. Click OK to close the Properties window. Choose OK again to close the Group Filters window.

FIG. 10.23
Newsgroup Filters
enable you to block
article subject lines as
well as the author's e-
mail address.

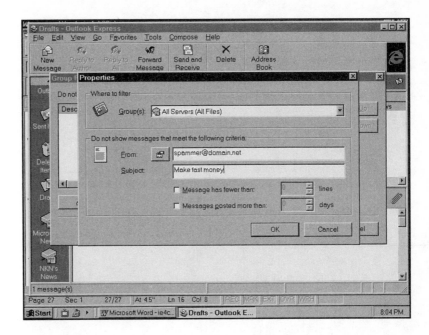

Your newsgroup filter is now set. You may find yourself creating many filters over time to block
known spammers and other postings that you do not wish to receive. You must realize, however, that you cannot block all unwanted messages and you should only spend a reasonable
amount of time trying to do so. Remember that UseNet newsgroups are a public forum for
exchanging ideas and the free nature of the Internet itself says that all messages can be freely
posted, no matter how out of place they seem to be. ●

In Depth: FrontPage Express

Back in Chapter 6, "Quick Start: FrontPage Express and the Internet Publishing Wizard," you learned how to get up and running with FrontPage Express—the Web page composition tool that comes bundled in the Internet Explorer software suite. You saw how to use FrontPage Express templates and wizards to get a quick start on certain types of pages, and you learned how to format text and add images and hyperlinks to your documents. Once your document was done, you read about how to use the Web Publishing Wizard to save your document to a remote server, thereby publishing it on the Internet.

The tasks you learned to complete in Chapter 6 are fundamental to HTML authoring, but they are by no means all that FrontPage Express can do for you. Remember that FrontPage Express is essentially the editor portion of FrontPage, a very powerful Web development tool. As such, it has many features that go beyond basic Web page composition. This chapter takes a closer look at some of these advanced features and shows you how to use them to make your pages more engaging and interactive.

The majority of this chapter is dedicated to discussing many of FrontPage Express's high-end abilities. Over the next several sections, you'll learn how to do the following:

Set global page attributes

FrontPage Express provides thorough support for controlling page attributes like backgrounds, link colors, and margins.

Create tables with ease

Setting up a table with FrontPage Express is as easy as filling out a dialog box. Once you set up the table, you can go back and tweak row and cell properties to customize the table to your needs.

Make use of Internet Explorer extensions

The Internet Explorer browser supports scrolling text marquees and inline playback of Audio Video Interleave (AVI) video clips. Find out how to use FrontPage Express to place these exciting and dynamic objects in your documents.

Go to the source

Even though it is a What-You-See-Is-What-You-Get (WYSIWYG) editor, you can still edit the raw HTML source code that FrontPage Express generates.

- Adjust the global properties of a page
- Add a background sound to a document
- Place a scrolling marquee on a page
- Display Audio Video Interleave (AVI) video clips
- Organize information using tables
- Create multiwindow layouts with frames
- Compose forms to gather information from users
- Write scripts that execute on either the server or the client side
- Embed precompiled content, such as Java applets and ActiveX controls
- Use FrontPage Express Web Bots to easily add interactivity to your pages
- Create a Web View folder
- Work with the raw HTML code that FrontPage Express generates

  ▶ **See** "Microsoft FrontPage and Image Composer," **p. 367**

Setting Page Properties

The HTML 3.2 standard includes a number of instructions that modify global page attributes. These new instructions give authors control over things like backgrounds, use of color, and, thanks to extensions by Microsoft, margins. You can specify all these attributes by using the FrontPage Express Page Properties dialog box shown in Figure 11.1. The dialog box is made up of four panels, each with its own set of page parameters that you can tweak. To access the dialog box, you can choose File, Page Properties or right-click your mouse on the page and select the Page Properties option from the pop-up menu.

FIG. 11.1

Control global page attributes from the Page Properties dialog box.

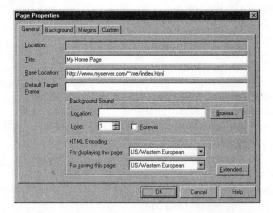

With the General tab of the Page Properties dialog box, you specify information typically found in the head of the HTML document. Specifically, you can give your document a title, specify its base URL (used as a basis for all relative URLs in the document), and any default target frame, if you're using a framed layout. You can also include a background sound and specify what kind of HTML encoding to use.

T I P Always make sure that your document is titled. Titles show up in the title bar of the Internet Explorer window, in the Favorite Places folder, and in History lists. Additionally, search engines dispatch roving programs called spiders to look at published pages, and one item for which spiders typically look is a title. Thus, a proper title helps the search engine index your page more accurately and efficiently.

From the Background tab, you can choose to use a solid color or an image as your document background. If you use a color, you can select from the drop-down list or click the Custom item in the list to choose your own color from the standard Windows Color dialog box. Images used for a background are tiled across and down the page, so be sure that the copies of the image fit together seamlessly. Otherwise, the tiled image pattern can be quite distracting.

N O T E Internet Explorer supports a background image being a "watermark," or a nonscrolling background. If you want your background image to stay in one place as readers scroll through your pages, be sure to click the Watermark checkbox. ▪

Other options in the Background tab enable you to choose colors for body text, unvisited hyperlinks, visited hyperlinks, and active hyperlinks. Choosing a color for one of these features is much like choosing a background color—simply select one from the drop-down list or pick a custom color.

Internet Explorer enables authors to specify a top and left margin in their documents so that there is a little breathing room along these edges of the browser window. You can set your margins from the Margins tab of the Page Properties dialog box by checking which type of margin you want to activate and then setting the number of pixels you want the margin to be.

Finally, with the Custom tab, you can set system and user variables, such as what program was used to generate the document or a list of document keywords to enhance searchability.

For instance, if you want to use the client pull technique to cause another document to load after a prescribed amount of time, you can specify the system variable HTTP-EQUIV to Refresh and the Value to the number of seconds of delay, followed by a semicolon (;), followed by the URL of the document to load next.

Including a Background Sound

In the previous section, you read that you can include a background sound on your pages by setting it up from the General tab of the Page Properties dialog box. The background sound can come from any file that stores sound in the WAV, MIDI, AU, or AIFF formats. You can browse for this type of file on your hard drive, or you can provide the URL of the sound file if you're pulling it off the Web.

Below the Background Sound Location field, you'll find two other items: Loop and Forever. Loop controls how many times the sound is played. If you're not satisfied with a finite number of times, you can check the Forever box and the sound will play for as long as a user is on the page.

Part
II

Ch
11

> **CAUTION**
>
> Think about whether you really want to use an infinitely looping sound. After a while, the repeating sound clip can become annoying to users and make them want to leave your page.
>
> Also, try to keep your sound files small. Large sound files can take a long time to download and users may leave your page before the sound has finished downloading.

Adding a Marquee

When Java first arrived, one early applet supported a scrolling text banner right in the browser window. Not too long afterward, Microsoft built this capability into Internet Explorer and proposed an HTML tag to support these banners. Microsoft called the banners marquees, and, using FrontPage Express, you don't have to worry about coding the marquee in HTML. You just need to choose Insert, Marquee and configure your marquee in the Marquee Properties dialog box (see Figure 11.2).

FIG. 11.2

Put your message in lights by using Internet Explorer's support for scrolling text marquees.

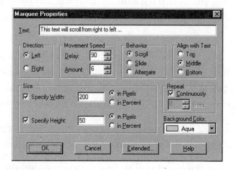

As you can see from the figure, a lot goes into setting up a marquee. The primary piece of information you need to specify is what text message you want to have scroll. Do this by typing the message into the Text field. From there, you can control whether the text moves to the left or to the right (Direction), how fast the text should move (Movement Speed), whether the movement behavior should be sliding, scrolling, or alternating (Behavior), and how other text should be aligned around the marquee (Align with Text).

A marquee will take up only as much space as is necessary. You can force a marquee to be a certain width and height by checking the Specify Width and Specify Height checkboxes, respectively. Once you activate these boxes, you can make the dimension a set number of pixels or a certain percentage of the available space in the browser window.

By default, the marquee message will keep scrolling as long as the user is on the page. You can make the message scroll a set number of times by deselecting the Continuously check box and specifying a number of times for the message to repeat. Finally, you can make the marquee background color different from the background of the rest of the page, which is a nice way to add contrast to your marquee so that your message stands out even more. Figure 11.3 shows a finished marquee scrolling across an open page.

FIG. 11.3
Marquees put text in motion across a page without any programming.

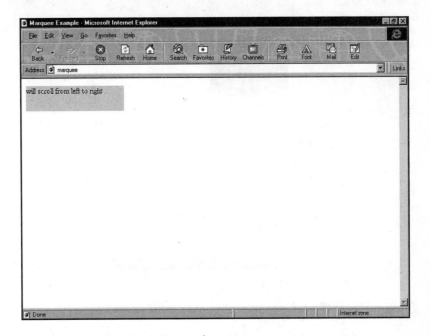

Inline Video Clips

When content developers first started putting video clips on their pages, users would need a separate helper application to view the video. Microsoft changed all that when it built inline support for Audio Video Interleave (AVI) files into Internet Explorer. This means that IE can play the movie right in the browser window without having to rely on a helper application.

To place an AVI video clip into a FrontPage Express document, choose Insert, Video. You can use an AVI file on a local drive or you can tell FrontPage Express where it can find the desired AVI file on the Internet. Once it knows from where to draw the AVI file, FrontPage Express makes a placeholder for it on your document.

From there, you can configure display parameters by right-clicking the space that FrontPage Express has reserved for the video clip and choosing the Image Properties option from the pop-up menu that appears. This menu takes you to the Video tab of the Image Properties dialog box . From this tab, you can change the URL of the AVI source file, if needed. You can also choose whether Internet Explorer displays a set of playback controls for the user (see Figure 11.4), how many times the clip should loop, how much delay there should be between playbacks, and when playback should start. By default, playback will start when the file opens, but you can also set it to occur when users pass their mouse pointers over the video clip.

FIG. 11.4
Playback controls enable the user to determine how and when to run the inline video clip.

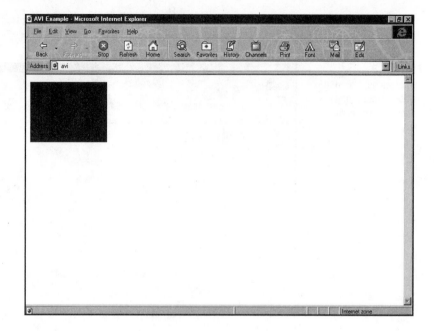

Creating Tables

Tables are useful page constructs for many reasons. You can use them to present tabular information in an easy-to-read form, align form fields so that your forms look streamlined and professional, and create interesting page layouts using the fine alignment control you get with tables. FrontPage Express's support for building and modifying tables can help you with each of these tasks.

You can add a table to your page quickly by clicking the Insert Table button on the bottom FrontPage Express toolbar. When you do, you'll see a five-by-five grid appear with a Cancel button under it. To create a table with five or fewer columns and five or fewer rows, simply drag your mouse from the upper left of the grid to fill out as many rows and columns you want your table to be. For example, as shown in Figure 11.5, if you want a table that's three rows and four columns, drag your mouse three spaces down the grid and four spaces across. When you release the mouse button, FrontPage Express will place an empty table of the size you specified in your document. Once the shell of the table is there, it falls on you to populate each of the cells of the table with content (see Figure 11.6).

If you need to make a table that has more than five rows or columns, you're better off choosing the Insert Table option under the Table menu. Figure 11.7 shows the dialog you get when choosing this option. You can set the dimensions of the table to be as many rows and columns as you want. Additionally, you can set some global table attributes, such as how the table is aligned relative to other elements on the page, how thick to make the table border, how much cellpadding (space between cell contents and the cell boundary) and cellspacing (space between adjacent cells) to leave, and how wide to make the table. Once you've set these parameters to your liking, FrontPage Express will create an empty table according to your specs.

FIG. 11.5
The Insert Table toolbar button enables you to specify a new table's size by dragging your mouse across a grid.

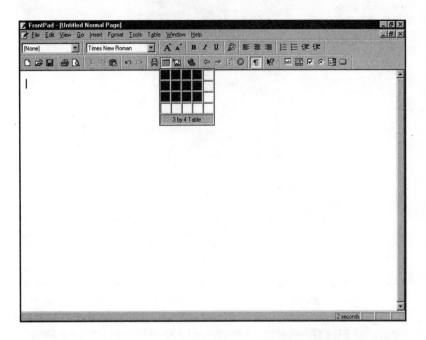

FIG. 11.6
Table cells can contain text, images, form fields, and even other tables!

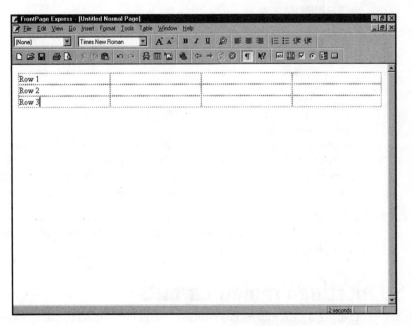

Part
II

Ch
11

FIG. 11.7
The Insert Table dialog box provides greater flexibility than the Create Table toolbar button.

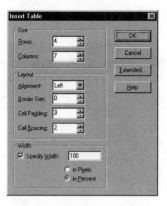

Even as you add content to your table, FrontPage Express continues to support you with an extensive set of options under the Table menu. You can insert more rows, columns, or cells into an existing table, and you can also put a caption on your table. For more intricate table requirements, you can merge multiple cells into one or split a given cell into multiple columns or rows.

N O T E If you choose the Insert Caption option, you'll see a cursor centered above the table where you can type in and format your caption. If you prefer your caption to be below the table, you can right-click the caption and choose the Caption Properties option you see on the pop-up menu. This menu will take you to a dialog box where you can change the caption position from above the table to below the table.

The next set of options on the Table menu enables you to highlight a particular cell, row, column, or the entire table. These options are useful if you want to selectively delete parts of your table or if you want to change the properties of just a few table sections.

Near the bottom of the Table menu, you'll find options for Caption Properties, Cell Properties, and Table Properties. The Caption Properties dialog box lets you change the position of the caption, as noted previously. You can modify the properties of a selected cell by making changes in the dialog box shown in Figure 11.8. Note in the dialog box how many attributes you can control—horizontal and vertical alignment, width, background color or image, border colors, and the number of rows and columns the cell should occupy. With this type of fine control, it should be no surprise to you that tables are a popular tool for Web page design.

If you call the Table Properties dialog box, you'll see that it contains all the same attributes as the Insert Table dialog did, plus the background and border color attributes you saw in the Cell Properties dialog box earlier.

Supporting Framed Layouts

Creating a page with frames requires a bit of planning on the author's part. First, you need to design the layout and produce the HTML code that will split the browser window into multiple frames. Then you must add content to those frames in a way that makes sense to the end user. For example, if you put a set of site navigation options in a frame near the bottom of the page, you'll want to set it up so that when a user clicks one of those links, the linked document is loaded in another frame, not the one in which the navigation links live.

FIG. 11.8

You can change a wealth of cell-related attributes to control behavior in the cell very precisely.

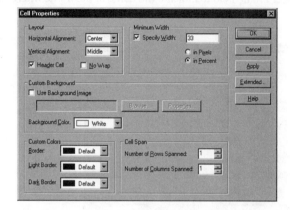

Though FrontPage Express does not have a facility for helping you create the basic framed layout, it can help you with the setup of content inside of a framed layout. In particular, FrontPage Express provides good support for *targeting* hyperlinks to a frame of a specific name. You've already read about one case of this in the Page Properties section of this chapter. The General tab of the Page Properties dialog box includes a field for entering a Default Target Frame (refer to Figure 11.1). When you place a frame's name in this field, every hyperlink in the document will target that frame. This means that when a link is clicked, the document to which it points will load in the specified frame.

The other time you specify frame names as targets is when setting up individual hyperlinks. To help with this, each tab in the Create Hyperlink (choose Insert, Hyperlink) dialog box (see Figure 11.9) contains a Target Frame field where you can specify the name of the frame where you want to display linked documents.

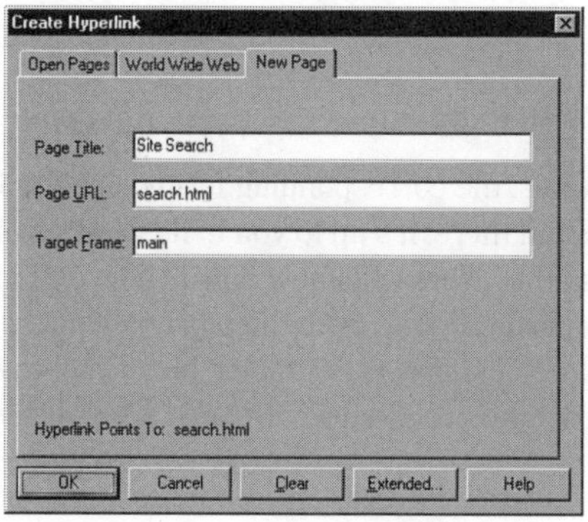

FIG. 11.9

You can target a frame in each of your hyper-links to make content appear where you want it to appear.

Part

II

Ch

11

A less familiar use of targeting is to route the output generated by a form submission to a particular frame. To set up this kind of target, you must access the Form Properties dialog box (see Figure 11.10) by right-clicking the form (FrontPage Express renders forms with dashed lines around them) and choosing the Form Properties option from the pop-up menu. Then move to the Target Frame field to indicate the name of the frame where the form-related output should appear.

FIG. 11.10
You can route output from a CGI script that processes a form to any named frame by setting up a target in the Form Properties dialog box.

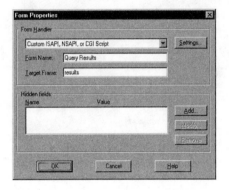

> **N O T E**   Targeting frames is also possible when you set imagemap links, though FrontPage Express does not provide dialog box support for this type of targeting. ■

Composing Forms

FrontPage Express helps you with form composition in three important ways. The most obvious is the Form Toolbar, which hosts buttons with which you can place the following:

- One-line text boxes
- Scrolling (multiple lines) text boxes
- Checkboxes
- Radio buttons
- Drop-down lists
- Action buttons (Submit or Reset)

When you click one of the buttons, the corresponding form control will appear in the FrontPage Express window. From there, it's up to you to do two things: Put some prompting text next to the form control so that users will know how to interpret it and right-click the control, select the Form Field Properties option from the pop-up menu, and fill out the dialog box that appears. When filling out the field properties dialog boxes, be sure that you're giving each field its own unique name so that the processing script can properly identify each piece of data a user submits.

Another way FrontPage Express helps you with forms is with the Insert, Form Field menu option. Choosing this will give you a list of form field controls that include those that you can place from the Form Toolbar *plus* the Image option. With the Image option, you can set up an image as a submit button rather than the standard gray, rectangular button.

Finally, FrontPage Express enables you to adjust global form parameters from the Form Properties dialog box (refer to Figure 11.10). In addition to specifying the target frame information you read about in the last section, you can also specify how the form is handled (by a CGI script or some other means), what the form's name is, and any hidden fields that should be included in the form.

Writing Client-Side Scripts

With the advent of browsers that can interpret and execute client-side scripts, authors needed a way to embed such scripts in their documents. FrontPage Express assists you with the Insert, Script menu option. When you choose Insert, Script, you see the dialog box shown in Figure 11.11. The first thing you must do in the dialog box is choose which language you want to use. VBScript and JavaScript are the two most popular languages, but you can also specify a different scripting language in the Other field. The rest of the space in the dialog box is dedicated to an area where you can type in the script code. When you click the OK button, the script shows up in your document as a yellow rectangle with an icon inside that suggests the scripting language you used.

▶ **See** "Enhancing Your Web Page with Scripts," **p. 541**

N O T E You can specify that a VBScript script should run on the server, rather than on the client. If you do this, make sure you're using a Microsoft Web server product, such as Personal Web Server or Internet Information Server. Other servers won't be able to process VBScript code. ■

FIG. 11.11
FrontPage Express takes the script code you type and incorporates it into the page on which you're working.

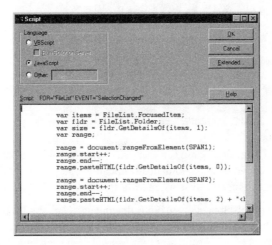

Using Web Bots

When Microsoft rolled out FrontPage, they also included a number of preprogrammed CGI-like functions called Web Bots. Web Bots were simple to use because a document author would simply drop the Web Bot into the documents and the server would know what to do with it. Initially, Web Bots only worked with Microsoft server products, but Microsoft later made FrontPage server extensions available for other servers and platforms so that Web Bots essentially became server independent.

Because it is a scaled-down version of the FrontPage editor, FrontPage Express retains some of the Web Bots that come with FrontPage, including the following:

- **Include**   The Include Bot enables you to include the contents from a separate file in your current document. When the document is served, the server will look at the included file and build its contents into the served document. An Include Bot is useful for standard page elements like navigation bars or copyright notices that appear on most pages. You can build in these elements easily using Web Bots and, if you need to edit one of the elements, you just have to edit it in the included file—the change is essentially made on every page.

- **Search**   The Search Bot puts a search form right on the page for you and then uses the user's search criteria to perform the search. When you configure the Search Bot, you can specify the search prompting text, how big the search criteria entry field should be, and how the Submit and Reset buttons should be labeled (see Figure 11.12). On the results side, you can control what word list to search and what information is presented with each match (file size, date of last change, and search score).

FIG. 11.12

Need a search engine? Just use a FrontPage Express Web Bot!

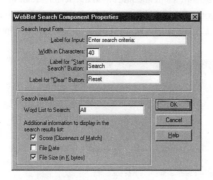

- **Timestamp**   The Timestamp Bot marks a document with the date and time that the page was last edited or last automatically updated. You have your choice of a number of different date and time formats when setting up this Bot.

To place any of these Web Bots in one of your documents, click the Insert WebBot Component button on the Standard Toolbar or choose Insert, WebBot Component menu option and then select the Bot you want to use. FrontPage Express will then present you with a dialog box that enables you to configure the Bot's options.

N O T E If you like FrontPage Express's Web Bot functionality, you should consider upgrading to FrontPage. FrontPage has noted the preceding Bots plus others for adding HTML markup, doing form validation, and setting up a table of contents. ▪

Placing ActiveX Controls and Java Applets

Embedded executables like ActiveX controls and Java applets have brought a whole new meaning to interactive Web pages. These precompiled chunks of programming bring pages to life and make a visit to your site a much more engaging experience. FrontPage Express supports placing several different types of "active" content into your documents, including the following:

■ **ActiveX Controls** When you choose Insert, Other Components and then select ActiveX Control, you see the dialog box shown in Figure 11.13. Once you choose a control to use, you can also set up layout properties such as height and width, border size, the amount of space to leave around the control, the way to arrange other page elements around the control, and the HTML that should be rendered if a user's browser cannot process the control.

Part
II

Ch
11

FIG. 11.13

You can select one of the many ActiveX controls that FrontPage Express knows about, many of which are installed when you install the Internet Explorer suite.

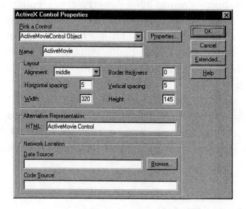

■ **Java Applets** Setting up a Java applet is similar to what you have to do for ActiveX controls. When you select Insert, Other Component, Java Applet, you are presented with the Java Applet Properties dialog box shown in Figure 11.14. Here you can give the location of the applet source code, its base URL, and the text that should be displayed by browsers that are not Java-enabled. If the applet requires any parameters, you can set them in the Applet Parameters portion of the dialog box. You can also configure many of the same layout properties that you could for an ActiveX control, such as width and height, alignment, and amount of white space to leave around the applet.

■ **Plug-ins** Content such as Macromedia Director movies are displayed in the Internet Explorer window by means of an add-on program called a plug-in. When you're placing content in your document that will be processed by a plug-in, you can choose the Insert,

Other Component, Plug-in option. The dialog you see next enables you to browse to the content file, to specify a text-based alternative for those users who do not have the plug-in, and to configure layout properties.

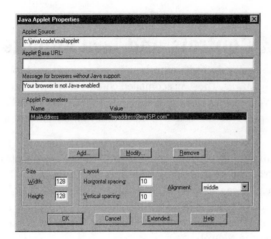

- ■ **PowerPoint Animation**   You can build PowerPoint presentations right into a page by placing the presentation as a PowerPoint animation. To do this, select Insert, Other Components, PowerPoint Animation and browse to the PowerPoint file you want to include. FrontPage Express asks you whether you want the file displayed via an ActiveX control or a plug-in. You should choose the type that will make the presentation visible to the greater number of users.

N O T E   For those knowledgeable of the HTML tags that support the placement of embedded active content, the following may help you keep the preceding options straight: ActiveX controls are placed with the `<OBJECT>` tag, Java applets with the `<APPLET>` tag, and plug-in content with the `<EMBED>` tag. ■

Creating a Web View Folder

Microsoft continues to blur the boundary between the Internet and your desktop by introducing the concept of a Web View Folder. With a Web View Folder, you can display the contents of folders on your machine via a Web page. With FrontPage Express, you can not only create Web View Folders, but you can also customize their appearance and even set up links to Internet mail and news!

To get started with a Web View Folder, the simplest thing to do is to choose File, New and then select the New Web View Folder from the dialog box that appears. When you do, you'll see a page that looks like that in Figure 11.15. The first two objects on the page are a JavaScript script that updates the folder listing whenever a selection changes, and an ActiveX control named "FileList" that does the work to gather the listing of folder contents. Below the script and the ActiveX control, you'll find a table with a black background in which a user would be able to select an item to see a description of it. The <?> items you see in the table are instances of HTML markup being applied.

FIG. 11.15
You can publish the contents of your computer by using a Web View Folder page.

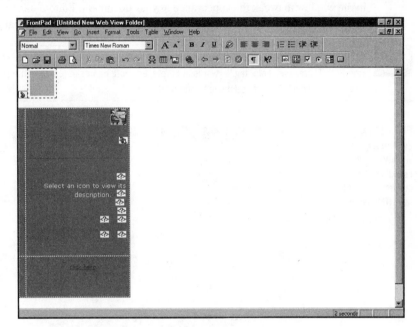

You get further Web View Folder support from the Insert menu. Choose Insert, Web View Folder Title to place a folder's title on your Web View page. The Web View Folder Contents option places the ActiveX control previously noted that generates the listing of folder contents. Finally, the Web View Shortcut to Mail and Web View Shortcut to News options place HTML markup that place links to Internet e-mail and news on the Web View.

> **CAUTION**
> The HTML markup placed by the Insert menu commands for Web View Folders relies on the FrontPage HTML Markup WebBot. This means you'll need to be running a Microsoft server product, or a different server with FrontPage extensions, for the Web View Folder page to work properly.

Working with Raw HTML Code

One of the biggest lamentations about the initial release of FrontPage was that you could not make changes to the HTML code FrontPage generates until after the code is saved in a file and then reopen it in a different editor. This changed in FrontPage97, when Microsoft included the option to view and edit the HTML code behind the WYSIWYG page on screen.

FrontPage Express users will be happy to know that it has inherited this capability as well. Anytime you're working on a page, you can choose View, HTML to call up a separate window that displays the corresponding HTML code (see Figure 11.16). You can edit any code you see in the window to tweak the appearance of your document. Editors often appreciate having this option because editing the code directly allows for finer control over many page attributes.

 T I P When you have the View or Edit HTML window open, be sure that you have activated color coding. FrontPage Express will color tag keywords in purple, attribute names in red, attribute values in blue, and regular text in black to assist you in editing the code.

FIG. 11.16

Even though it is a WYSIWYG editor, FrontPage Express will still let you edit the raw HTML code.

CHAPTER 12

In-Depth: NetMeeting

The Internet, through its ability to connect two or more physically separated people, has long been heralded as the vehicle through which long distance collaboration will become a reality. In the past several years, a variety of applications and standards have been developed to allow different kinds of information—text, graphics, audio, video, and application documents—to be shared in real time over the Internet. For example, Internet Relay Chat allows real-time text exchange and the Internet Phone does the same with audio.

With the release of NetMeeting, Microsoft has made freely available a tool that has the ability to share all these forms of information. Two or more NetMeeting users can connect over the Internet and share all sorts of information. Because NetMeeting uses established Internet standards for audio and video transmission, a NetMeeting user can also connect with users of other applications, such as the Internet Phone. Also, NetMeeting offers a unique application-sharing capability that enables multiple people to use an application, such as Microsoft Word or Excel, even when some of them don't have the application on their local system. ■

Install NetMeeting using the Active Setup Wizard

The Active Setup Wizard enables you to download and install NetMeeting on your system directly from the Internet.

Configure NetMeeting and optimize its performance for your system

NetMeeting's own configuration options and wizards, as well as the Intel Connection Advisor—which comes with NetMeeting—enable you to get the most out of NetMeeting on your system and with your Internet connection.

Establish discussions with others through directory services or directly over the Internet

You can make and receive calls in a number of ways with NetMeeting: either by using one of many directory services available or by calling directly using someone's IP name or number.

Communicate and collaborate with others using NetMeeting's many tools

NetMeeting enables you to exchange audio, video, text, and applications with any number of people, making it easy for many different people to cooperate over the Web.

Installing NetMeeting with the Active Setup Wizard

In Chapter 7, "Quick Start: NetMeeting," you learned how to download the NetMeeting application and install it on your local system. In this chapter, you find out how to use Internet Explorer 4's Active Setup Wizard to automatically download and install the application directly over the Internet without having to worry about temporary files or directories on your system.

▶ **See** "Up and Running with NetMeeting" for a description of how to download and install NetMeeting using its self-installing file, **p. 90**

N O T E Microsoft NetMeeting is included in the full installation option of the Internet Explorer 4 suite of applications. If that is the installation you used, NetMeeting will already be installed on your system. Look for a Microsoft NetMeeting entry on the Start menu under Programs and/or Programs, Internet Explorer. ■

The Internet Explorer 4 Active Setup Wizard is designed to take some of the pain out of keeping your system's Web and Internet applications up to date. You've probably noticed over the last couple of years, particularly with the Netscape versus Microsoft browser wars, that updates and new versions of Web browsers, as well as the other applications that support them, are released every couple of months. More often, sometimes. Downloading the 5, 10, or 20M necessary to completely update to the new version can get pretty annoying, and sometimes even expensive if you pay for your connect time by the minute.

Microsoft's ActiveX Controls technology addresses this issue for Web browser add-ins—a properly written Web page that uses ActiveX Controls will allow your browser to automatically download the latest version of the control if it isn't present on your system. The Active Setup Wizard, when run on your local system and connected to Microsoft's Web site, allows you to do the same with your Web browser and its components.

▶ **See** "The *CODEBASE* Attribute" to find out how Web pages can keep your system configured with the latest version of an ActiveX Control, **p. 584**

To use the Active Setup Wizard—specifically, in this case, to download and install Microsoft NetMeeting, but the process is the same for any other Internet Explorer component—follow these steps:

1. Start your Internet Explorer Web browser and go to **http://www.microsoft.com/ie/ ie40/download/** and look for the Internet Explorer 4.0 Suite Components and Add-ons page. The Windows 95 version of this page is currently located at **http:// www.microsoft.com/ie/ie40/download/b2/x86/en/download/addon95.htm**.

2. Viewing this page will automatically start the Active Setup Wizard on your local system, and you will get the alert box shown in Figure 12.1. Click Yes, and the Wizard will analyze your system to see what Internet Explorer components you have installed.

3. Figure 12.2 shows you an example of what the resulting screen might look like. Notice

FIG. 12.1

Internet Explorer 4's Active Setup Wizard can download and install NetMeeting and other needed components directly from the Web.

that NetMeeting is not currently installed. Check the box by the NetMeeting entry on this Web page to request that it be downloaded and installed on your system.

As you select items from the list presented to you on this Web page, the page automati-

FIG. 12.2

The Active Setup Wizard can estimate for you how long your download will take based on the total file size and connection type.

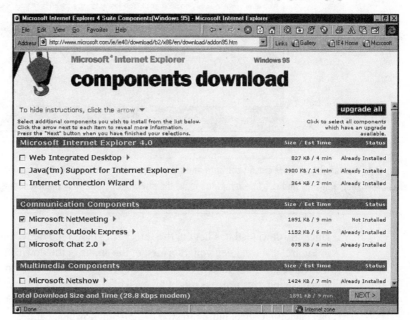

cally updates itself with the total size of the software download needed, as well as an estimate of how long the download will take. By doing this, you can tailor what components you wish to install and at what time to best use your time connected to the Internet.

Once you are done selecting components to download, click the NEXT button.

4. Once you have selected the components you wish to download and install—in this case, only the NetMeeting application—you can next choose which download site to use from the drop-down list shown in Figure 12.3. Once you have done this, begin the download and installation process by clicking the Install Now button.

FIG. 12.3
By selecting a download
location near you, you
can help to ensure a
good response time.

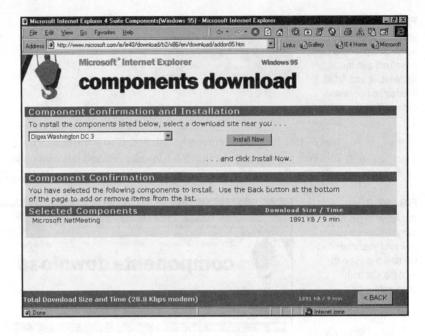

 TIP You can download Microsoft software and components from many sites. Pick one located close to you geographically and don't be afraid to restart the download from a new site if it seems to be going very slowly.

5. Once the download has begun, the Internet Explorer 4.0 Active Setup dialog box shown in Figure 12.4 will keep you informed of the status of the download and install process. Depending on your Internet connection speed and quality and how much you are downloading, this process might take a while. You can let it occur in the background while you go on to other tasks. If there seems to be a problem with the download, you can click the Cancel button to stop the current download and try again.

FIG. 12.4
The Active Setup
Wizard's progress dialog
box keeps you informed
of the status of the
download and
installation.

6. Once the desired components are downloaded—NetMeeting alone, in this example—they are installed on your system. When the entire process is complete, you will see an alert box similar to that shown in Figure 12.5. Click OK, and you're ready to go.

FIG. 12.5

After a successful download and installation, you are ready to use NetMeeting. Unlike some Internet Explorer 4 components, NetMeeting does not require you to restart your system to use it.

N O T E Some components, when downloaded and installed, require you to restart your system to complete the setup process. NetMeeting does not. If one or more of the components requires a restart, the Active Setup Wizard will inform you of this and give you the option of doing so immediately or later. ■

Configuring NetMeeting

As discussed in Chapter 7, "Quick Start: NetMeeting," the first time you run NetMeeting, it will lead you through a number of steps to configure it for use. There are a few additional notes to be made with respect to these steps.

▶ **See** "NetMeeting Installation and Setup" for a description of each of the steps necessary to run NetMeeting for the first time, **p. 90**

■ As shown in Figure 12.6, NetMeeting enables you to enter some of your personal information—name, e-mail address, location information, and a short comment. You are required to enter your first and last name and e-mail information to be listed in one of the Internet Locator Server (ILS) directory services.

If you want to be available to be contacted through a directory service but don't want to be listed, you can configure NetMeeting to do this (how to do this will be described in the "NetMeeting's Menus" section later in this chapter). In this case, someone would need to know your e-mail address to contact you.

■ Not only can you enter your personal information, but you can also classify it as personal, business, or adults-only. This classification will determine to whom you will be listed when other people connect to a directory (see Figure 12.7).

■ With the Audio Tuning Wizard, you can configure NetMeeting to transmit audio from your system over the Internet, optimized for your microphone, system speed, and connection speed. After you have performed the audio test (see Figure 12.8), NetMeeting should be configured for your system. If there is a problem with the test,

Part
II

Ch
12

NetMeeting will inform you. The most likely source of problems is not with NetMeeting itself, but with the setup of your microphone and sound card.

FIG. 12.6

You can use your personal information to determine what kinds of contacts you would like to make through ILS directory services.

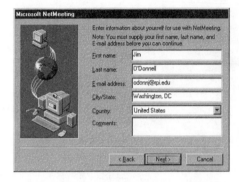

FIG. 12.7

NetMeeting enables you to determine what category of information you list and view.

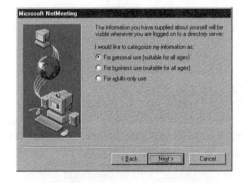

FIG. 12.8

You might feel silly speaking to your computer, but this test enables NetMeeting to set up your audio levels for optimal operation.

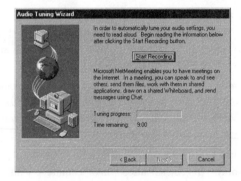

TIP If you have checked your sound card setup and microphone installation and are still having trouble getting your microphone to work, make sure its on/off switch, if it has one, is on! (Yes, I had this problem once.)

The simple configuration process you go through when you start NetMeeting for the first time should be enough to get you going. NetMeeting has a host of other ways in which you can configure it, which are available through its toolbars and menus.

Using the NetMeeting Toolbars

As with the toolbars on the Internet Explorer 4 Web browser, you can move the two NetMeeting toolbars around the application window. The movement is a little more restricted than with the Web browser because you can only move them with respect to one another. You can't individually enable or disable them or move them to other parts of the NetMeeting window. There are two NetMeeting toolbars that provide the following functions:

- **Main toolbar**   Has buttons for controlling some of NetMeeting's basic functions.
  - **Call**   Enables you to place a call to another NetMeeting (or other compatible application) user. See the "Placing a Call with NetMeeting" section later in this chapter.
  - **Hang Up**   Hangs up with one or more participants of your current discussion.
  - **Switch**   Allows you to switch where your audio and video output are going.
  - **Share**   Enables you to share one of your currently running applications with participants of your discussion.
  - **Collaborate**   Allows discussion participants to use shared applications on your system. See the "Application Sharing and Collaboration" section later in this chapter for more information on the difference between application sharing and collaborating.
  - **Chat**   Opens a chat window, allowing you to exchange text messages.
  - **Whiteboard**   Opens NetMeeting's whiteboard, a Microsoft Paint-like application that enables any participant in your discussion to draw and otherwise share graphics and text information.
- **Audio toolbar**   Contains settings to allow you to enable, disable, and adjust the volume of incoming and outgoing audio.

NetMeeting's Menus

NetMeeting has seven menus with selections for configuring and using the program. You can also access all the options available through NetMeeting's toolbars and windows through its menus. Also, NetMeeting shows its place as a component of the Internet Explorer 4 suite of applications with a menu for accessing other Internet and Web applications. NetMeeting has the following menus (in each case, more information about the specific functions will be given later in this chapter):

Part
II

Ch
12

■ **Call**   Using the selections in this menu, you can place a NetMeeting call, host a meeting, or control how you are listed through the ILS directory services.

■ **Edit**   This menu has selections for the Windows standard Cut, Copy, Paste functions.

■ **View**   The View menu enables you to control what you see in the main NetMeeting screen. You can enable or disable the toolbars or status line and choose which tab is shown in the NetMeeting window. You also control the local and remote video windows through this menu—you can either attach these windows to the main NetMeeting window or detach them into separate windows of their own.

■ **Go**   This menu allows you to connect NetMeeting to the other components of the Internet Explorer suite. With its selections, you can connect to the Microsoft's Web-based ILS directory or call up Internet Explorer to view a number of other pages on the Microsoft Web site. You can also initiate your selected Internet Mail or News client.

■ **Tools**   The selections of the Tools menu duplicate the buttons on the main toolbar, providing access to NetMeeting's most common applications. You can also access the other features of this application through this menu. Perhaps the most important selection in this menu, particularly for configuring NetMeeting, is the Options selection. The Options selection will be described in the next section, "Configuring NetMeeting's Options Dialog."

■ **SpeedDial**   Like most modern telephones, and any other good communications device, NetMeeting has a way to easily establish frequently-used contacts. Its SpeedDialer, which you can access through this menu, provides a way to establish a list of people, along with the necessary information for contacting them, through an ILS directory or directly across the Internet.

■ **Help**   With NetMeeting's Help menu, you can access helpful information that is both stored on your local system and available on Microsoft's Web site.

Configuring NetMeeting's Options Dialog Box

As I mentioned in the previous section, NetMeeting's Tools, Options menu selection will give you access to its Options dialog box. This dialog has six tabs with which you can configure many of NetMeeting's functions and abilities.

■ **General**   The options in this tab are divided into the following three categories:

   • **General**   This section controls some basic NetMeeting options, such as whether to run NetMeeting at system startup and whether to automatically accept incoming calls.

   • **Network bandwidth**   This drop-down list enables you to tell NetMeeting the speed of your Internet connection, in turn allowing NetMeeting to best configure itself for optimal transmission of audio, video, and the other information that you will exchange during a NetMeeting session.

   • **File transfer**   This option enables you to select the folder on your local system in which transferred files will be stored.

- **My Information**   This tab gives your personal information, and your categorization of it, that NetMeeting uses to list you in an ILS directory service.
- **Calling**   Using the selections on this tab, you control how and with which ILS directory you are listed (if any), and also you control how the NetMeeting SpeedDialer works.

 T I P The default ILS, **ils.microsoft.com**, is sometimes hard to connect to. Try a different Microsoft ILS, or one of the services offered by another vendor, for better results.

- **Audio**   This options tab enables you to configure NetMeeting's audio services, controlling how well you send and receive audio information. Through this tab, you can rerun the Audio Tuning Wizard and determine how the sensitivity of your microphone is set.

  NetMeeting recommends that you allow it to set your microphone sensitivity automatically. If, because of the placement of your microphone and/or speakers, you find you are having feedback or other problems, you might want to try to set the sensitivity yourself.

- **Video**   If you have configured a video camera with your system, you can use this options tab to control how NetMeeting handles the exchange of video information. These options give you the control of the quality versus transmission speed tradeoff—with them, you can control image size and video frame rate. If you have an ISDN connection or faster, it's probably worth it to increase the size and speed of your video image. Otherwise, its probably best for you to accept the defaults.

- **Protocols**   The Protocols tab enables you to configure the transmission protocol for your connection type. In reality, however, the majority of users will not need to adjust the settings under this tab.

Placing a Call with NetMeeting

When using NetMeeting to establish communication with one or more other people, you can use a few terms interchangeably to describe the session. You can call the session a conversation, a discussion, or a meeting. The difference is one mainly of semantics and type. If you are talking to one other participant on a personal basis, you are more likely to call it a conversation or discussion. If it involves multiple people and its purpose is oriented toward conducting business, it would be called a meeting.

Microsoft NetMeeting supports a variety of ways of using it to conduct conversations and meetings over the Internet. You can make your information available in a number of ways to make it easier for others to contact you. Once you have the necessary information for another person, you can contact them in a number of ways.

Direct Internet Calling

The most straightforward way to contact someone or to have them contact you is directly through the Internet because this way, you can establish communication with one or more people without having to go through an ILS directory service. To make a direct call, all you

Part
II

Ch
12

need is the host and domain name, or IP address, of the recipient of your call. With that information, you can click the Call toolbar button or select <u>C</u>all, <u>N</u>ew Call and get the dialog shown in Figure 12.9.

FIG. 12.9

If you know the IP name or number of the person you wish to contact, you can use NetMeeting to call them directly.

If you enter the desired recipient's IP name or number into this dialog and click the Call button, NetMeeting will attempt to contact that person and establish a conversation with them. This attempted connection will have one of several possible results:

- Due to transmission problems, your intended recipient may never receive your request or you may not receive their response. In this case, NetMeeting will inform you that your request has timed out and allow you to initiate the call or to make another one again.

- If your intended recipient is already involved in a meeting with others, he or she may reject your call on that basis or invite you to join the meeting already in progress. In either case, NetMeeting will inform you of that and, in the event that you are invited into his or her meeting, give you the option to join.

- Your intended recipient may reject your call. NetMeeting will inform you of this and allow you to attempt to make a different call.

- Your intended recipient will accept the call, and your conversation will be established.

If, instead of you initiating the call you are the one who is called, you will see an alert box similar to that shown in Figure 12.10. This button gives you the option to accept or reject the call, and the caller will be informed of your decision.

FIG. 12.10

If someone else calls you, you have the option of accepting or rejecting the call.

T I P You can select Tools, Options and check the Automatically accept incoming calls checkbox to allow NetMeeting to accept call requests without asking you.

Regardless of whether you or the other person (or persons) are the one who initiated the call, once the call is accepted, a conversation or meeting is established. The Current Call tab of the main NetMeeting window is updated to reflect that a meeting has been established. Figure 12.11 shows an example of this.

FIG. 12.11
Once you have established a connection, it is listed in the NetMeeting window along with both your and all the other participants' properties.

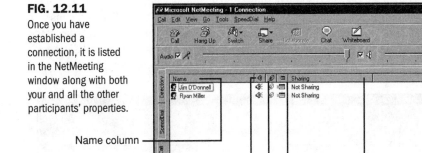

Name column

Audio column

Video column

File Transfer column

Sharing column

The columns for each entry on the Current Call tab mean the following:

- **Name** This column shows the name of the person or persons with whom you are conversing.
- **Audio** A speaker icon in this column indicates that the person has audio hardware and is capable of sending and receiving audio.
- **Video** A camera icon in this column indicates that the person has video hardware and is capable of sending and receiving video.
- **File Transfer** An icon in this column indicates that the person is running an application with file transfer, chat, whiteboard, and application sharing capabilities (such as NetMeeting).
- **Sharing** This column lists the applications each person is sharing.

Part
II

Ch
12

Internet Locator Server Directories

Unless you know someone's precise IP name or number, placing a call to him or her directly is impossible. Because many people connecting to the Internet through dial-up connections are assigned dynamic IP addresses—meaning that they will have a different IP address each time they connect—it is even more difficult to connect to them in this way. A way to get around this problem is to connect to someone through an Internet Locator Server (ILS) directory.

You can configure NetMeeting whenever you launch it to automatically connect you to any of several public ILS directory services. Some of those that are publicly available are shown in the drop-down list available on the Calling tab of the Tools, Options dialog box. Microsoft runs some of them, and others are run by other vendors. Whenever you connect to an ILS directory, the information from the other people to whom you're connected is downloaded and displayed in the Directory tab of your main NetMeeting window (see Figure 12.12).

FIG. 12.12
NetMeeting can connect you to any ILS directory server, giving you the ability to make calls to anyone else who is connected.

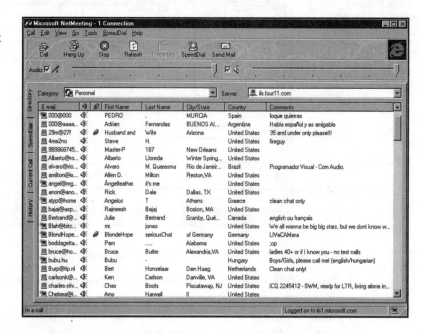

The columns in this directory are similar to those shown in the Current Call tab, described earlier in this chapter. In addition to seeing the name of the person, you can also see his or her other personal information, such as e-mail address, city, state, and comment. The audio and video columns display icons that mean the same thing as in the Current Call tab. In addition, a computer icon is displayed in the far left column. When this icon is displayed with a red asterisk, it indicates that the person is currently in a call.

Placing a call to someone listed in the directory service is easy. You can select that person's entry in the directory and click the Call button (or select Call, New Call) or right-click and select Call from the pop-up menu.

In addition to the ILS services available through NetMeeting, Microsoft maintains a Web page that also allows you to place NetMeeting calls. This Web page, located at **http://ils. microsoft.com**, displays the personal information of the people connected to Microsoft's **ils.microsoft.com** ILS directory and displays a hypertext link that will initiate a call to that person (see Figure 12.13). In addition to initiating the call, clicking this hypertext link will also launch the NetMeeting application, if it isn't already running.

FIG. 12.13

Microsoft hosts an ILS Web site—clicking the hypertext link automatically places a NetMeeting call to that person.

Note that this Web page is not a separate ILS directory but merely interfaces with the existing **ils.microsoft.com** directory. The Web page itself is dynamically created and used the **callto:** URL to initiate a NetMeeting call. The format of this URL will be discussed in the "NetMeeting Contact URL" section, a little bit later in this chapter.

Hosting a NetMeeting

By selecting Call, Host Meeting, you can establish a NetMeeting meeting to which you can invite other people or that others can attempt to join. You can invite people to join your meeting by calling them, using the same procedures for initiating calls discussed in the previous sections. People can attempt to join your meeting by calling you.

How, then, is hosting a meeting using this NetMeeting option different from the normal calling process? Using NetMeeting itself, there isn't much difference. The difference comes into play when you, or someone else, hosts a *named* meeting. With a named meeting connected through an ILS directory service, prospective participants can attempt to join the meeting by making a call to the meeting itself. NetMeeting supports named meetings by allowing you to join those that have been created. It is not possible to create a named meeting through NetMeeting, however.

Part
II

Ch
12

NetMeeting's SpeedDialer

With NetMeeting's SpeedDialer, you can save personal and contact information and then call your participants through the SpeedDial tab of the main NetMeeting window. SpeedDialer entries can be either direct Internet IP addresses or e-mail addresses needed to connect through a given ILS directory service.

SpeedDialer options are controlled through the Calling tab of the Tools, Options dialog box. You can configure NetMeeting to automatically add people who have initiated or received calls from you to the SpeedDialer. You can also set the parameters that NetMeeting uses to update the SpeedDial tab of its main window—this window displays the people for whom you have SpeedDial entries that are currently connected.

SpeedDial entries are implemented using the same **callto:** URL that you use in the Microsoft ILS Web page. One side effect of this implementation is that it is easy to send your SpeedDial entries to another person. In fact, NetMeeting's SpeedDialer includes an option to allow you to e-mail any of your SpeedDial entries to another person. In the SpeedDial entry dialog, just click the Send to mail recipient button, enter the e-mail address of the recipient, and the contact information will be sent to him or her.

An easy way to send your SpeedDial information to someone else is to select SpeedDial, Add SpeedDial, enter your own information, and click the Save on the desktop option. Then, you can e-mail anyone the information by right-clicking the desktop shortcut and selecting Send to, Mail Recipient from the pop-up menu.

NetMeeting Contact URL

As I mentioned in several previous sections, you use an URL format to implement contact information for NetMeeting calls. This NetMeeting contact URL has one of the following formats:

- For a direct contact:

  callto:IP_address

  For example, to contact me directly, the URL would be

  callto:dcc12258.slip.digex.net

- For a contact through an ILS directory:

  callto:ILS_address/e-mail_address

  For example, to contact me through Microsoft's **ils.microsoft.com** ILS directory, the URL would be

  callto:ils.microsoft.com/odonnj@rpi.edu

You can make your NetMeeting contact URL available by creating a Web page with a hypertext link to it, using the standard HTML tag (for example, `<A HREF="callto:ils.microsoft.com/odonnj@rpi.edu">`).

NetMeeting Audio and Video

Probably the two most important features of NetMeeting are also the features that are the hardest to show in a book such as this. These features are NetMeeting's audio and video capabilities. They're hard to show, of course, because you can't demonstrate audio in a book, and though it is possible to show still images, you can't really display true video.

Nevertheless, NetMeeting does have the capability of transmitting audio and video across the Internet. Most importantly, NetMeeting uses established Internet standards to transmit real-time audio and video, allowing users to use NetMeeting with other applications that support audio and video, such as the Internet Phone.

Figure 12.14 shows NetMeeting's Audio toolbar. This toolbar allows you to enable and disable your audio send and receive capabilities, as well as to adjust the volume of both incoming and outgoing audio. Using these controls and with the feedback of your recipient, it should be possible to set these adjustments for as clear audio as possible with your system and Internet connection speed.

FIG. 12.14

NetMeeting's audio display shows you the signal strength of incoming and outgoing audio.

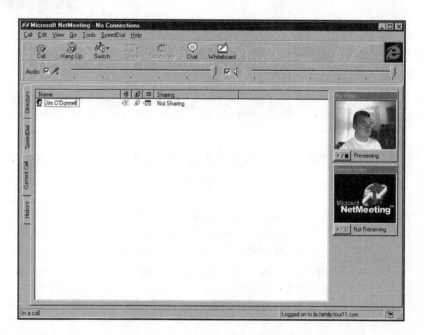

Part

II

Ch

12

As with audio, you can adjust NetMeeting's video capabilities for your particular system and connection. The Video tab of the Tools, Options dialog box gives you access to the options with which you can select the size and quality of the video signal. This capability allows you to get as much quality as possible given your connection bandwidth.

It is possible to attach or detach the video windows, both for your own local video as well as the remote video that you are receiving, from the main NetMeeting window. As shown in Figure

12.15, the local video window is attached to the NetMeeting window and the remote window is not. The remote window, then, would appear as a separate window on the Windows 95 Taskbar, and you could called it up independently of NetMeeting's main window.

FIG. 12.15

The local video window enables you to see what you are transmitting through NetMeeting.

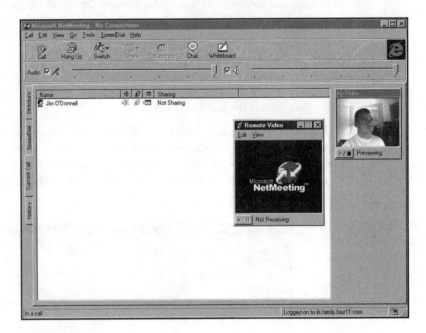

Consulting the Intel Connection Advisor

It is quite possible, if you are using NetMeeting to transmit audio and video over the Internet—particularly if you have a dial-up connection—that you will soon run into problems with bandwidth. Bandwidth is simply the amount of information you can send and receive over your Internet connection. Because audio and particularly video are fairly bandwidth intensive, it is sometimes hard to get a quality signal with a slow connection.

One way to get advice on how to deal with this issue if it becomes a problem is through the Intel Connection Advisor that installs on your system when you install NetMeeting. The Advisor has a system tray icon (which you can enable or disable by using the General tab of the Tools, Options dialog box). If you double-click the tray icon, you get the information alert box shown in Figure 12.16. This alert box shows you information about the processor load of your system, as well as how much audio and video information is being sent and received. The Advisor's Audio and Video tabs give you information about the audio and video data rates, as well as the percentage of information packets that are being lost.

If you find, either through the information given to you through the Connection Advisor or through the actual quality of the signals received, that you are having problems with bandwidth on your Internet connection, the Advisor might be able to help you. By clicking the Help button, you can read through some information on optimizing your system for getting the best audio and video transmission quality possible. By clicking the Home button, the Internet Explorer Web browser launches and the Intel Connection Advisor Web site loads (see Figure 12.17). You can consult this page for up-to-the-minute information on this subject.

FIG. 12.16

The Intel Connection Advisor gives you a way to optimize your system for audio and video transmission.

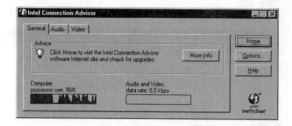

FIG. 12.17

The Intel Connection Advisor Web site enables you to stay up to date with the latest version of the Advisor.

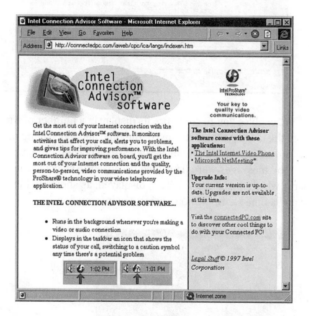

NetMeeting Chat—A Mini-IRC

For the remainder of this chapter, you will learn more information on using the other communications capabilities of Microsoft NetMeeting. The first of these, and the most straightforward, is NetMeeting Chat.

Through NetMeeting Chat, you are able to exchange text information with any person (or with multiple persons) with whom you are currently in a conversation. As shown in Figure 12.18, you simply need to type in a message and it will immediately be sent to the other members of the discussion. It is also possible to send a private message to only one member of the discussion, by selecting that person's name from the Send to drop-down list.

FIG. 12.18

In NetMeeting's Chat window, you can exchange text messages with the other members of your conference.

NetMeeting Chat enables you to configure its display in a number of ways (see Figure 12.19). You can change the display font that is used, the time and date stamp on incoming text messages, and the format in which these messages are displayed. In Figure 12.18, the names of the people sending the messages were truncated because the selected font was too big. By changing the format in which these messages are displayed, as shown in Figure 12.20, you can see the full name and a time stamp without losing any information.

FIG. 12.19

You can configure the fonts and style of the NetMeeting Chat window to make it easier to read and more informative.

Using the NetMeeting Whiteboard

NetMeeting's Whiteboard, like a whiteboard in a traditional meeting room, gives you a way to share more than simple text with the other members of your conference. At first blush, Whiteboard looks a lot like a simple graphics application like Microsoft Paint, but one in which it is possible for each member of the discussion to use simultaneously (see Figure 12.21).

Given this Paint-like interface, you might find it unlikely that you can transmit any real information across it. A number of features of the NetMeeting Whiteboard make it a lot more suitable for interchanging information, however. Some of these features follow.

FIG. 12.20

NetMeeting enables you to send private messages as well as messages to everyone in the discussion.

FIG. 12.21

The NetMeeting Whiteboard is a lot like Microsoft's Paint application, except that everyone in the discussion can use it simultaneously.

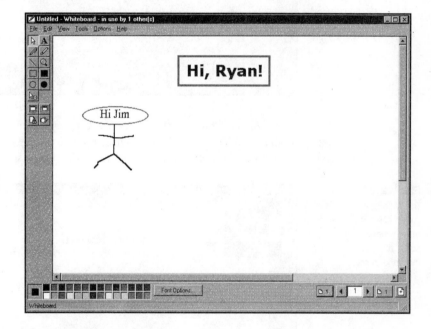

Part
II

Ch
12

- With the Remote Pointer On button, you can see the mouse cursor of the other participants of the Whiteboard, enabling you to see what they are doing and allowing them to point out things to you (see Figure 12.22).

- You can temporarily lock out other members of the discussion from working on the Whiteboard by clicking the Lock Contents button. When you do this, their cursors are displayed with a little lock, as shown in Figure 12.22, and most of their Whiteboard toolbar buttons are greyed out. This capability enables you to freeze the Whiteboard from others if you are doing something important on it.

FIG. 12.22

It is possible for one member of a discussion to lock the Whiteboard, preventing anyone else from changing it.

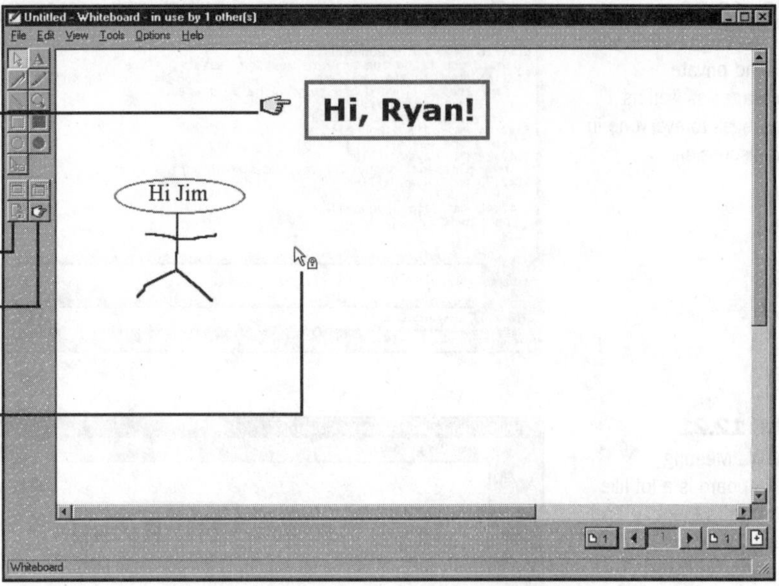

Remote Pointer ―

Lock Contents button ―

Remote Pointer On button ―

Locked cursor ―

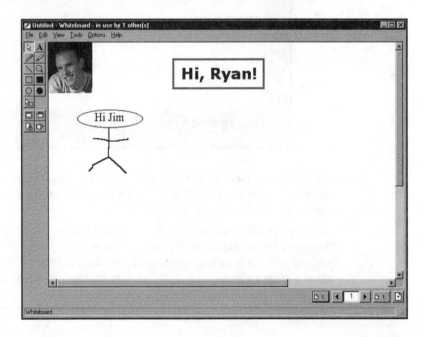

■ Using the Select Area button, you can select areas of other windows and paste them graphically onto the Whiteboard. Doing so enables you to display graphic images (see Figure 12.23) or show part of any of your other windows or screen.

FIG. 12.23

The Whiteboard enables you to clip out pieces of other windows and paste them up for everyone to see.

■ With the Select Window button, you can graphically paste the contents of an entire window onto the Whiteboard. Doing this, it is possible to show the other participants the current contents of an application on which you are working as a part of the meeting, as shown with the Excel window in Figure 12.24.

FIG. 12.24
You can even copy whole windows and share them and their contents with the other members of the discussion.

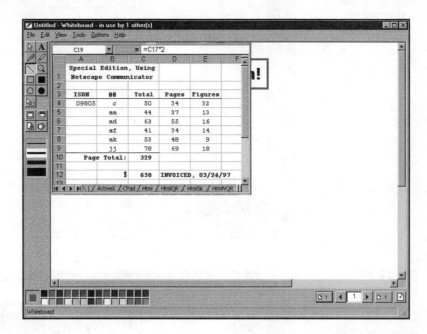

■ Unlike Microsoft Paint, objects you create on the Whiteboard are stored as objects. So, even after you create them, it is possible for you to pick them up and move them around. In Figure 12.24, multiple objects had been created and overlapped on the screen. Figure 12.25 shows the same Whiteboard after those items had been picked up and rearranged.

■ One last capability of the NetMeeting Whiteboard that makes it a good tool for multiple person information exchange is its highlighter. Using the highlighter, you can color *under* any area of the Whiteboard. Doing this enables you to set off these areas and make them more visible to the other members of the conversation (see Figure 12.26).

Transferring Files with NetMeeting

Frequently, when collaborating with others over the Internet, it is very helpful to be able to transfer files back and forth from your local system to theirs. NetMeeting has the capability to do this built in, so you don't have to maintain separate FTP sessions or find some other way to transfer files.

TIP Use NetMeeting's built-in file transfer capability to allow it to manage the bandwidth of your Internet connection. This will help prevent audio and/or video dropouts.

Part
II

Ch
12

FIG. 12.25
Each object on the
Whiteboard remains
separate from the
others, and you can
pick them up and
move them around.

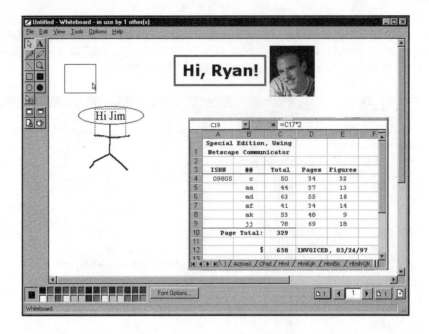

FIG. 12.26
The NetMeeting
highlighter enables you
to set off items by
coloring under them.

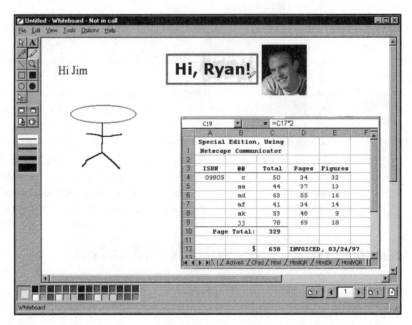

To send a file to another participant in a discussion, select Tools, File Transfer, Send File, or
press Ctrl+F. Doing so gives you a standard dialog box for selecting a file. Browse to the file on

your local system and select it, and the file transfer will be initiated. When the transfer has completed successfully, you will see an alert box similar to that shown in Figure 12.27.

FIG. 12.27

In NetMeeting, you can easily transfer files from your system to any participant in your discussion.

When another participant in a discussion wishes to send you a file, NetMeeting will display the dialog box shown in Figure 12.28. Note that though this dialog box gives you the option to Accept or Delete the incoming file, NetMeeting begins to download the file in the background. Even if the file contains a virus or other dangerous content, you are in absolutely no danger just because NetMeeting downloads it. You can still elect to Delete the file, either from this dialog box or through the Windows 95 Explorer. Unless you open the file, the virus (or whatever) won't be activated.

FIG. 12.28

A progress dialog box keeps you informed of files being transferred to your system.

Once the file has been completely downloaded, you can select Close, Open, or Delete. As before, Delete will delete the file without it ever opening it. The Close button will close the dialog box and leave the file in NetMeeting's received files folder (**C:\Program Files\ NetMeeting\Received Files**, by default), enabling you to review it later. If you click the Open button, the file will open and launch whatever application associated with files of its extension, just as though you had double-clicked the file within the Explorer (see Figure 12.29).

Application Sharing and Collaboration

NetMeeting's final capability is extremely powerful. When you are connected to other people in a NetMeeting discussion, you can actually share with them any of the applications you are currently running (see Figure 12.30). When you share your applications, the other participants on your discussion can see the application window, just as you see it, and observe you as you work within that application.

FIG. 12.29

Once you successfully transfer a file to your system, NetMeeting gives you the option of accepting or rejecting it—you can also elect to immediately open the file.

FIG. 12.30

Sharing an application enables the participants in your discussion to view the shared application as you make changes to it.

CAUTION

Conference participants can only correctly view shared application windows if the window is unobscured on your Windows desktop. Also, because the screen size and resolution of each of your participants' computers might vary, you will probably want to size the shared application window so that it will be small enough to fit all their screens.

In addition to sharing your application windows and allowing discussion participants to watch you as you make changes, NetMeeting enables you to *collaborate* with your participants using your shared application (see Figure 12.31). This collaboration allows any of the participants within your NetMeeting session to actually take control of the shared application and use it, regardless of whether he or she has the application on his or her own system. That participant actually uses his or her mouse and keyboard to control an application on your system, via NetMeeting.

Figure 12.32 shows an example of what you might see when a participant in your conversation takes control of a shared application when you have enabled collaboration. The cursor changes to show that person's initials to indicate that he or she is in control—you will no longer be able to move it around. To regain control, you can click your mouse button. In this case, however, the other participant can get control right back from you. To regain control of the application and disable collaboration, hit the Escape key.

FIG. 12.31

By collaborating within NetMeeting, other participants in your discussion can actually take control of applications on your machine.

FIG. 12.32

When another member of your discussion is in control of a shared application, the cursor changes to indicate that.

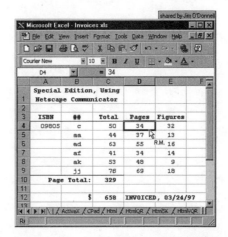

CAUTION

When you allow someone else to collaborate and use a shared application on your system, you make it possible for that person to do anything to your system that it is possible to do with that application. At the very least, this means he or she could overwrite any file or change any data or information that that application can read. Be very careful to make sure that the people with whom you are collaborating are who you think they are and that you trust them with your system.

Part
II

Ch
12

CHAPTER 13

In-Depth: Preferences

You can configure the applications that make up the Internet Explorer 4 suite in many ways to adjust how they work with the way you use them to access the Internet and the Web. Most of these options have been covered in the Quick Start and In-Depth chapters of these applications.

In this chapter, you will find out more than just *what* you can configure. Here you can find some tips, tricks, and ideas of *how* to configure the Internet Explorer Web browser, Outlook Express Mail and News client, and NetMeeting Internet conferencing program. Through these ideas, you will be better able to use your screen real estate, Internet bandwidth, and time spent connected to the Web efficiently. ▪

Configure Internet Explorer for best operation

Internet Explorer has many options that you can configure to set it up as you like. This chapter will show you how to configure some of those options to make your Web browsing experience as enjoyable as possible.

Use Internet Explorer's cookies and ratings

Find the best settings to use so your Web browser to use cookies and content ratings.

Learn efficient ways to use Outlook Express

This section will show you some techniques that can make your outgoing and incoming e-mail sessions as efficient and effective as possible.

Find out some tricks for using NetMeeting

NetMeeting's video, audio, and data conferencing can put a strain on your Internet connection. Find out how to set up your system to get the most out of it and to ease your communications in NetMeeting with others.

Setting Up Your Internet Explorer Toolbars

Internet Explorer has menus through which you can access and configure all the features and capabilities of the browser. Besides the menus and the dialog boxes that you access through them, there are also keyboard shortcuts that make many of your tasks much easier. Far and away, however, the most common interface through which you use the Web browser is the Internet Explorer toolbars.

Since the introduction of Netscape Navigator 2, the general layout of most Web browser screens has been very similar. At the top of the screen is the menu bar, directly underneath is a series of toolbars. Almost all these browsers, and Internet Explorer 4 is no exception, have three toolbars covering the following uses:

- **Web browser functions**   This toolbar has buttons with which you can control common navigation functions, such as those to move back and forward, load your Home Page, start a Web search, or refresh or stop loading the current page.

- **Internet address display and entry**   In this toolbar, you can see the URL of the Web page you are currently viewing, and enter a new URL to see a different Web page.

- **Shortcut buttons**   The last toolbar generally contains a number of buttons with which you can immediately load a number of Web pages.

Internet Explorer 4 has these same toolbars but also adds new abilities to configure them. You can move the toolbars around with respect to one another and with respect to the menu bar, change their size, and configure them on the Web browser, or even attach them to other parts of your system. With all these options, you might not know where to begin to configure them to use them to their fullest potential. The rest of this section will give you a few ideas for doing that.

▶ **See** "Using the Toolbars" for more information on using and configuring Internet Explorer's toolbars, **p. 112**

Links Bar Button Sizes

Similar to Netscape Navigator's Bookmarks, Microsoft uses Favorites to enable you to keep track of frequently visited places either on your own local system or on the Internet. Your favorites are available through Internet Explorer's Favorites menu or its Favorites Browser Bar (you can also access your favorites from the Explorer or the Start Menu, when you use Internet Explorer's Web Integration). You can organize your favorites into logical hierarchies using subdirectories within the Favorites folder.

▶ **See** "Manipulating and Using Favorites Through the Explorer Bar" to find out how to create and access your favorites, **p. 116**

▶ **See** "Web Surfing from the Start Menu" for how to access your favorites from the Windows 95 Start Menu, **p. 154**

Internet Explorer comes with one of these Favorites subdirectories preconfigured—the Links folder. Any favorites that you store in the Links folder will appear as buttons on the Internet Explorer Links bar. Figure 13.1 shows the Internet Explorer Links Bar with some of the default buttons replaced and a few new ones added.

FIG. 13.1

Internet Explorer 4 makes it easy for you to add and remove buttons from the Links Bar.

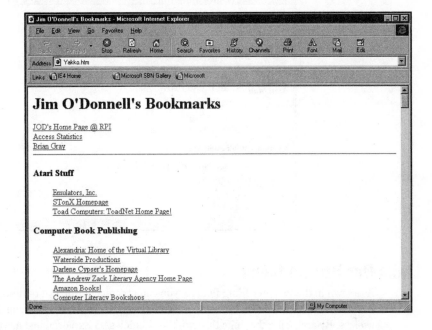

What might not be obvious from Figure 13.1 is that, with this Links Bar setup, you aren't getting the most you can get out of your Links Bar. Why not? *Internet Explorer sizes the Links Bar buttons based on the width of the widest button.* Because the button width is based on the length of the name, which, by default, is the name of the Web site to which the link points, a link with a long name will limit how many buttons can fit onto the Links Bar. You can get around this quirk by giving your Links Bar buttons shorter names, which you can do in one of two ways. First, when you originally make the favorite, you can rename it.

Microsoft favorites are stored in the **C:\Windows\Favorites** directory. Links Bar buttons are then in the **C:\Windows\Favorites\Links** directory. To rename a favorite, use the Windows 95 Explorer to browse to that directory, select the entry you wish to rename, and select File, Rename (or right-click the entry and select Rename from the pop-up menu). Then, give it a shorter name and press Return. The name of the Links Bar button will update immediately, but the buttons will not resize until the next time you start up Internet Explorer. As shown in Figure 13.2, your buttons will be a lot smaller, enabling you to fit more on the Links Bar.

Part

II

Ch

13

FIG. 13.2

If you're careful, you can fit 8 to 10 buttons on your Links Bar.

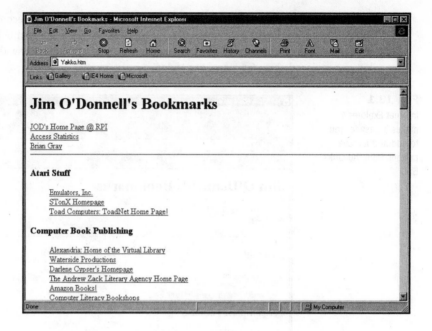

Links Bar Button Icons

As shown in the two preceding figures, you can create a number of buttons in the Links Bar. Each of these buttons uses the same icon, however, which makes the icon displayed pretty useless. By accessing the links through the Windows 95 Explorer, just as you did to rename them in the previous section, you can assign different icons to them. To assign a different icon to the Links Bar buttons, follow these steps:

1. Find the Links Bar entry with the Windows 95 Explorer in the **C:\Windows\Favorites\Links** subdirectory.

2. Right-click the desired entry and select Properties from the pop-up menu.

3. In the resulting Properties dialog box (see Figure 13.3), select the Internet Shortcut tab and click the Change Icon button.

4. Find the new icon you would like to use, select it, and click OK.

As shown in Figure 13.4, the icon for the Links Bar button is changed to your desired selection. The real benefit of changing the Links Bar button icons comes not from the Internet Explorer Web browser Links Bar, but when you attach the Links Bar to the Windows 95 Taskbar. When the Links Bar is there, you can disable its text label, leaving only the icon. By assigning different icons to each entry, you can add many buttons to the Links Bar.

FIG. 13.3
Because Links Bar button entries are just Windows 95 shortcuts, you can assign icons to them as with any other shortcut.

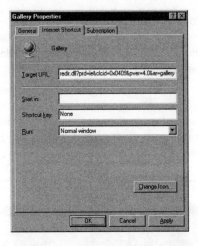

FIG. 13.4
Attaching different icons to Links Bar buttons allows each entry to have a unique appearance.

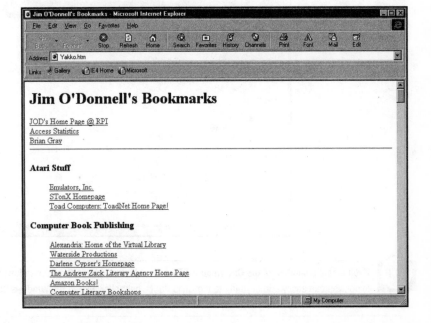

 These files, which should be on your system, are a good source of icons:

C:\WINDOWS\SYSTEM\Shell32.dll

C:\WINDOWS\SYSTEM\Url.dll

C:\WINDOWS\Moricons.dll

If you want to find new icons, a good place to look is the Windows95.com Web site, at

http://www.windows95.com/apps/icons.html

Part

II

Ch

13

Adding Other Types of Buttons to the Links Bar

Something that I mentioned in the previous section reveals another hidden capability of the Internet Explorer 4 Links Bar. The buttons for the Links Bar come from entries in the **C:\Windows\Favorites\Links** subdirectory, and these entries are just Windows 95 shortcuts.

Why, then, can't these entries be other types of shortcuts? As you might guess, they can! For instance, you can right-click and drag an application or application shortcut into the **C:\Windows\Favorites\Links** subdirectory, thus creating a new shortcut there that you should be able to use to launch the application. Figure 13.5 shows an example of this, with a shortcut to the NetTerm application embedded into the Links Bar. Clicking this button will launch the NetTerm application.

FIG. 13.5
You can put any kind of shortcut onto the Links Bar—not only Internet links, but also applications and other types of documents.

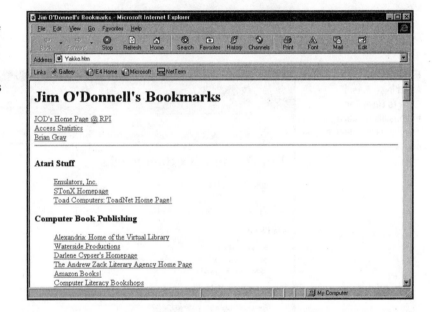

 If you create a shortcut of the **C:\Windows\Favorites\Links** folder in the **C:\Windows\Send To** folder, you can easily add anything to the Links Bar by right-clicking it in the Windows 95 Explorer or on the desktop, and selecting Send to, Links.

Optimal Toolbar Layout

The trend in today's computer market is that larger displays are becoming more common. Now, 17-inch monitors are the standard for many new desktop systems. Even so, plenty of 15-inch and even 14-inch displays are still out there, as well as the many laptop and notebook computers with even smaller screens.

All this can lead to your applications demanding a lot of screen real estate. In addition, Web browsing is a lot more fun (and effective) when you can see as much of the screen as possible. Short of buying a new monitor, you're stuck with the amount of area you have on your screen—what you want to do is use that area as effectively as possible.

Internet Explorer 4 offers you an unprecedented ability to adjust how your Web browser window looks. Previous versions of the Web browser allowed you selectively enable and disable toolbars. You could maximize the size of your Web browser window by disabling all the toolbars and the status bar along the bottom. Because so much is done with the toolbars, however, and the status bar relates a lot of important information, this is probably not the most effective way of setting up Internet Explorer.

As shown in the toolbars section of Chapter 8, "In-Depth: Internet Explorer 4," you can move Internet Explorer's toolbars *and* menu bar around with respect to one another. Figure 13.6 shows an effective setup, still displaying all three toolbars, the menu bar, and the status bar, but otherwise maximizing the available area for the Web browser window itself. To achieve this setup, follow these steps.

1. Right-click any toolbar and deselect the Text Labels entry, which removes the text labels from the Standard Toolbar, making it narrower and shorter.
2. Grab the Standard Toolbar handle and drag it up and to the right to put the toolbar on the same line as the menu bar. Because the entries on the menu bar don't go all the way across its length, you can cover a good part of it without losing functionality.
3. Slide the Standard Toolbar back and forth until all its buttons are visible.
4. Grab the Links Bar handle and drag it up to be on the same line as the Address Bar.
5. Slide the Links Bar back and forth until it's in its desired position.

 T I P If you don't have that many buttons on the Links Bar, you can show all of them and still have lots of room in the Address Bar. If you have lots of Links Bar buttons, you can slide it all the way to the left to keep it out of the way. Then, when you want to access one of the buttons, just click the Links Bar on the word Links, and it will expand across the line.

Through Internet Explorer 4's Web Integration, you have one more option for maximizing your available Web browser area even further while still retaining all the functions of the three toolbars. With Web Integration, you can place the Address Bar and the Links Bar on the Windows 95 Taskbar. By moving these toolbars, disabling them from appearing in the Web browser, and setting the Taskbar for Auto Hide, you get a little more screen with which to Web browse (with the added bonus of having the Address Bar available without needing to launch Internet Explorer. Figure 13.7 shows an example of this setup, with the Taskbar unhidden to enable you to make a selection.

▶ **See** "How to Add Toolbars to the Taskbar" to see what steps are needed to add the Address and Links Bars to the Taskbar, **p. 146**

Part

II

Ch

13

FIG. 13.6
By moving your toolbars around, you can make all their functions available and still see more of the Web browser window.

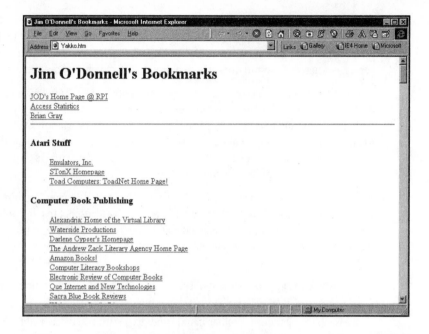

FIG. 13.7
Internet Explorer 4's Web Integration enables you to access any Web page at any time, whether your Web browser is running.

Choosing Your Web Browser Colors

As do most Web browsers, Internet Explorer 4 gives you the ability to select its default colors. These default colors are those that, in the absence of any instructions within the Web page itself, you would like your Web browser to use when rendering the page. The options for setting the default colors are located on the General tab of the View, Internet Options menu (see Figure 13.8). You would access this menu primarily by clicking the Colors button, but some color-control options are also under the Accessibility button.

FIG. 13.8

Internet Explorer enables you to select your default colors and font and to customize the appearance of Web pages that use the default values.

Figure 13.9 shows what the Colors dialog box looks like. You might want to adjust your default colors for a variety of reasons—one common reason is to reduce eye strain by changing the colors from the default black on white setting. More muted colors can be a lot easier on your eyes, as shown in Figure 13.10.

FIG. 13.9

Internet Explorer gives you the ability to control all your default colors.

Part
II

Ch
13

N O T E Figures 13.9 and 13.10 demonstrate another of Internet Explorer's abilities that you can customize—what it calls the "hover" color. *Hovering* is when the mouse is over a hypertext link. By setting a hover color, you can indicate that the link is there by allowing the whole link anchor to change to that color. In addition, you can enable or disable underlining of links or set them to be underlined only when the mouse hovers over them. ■

FIG. 13.10
You can select colors that are easier on your eyes. Make sure there is enough contrast to see all your text.

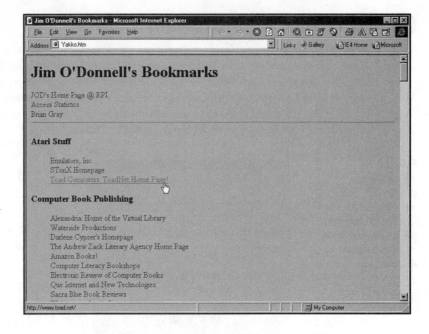

Internet Explorer Font Setup

The HTML 4.0 <FONT FACE> and <STYLE> tags enable Web authors to specify any font they would like for the text that appears on your Web browser. As long as you have that font on your system, the Web page will be displayed using it. Plenty of Web pages that use your Web browser's default font are still out there, however, with Internet Explorer, these defaults are Times Roman for proportional text and Courier New for fixed-width text.

The Fonts button on the View, Internet Options General tab enables you to set the font you would like your browser to use as a default. In addition, you can also set the default size of text to use (see Figure 13.11). Figure 13.12 demonstrates what the Web page will look like using the newly selected font.

FIG. 13.11
In the Fonts dialog box, you select the default fonts and font size Internet Explorer will use.

FIG. 13.12
You can select the fonts and sizes based on readability or on any other criterion that suits you.

CAUTION

Just as with the colors selections I discussed in the previous section, font selections made in this way only apply if the Web page uses the Web browser's defaults. If the Web page specifies its own colors or fonts, these values will override your selections. (You can override Web page specified fonts and colors, which I will show in the "User Style Sheets for Web Browsing" section later in this chapter.)

Viewing Foreign Language Web Sites

If you view foreign language Web sites, you must configure Internet Explorer to correctly render them. The Languages button of the View, Internet Options General tab enables you to do this. If you have the English language version of Internet Explorer 4, the only language that will likely be displayed in the Language Preference dialog box is U.S. English. To add others, click the Add button and select the desired language from the list that is shown (see Figure 13.13).

NOTE Configuring Internet Explorer's Language Preference only equips it to be able to correctly handle the character encoding it might encounter when you load a foreign-language Web page. You still must make sure you have the necessary fonts on your system for the pages to look right. ■

Part
II

Ch
13

FIG. 13.13
Internet Explorer 4 comes equipped to be able to render many languages you might find on the Web.

User Style Sheets for Web Browsing

Later in this book, Chapter 27, "Style Sheets," will show you how you can create Web pages with exactly the fonts, colors, and appearance you want, using what are known as style sheets (more formally as Cascading Style Sheets). Using these style sheets, you can control what font, size, weight, and foreground and background color are used by each and every HTML tag. The possibilities are endless.

▶ **See** "Style Sheet Tips and Tricks" for more information on what you can do with style sheets,
   p. 536

As a Web author, you can use not only style sheets, but you can also create a style sheet and set up Internet Explorer 4 to use it on all incoming Web pages. To do this, go to the General tab of the View, Internet Options dialog and click the Accessibility button (see Figure 13.14). By checking the Format documents using my style sheet box and entering the location of your style sheet into the text box below it, you can tell Internet Explorer to apply those formats. Figure 13.15 shows an example of a Web page with a user style sheet applied.

FIG. 13.14
You can use user style sheets to improve color contrast and font readability of Web pages and to make the Web more accessible to people with visual impairments.

Like the color and font selections you read about in previous sections of this chapter, your user style sheet will only be applied to Web pages that don't otherwise have their own <STYLE> information. You can override this behavior, however—for user style sheets, colors, and fonts—by checking some or all the boxes in the Formatting area of the Accessibility dialog box shown in Figure 13.14.

FIG. 13.15
You can specify a user style sheet to change any aspect of the way Web pages are displayed on your system.

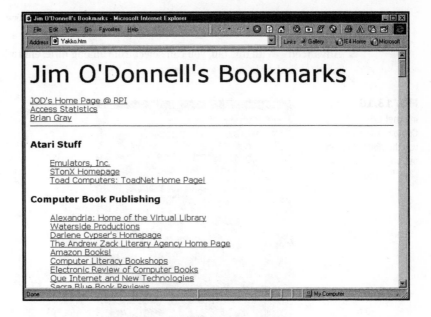

Using Internet Explorer's Content Advisor

There has been a lot of concern in the last year or two over the amount of adult material that is available over the Web and of finding ways to keep it away from children and others for whom it would not be appropriate. To support this idea, Internet Explorer implements the Platform for Internet Content Selection (PICS) standard, a definition of methods used to characterize the contents of information available on the Internet.

You can enable the use of PICS ratings by selecting the Content tab of the View, Internet Options dialog box and clicking the Enable key within the Ratings area. If you then click the Settings button, you will get the Content Advisor dialog box (see Figure 13.16).

The Content Advisor has three tabs that you can use to perform the following configuration functions:

- **Ratings**   With this tab, you can set the ratings for content in the categories of language, nudity, sex, and violence. Each category has five settings ranging, for example, from language level 0, inoffensive slang, through level 4, explicit or crude language.
- **General**   This tab, shown in Figure 13.16, enables you to change the supervisor password and enable the viewing of otherwise disallowed sites by entering the password.

  The last option on this tab is perhaps the most important at this time: You must decide whether to allow users of your Web browser to view unrated Web sites. Because the ratings system is voluntary and very new, many sites are unrated. To be completely safe, you should leave this box unchecked to safeguard against viewing an unrated site with adult content. If you do this, however, you can expect to see a lot of messages from the

Part

II

Ch

13

Content Advisor, like that shown in Figure 13.17, requiring a password to view an unrated site.

■ **Advanced** With this tab, you can select from among different ratings systems and services as they become available.

FIG. 13.16
Internet Explorer's Content Advisor gives you the ability to screen out adult-oriented Web sites from your browser.

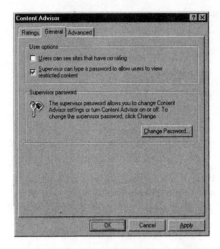

FIG. 13.17
Internet site ratings are a useful tool for screening out unwanted content from your system, but until more sites use them, they can cause a lot of added work.

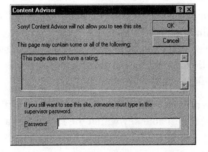

Configuring File Types for Internet Explorer 4

A familiar process to long-time users of Netscape Navigator is configuring helper applications to be used by that Web browser for dealing with the many different kinds of content that you are likely to find on the Web. Microsoft used a different approach with Internet Explorer, one that is easier to set up—almost requiring no setup at all—but that has a little less flexibility.

Under the Programs tab of the View, Options window is where you can configure Internet Explorer with the default program you would like to use for your Internet Mail and News, as well as Internet conferencing, calendar, and address book. These are the only file types/ content types that you can configure through the Internet Explorer Web browser. How, then, does it know how to deal with content other than the HTML and multimedia types that it supports?

Microsoft has released you from the need to configure each of the file types and content types that you wish to use with your Web browser by integrating it with the Windows 95 File Types database. Therefore, any document/application association about which your system knows—and they are usually automatically entered when a new application is installed—is also known by Internet Explorer 4. If you want to see what the associations are or change any of them, you can access the settings through the File Types tab of the Windows 95 Explorer's View, Folder Options tab (see Figure 13.18).

FIG. 13.18
Windows 95 shares its File Types database of applications and content types with Internet Explorer.

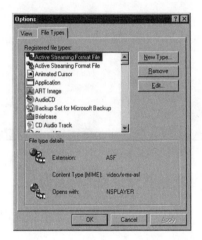

Web Browser Cookies

You may or may not have heard of "cookies." They're not the kind that you eat but the kind that can be passed back and forth between your Web browser and the Web servers to which it is connected. Cookies allow Web servers to collect and store information about your local system, enabling them to customize Web pages especially for you. Many Web sites allow you to set up custom Web pages, such as my customized Microsoft Network Web page, shown in Figure 13.19.

▶ **See** "Cookies" for more information of the uses of Web browser cookies, **p. 312**

Chapter 16, "In-Depth: Security," can tell you more about how cookies work. The cookie that enables the Microsoft Network to display the customized Web page shown in Figure 13.19 looks like that shown in Listing 13.1.

Part
II

Ch
13

FIG. 13.19
Cookies allow Web servers to set up customized Web pages for as many different people as they can support.

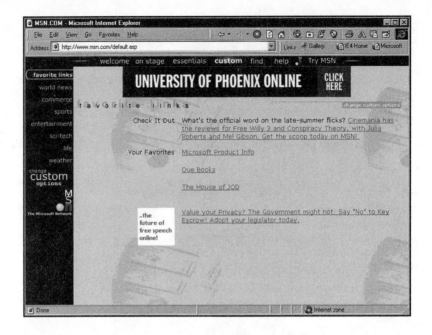

Listing 13.1 Cookies Contain Codes Set by Web Servers

```
MSN2.0Splash
2
msn.com/
0
3256846464
29212691
1416287968
29139267
*
MSN2.0FS1.0
3
msn.com/
0
3516846464
29212691
1416287968
29139267
*
MC1
GUID=23D1E17B0C5611D187800000F84A1409
msn.com/
0
1076911872
29212693
1429987968
29139267
*
```

Some privacy concerns have been raised about the information that cookies can transmit, but cookies are pretty benign, for the most part. If you still want to disable cookies on your machine, though, you can do so under the Advanced tab of the View, Internet Options dialog box.

N O T E You have a third option instead of accepting or rejecting all cookies—you can have Internet Explorer prompt you before accepting a cookie (see Figure 13.20). In general, this setting isn't very useful, however. Sites that use cookies sometimes use a lot of cookies. After visiting one or two such sites, you'll probably get very tired of clicking the Yes or No button. ■

FIG. 13.20
Internet Explorer gives you the final word on which cookies to accept onto your system.

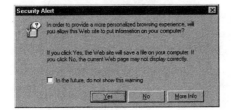

Explorer Web Integration

Internet Explorer 4 Web Integration brings Internet Explorer and the Windows 95 Explorer much closer together. You can use the Windows 95 Explorer to view either local or World Wide Web pages. You can use Internet Explorer to browse through your local system.

Microsoft Profile Assistant and Wallet Setup

Through the Content tab of the View, Internet Options dialog box, you can set up your personal information in Internet Explorer's Profile Assistant (see Figure 13.21) and also set up credit card payment information in Microsoft Wallet (see Figure 13.22). As Web sites that support these applications become more common, it will become easier for you to conduct business and interact with others over the Web.

▶ **See** "Using the Profile Assistant" for information on how you can standardize the personal information you make available, **p. 306**

▶ **See** "Using Microsoft Wallet" to find out more about how you can use Microsoft Wallet to make Internet purchases, **p. 307**

Part
II

Ch
13

FIG. 13.21

The Profile Assistant's standard form makes it easy for you to keep track of the information about yourself that you want to give out.

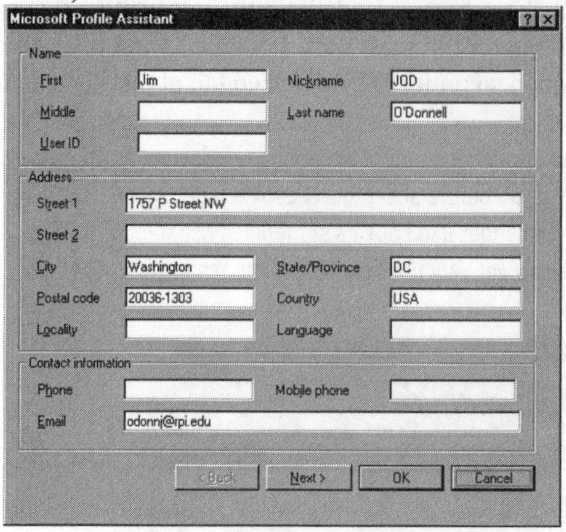

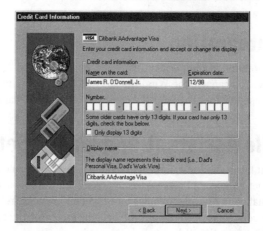

FIG. 13.22

Set up your credit card information ahead of time, and online purchases at compatible Web sites will be a snap.

As discussed in Chapter 16, "In-Depth: Security," the credit card information you include in Microsoft Wallet will only be passed over the Internet when you want it to and when you are connected to a secure, compatible Web site that is hosted by a Web site that uses Microsoft's Commerce Server or other compatible server software. To protect your credit card information at your end of the system, Microsoft Wallet requires you to set a password that it needs before it can use the information (see Figure 13.23).

FIG. 13.23
Secure servers protect
your credit card
information when it is
transmitted over the
Web. A user password
can protect it on your
local system.

Speeding Up Your Web Sessions

As the Internet and the Web has grown, it as been a constant race between the rapidly growing speed on Internet connections and the increased amount of information that must flow through those connections to support the Web's new multimedia capabilities. Despite your new, high-speed modem—or even the T1 line you might have at work—the Web will sometimes bog down.

There's an old trick that you can use to speed up your Web browsing, a trick that many people seem to have forgotten. By going into the Advanced tab of the View, Internet Options dialog box on Internet Explorer, you can selectively disable some or all multimedia content. Figure 13.24 shows the Microsoft Home Page when you disable all graphics, video, sound, and animations. It's not as exciting or visually appealing, but you still have access to all the site's content. This method can be a good way to quickly surf around to find the site for which you are looking. Then, you can re-enable any necessary multimedia content to correctly view that site.

Choosing Outlook Express Stationery

The Web browser is not the only application in the Internet Explorer suite of applications. Two of the other major applications that come with it also offer a number of options and ways with which you can configure the applications. The remainder of this chapter will discuss ways in which you can configure Outlook Express and NetMeeting for optimal and more effective operation.

Part
II

Ch
13

FIG. 13.24

If you disable graphics, be careful. This page looks okay, but many poorly designed Web pages will lose a lot or even all their content if their images don't show.

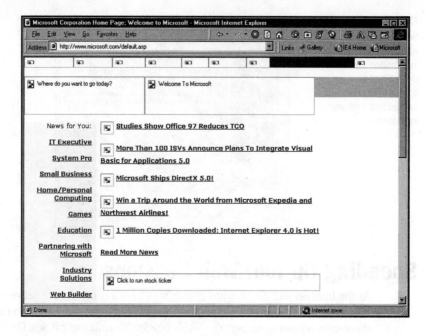

In addition to plain text e-mail messages and news postings, Outlook Express supports a rich text format. This format is actually HTML. You can make your HTML-formatted messages look better and communicate more effectively using Outlook Express's Stationery. This option, selected from the Tools, Stationery menu selection, enables you to select any GIF or JPEG image to use as a background for your image (see Figure 13.25).

FIG. 13.25

With Outlook Express's Stationery, you can add a personal touch to your outgoing mail and news postings.

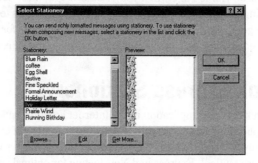

Outlook Express comes with a number of images that were especially designed to make effective backgrounds. By combining a suitable background with formatted text, you can make your e-mail a lot more attractive to its recipient (see Figure 13.26).

FIG. 13.26
Outlook Express will format and send this message as an HTML document and transmit it over the Internet.

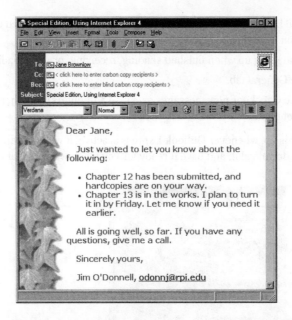

> **CAUTION**
>
> Make sure the recipients of your messages are using Outlook Express or another mail or news client that supports HTML message formatting. Far from being a more effective means of communication, HTML formatting makes your messages much less effective if the reader's software doesn't support it.

Periodically Checking Your Mail with Outlook Express

You can configure Outlook Express to check for new mail or news postings regardless of whether your computer is currently connected to the Internet. The Dial up tab of the Tools, Options dialog box enables you to set up the application to do this (see Figure 13.27). You can improve your productivity by configuring Outlook Express to automatically initiate an Internet connection, check for new mail or news, and terminate the connection afterward. This configuration enables you to download information while you aren't actually at your machine, enabling you to work more efficiently when you are at it:

The steps to set up Outlook Express for this operation follow.

1. Select Tools, Options.
2. Click the Dial up tab of the Options dialog box.

Part
II

Ch
13

3. Select the Dial this connection radio button and select the desired dial up networking connection from the drop-down list.

4. Check the Hang up when finished sending, receiving, or downloading button.

5. Click the General tab.

6. Check the Check for new messages every XXX minute(s) button, and select the desired number of minutes.

Once you set this up, whenever Outlook Express is active, it will periodically check for your mail and news, download it, and have it ready for you whenever you want to read it.

FIG. 13.27
By downloading mail and news when you aren't at the computer, Outlook Express enables you to be more productive when you are at the computer.

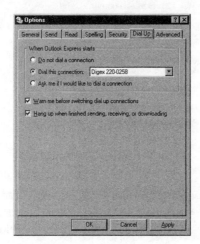

Outlook Express Inbox Assistant Tips

In Chapter 10, "In-Depth: Outlook Express Mail and News," you learned all about how to use Outlook Express's Inbox Assistant to automate receiving your mail, redirecting it into different folders, automatically forwarding it, and several other tasks. You can do other things with the Inbox Assistant, at least one of which could conceivably save you money.

▶ **See** "Using the Inbox Assistant to Automate Your Mail" to find out other ways to use Outlook Express's Inbox Assistant, **p. 157**

Though unlimited-access Internet accounts are becoming more common, there are still accounts that charge you for connect time. If you have such an account, the last thing you want to do is to download lots of unnecessary mail messages, particularly large ones. But, you still might want to use Outlook Express to automatically download your mail when you are not at your computer.

Fortunately, there is an option in the Inbox Assistant for dealing with this situation, as shown in Figure 13.28. By checking the boxes shown, you tell Outlook Express not to download messages larger than a certain size. If you want to be even more extreme, you can have the program delete such messages completely.

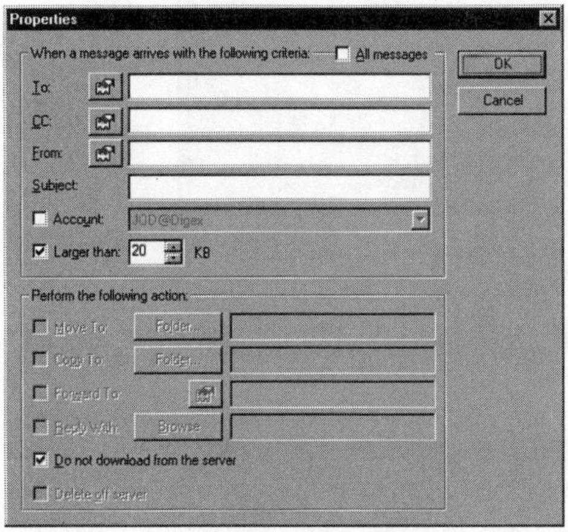

FIG. 13.28
The Inbox Assistant enables you to set up rules to control exactly which messages it downloads to your machine.

Configuring NetMeeting Audio

NetMeeting's two most desired features, transmitting real-time audio and video, are also its most problematic because, unless you have a direct connection to the Internet, sending audio or video will stress your Internet connection to the limit. Fortunately, NetMeeting has some options for mitigating this problem as much as possible.

Figure 13.29 shows the Audio tab of the Tools, Options dialog box. Through this dialog box, you can enable or disable full-duplex audio. With full-duplex audio and a sound card that is capable of supporting it, you can send and receive audio at the same time. If you are having trouble maintaining good quality audio transmission and reception with full-duplex set, try disabling it. By cutting the needed bandwidth in half, you are much more likely to transmit understandable speech.

Optimizing Video Transmission with NetMeeting

The options available for optimizing video transmission are a little different than with audio. You access these options through the Tools, Options Video tab, as shown in Figure 13.30. NetMeeting enables you to set the size and the desired quality of the image you send. Each of these settings affects the image-quality-versus-bandwidth tradeoff, and NetMeeting enables you to find the best settings for your system's hardware and Internet connection.

Part
II

Ch

13

FIG. 13.29
Use NetMeeting's audio options to configure your system for the best quality possible.

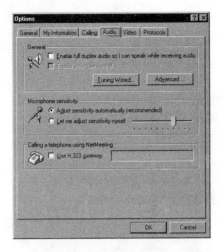

FIG. 13.30
Smaller versus larger images and the desired frame rate are some of the tradeoffs that affect image quality.

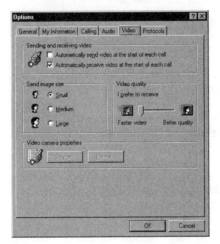

Exchanging Your NetMeeting SpeedDial Address

NetMeeting's SpeedDialer makes it easy for you to keep track of the addresses of people with whom you frequently converse. By properly setting the options in the Calling tab of the Tools, Options dialog box, you can even have NetMeeting automatically add people with whom you speak to your SpeedDialer. But what is a good way to provide your NetMeeting contact information to other people?

By selecting NetMeeting's SpeedDial, Add SpeedDial option, you can create a SpeedDial entry for yourself (see Figure 13.31). Rather than saving it to your SpeedDial list, check the Save on the desktop button to add your NetMeeting contact information to your desktop as a shortcut. Then, you can use Windows 95's Send to abilities to send it to anyone you want. Just right-click the desktop shortcut and select Se_nd to, Mail Recipient, as shown in Figure 13.32. Doing so will start Outlook Express (or whatever your Internet Mail client is) and enable you to enter the e-mail address of the person to whom you wish to send the information. Once that person receives it, he or she can enter it into his or her SpeedDial list or put it on his or her desktop. In fact, if he or she is using Outlook Express or other compatible application to read his or her mail, he or she will be able to double-click right on the shortcut within the mail message to initiate a NetMeeting call to you (if you are logged on).

FIG. 13.31
NetMeeting SpeedDial is a great way to keep track of frequent contacts.

FIG. 13.32
By putting a NetMeeting SpeedDial on the desktop, you make it a Windows 95 shortcut that you can easily send to other people.

 T I P You can put other SpeedDial entries on the desktop and initiate calls from the desktop. Or, you can move them from the desktop into **C:\Windows\Favorites\Links**, putting them right on your Links Bar.

Part
II

Ch
13

Speeding Up NetMeeting Startup

There are a lot of things that NetMeeting tries to do when it first starts executing that can really slow down its startup process. Depending on how it is set up, NetMeeting might try to log you on to your default directory server, download the information of everyone else who is on that server, and then go through the entire SpeedDial list to see if any or all of the people on the list are currently on the Internet. If you would like to speed the process up, you can disable any or all of the procedures through the Calling tab of the _T_ools, _O_ptions menu (see Figure 13.33). Then, once NetMeeting has started, you can manually initiate each one yourself.

FIG. 13.33

You can configure NetMeeting to skip some of its normal initial functions to speed up the startup process.

CHAPTER 14

In-Depth: Smart Favorites

With all the content out there on the Web, you're bound to come across a host of different documents and sites that really appeal to you. But when you're surfing, who has time to think about writing down the URL of a favorite Web page? You're far too engrossed in the experience to realize that you should record the page's address somewhere so you can get back to it later.

Fortunately, Internet Explorer comes to the rescue with support for recording the URLs of your favorite sites as you explore the Web. You can store the URLs in a simple list or organize them into folders by simply dragging and dropping them there. Then later, when you want to go back to one of these URLs, you just need to select it from your list—a task that's much easier than typing the URL from memory.

In Internet Explorer vernacular, these recorded URLs are called *favorites*. This chapter tells you how you can use Internet Explorer's Favorites menu to store and organize the URLs of the sites you plan to revisit. ■

Viewing your favorites

Internet Explorer gives you a number of different ways to access your list of favorite places on the Web, including the Favorites Bar—a graphic display of your favorites that appears right in the main browser window.

Managing your favorites

Adding a site to your list of Favorites is not the end of the story. You can organize Favorites into folders and even make changes to a Favorite's properties.

Favorites versus subscriptions

Subscriptions show under the Favorites menu, but they are different from Favorites in a number of important ways.

Favorites versus channels

You can also find Channels listed under the Favorites menu, but like Subscriptions, Channels are very different Favorite sites.

What Are Favorite Places?

The World Wide Web is a tapestry of millions of different documents and sites, all linked by means of references from other documents and sites. It is no surprise, then, that help was thought to be necessary for users exploring those links.

Because of the complexity of Web URLs, having to remember and manually enter every page's address each time you wanted to view it would be incredibly tedious. And while Internet Explorer enables you to save a page or an image to your hard drive for later offline browsing, you will likely have a great number of remote pages that you will want to access on a regular basis because they will be continually updated with fresh information.

Favorites take away the tedious task of having to write down or otherwise save each page's or document's URL. When you add an item to your list of Favorites, you make a record of that item's Internet address, along with a description of the item, and place it in a pull-down menu that you can access quickly from the Internet Explorer Favorites menu. When you want to visit that page, document, or image later on, you simply pull down the Favorites list and select the desired item. Internet Explorer automatically retrieves the item's URL and tries to access the address.

TIP If a link doesn't work, one reason may be that the file name on the remote server has changed or has been moved to another directory. To work around this, try typing in a truncated version of the full URL—perhaps just using the server name and nothing else. Doing so often gets you access to the hypertext documents on the remote machine from which you can rummage around and look for the file to which you wanted to link.

The Details of Storing Favorite Places

If you like to know specifics, here's the scoop on how Internet Explorer stores information on favorites. In Windows 95 and NT, the URL of a favorite is stored in its own file in the **C:\WINDOWS\FAVORITES** folder. If an author has given a document a title (which shows up at the top of the Internet Explorer window) and you record that document as one of your favorites, the file's MS-DOS name is the document's title (possibly compressed down to eight characters or fewer), followed by a .URL extension. In the absence of a title, the file's MS-DOS name is also the document's URL (again, possibly compressed and with reserved characters changed to dashes) followed by the .URL extension. Thus, if you add the document entitled Shareware Programs from **http://www.download-it.com/** to your favorites list, the URL would be stored in a file SHAREW~1.URL. If the document does not have a title, it is stored in a file name HTTP—~1.URL.

Inside the file, the URL is stored in the following format:

```
[InternetShortcut]
URL=http://www.download-it.com/
```

Knowing this, you could make your own favorites without Internet Explorer's assistance by creating a simple text file in the preceding format that includes the URL of the favorite place you want to record.

Additionally, because favorites appear in a Windows folder, you can use the Windows Explorer to manage your favorites, instead of using the tools that Internet Explorer comes with.

With a sense of what favorites are, you're now ready to learn how to use Internet Explorer to store and organize your favorite Web sites, the keys to which are the options you'll find under the Favorites menu.

The Favorites Menu

The options on the Internet Explorer Favorites menu are shown in Figure 14.1. The menu is divided into three different regions by separator bars. The top region contains the two options you'll use most frequently when managing your list of favorites. Specifically, these options enable you to add the page you're currently reading to your list of favorites and let you place related favorites into folders so that your list is better organized.

FIG. 14.1
The Favorites menu enables you to record and organize favorite URLs quickly and easily.

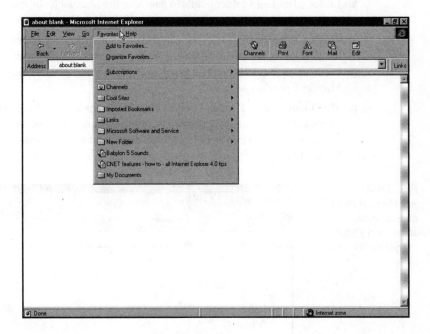

Below the first separator bar and above the second is the Subscriptions option. Internet Explorer subscriptions are not subscriptions in the traditional sense of the word. When you subscribe to a page using Internet Explorer, the browser will automatically check the page each time you start a new Web surfing session to see whether the page has changed. If it has changed, the browser will notify you and give you the option of going to the updated page. Thus, in the context of Internet Explorer, subscriptions refer to the browser proactively, going out to pages in which you're interested and checking them for new information.

▶ **See** "Subscriptions," **p. 391**

The area below the Subscriptions option is devoted to the storage of favorite places. In addition to favorites you add yourself, Internet Explorer prepopulates this menu with several standard folders:

Part
II
Ch
14

■ **Channels**   The Channels folder gives you quick access to the many Webcasting channels Microsoft has set up in conjunction with its content-provider partners. The Channels folder is organized into subfolders containing related channel links.

▶ **See** "Premium Channels," **p. 409**

■ **Cool Sites**   The Cool Sites folder contains a link to the Link Central page on the Microsoft Network (MSN) site. From there, you can jump to whatever MSN has designated as the cool sites of the day.

■ **Imported Bookmarks**   If you had an installation of Netscape Navigator in place when you installed Internet Explorer, Internet Explorer will import your Netscape bookmarks and make them available to you as Internet Explorer favorites.

■ **Links**   The Links folder points to pages on the Microsoft site that contain Microsoft product news and Microsoft's Best of the Web, Web Gallery, and Today's Picks.

■ **Microsoft Software and Service**   Favorites in this folder are set up to take you to the home pages of either the Microsoft Corporation or MSN. You can also learn how to speed up your connections by using an ISDN line and get specific information on Microsoft product support.

■ **My Documents**   The My Documents folder is the standard save location for the Microsoft Office suite of applications. Internet Explorer gives you easy access to this folder and you can browse it just as you would with the Windows Explorer (see Figure 14.2).

FIG. 14.2
Your Microsoft Office documents are automatically listed as Internet Explorer favorite places.

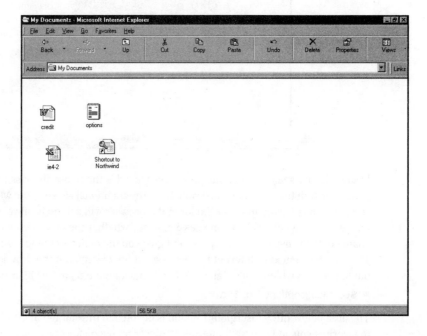

N O T E   If you double-click one of the documents in the My Documents folder, Internet Explorer will
launch the appropriate Office application and open the document there. ▮

Favorites, Channels, and Subscriptions

You can find favorites, subscriptions, and channels all under the Favorites menu, so you might wonder
what the relationship between them is. A *favorite* is simply the transcription of a page's title and URL
so that the browser can call up the page later. Favorites are not updated unless you do it, and it's up
to you to check your favorites regularly to see whether they're offering any new content.

A *subscription* is a favorite that Internet Explorer checks for new content according to a schedule that
you specify. If there has been a change to a favorite to which you've subscribed, Internet Explorer will
notify you of the change and ask whether you want to visit the updated page.

Channels broadcast content from a site that's been made Webcast-ready using Microsoft's Channel
Definition Format. By tuning in a channel with Internet Explorer, you pick up the channel's broadcast
and get to see the content being displayed there. Channel content is constantly changing, so it
doesn't make sense to try to subscribe to channel. Additionally, because channels get their own
Channel Bar, there's not much reason to store a channel under the Favorites folder.

You place any other items or folders in the bottom part of the Favorites menu as you add to and
organize your list of favorites. If you've created any favorites folders, you'll note that only the
topmost folders in your hierarchy show under the Favorites menu. Holding your mouse pointer
over a top-level folder reveals a list of favorites and subfolders stored under that top-level folder
(see Figure 14.3).

FIG. 14.3
Holding your mouse
over a folder reveals the
contents of that folder.

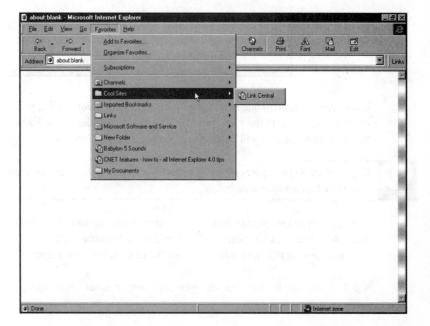

Other Ways to Access Your Favorites

Internet Explorer comes with a few other ways with which you can get at your list of favorites—most prominently, the Favorites button you see on the Internet Explorer toolbar. Figure 14.4 shows that clicking this button induces a substantial change in the Internet Explorer interface. The browser screen literally divides into two sections with your favorites shown in the section on the left (called the Favorites Bar) and the browsing area limited to the section in the right. This makes all of your favorites available to you all the time, rather than only when you've clicked the Favorites menu.

FIG. 14.4

You can display your list of favorites during your entire browsing session.

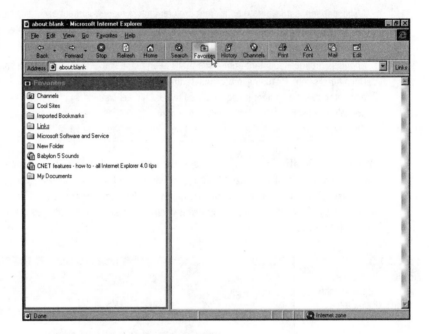

If you want to jump to one of the pages stored in your favorites list, you need only click the entry for that page in the Favorites Bar. To explore a folder in the Favorites Bar, just click the folder and its contents will be displayed below it (see Figure 14.5).

T I P   Click the black X in the upper-right corner of the Favorites Bar to close the window and return the Internet Explorer interface to normal.

You can also access your favorites using other components of the Windows 95 interface. For example, if you click the Start button, you'll see a Favorites option on your Start menu. Holding your mouse over this option reveals your list of favorites (see Figure 14.6).

N O T E   The favorites listing you see on the Start menu does not include the My Documents folder.

FIG. 14.5
You can expand or collapse the folders showing in the Favorites Bar.

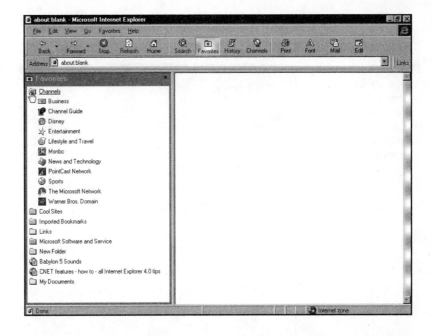

FIG. 14.6
Internet Explorer favorites are also accessible from your Start menu.

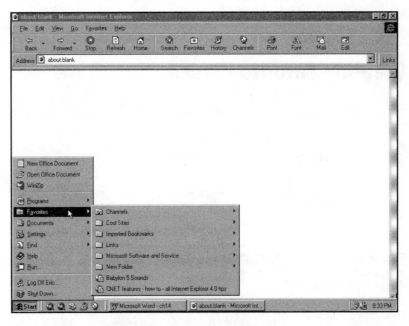

You can also use the Windows Explorer to navigate to the folder that holds your favorites. You'll find the Favorites folder as a subfolder of the Windows folder. When you open the Favorites folder, you'll see a screen much like that in Figure 14.7. The Windows Explorer view of your favorites reinforces the fact that favorites are stored in folders and files on your hard drive.

FIG. 14.7
You can see your favorites as individual files by browsing through the Favorites folder using the Windows Explorer.

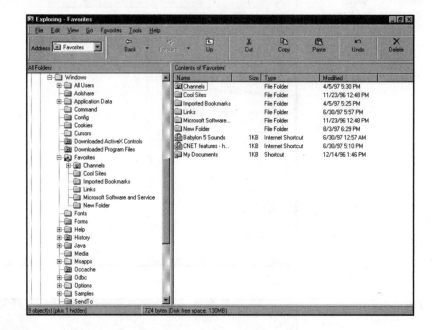

Creating Favorite Places

When you find a Web page that you really like, adding it to your list of favorites is easy. With the page loaded in the Internet Explorer window, you simply follow these steps:

1. Choose the Favorites menu.
2. Choose the Add to Favorites option.
3. The Add to Favorites dialog box will ask you to confirm the addition and whether you want to subscribe to the page (see Figure 14.8). Put a check in the Subscribe checkbox if you want to subscribe to the page and then click OK if you want to add the page to the top level of the Favorites folder.

FIG. 14.8
The Add to Favorites dialog box confirms your addition and enables you to subscribe to a page at the time you add it to your favorites.

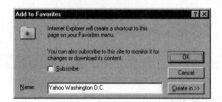

T I P The name under which the favorite is stored is the document's title. If you want the favorite stored under a different name, just type the new name into the Name field in the Add to Favorites dialog box.

4. If you want to store a favorite in a subfolder, click the Create In button in the Add to Favorites dialog box to reveal an expanded version of the box that displays the available subfolders (see Figure 14.9). You can choose to store the favorite in one of the subfolders or you can create a new folder for it by clicking the New Folder button. Once you're done selecting or setting up a subfolder, click the OK button to add the favorite to the subfolder. Once you clicked OK, the page is added to your favorites list. Simple!

FIG. 14.9
With an expanded version of the Add to Favorites dialog box, you can place the new favorite in a subfolder or create a new subfolder for it.

Another way to do the same thing is to use Internet Explorer's context-sensitive menu you get by right-clicking your mouse. You can add a page to your list of favorites by right-clicking at a point on the page where no hyperlinks and no graphics appear. The menu you see in Figure 14.10 will then appear and you can select the Add to Favorites option to open the Add to Favorites dialog box. From there, just follow the steps previously outlined to add the page to your favorites.

Organizing Favorite Places

As you accumulate a large number of favorites, it makes sense to organize them into logical groupings. You can store groups of related favorites together in folders that you create and name. Figure 14.11 shows a fair-sized list of favorites. Many of them are related, and, over the course of this section, you'll see how to arrange them into folders.

Part

II

Ch

14

FIG. 14.10

You can also add a page to your list of favorites by using the Internet Explorer right-click menus.

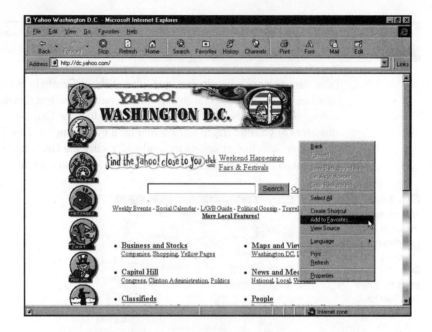

FIG. 14.11

In this list of favorites, many are candidates for being grouped into folders.

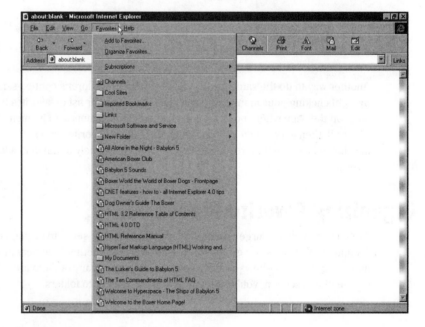

To begin organizing your favorites, you must first make some folders into which to put them. You can accomplish this by performing the following steps:

1. From the Favorites menu, select the Organize favorites option. The Organize Favorites dialog box appears (see Figure 14.12).

FIG. 14.12

The Organize Favorites dialog box resembles a standard Windows browsing dialog box, but it contains additional support for handling favorites.

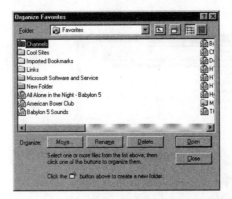

2. Right-click a blank spot in the Organize Favorites dialog box to produce a context-sensitive menu.

3. Move your mouse pointer over the New option to reveal a list of new items you can create (see Figure 14.13).

FIG. 14.13

Right-clicking in the Organize Favorites dialog box enables you to create folders for storing your favorites.

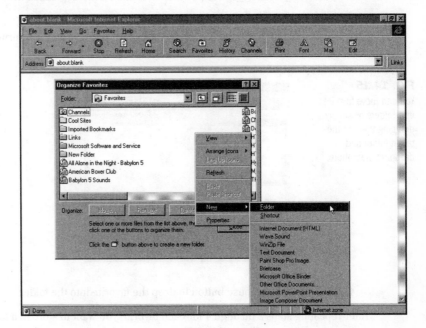

Part

II

Ch

14

4. Click the Folder option to place a new folder in the dialog box.

5. Type in an appropriately descriptive name for the folder and then press Enter.

You can repeat steps 2 through 5 to create and name as many new folders as you need. Figure 14.14 shows three newly created folders that you can use to organize the list of favorites shown in Figure 14.11.

FIG. 14.14

With these new folders created, you're ready to place individual favorites into each one.

Once you've created the new folders, storing favorites in them is as easy as dragging and dropping. Follow these steps to move a favorite into a folder:

1. Choose Favorites, Organize Favorites to call up the Organize Favorites dialog box.

2. Click the favorite you want to move.

3. While holding down the left mouse button, drag the selected favorite to the folder in which you want to store it (see Figure 14.15).

FIG. 14.15

You can move favorites into folders by simply dragging them to the target folder and dropping them there.

4. Release the left mouse button to drop the favorite into the folder.

After repeating steps 2 through 4 for each favorite you want to store in a folder, you'll see a screen like the one in Figure 14.16. To get to one of the favorites you just moved, you must open the folder in which you stored it by double-clicking the folder. Figure 14.17 shows the open HTML folder.

FIG. 14.16

The Favorites folder with most favorites organized into subfolders.

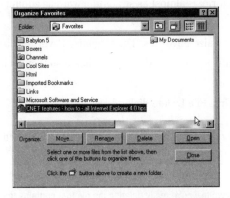

FIG. 14.17

Double-clicking the HTML folder reveals the favorites that it contains.

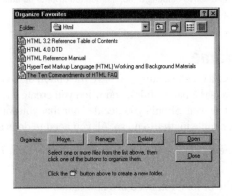

 T I P You can use the same drag and drop approach to moving favorites if you're managing them through the Windows Explorer.

N O T E If you don't like using drag and drop, you can move a favorite by highlighting it and clicking the Move button in the Organize Favorites dialog box. ∎

Changing Favorite Place Properties

The Web is a truly dynamic medium and content on the Web is changing all the time. Site administrators might remove pages whose contents are out of date or they might change the URL of a page as part of a site reorganization. Changes like these mean that you will very likely have to make changes to your favorites as some point, and Internet Explorer is well-equipped to assist you with this task.

Part
II

Ch
14

Deleting a Favorite

If a favorite page has been removed from a Web site, you should remove it from your Favorites folder as well. Deleting a favorite is almost as straightforward as adding one. To delete a favorite, follow these steps:

1. Choose Favorites, Organize Favorites. The Organize Favorites dialog box appears.

2. Navigate to the favorite you want to delete and click it so that it's highlighted.

3. Click the Delete button.

4. Click Yes in the Confirm File Delete dialog box.

 T I P   If you prefer using the right-click menus, you can right-click the outdated favorite and use the Delete option on the menu to remove the favorite.

N O T E   When you delete a favorite, you're really deleting the file that contains the URL information for the favorite. Because you're deleting a file, the deleted favorite actually goes into the Recycle Bin, so you can restore it from there if you haven't emptied the bin.

Changing a Favorite's Name

When you add a page to your list of favorites, you have the option of overriding the default name for the favorite (which is the page's title), and when you create a new folder to hold your favorites, you can name that as well. Should you decide later that you want to change the name of a favorite or folder, it is a simple matter to do so. All you need to do is follow these steps:

1. From the Favorites menu, choose the Organize Favorites option. The Organize Favorites dialog box appears.

2. Navigate to the favorite or folder in need of a new name.

3. Click the targeted favorite or folder and then click the Rename button.

4. Type in the new name for the favorite or folder, and then press Enter.

If you do a lot of file or folder renaming in the Windows Explorer, carrying out the preceding steps should remind you a lot of that process. That is, in fact, what you just did, because favorite information is stored in files in your hard drive's directory structure.

Changing a Favorite's URL

If a favorite page has moved to a new URL, you can edit the existing favorite and update the URL information. To update a favorite in your list, perform the following steps:

1. Choose Favorites, Organize Favorites to call the Organize Favorites dialog box.

2. Navigate to the favorite with the outdated URL.

3. Right-click the targeted favorite and select the Properties option from the context-sensitive menu that appears. You'll then see a dialog box similar to the one in Figure 14.18.

FIG. 14.18

Each favorite has a set of properties that you can change as you need.

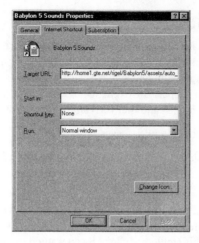

4. On the Internet Shortcut tab of the Properties dialog box, update the Target URL field with the updated URL information.

5. Click OK to save the change.

You probably noticed in Figure 14.18 that other tabs are on the Properties dialog box as well. The General tab provides general information about the file that contains the favorite: when it was created, when it was last updated, file size, MS-DOS name, what kind of attributes it has, and so on.

The other panel is the Subscription panel, shown in Figure 14.19, which will tell you whether you've subscribed to the page and what kind of download schedule you have set up for the page. If you haven't subscribed to the page, you can do so by clicking the Subscribe Now button you see on the tab.

FIG. 14.19

Subscription information is stored along with a favorite so it's easy to know if you've subscribed to a page or not.

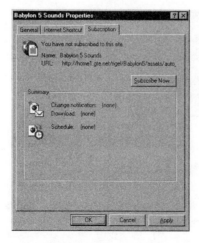

Part

II

Ch

14

Sharing Favorites with Others

In the course of your Web exploration, you're likely to compile an impressive list of favorites. Once this happens, you'll find that people with similar interests may want to get their hands on your list. Conversely, you may know someone who has a list of favorites that you wouldn't mind making part of your own. To help support the exchange of favorites in this situation, realize that all favorites are really stored in files and that you can pass files around accordingly.

You can do this file exchange in any number of ways:

- **Disk**   You can place the files or folders containing the favorites you want to swap on a disk and then hand the disk over to the person who is interested in your favorites.

- **Briefcase**   If you're trying to maintain the same set of favorites on two different computers, you can place them in a Windows 95 briefcase and use the automatic file synchronization feature. This would be helpful if you wanted to have the same favorites on both your PC and your laptop or if you and a colleague at work want to share favorites over a corporate LAN.

- **E-mail**   By attaching the desired favorites' files and folders to an e-mail message, you can send your favorites to anyone with an e-mail address.

- **Network file sharing**   You can set up file sharing from the Windows Explorer that enables other users on your network to have access to your Favorites folder. To do this, right-click the Favorites folder and then choose the Properties option. From there, click the Sharing tab to reveal the dialog box shown in Figure 14.20. On this tab, you can enable file sharing, choose which users have access to your favorites, and what level of access they have (read, write, delete, and so on). You can also enable HTTP sharing by clicking the Web Sharing button and making sure that the Share folder for HTTP box is checked (see Figure 14.21).

FIG. 14.20
Network users can share favorites easily once file sharing is enabled.

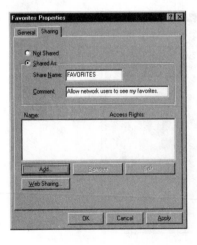

FIG. 14.21

You can also share favorites over an HTTP server, but access should be limited to read-only.

CHAPTER 15

In-Depth: Interacting with ActiveX Controls, Plug-Ins, Java, and Scripts

Y ou can view advanced content through some of the many technologies supported by Internet Explorer 4, such as ActiveX Controls, plug-ins, Java applets, and scripts. The nature of these technologies is to add new capabilities to your Web browser. Because they can add completely new capabilities and enable you to access content in many different formats, there is no fixed way to interact with them.

It is in the best interests of the developers of these controls and applets to make their use as intuitive as possible, however. The process of downloading, installing, and using advanced content and advanced technologies has become easier. ■

Increase Internet Explorer 4's capabilities with ActiveX Controls and Plug-ins

Microsoft's ActiveX Control technology, along with Internet Explorer 4's ability to use Netscape Navigator plug-ins, offers you an open-ended method to increase the capabilities of your Web browser.

How to interact with Java applets and scripts

Java applets and scripts are downloaded and executed within your Web browser at the same time as HTML and other Web content. Each applet and script determines the ways in which you can interact with it.

Use Internet Explorer 4's security settings to configure how it treats advanced content

If you're worried about what ActiveX Controls, plug-ins, or other applications or applets can do to your system, you can configure Internet Explorer to determine what is executed.

Learn where to find samples of advanced Web content

The Web is full of resources for finding samples and examples of all advanced content and technologies. You can find collections of some of the best URLs here.

Advanced Content in Internet Explorer 4

The four types of advanced content and advanced technologies discussed in this chapter perform several different types of functions. Some purposes that you can perform follow:

- **View multimedia content**   ActiveX Controls and plug-ins can give you the ability to view multimedia content beyond what is natively supported in Internet Explorer 4. For instance, you can install controls and plug-ins to view graphics, video, audio, and other animations, such as QuickTime and MPEG video and RealAudio audio content.

- **Provide new functionality**   ActiveX Controls, plug-ins, Java applets, and scripts enable Web page authors to provide you with functions that Internet Explorer 4 doesn't directly support. For example, Microsoft's ActiveX Marquee Control enables you to scroll text or graphics around the Web page or enables you to download Java applets, giving you a real-time clock on a Web page.

- **Provide interaction among Web page objects**   Internet Explorer 4 provides an extensive object model that enables ActiveX Controls, plug-ins, Java applets, and Web browser elements themselves to interact with one another. The VBScript and JScript/JavaScript scripting languages provide the glue that enables Web page authors to bring these elements together.

N O T E   JScript is Microsoft's implementation of Netscape's JavaScript language. ▓

Using Microsoft's ActiveX Controls

For most users, integrating ActiveX Controls is transparent because the controls open and become active whenever you open Internet Explorer. Furthermore, you often will not even see ActiveX Controls at work because most ActiveX Controls are not activated unless you open a Web page that initiates them. For example, after you install Macromedia's Flash 2 ActiveX Control, you will notice no difference in the way Internet Explorer functions until you come across a Web page that features Shockwave.

Once an ActiveX Control is installed on your machine and initiated by a Web page, it will manifest itself in one of these three potential forms:

- Embedded
- Full-screen
- Hidden

Embedded Controls

An embedded ActiveX Control appears as a visible, rectangular window integrated into a Web page. This window may not appear to be any different from a window created by a graphic, such as an embedded GIF or JPEG picture. The main difference between the previous windows supported by Internet Explorer and those created by ActiveX Controls is that ActiveX

Control windows support a much wider range of interactivity and movement and thereby remain live instead of static.

In addition to being able to react to mouse clicks, embedded ActiveX Controls also read and take note of mouse location, mouse movement, keyboard input, and input from virtually any other input device. In this way, an ActiveX Control can support the full range of user events required to produce sophisticated applications.

Full-Screen Controls

A full-screen ActiveX Control takes over the entire current Internet Explorer window to display its own content. This is necessary when a Web page is designed to display data that is not supported by HTML. An example of this type of ActiveX Control is the VRML ActiveX Control, available from Microsoft. If you view a VRML world using Internet Explorer with the VRML ActiveX Control, it loads into your Web browser like any other Web page, but it retains the look and functionality of a VRML world, with three-dimensional objects through and around which you can navigate.

Hidden Controls

A hidden ActiveX Control has no visible elements but works strictly behind the scenes to add some features to Internet Explorer that are not otherwise available. An example of a hidden control would be the Preloader Control, discussed later in this chapter. This ActiveX Control is used to preload a graphic, sound, or other element that the Internet Explorer user will subsequently view. Because the element is downloaded while the user is browsing through the current Web page, appearance response time is much greater.

Regardless of which ActiveX Controls you use and whether they are embedded, full-screen, or hidden, the rest of Internet Explorer's user interface should remain relatively constant and available. So, even if you have a VRML world displayed in Internet Explorer's main window, you'll still be able to access its menus and navigational controls.

Installing Internet Explorer 4 Components

Several ActiveX Controls are included in the set of components that are part of Internet Explorer 4. Loading these controls into your system is easily done by using the Active Setup Wizard that comes with the Web browser. You can begin this download process by going to **http://www.microsoft.com/ie/ie40/download/addon.htm**. When you follow the link there to download Internet Explorer 4 components, the Active Setup Wizard starts (see Figure 15.1).

FIG. 15.1
The Active Setup Wizard gives you an easy way to install components that are part of the Internet Explorer 4 suite.

The beauty of the Active Setup Wizard is that it is capable of analyzing your system to determine what components are already installed. Then, it is easy to download and install those components that you need. As shown in Figure 15.2, if you are interested in downloading some of the ActiveX Controls that are part of Internet Explorer components, you can check them off on this component's download page. Along the bottom of the Web page, a running total of the size and estimated download time of the desired components is maintained.

FIG. 15.2

You can select to install those components that aren't already in your system and keep an eye on how long the download will take.

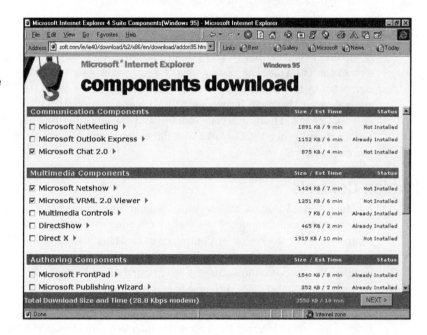

Once you have selected the components that you would like to download, the download begins (see Figure 15.3). Internet Explorer 4 and its Active Setup Wizard will automatically download and install the desired components onto your system. Once the download is complete, the Wizard will tell you what successfully downloaded (see Figure 15.4) and, depending on what you installed, may ask you to restart your system to complete the installation process.

FIG. 15.3

The Active Setup Wizard enables you to easily download and install Internet Explorer 4 components directly from the Microsoft Web site.

FIG. 15.4
When the download and installation is complete, the Wizard will inform you which components have been added to your system.

Streaming Media with Microsoft NetShow

One new component that is part of the Internet Explorer 4 suite is the NetShow ActiveX Control. NetShow, whose Web site is on the Microsoft site at **http://www.microsoft.com/ netshow/**, is Microsoft's technology for presenting streaming audio and video over the Web. NetShow uses Microsoft's own Active Streaming Format (ASF) to send audio and video from a Web server to one or more Web clients. The term *streaming* refers to the fact that content is displayed on your system as it arrives, without first having to wait for it all to download. NetShow supports most standard audio and video formats.

For you, the way you will use NetShow depends a lot on how the author set up his or her page that supports it. The NetShow Player that is used on your system to view NetShow content can either appear in a stand-alone window, as shown in Figure 15.5, or inline within a Web page, as shown in Figure 15.6.

FIG. 15.5
The stand-alone NetShow window displays its content while giving you controls to skip back and forth through the presentation.

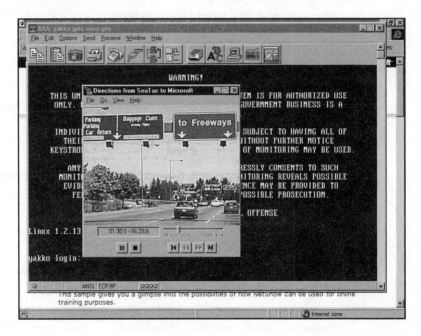

FIG. 15.6

When displayed inline within a Web page, you can control the NetShow Player by right-clicking the NetShow object.

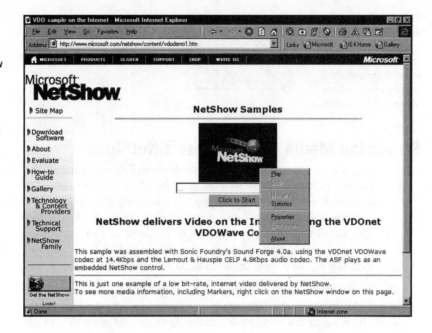

You can control the NetShow ActiveX Control through its controls and menu, in the event of a stand-alone window, or by right-clicking the inline NetShow Player. The standard controls enable you to go back and forth through the presentation. Most of the options of NetShow are accessed through the Microsoft NetShow Player Properties dialog box, which is brought up in a number of ways:

- Selecting File, Properties from the stand-alone NetShow Player window or right-clicking and selecting Properties from the pop-up menu brings up the Properties dialog box on the Details tab.

- Selecting View, Play Settings from the stand-alone window brings up the Properties dialog box on the Settings tab.

- Selecting View, Statistics from the stand-alone NetShow Player window or right-clicking and selecting Statistics from the pop-up menu brings up the Statistics dialog box on the Details tab (see Figure 15.7).

Six tabs are on the NetShow Player Properties dialog box, giving you access to the following information and functions:

- **General**   Gives you information about the title, author, and rating of the current multimedia content

- **Details**   Shows more technical information, including source, size, and other data

- **Statistics**   Gives you an idea of how well the current content is being received over the Internet

- **Codecs**   Shows you what *codecs* (coder-decoders) are installed in your NetShow Player

FIG. 15.7

The tabs on the Properties dialog box enable you to see information on the current content and enable you to configure the player.

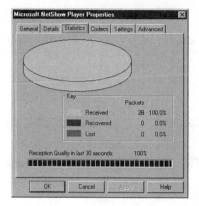

- ■ **Settings**   With the settings on this tab, you can control how often the content will be played, how large the NetShow window will be, and whether the player controls will be shown

- ■ **Advanced**   More advanced settings to determine how much information is buffered and what protocols the player is capable of using

 T I P   If you are experiencing poor quality with your NetShow Player, try increasing your buffering. It will take longer to start up, but the Player will be better able to maintain quality through data outages.

Figure 15.8 shows the same inline NetShow Player window that was shown in Figure 15.6 after its settings have been changed to double its size. Notice that even though the player is embedded in the Web page, it is able to have its size adjusted and the rest of the Web page adjusts around it.

Microsoft Chat Interactive Discussions

The Microsoft Chat application, formerly known as Comic Chat, is Microsoft's system for having interactive conversations over the Internet. Similar to Internet Relay Chat (IRC), the Microsoft Chat component of the Internet Explorer 4 suite enables you to type and receive messages in real time with other people all over the world. Unlike regular IRC, however, Chat also enables you to graphically present yourself. You can pick a comic character to represent yourself and then show appropriate facial expressions and motions as you have your discussions. Microsoft Chat's Web site is at **http://www.microsoft.com/ie/chat/**.

In addition to the Chat application, Microsoft has also created an ActiveX Control with which you can participate in interactive discussions within a Web page. This control gives a subset of the capabilities of the full Chat application right within a Web page.

N O T E   The Microsoft Chat ActiveX Control is different than the Chat application. As with all ActiveX Controls, if the Web page that uses them is correctly written, then the act of visiting the page will automatically download the most recent version of the control to your system, if it isn't

continues

continued

already there. Figure 15.9 shows the Security Warning dialog box that you get after the control is downloaded, which gives you the option of whether to install it. If you install it, you are immediately ready to go. ■

▶ **See** "Code Signing," **p. 304**

FIG. 15.8

You can dynamically resize Inline NetShow Player windows within the Web browser window.

FIG. 15.9

You can automatically download and install ActiveX Controls the first time you visit a Web page that uses them.

The Chat ActiveX Control enables a Web page to connect you to a Chat Server, and then you can have interactive conversations and discussions right within the boundaries of a Web page (see Figure 15.10). Not only can you send messages to all the other people in the chat, you also can "whisper" a message that will go only to one other person (see Figure 15.11).

FIG. 15.10
With the Chat ActiveX Control, you can access the text-based discussion capabilities of the full Chat application.

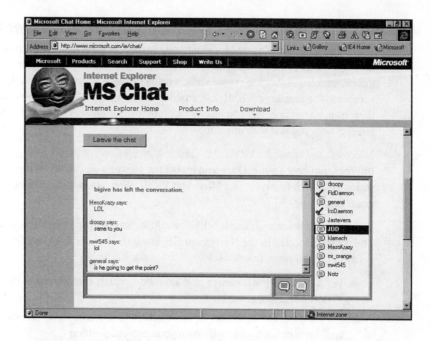

FIG. 15.11
You can either send messages to everyone in the room or just to one other person.

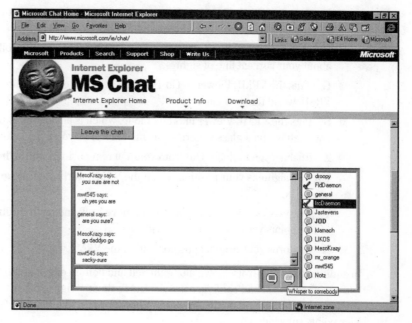

Viewing VRML Worlds with Microsoft VRML 2.0 Viewer

VRML is the Virtual Reality Modeling Language. It is used to create three-dimensional worlds through which you can move, navigate, and interact. VRML 1.0, the first version of the language, enabled authors to create static worlds through which a user could move. The second version of the language, VRML 2.0, enables authors to give objects behaviors and motions of their own, so not only can you interact with them, but objects within the VRML world can also interact with you and with one another.

Microsoft has created a VRML 2.0 Viewer ActiveX Control that is one of the components in the Internet Explorer 4 suite. Once you install the viewer, you can travel through VRML worlds within your Web browser. The Microsoft VRML Web site is located at **http://www.microsoft.com/vrml/**.

Figure 15.12 shows an example VRML world located at **http://idfx.com/idhome/vgz.html**. The controls located in the Navigation Bar along the left and bottom edges of the VRML world perform the following functions:

- **W** Puts the VRML Viewer in Walk mode, which enables you to navigate through the VRML world along one level
- **P** Puts the VRML Viewer in Pan mode, which enables you to slide the whole world up and down or back and forth from your current position
- **T** Puts the VRML Viewer in Turn mode, which enables you to turn the whole world about your current position
- **R** Puts the VRML Viewer in Roll mode, which enables you to roll the whole world about your current line of sight
- **G** Puts the VRML Viewer in Go To mode, which moves you directly to any object in the VRML world that you click
- **S** Puts the VRML Viewer in Study mode, which is analogous to the VRML world being enclosed within a glass sphere—this mode enables you to pick it up and study it
- **Z** Enables you to Zoom Out from your current position within the VRML world
- **Up** Straightens your position within the VRML world so that "up" is in the direction it should be
- **V** The two View arrows enable you to move back and forth through the predefined set of viewpoints within the VRML world.
- **R** Restores your original position within the VRML world

In addition to the controls shown along the left and bottom edges of the VRML Viewer window, you can also control and configure the viewer. To do this, right-click within the VRML Viewer window, which will bring up the pop-up window shown in Figure 15.13 (shown along with the Viewpoints subwindow).

FIG. 15.12
This example shows a virtual bathroom modeled in VRML.

FIG. 15.13
You access most of the VRML 2.0 Viewer configuration options through this pop-up menu.

The selections on the pop-up menu control the following configuration and control options:

- **Viewpoints** VRML 2.0 enables the VRML author to create a number of predefined viewpoints within a VRML world. This selection allows you to automatically move from one of these to another.

- **Graphics** The options in this menu enable you to increase or decrease the amount of detail shown to allow you to maximize the performance of a VRML world on your machine.

- **Speed**   With this menu, you can select the speed, and thus the degree of smoothness, with which you move from one point to another.
- **Movement**   This option provides another way to select from the control modes that are also shown in the Navigation Bar. One other option in this menu is the ability to enable collision detection. With detection on, you cannot move through VRML objects.
- **Show Navigation Bar**   This option enables you to turn the Navigation Bar on and off.
- **Help**   This option provides access to access help for the VRML 2.0 Viewer.
- **Options**   With this option, you gain access to a few miscellaneous options of the viewer.

As mentioned earlier in this chapter, in addition to being capable of modeling three-dimensional objects and enabling you to move among them, VRML 2.0 enables you to create behaviors and movement that you can attach to these objects. The VRML 2.0 Viewer supports these features—Figure 15.14 shows the viewer cursor, which appears with an outline when it is over an object to which a behavior is attached.

FIG. 15.14
The VRML 2.0 Viewer lets you know when you pass the cursor over an object that will do something when you touch it.

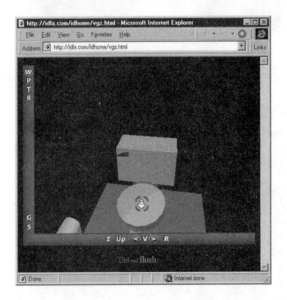

In this example, when you click the toilet seat in question, improbably enough, an ICBM streaks out of the bowl and rockets skyward (see Figure 15.15).

Interacting with the Microsoft Agent

In addition to the ActiveX Controls that are components of Internet Explorer 4 (and those that are installed automatically with the Web browser), Microsoft has other controls that you can use within Web pages. One of the most exciting controls is the Microsoft Agent, located at the Web site **http://www.microsoft.com/workshop/prog/agent/**. The Agent enables Web authors to add an animated figure to his or her Web pages. This figure can react to events on the Web page, such as when you click a button or enter data into a forms field.

FIG. 15.15

VRML 2.0 objects can react to events and move on their own through the VRML world.

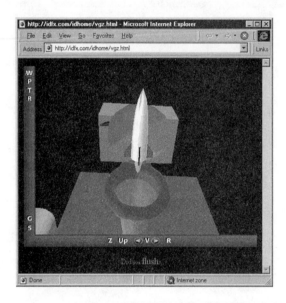

The most exciting feature of the Agent is its text-to-speech and voice recognition capabilities. Its text-to-speech capability enables Web authors to let it speak to you in response to your actions on the page. Adding voice recognition to this capability enables you to create Web pages with which you can interact completely through sound.

Figure 15.16 shows a very simple sample Web page that uses Microsoft Agent. This page does not use the voice recognition capabilities of the Agent; even so, it requires three pieces to be in place, two of which will be downloaded automatically.

- **Microsoft Agent ActiveX Control**   You can download this Control from the Agent Web site, or it will be downloaded automatically the first time you visit this sample page.

- **Centigram TruVoice Text-to-Speech Engine for Microsoft Agent**   This control will also be downloaded automatically, if needed (see Figure 15.17). This control provides the Agent with its capability to speak.

- **Microsoft Agent Character Data**   This character data is needed to provide the animation for the Agent.

When the Microsoft Agent is included in a Web page, the author can create scripts that allow the Agent to react to user inputs. Using its voice recognition capabilities, it can even respond to spoken commands, if properly programmed. In the sample page shown in Figure 15.18, the only user interaction is through the Speak button. Pressing that button causes "Robby" to appear, step forward and wave, and say "Hello, World!" before disappearing.

FIG. 15.16
With this simple sample, you can interact with the Agent through the Speak button.

FIG. 15.17
Microsoft Agent components will be downloaded and installed to be used in Web pages that include the Agent.

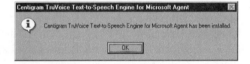

Using Macromedia's Flash 2 ActiveX Control

Obviously, Microsoft isn't the only vendor producing ActiveX Controls for Internet Explorer 4. If it were, the technology wouldn't go very far. The most popular plug-in produced for Netscape Navigator also has an ActiveX Control version: the Flash 2 ActiveX Control by Macromedia, used to view Shockwave for Director, Authorware, and FreeHand documents. Macromedia's Web site is at **http://www.macromedia.com**.

Using Macromedia's products, it is possible to build sophisticated animations, including coordinated graphics and sound. You can embed these animations seamlessly into a Web page and give them a high degree of interaction. Designed for presentation on the Web, these Shockwave animations can include embedded hypertext links.

As with other ActiveX Controls, downloading and installing the Flash 2 ActiveX Control is simplicity itself. By visiting the Macromedia Web site at **http://www.macromedia.com**, the control will automatically download and, if you allow, install on your system. Then the Macromedia Home Page will show, which includes a number of Shockwave animations (see Figure 15.19).

FIG. 15.18
The Microsoft Agent can respond to your inputs, speak to you, and even listen to your requests, when programmed.

FIG. 15.19
You can embed Shockwave animations into a Web page inline with other Web content.

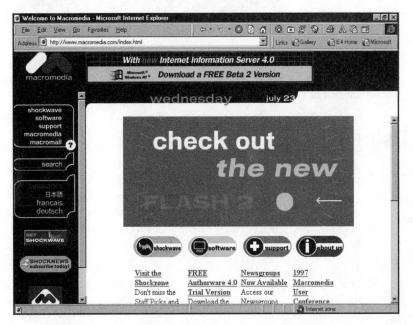

Figure 15.20 shows the California Coast Online Network Web site at **http://www. calcoast.com/new/new.htm**, which includes a number of Shockwave animations. The black menu bar in the Web page is an example of such an animation. As the mouse cursor is passed

over each entry in the menu, the text on the right side of the screen is changed to reflect the menu entry.

FIG. 15.20
Shockwave animations can change dynamically in response to mouse movements and actions.

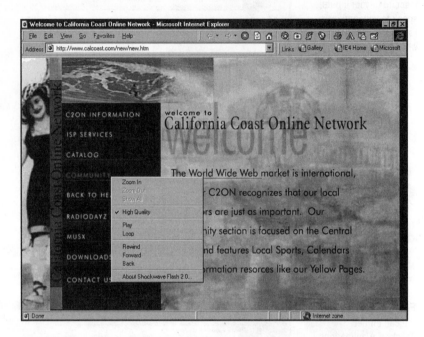

To configure the Flash 2 ActiveX Control, right-click the animation. Figure 15.20 shows the options available from this menu. Figure 15.21 shows the same animation after it has been zoomed in a couple times.

Using Plug-Ins with Internet Explorer 4

As I mentioned earlier in this chapter, there is less and less need for using Netscape Navigator plug-ins with Internet Explorer 4 as more and more ActiveX Controls become available. Nevertheless, Internet Explorer supports many plug-ins. The process of downloading and installing plug-ins is a little more complicated than that of downloading and installing ActiveX Controls. In this section, you'll see an example of how to download and install a plug-in to use with Internet Explorer.

The plug-in you will use as an example is the AnimaFlex plug-in from RubberFlex Software, located at **http://www.rubberflex.com** (see Figure 15.22). With this plug-in, you can view AnimaFlex animations, which you can use to achieve similar effects to animated GIFs at a fraction of the file size.

The download and install process for the AnimaFlex plug-in consists of the following steps.

1. Download the self-executable program for the AnimaFlex plug-in. Look for the download link on the RubberFlex Home Page, and follow the instructions.

FIG. 15.21
Shockwave animations can be zoomed in and out, panned, and the animations can be replayed and looped.

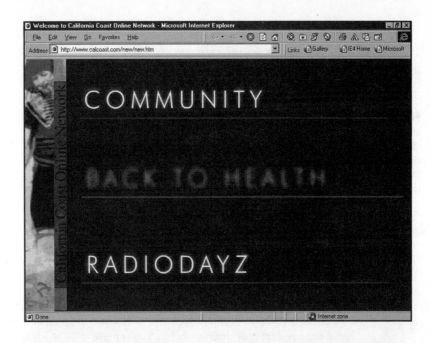

FIG. 15.22
RubberFlex's AnimaFlex enables you to view animations created with their RubberWeb or RubberWeb Composer products.

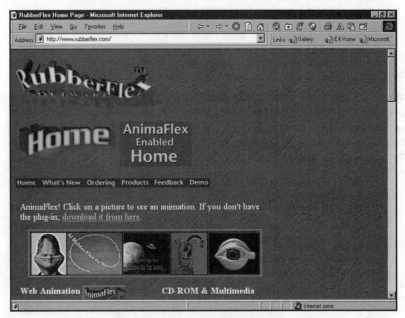

2. Execute the program to begin the installation.

3. The Install Wizard will ask you to select the installation directory.

N O T E Internet Explorer 4 is capable of using Netscape Navigator plug-ins either in the Navigator or the Internet Explorer plug-in directory. If you have Netscape Navigator installed on your system, you should probably install the plug-in in its directory. Otherwise, you can install it in Internet Explorer's plug-ins directory (see Figure 15.23). ■

FIG. 15.23

Internet Explorer can use plug-ins stored in either its own or in Netscape Navigator's plug-ins directory.

4. After the installation is complete, if you wish to use the plug-in with Netscape Navigator, you must restart your machine before you can use it. To use it in Internet Explorer, the plug-in is ready to go without restarting.

Figure 15.24 shows an example of the use of the AnimaFlex plug-in, showing a morphing animation of a picture. The plug-in displays itself inline within the Web browser window and functions perfectly within Internet Explorer.

FIG. 15.24

AnimaFlex animations appear directly within Internet Explorer 4 using the plug-in.

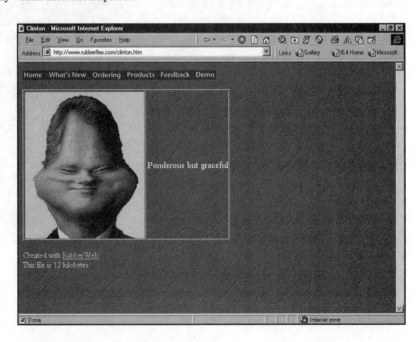

Internet Explorer 4 and Java

Since Internet Explorer 3, Microsoft's Web browser has included full support for applets written in Sun's Java language. An applet is just an application (typically small, though it doesn't need to be) that can only be executed within an appropriate environment. So, for Java applets, they cannot be executed on their own, but they can be executed by Netscape Navigator, Microsoft Internet Explorer, and other Java-compatible browsers and applications.

Not only does Microsoft support the Java language, but the Java Virtual Machine (VM) that runs within Internet Explorer normally executes Java applets faster than any other Web browser or applet viewer currently available. Applets that Internet Explorer executes typically do so measurably faster than in any other browser. Also, Microsoft includes its J/Direct technology, which allows Java applets to directly access Windows functionality, thus increasing the number of things that a Java applet can do.

Microsoft's J/Direct versus Sun's 100% Pure Java

Microsoft's J/Direct, which enables the integration of Java applets with Windows system functions, is accompanied by some controversy. One original benefit to the Java language is that it is platform independent. Normally, a Java applet would function the same way in any computer platform that supported the Java language itself.

A Java applet that accesses Windows functions is no longer platform dependent, however, though the tradeoff is greater performance and increased functionality. Sun Microsystems, creators of Java, have launched its "100% Pure Java" campaign to encourage the continued development of platform-independent Java applications.

What does this mean for you? Not much, at this point. Depending on your platform, much of this discussion will be largely transparent to the end user. In the long term, however, if multiple "flavors" of Java become common, it will decrease Java's usefulness as a platform-independent language.

Unlike ActiveX Controls and plug-ins, a Java applet is downloaded with a Web page each time the page is viewed (though vendors are working on ways to cache applets so they don't need to be downloaded every time). There is no set way to determine how you will interact with the applets—each applet carries its own user interface along with itself. To get an idea of what types of applets are available, a good place to look is the Gamelan Web site at **http://www. gamelan.com** (see Figure 15.25).

So, how to interact with Java applets varies from applet to applet. Figure 15.26 shows an example of a Java theory that explores the relationship between music and set theory. This applet, located at **http://php.indiana.edu/~ltomlin/settheory/**, combines graphics, user input through the buttons and images, and sound, all coordinated through a Java applet, to perform its functions.

FIG. 15.25
Gamelan has long been the central repository of Java applets and information on the Web.

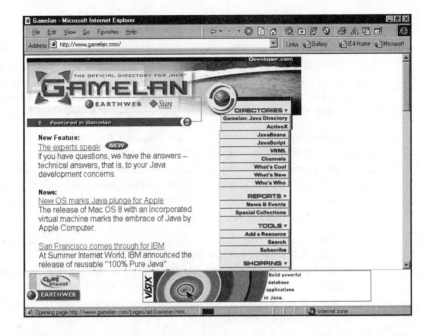

FIG. 15.26
Java applets can include very complicated user interfaces for performing their functions.

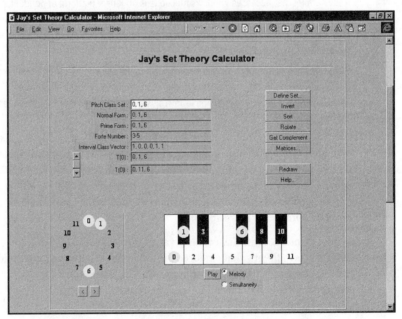

By contrast, **http://stuwww.kub.nl/~s141003/lsd_javapage.html** shows a Web site with a very simple Java applet. This applet allows for the creation of images that are used as hypertext links, where the images can change dynamically as the mouse cursor passes over them. Figure

15.27 shows a composite screen shot of a navigation bar created using these applets. As the mouse cursor is passed over different buttons, the display changes.

FIG. 15.27
Java applets can provide small, very special purpose focused functions within a Web page.

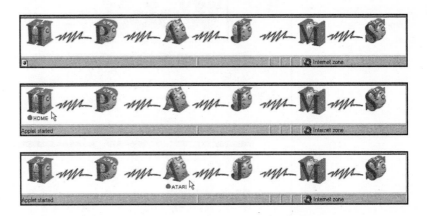

Interacting with JavaScript, JScript, and VBScript

The last example of advanced content and advanced technology supported in Internet Explorer 4 is the script. Internet Explorer supports Visual Basic Scripting Edition (VBScript) and JScript, Microsoft's implementation of Netscape's JavaScript language.

Unlike the topics discussed previously in this chapter—ActiveX Control, plug-ins, and Java applets—scripts do not add new capabilities to the browser. Rather, they add a predetermined set of new functions to the Web browser and serve as the glue that a Web author uses to allow you to interact with other portions of the Web page.

Figure 15.28 shows an example of a Web page that implements the dice game Yahtzee using VBScript. This Web page is located on the Microsoft VBScript Web site at **http://www. microsoft.com/vbscript/us/samples/webzee/webzee.htm**. In this Web page, VBScript is used to implement the random number generator used to specify the dice rolls and to keep track of your score. The VBScripts are attached to the HTML Forms buttons and can also change the properties of those buttons. For instance, Figure 15.28 shows the caption of the button next to Player One's Webzee score being changed to 50 to indicate the new score for that player's last turn.

You can also create other page elements using VBScript, as shown by the alert box in Figure 15.29. This box was displayed on the page to indicate the winner of the game of Webzee.

One of Netscape Navigator's features that was not supported in Internet Explorer until version 4 was the Image array. Using this array, you can dynamically change images. Combined with scripting languages, these images can be changed in response to other events, either user input or as a function of time.

FIG. 15.28
You can use Vbscripts to respond to your actions and change elements on the Web page.

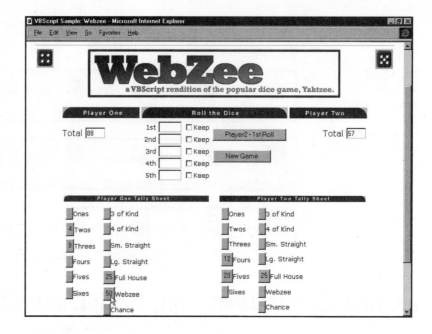

FIG. 15.29
VBScript can display alert boxes to provide choices and informa-tion.

Figure 15.30 shows a Web site located at **http://www-leland.stanford.edu/~dmiller/geir2sml.html**. This Web site enables you to request an animation to be built based on current weather radar data. Once the images are loaded and displayed, JavaScript animates the display by stepping through the images. You can click the Slower or Faster buttons to speed up or slow down the animation.

Advanced Content Resources on the Web

The nicest thing about the advanced content technologies that are becoming available for the Web is that the vast majority of them are completely free to you, the user. The model that cre-ators of the different multimedia techniques are using, as demonstrated by the examples of the Macromedia Flash 2 ActiveX Control and the RubberFlex AnimaFlex Plug-In, is to supply free viewers for their content. By making these viewers freely available, they hope to use the tech-nology as widespread as possible. Their commercial products are then the applications to *produce* the advanced content that their viewers are used to display. In the previous examples, these applications would be Macromedia's Director, Authorware, or FreeHand and RubberFlex's RubberWeb and RubberWeb Composer.

FIG. 15.30
Internet Explorer 4 can successfully execute most JavaScript-enabled Web pages using its JScript language.

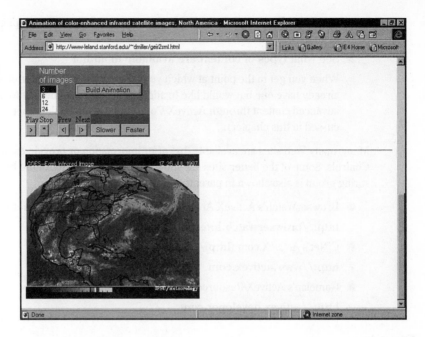

Because of this stress on free viewing applications, ActiveX Controls, and plug-ins, it is easy for you to configure your Web browser for displaying a wide variety of advanced and multimedia content. Following are a sampling of Web sites that you can use to begin looking for either ActiveX Controls and plug-ins that you can install into your system or Web sites with example Java applets and scripts.

ActiveX Controls

Because of the nature of ActiveX Controls, it is not usually necessary to preconfigure Internet Explorer 4 with a given ActiveX Control for viewing a specific type of content or for performing a given function. The reason for this is that, unlike plug-ins, Web pages that use ActiveX Controls can be written in such a way that causes the appropriate control to be automatically downloaded when a compatible browser views the page.

There are some good reasons for taking a look at the resources for ActiveX Controls on the Web. These reasons include the following:

■ **Preconfigure your Web browser**

Even though you can automatically download ActiveX Controls, this process can take some time, particularly for larger controls. By using a sample page of other Web resource to preconfigure your Web browser with the control, there will be no delay when you actually need to use it.

■ **See what content is available to view**

Part of the fun of Web browsing is to see what you can do. With all the new technologies available, the possibilities are endless. This is particularly true for ActiveX Controls (as well as plug-ins and Java applets), which you can use to add completely new capabilities to your Web browser.

■ **See what types of content are available to author**

When you get to the point at which you are ready to create your own Web page or if you already have one but would like to add a little zest to it, one way to do this is to add advanced content through ActiveX Controls (or some of the other technologies discussed in this chapter).

Many, many Web sites are available that offer information or provide examples of ActiveX Controls. Some of the better sites are shown following (the URL of the home page of the sponsoring group is also shown in parentheses):

■ BrowserWatch's ActiveX Arena (**http://browserwatch.internet.com**)
  http://browserwatch.internet.com/activex.html

■ C|Net's ActiveX.com (**http://www.cnet.com**)
  http://www.activex.com

■ Gamelan's ActiveX Resources (**http://www.gamelan.com**)
  http://activex.developer.com

Plug-Ins

As more and more ActiveX Controls become available, you will want to add fewer plug-ins to your system because more and more plug-ins are also becoming available in ActiveX Control versions. As with the Macromedia Flash 2 example shown previously, why download and install a plug-in when you can automatically download the ActiveX Control just by visiting a Web page?

■ BrowserWatch's Plug-in Place (**http://browserwatch.internet.com**)
  http://browserwatch.internet.com/plug-in.html

■ C|Net's Browsers.com (**http://www.cnet.com**)
  http://www.browsers.com

Java

The number one repository for Java samples and applets has always been EarthWeb's Gamelan Web site. Recently, Gamelan has branched out and become a resource for other technologies such as ActiveX and JavaScript, but their Java resources are still the most complete. Here is their site information:

Gamelan's Java Resources (**http://www.gamelan.com**)
http://java.developer.com

Scripts

One script characteristic that is not true with ActiveX Controls, plug-ins, or Java is its accessibility. In other words, if you come across a script in a Web page that you find useful, it is easy to look at the script itself through Internet Explorer's View, Source menu selection. If you are also a Web page author, this is a good way to adapt good ideas you come across on the Web to your own purposes.

- Microsoft VBScript Web Site (**http://www.microsoft.com**)

  http://www.microsoft.com/vbscript/

- Microsoft JScript Web Site (**http://www.microsoft.com**)

  http://www.microsoft.com/jscript/

- Gamelan's JavaScript Resources (**http://www.gamelan.com**)

  http://javascript.developer.com

In Depth: Security

Security continues to be a key concern for most Internet users. Users want to be able to use high-powered applications developed in Java, ActiveX, and other languages, but they are concerned that such executable code might compromise their systems by erasing essential files, transmitting harmful viruses, or rebooting their machines at inopportune times.

These same users also want their information to stay secure not only as it sits on their computers, but also as it is transmitted across the Internet. This is particularly true of personal and financial data like Social Security numbers, credit card information, and bank account numbers.

This highly constrained situation has made it difficult for Web commerce to really take off because so many people are leery about using the shopping interfaces on the Web and are even more concerned about providing information that, if intercepted, could cause them great financial loss.

The basic question each user must ask himself or herself is: *Whom do you trust?* Once you decide that you trust a site and its security configuration, you should be able to go to the site, download software from it, or provide personal information to it without those pesky browser messages reminding you that "You're about to send information over the Internet…" and so on. Conversely, for the sites you don't trust, you *do* want those pesky messages

Get into the zone

Microsoft has introduced the concept of security zones—lists of different sites in which you have varying levels of trust—in Internet Explorer 4.

Working with digital certificates

Internet Explorer simplifies certificate management and gives you control over whose software can run on your browser.

Verifying who authored a piece of code

Microsoft's Authenticode checks a piece of downloadable code to see who wrote it and to determine whether it has been tampered with.

Controlling your applets

Internet Explorer enables you to specify where applets can run on your machine. You can restrict applets from an unknown source to a certain safe area of your computer while allowing greater access to trusted applets.

Transaction security

Find out how you can go shopping on the Web without the risk of an ill-intentioned hacker finding out your credit card number or other personal data.

telling you that the Web server is trying to place a cookie on your machine or that the ActiveX control you're about to download has been altered from its original state. But how can you have it both ways?

The answer is Internet Explorer security zones. Zones let you group trusted sites together and reduce the number of security precautions the browser uses when interacting with those sites. Similarly, you can set up a zone for sites you don't trust and have Internet Explorer use all its security measures when you visit one of those sites.

And version 4.0 of Internet Explorer has plenty of security measures. In addition to security zones, Internet Explorer supports many key security functions, such as the following:

- Signed digital certificates, electronic documents that testify to the authenticity of a source on the Internet
- Checking of downloaded code to its source and whether it has been changed in any way
- Security protocols that use encryption to keep transmissions private
- Management of personal and financial data
- Working with proxy servers to handle communications between your protected network and the rest of the Internet

Clearly, Microsoft has been listening to the concerns the Internet community has about security and has built some high-powered security features into its latest browser product. This chapter introduces you to those features and helps you to understand how to configure them to provide an Internet experience that maximizes your use of online applications while minimizing risk and privacy concerns.

N O T E   Microsoft has demonstrated an ongoing sensitivity to users' concerns about Internet security and is continuously publishing white papers on the Security portion of its Web site. You can check out Microsoft's latest efforts to ensure that its products are secure at **http://www.microsoft.com/security/**.

Configuring Internet Explorer Security Zones

Internet Explorer comes preconfigured with four different Internet security zones:

- **Local intranet zone**   For sites on a corporate intranet
- **Trusted sites zone**   For sites you trust that are outside your intranet
- **Internet zone**   For general Web browsing
- **Restricted sites zone**   For sites of which you are wary

To view the list of zones, choose View, Options and click the Security tab in the dialog box that comes up (see Figure 16.1). The different zones are in the drop-down list labeled Zone.

FIG. 16.1

Internet Explorer recognizes four different security zones for trusted and nontrusted sites.

Each zone has a particular security level setting associated with it. You have your choice of four settings, including:

- **High**   In which any potentially damaging content will not be downloaded to your machine
- **Medium**   In which Internet Explorer will prompt you before running any potentially harmful content
- **Low**   To skip any warnings about potentially harmful content
- **Custom**   For very fine control over security settings for a zone

When you install Internet Explorer, each zone is assigned a default security level. The Internet zone and the Local intranet zone have security settings of Medium, the Trusted sites zone has a security setting of Low, and the Restricted sites zone has a setting of High. All these make sense, though you may want to think about changing the security setting for your Local intranet zone to Low if you feel confident that your intranet administrator is doing a good job of making only trusted content available.

When you first run Internet Explorer, all the zones are empty, meaning that no Web sites have been assigned to them. It's up to you to place the various sites you visit into different zones as it becomes appropriate. To add a site to a zone, select the zone from the drop-down list on the Security tab (refer to Figure 16.1) and then click the Add Sites button. Depending on which zone to which you're adding, you'll see one of two dialog boxes. If you're adding to the Local intranet zone, you'll see the box shown in Figure 16.2. In this case, you're not adding a site URL but rather specifying what kinds of sites you want to be considered as part of your intranet zone. You can choose from:

- Any local site that has not been placed explicitly in one of the other zones
- Any site that is not accessed via your proxy server

FIG. 16.2

Your Local intranet zone is made up of all sites on your local network, unless you've placed one of the sites in another zone.

If you're adding to the Trusted sites zone or the Restricted sites zone, you'll see the dialog box shown in Figure 16.3. From here, you can remove any sites that are already in the zone or provide a URL to add to the zone. You can also require that https: verify the server when you initiate contact with one of the sites in the zone. This assures you that the server you've reached is the server you intended to reach.

FIG. 16.3

You can add or remove sites from your Trusted and Restricted sites zones as you need to.

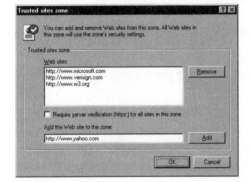

N O T E   You cannot add sites to or remove sites from the Internet zone. The Internet zone is a "catch-all" for sites that are not explicitly placed in one of the other zones. ▪

Selecting security settings for your different zones is fairly straightforward unless you decide to use the Custom option, in which case it is up to you to configure a number of different security parameters. If you choose the Custom security option for a particular zone, the Settings button will light up. Clicking this button takes you to the dialog box you see in Figure 16.4. In this dialog box, you can enable, disable, or require user prompting for a whole host of potentially harmful actions, including:

- Running ActiveX Controls and plug-ins
- Downloading signed ActiveX Controls
- Downloading unsigned ActiveX Controls
- Initializing and scripting ActiveX Controls not marked as safe
- Using active scripting
- Scripting Java applets

- Downloading files
- Downloading fonts
- Sending form data unencrypted
- Launching helper applications and files
- Installing desktop items
- Dragging and dropping or copying and pasting files

In addition, you can set Java security permissions to high, medium, or low, or you can disable Java altogether.

FIG. 16.4

Expert users can exercise very fine control over their security settings by using the Custom security option.

N O T E The High, Medium, and Low security settings are actually just different configurations of the preceding parameters. To see what each setting equates to in terms of the parameters, choose the setting in the Reset to drop-down list, and the parameter configurations will set themselves to the values used for that setting. ■

One really nice thing about using the Custom option is that you can use the settings to eliminate those annoying pop-up boxes that warn you about a potentially insecure action when you're dealing with a trusted site. Similarly, you can turn on all warnings for sites in the Restricted zone and be aware of security risks every step of the way.

N O T E Security zones should not be confused with content ratings. Internet Explorer is able to read voluntarily placed content ratings from a Web site and filter inappropriate content so that younger users are not exposed to it. Security zones protect your computer from potentially damaging active content and have nothing to do with the nature of the content. Voluntary content rating is covered later in this chapter. ■

T I P You can use the Internet and Restricted sites zones in Outlook Express to control whether scripts embedded in HTML messages can be run. To set up your zone permissions in Outlook Express, choose Tools, Options, and then select the Security tab.

Handling Digital Certificates

Signed digital certificates are an assurance that the person or site on the other end of your connection is who or what he or she says it is. Certificates are typically issued by a certificate authority that has taken an explicit set of steps to verify the authenticity of the certificate holder.

Internet Explorer makes it easy to manage the three main types of certificates used on the Internet:

- Personal certificates
- Site certificates
- Publisher's certificates

You can look at each type of certificate by choosing View, Options and selecting the Content tab. In the middle of the tab, you'll find the Certificates section with three buttons from which to choose (see Figure 16.5):

- Personal, for certificates you can use to prove your own identity
- Sites, for certificates you'll accept from Web sites to prove their authenticity
- Publishers, for those software publishers whose code you've decided that you trust

FIG. 16.5

Digital certificate management takes place from the Content tab of the Options dialog box.

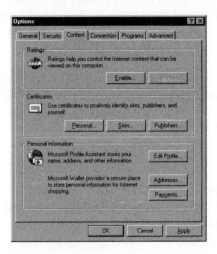

The specifics of each of these certificate types are discussed in the sections that follow.

Personal Certificates

A personal certificate is an electronic document that assures another party that you are who you say you are in the course of a transaction over the Internet. A Web site you're visiting might ask Internet Explorer for a personal certificate or you can use a personal certificate when sending mail with Outlook Express. To look at your set of personal certificates, click the Personal button to reveal a dialog box that looks like the one you see in Figure 16.6. Here you'll find a listing of all of your personal certificates and you have the option of viewing each one.

FIG. 16.6

Internet Explorer keeps a catalog of your personal digital certificates.

If you don't have a digital certificate, don't despair. Microsoft has an arrangement with VeriSign, a leading issuer of digital certificates, to provide a free trial certificate for users of Outlook Express. To request your digital ID, follow these steps:

1. Start up Outlook Express.
2. Choose Tools, Options, and then select the Security tab.
3. Click the button labeled Get Digital ID you see near the bottom of the tab.
4. Microsoft Internet Explorer will open and walk you through a series of pages that gather information for your certificate. Enter the requested information as needed.
5. Once your request is processed by VeriSign's server, an HTML mail message will appear in your Inbox. Read this message and click the Next button to complete the issuing of your digital ID.

N O T E You can also opt to pay $9.95 for a one-year, fully supported digital ID rather than getting the free, six-month trial ID. ■

 T I P If you read the message sent to you by VeriSign in a mail reader that can't handle HTML-based messages, save the HTML attachment to your hard drive and open that file with Internet Explorer to complete the process.

Sites

A firm that hosts a Web site can apply for a digital certificate just as you can. In this case, though, the certificate testifies the authenticity of the firm's Web server. That is, it assures you that the Web server with which you're communicating belongs to whom it says it does. This is important because these days it is possible for a resourceful hacker to spoof an entire site!

When you click the Sites button on the Content tab, you're presented with a dialog box, as shown in Figure 16.7. The box lists the names of several well-known site certificate issuers. By checking the box next to an issuer's name, you say that you trust any certificate provided by that issuer. You can also view the details of any certificate or certificate issuer contained in the dialog box.

FIG. 16.7

You can pick and choose which providers from which you want to accept certificates.

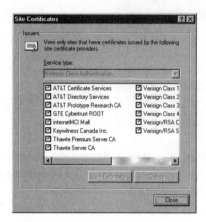

Code Signing

When interacting with a site requires you to download a piece of code and run it locally, it's reassuring to be able to verify that the purported author of the code is who actually wrote it and that no one has tampered with the code since it was made available. This is the purpose of code signing. A certificate from a code publisher is an assurance that the code is genuine and intact.

Clicking the Publishers button on the Content tab takes you to a listing of those software certificate providers you have decided to trust (see Figure 16.8). Code that bears a certificate from one of these providers will not require your confirmation that it is okay to download the code.

N O T E Sometimes code will bear a certificate from a provider that is not on your trusted provider list. In this case, Internet Explorer will provide you with the information on the certificate and ask you to make a download decision based on the certificate's contents. ∎

FIG. 16.8

If you're downloading code with a certificate from a trusted provider, you won't be asked to confirm the download.

> **CAUTION**
>
> Handle code that does not have a certificate with the greatest of care, if you download it at all. Download it to a separate folder (or drive partition, if you have one) and make sure your system is completely backed up before running it.

Certificate Authorities

More and more companies are offering services as digital certificate authorities. Some of the larger ones include:

- VeriSign
- AT&T
- MCI
- GTE
- Thawte Consulting (South Africa)
- Keywitness Canada, Inc.

Of these, VeriSign is original and is recognized by Microsoft as an official certificate provider. VeriSign certificates come in one of four different classes:

- **Class 1** Provides a low level of assurance; to be used for secure e-mail and casual browsing. Noncommercial and evaluation versions are available free of charge. A fully supported certificate requires an annual fee.
- **Class 2** Provides a higher degree of trust and security, used for access to advanced Web sites.
- **Class 3** Provides an even higher level of assurance for valued purchases and intercompany communications.
- **Class 4** Provides the maximum level of identity assurance for high-end financial transactions and trades.

The fully supported Class 1 certificate and certificates for all other classes have some kind of fee associated with them. For the most up-to-date fee structure, consult VeriSign's Web site at **http://www.verisign.com/**.

Using the Profile Assistant

Much of the discussion thus far has focused on how to keep ill-intentioned executables off your machine, but that is not the only facet of Internet security that worries users. Another big concern is how to keep personal data private, whether it's being transmitted over the Internet or it's just sitting on your system. Internet Explorer is capable of helping you keep your personal information private with two different components:

■ The Profile Assistant, for managing personal data like name, address, and birth date

■ Microsoft Wallet, for storing credit and ATM card information

You can access the Profile Assistant from the same tab you use to access the digital certificates. At the bottom of the Content tab of the Internet Explorer Options dialog box, you'll find a Personal Information section. The first item in that section is for the Profile Assistant. If you haven't set up your profile yet or if you need to change your existing profile, click the Edit Profile button to go the Assistant's first dialog box (see Figure 16.9).

FIG. 16.9

The Profile Assistant is a secure storehouse for personal information.

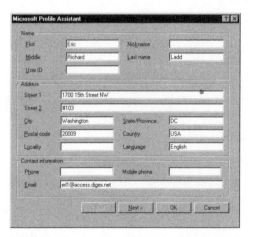

This first dialog box collects basic information, such as name, address, and contact information (both phone and e-mail). You're free to omit any pieces of information you'd rather not give. Once you've provided information in the fields you wanted to fill out, click the Next button to move to the second dialog box (see Figure 16.10).

FIG. 16.10

You can also store information about your education, occupation, and family size.

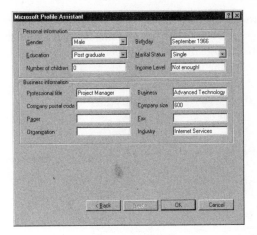

The fields in the second dialog box are optional as well, though you may want to take care of the items that appear as drop-down lists. Otherwise, you'll be cataloged as a single female with a high school education. When you've finished with the second dialog box, click the OK button. The Profile Assistant will present a list of the items you've either filled out or modified. Should you not wish to build a piece of the new information into your profile, just uncheck the box next to that piece.

Once the Profile Assistant is set up with your personal data, it acts as the gateway for the disclosure of any of the data. When a Web site requests personal information from you, the Profile Assistant will let you know and let you decide which pieces of information to give out. You can even encrypt the data as the Assistant transmits it or even as it sits on your hard drive.

N O T E The Assistant supports the World Wide Web Consortium's (W3C's) proposed Platform for Internet Content Selection (PICS), which specifies privacy standards for information transmitted over the Internet, so you can feel secure about it managing your personal data.

Using Microsoft Wallet

Anything that you would put into your own wallet you can put into Microsoft Wallet as well. Though it is primarily designed as a tool to assist with Internet purchase transactions, it is also a place to store personal information you want to keep private.

You'll find the Wallet right below the Personal Assistant on the Content tab of the Internet Explorer Options dialog box. You can work with one of the two sides of the Wallet—Addresses and Payments—by clicking the appropriate button on the tab.

The Addresses side of the Wallet is like your "little black book." It stores address information for family members, business colleagues, and creditors. When you click the Addresses button, you'll see a list of addresses available through the Wallet. You can edit or remove an existing address or you can choose to add a new one. Clicking the Add button takes you to the dialog box shown in Figure 16.11. Note that you can import an address from the Windows Address Book or type it directly into the fields provided.

FIG. 16.11

You can stash address information for friends and co-workers easily in your Microsoft Wallet.

 TIP Make sure you check the box that enables warnings when address information is requested over the Internet. This way, Internet Explorer will notify you when someone tries to get address information from your Wallet.

On the Payments side, you can click the Payments button to reveal which of your credit cards you have configured for use with the Wallet. You can edit or remove any of the cards that are available or you can add a completely new card by clicking and holding down the Add button. When you do, you'll see a drop-down list of different types of credit cards. After selecting the type of card you want to enter, a set-up wizard will walk you through the steps required to configure the card (see Figure 16.12). You will need to provide:

- Name on the card, account number, and expiration date
- Billing address
- Password to authorize use of the card

N O T E Microsoft Wallet only allows Visa, MasterCard, American Express, and Discover cards. There is no support for specialty or store credit cards. ▦

Another option you have on the Payments side of the Wallet is to disable a certain type of credit card altogether. For example, if you know you're close to your limit on your Visa card, you can disable the Wallet's use of any Visa card by clicking the Methods button in the Payment Options dialog box and unchecking the box next to the Visa option (see Figure 16.13).

FIG. 16.12
Microsoft Wallet gathers credit card information from you and then keeps it protected by a password.

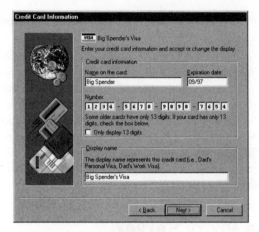

FIG. 16.13
If there's a certain type of card you don't want in your Microsoft Wallet, you can simply turn that card type off.

Microsoft is touting the Wallet's extensibility, so you should expect to see its capabilities grow as electronic payment methods become more diverse. One option that's close to implementation is the idea of *digital money*. In its most basic form, digital money involves the transmission of an encoded electronic packet of information that is as secure and as difficult to counterfeit as a dollar bill. Some of the companies to watch on the digital money front include the following:

- **CyberCash** CyberCash has proposed both credit and debit systems, but it is the debit system that is equivalent to the digital money idea. In the CyberCash scheme, participating banks let customers open accounts that amount to "electronic purses." Using the company's software, a customer moves money from his or her checking account to the purse. As with an automatic teller machine, the customer then withdraws digital tokens from the purse and uses them to buy things over the Internet. On receipt of a token, the seller queries CyberCash to verify the authenticity of the token and tells CyberCash where to deposit the money.

  To use the CyberCash system, you have to install the client version of the CyberCash software to work with Internet Explorer. It also requires that the Web server handling the transaction use the CyberCash system to decrypt the order information.

- **DigiCash** DigiCash operates a debit system that is similar to an electronic checking account. To set up a DigiCash account, you deposit money in a bank that supports the

DigiCash system and you are issued Ecash that you can use to make purchases on the Internet.

One interesting component of DigiCash's philosophy is that records of electronic transactions should not be kept. DigiCash sees these records as a threat to the privacy of the person doing the shopping. To this end, it has developed a way to spend completely untraceable, anonymous digital cash. DigiCash's electronic tokens can be trusted regardless of who is spending them and its double-blind encryption algorithm makes it impossible to trace the transaction unless there is mathematical proof that fraud has occurred. Though those who favor privacy are cheering DigiCash's approach, banks and governments are fearful that total anonymity would provide a haven for money laundering and other illicit activities.

Connecting via a Proxy Server

A *proxy server* is a program that handles communications between a protected network and the rest of the Internet. Many corporations use them because they provide a useful insulating layer between your system and potentially harmful applications on the Internet. You can instruct Internet Explorer to use a proxy server while browsing by choosing View, Options and selecting the Connection tab. The proxy server section is just below the middle of the tab (see Figure 16.14).

FIG. 16.14
Internet Explorer can work through a proxy server to keep your network protected from direct contact with other computers on the Internet.

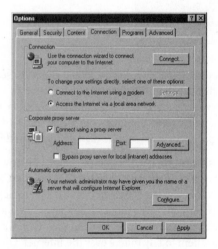

To specify a proxy server, enter its address and port number in the fields provided. You can opt not to use the proxy when connecting to sites within your corporation's network, which makes sense because servers for those sites are presumably on the same network you are.

You can take things a step further by specifying a proxy server for each Internet service that Internet Explorer can handle. By clicking the Advanced button, you open the Proxy Settings dialog box (see Figure 16.15), where you can supply a server address and port number for all your Internet services (HTTP, FTP, Gopher, and so on). You can also enter a list of sites that do not require connection through a proxy. These sites should be those that you trust completely and preferably are sites within your corporation.

FIG. 16.15
You can set up separate proxies for each Internet service that Internet Explorer supports.

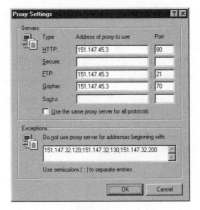

Part II
Ch
16

Enabling Security Protocols

Now that you have security of downloaded executables and your own personal data well in hand, you can look at the other security features Internet Explorer provides. These features are found on the Advanced tab of the Options (choose View, Options) dialog box.

If you scroll down the list of parameters on the Advanced tab, you'll come to a set labeled Security (see Figure 16.16). The first three items in the list refer to different encryption protocols that Internet Explorer supports, which follow:

- **Secure Sockets Layer (SSL) 2.0 and 3.0**   Netscape Communications Corporation developed the Secure Sockets Layer (SSL) protocol in response to the need for secure transmission of data over the Web. SSL is an application-independent protocol that provides *encryption* (a secure channel into which others cannot tap), *authentication* (use of digital certificates to verify the identities of the parties at either end of the connection), *and message integrity* (assures that a message in not altered while in transit).

  SSL is layered beneath application protocols, such as HTTP or FTP, but above the connection protocol TCP/IP. This strategy enables SSL to operate independently of any of the Internet service protocols. With SSL implemented on both the client and the server, your Internet communications are transmitted in encrypted form, ensuring privacy.

  Internet Explorer supports both SSL 2.0 and 3.0, and you can activate either or both from the Advanced tab. SSL 2.0 creates a secure, encrypted channel and authenticates servers so that you know you're getting information from a genuine source. SSL 3.0 adds the ability to authenticate a server or a client and lets either one request authentication of the other. When authentication of your client is requested, Internet Explorer will present your personal digital certificate to the server. If you have more than one certificate, Internet Explorer enables you to decide which one to present.

■ **Private Communication Technology (PCT) 1.0** Internet Explorer also supports the Private Communication Technology (PCT) 1.0 security standard developed by Microsoft. Like SSL, PCT is layered between application protocols like HTTP and the TCP/IP connection protocol. PCT encrypts messages, authenticates servers to ensure that you are in contact with your intended party, and allows servers to request client authentication just as SSL 3.0 does. Microsoft claims that PCT 1.0 is superior to SSL 3.0, however, particularly in the handshaking step during which the client and server negotiate the secure connection. Internet Explorer supports all aspects of PCT, including the presentation of certificates during client authentication.

You can activate any or all of these secure protocols by checking the box that appears next to each one.

FIG. 16.16

The Advanced tab in the Options dialog box plays host to a number of additional Internet Explorer security features.

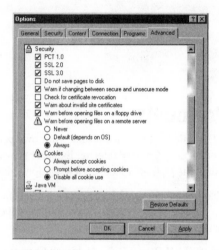

Cookies

Cookies are bits of text-based information that a server places on your hard drive. They are typically referenced by the server when you return to the site so that it can know where you've been, what your site log in name is, or how it should present a customized page to you.

Even though cookies are just text, they are a security concern because a Web server instructs your browser to write something to your hard drive. Though most sites that use cookies do so in a responsible way, it is still conceivable that there are servers in the world that are configured to dispense bad cookies that could damage your system. Internet Explorer gives you control over the placement of cookies through options on the Advanced tab. You can always accept any cookie, receive a warning message before a cookie is placed and decide to accept or reject the cookie, or you can disable the use of cookies altogether (refer to Figure 16.16).

 TIP Cookies are placed in text files under the C:\WINDOWS\COOKIES folder on your PC. You can look at any cookie files using Notepad and delete any cookie file you don't want there.

Other Security Settings

The Security section on the Advanced tab provides for a number of other parameters you can set to really lock down your machine. These parameters include the following:

- Suppressing the saving of files to a local drive
- Showing a warning when you're switching between secure and unsecure connections
- Checking for certificate revocation by the certificate authority
- Showing a warning when an invalid site certificate is encountered
- Showing a warning before opening files from a floppy drive
- Showing a warning before opening a file on a remote server

Any of these events could signal a potential security problem. By not downloading any files, you eliminate the risk of a virus or destructive pieces of code. If you encounter a site with a revoked or an invalid certificate, you should think twice about visiting it. And opening files from a source over which you don't have control, such as a floppy or an untrusted remote machine, means that you're exposing your system to potentially harmful content.

You should consider each element in the Advanced tab's Security list and activate any of the items that you think is applicable to your system's configuration. For example, if you're using Internet Explorer at work and are downloading files from an intranet server, you can probably turn off the warning before opening a file on a remote server because you should be able to trust the servers in place where you work. Conversely, if you're browsing on the open Internet, you would most likely want to leave the warning turned on.

Java Virtual Machine (VM)

A little further down the Advanced tab, you'll find two options under the heading of Java VM (Virtual Machine). The first enables Internet Explorer's Just In Time (JIT) Java compiler. This compiler lets Internet Explorer create all Java applets by using its own internal compiler.

The other option is to enable Java logging, which is important to the security of your machine because the logs may provide you with clues about a rogue applet. Unfortunately, logs usually only help after something bad has happened, but at least with logging turned on, you'll have some kind of audit trail you can use to troubleshoot the problem.

Web Page Security Properties

If you're ever in doubt about whether a page you're viewing is secure, you can use clues that Internet Explorer provides to make the determination. The most obvious way to tell is to look at the Explorer status bar. If you see a lock near the right-hand side of the status bar (see Figure 16.17), that means the page you're viewing is secure.

FIG. 16.17

A lock icon on your status bar means that you're looking at a secure document.

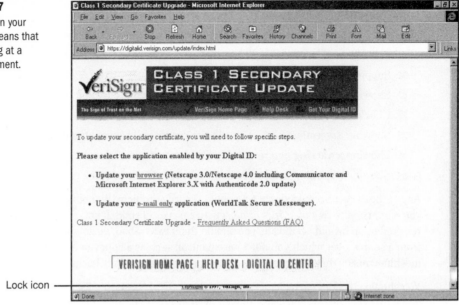

Lock icon ——

You can find out more information about a page's security setup by choosing File, Properties and looking at the Security tab. If you're viewing the document over a secure connection, you'll see certificate information presented in the scrollbox on the tab (see Figure 16.18).

FIG. 16.18

A secure document's certificate information is readily available from the document's Properties listing.

Sending Secure E-Mail

Security concerns aren't limited to Web browsing. When you send an electronic mail message, it is passed through several computers before it reaches its destination. Each computer that participates in routing the mail is a potentially security threat because a user of that machine may be able to intercept and read your messages. In response to concerns over e-mail security, the Secure Multipurpose Internet Mail Extensions (S/MIME) were introduced in 1996 to support the secure transmission of mail messages.

The Internet Explorer suite's mail client, Outlook Express, is fully S/MIME-compliant and can also use your personal digital certificate to authenticate you as the sender of a message. To access Outlook Express's security options, choose Tools, Options and then select the Security tab. The resulting dialog box is shown in Figure 16.19.

FIG. 16.19

Outlook Express also supports encryption and authentication to keep your mail messages secure.

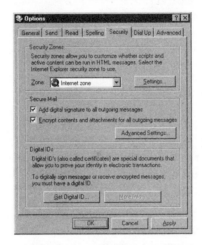

You can do a number of things from this tab, the first of which is to suppress the running of active content contained in HTML messages. To do this, use the same security zones as those you set up for Internet Explorer. If there's a mail source that you trust, you can add that server to your Trusted sites zone and not worry about any destructive content. Similarly, if you get word of a mail source that's sending out something harmful, you can add that source to your Restricted sites zone and disable all active content.

N O T E   Mail sources not in the Trusted sites zone or the Restricted sites zone are taken to be in the Internet zone, so make sure your Internet zone security setting is set to at least Medium, if not High. ▨

The Secure Mail area in the center of the Security tab is where you can activate:

- ▨ Inclusion of your personal digital certificate with each message
- ▨ Encryption of all message contents and attachments

Your digital certificate is an assurance that the mail message is really from you and not someone posing as you. If you encrypt your outbound mail messages, you are scrambling them so that if someone intercepts the message along the way, it will be nearly impossible for him or her to read it.

Part II

Ch 16

You can digitally sign and encrypt messages on a case-by-case basis, too. While you're composing a message in Outlook Express, you can choose Tools, Encrypt to activate encryption and Tools, Digitally Sign to add your digital signature.

The bottom section of the tab reminds you that you need a personal digital certificate to digitally sign messages or to receive encrypted mail. Fortunately, if you don't have a certificate, you can click the Get Digital ID button to learn how you get a free trial certificate from VeriSign. The trial certificate is good for six months, after which you'll have to pay an annual fee to VeriSign for a fully supported certificate.

N O T E   In addition to signing and encrypting your outbound messages, Outlook Express can verify the sender of and decrypt your signed and encrypted inbound messages. ■

Content Rating

A different security concern many parents share is how to protect their children from viewing offensive content on the Internet. To assist parents in this regard, Internet Explorer comes equipped with the ability to detect voluntary *content ratings*—information embedded in a HTML document that describe the nature of any potentially offensive content in the document—and take appropriate actions, based on how parents set up content filtering.

To use Internet Explorer's content rating detection feature, you first need to turn it on. You do this by choosing View, Options, and then selecting the Content tab (refer to Figure 16.5). At the top of the tab, you'll see the Ratings section. Initially, the detection is shut off, so you should click the Enable button to activate it. When you do, you are prompted to enter a content supervisor's password for use when enabling, disabling, or reconfiguring the rating detection feature. After you enter the password, you're shown the Content Advisor dialog box you see in Figure 16.20.

The initial tab you see in the Content Advisor is the Ratings tab. Internet Explorer comes with the Recreational Software Advisory Council's (RSAC) rating scheme built in. This scheme classifies various levels of potentially offensive language, nudity, sexual content, and violence along a numerical scale with values ranging between 0 and 4. Parents can select one of the ratings categories and then move the slider bar seen in Figure 16.20 to the filter level of their choosing.

The General tab of the Content Advisor (see Figure 16.21) is where parents can specify what Internet Explorer should do when it detects a page with offensive content. They have the option of letting all users see any page that is not rated and of being able to type in the supervisor's password before Internet Explorer displays a potentially offending page. There is also a button on this tab that enables parents to change the content supervisor's password.

FIG. 16.20
Internet Explorer can scan documents for information about potentially offensive content and prevent children from seeing such documents.

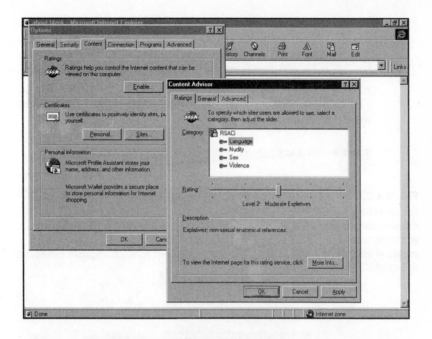

FIG. 16.21
You tell Internet Explorer how to handle pages with offensive content from the General tab of the Content Advisor.

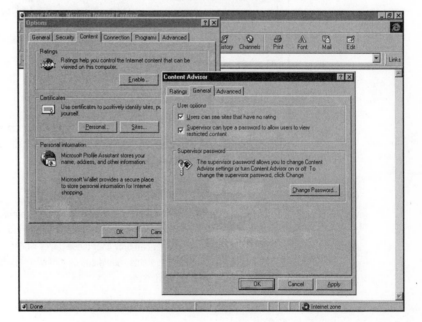

The Content Advisor's Advanced tab (see Figure 16.22) enables parents to select from ratings services other than the RASC or to invoke the use of a ratings bureau to access ratings systems. Content rating systems are based on the World Wide Web Consortium's Platform for Internet Content Selection (PICS) and anyone is welcome to propose a rating system that adheres to the PICS standard. To learn more about PICS, consult **http://www.w3.org/PICS/**. To see a list of current PICS-based rating systems, direct Internet Explorer to **http://www.classify.org/pics.htm**.

N O T E   Using a rating bureau tends to slow down your download times. ■

FIG. 16.22
You can enlist a different rating scheme or a rating bureau instead of using the default RASC ratings.

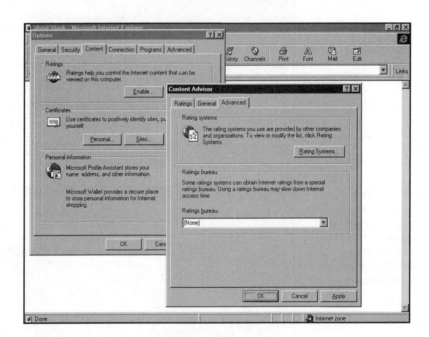

CAUTION
While Internet Explorer's content rating detection feature is a great way to help protect kids from lewd content, there is still no substitute for parental supervision while children are exploring the Web. Content rating is a voluntary activity and Internet Explorer can only filter those pages whose authors have placed content rating information in them. Concerned parents should still continue to supervise their children since there are many unrated, offensive pages on the Internet.

Help

A lot of online resources are out there to help you with security related issues. You can use Internet Explorer to check out any of the following:

- Microsoft is actively promoting the security support provided by its software products. You can read Microsoft's Internet Security white paper at **http://www.microsoft.com/ ie/ie3/securewp.htm**. A more general treatment of Microsoft software security features can be found at **http://www.microsoft.com/security/**.

- VeriSign is a digital certificate authority that provides services to individuals, corporations, and software publishers. You can learn more about digital certificates and sign up for one of your own at **http://www.verisign.com/**.

- Rivest-Shamir-Aldeman (RSA), Inc. developed the cryptographic schemes that are at the heart of SSL. RSA also maintains information and links that pertain to encryption. You can find RSA on the Web at **http://www.rsa.com/**.

- RSA, Inc. maintains an S/MIME Frequently Asked Questions (FAQ) at **http:// www.rsa.com/rsa/S-MIME/html/faq.htm**.

- Digital money leaders CyberCash and DigiCash can be found online at **http:// www.cybercash.com/** and **http://digicash.support.nl/**, respectively.

- SSL creator Netscape Communications Corporation maintains an SSL page at **http:// www.netscape.com/assist/security/index.html**.

- The World Wide Web Consortium (W3C) maintains a comprehensive list of security-related links at **http://www.w3.org/Security/**.

- The UseNet comp.security newsgroups are always active with discussions of very current security issues. You can look at the newsgroup hierarchy by pointing Outlook Express to **comp.security**.

Internet Explorer 4 and Related Microsoft Applications

CHAPTER 17

Web Browsing with Microsoft Office 97

With the Office 97 release of their productivity suite of programs—Word, Excel, PowerPoint, Access, and Outlook—Microsoft has further integrated Internet and Web functionality right into the its applications. Each application now has a Web Toolbar, which gives you access to many functions of its Internet Explorer Web browser, without first having to start the application.

In addition to the Web Toolbar, the Office applications have a few other ways in which you can access the Web. You can load Office format documents right off the Web, either into their own applications or into Internet Explorer. Also, the Office 97 and Internet Explorer 4 versions of Microsoft Word, Outlook, and Outlook Express have a few special Web capabilities of their own. ■

Use the Office applications' Web Toolbar

All the applications in the Microsoft Office 97 suite now include the Web Toolbar, with which you can access the Web any time you are using any of the programs.

Learn how to load Office documents from the Web

Using either the Web Toolbar or the regular document-opening capabilities in the Office 97 applications, you can open Word, Excel, and other documents that are stored on the Web and the Internet.

Find out about Microsoft's ActiveX Documents

Microsoft's ActiveX Document technology enables you to open and edit Office documents within the Microsoft Internet Explorer Web browser.

Access the Web with Outlook and Outlook Express

Microsoft Outlook and Outlook Express include a few of their own capabilities with which you can access parts of the Web.

Using the Microsoft Office Web Toolbar

Figure 17.1 shows two toolbar buttons that are present on the standard toolbar of all of the Office 97 applications (shown, in this example, in Excel 97). The Insert Hyperlink button enables you to place a hypertext link into any Office application—the use of this button will be covered in Chapter 18, "Web Publishing with Microsoft Office 97."

▶ **See** "Adding Hypertext Links" to find out how to add hypertext links into Word, Excel, and other Office documents, **p. 345**

FIG. 17.1
The Web Toolbar can be accessed in any Office application, giving you a consistent way to access the Web.

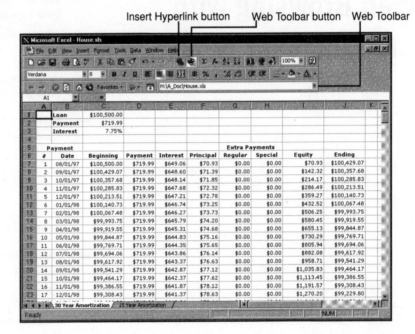

Clicking the Web Toolbar button enables the Web Toolbar in the Office application that you are using, as shown in Figure 17.1. This Web Toolbar gives you a subset of the applications that are available in the Internet Explorer 4 Web browser toolbars. The buttons in the Web Toolbar give you the following abilities:

- **Back** and **Forward**   These buttons enable you to navigate back and forth through documents opened through the Address area of the Web Toolbar.

- **Stop Current Jump** and **Refresh Current Page**   These two buttons enable you to stop the current page from loading, or refresh the page that is currently displayed.

- **Start Page**   Clicking this button loads your Start Page.

- **Search the Web**   Clicking this button loads the Web page that is configured on your system for Web searches.

■ **Go** The Go button enables you to open documents and go to or set the address of your Start or Search page. As shown in Figure 17.2, you can use the Set Start Page entry to set the Start Page to the current page you are viewing.

FIG. 17.2

You can set your Start Page through the Web Toolbar. This change affects all applications, including the Internet Explorer Web browser, that make use of the Start or Home Page.

The Open entry under the Go button allows you to access and open documents that are on the Web (see Figure 17.3).

FIG. 17.3

You can use the Web Toolbar to enter an Internet address and open any document on the Web.

■ **Favorites** This Web Toolbar entry gives you access to your Favorites menu. Figure 17.4 shows the use of the Favorites, Add to Favorites entry to add an Office document to the Favorites list.

If you add such a document to your Favorites list through an Office application, and then look at your Favorites in the Internet Explorer Web browser, you can see that all of the applications utilize the same database (see Figure 17.5).

■ **Show Only Web Toolbar** Clicking this button disables the other toolbars in the Office application you are using, other than the Web Toolbar.

■ **Address** This area gives you the ability to see and enter addresses for loading documents into your application and behaves the same way as the Internet Explorer Address Bar.

Loading Office Documents from the Web

In the previous section, Figure 17.3 showed you how you can use the Web Toolbar Go, Open entry to open a document on the Web. If the address you enter is an HTML document, then regardless of the Office application you are using, your Internet Explorer 4 Web browser will launch and load that document. (In the "Web Browsing with Microsoft Word" section later in this chapter, you will find out how you can use Word 97 to directly load HTML Web pages.)

FIG. 17.4

Local documents, as well as documents located on the Internet, can be added to your Favorites list.

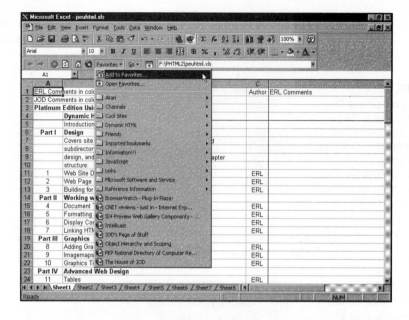

FIG. 17.5

Microsoft's integrated Internet approach enables you to access the same group of Favorites from any of their applications.

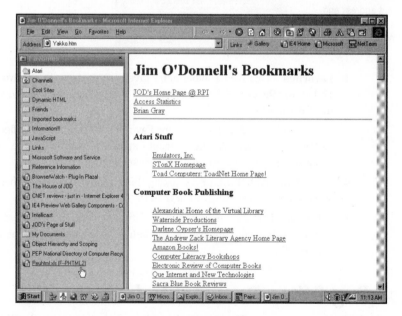

As shown in Figure 17.3, you can also load Office documents directly off the Web—in this case, use the Web Toolbar in Excel 97 to load an Excel document. The document will be downloaded directly from its location, as long as your Internet connection is active, and will load into Excel. Depending on your security settings, you will probably get an alert box similar to that shown in Figure 17.6. Make sure that the document is coming from a trusted source before you agree to open it.

FIG. 17.6
Microsoft Office
documents can contain
macros that might
be harmful to your
system—make sure you
know and trust where
they are coming from.

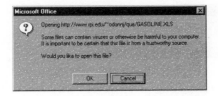

By being able to load documents right off of the Web, the Microsoft Office 97 applications
make it much easier for you to make your documents available to other people. Figure 17.7
shows the Web-based Excel document once it has been downloaded and opened in Excel 97.
There are a couple of things to note in this figure:

- **Microsoft Office 97 application title bar**   The full Internet address of the document
  is shown in the title bar, along with the notation "[Read Only]". Because the document
  was loaded from the Web, it cannot be saved directly back to that location (see Figure
  17.8). You can edit it at will and save another copy of it to your local system.

- **Web Toolbar navigation buttons**   Once you have loaded a document via the Web
  Toolbar, either through any of the Web Toolbar buttons or through the Address area,
  the Back button becomes active. If you use the Back button to move back through the
  opened documents, the Forward button will also become active.

- **Web Toolbar Address area**   The location of the current document is listed in this
  area, regardless of whether or not the document was loaded from the Web or from the
  local system.

FIG. 17.7
Microsoft Excel 97, and
the other Office 97
applications, can load
compatible documents
right off of the Web.

Navigation buttons—

Title Bar   Address area

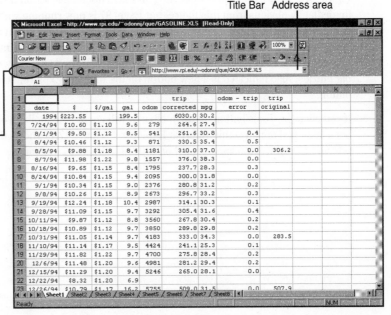

FIG. 17.8
You can edit and save
them on your local
system, however.

Though this example used Microsoft Excel 97, it would work just as well with any Office 97 application. In fact, you can use the Web Toolbar to load documents from other Office applications. For instance, if you use the Web Toolbar from Excel 97 to attempt to load a Word 97 document from the Web, it will work just fine—the download will initiate and, if you opt to open the document, Word 97 will be launched (if neccesary), and the document will open within it.

ActiveX Documents: Office Documents in Internet Explorer

In addition to directly using the Office 97 applications to open Office format documents over the Web, you can also open these documents through Internet Explorer 4. While you are using the Web browser, however, you will *also* be using the appropriate Office application through a technology Microsoft calls ActiveX Documents.

When you use your Internet Explorer Web browser to load an Office document or a document from any application that supports the ActiveX Document technology, Internet Explorer will actually launch that application and open the document *within the Web browser window*. Your Web browser becomes a container in which you can use the Office application to look at and edit the document.

Figure 17.9 shows the results of loading an Excel document within Internet Explorer 4. It is not immediately obvious from this figure, but Excel 97 is now running within Internet Explorer 4, and the full functionality of both applications is available to you. If you look at the menu bar, you can see that the entries on it are a combination of entries of the Internet Explorer (Go, Favorites) and Excel 97 menu bars (Insert, Format, Tools, Data), as well as the standard menu bar entries. Also indicated is a new button on the Internet Explorer standard toolbar, the Tools button.

If you click the Tools button on the toolbar, it will enable the toolbars of the application that has been launched to run within Internet Explorer 4. Figure 17.10 shows the results, with the Internet Explorer 4 toolbars located on top of the Excel 97 toolbars.

FIG. 17.9
ActiveX Document technology enables Internet Explorer 4 to load Office documents within the Web browser.

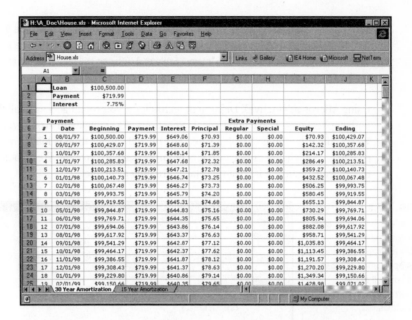

FIG. 17.10
The application menus and toolbars are available within Internet Explorer, enabling you to edit the document just as if it had been loaded directly.

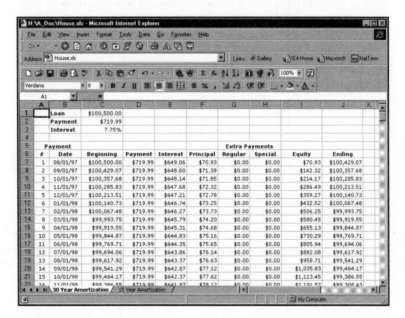

N O T E You can rearrange the toolbars in both Internet Explorer 4 and the Office 97 applications (Excel 97 in Figures 17.9 and 17.10), can be rearranged relative to one another. When you open an Office 97 application within Internet Explorer 4, you can still rearrange the toolbars, but it is not possible to mix the toolbars from the Web browser and the application. ▨

Using Microsoft's ActiveX Document technology, you retain access to all the capabilities of both applications, with some logical exceptions. As shown with Word 97, in Figure 17.11, the Web Toolbar button is disabled when an Office 97 application is loaded within the Web browser container. This happens because it is not necessary to have the Web Toolbar available when the full capabilities of Internet Explorer are fully available.

FIG. 17.11

In addition to being able to edit and view an Office document using its application, you can still use all of the Internet Explorer functions.

Web Toolbar

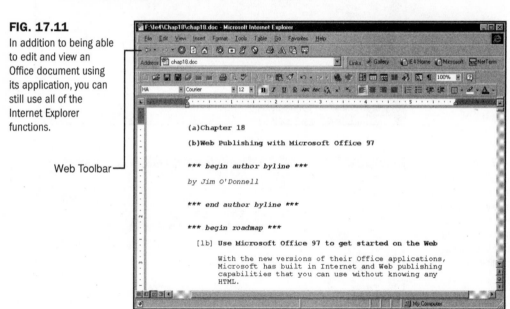

The functions of the Web browser and the contained application are both available, and mixed to some extent, but they are also kept separate. As shown in Figure 17.12, if you right-click in the Internet Explorer 4 toolbar area, you will get access to its toolbar popup menu, allowing you to enable and disable any of the Web browser toolbars. On the other hand, if you right-click in the application toolbar area, as shown in Figure 17.13, you can access the application's toolbars.

FIG. 17.12
You can enable or disable Internet Explorer 4's toolbars individually, even when looking at an Office document.

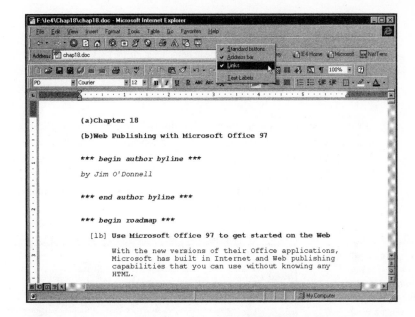

FIG. 17.13
When looking at a Word document within Internet Explorer, you can use Word 97's menus and toolbars to review and edit the document.

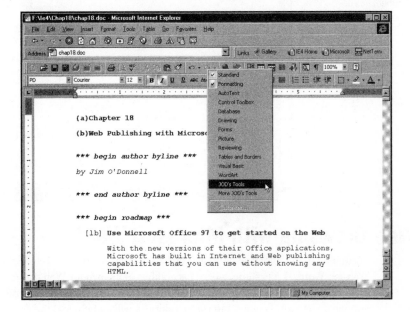

Part
III

Ch
17

CAUTION

As shown by the greyed-out popup menu entry in Figure 17.13, there are some things you can't do when an Office 97 application is opened within Internet Explorer 4. For instance, in this case you can enable or disable any of the toolbars, but you don't have access to the functions for customizing any of the toolbars.

One final good example of the way that the Web browser and application capabilities and information are merged when using the ActiveX Document technology is shown in Figure 17.14. The Internet Explorer 4 Help menu shows all the selections normally present within the Web browser. In addition to those selections is an entry for Microsoft Word Help, however. That entry is a submenu that, in turn, contains all of the selections normally included within Microsoft Word 97's Help menu.

FIG. 17.14

You can get help, either from local or Web sources, for either Internet Explorer or Word 97, when a Word document has been loaded.

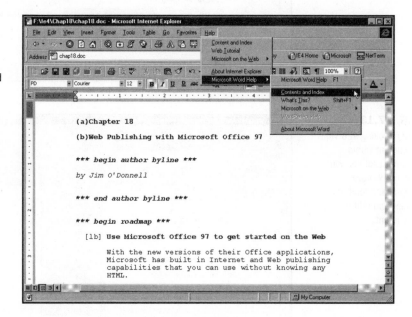

Web Browsing with Microsoft Word

In addition to the interface of the Office 97 applications with the Internet Explorer 4 Web browser, Word 97 has some special capabilities of its own for Web browsing. As mentioned earlier in this chapter, if you use Word 97 to try to open an HTML document using any of the buttons on its Web Toolbar, Internet Explorer 4 will launch, and the document will load into the Web browser.

You can load an HTML document directly into Microsoft Word 97, and edit it there. Doing so is possible because Word 97 possesses the capability to read and write HTML documents, allowing you to create HTML documents from Word files, but also allowing Word to load HTML documents and convert them back into a format that you can view and edit within the Word application.

Loading an HTML document directly into Word 97 rather than into the Internet Explorer Web browser is a simple, two step process.

1. Select File, Open, click the Word 97 standard toolbar Open button, or press Ctrl+O to get the Open dialog box shown in Figure 17.15.

2. In the File name area, enter the local location or Internet URL of the HTML Web page that you'd like to load.

FIG. 17.15

Using the File, Open selection, you can load an HTML document directly into Word 97.

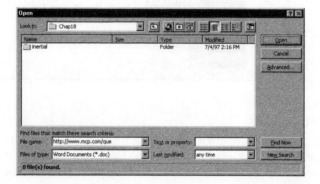

If you download an HTML Web page from the Internet and load it into Word 97 this way, you will see the document transfer to your local system, as shown by an alert box similar to that shown in Figure 17.16. Once the file is downloaded, it will be displayed within Word, as shown in Figure 17.17.

FIG. 17.16

You must download HTML documents located on the Web to your local system before you can load them into Word 97.

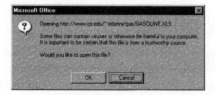

FIG. 17.17

You can view and edit HTML documents directly with Word 97 without using Internet Explorer 4 or a Web authoring program, such as FrontPage Express.

> **CAUTION**
>
> When editing HTML documents in Word 97, remember that HTML does not support some Word formatting options, and that some HTML and Web capabilities are not supported in Word 97. If any of these capabilities are used on either end, the Web page will lose something in the translation back and forth.

As with opening Office documents over the Web, if an HTML document is opened from the Web using Word 97, it cannot be saved directly back to its Internet location. If you wish to edit the document within Word 97, you will need to save it locally and use some other means to upload it to back to its original location.

Outlook and Outlook Express

In addition to the Web Toolbar capabilities of all of the Office 97 products, and the special capabilities of Microsoft Word 97, there are a couple of capabilities of Microsoft Outlook, and its smaller cousin, Outlook Express, that give you other Web browsing abilities.

As shown in Figure 17.18, if you click the Other button in Outlook's left pane menu, you get another method of accessing your Internet Explorer 4 Favorites database. If you select and double-click any of the entries in this area, if the entry corresponds to a Web page, Internet Explorer 4 will launch and the document will load.

FIG. 17.18
Microsoft Outlook gives you another way to access the entries in your Favorites folder.

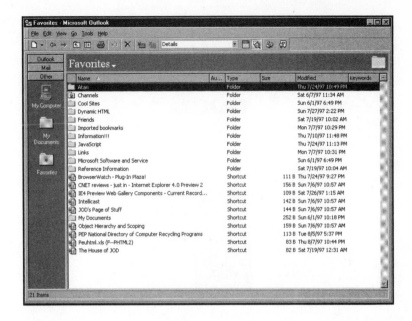

Unlike its otherwise more full-featured "older brother," you can actually use Microsoft's Outlook Express to view Web pages, albeit indirectly. By selecting File, Send a Web Page, you can enter the URL of an HTML Web page and actually send the Web page to someone else. As shown in Figure 17.19, the page is loaded and shown in the message composition window.

FIG. 17.19
Outlook Express uses HTML to format its messages, so you can also use it to view Web pages.

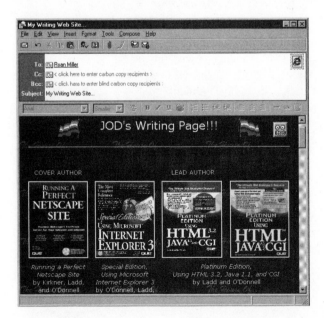

CHAPTER 18

Web Publishing with Microsoft Office 97

Developing and making available its Internet Explorer Web browser, and other associated applications, is only part of Microsoft's strategy for exploiting interest in the Internet and the Web. Obviously, if the only product it created for the Internet was a free one, it wouldn't go very far toward helping its corporate bottom line.

The technologies in Internet Explorer have served as a starting point as Microsoft seeks to integrate Internet and Web technologies into all of its software products. This chapter teaches you how to produce Web pages and format information for the Web using Microsoft Office 97. ■

Use Microsoft Office 97 to get started on the Web

Microsoft has built in Internet and Web publishing capabilities that you can use without knowing any HTML.

Create Web pages and add information

Just about all of the Office 97 applications include capabilities for creating Web pages, as well as the ability to export data and other information to include in existing pages.

Add Internet capabilities to Office 95

If you haven't upgraded to Office 97, you don't have to miss out on its Internet functions; Microsoft has created free Internet Assistants that can be added to your Office 95 programs.

Use Microsoft Publisher to work on the Web

You can also use the Microsoft Publisher desktop publishing program to create Web pages.

Internet Publishing with Office 97

Last year, Microsoft released a series of freeware add-ons to its Office 95 applications, called Internet Assistants. These add-on products gave these applications additional abilities to access and prepare information for the Web. With Office 97, Microsoft has built these abilities into its suite of productivity applications.

The Office 97 suite features the following applications that can be used to prepare Web pages and other HTML documents, or to prepare information for the Web:

- **Word 97**   Microsoft Word is the Office application with the greatest ability to produce Web pages. It gives you the ability to create and format documents for the Web without knowing HTML. It's not quite as "What You See Is What You Get" (WYSIWYG) as a product like Microsoft FrontPage 97, but it does allow you to see some formatting such as bold and italics.

  Additionally, some existing Word features translate nicely to the creation of Web pages. These include the ability to insert pictures into a document and the use of Word tables. Also, some abilities have been added especially for the creation of Web pages, such as inserting hypertext links and HTML Form elements.

- **Excel 97**   Excel's Web publishing abilities are more limited than Word's, but are very appropriate for its nature. With Microsoft Excel, you can select any region within a spreadsheet, and either create a Web page out of it or create the code necessary to include that region as an HTML Table in an existing page. Excel also supports adding hypertext links, and the creation of HTML Forms.

- **PowerPoint 97**   PowerPoint 97 supports two methods of producing Web versions of PowerPoint presentations. The first creates GIF or JPEG images for each slide in the presentation and builds the Web page framework around them. The second uses the PowerPoint Animation Player ActiveX Control to create a Web-based PowerPoint presentation that includes all of the animated slide transition effects, audio, and video possible within PowerPoint itself.

- **Access 97**   Microsoft Access 97 allows you to create Web pages that present the information present in Access databases, tables, forms, and queries. Not only is it possible to create static Web pages based on this information, but you can make use of Microsoft's Internet Information Server and/or Active Server Pages to make dynamic, database-driven Web sites and pages.

Microsoft Word 97

As the word processor in Office 97, Microsoft Word is the primary application for the creation of Web pages. While Word is not a true WYSIWYG Web page or HTML document processor, it does allow you to create pages with many different elements without knowing any HTML. Think of HTML as just another format that Word supports.

Converting Word Files to HTML

If you have any Word documents that you would like to make available on the Web, the ability of Microsoft Word to convert its documents into HTML will come in very useful. While Internet Explorer is capable of opening Word documents directly, using its ActiveX Documents technology by converting them to HTML, you can make them more widely and easily available.

▶ **See** "ActiveX Documents: Office Documents in Internet Explorer" **p. 328**

Figure 18.1 shows an example of a Word document. Figure 18.2 shows the same document in Word after it has been converted to HTML format. You will notice that the major features of the document format—font, bold, italic, some indenting—have been preserved.

FIG. 18.1

Existing Microsoft Word files can be saved as HTML documents by selecting the File, Save As HTML menu option.

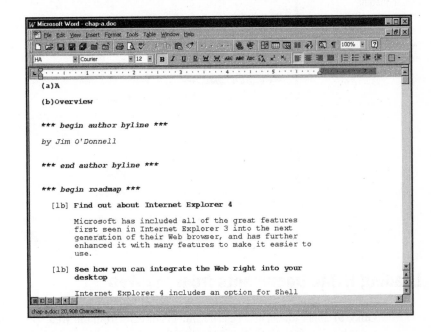

Figure 18.3 shows the HTML version of this document as viewed in Internet Explorer. As hoped, most of the formatting of the original document is preserved.

Some of the differences you are likely to see when doing this conversion, and the reasons they occur, are as follows:

■ **Fonts** When converting files to HTML, Word makes use of the FACE attribute of the <FONT> tag to retain the font of the original file. You should be aware, however, that not all browsers support this attribute, and, even if they do, the desired font might not be available on your user's machine. This causes the document to appear differently.

Part

III

Ch

18

■ **Horizontal Spacing**   Word uses HTML tags such as `<DIR>` to create indented sections of text. However, it is not possible with these tags to position tab stops as precisely as in Word, so horizontal spacing is likely to change when moving to HTML.

■ **Vertical Spacing**   Again, Word uses HTML tags such as `<P>` and `<BR>` to add vertical spacing within a document converted into HTML. Not only is this not as precise as is possible using Word format, but different browsers also interpret these tags differently.

FIG. 18.2

Documents converted to HTML within Microsoft Word retain most of their formatting; limitations in HTML, however, mean that the two versions will not be exactly the same.

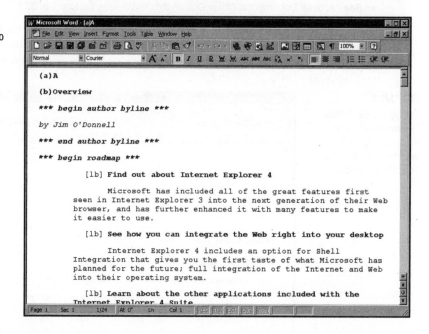

Loading HTML Documents from the Web

As discussed in the previous chapter, it is possible to use Microsoft Word, as well as the other Office 97 applications, to access documents directly from the Web. This is important for Web publishing, because it allows you to directly access existing Web pages and other HTML documents on the Internet, and import them right into Microsoft Word.

▶ **See** "Web Browsing with Microsoft Word," **p. 332**

Once these documents are in Word, you can do a number of things with them, including:

■ Edit them in HTML format and republish them onto the Web.

■ Save them in Word format and use them as a starting point for enhanced, Microsoft Word versions of the same document.

■ Use them as a starting point for a new Web page. This would allow you to create a common document template for all of your Web pages, or to make use of existing pages or techniques and expand and refine them for your own use.

FIG. 18.3

Word documents converted into HTML format are subject to the formatting limitations of HTML, and so will not appear exactly the same on the Web as they will in Word.

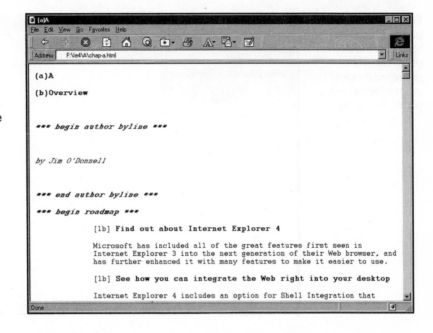

As shown in Figure 18.4, loading in an HTML document right from the Web is no harder than loading any other document. In the place of location of a local file, all you need to do is type in the URL of a Web page. Word will then access the document from the Web, transfer it to your system, and make it available for editing (see Figure 18.5).

FIG. 18.4

Word 97 gives you access to files and documents from all over the Internet, not just on your local system.

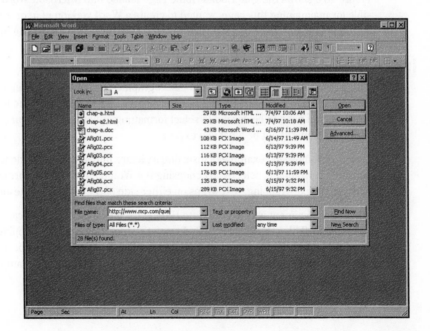

FIG. 18.5
Loading a document from the Web is a simple matter of transferring the file to your local system and loading it for editing.

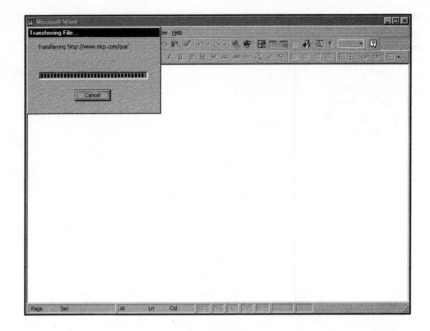

TIP HTML Web documents opened by Word are stored in your Windows\Temp directory. If you want to keep them, use File, Save As to store them in a more permanent location.

Figure 18.6 shows the Que Books Home Page loaded into Microsoft Word. If I were responsible for maintaining this page, wanted to create a Word version of it, or wanted to use it as a starting point for a page of my own, it would now be available for editing in Microsoft Word.

Including Graphics

Just as Microsoft Word allows you to insert graphics and pictures within its documents, if you are editing HTML documents you can do the same. As with many of the features of Word, however, you need to be careful to select formatting options that are compatible with HTML, or your results might not be what you expect.

Figure 18.7 shows an example of inserting a picture into a Word document. This picture uses Square text wrapping, selected by choosing the Wrapping tab of the Format, Picture menu. In this type of text wrapping, text wraps on either side of the picture in question.

When this document is converted into HTML, its appearance is significantly different (see Figure 18.8). This is because HTML does not support square text wrapping. As shown by the decreased number of options in the Picture Toolbar, you can either choose no wrapping, or text can wrap to the left or the right of the picture. Figure 18.9 shows an example of right wrapping.

▶ **See** "Using Tables in Page Design," **p. 486**

▶ **See** "Placing Content in Your Frames," **p. 490**

▶ **See** "Style Sheet Tips and Tricks," **p. 536**

FIG. 18.6
Once in Word, HTML documents can be viewed, edited, and changed to suit your needs.

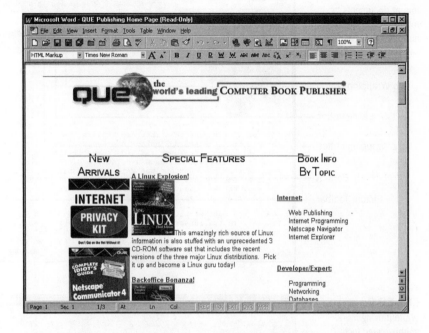

FIG. 18.7
Microsoft Word gives you many options for formatting text and graphics together in a document, not all of which are supported in HTML.

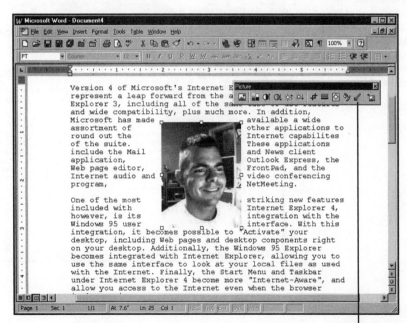

Word Format
Picture Toolbar

Part
III

Ch
18

FIG. 18.8

The Picture Toolbar changes for HTML format documents to reflect the decreased number of options supported in HTML.

No Wrapping button——

Left Wrapping button——

Right Wrapping button——

HTML Format——

Picture Toolbar——

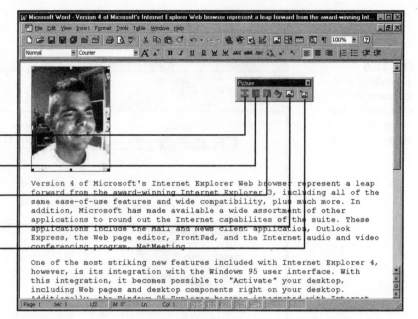

FIG. 18.9

Without using more sophisticated techniques such as frames, tables, or style sheets, text can only be wrapped around images in HTML to the right or to the left.

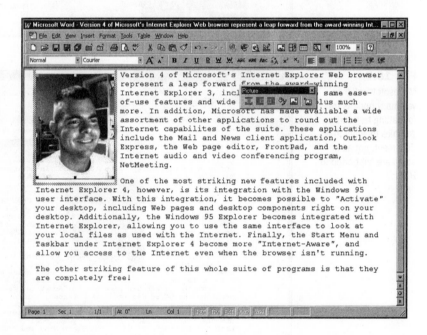

Adding Hypertext Links

Of course, no HTML publishing application would be complete without a way to insert and define hypertext links; it is the existence of these links that defines the very nature of the Web. Inserting links using Word 97 (which refers to them as *hyperlinks*) is a simple, two-step process.

1. First, select the text within the document that you wish to use as the hypertext link anchor. This is the text and/or picture that will be clicked to activate the link.

2. Next, select Insert, Hyperlink or press Ctrl+K. This gives you the dialog box shown in Figure 18.10. From here, you can type in the URL of the link, as well as enter a named position within that file (if desired). When you are done, click OK and the link is created.

FIG. 18.10

You can easily create and edit hypertext links within Word or HTML documents using Microsoft Word 97.

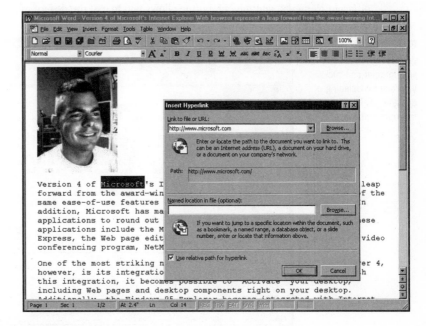

Adding HTML Form Elements

When it comes to editing and creating HTML documents, Word is not limited to simple text and graphics but also has tools for creating more sophisiticated HTML elements. Additionally, some native Word formatting options, such as bold and italics, also translate very well into HTML.

CAUTION

You should be warned that, just as there are some Word elements that don't translate into HTML, there are some HTML elements that can't be placed into Word documents. As a result of this, the Word menus change depending on what type of document you are editing. So, when you read about creating an HTML form using the View, Form Design Mode or Insert, Forms menu selections, don't be surprised when you can't find these options when editing a Word document—they are only available when editing a document formatted for HTML.

One HTML series of elements that can be included into an HTML document using Word 97 is HTML Forms. Figure 18.11 shows the result of a simple forms design, initiated by selecting View, Form Design Mode. In this mode, you can enter any of the HTML Forms elements into your document, within the confines of the form. The Control Toolbox gives you access to the different elements, and the exit button allows you to exit the design mode.

FIG. 18.11

Word 97 gives you a simple point-and-click interface for including designing HTML Forms for your documents.

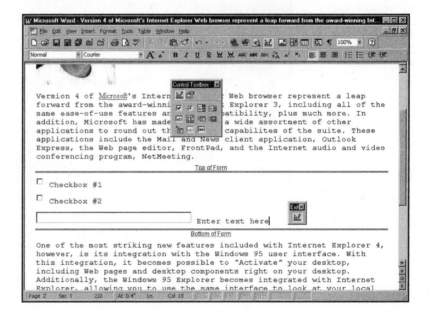

Figure 18.12 shows the resulting HTML Form within the Web page. Notice that you can also see the hypertext link inserted in the previous section.

▶ **See** "Passing Form Data to the Server," **p. 519**

FIG. 18.12
HTML Forms are a good way to solicit user input within your Web pages.

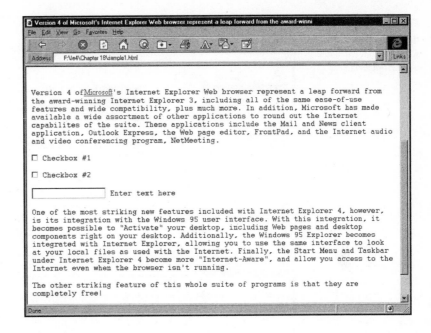

Using Word and HTML Tables

An existing feature of Word that translates well into HTML is Word Tables. If you wish to create a table and use it in an HTML document, the procedure you use is identical to that used when creating one in Word. There are a number of standard ways in Word to begin the process of creating a table, including the following (all selections under the Table menu):

- Draw Table
- Insert Table
- Convert Text to Table

Once you have created the framework of the table, populating its cells is simply a matter of clicking within the appropriate cell and placing whatever you would like there. HTML tables can be used for many different things—to hold text or graphics, to lay out objects on a page, and to format the appearance of HTML Forms. Figure 18.13 shows a table design in progress, with a series of HTML Form radio buttons being placed within the cells of the table.

N O T E   Figure 18.13 also illustrates another important point, something you might miss the first time around since Word shields you from a lot of the details of the underlying HTML in the Web pages it helps you design. Radio buttons work such that only one button can be selected at a time. When using radio buttons in an HTML Form, in order for them to work properly, all of the buttons must be given the same NAME attribute. This is done by selecting each radio button in turn, then clicking the Properties button, and giving each one the same HTMLName.

FIG. 18.13

HTML Tables are a good way to format forms and other HTML elements.

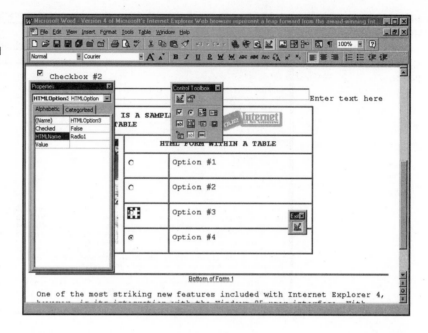

Figure 18.14 shows the final format of the table as shown in Internet Explorer. Notice that the HTML Table properties such as text alignment, borders, and the others can also be set when editing tables in Word.

FIG. 18.14

Merging cells when editing tables in Word creates the correct ROWSPAN and/or COLSPAN attributes to allow elements to cover multiple rows or columns.

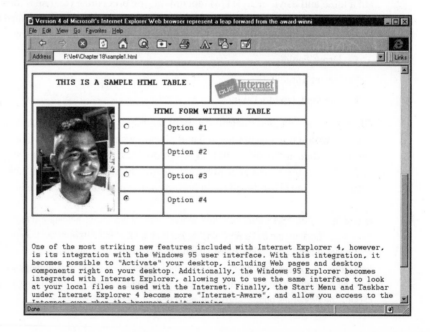

Adding Scrolling Marquees

Another HTML-specific feature that is supported by Word—in fact, this is an Internet Explorer specific HTML tag—is the ability to include scrolling into an HTML document. This is done by selecting Insert, Scrolling Text (see Figure 18.15). The text, as well as the other scrolling parameters, can be set here. Then, when viewed in Internet Explorer, the scrolling text will be shown.

FIG. 18.15
Word 97 gives you the ability to add Microsoft's <MARQUEE> tag into your Web pages.

Microsoft Excel 97

The Web publishing abilities of Excel 97 are more limited than those of Word, and more specific to the export of spreadsheet data into new or existing pages on the Web. Excel 97 does, however, include a Web Forms capability which, when used along with some of Microsoft's Web server applications, can be used to allow more dynamic, interactive interfaces with spreadsheet data.

Creating Web Pages from Excel Spreadsheets

Creating Web pages from Excel is a simple process involving the following steps:

1. Load the desired spreadsheet into Excel 97.
2. Select File, Save as HTML. This brings up the Internet Assistant Wizard (see Figure 18.16).
3. The Internet Assistant Wizard makes a guess at what region it thinks you might want to export. If this region is correct, click Next. If it isn't, click Add in order to create another region. You can do this by either typing in the range in standard Excel format, or by clicking and dragging within the spreadsheet.
4. In this step, you can choose to either Create a new Web page, or to Insert that data into an existing Web page. In this example, we are creating a new one (see Figure 18.17).

FIG. 18.16

The Excel Internet Assistant Wizard gives you a simple interface for exporting spreadsheet data onto the Web.

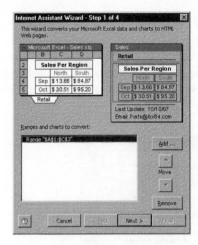

FIG. 18.17

It is possible to create an entirely new Web page from spreadsheet data, or to insert the information into an existing page.

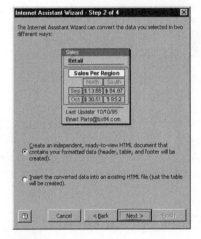

5. The next step, as shown in Figure 18.18, allows you to add additional information to a new Web page, including title and heading, as well as identifying information to be included on the bottom of the page.

6. In the final step, you can choose to either create a new HTML file, or to add the new Web page to an existing FrontPage Web (see Figure 18.19).

The resulting Web page will be shown in Figure 18.22, after you find out how to do a few more things in Excel that can be exported into HTML.

FIG. 18.18
Identifying your Web pages is a good idea, as it will allow your users to contact you, if they wish.

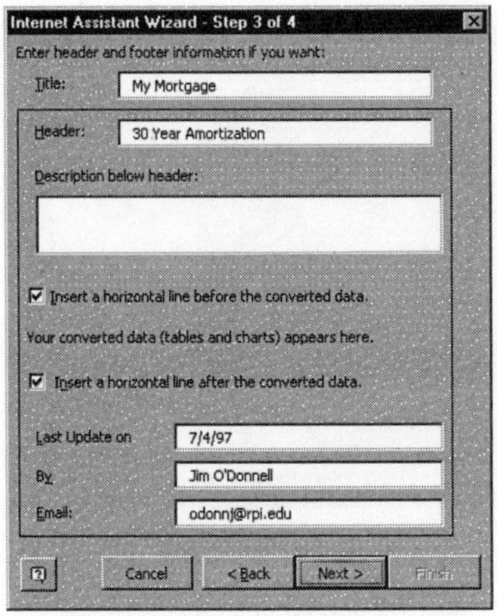

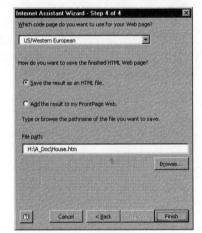

FIG. 18.19
Excel's Internet Assistant Wizard supports the FrontPage Web setup, and can export documents directly into a Web.

Adding Hypertext Links

As with Microsoft Word, Excel includes the ability to place hypertext links within a spreadsheet. Figure 18.20 shows the dialog box brought up by selecting Insert, Hyperlink, or pressing Ctrl+K. From this dialog box, it is easy to attach a hypertext link to any cell or series of cells in your spreadsheet. As shown in Figure 18.21, this link shows up as a link while in Excel as well.

FIG. 18.20
Any application used to create Web pages must be able to create and edit hypertext links.

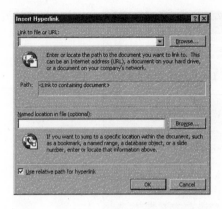

FIG. 18.21
Hypertext links within Excel appear as expected; when you move the mouse over them, the cursor changes and a tooltip appears showing the link.

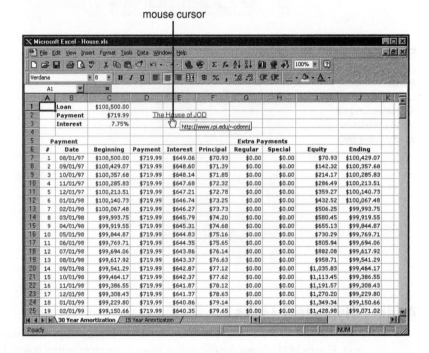

When this spreadsheet is used to create a new HTML document, the result is shown in Figure 18.22. Notice that one other thing was done to this spreadsheet that translated into the resulting HTML. The hypertext link attached to "The House of JOD" was placed in two cells using the Merge and Center formatting button in Excel. When this spreadsheet is used to create a Web page, the two cells in question have also been merged, using the HTML COLSPAN attribute of the <TD> tag.

FIG. 18.22

Excel's Internet Assistant is a great way to format and export spreadsheet data to make it available on the Web.

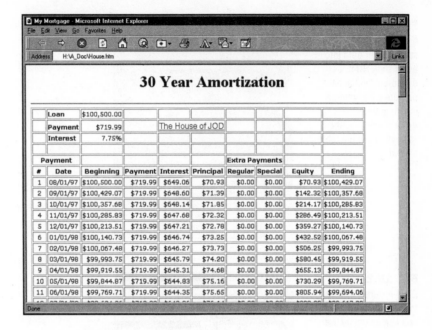

Exporting Excel Data to Existing Web Pages

Rather than creating a new Web page, you can export spreadsheet data into a table in an existing HTML document. The steps are similar to those shown above:

1. Load the desired spreadsheet into Excel 97.
2. Select File, Save as HTML. This brings up the Internet Assistant Wizard.
3. Select the region you would like to export.
4. Choose to Insert the data into an existing Web page.
5. Choose the file into which you would like the data inserted as an HTML Table. This HTML document should include the HTML comment `<!--##Table##-->` to tell Excel where to place the table (see Figure 18.23).
6. In the final step, you can choose to either create a new HTML file, or to add the new Web page to an existing FrontPage Web.

Creating Web Forms

Microsoft Excel 97 also includes a Web Form Wizard (see Figure 18.24), accessed by selecting Tools, Wizard, Web Form. This allows you to set up a spreadsheet to be used as an HTML Form for interacting with a Microsoft Access database. Creating an interactive database in this manner is a complicated process. For more information about this process, check out Que's *Platinum Edition Using Microsoft Access*.

Part
III

Ch
18

FIG. 18.23

If you want to export spreadsheet data into an existing HTML document, you must prepare it beforehand, inserting the <!— ##Table##—> where you would like the table placed.

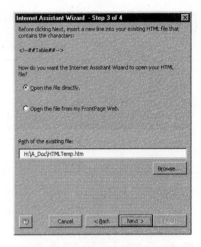

FIG. 18.24

Excel includes a Wizard to ease the process of building an interactive database over the Web.

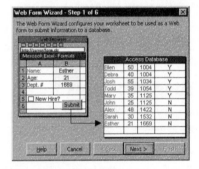

Microsoft PowerPoint 97

Presentations prepared with Microsoft PowerPoint 97 are especially appropriate for export to the Web. By their very nature, PowerPoint presentations, such as that shown in Figure 18.25, are prepared to be shown to other people. It is a logical extension of this idea to include the tools to easily convert these presentations so that they may be viewed on the Web. This allows them to be shown to as wide an audience as possible.

Exporting PowerPoint to the Web

Once a PowerPoint presentation is created, the process of exporting it to the Web is fairly straightforward. The steps involved are:

1. Make sure the desired PowerPoint presentation is loaded, and select File, Save as HTML. This brings up the dialog box shown in Figure 18.26. This dialog box will lead you through the process of exporting your presentation to the Web.

FIG. 18.25
PowerPoint presentations can reach as wide an audience as possible by exporting them to the Web.

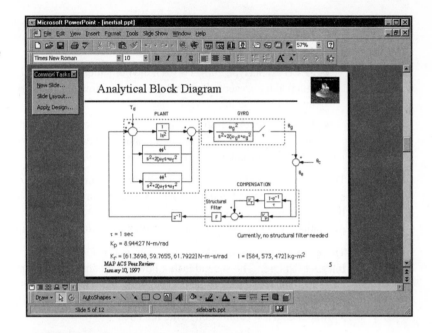

FIG. 18.26
PowerPoint leads you step-by-step through the process of creating a Web version of your presentation.

2. In the first step, you are given the option of choosing an existing layout selection. A layout, in this context, is a way of exporting a PowerPoint presentation to the Web. If this is the first time you have exported a PowerPoint presentation, you won't have any existing layouts. Note that, at the last stage of this process you will be given the option of saving your current selection of options into a layout.

3. Next, you can choose to select a standard Web page presentation, or one using frames.

   ▶ **See** "Placing Content in Your Frames," **p. 490**

4. The next step is an important one. Select what type of graphics you would like to use when exporting your presentation to the Web. You have three options, and each has its advantages and disadvantages (see Figure 18.27).

- **GIF**   With this type of presentation, each of the slides in your presentation will be converted into a GIF image. GIFs are best for presentations that are primarily text and line graphics.

- **JPEG**   This type converts each of your slides into a JPEG image. JPEGs are most suitable for presentations that use scanned images, or other graphics that make use of a lot of color.

- **PowerPoint Animation**   If you make this selection, your presentation is made into a PowerPoint Animation presentation, which is displayed using the PowerPoint Animation Player ActiveX Control.

The advantages of this format are that it allows you to include audio and visual animation effects, including text building within a slide, and animated transitions from slide to slide. If a user attempts to view this presentation using Internet Explorer but does not have the Animation Player installed, it will be automatically downloaded and installed.

There are two big disadvantages, however, to this format. The first is that it requires Internet Explorer. The second is that PowerPoint animations, particularly ones that use a lot of audio or visual effects, tend to be pretty big. This method is probably best in a corporate environment, when you know that most of your users have the correct software and a fast connection to the Internet.

FIG. 18.27

Because this presentation consists mainly of text and line graphics, the best format for it is GIF.

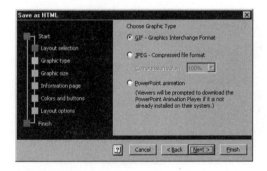

5. Select the resolution that you expect most of your users will be using, and how much of the browser window you wish to use for the images, as shown in Figure 18.28. The bigger the image and the bigger a percentage of the browser window is used, the more detail can be shown. However, each slide will then also be larger and take longer to transmit.

6. Add in your e-mail and URL information, to be included in the presentation.

7. Select the color scheme to use (or allow the default browser colors to be used).

8. Select the type of buttons to be used by the user to control the presentation.

9. Select the layout of the buttons relative to where the slide images are shown, either to the right or left, top or bottom.

FIG. 18.28

Select the size of your presentation based on a trade-off between the amount of detail you need to show, and how big you want the presentation to be.

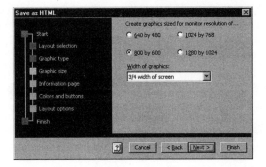

10. Select where to save the resulting Web pages for the presentation. This should be a folder on your system, in which a series of Web page will be created. For GIF and JPEG formats, in addition to the images used for the button controls and the index page, three files get created for each slide—the image file, the HTML file used to show the image, and an HTML file showing a text version of the slide. For PowerPoint Animations, only the index page and the presentation file need to be created.

11. This concludes the creation of your PowerPoint Web presentation. In this last step, you have the opportunity to save the selection of options that you used to create this presentation as a layout so that you can use it again later.

PowerPoint Web Presentations

Figure 18.29 shows the index page of a PowerPoint Web presentation. This page is used to show the identifying information of the person who created the presentation, as well as a table of contents of all of the included slides.

FIG. 18.29

The index page of the PowerPoint Web presentation is the best starting point for your presentation, giving your users access to any of your slides.

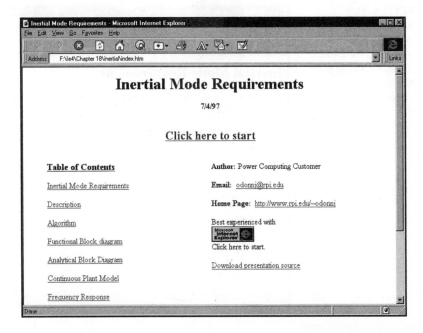

Part
III

Ch
18

By selecting one of the slides from the table of contents, or by stepping through the slides one by one, you can see all of the presentation (see Figure 18.30). As shown in Figure 18.31, PowerPoint's Web export also automatically creates text versions of all of your slides, to support people with text-only browsers.

FIG. 18.30

At this resolution and screen size, some of the detail in this slide was lost; this could be improved at the cost of increased file sizes.

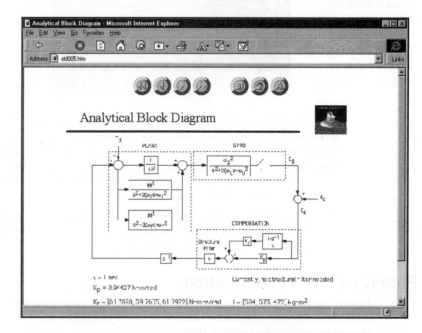

FIG. 18.31

By automatically creating text versions of your slides, PowerPoint makes it easier for you to support a wider audience.

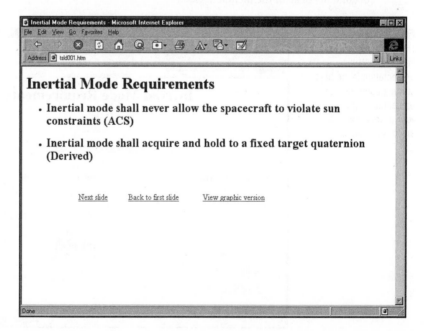

Microsoft Access 97

The final Office 97 application with significant Web publishing capabilities, Microsoft Access 97, includes significant tools for creating a dynamic, interactive database-driven Web site. Setting such a site up allows you to create Web pages that can access and be customized by your Access databases. In this section, you can find out how to export your database to the Web.

Publishing to the Web

This section shows a quick example of how you might export an Access database to the Web. Certainly, much more is possible than this, but this gives you an idea of how Access tries to simplify the process.

1. Make sure the desired Access database is loaded and select File, Save as HTML. This starts up Access 97's Publish to the Web Wizard (see Figure 18.32).

FIG. 18.32
The Publish to the Web Wizard simplifies the process of exporting data to HTML for publication on the Web.

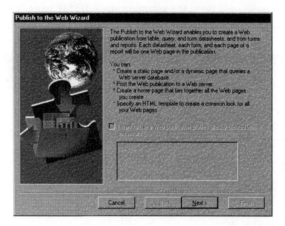

Part
III

Ch
18

2. If you have a profile of options saved from a previous HTML export, you can select that profile now to establish the defaults for the rest of the process.

3. Select what aspects of your database to export. You can select any or all of the table, query, or form datasheets that are part of your database.

4. If you have an existing HTML template file to use to structure the data export, select it in this step.

5. Then, you get the choice of creating a static HTML Web page, or using Microsoft's Internet Information Server or Active Server Pages to create a dynamic Web page (see Figure 18.33).

6. Choose where to publish the Web pages created in the export process.

7. Select whether or not you want a home page created for this database HTML export, which will summarize the Web pages created.

8. Lastly, you are given the option of saving your profile of options used to create this HTML export so that you can use it again in the future.

FIG. 18.33
Using Microsoft's Web server products, you can create dynamic, database-driven Web sites.

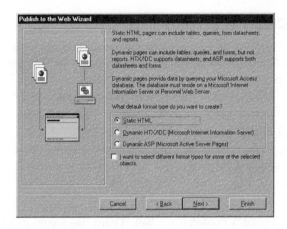

For the simple example used here, the resulting static HTML page created showing the database table is shown in Figure 18.34.

FIG. 18.34
Data, queries, and forms in Access databases can be used to create Web pages.

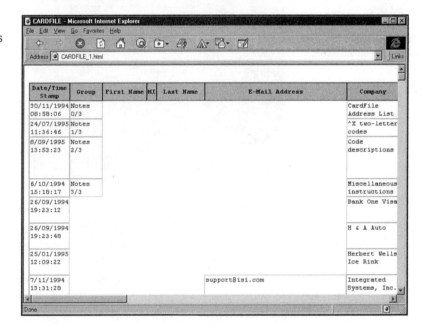

Using ActiveX Controls

As shown in Figure 18.35, Microsoft Access allows you to build ActiveX Controls directly into your databases. This gives you the ability to add incresed functionality, just as when they are used with Web pages. Also, through the controls in the Internet Control Pack, you can add Internet functionality directly into your databases.

FIG. 18.35

You can place ActiveX Controls directly into your databases, increasing the number of ways you can interact with them.

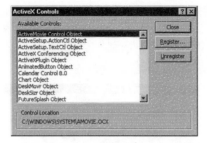

Internet Assistants for Office 95

As mentioned at the opening of this chapter, most of the Internet and Web capabilities built in to the Office 97 applications made their debut as Internet Assistant add-ons, freely available for Office 95. If you would like to use these capabilities, and haven't upgraded from Office 95 to Office 97 yet, you can still download these add-ons through the Microsoft Office Web site, starting at **http://www.microsoft.com/officefreestuff/office/office95.htm**.

Using Microsoft Publisher's Web Site PageWizard

While not a member of Microsoft's Office 97 suite of applications, there is one other Microsoft program that should be mentioned in this chapter—Microsoft Publisher. Publisher is Microsoft's desktop publishing program, but it also has some built-in Web publishing capabilities of its own. It has a special template and PageWizard that you can use to lead you through the steps of designing a Publisher document meant to be converted into an HTML Web site. It also has a companion capability to take such a publication—or any other publication that you can design with Publisher—and do the necessary HTML conversion.

To use the PageWizard to help you design your own Web site, select File, Create New Publication, and select the Web Site template from the PageWizard tab. This will start the Web Site PageWizard, which will ask you to make the choices involved in the following steps:

1. Select the type of Web site you would like to produce, Business, Community, or Personal (see Figure 18.36). The PageWizard will ask you for different information depending on what type of site you select. In this example, you'll see what steps are involved in a Personal Web Site—they'll be similar for the other types.

2. Choose to set up either a one- or multiple-page Web site.

3. Select the types of pages you would like to have included in your site. The PageWizard gives you some choices for pages commonly seen on a Web site of the type you are creating. For instance, a Personal Web site typically has an "About Me" page or a "Photo Album" page, among others.

4. Choose from a number of predefined styles, as shown in Figure 18.37, that Microsoft Publisher offers for you Web site "look." This selection, along with the next two, are global decisions for every page in your site, and enable you to create a consistent look throughout.

FIG. 18.36
Publisher has templates
for a variety of different
kinds of Web sites.

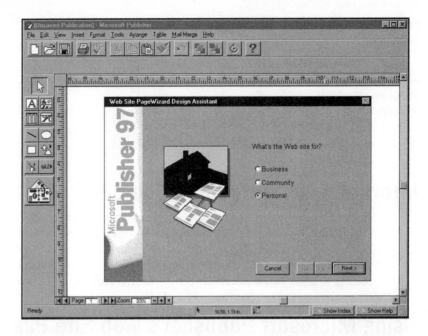

FIG. 18.37
The Publisher Web Site
PageWizard helps you to
establish a framework
that will hold true
across all of the pages
of your Web site.

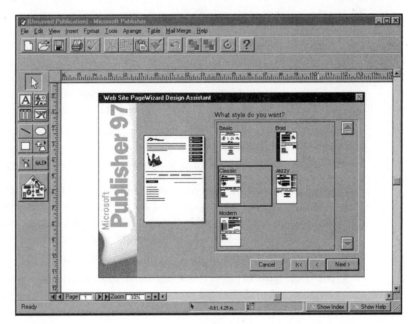

5. Decide which background you would like for the pages in your site.

6. Select the types of navigational hypertext links you would like to use, either textual, icons with text, or image buttons with text.

7. Enter the heading for the initial page in your Web site.

8. Tell the PageWizard whether or not you would like a postal address listed on your site—if so, enter the address information.

9. Finally, enter your phone number, fax number, and e-mail address to be displayed on the page.

When you have finished going through the Web Site PageWizard steps shown above, you will have a finished *format* for your Web site, but not very much content. As shown in Figure 18.38, you can get further help from Publisher in adding your own content to the resulting framework. You can choose not to use Publisher's step-by-step help, and add material just as you would with any Publisher document.

FIG. 18.38
Once you have your framework established, you can even get help from Publisher filling it with your information.

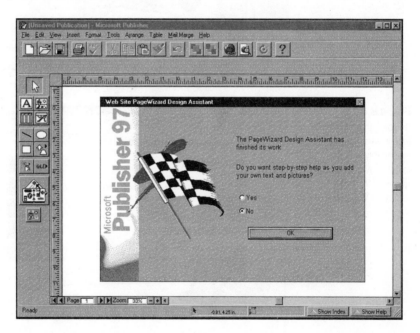

Part
III

Ch
18

Figure 18.39 shows what the resulting framework document looks like within the Publisher window. The text and graphics included within the document are placeholders only; you can add your own into the appropriate places. At any time, you can select File, Preview Web Site to see what the document will look like when rendered into HTML and viewed within a Web browser (see Figure 18.40).

FIG. 18.39

The placeholders included in the PageWizard created framework give you an easy way to determine where to best add your own content.

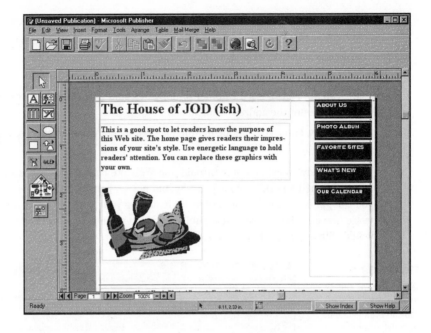

FIG. 18.40

By going through the PageWizard, you can be reasonably sure that the resulting Web publication will look good through a Web browser.

Converting Publisher Publications for the Web

The final step in creating a Web site, which can be done with a Publisher document especially meant for the purpose, or with any other document, is to convert it into a Web site. There are a few steps to this process, mainly concerned with making sure that the elements in your Publisher document will be translated correctly into an HTML Web page.

1. The first step in the conversion process to HTML is your option to invoke the Design Checker. As shown in Figure 18.41, this procedure allows you to review elements in your Publication document that may cause problems, or might not look good in a Web-based version.

FIG. 18.41

Publisher gives you a great deal of control over how your documents look; some of what you can do won't look right in HTML.

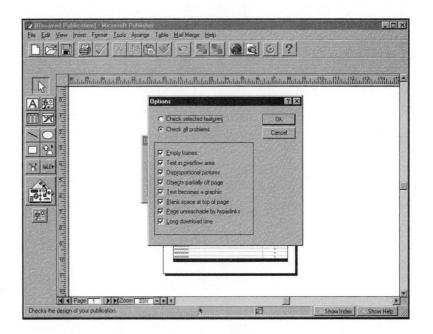

2. After the Design Checker has finished its format check, you can ask it to check the relative size of the Web pages you are creating, to see if they will download in a reasonable amount of time over the Web.

3. Finally, you can decide whether or not you want to publish the Web versions of your publications right to the Web—if you have the Web Publishing Wizard installed on your system—or to a local directory on your hard drive.

CHAPTER 19

Microsoft FrontPage and Image Composer

When you read about FrontPage Express in Chapters 6, "Quick Start: FrontPage Express and the Internet Publishing Wizard," and 11, "In-Depth: FrontPage Express," you learned how to use what is essentially a WYSIWYG Web document editor. FrontPage Express's sole purpose is to create publishable pages for the Web. It is capable of accomplishing this in a much more high-powered fashion than most WYSIWYG editors, due in large part to its borrowing of features from its "big brother," the FrontPage Editor. In this chapter, you take a closer look at FrontPage Express's older sibling and, in fact, the rest of the FrontPage family. The key thing to remember with FrontPage is that it does more than just WYSIWYG page creation—it is a full-fledged Web site management tool.

Managing your site with the FrontPage Explorer

The FrontPage Explorer is a Webmaster's tool for setting up, testing, and maintaining an entire Web site.

Maintaining content with the FrontPage Editor

If you've checked out FrontPage Express, you'll find the FrontPage Editor to be very familiar, yet much more capable, thanks to its expanded set of features.

Creating and editing graphics with Microsoft's Image Composer

The FrontPage suite integrates seamlessly with Microsoft's Image Composer, enabling you to make changes to your graphics from within the FrontPage environment.

Using other FrontPage support

FrontPage comes bundled with some other features that round out its total support for site management. Plus, you can download FrontPage server extensions from Microsoft if your server doesn't know how to work with FrontPage's preprogrammed functions.

Specifically, you will learn about each component of the FrontPage suite of programs, including:

- The FrontPage Explorer
- The FrontPage Editor
- Microsoft's Image Composer
- Microsoft's Personal Web Server
- The FrontPage TCP/IP Test

Using the FrontPage Explorer

When you start up the FrontPage Explorer and load a site, you will see the screen shown in Figure 19.1. At start up, Explorer displays the Hyperlink View and the two major areas of the window—All Hyperlinks and Hyperlinks for "My Home Page"—provide two very different ways of looking at the Web site or, in FrontPage vernacular, the *Web*. With no Web loaded, the Explorer window is largely empty, so your first step in creating your own Web is to give yourself something with which to work.

N O T E Before you start working on a Web, make sure you have a Web server program running. The Personal Web Server that comes bundled with FrontPage is fine for this purpose. Versions 1.1 and later of FrontPage will launch the Personal Web Server automatically when it is needed. ■

N O T E You can get the Explorer to run without a Web server present, but you will lose the preprogrammed functions if you do. ■

Creating a New Web

To start a new Web, choose File, New, FrontPage Web or click the New Web toolbar button. You will then see the dialog box shown in Figure 19.2. From the box, you can choose one of six Web templates or one of three Web wizards, which include the following:

- **Normal Web** This simple Web is made up of only one page. You can make this page a home page and build the rest of the Web around it.

- **Customer Support Web** If you're planning to provide customer support over the Internet, you may wish to investigate this Web, which is especially useful for companies supporting software products.

- **Empty Web** Choose this option to start completely from scratch. An Empty Web is useful if you have a pre-existing page done in the Editor or in another authoring program and want to incorporate it into a Web.

- **Import Web Wizard** By stepping through the dialog boxes in the Import Web Wizard, you can create a Web from files in a local or shared directory.

FIG. 19.1

FrontPage Explorer gives you two different ways to look at the hyperlinks in a site—a tree structure on the left and arrows pointing to a page on the right.

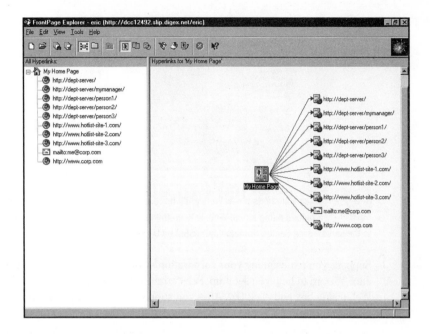

- **Personal Web**   The Personal Web is much like the average person's résumé. It has information fields and hypertext links that you can customize or delete as you please.

- **Project Web**   Corporate intranet users can put project management online with the Project Web. The Web helps to track individual tasks and progress toward the goals of the project.

- **Learning FrontPage**   If you're just learning FrontPage or if you want to make online support available to those who are, you can use the Learning FrontPage Web to help you attain your goal.

- **Corporate Presence Wizard**   By walking you through several dialog boxes, this Wizard collects information that is typically found on a corporate Web site and builds a Web with the responses you provide.

- **Discussion Web Wizard**   This Wizard also takes you through a series of dialog boxes that create a Web to support threaded discussions and a full-text search.

If you're creating a Web with a purpose that's consistent with one of the templates or Wizards, you should choose the appropriate one. If you have existing pages that you want to assemble into a Web, your best bet is to choose the Empty Web and place your pages into it. To begin with a blank page on which you can place content, select the Normal Web option.

N O T E   The Normal Web template is the default choice when creating a new Web. ■

Part
III

Ch
19

FIG. 19.2
Explorer gives you nine different options when creating a new Web.

N O T E   When you create a new Web, you'll be required to supply the IP address of your server and a unique name for the Web. To keep things secure, you also have the option of connecting to the server using Secure Sockets Layer (SSL) encryption. ▦

Suppose you're designing your corporation's Web site and you want to use the Corporate Presence Wizard to help you set it up. Select the Corporate Presence Wizard option in the New Web dialog box and click OK. After you supply the server address and a Web name, Explorer walks you through a series of dialog boxes that poll you for the following information:

- ▦ **What kind of pages you want in the Web**   You have a choice of the most popular page types found on corporate sites, including Table of Contents, What's New, Products and Services, Search, and Feedback pages.

- ▦ **What kind of content you want on each page**   This option might take you some time, depending on how many pages you choose to have in your Web. For example, if you opt for a feedback page, you will be asked what fields to include on the form. You can choose from the respondent's name, title, company, mailing addresses (postal and e-mail), telephone number, and fax number.

- ▦ **Standard page elements**   You can set up standard headers and footers for things like your logo, site navigation links, copyright notices, and Webmaster contact information when you configure your Corporate Presence Web.

- ▦ **Presentation style**   Explorer supports page designs that are plain, conservative, flashy, or cool!

- ▦ **Color scheme**   Choose colors for body text and hypertext links, as well as a color or pattern for your background.

- ▦ **Under construction graphics**   These familiar yellow signs have been overused to the point that they're more trite than illustrative. Think twice—three times even—before you use them.

- ▦ **Company information**   You can build in the standard complement of information like name, address, telephone, and fax numbers, plus e-mail addresses for the Webmaster and general information.

- ▦ **To Do List**   If you're managing a team that is responsible for a large Web site, the FrontPage To Do List is an invaluable tool for tracking tasks to be done and assigning who is responsible for each task. When you create a Corporate Presence Web, you can choose to present the To Do List whenever you load the Web into Explorer.

N O T E Most of the information you supply to the Wizard will be used to create a structure for the Web. It's up to you to go back in and add the content. ■

With the exhausting sequence of dialog boxes complete, the Explorer now has enough information to compose your Web. If you asked for the To Do List to display each time the Web is loaded, you'll see the dialog box in Figure 19.3, showing you what pages are left to complete. The Explorer puts these tasks in the list automatically, but you're free to add other tasks to the list as you encounter them.

FIG. 19.3

The Explorer's To Do List tracks unfinished tasks and who is responsible for completing them.

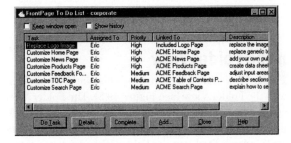

Once you close out the list, you will see the Explorer window shown in Figure 19.4. The default display shows the Hyperlink View of your newly created Web.

FIG. 19.4

The Corporate Presence Wizard builds this Web based on your input.

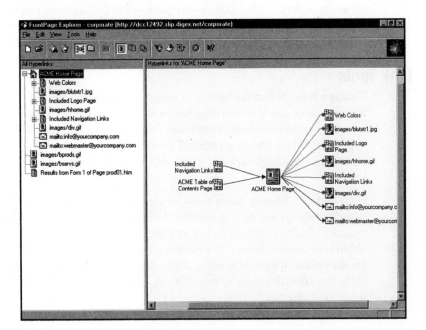

Part **III**

Ch **19**

Viewing a Web in the Hyperlink View

Once you have loaded a Web into the Explorer, you can examine it in two different ways: the Hyperlink View and the Folder View. The Hyperlink View is the default view in the Explorer window (refer to Figure 19.1). This view depicts your site more graphically, illustrating with arrows links to other pages within the site and off the site. You can click items whose icons have a plus (+) sign to expand the Link View further.

The Link View makes it easy to see how your documents are linked together and where you might be missing some critical links. Also, if you're looking for broken links pointed out by the Explorer link checker, this is the view you want to use.

 TIP Clicking a page on the left side of the Hyperlink View moves it to the center of the pane on the right side.

Viewing a Web in the Folder View

By clicking the Folder View toolbar button or by choosing View, Folder View, you change the Explorer window to the Folder View (see Figure 19.5). The Folder View is very much like the Windows Explorer window because it details document-specific information such as titles, file names and sizes, last change dates, who made the most recent edits, and the document's URL. Also like the Window's Explorer, the Folder View displays a tree of the folders and files that comprise the Web.

The Folder View can be handy in a number of situations. The last change date information can tell you how "fresh" information is on a page or whether a person responsible for an update has made the necessary changes. File size information is important for graphics and multimedia files and the Folder View can help you identify files that are too big to be part of your Web.

Link Tools

Visiting a Web site that has broken or outdated links can be one of a Web surfer's most frustrating experiences. It's frustrating for the site administrator, too. Keeping track of all links on a large site requires incredible attention to detail. Keeping track of links to other sites is all but impossible without checking each link individually on a regular basis. Fortunately for both parties, the FrontPage Explorer comes with some link utilities that help to alleviate these problems.

Verify Links Choosing Tools, Verify Hyperlinks instructs the Explorer to perform a check on all of the links in your Web, including links to pages that are not on your Web. The Explorer reports its findings back to you in a window like the one you see in Figure 19.6. Links to pages within your site are shown with a red circle and the word "Broken" if they are broken or are not shown at all if they are working. Links that couldn't be checked are shown with a yellow circle and a question mark in front of them. To verify these links, click the Verify button you see in the dialog box.

FIG. 19.5
The Summary View gives you all the details on all the component files in a Web site.

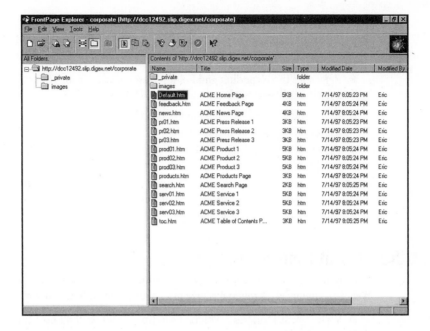

You can verify each external link by selecting it in the window and clicking the Verify button. If an external link is verified, the Explorer places a green circle with "OK" in front of the link. If an external link is broken, it gets a red circle with "Broken."

 TIP If you're using a To Do List to track your site management tasks, you can select a broken link and click the Add Task button to assign the task to a member of your team. Or, if you're working by yourself, you can use the Edit Link or Edit Page buttons to repair the broken link.

FIG. 19.6
You can generate a report on the integrity of all internal and external links by choosing Tools, Verify Hyperlinks.

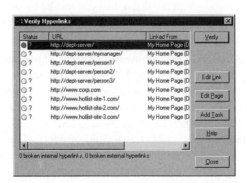

Checking your links frequently is a critical site maintenance activity that can't be stressed enough. When a user hits a dead link, it's like slamming into a wall. If users come to associate that type of experience with your site, it's unlikely that they will return during later browsing sessions.

Part
III

Ch
19

Recalculate Links   The Recalculate Links command (choose Tools, Recalculate Links) updates the displays in each of the three views to reflect any changes made by you or other authors. Specifically, the Recalculate Links command does the following three things:

- Refreshes the Hyperlink and Folder Views of your Web. The refreshed views will reflect any changes made by you or by others who have author access to the pages.

- Regenerates all *dependencies* in the open Web. Dependencies are items that are read into a page like images or Include bots.

- Updates the index created by the Search bot.

N O T E   Link recalculation actually occurs on the Personal Web Server, which comes as part of the FrontPage suite, or on any server using FrontPage extensions. Once the server has finished recalculating, control returns back to the Explorer. ▪

Other Useful Explorer Features

The FrontPage Explorer comes with some other handy features that can make your life as a Web site administrator much easier. These features include the following:

- **View Menu Options**   The Links to Images, Repeated Links (multiple links to the same page), and Links Inside Page (links from one point to another point on the same page) options under the View menu, toggle the display of these types of links on and off. When these options are on, it modifies the Hyperlink view to show the type of link selected. You can toggle these options from the Explorer toolbar as well.

- **User Databases**   You can set up users and groups of users so that they have different levels of access to each Web. This gives you control over who can look at and/or modify the Web. To set up a user database for your Web, choose Tools, Permissions and complete the three tabs in the Permissions dialog box accordingly.

- **Configuration Options**   With the dialog box you invoke by selecting Tools, Options, you can specify general program parameters, proxy servers, and which editing programs to launch for a certain kind of file extension.

- **Import/Export of Individual Documents**   You can import an existing document into the Web you're working on by selecting File, Import. You want to use this feature if you start with an Empty Web and want to incorporate an existing page into it. The Import feature is especially nice because you can choose to read in individual files or entire folders of files. Further, the files do not necessarily have to be Web-related files—you can import files from any of the other Microsoft Office products. Likewise, choosing File, Export, exports a selected document so that you can have a stand-alone version of it.

CAUTION

Be careful when importing documents, though, because some page element properties may need to be manually edited for FrontPage to recognize them. This is particularly true for images.

With your Web created, it's time to put some content on its component pages. You do this using the FrontPage Editor—a full-featured, WYSIWYG page composition program.

Using the FrontPage Editor

When you fire up the FrontPage Editor, you see a WYSIWYG environment in which you can create your Web documents—all without even typing an HTML tag. If you've used the FrontPage Editor, you may find yourself looking at something very familiar because the FrontPage Express Editor is really just a scaled-down version of the FrontPage Editor. For this reason, much of the discussion in this section will focus on the different features that are available in FrontPage but not in FrontPage Express.

 T I P If you are a veteran HTML programmer who's used to having access to the source code you write, you may find using the FrontPage Editor a little frustrating. When you work with the Editor, you rarely see an HTML tag. You can look at and edit the code that the Editor has generated for you by choosing View, HTML.

Starting a New Document

When you select File, New to start a new document, you don't just get a blank screen in which to work. Rather, you are given the option to activate one of the Editor's many templates and page creation wizards. Templates give you a structured document with several informational "holes" that you can fill in with appropriate text (see Figure 19.7). Page creation wizards collect information from you through a series of dialog boxes and then use the information you supply to author a page.

The FrontPage Editor makes substantially more templates and wizards available to you. Indeed, the FrontPage Express Editor supports only four templates and two wizards while the FrontPage Editor gives you access to 26 templates and four wizards!

Figure 19.8 shows a dialog box from the Frames Wizard—a useful feature for developing framed pages without having to worry about all of those confusing tags. There are only a few standard framed layouts from which to choose, though, so you may not find your desired layout prepackaged in FrontPage. In this case, you can set it up yourself choosing the Make a Custom Grid option you see in the first Frames Wizard dialog.

> **CAUTION**
> The Frames Wizard will try to save the framed layout to an open Web in the FrontPage Explorer, so make sure that you have such a Web open.

Part
III

Ch
19

FIG. 19.7

The Employment Opportunities template gives you a structure into which you can enter the job openings available at your company.

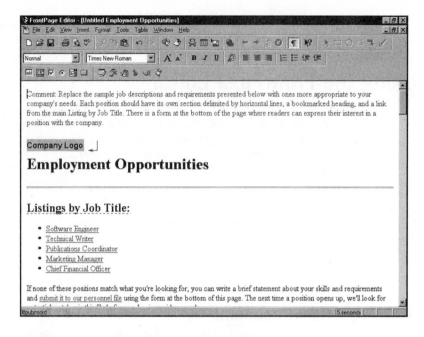

FIG. 19.8

Frames can be simple when you use the FrontPage Editor's Frames Wizard.

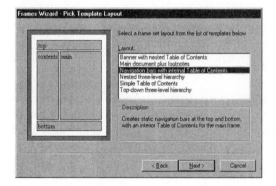

The FrontPage Editor comes with three other wizards: Forms Page, Personal Home Page, and Database Connector. The Forms Wizard is quite handy and can spare you much of the drudgery of coding a form. Many common form fields come prepackaged and all you need to do is place them on your form. This isn't very helpful if the prepackaged form fields don't include the types of fields you need, but FrontPage also lets you build a customized form from the ground up. You can pass the form results to a CGI script or you can use the FrontPage Save Results bot to write the form data to a file. You can save results in HTML, plain text, or rich text formats.

The Personal Home Page Wizard walks you through a sequence of dialog boxes to gather information to create a personal Web page. The personal page FrontPage can generate for you is more like a résumé than your average Web page because it includes page elements like "Employee Information" and "Current Projects." If you want to author a more typical home page, you might want to skip FrontPage's Home Page Wizard.

Finally, the Database Connector Wizard walks you through a connection to a back-end database. The information gathered by the wizard will set up an Internet Database Connector (.idc) file that the Microsoft's Personal Web Server or Internet Information Server can use to connect to an Open Database Connectivity (ODBC)-compliant database.

In addition to the wizards, FrontPage can get you started with more than 20 standard page templates, including the following:

- Bibliography
- Directory of Press Releases
- Employee Directory
- Feedback Form
- Frequently Asked Questions
- Glossary
- Guest Book
- Meeting Agenda
- Press Release
- Table of Contents
- What's New

Corporate site designers can use a good number of these templates. Specifically, press releases and press release directories, guest books, tables of contents, and What's New pages are frequently found on corporate sites.

Editing Your Document

Once you have a document started or have loaded one in from an existing Web, you can use the Editor's many useful features to create or change the page.

Figure 19.9 shows the Editor with all its toolbars active. Many are just like the toolbar buttons you would see in other Microsoft Office applications. Others that are more specific to HTML authoring are labeled with callouts in the figure.

Because they are not available in FrontPage Express, the Image toolbar and the Advanced toolbar are of particular note. When you select an image on the page, the Image toolbar becomes active and enables you to trace hot regions for image maps or to make a color in the image transparent. The Advanced toolbar is home to buttons that enable you place unsupported HTML, Java applets, ActiveX controls, scripts, and database connections into your documents.

Part
III

Ch
19

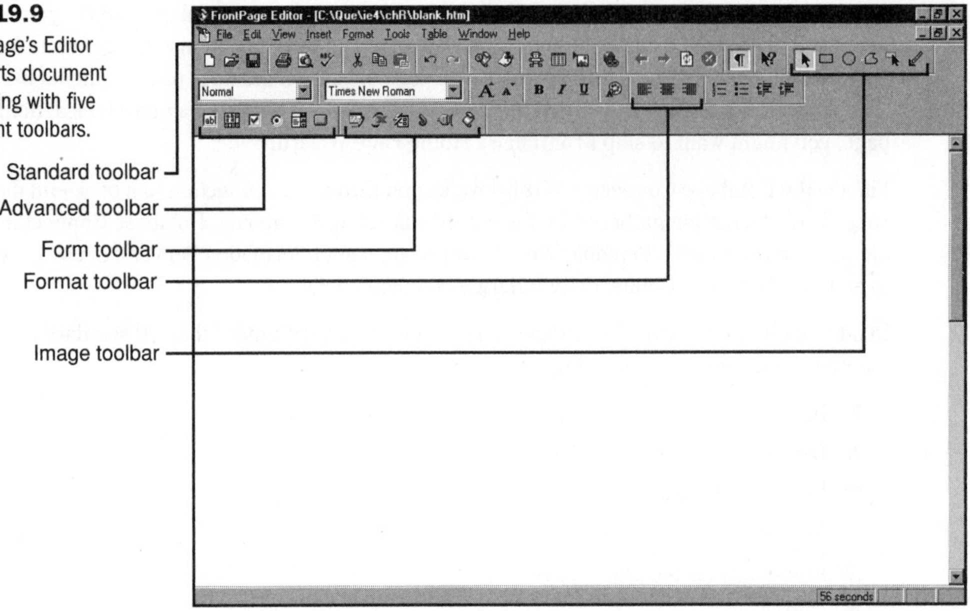

FIG. 19.9

FrontPage's Editor supports document authoring with five different toolbars.

Standard toolbar

Advanced toolbar

Form toolbar

Format toolbar

Image toolbar

T I P You can toggle the display of any of the toolbars under the Editor View menu.

Formatting Text   Text formatting with the FrontPage Editor is virtually the same as it is with FrontPage Express. The physical styles (bold, italic, underline) are available near the center of the middle row of toolbars. All you need to do is highlight the text to format and click the appropriate button. The Style drop-down box works similarly and gives you access to a much greater range of styles, including heading and list styles. Also on the middle toolbar are the Text Color button, with which you can paint highlighted text with a different color, and the Increase/Decrease Text Size buttons.

For several formatting options at once, select Format, Font to reveal the dialog box you see in Figure 19.10. Clicking different properties and styles on either tab of this box applies them to highlighted text.

Though most text formatting in the editor is straightforward, you should keep a few issues in mind. For example, when you cut a piece of text and paste it somewhere else, the formatting is not always retained, meaning you'll have to go back through and reformat it. This suggests that you might want to get all of your *plain* text where you want it first and then apply your formatting.

FIG. 19.10
The Format, Font dialog box gives you a lot of formatting options that correspond to different HTML formatting tags.

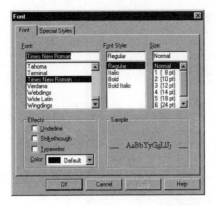

Another issue is text color. Text colors may not be displayed correctly in FrontPage, depending on what color resolution you're using in Windows 95. You may have to experiment with the Windows color palette, switching between 256 colors and high color, to paint your text with the color you want. If you're using 16 colors, you may have trouble getting page elements painted on-screen exactly as you want them. In this case, you should check the page on a browser running on a system with more colors.

N O T E Even with a WYSIWYG editor, you need to test your pages often in Web browsers—Microsoft Internet Explorer and Netscape Navigator, as well as other browsers you suspect will be used to view your site's pages. Not only will different browsers interpret the color palette somewhat differently, but text formatting may also vary. ▓

When you want to insert vertical space between page elements and you use the Enter key to do it, it will be interpreted as a paragraph break (or <P> tag) in your HTML code. If you just want a line break (or <BR> tag), you have to insert that manually by choosing Insert, Break.

Inserting Images To place an image on your page, choose Insert, Image to open the dialog box you see in Figure 19.11. In the box, you get the option to load the file from a local drive or from an URL, so you can pull down any image you want from the Web. FrontPage also comes with a collection of clip art that you can browse and from which you can select images.

By default, the image is placed at the current cursor location and is left-justified with an ALIGN value of BOTTOM (text next to the image will line up with the bottom of the image). You can exercise greater control over the placement of the image in the image's Properties box. To reveal the image's properties, double-click the image or right-click the image and select the Properties option you see in the context-sensitive pop-up menu. The Image Properties dialog box, shown in Figure 19.12, allows you to specify image alignment, border size, horizontal and vertical spacing, low-resolution and text alternatives for the image, and if it is hyperlinked, what URL to which it is linked.

Part
III
Ch
19

FIG. 19.11

You can place images from local or remote sources in your FrontPage Editor document.

FIG. 19.12

An image's Properties dialog box gives you finer control over image attributes.

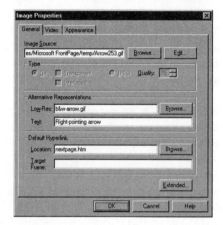

> **CAUTION**
>
> If you tweak your HTML code in a plain text editor, you may encounter some problems. FrontPage sets image WIDTH and HEIGHT attributes automatically. If you change the SRC attribute of any tag in a text editor without changing the WIDTH and HEIGHT, the image will be displayed with the dimensions of the previous image and look distorted! Be sure to change WIDTH and HEIGHT values if you change the image file you're using. Alternately, you can reload the changed file into FrontPage and it will automatically reset these attributes.

Image handling in the FrontPage Editor requires a bit of explanation. If you click an image once, you have selected it. Once selected, you can copy or cut the image, trace out image map hot regions on the image, or choose a transparent color. To delete the image, however, you must highlight it (pass over it from left to right with the cursor and the mouse button held down) first and then press the Delete key.

Setting up Hyperlinks   Placing hyperlinks with the FrontPage Editor involves the same steps as placing them with FrontPad. To create hypertext, highlight the text to serve as the anchor and click the Create or Edit Link toolbar button. You'll then see a dialog box like the one in Figure 19.13. In the box, you can choose to link to a page that is currently open in the Editor, a page that is part of the Web that you're working on, any page on the World Wide Web, or a page that you ask the Editor to create for you.

FIG. 19.13

The Create Link dialog box enables you to link to files on your site, files out on the Web, or files you have yet to create.

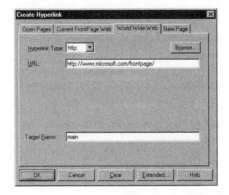

If you need to change the attributes of a link, you can right-click it and select the Properties option from the popup menu you see.

Setting up a linked image is virtually the same as setting up linked text. Simply click the image you wish to link and then click the Create or Edit Link button to open the dialog box, as shown in Figure 19.13. If you're setting up an image map, click the image once to select it and then use the tools on the Image toolbar to set up the different hot regions. After you trace out a hot region, the Editor will display the same dialog box you saw in Figure 19.13 so you can enter the URL to associate with the hot region.

NOTE   The FrontPage Editor uses client-side image maps. If you need to implement a server-side image map, look at the HTML source code to get the hot region coordinates and then type out your map file manually. ▪

Part
III

Ch
19

Using Web Bots

Web bots are preprogrammed dynamic objects that run when you save a file or when a user views your file online. The FrontPage Editor comes with eight bots—five more than FrontPad—that you can build into your pages, including the following:

▪ **Confirmation Field**   To confirm the contents of a key form field, you can build a Confirmation Field bot into the confirmation page.

▪ **Include**   The Include bot reads in the contents of another file and displays them on the page. This is useful if you're including a standard element on every page, like a mailto link to your Webmaster or a navigation bar. By using the Include bot to place standard items on pages, you can keep these items in one file, and changes made to that file will be enough to make changes throughout your entire site.

- **Scheduled Image** If you want an image to appear on a page but only for a certain amount of time, you can use the Scheduled Image bot to do it. You tell the bot what image to use, when to start displaying it, when to stop displaying it, and what it should display outside of the scheduled period.

- **Scheduled Include** The Scheduled Include bot works the same way as the Schedule Image bot, except it displays the contents of another file during the scheduled period.

- **Search** The very useful Search bot gives you a simple way to set up full text searching capabilities on your Web. The bot generates a query form and then does the search based on the user's input. FrontPage lets you specify the prompting text, the width of the input field, and the labels on the submit and reset buttons. You can also customize the search output with a given match's search score, file date, and file size.

- **Substitution** A Substitution bot is replaced with the value of a page variable such as Author, ModifiedBy, Description, or Page-URL.

- **Table of Contents** The Table of Contents bot prepares a table of contents for your site, starting from any page you choose. It will even recalculate the table when pages are edited, if you tell it to do so while setting it up.

- **Timestamp** The Timestamp bot is particularly useful if you intend to note the time and date of the most recent changes to a page. The Timestamp bot gives you the choice between the date the page was last updated or the date that the page was last automatically updated.

Bots are unique in that their functionality is built right into FrontPage. This is very different from programming that supports similar functions because these programs are typically written separately from the coding of the HTML. FrontPage integrates these two activities into one.

Saving Your Document

To save your document for the first time, select File, Save As to open the dialog box shown in Figure 19.14. Notice that in this box you can save the document as a normal file or as a document template. Clicking OK will save the file to your current Web. If you want to save the page as a separate file, click the As File button and specify the name of the file to which to save the page.

FIG. 19.14

When saving for the first time, you can make your document into a template for reuse at a later time.

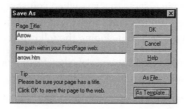

Using Microsoft's Image Composer

If you've purchased a copy of FrontPage with the Bonus Pack option, you've also bought yourself a handy image editing tool. Microsoft's Image Composer is a full-featured, image-editing program that integrates seamlessly with the FrontPage Explorer and Editor to give you complete support when preparing documents for the Web.

You can invoke Image Composer from either the Explorer or the Editor by first selecting an image and then choosing Tools, Show Image Editor or by clicking the Show Image Editor toolbar button. When you do, the Image Composer will launch and load the selected graphic, as shown in Figure 19.15.

FIG. 19.15
FrontPage automatically starts the Image Composer when you want to edit an image.

Image Composer breaks new ground in developing graphics for Web documents by introducing the notion of *sprites*. Put simply, a sprite is an image whose shape is not necessarily rectangular (as it would be in any other image program). Instead, a sprite's shape is exactly the shape of the object in the image. As an example, consider the fishbowl image in Figure 19.16. The sprite that holds the stop sign has a rectangular bounding box, but its shape is that of the stop sign. To achieve a similar effect with a traditional image editor, the image would have to be rectangular with the bounding box "removed" by making its color the transparent color for the image. This doesn't really get rid of the bounding box though—it just makes it so you can't see it.

Part
III

Ch
19

CAUTION

Macromedia Director users should not confuse Image Composer sprites with Director sprites. Director sprites are cast members that have been placed into the score, and Image Composer sprites are images that have the shape of the object in the image.

FIG. 19.16

By overlaying different sprites, you can produce eye-catching image compositions.

Sprite

Sprites are made possible by an Image Composer feature called the *alpha channel*. Every sprite has a built-in, 8-bit (256 color) alpha channel that stores transparency information. This channel means that you can have up to 256 levels of transparency—a level of flexibility that is much greater than that of a single transparent color in a transparent GIF. With these multiple levels of transparency, you can overlay several sprites easily to create effects that would require immense effort to produce with other image editors. And once you're done overlaying sprites, you can export the whole thing as a GIF or a JPEG and place it in any of your Web documents.

Beyond sprite technology, Image Composer offers many things you'd want in a graphics program. It saves images in both GIF (including transparent GIF) and JPEG formats. You get all of the standard image creation tools like paint, fill, text, and shapes. Further, you get more than 500 special effects filters, including:

- Angled Strokes
- Dry Brush
- Fresco

- Halftone Screens
- Neon Glow
- Pencil Sketch
- Stained Glass

Additionally, Image Composer can work with most Adobe-compatible plug-ins such as Kai's Power Tools, KPT Convolver, and Andromeda Series 1 Photography. The Impressionist plug-in package is shipped with Image Composer and the effects found in the Adobe Gallery 1.51 already reside in Image Composer. To get the full scoop on Image Composer, including a gallery of free, downloadable images, point your browser to **http://www.microsoft.com/ imagecomposer**.

 T I P Microsoft Image Composer also integrates seamlessly with Microsoft's GIF Animator, if you're developing animated GIFs for your site.

Setting Up a Server to Work with FrontPage

It's essential to run FrontPage with a Web server, as noted earlier in the chapter, to get the full benefit from the program. For this reason, the FrontPage with Bonus Pack suite comes with a copy of Microsoft's Personal Web Server and FrontPage server extensions so that you can install such a server right on your own machine. This final section of the chapter looks briefly at the Personal Web Server and some of the supporting applications that help create the server environment you need with FrontPage.

Microsoft's Personal Web Server

A Web server program's main responsibility is to field requests for Web pages from client programs such as Internet Explorer and to send the pages to the requesting program. Because this isn't a highly visible activity, a Web server often runs "in the background" with no on-screen display of what's going on.

This is the case with FrontPage's Personal Web Server program. When it is active, it usually sits on your Task Bar. If you click the Task Bar item for the Personal Web Server, you'll see the dialog box shown in Figure 19.17. With the various tabs in the figure, you can configure the Personal Web Server according to your preferences.

Your best use of the Personal Web Server is as a way to test your Webs before you make them publicly available. Using the Personal Web Server to view your Web in a browser is the important final test of your site. Once a Web is ready to go, you may want it served by a server with a little more "horsepower," like the Microsoft Internet Information Server.

▶ **See** "Microsoft Servers," **p. 599**

Part
III

Ch
19

FIG. 19.17
You can set up the basic
configuration of your
Personal Web Server
or you can launch the
Administration panel
from this dialog box.

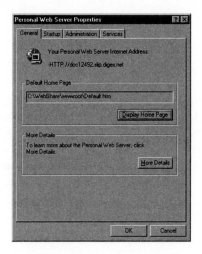

Even though the Personal Web Server doesn't seem to be as "high-profile" as the Editor or the
Explorer, it does have some desirable features, including the following:

- Complete support of HTTP and CGI standards

- Supports *multi-homing* (assigning multiple domain names to the same machine) so that
  more than one Web can be served by a single machine

- Recalculation of links when requested by the Explorer

FrontPage Server Extensions

To harness the full functionality of FrontPage, you must install FrontPage server extensions.
By communicating with the extensions through the Common Gateway Interface (CGI), the
FrontPage client software is able to invoke the FrontPage server-side components that support
things such as Web Bots and different viewing and editing permissions for different users.

Initially, Microsoft charged $200 for each set of server extensions, but now they are available
free of charge. The server extensions currently available are shown in Table 19.1.

Table 19.1 FrontPage Server Extensions	
Operating System	**Web Servers**
Solaris 2.4, 2.5	NCSA 1.5.2; CERN 3.0; Apache 1.0.5, 1.1.1, and 1.1.3; Netscape Commerce Server 1.12; Netscape Communications Server 1.12; Netscape Enterprise 2.0; Netscape FastTrack 2.0
SunOS 4.1.3, 4.1.4	NCSA 1.5.2; CERN 3.0; Apache 1.0.5, 1.1.1, and 1.1.3; Netscape Commerce Server 1.12; Netscape Communications Server 1.12; Netscape Enterprise 2.0; Netscape FastTrack 2.0

Operating System	Web Servers
IRIX 5.3, 6.2	NCSA 1.5.2; CERN 3.0; Apache 1.0.5, 1.1.1, and 1.1.3; Netscape Commerce Server 1.12; Netscape Communications Server 1.12; Netscape Enterprise 2.0; Netscape FastTrack 2.0
HP/UX 9.03, 10.01	NCSA 1.5.2; CERN 3.0; Apache 1.0.5, 1.1.1, and 1.1.3; Netscape Commerce Server 1.12; Netscape Communications Server 1.12; Netscape Enterprise 2.0; Netscape FastTrack 2.0
BSD/OS 2.1	NCSA 1.5.2; CERN 3.0; Apache 1.0.5, 1.1.1, and 1.1.3; Netscape Commerce Server 1.12; Netscape Communications Server 1.12; Netscape Enterprise 2.0; Netscape FastTrack 2.0
Digital UNIX 3.2c, 4.0	NCSA 1.5.2; CERN 3.0; Apache 1.0.5, 1.1.1, and 1.1.3; Netscape Commerce Server 1.12; Netscape Communications Server 1.12; Netscape Enterprise 2.0; Netscape FastTrack 2.0
Linux 3.0.3	NCSA 1.5.2; CERN 3.0; Apache 1.0.5, 1.1.1, and 1.1.3; Netscape Commerce Server 1.12; Netscape Communications Server 1.12; Netscape Enterprise 2.0; Netscape FastTrack 2.0
AIX 3.2.5, 4.x	NCSA 1.5.2; CERN 3.0; Apache 1.0.5, 1.1.1, and 1.1.3; Netscape Commerce Server 1.12; Netscape Communications Server 1.12; Netscape Enterprise 2.0; Netscape FastTrack 2.0
Windows 95	Microsoft Personal Web Server, FrontPage Personal Web Server, O'Reilly and Associates WebSite, Netscape FastTrack 2.0
Windows NT, Intel x86	Internet Information Server 2.0, 3.0; O'Reilly and Associates WebSite; Netscape Commerce Server 1.12; Netscape Communications Server 1.12; Netscape Enterprise 2.0; Netscape FastTrack 2.0; FrontPage Personal Web Server
Alpha NT Server 4.0	Internet Information Server 2.0, 3.0; Microsoft Peer Web Services

Part III
Ch 19

Once you install the appropriate set of server extensions, it is simple to copy a Web between platforms and to other servers while preserving all programming, access controls, and imagemaps. To find out about the most current sets of server extensions, direct your browser to **http://www.microsoft.com/frontpage/wpp.htm**.

The FrontPage TCP/IP Test

The FrontPage TCP/IP Test program does a quick check for your machine's host name, IP address, and other information required for it to act as a Web server on the Internet. To start the TCP/IP Test, select the Help menu in the FrontPage Explorer and then choose the About Microsoft FrontPage Explorer option. In the dialog box that pops up, click the Network Test button to open the FrontPage TCP/IP Test box. To start the test, click the Start Test button.

When the test has finished, the empty boxes on the left side of the dialog box fill with the words "Yes" or "No," depending on the program it was able to find (see Figure 19.18).

FIG. 19.18

The TCP/IP Test program explains the test results to you in easy-to-understand terms.

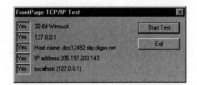

Webcasting

CHAPTER 20

Subscriptions

You know what subscriptions are in the traditional sense of the word. You pay a certain amount of money to have some periodical, typically a newspaper or a magazine, delivered to your home. Delivery usually occurs on a regular schedule—daily for the newspaper, weekly or monthly for a magazine—and sometimes it becomes necessary to modify your subscription, possibly due to an address change or an absence for a vacation.

When you shift your focus to Internet Explorer though, the essence of what a subscription is changes dramatically. Internet Explorer subscriptions are the simplest form of Webcasting—a set of approaches to managing Web content and controlling how users see the content in which they're interested. You don't have to pay for an Internet Explorer subscription either—they're all completely free!

For all the differences between traditional subscriptions and Internet Explorer subscriptions, you should also realize that there are some important similarities. Internet Explorer subscriptions bring information to your desktop just as a newspaper carrier brings the daily paper to your home. Internet Explorer subscriptions are updated according to a regular schedule, though it is you who determines the update frequency rather than someone else. And finally, you can make changes to your Internet Explorer subscriptions to make them more consistent with your Web browsing habits.

Understanding the different kinds of Webcasting

Subscriptions are just the first level of Webcasting as defined by Microsoft. Learning about Microsoft's Webcasting philosophy will help you to better understand the chapter.

Subscribing to Web pages

When you subscribe to a Web page, Internet Explorer will notify you about any changes to the page so you can check out the new content.

Subscribing to Webcast channels

Channel subscriptions work the same way as Web page subscriptions, but there are important differences in how you set them up.

Managing your subscriptions

Subscriptions have properties that you can change to alter how frequently the subscriptions are updated and how you are notified about content changes.

This chapter introduces you to the use of Internet Explorer subscriptions and offers tips on how you can use the subscriptions intelligently to enhance your Web experience. ■

Microsoft's Approach to Webcasting

You've probably heard a lot these days about "push technology" and how it is used to actively send content to a user's desktop. Ideally, users should be able to determine the content they want showing up on their computers, though you can be sure that someone will find a way to litter push delivery with unwanted content the same way junk mail shows up in your mailbox. Push technology has even found a role in corporate intranets as it gives system administrators an easy way to distribute software updates to all users.

But what exactly is push technology? In many cases, what some people call "push" is actually a misnomer. That's why Microsoft has proposed a three tiered model of what it calls Webcasting. Push technology is part of this model, as are some simpler, less "intelligent" ways of managing content delivery.

The three components of the Microsoft Webcasting model follow:

- ■ **Subscriptions**   the most basic form of Webcasting in which a user subscribes to a specific Web page and is notified by Internet Explorer whenever the page changes.
- ■ **Channels**   an intermediate form of Webcasting in which content providers can create a "channel" from their existing content, allowing them to manage what users see and how frequently updates are made
- ■ **Push technology**   true push technology, content delivery handled completely on the server side, is the highest form of Webcasting.

According to Microsoft, the first two tiers of the model do not represent true push technology. Rather, they are more accurately described as an "intelligent pull" of content. "Pull" suggests that the movement of content is initiated by the browser, rather than by a server and the intelligence comes in through regularly scheduled site crawls that look for information that has changed.

N O T E   For a full treatment of Microsoft's take on Webcasting, consult their Webcasting white paper
at http://www.microsoft.com/ie/press/techinfo-f.htm?/ie/press/
whitepaper/pushwp.htm. ■

The next few sections take a closer look at each of these tiers.

Subscriptions

When users subscribe to a page, they're really giving Internet Explorer instructions to look for changes to the page on a regular basis. If any changes are found, Internet Explorer can notify the users in one or both of two ways:

- By placing a red asterisk or gleam at the upper left corner of an updated favorite's icon
- By sending an e-mail message

N O T E Internet Explorer assumes that if you like a page enough to subscribe to it, it will also have a place in your Favorites folder. That's why a change in a page to which you've subscribed shows up as a gleam in the favorites listing. ■

Either way, users find out about the changed content and decide whether to go back to the page and check out what's been updated. If they don't want to look at the page right then, Internet Explorer can download it and store a copy locally for later offline browsing. This can save you big bucks in connect time charges if your Internet service provider charges you based on how long you've been connected.

Subscriptions, though considered to be the most basic form of Webcasting, have several inherent advantages:

- They're free and easy to use.
- Users have complete control over how often Internet Explorer checks a page for changes.
- Downloading of updated pages allows portability of content to a laptop, meaning you can take the pages with you.
- Site administrators don't have to make any changes to their sites for users to be able to subscribe to them.
- Internet Explorer, rather than a separate add-on program, maintains subscriptions.

The major drawbacks to subscriptions center around the fact that Internet Explorer has to do a site crawl to determine if a page has changed. A site crawl might generate too much information, leaving users to sift through everything Internet Explorer found to figure out what was relevant. Additionally, some sites do not permit site crawling programs (frequently called *spiders*) to access them at all, so even if you do subscribe to a page, Internet Explorer can't check to see whether there are any updates.

Channel

To overcome some of the limitations associated with subscriptions, Microsoft has developed the notion of a Webcast channel that starts with the content provider, rather than with the user. Channels enable content providers to better manage what they put out on the Web and when they do, just as a television station manages its programming and schedule. Users tune in to Webcast channels using Internet Explorer just as they would use their television sets to tune into a TV broadcast channel. Figure 20.1 shows a Webcast channel produced by E! Entertainment Television.

Part
IV

Ch
20

FIG. 20.1

Even popular cable TV channels are going online with Webcast channels.

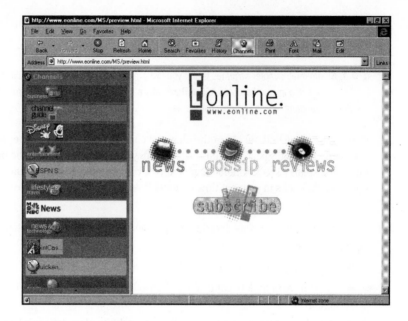

Channel authoring begins with Microsoft's Channel Definition Format (CDF), a markup language based on the eXtensible Markup Language (XML) standard. A CDF file defines a channel by specifying the following:

- Basic channel information such as its title, a descriptive statement of the channel's content, and what iconography and graphics to use to represent the channel
- What Web pages on a site should be part of the channel
- How frequently the channel should be updated

This information is stored in a file ending with the .cdf extension. When a user tunes in to a channel and subscribes to a channel, Internet Explorer accesses the CDF file and notes the pages and update schedule specified there. Users don't need to know exactly to which pages they're subscribing and don't have to guess at what an appropriate update schedule is because all that is now supplied by the content provider (who would know best about what pages are essential to a channel and when those pages might change).

Channels allow for another important benefit as well. Because the server can generate CDF Files on the fly, it's possible for channels to be customized to a user's preferences. A user would specify these preferences when subscribing to the channel and the Web server would store the preferences in a cookie file on the user's machine. Later, when the channel is accessed again, the cookie file is retrieved and the information there is used to display channel content according to the user's liking.

▶ **See** "Microsoft's Channel Definition Format," **p. 428**

Push Technology

Though they represent a more advanced form of Webcasting than subscriptions, channels are also examples of "intelligent pull" rather than "push" technology because the browser is still initiating the update step (though with channels, the intelligence is based on information from the content provider, rather than the user). True push technology in the Microsoft Webcasting scheme involve the use of *multicast* (one server broadcasting to many client) protocols. These special protocols make efficient use of available bandwidth to distribute content across a network. Note that this is very different from subscriptions or channels because they only involve an interaction between one server and one browser.

Internet Explorer provides an open architecture for the implementation of push technology client software. While there are many such client programs provided by third-part vendors, you could also use Microsoft's NetShow client to tune into a true push broadcast.

On the server side, your common, everyday HTTP server alone cannot provide push delivery. Rather, you'd have to use some kind of streaming media server that knows the Multicast File Transfer Protocol (MFTP). Microsoft's NetShow Server is one such server product.

N O T E   For more information about the NetShow server or client, visit the NetShow Web site at `http://www.microsoft.com/netshow/`. ▨

Because this book focuses on the Internet Explorer client program, the balance of this chapter will focus on the first two tiers of Microsoft's Webcasting model—subscriptions and channels rather than considering true, server-based push technology. In the sections that remain, you'll see how to subscribe to Web pages and to Webcast channels. You'll also learn how to make changes to a subscription once you've set it up.

Subscribing to Web Pages

Once you've identified a Web page that interests you enough to make you want to subscribe, it's very easy to set up the subscription. With the page loaded in Internet Explorer, just follow these steps:

1. Click the Favorites menu to reveal the set of options stored there.
2. Place your mouse point over the Subscriptions option to call up a set of subscription-related choices (see Figure 20.2).
3. Choose the Subscribe option to call up the Subscribe dialog box you see in Figure 20.3.

Part

IV

Ch

20

FIG. 20.2

The Subscriptions option under the Favorites menu is your gateway to performing several different subscription support tasks.

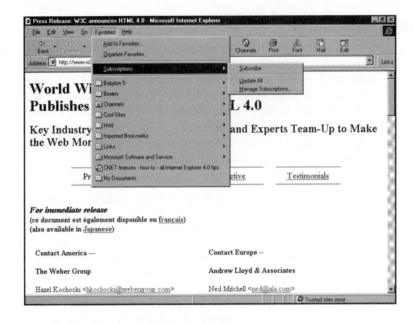

FIG. 20.3

All subscription information is coordinated from the Subscribe dialog box.

4. Make sure that your subscription has a descriptive name. The Name field in the dialog box is automatically populated with the Web page's title, but you're welcome to change it to something else.

5. Next check the Summary box to see whether you are happy with the Notification, Download, and Schedule settings. If you are, skip ahead to step 10. If you're not, click the Customize button to invoke the Web Site Subscription Wizard (see Figure 20.4).

FIG. 20.4

The Web Site Subscription Wizard walks you through the configuration of several different subscription parameters.

6. In the first Wizard dialog box, you're asked about which download option you want. You can choose to simply be notified in the event of a change to a page or you can elect to have Internet Explorer download the page or the page together with pages linked to it. The download feature is useful if you plan to view pages offline, so be sure to choose one of the two download options if this is how you plan to view content.

7. You specify how you want to be notified about changes to a page in the next Wizard dialog box. The default notification method is to put a "gleam" (a small red star) on the upper left of a subscription's icon, but you can also choose to have Internet Explorer send you an e-mail message telling you about the change. If you choose this option, be sure to click the Change Address button to make sure Internet Explorer has the proper e-mail address for you.

8. The final Wizard dialog box asks if you need to log in to the site to access the content. If you do, click the Yes option and type in your User Name and Password for the site.

9. Click the Finish button to close out the Wizard and return to the Subscribe dialog box.

10. Click OK in the Subscribe dialog box to complete the subscription.

N O T E Subscriptions are automatically set for an AutoSchedule update schedule. Though there's no way to change this when setting up the subscription, you'll learn how to do it later in the chapter when you read the section "Changing Subscription Properties." ▪

Part

IV

Ch

20

Your subscription set-up information is stored in a file in the C:\WINDOWS\SUBSCRIPTIONS folder on your hard drive. If you look at this folder in the Windows Explorer, you'll find that it is labeled as an "Offline Object Folder," meaning that it is meant to hold content for later viewing offline.

Once you've subscribed to a page, Internet Explorer will periodically check the page against the version stored on your hard drive to see if there are any changes. If there are, you'll be notified by the method you specified when you established the subscription. When you receive a notification, it's up to you to determine whether you want to check out the updated page or not.

There are some other, less obvious ways you can set up a Web page subscription as well. These include the following:

■ **Pages already stored as a favorite**   If you have a page stored as a favorite, you can right-click it to call up a context-sensitive menu. One of the options on the menu is Subscribe (see Figure 20.5). Choosing this option takes you to the dialog box you saw in Figure 20.3.

FIG. 20.5

If you've made a page a favorite, it's likely you'll want to subscribe to it, too.

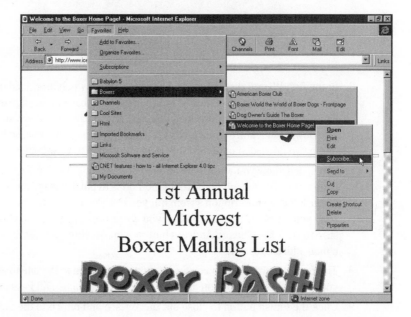

■ **Pages you're designating as a favorite**   When you choose Favorites, Add to Favorites, you see the dialog box shown in Figure 20.6. Note that the dialog box has a checkbox labeled Subscribe. If you put a check in the box, you'll be taken to the Subscribe dialog box once you click OK.

FIG. 20.6

You can make a page a favorite and subscribe to it all in one shot.

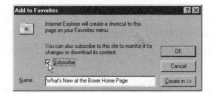

Subscribing to Webcast Channels

Because channels are different from standalone Web pages, subscribing to them is a slightly different process. Probably the biggest difference is that you are *obliged* to subscribe to a channel, whereas you can choose to subscribe (or not) to a Web page. The mandatory nature of channel subscriptions is based on the fact that channel authors embed update schedule information into the CDF files they use to define their channels and it would be impossible for Internet Explorer to capitalize on this schedule if it weren't subscribed to the site.

Webcast channels always have some kind of "gateway" page that introduces you to the channel and gives you the option to subscribe. Many channels will have the button you see called out in Figure 20.7 somewhere on the gateway page to provide you with the option to subscribe. But whether they use this button, channel authors have to give users something to click to initiate the subscription process.

FIG. 20.7
There will always be some kind of Subscribe option on a channel's initial page.

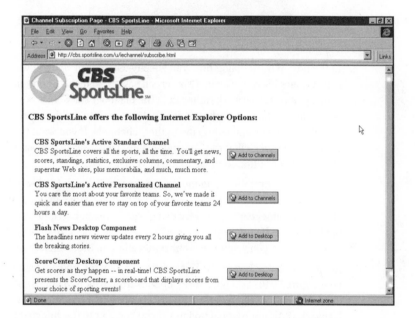

Once you've identified the graphic or link you need to click to subscribe, click it and then follow these steps to set up your subscription:

1. Clicking the subscribe button prompts Internet Explorer to open the Subscribe dialog box you see in Figure 20.8. The Name and URL fields of the dialog box are automatically populated with the title and URL of the channel and cannot be changed.

2. Check the Summary information in the dialog box to see if the Notification, Download, and Schedule configurations are to your liking. If they are, skip ahead to step 8. If they are not, click the Customize button and proceed to step 3.

3. Clicking the Customize button launches the Channel Subscription Wizard, a series of dialog boxes that walks you through the configuration of subscription parameters. The first Wizard dialog box asks you if you want the channel content downloaded for offline viewing or if you just want to be notified about content changes. If you plan to do some viewing offline to save a few dollars on your Internet service provider bill, be sure to click the Yes option. Once you've chosen your download option, click the Next button to continue.

FIG. 20.8

Channels get their own Subscribe dialog box, but it is subtly different than the one you see when subscribing to a Web page.

4. In the next Wizard dialog box, you specify whether or not you want to add the channel to your Channel Screen Saver. This screen saver can display content from each channel to which you've subscribed, rather than the plain old starfield screen saver that so many people use. In fact, a number of channel authors are making special screen savers available to those who subscribe to their channels. If you want the channel to be part of your screen saver, click the Yes option. Otherwise, leave the No button selected and click the Next button to move to the next dialog box.

5. You choose your notification method in the next Channel Subscription Wizard dialog box. Just as you could for Web page subscriptions, you can opt to be notified about changed channel content by way of a gleam in the subscription's icon or by an electronic mail message. If you want to be notified by e-mail, be sure to provide an accurate address. Once you've chosen your notification method, click the Next button to continue.

6. In the final dialog box in the Wizard, you specify the update schedule for the channel (see Figure 20.9). You have three options from which to choose: AutoSchedule, which does automatic daily updates if you're connected to the Internet via a Local Area Network (LAN) or manual updates if you connect to the Internet by modem; Custom Schedule, which enables you define your own update schedule; and Manually, which updates the subscription only when you tell Internet Explorer to do so. If you choose AutoSchedule or Manually, you can just click the Finish button to complete the Wizard and then move on to step 8. If you select the Custom Schedule option, you'll notice that the Finish button becomes a Next button. Click the Next button and then proceed to step 7.

7. To set up your custom update schedule, first take note of the existing update schedule shown in the status bar of the dialog box (see Figure 20.10). If you want to modify the frequency of the update, you have several options. You can switch among daily, weekly, and monthly update schemes just using the drop-down list you see on the dialog box. If you want to edit the existing update schedule, you can click the Edit button to open a dialog box that lets you modify the days and times that your updates occur (see Figure 20.11). The New button works almost the same way, except that the new schedule you create will displace the existing one.

FIG. 20.9

A channel subscription can be updated according to one of three types of schedules.

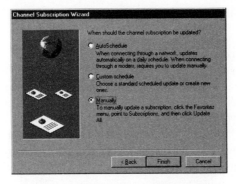

FIG. 20.10

You can change some update schedule parameters from this initial custom schedule dialog box ...

FIG. 20.11

... but you can specify your schedule requirements in greater detail by using this expanded scheduling dialog box.

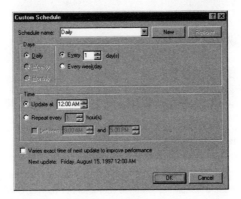

Part
IV

Ch
20

Note in Figure 20.10 that you can permit the computer to call up your Internet service provider to perform updates without you being there. If you don't want your computer calling out without your oversight, be sure to uncheck the box. When you're finished setting up your custom schedule, click the Finish button to close out of the Channel Subscriptions Wizard.

8. Finally, click OK in the Subscribe dialog box to complete the channel subscription process.

When you subscribe to a channel, it is added to a number of places in the Internet Explorer interface. The channel is added to the C:\WINDOWS\SUBSCRIPTIONS folder, just as Web page subscriptions are. It also appears in the Channels folder which you can access by selecting the Favorites menu and then holding your mouse pointer over the Channels folder. Additionally, the channel will also now show up on your Channels Bar. You can activate the Channels Bar by clicking the Channels button on the Internet Explorer toolbar. This will split the browser window into two sections that very much resembles a framed layout (see Figure 20.12). The left-hand section contains a list of your channels and the right-hand section displays channel content.

FIG. 20.12

The Channels Bar plays host to all of your channel subscriptions

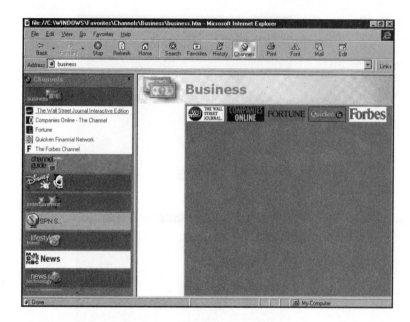

What are Channel Desktop Components?

As you explore the different content channels out there, you may find some that have a button that says "Add to Desktop" (see Figure 20.13). What the button means is that the channel has an Active Desktop Component that you can download to enhance your channel viewing experience. For example, a business related channel might have a stock ticker that displays continuous updates on prices for the stocks in your portfolio. Or, if you're a sports fanatic, you can have the your favorite teams' scores delivered right to your desktop with a scoreboard component.

Though they are not meant to replace the content on a channel, downloadable channel components can be a lively and interesting addition to your Internet desktop.

FIG. 20.13

Some Webcast channels come with Active Desktop components that keep a continuous feed of information coming to your computer.

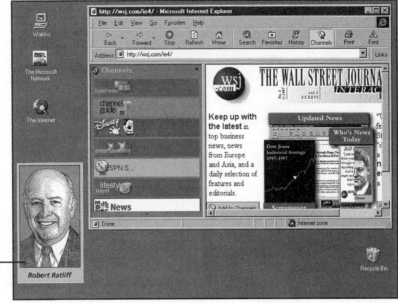

Desktop Component ⎯ Robert Ratliff

Managing Your Subscriptions

Regardless of whether you subscribe to a Web page or a channel, the subscription ends up in the C:\WINDOWS\SUBSCRIPTIONS folder on your computer. Should you ever need to do any maintenance on a subscription, you can begin by clicking the Favorites menu, holding your mouse pointer over the Subscriptions option. When you do, you'll see a pop-up menu with three options appear. You've already seen how to use the Subscribe option to set up a subscription to a page. When it comes to maintaining your subscriptions, you'll be more interested in the other two options:

- Update All, which checks your Web page subscriptions for changes and your channel subscriptions for fresh content, and

- Manage Subscriptions, which gives you access to all of the subscriptions in the C:\WINDOWS\SUBSCRIPTIONS folder.

The chapter closes with instructions on how to use each of these options to keep your subscriptions current and accurate.

Updating Your Subscriptions

If you choose the Update All option, you'll launch a Download Progress dialog box that will show you how the update is proceeding. If you want the full scoop on what's going on, you can click the Details button to reveal a larger version of the dialog box that looks like the one shown in Figure 20.14. The lower section of the dialog box shows each of your subscriptions and tells you whether the update succeeded, failed, or is pending.

Part

IV

Ch

20

FIG. 20.14
You can track the
progress of your
subscription updates as
they happen.

Updating subscriptions should not be an issue for Internet Explorer users with constant access
to the Internet via a corporate LAN. Those users can just use the AutoSchedule or Custom
Schedule update option to specify how frequently they want downloads to occur and then kick
back and enjoy automatically updated subscriptions. If you're accessing the Internet by a modem, you will need to update your subscriptions manually by using this menu option.

Changing Subscription Properties

When you invoke the Manage Subscriptions option, you call up the Explorer window you see in
Figure 20.15. The window lists the contents of the C:\WINDOWS\SUBSCRIPTIONS folder and
shows you detailed information about each subscription including the following:

- When it was last updated
- The status of the last update (succeeded, failed, or stopped)
- When the next scheduled update is
- The URL to which the subscription points
- The kind of update schedule the subscription uses,
- How big the downloaded file is
- The subscription's update priority.

To change the properties of a subscription, simply right click it to call up a context-sensitive
menu that includes the Properties option. Choosing this option calls up the Properties dialog
box you see in Figure 20.16. The dialog box tabs are the same for both Web page and channel
subscriptions, though the content on each tab may vary slightly due to the differences between
the two types of subscription.

FIG. 20.15

You manage your subscriptions from an Explorer type of window which gives you details about the subscription at a glance.

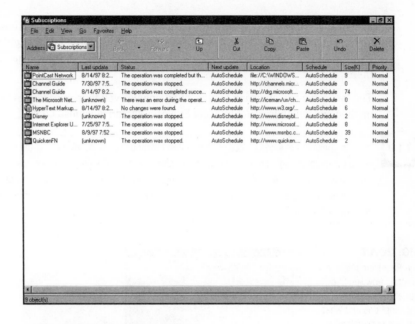

FIG. 20.16

You can change subscription parameters after you've set up the subscription from the subscription Properties dialog box.

The first tab you see is the Subscription tab, from which you can do three things:

- Unsubscribe to the Web page or channel by clicking the Unsubscribe button
- Read the subscription summary information which includes change notification method, what to download, the schedule, and the date and results of the last update
- Add or update login information if the page or channel requires a username and password

Note that you can't modify the subscription's URL or title in this dialog box. To change the title, you can change the Name field in the Subscriptions Explorer, but changing the URL would require going into the file where the subscription information is kept and making the update there.

The Receiving tab, shown in Figure 20.17, enables you to make changes to your notification method and whether or not Internet Explorer should download content for offline viewing.

 You can specify what kinds of files you do or don't want to download by clicking the Advanced button in the Downloading section of the Receiving tab. This calls up a dialog box where you can filter images, video and sound files, ActiveX controls, Java applets, and channel screen savers. You can also give your subscriptions a higher update priority and set an upper bound on the amount of information downloaded per update.

FIG. 20.17

The Receiving tab controls how you find out about updated subscriptions and what content is downloaded during an update.

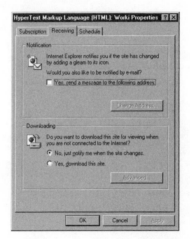

Finally, the Schedule tab (see Figure 20.18) presents you with the three main types of update schedule: AutoSchedule, Custom Schedule, and Update Now (which corresponds to the Manual option you saw earlier in the chapter). You can switch a subscription's update schedule from one to the other from here, but keep in mind that you should base your schedule decision, at least in part, on what kind of Internet connectivity you have. You can also click the Update Now button to have the selected subscription updated on the spot.

FIG. 20.18
Need to update a
subscription more
frequently? Change its
schedule from this
dialog box.

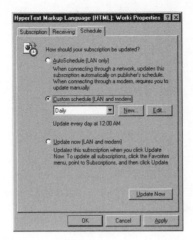

CHAPTER 21

Premium Channels

The onset of content push delivery was bound to happen. Consider mail delivery: Once it was perfected, companies everywhere began to use the medium to reach potential customers, sending their product and service information directly to people's mailboxes. The same is true for the telephone, as anyone who has been called by a tele-marketer knows. What happened with both of these media is that someone got the idea to make the use of them *active* to get the word out, rather than waiting for users of the media to write or call for information.

The same now holds true for the Web. Content providers can now create Web channels in which they broadcast their information over the Internet, a process commonly referred to as *push delivery* or *Webcasting*. Users then use a client program called a *tuner* to tune in to the Webcast channel and view the content. Initially, tuners were available only as separate programs, but now they are being built right into browsers, allowing users to call up their favorite channels through the same interface that gives them access to the rest of the popular services of the Internet.

This chapter introduces you to Webcasting from two angles. First, you'll learn about it from the user's perspective and see what features Internet Explorer has available to make your Webcast viewing more enjoyable. Additionally, you'll read about the many premium content channels that Microsoft's content provider partners have created.

Understanding push technology and Webcasting

Rather than leaving content on a server and letting users request it, you can employ Webcasting, the act of actively broadcasting your content over the Internet.

Subscribing to and managing channels

You must subscribe to a channel to view its content, and, should the need arise, you may have to change some of the channel's properties as channel content changes.

Tune in to dozens of Web channels

In addition to its capability to take you anywhere on the Web, Internet Explorer can also act as your "Internet television set" and tune you in to one of the many special Webcast channels already in existence.

Preparing your site to be Webcast

Microsoft's Channel Definition Format (CDF) enables Webmasters to use their content to author a channel for their site.

Then, you'll take the perspective of a site administrator and see how you can make your site ready for Webcasting and how to author a channel using Microsoft's Channel Definition Format (CDF).

Are Server Push and Push Delivery the Same Thing?

Though they both have the word "push" in common, server push and push delivery aren't really the same thing. *Server push* is a CGI-driven process that actively pushes content down an open HTTP connection. Once it arrives at the browser, it replaces a set of content that was previously loaded there, presumably to update or refresh it. Many amusing examples of server push have been on the Web, including pages that show pictures of someone's fish tank (with the picture updated every few seconds) or the National Debt Clock, which was updated periodically with a new grand total for the country's debt level. Additionally, in the days before animated GIFs, server push was a valuable way to create animations because it is fairly simple to write a CGI program that sends the component frames of an animation to the browser.

Push delivery refers to the active broadcast of the content on an entire site, rather than a constant update to a specific part of an otherwise static page. Using push delivery doesn't require a special CGI program, though as noted at the start of the chapter, users who want to tune in to a push delivery channel must have a tuner or a browser like Internet Explorer that can act as a tuner.

Using Internet Explorer as a Channel Tuner

Internet Explorer gives you a couple of different ways to look at Webcast channels, depending on whether you have the browser open. If you have Internet Explorer open, the simplest thing to do is to click the Channels button on the toolbar to open the Channels Bar, an area on the left side of the browser window that lists all the channels stored in the Channels subfolder of your Favorites folder (see Figure 21.1). Internet Explorer comes preconfigured with more than 20 channels already organized by topic in the Channels folder.

 As you discover other Webcast channels that you like, you can add them to your list of favorites and place them in the Channels subfolder. Doing so makes the channel available in the Channels bar whenever you call it up.

With the Channels Bar open, changing from one channel to another is simply a matter of clicking the channel you want to watch. In some cases, clicking a channel will reveal a more detailed set of options, meaning that the channel is more like a "channel subfolder" in which you can store channels of a certain type. For example, Figure 21.2 shows that when you select the Entertainment channel, you can choose from Hollywood Online, the AudioNet Channel, and the Comics Channel. You can use these channel subfolders to store favorite channels that you find later.

FIG. 21.1

The Channels Bar is like a remote control for the Internet Explorer tuner.

FIG. 21.2

Some channel selections are menus to even more channel choices.

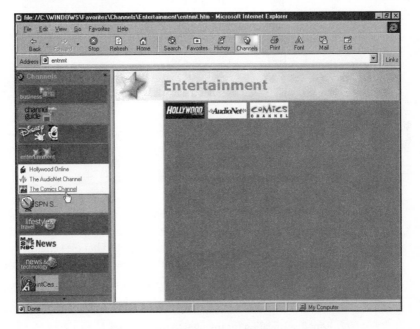

If you haven't fired up Internet Explorer and want to see Webcast channels, click the satellite dish icon on the Windows 95 Task Bar (see Figure 21.3). This icon launches the Active Channel Viewer, a modified version of Internet Explorer that is specifically designed for surfing Web channels. Figure 21.4 shows that the Active Channel Viewer has a Channels Bar on the left side of the screen and room on the right side for channel content. Note in the figure that the standard Internet Explorer toolbars are available along the top left of the screen. You can also right-click any point along the bar across the top of the screen and get a context-sensitive menu with which you can display the Internet Explorer menus, the Address Bar, and the Links Bar. You can also choose to Auto Hide the top bar when your mouse pointer isn't over it.

FIG. 21.3

You launch the Active Channel Viewer by clicking the View Channels button on the Task Bar.

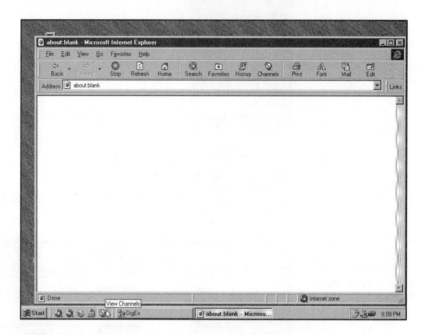

 TIP If you don't like the Active Channel Viewer interface, just minimize the Channel Viewer's window and then maximize it, which makes the Channel Viewer revert back to the standard Internet Explorer interface (see Figure 21.5).

One important thing to realize when you visit a channel for the first time is that you have to subscribe to the channel. Many of Microsoft's channel content providers make subscribing simple by placing a button on the main screen that you can click to initiate the subscription (see Figure 21.6). The Channel Subscription Wizard handles channel subscriptions by walking you through the components, including the following, of a channel subscription:

- Whether you want to download the channel content for offline viewing
- Whether you want the Channel Screen Saver to display content from the channel
- E-mail notification for updates to the channel
- How frequently you want the subscription updated

You have the option of AutoScheduling your subscription updates, setting up a custom updating schedule, or updating the subscriptions manually (see Figure 21.7).

FIG. 21.4

The Active Channel Viewer is another way of looking at what's in your Channels folder.

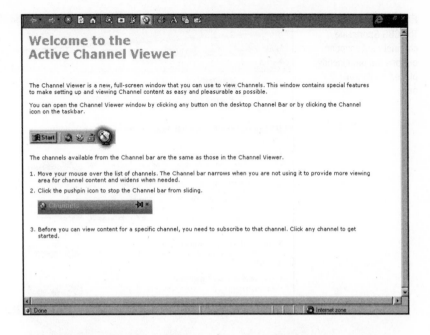

FIG. 21.5

The Active Channel Viewer is really just Internet Explorer dressed up a little differently.

Part

IV

Ch

21

FIG. 21.6

The CBS SportsLine channel's subscription buttons are prominently placed on its main page.

FIG. 21.7

When subscribing to a channel, you may choose how often the subscription is updated.

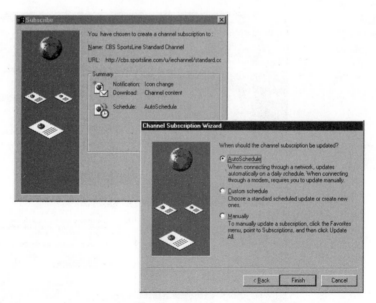

CAUTION

Some channels will attempt to write cookies to your hard drive when you subscribe to them. If you're concerned about cookies on your machine, instruct Internet Explorer to warn you whenever a site or channel tries to place a cookie on your hard drive. You do this by choosing View, Options, and selecting the Advanced tab. There, you'll find a section on cookies in which you can specify how you want Internet Explorer to handle them.

Once you've subscribed to a channel, you may need to do a little maintenance on it to keep things as current as possible. The easiest way to handle these tasks is by right-clicking the channel on the Channel Bar that needs attention and selecting options from the context-sensitive menu that appears. A number of the helpful options include the following:

- **Update Now**   When you subscribe to a channel, you tell Internet Explorer how frequently you want the channel to be updated. If you don't want to wait until the next scheduled update, you can choose the Update Now option to instruct Internet Explorer to download the changes to the channel.

- **Refresh**   The Refresh option resets the information stored in the channel shortcut on your hard drive. This is useful, for example, when a channel changes its URL. Once you get to the new URL, you can choose the Refresh option so that the new address is stored in the shortcut file.

- **View Source**   This option enables you to see the markup code behind the channel. As you'll see later in this chapter, this is the code that is defined by Microsoft's Channel Definition Format.

- **Properties**   A channel's Properties dialog box has five different tabs in it, though the three in which you're probably most interested are the Subscription, Receiving, and Schedule tabs. From the Subscription tab, you can unsubscribe from the channel or update your channel login name and password. You can activate e-mail notification in the event of content change on the channel from the Receiving tab, as well as download the entire channel for offline viewing. Options on the Schedule tab enable you to vary the update schedule for your channel subscription.

N O T E   Remember that you should use the AutoSchedule update option only when you're connected to a LAN that has constant Internet access. If you're dialing from home, make sure you choose either the Custom Schedule or the Update Now option.

Now that you know how to subscribe to and maintain channels, it's time to investigate some of the channels Microsoft has developed with its Webcasting partners. The next section is your "TV Guide" for the Web and covers each of the premium channels that Microsoft and its partners have established.

Part

IV

Ch

21

Microsoft's Premium Channels

You wouldn't turn on your television set if there were nothing on. Knowing this, Microsoft put several Webcasting channels in place before the production release of Internet Explorer ever became available. Indeed, Internet Explorer comes configured with a Channels folder under the Favorites menu that contains links to the more than twenty channels that Microsoft's content-providing partners support.

The Channels folder is subdivided into several areas in an effort to group channels with similar content together. The subdivisions with which Internet Explorer comes include the following:

- Business
- Channel Guide
- Disney
- Entertainment
- ESPN SportsZone
- Lifestyle and Travel
- MSNBC
- News and Technology
- PointCast Network
- Sports
- The Microsoft Network
- Warner Brothers

As you discover other Webcast channels that you like, you're free to store links to those channels in one of the previously mentioned folders, or you can set up your own custom folder. For now, you can get started with your Web channel surfing by checking out the channels for which Internet Explorer has links. These channels are profiled throughout the course of this section.

Business

The Business folder provides you with the following five links to channels that can help you with investing and personal finance information:

- ***The Wall Street Journal* Interactive Edition** An online version of the immensely popular daily paper, *The Wall Street Journal* Interactive Edition features continually updated financial news, stock prices, and coverage of events that have an impact on the business world. You can even download a screensaver that shows you how the Dow Jones Industrial Average has grown over the past 10 years and tells you the reasons for its growth. Note in Figure 21.8 that there are buttons with which you can subscribe to the channel and add the channel to your Active Desktop.

FIG. 21.8
The Wall Street Journal Interactive Edition keeps you apprised of financial happenings around the world.

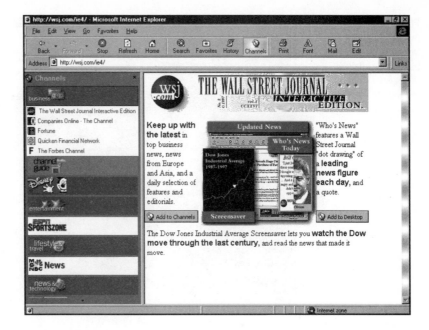

- **Companies Online: The Channel** is a service of Dun and Bradstreet, a firm noted for its analysis of corporations and industry groups, and Lycos, the popular search engine. You can use this channel to gather information about any one of the Fortune 1000 companies that Dun and Bradstreet tracks.

- *Fortune* The famous financial magazine is now available via a Webcast channel. Focused on information of interest to investors, *Fortune* provides business news and analysis with investment tips to help you maximize your returns.

- **Quicken Financial Network** Quicken's renown stems from its popular PC software product for personal finance management. Now Quicken sponsors the Quicken Financial Network Channel, a place where you can read the latest financial news and check up on your favorite stocks (see Figure 21.9).

- **The *Forbes* Channel** Drawing from *Forbes* magazine and other Forbes publications, the Forbes channel puts a wealth of information and business tools at your disposal. You can browse the list of the Richest People in the World or you can check the Mutual Fund Information Center for tips on how to choose the fund that's right for you.

Channel Guide

The Channel Guide is a Microsoft service that keeps you up-to-date on any new channels that become available. When you first tune in to the Channel Guide, you'll see the "Random Preview Page" that features a channel that recently has come online (see Figure 21.10). You can also check out the What's New section for other channels that just started broadcasting and the Coming Soon section for channels that are expected to be operational in the near future.

Part
IV

Ch
21

FIG. 21.9
Quicken Financial Network's Watch List contains ticker symbols for stocks that you want to track.

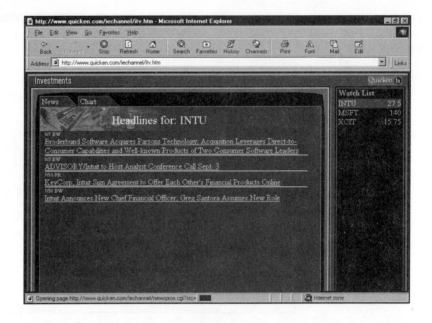

FIG. 21.10
New channels are starting all the time. Tune in to the Channel Guide to find out where they are.

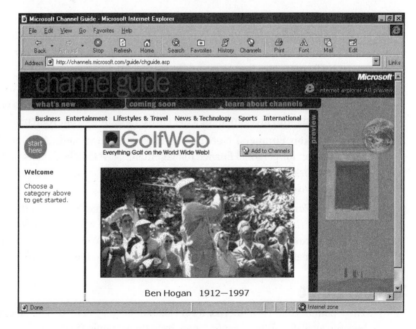

The Channel Guide also comes with a set of topic headings like Business, Entertainment, Sports, and so on. Many of these topics are expanded versions of the same topics that were preconfigured in your Internet Explorer browser. Be sure to check these topics and, if there's a new channel there that you like, you can add it to the appropriate Internet Explorer folder.

Disney

Walt probably never imagined having a Web channel named after him, but he does! The magical world of Disney goes online with four major content areas to check out:

- **Daily Blast** This section is devoted to fun, games, and activities (see Figure 21.11). The blast is new everyday, so be sure to set up your subscription accordingly.

- **Disney.com** This area is a Webcast version of the popular Disney Web site. Check the link to Disney Interactive for links to games and activities that the kids will enjoy.

- **Family.com** Disney sponsors **www.family.com**, a site devoted to things the whole family can enjoy. Choose from food, travel, computing, parenting, and learning.

- **Shopping** If you can't make it to your local Disney Store, fear not! The Shopping part of the Disney channel takes you to the Disney Store Online where you can choose from clothes, books, videos, CDs, animation art, toys, and other gifts.

FIG. 21.11

Get blasted with your Disney Daily Blast!

N O T E An important thing to know about the Disney channel is that it will download Macromedia's Flash and Shockwave products to enhance your viewing experience. On your first visit, these two components will be downloaded and installed automatically if they are not detected on your machine. This process can take a while, so be patient during the download.

Flash and Shockwave are useful when viewing other channels and Web sites as well, so waiting for them to download and install is generally worth it. If you don't want these components to load, click the "Continue" link on the screen to tell you whether Flash and Shockwave are loading, but keep in mind that without them, you will not be able to appreciate fully all the content on the channel. ■

Part

IV

Ch

21

Entertainment

The Entertainment folder comes with three preset channels, including the following:

- **Hollywood Online**   Feel like checking up on your favorite movie star? The Hollywood Online channel takes you behind the scenes of today's blockbusters as well as yesterday's favorites. You can take a multimedia tour of selected films by checking this channel's online photos, video clips, and audio clips. If you want to know what's playing in your area, check the ShowTimes option to get a list of movies being shown in your zip code.

- **The AudioNet Channel**   Turn on your speakers for this channel. The AudioNet Channel gives you access to CDs, continuously streamed music, audio books, and live TV and radio. AudioNet also brings you news and opinions on a wealth of subjects of popular interest.

- **The Comics Channel**   Delve into the hilarious world of the Universal Press Syndicate's (UPS) comic strip characters. You can choose to have strips like *FoxTrot*, *Garfield*, *Adam*, or *Doonesbury* delivered to you daily or made part of your Active Desktop. Additionally, you can purchase merchandise with your favorite characters on it and check UPS archives to catch up on older strips.

FIG. 21.12

Garfield comes to your desktop thanks to the Comics Channel from Universal Press Syndicate.

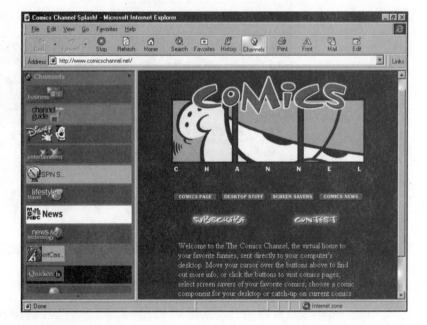

ESPN SportsZone

The latest scores, stories, and highlights are pushed right to your desktop when you tune in to the ESPN SportsZone channel. Scores are continuously displayed in the left side of the channel window (see Figure 21.13) and each score contains a link to a story about the game as it progresses or to a recap of the game if it is over. The large window in the center presents the top sports headlines and story synopses. To receive more detail on any of the stories, click its accompanying link. Plus, be on the lookout for links to fantasy sports leagues and to channel-sponsored games and contests!

FIG. 21.13
Go team! The ESPN SportsZone is a Webcasted version of the well-known television show and Web site.

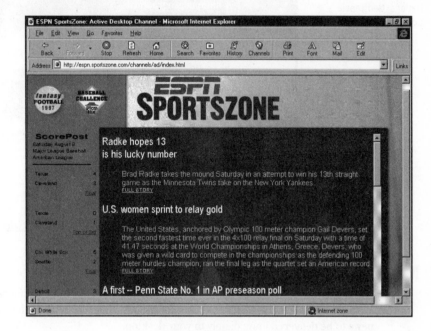

Lifestyle and Travel

The Lifestyle and Travel folder comes set up with two channels initially, though both are first rate!

- **Epicurious Food and Travel**   Epicurious actually brings you two different channels in one—one for food and one for travel. The Food channel is a great place to find gourmet recipes and tips for putting on a fabulous dinner party. If you're planning a vacation, the Travel channel has some great ideas for exotic trips that won't wreck your budget.

- *National Geographic*   *National Geographic* has ported its **nationalgeographic.com** site as a Web channel as well. Here, you can read feature articles from the current issue of *National Geographic* magazine, learn about the activities of the National Geographic Society, or shop the NGS Store, where you can pick up some of the highly detailed maps for which the Society is famous (see Figure 21.14).

Part
IV

Ch
21

FIG. 21.14
Books, maps, globes, and other geography-related merchandise waits for you at the National Geographic Society's online store.

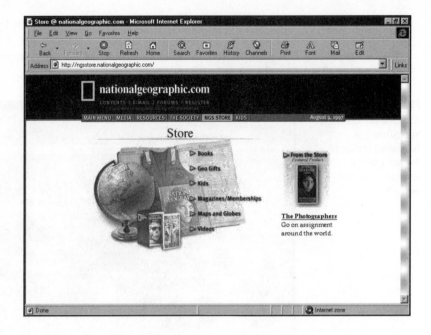

MSNBC

A joint venture of Microsoft and NBC, MSNBC is the first 24-hour online news source. A Webcast channel is the perfect medium for MSNBC because it allows for updated and breaking news to be delivered immediately to your desktop.

When you subscribe to MSNBC, you'll find that the MSNBC folder on your Channel Bar expands to include selections on World News, Commerce, Sports, Science and Technology, Life Today, and Opinion. Clicking any of these options reveals the component articles in the section. The icons used in rendering these topic-specific areas of the MSNBC folder very much resemble those used in a standard Windows application's Help section (see Figure 21.15)

News and Technology

The News and Technology folder is a little heavy with channels related to technology, but the sole news source is a biggie: *The New York Times*. These are the channel links you'll find:

- **CMPnet** CMP is well-known for its host of Internet-related print publications, as well as its online technology information site TechWeb. On the CMPnet channel, you can browse TechWeb or CMP's NetGuide, a site designed to help you find the best Web sites related to a particular topic. CMP also hosts File Mine, a one-stop shop for downloadable software, and GamePower, a site devoted to the PC gamer.

- **Live *Wired*** If you've read *Wired* magazine, you'll find Live Wired to be just as hip and irreverent. The Live Wired channel brings you news stories, factoids, and information—all with a technological edge.

FIG. 21.15
When you update your MSNBC channel, it refreshes the list of stories available under each major content section.

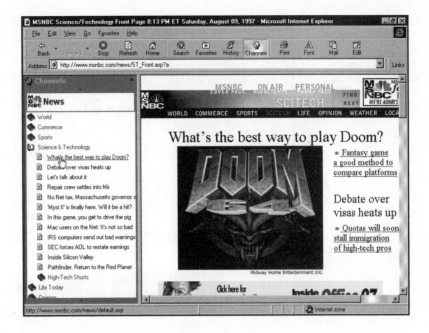

- **The CNET Channel**   CNET is a popular network of sites for technology enthusiasts. The CNET Channel brings together all the component CNET sites, including **cnet.com**, **news.com**, **gamecenter.com**, **mediadome.com**, **download.com**, **shareware.com**, **activex.com**, **search.com**, and **buydirect.com**.

- *The New York Times*   The most respected of all daily newspapers joins the ranks of the Webcasters by producing *The New York Times* channel. Here, you can check the latest headlines and related articles (see Figure 21.16), browse **www.nytimes.com**, and check some of the extras that NYT makes available only over the Web.

  N O T E   The New York Times site requires that you have a user login and password to view content. You can register for your login name online and even store it as a cookie on your computer. ■

- **ZDNet**   ZDNet, produced by Ziff-Davis, brings you the insight and experience of hundreds of computer journalists. Technology lovers can find product reviews, information about the Web, games, and a software download library. Macintosh users will be pleased to know that there is an entire section dedicated to news, tips, tricks, and software for the Mac.

PointCast Network

PointCast was the leader in desktop newscasting and had a news service in place more than a year ago. Now PointCast is sponsoring the PointCast Business Network channel, where you choose from more than 20 different news sources to create your own personalized news channel.

Part
IV

Ch
21

FIG. 21.16
Continuously updated headlines scroll over the New York Times' masthead, giving you instant access to the latest happenings.

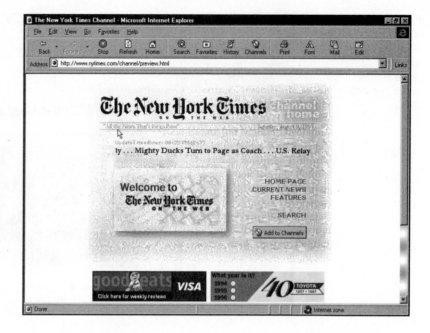

To start with the PointCast channel, you'll need to download some ActiveX Controls that support its incorporation to your Active Desktop. Once you download the controls, you'll be prompted to register with PointCast by providing some basic demographic information. Finally, you can choose the news sources you want to provide information to your PointCast channel. Figure 21.17 shows that you can choose from providers of news, technology, business, living, and regional information.

 T I P Make sure your Internet Explorer security options allow for downloading and use of ActiveX Controls if you want to be able to view the PointCast channel.

Sports

If watching sports on a television channel isn't enough, you can tune in to one of Internet Explorer's three preset sports channels, which include the following:

- **CBS SportsLine** CBS Sports brings you two different channels to which you can subscribe and also gives you two desktop components that bring you all the sports scores and headlines in real time. The SportsLine Active Standard Channel covers all sports by bringing you the stories, scores, and statistics from each game. If you're interests are more focused, you can subscribe to the SportsLine Active Personalized Channel, with which you can configure to track only your favorite teams.

  The available SportsLine Desktop Components are the cyber-equivalent of the scrolling headlines and scores that you see on your television. The Flash News Desktop Component is refreshed every two hours with the latest sports headlines, and the ScoreCenter Desktop Component keeps you on top of the scores of any games that your favorite teams are playing.

■ **ESPN SportsZone**   This channel is a duplicate link for the ESPN SportsZone you read about earlier (refer to Figure 21.13).

■ **MSNBC Sports**   MSNBC returns, though this time with a focus on sports. If you've already subscribed to MSNBC, you'll have access to Sports news in the MSNBC subfolders (refer to Figure 21.25), and you may want to pass on a subscription to this channel. Conversely, if you're a sports nut who hasn't subscribed to MSNBC, this is an ideal channel to which to subscribe.

FIG. 21.17
You build your PointCast news channel from more than 20 different news sources.

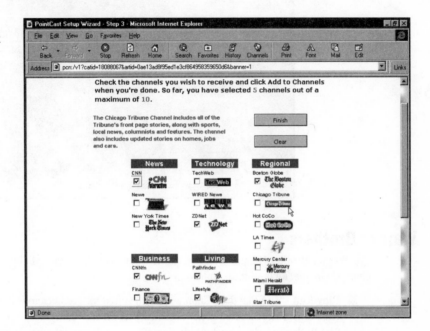

The Microsoft Network

Microsoft isn't just encouraging other corporations to produce Webcasting channels, it is doing it itself as well. The Microsoft Network (MSN) channel gives you access to seven major content areas of the MSN Web site, including

■ News

■ Discovery

■ Entertainment

■ Self

■ Travel

■ Local

■ Custom (for customizing your MSN experience)

Part
IV
Ch
21

Figure 21.18 shows you the Self main page, a repository of information to help you with the "necessities of life."

FIG. 21.18
Tune in to the Microsoft Network for the scoop on just about anything.

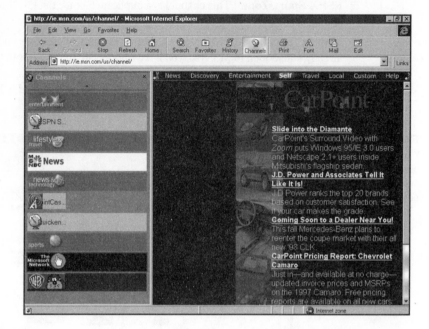

Warner Brothers

The Warner Brothers channel, called the Warner Brothers Entertaindom, is actually three channels in one, including the following:

- **Playdom** The Playdom Channel is well-suited for kids because it covers the world of Warner Brothers animated features like Bugs Bunny and the Animaniacs (see Figure 21.19). You can also check Animation 101 to see how cartoons are created and even send Looney Tunes Web Card to a friend.

- **Screendom** Warner Brothers feature films and television shows are the cornerstone of the Screendom Channel. Go behind the scenes of your favorite blockbusters to meet the cast, directors, and producers or to learn more about popular weekly shows like "ER," "Friends," and "Babylon 5."

- **Tunedom** Warner Brothers is also known for its record labels and the Tunedom Channel focuses on Warner Brothers artists and their latest releases. For the best experience with the Tunedom Channel, you should make sure you have Microsoft NetShow installed because many of the previews are done with streamed audio and video.

FIG. 21.19
The Warner Brothers Playdom channel allows WB animated features to invade your desktop.

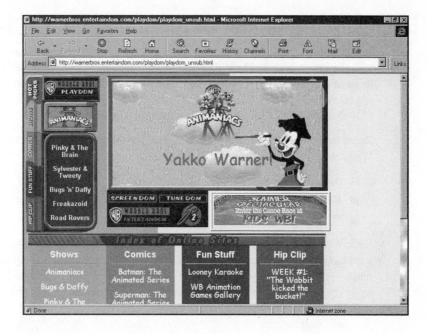

The channels covered in this section are only the beginning. Microsoft is working with many other content providers to set them up with a Webcast channel. Some of the new channels that are in place include

- *Better Homes and Gardens*
- Black Entertainment Television
- Discovery Channel Online
- Dow Jones Markets
- E! Online
- Excite
- Gartner Group
- Happy Puppy
- LEXIS-NEXIS
- MTV Online
- Paramount Digital Entertainment
- *Rolling Stone Magazine*
- Science Channel
- Women's Wire

Be sure to check the Channel Guide frequently to see what new channels are being made live each day.

Part
IV
Ch
21

Microsoft's Channel Definition Format (CDF)

In the course of subscribing to some channels, you may have seen some file names that ended with the extension .cdf. These files are Channel Definition Format (CDF) files and are at the heart of Internet Explorer Webcasting. Microsoft developed the CDF standard so that content providers could quickly and easily author Webcast channels. This section introduces you to CDF and how you can use it to create a channel of your own.

Recall from Chapter 20, "Subscriptions," that there are three levels to Internet Explorer Webcasting:

- Basic Webcasting
- Managed Webcasting
- "True" Webcasting

Basic Webcasting refers to the use of subscriptions. A user subscribes to a site and Internet Explorer proactively checks the site for updates. If there has been an update, the browser notifies you and gives you the option to visit the updated page. This type of Webcasting is not really "push" technology because it is the browser, on instructions from the user, that goes on to the Internet and scans for changed content, rather than the changed content that a server to the user's desktop pushes.

Managed Webcasting is where CDF comes in. By allowing the content developer to decide what content to deliver and when, the situation becomes more akin to a television station making decisions about a broadcast schedule. Accordingly, sites whose content is managed in this way are referred to as *channels*. Site administrators create channels out of their sites by simply authoring a CDF file to support the channel. No change to the HTML files that comprise the site are necessary.

CDF, a markup language based on the widely supported Extensible Markup Language (XML), is intended to be an open, scaleable solution for creating managed content channels. A CDF file provides a map of the information on a site, grouped into logical categories. Along with the information map, the CDF file also specifies which information should be Webcast and when, giving a site administrator complete control over what content becomes part of the channel. The basic elements of CDF are discussed over the next several sections.

The <*CHANNEL*> Element

The <CHANNEL> element or tag is used to define a channel in a CDF file. The <CHANNEL> element is a container tag, meaning that it has a companion tag, </CHANNEL>. All content between these two tags go toward defining the properties of the channel.

The <CHANNEL> tag can take several different attributes, as shown in Table 21.1.

Table 21.1   Attributes of the <*CHANNEL*> Tag

Attribute	Purpose
BASE="url"	Specifies the base URL of the channel (for resolving relative references later in the CDF file)
HREF="url"	Denotes the channel's cover page, a document that prompts the user to subscribe to the channel
LEVEL="n"	Specifies how many levels below the cover page the browser should look for important content

Of the three attributes in Table 21.1, only HREF is really required. The default value of LEVEL is 0.

One important thing to note is that you can nest <CHANNEL> tags, meaning you can have one <CHANNEL></CHANNEL> pair inside another. By nesting channels, you can set up subchannels to your main channel and better organize your content.

> **N O T E**   A nested <CHANNEL> tag should not have an HREF attribute because subchannels are not permitted to have their own cover page. If you specify a BASE attribute in a nested <CHANNEL> tag, it will override a BASE specified in the parent <CHANNEL> tag. ■

So far, then, if you were setting up a channel, your CDF file might look like the following:

```
<CHANNEL HREF="http://www.myserver.com/channel/subscribe.html" LEVEL=4>
...
</CHANNEL>
```

As you might guess, there's still some work to do. Specifically, you need to specify the content that goes into the channel and how frequently it should be updated. Before getting in the CDF elements that handle those duties, though, you have a few other channel housekeeping chores to which to tend—giving the channel a title, an abstract, and a logo.

The <*TITLE*> Element

The CDF <TITLE> tag is much like the corresponding tag in HTML: it is a container tag used to specify the title of the channel. Just as when you title an HTML document, you should make the title sufficiently descriptive without exceeding 40 or so characters. Longer titles will be cut off when displayed on the Internet Explorer title bar.

Once you give your developing channel a title, the corresponding CDF code would look like the following:

```
<CHANNEL HREF="http://www.myserver.com/channel/subscribe.html" LEVEL=4>
  <TITLE>My First Channel</TITLE>
...
</CHANNEL>
```

Next, you'll see how to give your channel an abstract—a detailed statement of what's available to users when they subscribe to your channel.

Part
IV

Ch
21

The *<ABSTRACT>* Element

The abstract of a paper gives a brief overview of the entire paper's content. A channel abstract does the same thing for a Webcasting channel. The <ABSTRACT> tag is a container tag that contains a statement describing the nature of your channel's content. You can be a little more verbose here than you were in the title, but you should still keep your abstract fairly brief because this text will appear in the pop-up box users see when they hold their mouse pointers over the icon for your channel. These pop-up boxes can only accommodate so much text before cutting off the message.

Updating your CDF code to include a title, you might have something like the following:

```
<CHANNEL HREF="http://www.myserver.com/channel/subscribe.html" LEVEL=4>
    <TITLE>My First Channel</TITLE>
    <ABSTRACT>This channel allows you to check out the three major
    content areas of my site: press releases, products, and
    customer service.</ABSTRACT>
...
</CHANNEL>
```

The last housekeeping item to complete before giving the channel some content and an update schedule is to provide a logo that Internet Explorer can use when displaying the channel on the Channel Bar.

The *<LOGO ... />* Element

The <LOGO ... /> tag is a stand-alone tag that tells Internet Explorer where it can find an image file containing the logo for your site. The <LOGO ... /> tag's syntax is

```
<LOGO HREF="url_of_image" STYLE="ICON"¦"IMAGE"/>
```

The HREF attribute is set to the logo image's URL, enabling Internet Explorer to download it. The STYLE attribute denotes the context in which the image will be used. If you choose the ICON style, your image must be 16 pixels wide by 16 pixels high. It will be used with the channel title to identify the channel in places like the Internet Explorer title bar. If you go with the IMAGE style, the image must be 80 pixels wide by 32 pixels high. This type of image is what users see in the Channels Bar.

N O T E   The slash (/) you see at the end of the <LOGO ... /> tag is not a typo. It is part of the syntax for standalone CDF tags. ■

With a logo added, your CDF code now changes to

```
<CHANNEL HREF="http://www.myserver.com/channel/subscribe.html" LEVEL=4>
    <TITLE>My First Channel</TITLE>
    <ABSTRACT>This channel allows you to check out the three major
    content areas of my site: press releases, products, and
    customer service.</ABSTRACT>
    <LOGO HREF="http://www.myserver.com/channel/images/chanlogo.gif"
        STYLE="ICON"/>
...
</CHANNEL>
```

TIP You can specify both an ICON and an IMAGE logo for your channel by having two <LOGO ... /> tags—one with the STYLE set to ICON and the other with STYLE set to IMAGE.

With the channel structure and supporting items in place, you're now ready to put some content in the channel. As noted in the abstract, there are three major content areas to your channel: press releases, products, and customer service. You'll see how to add each of these in the next section.

The <*ITEM*> Element

The <ITEM> element is a container tag that you use to place content in your channel. Each <ITEM></ITEM> tag pair corresponds to one page of your site, so each page you want as part of the channel will need its own <ITEM> tag.

The <ITEM> tag takes the mandatory HREF attribute, which is set equal to the URL of the document you want to include in the channel. You can modify the <ITEM> tag further by using one of the attributes shown in Table 21.2.

Table 21.2 Attributes of the <*ITEM*> Tag

Attribute	Purpose
HREF="url"	Specifies the URL of the document to add to the channel
LASTMOD="date"	Denotes when the document was last modified; date is given in ISO 8601:1998 format (YYYY-MM-DDTHH:MM+HHMM)
LEVEL="n"	Tells the browser how many levels below the document it should look and precache content
PRECACHE="YES" ¦ "NO"	Indicates whether the browser should precache content

N O T E The T in the ISO 8601:1998 date format separates date and time information. To learn more about ISO 8601:1998, consult **http://www.mcs.vuw.ac.nz/comp/Technical/ SGML/doc/iso8601/ISO8601.html.** ■

N O T E If you set PRECACHE to NO, Internet Explorer will ignore the LEVEL attribute. ■

You read that <ITEM> is a container tag, so you may wonder what you can put between <ITEM> and </ITEM>. The answer is that you can give the item its own title, abstract, and logo using the tags discussed in the previous few sections. Thus, a full-blown <ITEM> specification might look like

```
<ITEM HREF="http://www.myserver.com/press/index.html">
    <TITLE>Press Room</TITLE>
    <ABSTRACT>Press Releases About the Company</ABSTRACT>
```

Part

IV

Ch

21

```
    <LOGO HREF="http://www.myserver.com/channel/images/press.gif"
    STYLE="ICON"/>
</ITEM>
```

If you build an <ITEM> like the preceding tag for the other two areas of your site, your CDF code now looks like

```
<CHANNEL HREF="http://www.myserver.com/channel/subscribe.html" LEVEL=4>
    <TITLE>My First Channel</TITLE>
    <ABSTRACT>This channel allows you to check out the three major
    content areas of my site: press releases, products, and
    customer service.</ABSTRACT>
    <LOGO HREF="http://www.myserver.com/channel/images/chanlogo.gif"
        STYLE="ICON"/>

    <ITEM HREF="http://www.myserver.com/press/index.html">
        <TITLE>Press Room</TITLE>
        <ABSTRACT>Press Releases About the Company</ABSTRACT>
        <LOGO HREF="http://www.myserver.com/channel/images/press.gif"
        STYLE="ICON"/>
    </ITEM>

<ITEM HREF="http://www.myserver.com/products/index.html">
        <TITLE>What We Make</TITLE>
        <ABSTRACT>The Company Product Line</ABSTRACT>
        <LOGO HREF="http://www.myserver.com/channel/images/products.gif"
        STYLE="ICON"/>
    </ITEM>

<ITEM HREF="http://www.myserver.com/service/index.html">
        <TITLE>At Your Service</TITLE>
        <ABSTRACT>Our Customer Service area is standing by to help.
        </ABSTRACT>
        <LOGO HREF="http://www.myserver.com/channel/images/press.gif"
        STYLE="ICON"/>
    </ITEM>
...
</CHANNEL>
```

Now that you have content in your channel, there's one issue left to complete: setting up the update schedule.

The *<SCHEDULE>* Element

The <SCHEDULE> tag is a container tag that specifies the update schedule for content you place in your channels. You can specify a <SCHEDULE> for the entire channel by placing it after the top-most <CHANNEL> tag and before the first nested <CHANNEL> tag. You can also assign a <SCHEDULE> to each <ITEM> by placing the <SCHEDULE></SCHEDULE> tag pair inside the <ITEM></ITEM> tag pair.

The <SCHEDULE> tag takes two attributes: STARTDATE indicates the date on which the update schedule should take effect and ENDDATE indicates when the schedule should terminate. Both STARTDATE and ENDDATE are set equal to dates in the ISO 8601:1988 format (YYYY-MM-DD).

Between the `<SCHEDULE></SCHEDULE>` tags, you can have one of three different stand-alone tags:

- `<INTERVALTIME ... />` Specifies the time interval between updates
- `<EARLIESTIME ... />` Indicates the earliest time during an interval that an update can occur
- `<LATESTTIME ... />` Indicates the latest time during an interval that an update can occur

Each of the preceding stand-alone tags can take one of the following attributes: DAY, HOUR, or MIN. You set these attributes to the number of days (values of 1 through 7), hours (values of 1 through 23), or minutes (values of 1 through 59) that are appropriate to your scheduling needs. For example, to do an update every half hour, you would use

```
<INTERVALTIME MIN=30/>
```

To ensure that an update happens sometime in the 10 minutes before each hour, you would use

```
<INTERVALTIME HOUR=1/>
<EARLIESTTIME MIN=50/>
<LATESTTIME HOUR=1/>
```

Inserting a schedule that calls for a weekly update every Monday morning at exactly 8 a.m. into the channel you're building, you'd have the following code:

```
<CHANNEL HREF="http://www.myserver.com/channel/subscribe.html" LEVEL=4>
   <TITLE>My First Channel</TITLE>
   <ABSTRACT>This channel allows you to check out the three major
   content areas of my site: press releases, products, and
   customer service.</ABSTRACT>
   <LOGO HREF="http://www.myserver.com/channel/images/chanlogo.gif"
       STYLE="ICON"/>

   <SCHEDULE STARTDATE="1997-10-06"> <!-- 10/6 is a Monday -->
      <INTERVALTIME DAY=7/>  <!- Weekly update -->
      <EARLIESTTIME DAY=7 HOUR=8/> <!-- Not earlier than 8 on Monday -->
      <LATESTTIME DAY=7 HOUR=8/>  <!-- Not later than 8 on Monday -->
   </SCHEDULE>

   <ITEM HREF="http://www.myserver.com/press/index.html">
      <TITLE>Press Room</TITLE>
      <ABSTRACT>Press Releases About the Company</ABSTRACT>
      <LOGO HREF="http://www.myserver.com/channel/images/press.gif"
       STYLE="ICON"/>
   </ITEM>

<ITEM HREF="http://www.myserver.com/products/index.html">
      <TITLE>What We Make</TITLE>
      <ABSTRACT>The Company Product Line</ABSTRACT>
      <LOGO HREF="http://www.myserver.com/channel/images/products.gif"
       STYLE="ICON"/>
   </ITEM>
```

```
<ITEM HREF="http://www.myserver.com/service/index.html">
    <TITLE>At Your Service</TITLE>
    <ABSTRACT>Our Customer Service area is standing by to help.
    </ABSTRACT>
    <LOGO HREF="http://www.myserver.com/channel/images/press.gif"
     STYLE="ICON"/>
</ITEM>
...
</CHANNEL>
```

The preceding code completes your channel setup. Note that you did not have to recode your content in any way. This is a key feature of CDF—it is content independent so there is no need to overhaul your content as you would need to do with channel authoring for other software.

Other, more advanced CDF tags have been proposed to support software distribution. Because Webcasting is becoming an important way for businesses to distribute new software releases on corporate intranets, you can expect that these tags will earn widespread support.

N O T E Microsoft has submitted its CDF specification to the World Wide Web Consortium (W3C) for consideration as a standard. You can view the CDF spec online at **http://www.w3.org/ pub/WWW/TR/NOTE-CDFsubmit.html**.

Additionally, Microsoft maintains an updated list of CDF elements at **http://www.microsoft.com/ standards/cdf.htm**. ▨

CDF-Compliant Software

So that users can fully appreciate the work you put into creating your channel, they must have a client program that is CDF compliant. Internet Explorer is an obvious choice for this compliance, but other push technology vendors have embraced CDF as the way to go for authoring managed content channels. Some of these companies include the following:

- AirMedia
- BackWeb
- DataChannel
- FirstFloor
- Torso
- Wayfarer

Additionally, PointCast has put its support behind the CDF specification. Netscape's Netcaster can support CDF in a limited way, owing to a less powerful site-crawling scheme. ●

Webmaster Section

CHAPTER 22

HTML Primer

HyperText Markup Language, or HTML, is at the heart of just about every Web document. A document's content is really just words. Imagine these words just sitting in a file in plain-text format. Pretty boring, right? HTML instructions let you dress up the content so that it comes alive and imparts meaning more easily. A reader will most certainly be able to pick out a word in boldface or a centered heading in a sea of text and take these formatted elements to have special significance.

HTML formatting instructions are easy to give. You simply embed them in the informational content. As a browser reads your document's file, it will parse out and execute the HTML instructions and render your content in a nicely formatted way.

This chapter introduces you to the basics of HTML, including how an HTML document is structured and how to apply formatting instructions at the character and block levels. By mastering these fundamental instructions, you'll be able to turn your ordinary, plain-text documents into engaging and interesting Web pages.

Before you dive right into authoring HTML documents, some introductory information is in order. You've already read that HTML formatting instructions are embedded in the informational text of a document. These instructions come in one of two flavors:

The building blocks of HTML

HTML provides formatting instructions to a browser in two important ways: tags and entities.

HTML documents have a set structure

Every HTML file should contain a few key tags that set up the different sections of the document.

Formatting characters and words

HTML character formatting can indicate either a typographic effect or the meaning of the characters in the context of the document.

Breaking up your document

HTML provides for ways to break up large blocks of text and make your document easier to read and understand.

- ■ **Tags**   HTML tags are instructions that are contained between angle brackets (or "greater-than" and "less-than" signs). Tags govern the application of a particular formatting effect or the placement of an element on a page.

- ■ **Entities**   HTML entities are used to place special characters in a document. These characters include those that are not on a standard keyboard and those that are reserved to support HTML syntax. Entities begin with an ampersand (&) and end with a semicolon (;).

Each type of instruction is discussed in greater detail in the following sections. ■

Tags Are the Basis of HTML

HTML tags are the type of instruction you'll use more often than not. Dozens of different tags do everything from italicizing text to placing a graphic to setting up a framed layout. You'll learn about many of these tags as you progress through the next four or five chapters, but there are some general things to know that will help you understand these tags a little better.

Each HTML tag starts with a less-than sign (<) and ends with a greater-than sign (>). Between these two characters, you will always find a keyword that indicates the major function of the tag. For example, the IMG keyword in the <IMG> tag indicates that the tag is placing an image in the document. By varying the keyword between the less-than and greater-than signs, you can create a wide variety of formatting effects.

Container and Stand-Alone Tags Provide Basic Formatting Instructions

Many HTML tags, particularly those that produce special formatting, occur in pairs. The first tag in the pair activates the effect and the second tag in the pair terminates it. For example, you might use the <I> tag to turn on italics formatting. When you're ready to turn it off, you place </I> tag in the document. The slash (/) before the I keyword means to discontinue the effect controlled by that keyword. The first tag in a pair is often called the *opening tag* and the second is called the *closing tag*. Tags that occur in pairs are also referred to as *container tags* because they flank and contain the text being formatted. For example, in the following HTML code:

```
HTML tags are <I>very important</I>.
```

the <I> and </I> tags contain the text "very important."

Other HTML tags occur by themselves and are called *stand-alone tags*. These tags usually govern one-time formatting instructions like the placement of an image, a horizontal line, or a line break.

Tag Attributes Change the Way a Tag Works

Beyond the keyword that each HTML tag is obliged to have, you can also include attributes with some tags to modify the effect of the tag. Consider the <HR> tag, which places a single horizontal line across the width of a page. This tag has several attributes that you can use to change how the line looks. For example, you could use the WIDTH attribute to make the line reach only halfway across the screen (WIDTH=50%) or the SIZE attribute to modify the thickness of the line (SIZE=4; the default size is 1).You don't need to set other attributes to anything. The NOSHADE attribute of the <HR> tag removes the drop-shadow that a browser will typically render behind a horizontal line.

Attributes are generally what make HTML authoring fun and interesting. By tweaking attribute values, you can experiment with different designs in search of that perfect document layout.

 TIP Many HTML authors find it useful to put their tag keywords and attributes in uppercase letters. This makes them stand out more while editing.

Entities Enable You to Display Special Characters

You use HTML entities to place reserved or special characters on a page. The HTML reserved characters and their respective entities are given in Table 22.1. The double quote is reserved for use with specified values for tag attributes. The ampersand (&) is a reserved character because it is used to start each entity.

Table 22.1   HTML Reserved Characters and Their Entities

Character	Appearance	Entity
Less-than sign	<	&lt;
Greater-than sign	>	&gt;
Double quote	"	&quot;
Ampersand	&	&amp;

Whenever you want to use one of these reserved characters in your document, you simply use its entity rather than the character itself. For example, the following HTML:

```
The expression (4&lt;3 &amp; 7&gt;3) is <B>FALSE</B>.
```

results in the screen you see in Figure 22.1.

The other characters that require entities to represent them are those with diacritical marks. HTML uses the ISO-Latin1 character set, which includes characters from the alphabets from the Latin-based languages. Because these characters are not readily available on an English-language keyboard, you must use HTML entities to place them in a document. Table 22.2 lists the foreign language characters you can render in HTML along with their corresponding entities.

FIG. 22.1
Entities enable you to
reproduce characters
that support HTML
syntax.

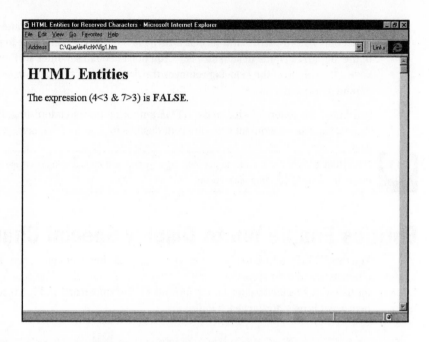

Table 22.2   HTML Entities for Foreign Language Characters

Character	Entity
Æ, æ	&Aelig;, æ
Á, á	Á, á
Â, â	Â, â
À, à	À, à
Å, å	Å, å
Ã, ã	Ã, ã
Ä, ä	Ä, ä
Ç, ç	Ç, ç
Ð, ´	Ð, ð
É, é	É, é
Ê, ê	Ê, ê
È, è	È, è
Ë, ë	Ë, ë
Í, í	Í, í
Î, î	Î, î

Character	Entity
Ì, ì	Ì, ì
Ï, ï	Ï, ï
Ñ, ñ	Ñ, ñ
Ó, ó	Ó, ó
Ô, ô	Ô, ô
Ò, ò	Ò, ò
Ø, ø	Ø, ø
Õ, õ	Õ, õ
Ö, ö	Ö, ö
ß	ß
Ú, ú	Ú, ú
Û, û	Û, û
Ù, ù	Ù, ù
Ü, ü	Ü, ü
Ý, ý	Ý, ý
Ÿ, ÿ	Ÿ, ÿ

In addition to reserved and foreign language characters, you should know about two other types of HTML entities. The first type is using entities to produce any character by referencing its ASCII value. To produce a given character on the browser screen, you can use an entity that starts with an ampersand (&), followed by the pound sign (#), followed by the character's ASCII number, and then ended with a semicolon (;). For example, the copyright symbol (©) has an ASCII value of 169. Thus, its corresponding HTML entity would be **©**.

The other special type of entity is ** **. This entity inserts a *nonbreaking space* wherever it is placed in the document. Nonbreaking spaces are typically placed between two words when you don't want a browser to break a line between those two words.

Marking Up Content

Now that you have an idea about each of the two major HTML components, you're ready to consider how to do HTML markup. The idea is simple: to format a plain-text document for an on-screen presentation, you just insert the HTML tags and entities that support the desired presentation effects right into the document's text file. Thus, HTML is a completely text-based language, meaning that all you really need to compose an HTML document is a plain-text editor, like Notepad. Many document authors opt for a higher-end tool, though, and end up using their favorite word processing package or a program like Microsoft's FrontPage Express, which was specifically written for HTML.

▶ **See** "Quick Start: FrontPage Express and the Internet Publishing Wizard," **p. 73**

▶ **See** "In Depth: FrontPage Express," **p. 185**

As you embed HTML instructions in your plain-text content, you should keep in mind a few rules about how a browser interprets HTML code. These rules follow:

■ **Case doesn't matter in tags**   You can use uppercase, lowercase, or mixed-case lettering in your HTML tags. For example, the tags <IMG>, <img>, and <Img> would all be taken by a browser to mean the same thing. Recall, though, that it is usually a good idea to make you tag keywords and attributes uppercase so they're easier to see while editing.

Case does matter, though, if the text is contained between double quotes. Such text is interpreted literally, meaning that differences between upper- and lowercase will be preserved. This means, for example, that the two <Img> tags

```
<IMG SRC="banner.gif">
```

and

```
<IMG SRC="Banner.gif">
```

would place different images on the browser screen as long as there were differences between the graphic in the **banner.gif** file and the **Banner.gif** file.

■ **Extra white space is ignored**   A browser will recognize the first space character in a sequence of many. After the first, however, the browser will ignore any others.

 TIP   If you need to have multiple spaces rendered on a browser screen, you can force the issue by using nonbreaking space entities (** **) instead of the normal space character.

Browsers also ignore other white space characters like carriage returns and tabs. This can often create confusion for first-time authors who put carriage returns in their HTML source code and wonder why they don't create corresponding line breaks in what they see on-screen. As you'll learn later in the chapter, there is a specific HTML tag you must place in your document wherever you want a line break to occur.

To give yourself a better idea of how these embedded formatting instructions mesh with the informational text of a document, consider Figures 22.2 and 22.3. Figure 22.2 shows a popular Web page on the Internet, and Figure 22.3 is what you would see if you chose View, Source in Internet Explorer. The callouts on the figures will help you identify which tags produce which on-screen effects.

Now that you understand some of the underlying concepts behind HTML, you're ready to start learning the tags you'll use to author your documents.

title   image   table

FIG. 22.2
Yahoo's home page is
well-known to denizens
of the World Wide Web,
but how do you
produce a page like
this?

hypertext

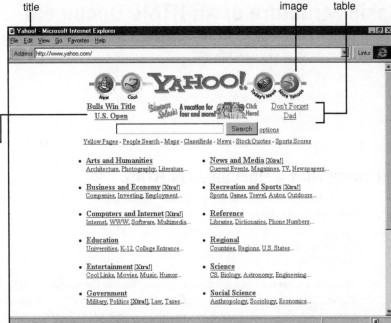

title

FIG. 22.3
Looking at a
document's source
code is a great way to
expand your knowledge
of HTML.

image

start of table

hypertext

Basic Structure of an HTML Document

Every HTML document has a very particular structure. The three main parts of the document you must always include follow:

- The HTML declaration
- The document head
- The document body

The next three sections discuss each of these document components.

Declaring That a Document Is HTML

This component is the easiest part of the three to build into your document. All you need to do is start your document with the <HTML> tag and end it with the </HTML> tag, like so:

```
<HTML>
... rest of the document ...
</HTML>
```

Thus, these two tags will contain everything else in the document. The HTML declaration is important because it alerts the application that has to display the document to what kind of markup is being used. Most browsers already know that they're reading HTML files, so you can get away with leaving these tags out. It is good style to include them, however, and it's an easy matter to build these tags into a standard template that you can use for all of your HTML files.

What Is in the HTML Document Head?

The document head contains information about the document that is typically not for consumption by the person reading the document. You start the document head using the <HEAD> tag and end it with the </HEAD> tag.

You can place many different kinds of information between the <HEAD> and </HEAD> tags, but the single most important item you should always include is a title for the document. Titles appear at the top of the browser window and in favorite place listings. The spider programs that rove the Web and build the databases used by the major search engines also index them. To title your document, place the title between the <TITLE> and </TITLE> tags.

 Make your titles descriptive, but keep them to 40 or fewer characters. This way, you don't run the risk of having a title that is so long that a browser can't display it completely.

Other HTML tags live in the document head as well. Table 22.3 lists those tags you can use between the <HEAD> and </HEAD> tags. The table also tells you what each tag does, though most of them are described in greater detail in subsequent chapters.

Table 22.3   HTML Tags Permissible in the Document Head

Tag	Type	Function
`<BASE>`	Stand-alone	Specifies base document address or frame targeting information
`<META>`	Stand-alone	Allows for specification of document meta-information, such as keywords
`<STYLE>`	Container	Contains style sheet information
`<SCRIPT>`	Container	Contains script code for the browser to execute
`<LINK>`	Stand-alone	Defines linking relationships with other documents
`<ISINDEX>`	Stand-alone	Denotes that the document is a searchable index
`<TITLE>`	Container	Contains a descriptive title for the document

At this point, you can begin to see more of an HTML document's basic structure. From what you know so far, every HTML document should have the following tags:

```
<HTML>
<HEAD>
<TITLE>Descriptive title goes here</TITLE>
... other tags appropriate to the document head ...
</HEAD>
... rest of the document ...
</HTML>
```

All that remains to be done is to fill in the document body. This is where most of the action occurs because the body is what contains the content that the user will actually read.

What's in the HTML Document Body?

The third major part of an HTML document is the body. The body immediately follows the document head and is contained between the `<BODY>` and `</BODY>` tags. The `<BODY>` tag should come immediately after the `</HEAD>` tag and the `</BODY>` tag should occur right before the `</HTML>` tag. It is between these tags that you put the information that users will actually see displayed on-screen and the HTML instructions.

The `<BODY>` tag can also take several attributes that you can set to give your document a more interesting look and feel. These attributes include the following:

- ■ **TEXT** TEXT is set equal to the color in which you want the body text to be rendered. The default color is black.

- ■ **BGCOLOR** If you don't like the standard gray background sported by most browsers, you can set BGCOLOR equal to the color that you want to paint the background.

- ■ **BACKGROUND** If you'd rather use an image for your background, you can do so by setting the BACKGROUND attribute equal to the name of the file you want to create the background. The browser will read in the image file and tile it horizontally and vertically to fill in the entire background. Because the image will be tiled, you should take steps to ensure that it occurs seamlessly. Sloppy tiling will detract from your document's impact.

■ **LINK, VLINK, and ALINK**   These attributes control the colors of unvisited, visited, and active hyperlinks, respectively.

You have two options when setting attributes that control color. The first is to use one of the 16 reserved English-language names to reference a color. The 16 names correspond to the 16 colors in the standard Windows palette. These colors include: AQUA, BLACK, BLUE, FUCHSIA, GRAY, GREEN, LIME, MAROON, NAVY, OLIVE, PURPLE, RED, SILVER, TEAL, YELLOW, and WHITE.

If you want to use a color that's not represented in the preceding list of 16, you'll need to determine the color's RGB (Red/Green/Blue) hexadecimal triplet. The triplet provides a measure of how much red, green, and blue contribute to the desired color. Browsers can take these triplet values and use them to estimate the desired on-screen color. To determine a color's RGB hexadecimal triplet, just follow these steps:

1. Determine the color's red, green, and blue contributions in decimal (base 10) numbers, which is often easy to do in a graphics program. All contribution values will be between 00 and 255.

2. Convert each value to a hexadecimal (base 16) number. The Windows calculator used in scientific mode is particularly handy for this conversion.

3. List the three hexadecimal numbers together in red/green/blue order. The resulting six-digit hexadecimal number represents the color.

For example, suppose your desired color had values of 124 red, 178 green, and 56 blue. Converting each number to hexadecimal, you get 7C red, B2 green, and 86 blue. Joining these values together, you get the hexadecimal triplet

```
7CB286
```

which you can use in a tag like

```
<BODY BACKGROUND="WHITE" TEXT="#7CB286">
```

Once the `<BODY>` and `</BODY>` tags are in place, you can mark up the content between them with other HTML instructions so that the information the user sees is formatted the way you want it to be. The balance of this chapter, along with the next four chapters, are largely devoted to discussing tags that can occur in the document body. But before moving on, we should update our standard document template one last time. Once we include the `<BODY>` and `</BODY>` tags, our template looks like this:

```
<HTML>
<HEAD>
<TITLE>Descriptive title goes here</TITLE>
</HEAD>
<BODY>
... information ...
</BODY>
</HTML>
```

This is a useful piece of code that you can save into a file and use each time you start a new HTML document. Doing so ensures that every document you prepare will be set up with the appropriate structure.

Part V

How to Use Character Formatting

If you never applied any HTML instructions to the content in the document body, it would all appear as plain text. Because that would make for a very boring page, you must be familiar with some ways to format the content. HTML provides you with two basic ways to format your document. You can apply effects at the character level (individual characters or groups of characters) or at the block level (to create block structures like paragraphs or lists). This section focuses on character-level formatting. The final section of the chapter takes you through the different ways to block format your document.

Being Specific About How to Display Text: Physical Styles

The first approach to character-level formatting is to alter the typographical attribute of the text you're formatting. When you apply a style like this, it is referred to as a *physical style*. Table 22.4 summarizes the physical styles available through HTML 3.2 and their effects. Each tag shown is a container tag; closing tags are left out in interest of space.

Table 22.4   HTML 3.2 Physical Styles

Tag	Effect
<B>	Boldface
<BIG>	Text in a large font
<I>	Italics
<SMALL>	Text in a small font
<STRIKE>	Strikethrough text
<SUB>	Subscript
<SUP>	Superscript
<TT>	Typewriter text (fixed-width font)

Some may argue that the <U> tag, which produces an underline style, should be present in Table 22.4 as well. Though the <U> tag is not part of the HTML 3.2 standard, many browsers, including Internet Explorer, support it. You should use the <U> tag with care, however, because most Web users are accustomed to underlined text indicating a hyperlink to another document. If you use the underline style, you may discover that users try to click text that isn't really hypertext.

Figure 22.4 shows some text marked up with some of the physical styles. The corresponding HTML is as follows:

```
When working with type, you should introduce variety into your
documents by using <B>boldface</B>, <I>italics</I>, or
<TT>fixed-width characters</TT>, as appropriate.  You can even
apply these styles to <SUP>superscripts</SUP> and <SUB>subscripts</SUB>.
```

FIG. 22.4

The physical styles create changes in the typographical properties of the text to which they're applied.

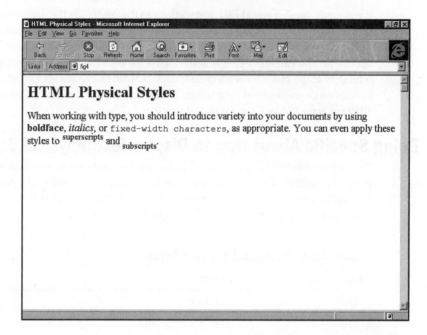

 T I P You can nest physical styles inside each other to combine effects. For example, you can produce bold italics by using `<B><I>bold italics</I></B>`.

Identifying Special Text: Logical Styles

The logical styles are different from the physical styles in that they denote the *meaning* of the text they contain. When rendered on-screen, the logical styles do produce modified typographical properties, but these can vary from browser to browser. Table 22.5 lists the logical styles and how they are rendered by Internet Explorer. Again, each tag is a container tag and closing tags are omitted.

Table 22.5 HTML 3.2 Logical Styles

Tag	Meaning	IE Rendering
`<ADDRESS>`	E-mail or postal address	Italics
`<CITE>`	Citation	Italics

Tag	Meaning	IE Rendering
<CODE>	Computer code	Fixed-width fon
<DFN>	Definition	Boldface
<EM>	Emphasized text	Italics
<KBD>	Keyboard input	Fixed-width font
<SAMP>	Sample text	Fixed-width font
<STRONG>	Strongly emphasized text	Boldface
<VAR>	Variable	Italics

Figure 22.5 shows some text marked up with HTML logical styles, with the corresponding HTML shown in Figure 22.6.

FIG. 22.5

Logical styles indicate the meaning of text, but they do produce differences in on-screen appearance as well.

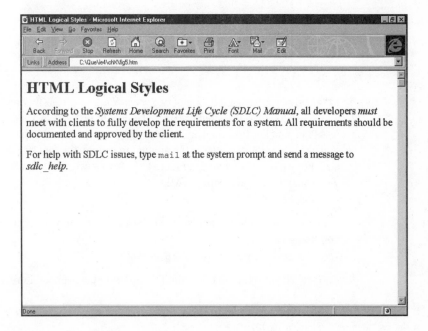

Controlling the Font Using the *<FONT>* Tag

The <FONT> and </FONT> tags were originally introduced as a browser-specific extension to HTML, but they were incorporated into the HTML 3.2 standard and now most browsers can handle these tags, as well as any other. The <FONT> tag can take two attributes:

- **COLOR**   You can change the text color from its default value to whatever you choose by using the COLOR attribute. By setting color equal to one of the reserved color names or a hexadecimal triplet, you instruct a browser to render text in that color. The color reverts back to the default once you apply the </FONT> tag.

FIG. 22.6

The source code for Figure 22.5 reveals the logical style codes used, though you could have used physical style tags to achieve the same on-screen effects.

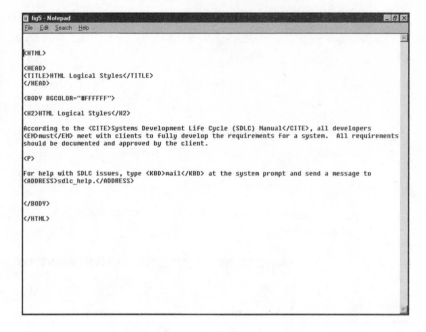

```
<HTML>

<HEAD>
<TITLE>HTML Logical Styles</TITLE>
</HEAD>

<BODY BGCOLOR="#FFFFFF">

<H2>HTML Logical Styles</H2>

According to the <CITE>Systems Development Life Cycle (SDLC) Manual</CITE>, all developers
<EM>must</EM> meet with clients to fully develop the requirements for a system.  All requirements
should be documented and approved by the client.

<P>

For help with SDLC issues, type <KBD>mail</KBD> at the system prompt and send a message to
<ADDRESS>sdlc_help.</ADDRESS>


</BODY>

</HTML>
```

■ **SIZE** SIZE can be used in one of two ways. You can set SIZE equal to a value between 1 and 7, in which 1 is the smallest size. The default text size is 3, so setting size to a value less than 3 makes text smaller, and changing to a size greater than 3 makes text larger. You can also set SIZE equal to the amount to change the font size relative to the current size. For example, to change a font to a size that's two sizes smaller than the current size, you would use the following HTML:

```
<FONT SIZE=-2>two sizes smaller</FONT>
```

Similarly, to increase the font size to one that is three times larger than the current size, you would use

```
<FONT SIZE=+3>three sizes larger</FONT>
```

The size change stays in effect until the </FONT> tag is encountered.

N O T E The default font size is 3, but you can reassign this using the <BASEFONT> tag. For example, the HTML:

```
<BASEFONT SIZE=1>
```

sets the default font size to 1 and all changes to the font size are made relative to the new value. ■

Keeping the Formatting You Already Have with Preformatted Text

Text contained between the <PRE> and </PRE> tags is treated as preformatted text. Though that might not have much meaning for you, there are two important things to remember about preformatted text:

- Preformatted text is rendered in a fixed-width font.
- White space characters are *not* ignored.

This means that text marked up as preformatted text will be rendered on-screen *exactly* as it looks in the source file. Before the advent of HTML table tags, preformatted text was the best way to put information into tabular form on a Web page. It was an easy task to get text to line up in columns because all characters (including spaces) have the same width. For example, the HTML:

```
<PRE>
Payment Number        Due Date         Amount
- - - - - - - - - - - -        - - - - - - - -         - - - - - -
            1             4/15/97          $506.50
            2             6/15/87          $556.75
            3             9/15/97          $562.00
            4             1/15/98          $557.25
</PRE>
```

produces the screen you see in Figure 22.7. Note how the carriage returns and all the spaces between table entries are preserved.

FIG. 22.7

You can create simple tables with preformatted text, provided you don't mind them being rendered in a fixed-width font.

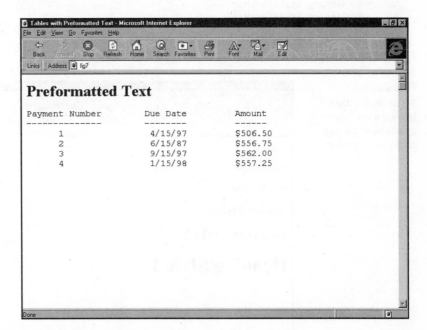

In addition to the text-level formatting you've read about so far, there is one other major type of formatting instruction that HTML supports: block-level formatting. This type of formatting refers to how you format large chunks of your documents rather than how you format individual characters or words. HTML provides you with several different ways to block format a document, including:

- Headings
- Paragraph and line breaks
- Lists
- Blockquotes
- Horizontal rule

The next five sections discuss each of these formatting options in detail.

Using the Heading Styles

HTML provides for six different heading styles, each of a different size. The styles are numbered 1 through 6, 1 being the largest. To format text in a heading style, simply enclose it between <H#> and </H#> tags, in which # is replaced by the number of the style you want. Figure 22.8 shows you how Internet Explorer renders all six heading styles. The corresponding HTML is:

```
<H6>Heading Style 6</H6>
<H5>Heading Style 5</H5>
<H4>Heading Style 4</H4>
<H3>Heading Style 3</H3>
<H2>Heading Style 2</H2>
<H1>Heading Style 1</H1>
```

FIG. 22.8

The six heading styles give you a way to break up and name the major sections of a document.

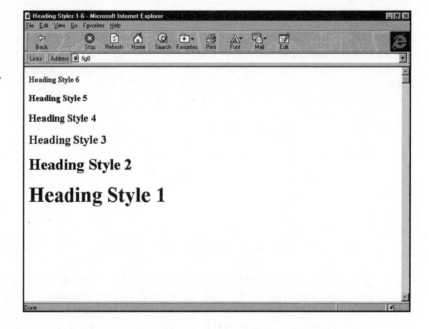

N O T E When a browser renders an HTML heading, it typically leaves some extra white space above and below the heading. ■

Breaking Text Apart Using Paragraph and Line Breaks

The <P> tag is used to indicate the start of a new paragraph. Before the advent of HTML 3.2, the <P> tag was frequently used as a stand-alone tag, but now <P> can take the ALIGN attribute if you want to specify an alignment other than the default left-justification. For example, it is now permissible to use

```
<P ALIGN=RIGHT>
This text is right-justified!
</P>
```

Because the browser needs to know when to stop using the prescribed alignment, the </P> tag becomes essential. Thus, the <P> tag is now best treated as a container tag.

> **N O T E** Paragraphs are separated by blank lines, but there is no indentation at the start of a new paragraph.

If you simply want to break to a new line, you can avail yourself of the HTML <BR> tag. Many first-time HTML authors expect that if they put a carriage return in the documents, it will correspond to a carriage return on the browser screen. But you know better because you read earlier in the chapter that carriage returns are ignored. What you need to use instead is the <BR> tag. Having to insert a <BR> tag wherever you want a line break takes some getting used to, but it's the only way to cleanly start a new line.

One place in which <BR> tags are handy is when you're entering an address. You might initially try to put an address into a document with code such as the following:

```
The Microsoft Corporation
One Microsoft Way
Redmond, WA 98052
```

but this would produce the result you see in Figure 22.9. The carriage returns in the code do not produce breaks to new lines on the browser screen. Instead, you need to use the HTML

```
The Microsoft Corporation<BR>
One Microsoft Way<BR>
Redmond, WA 98052
```

Displaying Lists

HTML supports five different type of lists, each of which is an easy and attractive way to present a lot of information. All HTML lists require a pair of tags to set up the list and a pair of tags to denote each item in the list. Table 22.6 catalogs the tags you need for each type of list.

FIG. 22.9
Carriage returns aren't enough to produce line breaks in your documents. You need to use the <BR> tag.

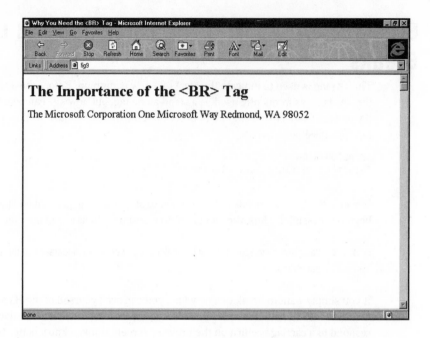

The Importance of the
 Tag

The Microsoft Corporation One Microsoft Way Redmond, WA 98052

Table 22.6 HTML List Tags

List Type	List Tags	Item Tags
Ordered	<OL></OL>	<LI></LI>
Unordered	<UL></UL>	<LI></LI>
Description	<DL></DL>	<DT></DT>,<DD></DD>
Menu	<MENU></MENU>	<LI></LI>
Directory	<DIR></DIR>	<LI></LI>

The browser automatically numbers items in an ordered list, starting with the number one. The automatic numbering is convenient because it spares you from having to do it if you add or delete an item from the list. The <OL> tag also supports two attributes: the TYPE and START attributes. You can set the TYPE attribute to 1, A, a, i, or I, depending on whether you want to use numbers, upper- or lowercase letters, or upper- or lowercase Roman numerals to show the order in your list. You can use the START attribute to commence the numbering of the list at a value different than one. For example, if you had set TYPE="A" and used a START value of 3, the first item in the ordered list would be labeled with a "C."

Unordered lists are bulleted rather than numbered. The <UL> tag also supports a TYPE attribute that enables you to change the bullet character from the default solid disk to an open circle (TYPE="CIRCLE") or to a square (TYPE="SQUARE").

With description lists, also called definition lists, you can present a term, followed by a description or definition below and indented from the term. Terms are enclosed in <DT> and </DT> tags and the descriptions/definitions are contained between <DD> and </DD> tags.

Menu lists and directory lists are rendered as bulleted lists and are generally taken to have shorter list elements. The popularity of these two types of list is fading and not all browsers continue to support them.

Figure 22.10 shows how Internet Explorer renders ordered, unordered, and description lists. The HTML to produce the figure follows:

```
<H2>Ordered Lists</H2>
<OL>
<LI>Numbered list items</LI>
<LI>List items are indented</LI>
</OL>
<H2>Unordered Lists</H2>
<UL>
<LI>Bulleted list items</LI>
<LI>List items are indented</LI>
</UL>
<H2>Description Lists</H2>
<DL>
<DT>First term</DT>
<DD>Description of first term</DD>
<DT>Second term</DT>
<DD>Description of second term</DD>
</DL>
```

FIG. 22.10
HTML lists are simple to use and display information in an easy-to-read format.

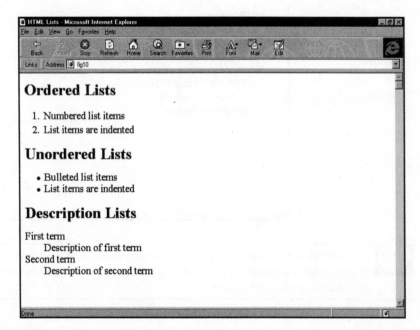

You can also nest lists one inside the other. For example, by nesting ordered lists and making diligent use of the TYPE attribute, you can create an outline format. You can also nest lists of different types, as shown in the following HTML code:

```
<H2>Nested Lists</H2>
<UL>
<LI>HTTP Servers</LI>
<OL>
<LI>Microsoft Internet Information Server</LI>
<LI>Netscape Enterprise Server</LI>
<LI>O'Reilly Web Site</LI>
</OL>
<LI>Web Clients</LI>
<OL>
<LI>Microsoft Internet Explorer 4</LI>
<LI>Netscape Navigator 4</LI>
<LI>Quarterdeck Mosaic</LI>
</OL>
</UL>
```

The preceding code produces the screen you see in Figure 22.11.

FIG. 22.11

Nesting lists inside each other gives you increased flexibility in how you present information.

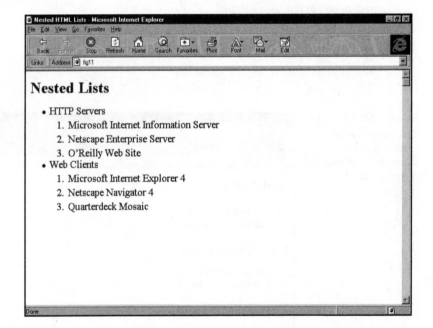

 If you want some white space between your list elements, you can put a <P> tag after each </LI> tag to place a blank line between each item. Because you're using the <P> tag for its spacing properties, the use of a </P> tag is not required.

Using Blockquotes

The <BLOCKQUOTE> and </BLOCKQUOTE> tags are used to contain a quoted passage. What's nice about these tags is that they render the quoted text with indents on both the left and right sides of the browser screen. Many HTML authors have harnessed this behavior for use in other parts of their sites. For example, some authors will place their entire documents inside of <BLOCKQUOTE> and </BLOCKQUOTE> tags so that left and right indent is present everywhere, thereby creating the effect of left and right margins. The extra white space on the sides tends to make documents easier to read.

N O T E Internet Explorer supports LEFTMARGIN and TOPMARGIN attributes of the <BODY> tag. These attributes give you another way to put margins in your documents, if you know that your audience is using Internet Explorer. ■

Creating Horizontal Lines

One other way to break up sections of your documents is to do so graphically. The simple <HR> tag places a horizontal line across the entire width of the browser screen, minus a few pixels on each side (see Figure 22.12).

FIG. 22.12

Horizontal lines give the eye a break from lines and lines of text.

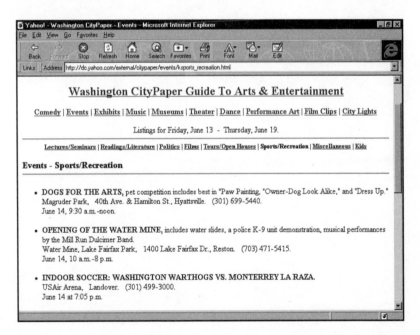

When HTML 3.2 was introduced, it included a number of useful attributes of the <HR> tag with which you can control horizontal line properties. These attributes are listed in Table 22.7.

Table 22.7 Attributes of the *<HR>* Tag

Attribute	Purpose
SIZE=n	Changes the thickness of the line to *n* (default thickness is 1)
WIDTH=pixels ¦ percent	Makes the line width a certain number of pixels or a percentage of the screen width
ALIGN=LEFT ¦ CENTER ¦ RIGHT	Aligns the line on the browser screen (default is CENTER)
NOSHADE	Suppresses the default shading effect

Because you can't know the exact width of every user's screen, you should specify a line's width as a percentage whenever possible.

CHAPTER 23

Links, Graphics, and Advanced Graphics

Before the advent of the Web, content was published on the Internet by means of Gopher services. Gopher documents were simple, plain-text documents that were accessed by menus of folders and files, not unlike what you see in the Windows Explorer in Windows 95. And though their publications were rather ordinary looking, Gopher servers were a very efficient means of getting information out to people. Indeed, many Gopher servers are still operating today.

Once the Web came along, it very quickly became the service of choice for electronic publishing. Two important features about the Web distinguished it from Gopher and propelled its rise to prominence. The first is the capability to link related documents together with hypertext. By pointing at and clicking a piece of hypertext, a user instructs the browser to load the document associated with that piece of hypertext. This was much more attractive than Gopher navigation, which had to be done by means of menus.

The other key feature the Web had going for it was the capability to include inline images in a document. This, combined with browsers' capacity to render text in different fonts and to apply different typographical effects, gave Web documents a much more compelling look than plain-text Gopher documents.

Setting up hypertext links

The intertangling of publications called the Web wouldn't be possible if it weren't for the ability to link related documents to one another. Find out how to set up links not only to other documents but to other Internet services as well.

Placing graphics in your documents

The Web's powerful visual appeal springs from the graphics you see on most Web pages. HTML allows for two different types of image formats to be placed in a publication, all with the use of a simple tag.

Creating special image effects

By using effects like transparency, interlacing, and animation, you can give your images even greater impact.

Keeping graphics files small

Some users are put-off by the long download times required for some graphics files. You should strive to keep file sizes to a minimum, and there are a number of techniques you can try to accomplish this.

This chapter explores the HTML that supports the placement of hyperlinks and inline images in a Web document. The first section discusses links to not only other Web publications, but to other Internet services as well. Then you'll read about the basics of Web graphics and how to include such images in your documents. The final section of the chapter takes images a step further by looking at some of the special effects that are possible with both major types of Web graphics. ■

URLs

To render a piece of hypertext, a browser has to know two things: what text should be clickable and the Web address of the document that should be loaded when the hypertext is clicked. A document's Web address is called its Uniform Resource Locator, or URL. URLs have a very particular structure, so before delving into how to set up a link, the next section takes you through a quick review of URL syntax.

An URL is a way of compactly and completely identifying any document on any type Web-compatible server anywhere in the world. A document's URL consists of four parts: a protocol, a server name, a port number, and a file name. With the exception of a News URL, the general format for an URL is ***protocol://server_name:port_number/file_name***.

The protocol used to serve most Web documents is http, which stands for HyperText Transfer Protocol. A list of other valid protocols is given in Table 23.1. The server_name is the English-language name or Internet Protocol (IP) address of the computer on which the Web server is running and usually has the form "www.servername.com". Specifying a port_number is typically not required because most Web servers listen at port 80. Some servers may not use port 80, though, and URLs for these servers would have to include the port number that the server is configured to use. The file_name includes both the directory path to the file and the name of the file itself.

Table 23.1   Commonly Used Internet Protocols

Protocol	Name
http	HyperText Transfer Protocol
https	Secure HyperText Transfer Protocol
ftp	File Transfer Protocol
gopher	Gopher
wais	Wide Area Information Service
telnet	Telnet session
news	UseNet newsgroup protocol
mailto	Electronic mail

An URL that specifies a protocol, server name, and a file name is said to be an absolute or fully qualified URL. In some cases, it is convenient to specify an URL relative to a base URL, resulting in a relative or partially qualified URL. For example, suppose your base URL is **http://www.yourfirm.com/products/pricing/prices.html** and you want to reference the file profiles.html in the services directory (two directory levels up). To do this, you could use the fully qualified URL **http://www.yourfirm.com/services/profiles.html** or you can save some typing by using the partially qualified URL **../../services/profiles.html**. The two dots followed by the forward slash (../) are an indicator to move up one directory level. If you needed to specify the URL of the file schedule.html in the discounts directory, a subdirectory of the pricing directory, you could use the partially qualified URL **discounts/schedule.html**.

 TIP An even quicker way to reference the profiles.html file would be with the URL **/services/profiles.html**. The forward slash (/) before the services subdirectory instructs the browser to look at the Web server's root directory.

NOTE You might sometimes see a URL like **http://www.microsoft.com/** that lacks a file name. For this type of URL, the server is configured to automatically serve a file of a specific name. For many servers, the name of this file is index.html. For Microsoft servers, the name is default.htm or default.asp. ▦

NOTE The base URL is the URL of the document that is currently loaded into the browser. You can override that by using the <BASE> tag in the document head. For example, the HTML

```
<BASE HREF="http://www.other_server.com/">
```

sets the base URL to **http://www.other_server.com/**. ▦

Linking to Other HTML Documents

Now that you know how to compose a Web URL, you're ready to learn how to set up a hyperlink. You read earlier in the chapter that you need two things need to define a piece of hypertext: what text should be clickable and the address of the document that is loaded when the hypertext is clicked. You now know that the address of the associated document is the document's URL. All that remains is to define what text should be the hypertext. Because the text that serves as hypertext is frequently referred to as the link anchor, you use the <A> and </A> (A stands for anchor) tags to contain the text that is to be denoted as hypertext. Any text can be a hypertext anchor, regardless of its size or formatting. An anchor can be a single character, a few words, or entire lines of text. Hypertext anchors are underlined and rendered in a different color by Internet Explorer.

Putting the two elements of a hypertext link together, you get the following format for setting up a link in HTML:

```
<A HREF="URL">anchor text</A>
```

The HREF attribute in the <A> tag stands for "hypertext reference" and is set equal to the URL of the document to which you want the hypertext to point. Everything sandwiched between the <A> and </A> tags forms the anchor and will appear colored and underlined in the Internet Explorer window.

TIP If a link doesn't seem to be working right, check to make sure that the URL in the <A> tag is completely contained in quotes. Omitting the final quotation mark is a common coding mistake.

You can use other formatting codes in conjunction with hypertext anchors. For example, to make a heading into a link, you could use the following HTML:

```
<A HREF="URL"><H1>Linked level-1 heading</H1></A>
```

The order in which you apply these tags is not important. You could equivalently use

```
<H1><A HREF="URL">Linked level-1 heading</A></H1>
```

The <A> tag most commonly takes the HREF attribute, but it can also take the attributes listed in Table 23.2. The NAME attribute is essential for setting up links that target positions within the same document (see next section).

Table 23.2   Attributes of the <A> Tag

Attribute	Purpose
HREF	Specifies the URL of the Internet resource to which you're linking
NAME	Establishes a named anchor within a document that an HREF can target
REL	Specifies a forward link relationship
REV	Specifies a reverse link relationship
TITLE	Supplies an advisory title for the linked document

N O T E A forward link relationship describes how the file being linked to relates to the file being linked. For example, if you're linking from a product index page to a page with details about a particular product, you could set REL="Product detail" to indicate that you're linking to a document that has more information about a particular product.

Reverse link relationships are similar, but work in the opposite direction. ■

Linking Within a Given Document

When you click a piece of hypertext, Internet Explorer will load the document to which the hypertext points, starting from the top of the linked document. This is fine, unless the document is long and the information you really want displayed isn't near the top. In this case, users have to scroll through the document to find the information you wanted them to see. An alternative to burdening your visitors is to set up named anchors in longer documents and then have your hyperlink references point directly to the named anchors.

As an example, suppose you have a four-part document stored in the single file longdoc.html and each section has its own level-one heading. You can set up named anchors on each of the headings by using the `<A NAME="anchor_name">` and `</A>` tags as follows:

```
<A NAME="one"><H1>Part One</H1></A>
```

With anchors set up at each heading, you can instruct a browser to link to a specific anchor by appending a pound sign (#) and the anchor's name at the end of the document's URL, as in the following code:

```
Read <A HREF="longdoc.html#four">Part Four</A>.
```

When a user clicks the hypertext Part Four, the browser loads the document longdoc.html and begins displaying it from the heading for Part Four. This spares the user from having to scroll all the way through the document just to get to where you want them.

Named anchors are useful within a single document for setting up a table of contents at the top of document with links pointing to the different major sections (see Figure 23.1).

FIG. 23.1
Users appreciate tables of contents for long documents so they don't have to scroll a lot.

Linking to Other Internet Services

When setting up hyperlinks, you're not restricted to linking only to other Web documents. You can point your hyperlinks at other Internet services as well. This section of the chapter closes with a quick look at some of these types of links.

- **mailto**   E-mail addresses are frequently hyperlinked so that when users click the address, they go into a mail program that enables them to compose an e-mail message to that address. For example:

```
E-mail the President at <A HREF="mailto:president@whitehouse.gov">
➥president@whitehouse.gov</A>.
```

- **FTP**   If you're linking to a file that's intended for downloading only, you may want to set it up on an FTP server and then point your hyperlink there. A link to an FTP server might look like

```
Download the <A HREF="ftp://ftp.your_firm.com/pub/bin/program.exe>self-
➥extracting executable (6.2 MB)</A>.
```

  Be sure to include the size of the file so that users will have some idea of how long it will take for the file to download.

- **Gopher**   As noted at the start of the chapter, Gopher sites are still very much around. By setting an HREF attribute equal to a URL that uses the Gopher protocol, for example

```
Connect to the <A HREF="gopher://gopher.micro.umn.edu/">Mother Gopher</A>,
```

  you can direct a browser to act like a Gopher client and display the menus of folders and files on the server.

- **UseNet**   UseNet newsgroups number in the thousands and cover topics that range from being a Star Trek fan to psychology of personality. They are referenced using a hierarchy that begins with general terms and works down to more specific ideas. The URL for a UseNet newsgroup is somewhat different than the other URLs, as seen in the following code:

```
Read about <A HREF="news:sci.psychology.personality">Personality Theory
➥</A>.
```

N O T E   For a browser to work properly with a mailto or UseNet newsgroup link, it has to be configured to use mail and news clients, respectively. Internet Explorer 4 comes complete with this kind of integration. ◼

Web Graphics Formats

In the last section, you learned that any text you can place between <A> and </A> tags you can make into hypertext. Then by clicking the hypertext, you can visit its associated URL. Text isn't the only thing that can serve as a hyperlink anchor, however—images can as well! But before you can learn how to hyperlink images, you must learn how to put them on your pages. That is the focus of the following two sections.

If you've done much work with computer graphics, you probably know that graphic data is stored in several different formats. When you shift your focus to the World Wide Web, however, the field narrows to just two formats: GIF and JPEG.

GIF

GIF, or Graphics Interchange Format, was originally developed by CompuServe as a standard for storing and transmitting images. GIF is an 8 bit format, meaning that GIF images are limited to 2^8, or 256, colors. The current GIF specification is GIF89a, released by CompuServe in 1990.

Part
V
Ch
23

Image data in the GIF format are organized into related blocks and subblocks that you can use to reproduce the graphic. When transmitting a GIF, a program called an *encoder* is used to produce a GIF data stream of control and data blocks that are sent along to the destination machine. There, a program called a *decoder* parses the data stream and reassembles the image.

GIF employs a compression scheme called LZW compression to reduce the amount of data it needs to send to describe an image completely. LZW compression works best on simple images like line drawings or graphics with just a few colors. For more color-rich images, LZW is less robust, producing compression ratios of around 2:1 or less.

The GIF89a standard supports three desirable Web page effects:

- **Interlacing** In an interlaced GIF, nonadjacent parts of the image are stored together. As a browser reads in an interlaced GIF, the image appears to "fade in" over several passes rather than be read in from top to bottom. This is useful because a visitor can then get a sense of what the entire image looks like without having to wait for the whole file to load.

- **Transparency** With transparent GIFs, one color is designated to be the transparent color. When the GIF is rendered, a pixel that should be painted with the transparent color is instead painted with the background color. Figure 23.2 illustrates a transparent and nontransparent GIF. Note in the nontransparent GIF that the bounding box around the text "Hi there!" is visible. By making the color of the bounding box transparent, the background color shows through and the text appears to float over the page.

    Transparent GIFs are very popular because of the "floating" effect they create. With most graphics programs available today, you can create transparent GIFs easily either as part of the program's normal functioning or through plug-in filters.

- **Animation** Animated GIFs are created by storing the sequence of images used to produce the animation in one file. A browser that fully supports the GIF89a standard will know to render each of these images in sequence, thereby creating the animation. The programs that let you store the multiple images in a GIF file also let you specify how much delay there should be before starting the animation and how many times the animation should repeat.

FIG. 23.2
A transparent GIF appears to hover over the page.

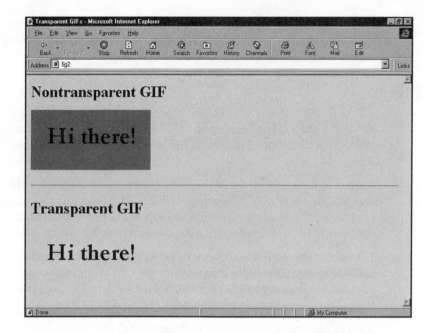

GIF is the more popular format for inline images because all graphical browsers support it and because it is the only format that supports all of the effects previously noted. The GIF format is best suited for the following types of images:

- Black-and-white line art and text
- Images with a limited number of distinct colors
- Graphics that have sharp or distinct edges (most buttons fit into this category)
- Graphics that are overlaid with text

JPEG

The JPEG (Joint Picture Experts Group) format refers to a set of standards for compressing full-color or grayscale still images. JPEG's ability to work with full-color (24-bits per pixel, 16.7 million colors) make it preferable to the GIF format (8 bits per pixel, 256 colors) for working with photographs, particularly nature-related images, in which the entire spectrum, not just a few colors, is in play.

JPEG can handle so many colors in a relatively small file because it compresses the image data. You can control how big or small the file ultimately is by adjusting the parameters of the compression. A highly compressed file can be very small, but the quality of the image rendering will suffer for it.

When you decompress a JPEG image, there is always some amount of loss, meaning that some pixels will not be painted with the color they originally had. Fortunately, JPEG's compression/decompression scheme is such that lost image data occurs in the higher color frequencies where it is harder for the human eye to detect the differences. In spite of this loss, you can use JPEG compression to achieve ratios between 10:1 and 20:1 without appreciable change in the image. This means you've gone from storing 24 bits per pixel to 1 or 2 bits per pixel—a rather impressive savings! Again, you can compress the file further, but you risk reducing the image quality on the user's browser screen.

The JPEG format supports an effect similar to interlacing with GIFs. A *progressive JPEG* (or p-JPEG) is much like an interlaced GIF in that the image is stored as a series of scans. The first scan, or layer, of the progressive JPEG will appear in the browser window as soon as the download begins. Subsequently downloaded layers clarify the image until it is finally rendered in its finished form. Transparency is not possible with JPEGs because of the loss that tends to occur during compression. If a pixel originally colored with the transparent color is assigned a different color during decompression or if a nontransparent pixel is painted with the transparent color, the onscreen results would be confusing and unappealing!

Part
V

Ch
23

The JPEG format is best suited for the following kinds of images:

- Scanned photographs (full-color or black-and-white) and ray-traced renderings
- Images that contain a complex mixture of colors
- Any images that require a palette of more than 256 colors

The Windows Bitmap (BMP) Format

Internet Explorer takes Web graphics one step further by supporting the Windows Bitmap or BMP format. This format is typically used by Windows-specific graphics like background wallpapers. Because Internet Explorer and Windows are both Microsoft products, it was probably a fairly simple matter for Microsoft to build BMP support into Internet Explorer.

If you know that the vast majority of your audience will be using Internet Explorer, you could consider using the BMP format for graphics on your Web pages. People with browsers that don't support BMP will not be able to view these images, however, and you need to be careful not to alienate these folks, especially of they comprise a significant fraction of the visitors to your pages. Additionally, bitmapped files can't be compressed, so even if a user has a browser than can display BMP files, it may take longer for the file to download.

N O T E For a good reference on Web image formats, consult the World Wide Web FAQ at **http://www.boutell.com/faq/**. ■

Placing Graphics in Your Documents

You must save images in separate files even though they are references and are displayed inside an HTML document. To place an image on a page, you need to use the `<IMG>` tag. The `<IMG>` tag is a stand-alone tag that, in its simplest form, has the syntax

```
<IMG SRC="URL_of_image_file">
```

SRC is a mandatory attribute and specifies the URL of the graphics file. Because URLs can point anywhere, you can reference images on a remote server as well as on your own server. You can even read in images stored on other types of servers, such as FTP and Gopher, as long as your browser supports these protocols.

The beauty of the <IMG> tag is that it has several very useful attributes that give you a lot of design freedom when placing an image on a page. Table 23.3 lists these attributes and what each does. Many of these attributes were introduced as a browser-specific extension to HTML, but now they are all accepted as part of the HTML 3.2 standard.

Table 23.3   Attributes of the <IMG> Tag

Attribute	Purpose
ALT	Specifies a text-based alternative for the image
ALIGN	Controls alignment of text surrounding the image
BORDER	Specifies the size of the border to place around the image
HEIGHT	Denotes the height of the image in pixel
HSPACE	Controls the amount of white space to the left and right of the image
ISMAP	Designates the image as being used in a server-side imagemap
SRC	Specifies the URL of the image file
USEMAP	Designates the image as being used in a client-side imagemap
VSPACE	Controls the amount of white space above and below the image
WIDTH	Denotes the width of the image in pixels

The ISMAP and USEMAP attributes are detailed in Chapter 25, "Building Navigational Imagemaps." The remaining attributes are discussed in the sections that follow.

▶ **See** "Building Navigational Imagemaps," **p. 493**

 When placing more than one image on a Web page, try to make sure that images' pallets are all the same. This prevents that annoying "pallet flashing" that can occur when a browser is trying to cope with multiple pallets.

ALT

With the ALT attribute, you can specify a line of text the browser can use in place of the image if it can't load the image or if the user has image loading turned off. Also, don't forget that some users don't have graphical browsers and can't see images at all. Using the ALT attribute judiciously is an important courtesy to these users. Finally, Web robots can't parse images, so they often use the ALT text in <IMG> tag to index an image.

N O T E When Internet Explorer renders a page, it will display the ALT text as a placeholder for the image until it has completely loaded. ■

ALIGN

The ALIGN attribute can take on any one of five different possible values. All values have something to do with how text around the image is aligned, but two of them behave in a substantially different way. We'll begin by looking at the TOP, MIDDLE, and BOTTOM values and then examine the LEFT and RIGHT values.

When you set ALIGN equal to TOP, MIDDLE, or BOTTOM, text subsequent to the image is aligned with the top, center, or bottom of the image, respectively (see Figure 23.5). One thing to note with TOP and MIDDLE alignments is that if the text following the image runs too long, it will break to a new line that starts *below* the image. In many cases, this may look unattractive.

FIG. 23.5

You can align text that follows an image along the top, middle, or bottom of the image.

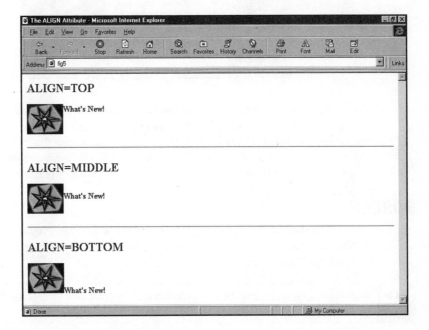

Setting ALIGN equal to LEFT or RIGHT causes the image to "float" in the left or right margin, respectively. The floating allows text to wrap around the image, thereby making the image appear to be embedded in the text. This capability has opened the way to many creative and interesting layouts (see Figure 23.6).

FIG. 23.6
The text of this CNN story wraps around the image floating in the right margin.

The advent of floating images created a need for a way to break to the first left or right margin that is clear of floating images. To satisfy this need, the CLEAR attribute was added to the <BR> tag. Setting CLEAR to LEFT causes a break to the first left margin that's clear of floating images. Setting CLEAR=RIGHT does the same thing, only it breaks to the first open right margin. Setting CLEAR=ALL clears to the first point where both margins are free of floating images.

BORDER

The BORDER attribute gives you an easy way to place a border around an image. The BORDER attribute is set equal to the number of pixels wide you want the border to be. By default, images are rendered without a border.

 When hyperlinking images (see the next section), it is useful to set BORDER=0 to suppress the colored border that would normally appear around the image.

HEIGHT and WIDTH

By providing image HEIGHT and WIDTH information, you speed up the page layout process and enable users to see the final page much more quickly. A browser uses HEIGHT and WIDTH information to allocate an appropriate amount of space for an image as it lays out the page. The image shows up in this reserved space once it has downloaded. Without these two attributes, a browser would have to download the entire image, compute its size, place it on the page, and then continue with the layout of the rest of the page. If a page has several images, the series of delays to load, size, and place all the images could be a source of annoyance to your visitors.

 TIP You can usually get an image's HEIGHT and WIDTH pretty easily from a graphics program. Also, if you're using a WYSIWYG editor like FrontPage Express, it will most likely determine the HEIGHT and WIDTH information for you and build it into its HTML output automatically.

HSPACE and *VSPACE*

White space around an image is called gutter space or runaround. Leaving a little extra white space around an image is a good way to give it some breathing room and make it stand out better. Runaround is also useful with floating images that have text wrapping around them. Text that is jammed right up against a floating image is often hard to read, but placing some runaround around the image usually clears this problem.

Runaround is controlled by the HSPACE and VSPACE attributes of the <IMG> tag. Each is set equal to the number of pixels of white space to leave to the left and right of the image (HSPACE) or above and below the image (VSPACE).

Making a Graphic into a Hyperlink Anchor

You can hyperlink graphics to create button-like effects and to provide an alternative to always clicking hypertext. The syntax for setting up a graphical anchor is the same as for setting up a text anchor. Instead of placing text between the <A HREF="URL"> and </A> tag, however, you place an <IMG> tag between them instead, as in the following example:

```
<A HREF="pub.html"><IMG SRC="cheers.jpg"></A> Visit the Pub!
```

Figure 23.7 shows the linked HTML produced by the preceding code. Clicking the image is an instruction to the browser to load the document specified in the HREF attribute. Note that the linked image has a border colored the same as hypertext links, even though the BORDER attribute is not specified in the <IMG> tag.

There are times when you don't want a colored border to be placed around a linked image. This is particularly true when the image is a transparent GIF because the border will trace out the bounding box and ruin the transparency effect (see Figure 23.8). To get rid of the colored border around a hyperlinked image, be sure to use the BORDER=0 attribute in the <IMG> tag that places the image.

FIG. 23.7
Hyperlinked images are rendered with a colored border, even if you don't use the BORDER attribute.

FIG. 23.8
Having a border around a transparent GIF tends to detract from the transparency effect.

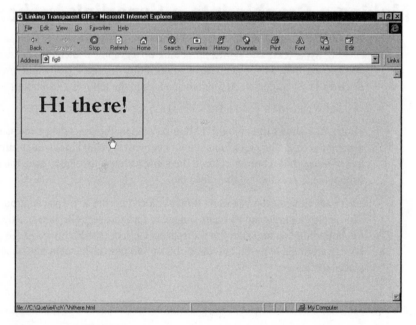

Internet Explorer Extensions to the *<IMG>* Tag

Microsoft has extended the <IMG> tag to support the placement of inline video clips stored in the Audio Video Interleave (AVI) format. The extended attributes are shown in Table 23.4.

Table 23.4 Microsoft Extensions to the *<IMG>* Tag

Attribute	Purpose
DYNSRC="URL"	Specifies the URL of the AVI file
CONTROLS	Places a set of playback controls in the browser window so the user can control the playing of the clip
START=FILEOPEN¦MOUSEOVER	Specifies what event should trigger the playing of the video clip
LOOP=n¦INFINITE	Controls how many times the video clip is played
LOOPDELAY=n	Specifies how many milliseconds to wait before replaying the clip

For example, the following HTML

```
<IMG DYNSRC="B5.AVI" CONTROLS START=MOUSEOVER LOOP=5>
```

will play the video clip B5.AVI five times once a user moves his or her mouse over the playback area. A control panel will be present while the clip is playing so a user can rewind or fast-forward.

Transparency

In the last section, you read a little bit about the desirable effects the GIF and JPEG formats support. To close this chapter, we look at how you can create these effects with your own images and how you can keep image file sizes to a minimum.

You were introduced to transparent GIF back in Figure 23.2. With the nontransparent image in that figure, the bounding box around the text shows up against the gray background. The transparent version of the same image designates the bounding box color as transparent, allowing the gray background to show through. This gives the text the appearance of floating on the background.

You can convert GIFs to transparent GIFs by using a number of commercial or shareware programs. The shareware program LViewPro, developed by Leonardo Loureiro, is one such utility. To create a transparent GIF using LViewPro, follow these steps.

1. Open LViewPro by choosing it from your Start menu.
2. Choose File, Open; in the Open dialog box, highlight the image you want to make transparent, and then click OK.

3. Select <u>R</u>etouch, Color <u>D</u>epth. To save as a GIF, your image must be a palette image, meaning it must have a color depth of not more than 256 colors. You can accomplish this (if it's not a palette image already) by selecting the <u>P</u>alette Image radio button in the Color Depth dialog box (see Figure 23.10). Next you see options for palette creation and quantizing. Select <u>2</u>56 colors, uncheck the <u>D</u>ithering option, and click OK.

N O T E *Dithering* refers to a process whereby a program simulates a color that's not in an image's palette with colors that are in the image's palette. Frequently though, dithering does not provide a good color match, so you should avoid using it where you can. ■

FIG. 23.10

Before you can make an image transparent, you must make sure it has a palette of not more than 256 colors.

4. Next, you need to identify the transparent color. Select <u>R</u>etouch, Bac<u>k</u>ground Color, and you'll see the Select Color Palette Entry dialog box. This dialog box shows you all of the colors in the image's palette (see Figure 23.11).

FIG. 23.11

You pick one color from the image's palette to behave as the transparent color.

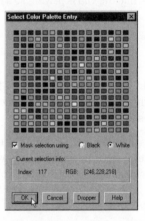

5. If you can identify the color you want to make transparent, click that color once in the Select Palette Entry dialog box and check the Mask selection box with either the Black or White options. This masks your selection with either black or white and enables you

to see whether you made the correct choice for the transparent color. The mask does not change any colors in the actual image—it's just a helpful way of showing you the transparent selection.

6. If you have trouble picking out the exact color you want to make transparent, you can click the Dropper button in the Select Color Palette Entry dialog box. You can then move the dropper over the image and sample different colors to be the transparent color. When you click the dropper, it disappears from the screen and the color you clicked is highlighted in the dialog box. You can then test your transparency selection by choosing a mask of black or white. If you chose the correct color, click OK; otherwise, select the Dropper again and try choosing another color.

7. Choose File, Properties and then select the GIF tab from the Properties dialog box. If it's not selected already, put a check in the box next to Save Transparent Color Information to GIF89a Files.

8. Choose File, Save As to save the file. In the Save Image As dialog box, be sure to select the GIF89a file type and then click Save to save the file.

Interlaced GIFs and Progressive JPEGs

Recall from earlier in the chapter that interlaced GIFs and progressive JPEGs were alike in that they fade onto the page gradually, giving the viewer a quick, overall sense of what the image looks like. You can easily make your GIFs interlaced or your JPEGs progressive by using LViewPro.

To save a GIF as interlaced, perform the following steps.

1. Open LViewPro by selecting it from your Start menu.

2. Choose File, Open; in the Open dialog box, highlight the image file you want to convert to interlaced and then click OK.

3. Choose File, Properties and select the GIF tab. Put a check in the box next to Save Interlaced.

4. Save the image as an interlaced GIF by selecting File, Save As. In the Save Image As dialog box, select the GIF89a file type and then click the Save button.

Creating a progressive JPEG with LViewPro is just as easy, as illustrated in the following steps.

1. Open LViewPro by selecting it from your Start menu.

2. Choose File, Open. In the Open dialog box, highlight the JPEG file you want to convert to progressive and then click OK.

3. Choose File, Properties and select the JPEG (Normal) tab. Put a check in the box next to Progressive Compression (see Figure 23.12).

4. To save the image as a progressive JPEG, select File, Save As. In the Save Image As dialog box, select the JPEG file type.

FIG. 23.12
Progressive compression is one of the many options you can set from the JPEG (Normal) tag of the Properties dialog box.

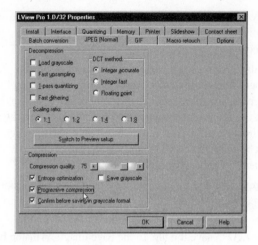

Animated GIFs

You can create simple animations using GIF files as well. Recall that the GIF89a standard enables you to store all the still images that comprise the animation in a single file. When a decoder detects a file containing multiple images, it presents them in sequence to produce the animation.

In addition to storing the individual frames of the animation, the GIF file can also contain information about how to present the frames. You can specify such parameters as the following:

- How much delay there should be between frames
- Waiting for user input before starting the animation
- Whether you want the last frame of the animation to stay on the screen

More and more programs are becoming available to help you prepare animated GIFs. If you're using Microsoft's Image Composer, you should check out Microsoft's GIF Animator at **http://www.microsoft.com/imagecomposer/gifanimator/gifanin.htm**. Another popular product is Alchemy Mindwork's GIF Construction Set for Windows. You can learn more about the GIF Construction Set at **http://www.mindworkshop.com/alchemy/alchemy.html**.

Keeping File Sizes Manageable

Some of us may get spoiled by the T1 or faster access to the Internet we have at work or school. If you have such a connection, you probably don't often experience the frustration of waiting for a large image file to download. But dial-up users from home, who typically have a 14.4Kbps or 28.8Kbps connection, may have to wait several minutes for the same files to download. For this reason, it's an important end-user courtesy to make your image files as small as possible. The chapter closes with a quick look at some things you can do to keep your file sizes to a minimum.

■ **Resizing the image**   Simply stated, a larger image has more pixels and, therefore, more color information that has to be stored. By making your image's width and height as small as possible, you contribute to a smaller file size.

■ **Use thumbnails**   A thumbnail is a very small version of an image, typically a photograph. Because they are so much smaller than the original, they take up less disk space. Thumbnails are usually hyperlinked to the full-sized version of the image so that users can see the full image if they want.

■ **Increasing JPEG compression**   The higher you crank the JPEG compression level, the smaller your file size becomes. But don't forget that high compression can lead to poor image quality when the JPEG is decompressed and rendered on screen.

 You can adjust the JPEG compression level in LViewPro from the JPEG (Normal) tab of the Properties dialog box (refer to Figure 23.12).

■ **Reducing color depth**   A GIF can store as many as 256 colors, but if you have a very simple image with just a handful of colors, there's no need to use 8 bits per pixel to store color information. By reducing your color depth to the minimum number of bits per pixel needed to account for all the colors in the image, you can substantially reduce overall file size.

■ **Suppress dithering**   Dithering uses combinations of colors in an image's palette to simulate colors that aren't in the palette. Activating dithering tends to increase the file size, so if you can get by without it—and you usually can because dithering often makes an image look grainy—you should suppress dithering to prevent a file from becoming unnecessarily large.

Part

V

Ch

23

CHAPTER 24

Organizing Content with Tables and Frames

As Web documents evolved into more a complicated type of publication, HTML was forced to evolve to accommodate new publishing requirements. One product of this evolution was the advent of the HTML table tags. These tags enabled authors to organize data into rows and columns, making it easier for readers to understand the meaning of the data in the table. Shortly after the table tags were introduced, clever HTML authors saw another use for them—as a means or producing more elaborate layouts than had been previously possible. Now part of the HTML 3.2 standard, the table tags are an integral part of document markup because, no matter how you use them, they greatly enhance document readability.

Another critical product of HTML's evolution is the idea of a framed document. By splitting the browser window into two or more smaller windows called frames, document authors can present more than one document at a time to a reader. And even though the frame tags have yet to be adopted by the World Wide Web Consortium as part of the HTML standard, frames have been implemented on many sites to give visitors a better interface to content.

This chapter discusses the HTML tags you need to know to create tables and frames and also points out some intelligent ways to use each kind of element in your site design.

Creating a simple table

HTML's table tags give you the ability to put information in tabular form without having to use preformatted text.

Using tables as a design tool

Because you can precisely align the elements that you place in them, tables are an excellent way to compose well-designed pages.

Setting up a framed document

By breaking up the browser window into multiple smaller windows, you can display more than one document at a time.

Targeting your content

Once you introduce a framed layout, you must take steps to ensure that content shows up in the frame in which you want it to.

Before HTML 3.2, the only means at your disposal for creating tables was to use preformatted text. But the HTML standard now supports several table tags that make it possible to build tables on Web pages without having to convert everything to a fixed-width font. Many browsers, including Internet Explorer, had implemented these tags even before they became part of the standard.

This first part of this chapter is devoted to introducing you to the HTML table tags so you can use them not only to format tabular data, but also to format entire Web documents. ■

Basic Structure of a Table

To better understand the table tags, it helps to take a moment to consider how HTML tables are structured. The fundamental building block of an HTML table is a table *cell*. Cells can contain a data element of the table or a heading for a column of data. Related cells are logically grouped together into a table row. The rows, in turn, are taken together to produce the entire table. If you keep this structure in mind as you read the next few sections, the syntax of the table tags will make much more sense to you.

Creating a Simple Table

To start a table, you must use the `<TABLE>` tag. The `<TABLE>` tag has a companion closing tag, `</TABLE>`, and together these tags contain all of the other tags that go into making a table. The `<TABLE>` tag can take the `BORDER` attribute. By setting `BORDER=n`, you create an *n* pixel border around the table. By default, a table has no borders.

 When space on the browser screen is at a premium, you can also set BORDER=0. Not only will this produce no border, but it will recapture the space that a browser automatically reserves for a table border.

Defining the Table Rows

Because tables are built of rows, you next must know how to define a row. The `<TR>` and `</TR>` tags contain the tags that comprise a row of a table. The `<TR>` tag can take the `ALIGN` and `VALIGN` attributes. The `ALIGN` attribute controls the horizontal alignment of cell contents in the row and can be set to `LEFT`, `CENTER`, or `RIGHT`. The `VALIGN` attribute controls the vertical alignment and can be set to `TOP`, `MIDDLE`, or `BOTTOM`. Values of `ALIGN` or `VALIGN` prescribed in a `<TR>` tag apply to each cell in a row and will override any default alignments.

Setting Up Table Cells

With a row defined, you next must be able to construct the cells in that row. If a cell contains a heading for a column of data, you use the `<TH>` and `</TH>` tags to contain the heading. Text placed between these tags will automatically be rendered in boldface type and will be centered over the column of data.

If you're not creating a heading, you should use the <TD> and </TD> to contain the contents of a cell. Ordinarily, you'll be putting some kind of text between these two tags, but that's not all you're limited to doing. You can place an image in a cell by inserting an <IMG> tag between the <TD> and </TD> tags. Similarly, you can have a blank cell by putting nonbreaking space between the tags (<TD> </TD>) or by putting nothing between the tag (<TD></TD>). In fact, you can place just about any page element into a table cell—even another table! Nested tables can be tough to code though, so you should take some time to plan out the table before trying to write the HTML that produces it.

Default horizontal and vertical alignments are associated with each kind of cell. Both types of cells have a vertical alignment of MIDDLE. Data cells have a default horizontal alignment of LEFT, and header cells have the before-mentioned CENTER alignment. You can override any of these defaults and any alignment instructions specified in a <TR> tag by including the desired ALIGN or VALIGN attribute in a <TD> or <TH> tag, as show in the following code:

```
<H2>U.S. Open Scores - First Round</H2>
<TABLE BORDER=1>
  <TR>
    <TH></TH>
    <TH>Colin Montgomerie</TH>
    <TH>Tiger Woods</TH>
    <TH>Tom Lehman</TH>
  </TR>
  <TR ALIGN=CENTER VALIGN=TOP>
    <TD VALIGN=MIDDLE><H2>Score</H2></TD>
    <TD ALIGN=RIGHT VALIGN=BOTTOM>65</TD>
    <TD>74</TD>
    <TD ALIGN=LEFT VALIGN=MIDDLE>67</TD>
  </TR>
</TABLE>
```

Figure 24.1 shows how Internet Explorer renders the table in the previous listing.

Note in the <TR> tag that the alignment for the entire second row of the table is set to a CENTER horizontal alignment and a TOP vertical alignment. In the first data element of the second row, these alignments are overridden by the ALIGN and VALIGN attributes specified in the <TD> tag. Thus, Colin Montgomerie's first round score shows right-justified and flush along the bottom of the cell. The <TD> tag that defines the cell with Tiger Wood's first round score has no alignment instructions, so the alignments specified in the <TR> tag prevail. Finally, the third cell changes the horizontal alignment to LEFT and the vertical alignment to MIDDLE so that Tom Lehman's score shows up with the default alignment for any data cell (though it was necessary to undo the alignment instructions in the <TR> tag to accomplish this).

Aligning data elements and headers in your tables may seem a bit confusing, but if you keep the following rules in mind, you can master table alignment quickly:

- Alignments specified in <TD> or <TH> tags override all other alignments but apply only to the cell being defined.
- Alignments specified in a <TR> tag override default alignments and apply to all cells in a row unless they are overridden by an alignment instruction in a <TD> or <TH> tag.

FIG. 24.1

You can control table
alignments right down
to the cell level.

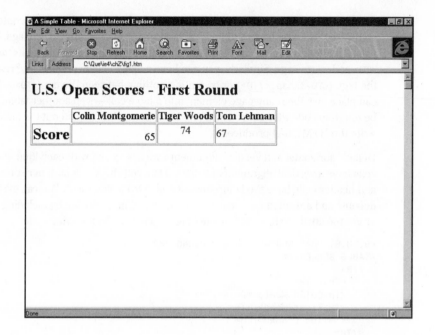

■ In the absence of alignment specifications in the <TR>, <TD>, or <TH> tags, default
alignments are used.

Putting together everything you've read so far, you can construct the following table template.
You can use this template as a starting point for building any HTML table. Depending on your
needs, you'll have to modify the template by adding or deleting the appropriate tags and attributes:

```
<TABLE BORDER=1>
<TR>  <!-- Row 1-->
            <TD>...</TD>
            <TD>...</TD>
            ...
            <TD>...</TD>
      </TR>
<TR>  <!-- Row 2-->
            <TD>...</TD>
            <TD>...</TD>
            ...
            <TD>...</TD>
      </TR>
...
<TR>  <!-- Row m-->
            <TD>...</TD>
            <TD>...</TD>
            ...
            <TD>...</TD>
      </TR>
</TABLE>
```

Fine Tuning Your Tables

In addition to tweaking alignments, you can polish your tables by making use of some other table-related tags and attributes. In particular, you can:

- Add a caption to a table
- Increase or decrease the width of a table
- Increase or decrease the spacing within and between cells
- Make a cell occupy more than one row or column

The next four sections discuss these table features and the HTML you need to know to produce them.

Adding a Caption to a Table

You can add a caption to your tables by enclosing the caption text between the `<CAPTION>` and `</CAPTION>` tags. Captions will appear centered over the top of the table unless you use the `ALIGN=BOTTOM` attribute of the `<CAPTION>` tag, in which case the caption is centered below the table. Caption text can be formatted with any of the HTML physical styles as well.

 TIP Put your caption immediately after the `<TABLE>` tag or immediately before the `</TABLE>` tag so you don't run the risk of it accidentally becoming part of a cell.

Table Width

When a browser renders a table, it only uses as much of the screen width as necessary to accommodate the table. You can force the browser to use more or less of the screen by using the WIDTH attribute of the `<TABLE>` tag. For example, the table in Figure 24.1 only took up part of screen width that Internet Explorer had available. By changing the source code to use the `<TABLE>` tag, as follows:

```
<TABLE BORDER=1 WIDTH=100%>
```

Internet Explorer is compelled to use the entire screen width to render the table (see Figure 24.2). The alignment of the data elements has been changed to CENTER and MIDDLE for easier readability.

You can set WIDTH to a percentage of available screen width or a specific number of pixels. Because you typically don't know the screen width settings of every user's computer, however, you should use percentages whenever possible. The only exception to using percentages is when the table has to be a certain number of pixels wide to accommodate an image in one of its cells.

Changing Cell Padding and Cell Spacing

Cell padding refers to the amount of space a browser leaves between the data element in a cell and the edges of the cell. If your table looks crowded and you want to open it up with some white space, you can increase the CELLPADDING attribute of the <TABLE> tag from its default value of 1 to a higher value. Figure 24.3 shows our golf score table with the following <TABLE> tag:

```
<TABLE BORDER=1 WIDTH=100% CELLPADDING=8>
```

FIG. 24.2

The WIDTH attribute of the <TABLE> tag gives you control over how much screen real estate a table occupies.

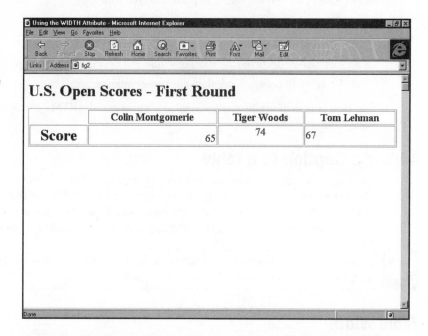

FIG. 24.3

Give your table some room to breathe by increasing the amount of cell padding.

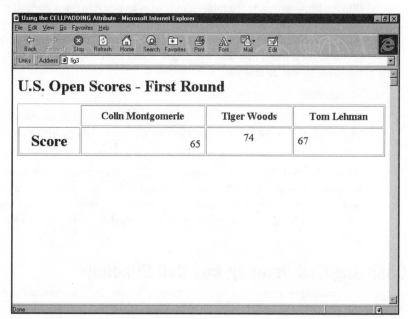

The amount of space a browser leaves between adjacent cells is called *cell spacing*. You can control this table property as well by making use of the CELLSPACING attribute of the <TABLE> tag. Figure 24.4 shows the golf scores table with the following <TABLE> tag:

```
<TABLE BORDER=1 WIDTH=100% CELLSPACING=8>
```

Note in Figure 24.4 how the border appears to grow thicker to account for the additional space between cells.

FIG. 24.4
You can push cells farther apart from each other by increasing the CELLSPACING attribute.

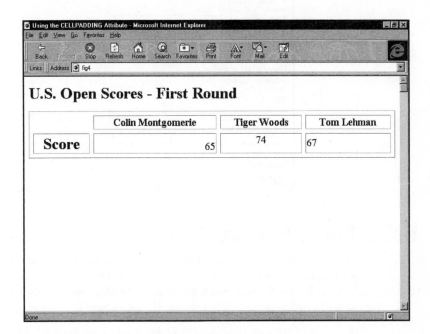

Part
V

Ch
24

Spanning Multiple Rows and Columns

By default, a table cell occupies or *spans* one row and one column. This default is fine for using tables to present rows and columns of data, but once tables found a role in page design, it became necessary to allow cells to span multiple rows or columns. HTML 3.2 supports attributes of the <TD> and <TH> tags that create this effect.

You use the COLSPAN attribute when a cell needs to span more than one column in a given row. Set the COLSPAN attribute to the number of columns you want a cell to occupy. This attribute comes in handy when you have one row in a table with substantially more data elements in it than the others (see Figure 24.5). That one row will determine the total number of columns needed for the table. Because the rows with fewer data elements don't require as many columns, you can make cells in those rows span more than one column so that they occupy all of the columns available.

The ROWSPAN attribute works similarly for cells that must occupy more than one row. Just set ROWSPAN equal to the number of rows you want the cell to take up.

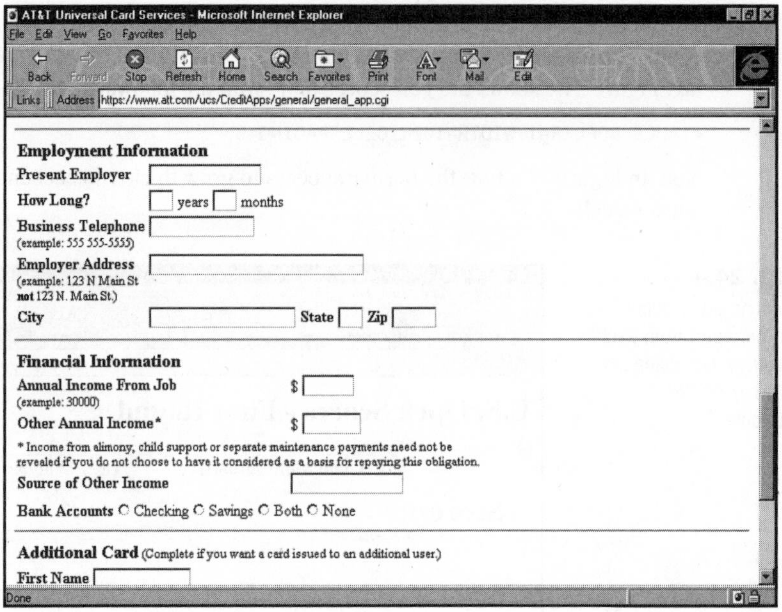

FIG. 24.5
AT&T's online Universal Card application uses the COLSPAN attribute to make form fields occupy more than one column.

Using Tables in Page Design

So far you've only read about tables in the context of presenting tabular data, but you've probably also deduced from the reading that you can use tables for much more than that. HTML tables also serve as the framework for creating complex page layouts that aren't otherwise possible. There are at least three reasons why tables have become so popular for page design:

- You can finely control alignment all the way down to the cell level.
- You're not limited to placing just text in a table cell. You can place other page elements, like images and form fields, in cells, too.
- You can make cells occupy more than one row or column.

To close this section of the chapter, here are a few situations in which tables make a handy design tool:

- **Creating multicolumn layouts** Suppose you wanted to create a three-column layout. All you need is a table with one row and three columns. Because there is no limit to how far down the page a column can run and because you can place any kind of page element you want in the table, producing the three-column layout is just a matter of populating each of the table cells with the appropriate content.

- **Aligning form fields** A form field isn't much good without some text in front of it that tells the user what information he or she should enter in the field. The problem is that the prompting text for adjacent form fields is rarely the same length, which means that the left-most edges of the form fields will occur at different positions on the screen.

Couple that with the fact that form fields aren't usually the same length, and you can end up with a very unattractive form!

A two-column table can remedy this situation. By placing the prompting text in the first column and all of the form fields in the second column, you can create a form with greater visual appeal (see Figure 24.6).

FIG. 24.6
Aligning form fields creates a better looking form that users will be more likely to read and fill out.

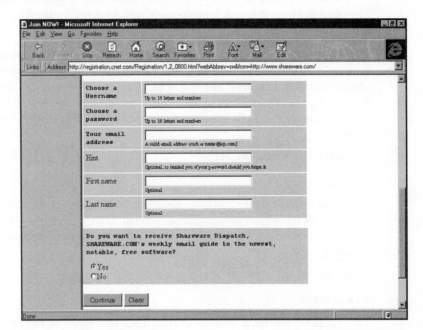

- **Aligning images**   It's always been difficult to get an image exactly where you want it to go on a page. This is especially true if you use an image as a bullet in an unordered list. The list items are usually too close to the image, and, if they break to a new line, they wrap to a point below the image rather than lining up with the first line of text. By putting the bullet images in one column of a two-column table and putting the list items in the second column, you can take care of bullet/text alignment and spacing and the text wrapping issues all at the same time.

Setting Up the Framed Layout

Frames were introduced as an extension to HTML a few years ago, and, in spite of the fact that they are still not part of standard HTML, Internet Explorer and other browsers still support their implementation. Using the frame tags, you can break up the browser window into multiple areas that can each display its own HTML document. The ability to display multiple documents simultaneously has proved most useful in situations where authors have wanted to display smaller, static items like navigation aids in their own permanent windows while still leaving a lot of space for changing content. This capability enables users to move through a site while still having constant access to the navigation aids.

The balance of this chapter is devoted to a discussion of the frame tags as implemented by Internet Explorer and how you can build framed documents into your Web site.

The first step in creating a framed layout is to split the Internet Explorer window into the regions you want. You accomplish this with an HTML file that uses the <FRAMESET> and </FRAMESET> tags instead of the <BODY> and </BODY> tags. <FRAMESET> and </FRAMESET> are more than just container tags, though. The attributes of the <FRAMESET> tag specify how the screen is split up.

The <FRAMESET> tag can take one of two attributes: ROWS, to split the screen into two or more rows; or COLS, to split the screen into two or more columns. Each attribute is set equal to a list of values that tells Internet Explorer how big to make each row or column. The values can be a number of pixels, a percentage of the available space, or an asterisk (*), which acts as a wildcard character and tells Internet Explorer to use whatever space it has left. For example, the HTML:

```
<FRAMESET ROWS="25%,40%,35%">
...
</FRAMESET>
```

divides the browser screen into three rows. The first row occupies 25 percent of the available screen depth, the second row occupies 40 percent, and the third row occupies the remaining 35 percent. Similarly, you can split the screen into columns by using a <FRAMESET> such as the following:

```
<FRAMESET COLS="55,120,2*,*">
...
</FRAMESET>
```

The preceding code splits the browser screen into four columns. The first column is 55 pixels wide and the second is 120 pixels wide. The remaining screen width is divided between the third and fourth columns, with the third column being twice as large (2*) as the fourth (*).

By default, frames are separated by a small amount of space. You can increase the amount of space between frames by using increasing values of the FRAMESPACING attribute of the <FRAMESET> tag. The <FRAMESET> tag also takes the FRAMEBORDER attribute, which is used to control the thickness of the visible border between frames. Many authors make their frames appear seamless by setting FRAMEBORDER=0.

You can create complex layouts by nesting <FRAMESET> and </FRAMESET> tags. Suppose you want to set up a layout in which the right-most two-thirds of the browser window is dedicated to displaying changing content and the left-most one-third is for a 75-pixel high corporate logo and a table of contents. You can begin to construct this layout with the following HTML:

```
<FRAMESET COLS="33%,67%">
...
</FRAMESET>
```

This HTML splits the screen into two columns—the left column is one-third of the available width and the right column occupies the other two thirds (see Figure 24.7).

FIG. 24.7

The first step in producing your complex layout is to split the screen into two columns.

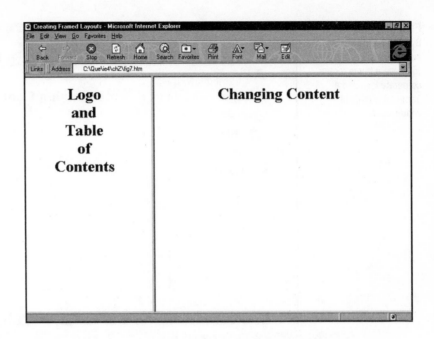

At this point, part of your layout requirements are met, but you still need to allocate space in the first column for the logo and the table of contents. You can do this by splitting the first column into two rows—one that is 75 pixels high (to accommodate the logo) and one that takes up the rest of the available space. Figure 24.8 shows that you can accomplish this with the following HTML:

```
<FRAMESET COLS="33%,67%">  <!-- Split screen into two columns. -->
  <FRAMESET ROWS="75,*">  <!-- Split column 1 into two rows. -->
    ...  <!-- Placeholder for content to go into the two rows. -->
  </FRAMESET>
  ...  <!-- Placeholder for content to go into column 2. -->
</FRAMESET>
```

The preceding code splits up the screen into the frames that you want. What remains for you to do is to place content into each of these frames. To do this, use the <FRAME> tag, which is the topic of the next section.

If you're not sure whether to do the ROWS or the COLS first when doing a nested <FRAMESET>, try this approach. Make a sketch of what you want the finished frame configuration to look like. If you have unbroken horizontal lines that go from one edge of the screen to the other, do your ROWS first. If you have unbroken vertical lines that go from the top of the window to the bottom, do your COLS first. If you have unbroken horizontal and vertical lines, it doesn't matter which one you do first.

FIG. 24.8

By splitting the first column into two rows, you have a frame for the corporate logo and a frame for a table of contents.

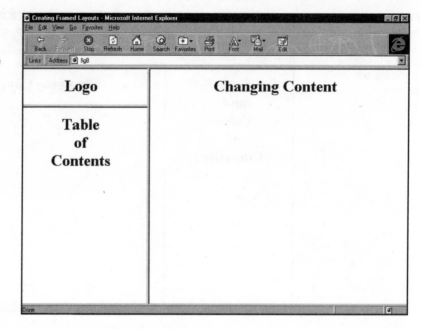

Placing Content in Your Frames

With your frames all set, you're ready to place content in each one with the <FRAME> tag. The <FRAME> tag takes the mandatory SRC attribute, which tells Internet Explorer the URL of the document you want to load into the frame. Table 24.1 summarizes the other attributes of the <FRAME> tag. Though none of them are mandatory, they go a long way to making a framed layout more user-friendly.

Table 24.1   Attributes of the _<FRAME>_ Tag

Attribute	Purpose
FRAMEBORDER=n	Specifies the width to use for the border between frames (0 is acceptable)
MARGINHEIGHT=n	Specifies the number of pixels of white space to leave at the top and bottom of the frame
MARGINWIDTH=n	Specifies the number of pixels of white space to leave along the sides of the frame
NAME="name"	Gives the frame a unique name; names must begin with an alphanumeric character
NORESIZE	Disables the user's ability to resize a frame by dragging its border to a new position

Attribute	Purpose
SCROLLING=YES ¦ NO ¦ AUTO	Controls the appearance of horizontal and vertical scrollbars in the frame; the default is AUTO, in which case the browser places the scrollbars if they are needed

Going back to the example from the previous section, you can add <FRAME> tags to place the corporate logo, the table of contents, and the site's main page into their respective frames:

```
<FRAMESET COLS="33%,67%">  <!-- Split screen into two columns. -->
  <FRAMESET ROWS="75,*">  <!-- Split column 1 into two rows. -->
    <FRAME NAME="logo" SRC="logo.html">  <!-- Place the logo into
                                               the first row. -->
    <FRAME NAME="toc" SRC="tableofcontents.html">  <!-- Place the
                                               ToC into the second row. -->
  </FRAMESET>
  <FRAME NAME="main" SRC="homepage.html"> <!-- Initial document for
                                               changing content frame. -->
</FRAMESET>
```

Note in the preceding code that each frame was given a NAME. Unique frame names are important when you're targeting links to point at a particular frame. For example, the table of contents links will all be in the frame named "toc." Thus, when you click one of the links, it will load the linked document into the "toc" frame. But this is not the effect you want! You created a large frame named "main" to hold the changing content. What you need to do is set up the links in the table of contents so that they target the frame named "main." To do this, add the TARGET attribute to the <A> tag in your hyperlinks, as in the following HTML:

```
<A HREF="stockholders.html" TARGET="main">
Message to Stockholders
</A>
```

With the preceding code, the file stockholders.html is loaded into the frame named "main" when a user clicks the **Message to Stockholders** hypertext. Thus, the changing content goes into the big frame and the table of contents stays put in the smaller frame.

 TIP If all of the hyperlinks in a file are targeting one particular frame, you can set up a "global" target using the <BASE> tag in the document head. In the table of contents file, you might have code such as the following:

```
<HEAD>
<TITLE>Site Table of Contents</TITLE>
<BASE TARGET="main">
</HEAD>
```

This code tells Internet Explorer that every hyperlink in the file should target the frame named "main."

The TARGET attribute isn't limited to just the <A> tag. You can use it in the <FORM> tag to display the response from a form submission in a particular frame. Also, you can use it in the <AREA> tag when creating a client-side imagemap so that documents associated with the hot regions on your imagemap can be loaded into the frame of your choosing.

N O T E Some reserved frame names are useful in conjunction with the TARGET attribute. These include:

- "_blank"   Targets a new blank window.
- "_self"   Targets the frame where the hyperlink is found.
- "_parent" Targets the parent <FRAMESET> of the frame where the hyperlink is found. The "_parent" name defaults to "_self" if there is no parent <FRAMESET>.
- "_top"   Targets the full window before any frames were introduced. This is a good way to jump completely out of a <FRAMESET>. ◼

Respecting Frames-Challenged Browsers

The frame tags discussed in this section are not part of standard HTML, so it's reasonable to assume that not all browsers will support them. For this reason, you must include a version of your pages that these "frames-challenged" browsers can process. To do this, you can place alternative HTML code between the <NOFRAMES> and </NOFRAMES> tags. Any HTML between these tags will be ignored by Internet Explorer but will be understood and rendered by the frames-challenged browsers.

One nice thing about the <NOFRAMES> and </NOFRAMES> tags is that you can typically place existing code between them. For the example discussed in this section, you have presumably created several files that would be displayed in the frame named "main." You can recycle this same code and place it between <NOFRAMES> and </NOFRAMES> so that users with frames-challenged browsers will see the exact same content as those with frames-capable browsers.

> **CAUTION**
>
> The <NOFRAMES> and </NOFRAMES> tags must occur after the initial <FRAMESET> tag but before any nested <FRAMESET> tags.

CHAPTER 25

Building Navigational Imagemaps

When you visit the initial page of a Web site, more often than not you are greeted by a fairly large image that presents you with several different site navigation options (see Figure 25.1). By clicking different areas of the image, you can instruct Internet Explorer to load one of a number of different pages. Such a multiply linked image is called an *imagemap*.

An imagemap is different from an ordinary hyperlinked image in that the image is subdivided into regions called *hot regions*, and each hot region is linked to a different document. Because you're designating one image to act as a gateway to many different pages, setting up an imagemap is not as simple as setting up a single hyperlinked image as you learned how to do in Chapter 23, "Links, Graphics, and Advanced Graphics." Rather, you'll need to define where the hot regions on the image are and associate each hot region with a different URL.

Creating server-side imagemaps

Server-side maps were the first kind of imagemap and are still a perfectly good approach to creating a multiply linked image.

Shifting the computational burden to the browser

A client-side imagemap is one that is processed by Internet Explorer. To accomplish this, you must first learn how to pass map information in your HTML documents.

Tips for creating good imagemaps

Like any Web page element, imagemaps require careful planning and thoughtful execution. This chapter shares some suggestions for producing quality imagemaps that also respect bandwidth and browser limitations.

Tools for building imagemaps

Early Web page authors had to code imagemaps manually, but developers today have a wealth of tools at their disposal to assist in the creation of both server-side and client-side imagemaps.

FIG. 25.1

Imagemaps are commonly used to present users with links to all major content areas of a Web site.

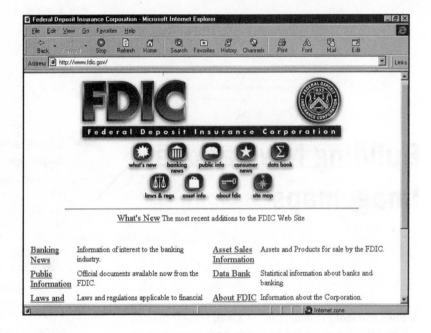

Currently, HTML 3.2 supports two different approaches to imagemaps. The original type of imagemap on the Web is the *server-side imagemap*. When a user clicks a server-side imagemap, the coordinates of the click are sent to the Web server and a program running on the server determines what hot region the user clicked. Then, the server sends the URL of the document associated with that hot region to the browser and the browser makes an HTTP request for that document. Though server-side imagemaps work just fine, they are generally thought to be slow because of the data exchange that has to occur between the server and the browser. Additionally, they place extra overhead on the server because the server has to do the computations to determine which hot region the user clicked.

The other approach to imagemaps is the *client-side imagemap*. In this case, the information that defines the different hot regions and their associated documents is sent to the browser as part of the HTML code for the page that contains the imagemap. Once the browser has this information, it can do all of the computations to figure out which URL to load based on a user's mouse click. This eliminates the need for additional transactions between the browser and the server and, in most cases, greatly reduces the time between the user clicking the map and the next page loading.

This chapter illustrates both imagemapping methods and introduces you to the HTML you will need to know to implement one approach or the other. Additionally, you'll pick up some handy tips on creating a good imagemap and you'll learn about some software tools available to developers to help with imagemap composition. ■

Server-Side Imagemaps

As you read earlier, server-side imagemaps are the original type of map on the Web. They continue to have their place in the Web world because there are still browsers that do not yet support the HTML 3.2 tags used to create a client-side imagemap. This section walks you through the process of creating a server-side imagemap.

What You'll Need

A server-side imagemap has three main components:

■ **An image**   This component is the only part of your imagemap that the user will see. Your imagemap image should be a GIF or a JPEG image designed so that it is easy to visually discern the different hot regions.

■ **A map file**   The map file resides on the server and contains information that defines the hot regions on the image and which document is associated with each hot region.

■ **Proper setup in the HTML file**   When setting up an imagemap in your HTML code, you have to take some special steps to let the browser know that it is rendering an imagemap.

Additionally, you'll need access to the server so you can place the map file there. If you don't have server access, you should become friends with the server administrator so that he or she can help you when the time comes to put your map file on the server.

N O T E   You may wonder whether you also need a program on the server that takes the coordinates of a user's mouse click and determines in which hot region the click occurred. Fortunately, every Web server comes with a built-in program to handle this task. ■

Setting Up the Map File

A map file is simply a text file that contains enough information to define the image hot regions and the URLs of the documents that you are linking to the hot regions. For this reason, you need to create a separate map file for each imagemap you're preparing.

Types of Hot Regions   Hot regions are named for their geometric shapes. Each permissible shape has a keyword associated with it and a specific number of points that are required to completely define the region. Points are specified by (x,y) coordinate pairs measured from the upper left corner of the image, which is taken to have the coordinates (0,0). A list of the valid types of hot regions, their keywords, and the coordinates needed to define them follows:

Part

V

Ch

25

- **Rectangle** A rectangular hot region is denoted by the keyword **rect** in the map file. You only need two sets of coordinates to define a rectangle: those for the upper-left and lower- right corners.

- **Circle** You can define a circular hot region by using the keyword **circle** in the map file and by providing the coordinates of the center of the circle and of one point on the circle itself.

- **Polygon** Polygons are nice to have as hot regions because they can take on a wide variety of appearances. To define a polygonal hot region, you use the keyword **poly**. When it comes to defining the polygon, you must provide the coordinates of every vertex of the polygon—a list that can grow very long sometimes! Polygonal hot regions can have as many as 100 vertices.

- **Point** You can make a single point in the image into a hot region by using the **point** keyword and specifying the coordinates of the point. A point is considered to be clicked if the click occurs closest to that point on the graphic while not being in any other hot region.

- **Default** The default keyword is a catch-all for any points on the image that are not part of an otherwise defined hot region.

In addition to the hot region's keyword and defining coordinates, you'll also need to provide the URL of the document you're linking to the hot region when you set up the map file. Map file URLs should be fully qualified—that is, they should include a protocol, server name, directory path, and file name.

Types of Map Files Now that you know the three key pieces of information that must go into a map file, you can turn to the issue of how to order that information in the file. You can use two map file formats: one for CERN server imagemaps and one for NCSA server imagemaps. Each format uses the same pieces of information, but the order is different in each. You should consult with your server's administrator to determine which format is appropriate for use with your server.

A line in a CERN server map file has the following syntax:

```
region_keyword coordinates URL
```

The coordinate pairs must be in parentheses and the x and y coordinates are each separated by commas. A sample circular hot region definition in a CERN-style map file might look like this:

```
circle (101,75) (88,62) http://www.circles.com/index.html
```

NCSA server map files order the information as follows:

```
region_keyword URL coordinates
```

In addition to the different ordering, the coordinate pairs do not have to be contained in parentheses. The x and y coordinates still must be separated by commas, though. The NCSA equivalent of the preceding circular hot region definition would be

```
circle http://www.circles.com/index.html 101,75 88,62
```

N O T E Most servers in use today, including all Netscape and Microsoft server products, follow the NSCA format. ◼

Setting Up the Imagemap in Your Document

Having defined and placed the map file on your server, you're now ready to set up the call to the imagemap in your HTML document. Because of differences in how individual servers process imagemaps, you have two different set up options.

CERN and NCSA Servers   Once you've created the map file in the appropriate format, you must make the imagemap graphic an anchor with the `<A>` tag, as follows:

```
<A HREF="/cgi-bin/imagemap/navigation">
<IMS SRC="nav_footer.gif" ISMAP></A>
```

The HREF attribute points to the imagemap script on the server (located at **/cgi-bin/ imagemap**). The call to the script is followed by a slash (/) and the name of the map file's entry in the **imagemap.conf** file on the server. The `<IMG>` tag places the graphic and the ISMAP attribute indicates to the browser that the graphic is to be used as an imagemap.

The **imagemap.conf** file on the server contains a listing of imagemap names and the location of the corresponding map file. For the imagemap previously named navigation, the line in the **imagemap.conf** file might look like

```
navigation : /maps/navigate.map
```

This entry would allow the imagemap script to find the map file **navigate.map** located in the map's directory. You need to have a line like the previous one in the **imagemap.conf** file for each imagemap you want the server to be able to process.

Netscape and Microsoft Servers   Netscape and Microsoft servers make it much easier to set up the link to an imagemap. In either of these cases, you simply make the HREF attribute in the `<A>` tag point directly to the map file (done in NCSA format). For example

```
<A HREF="/maps/navigate.map">
<IMS SRC="nav_footer.gif" ISMAP></A>
```

would replicate the set up noted earlier for CERN and NCSA servers. Netscape and Microsoft servers don't use an **imagemap.conf** file.

Client-Side Imagemaps

As Web browsers became more sophisticated, they also became better able to handle more complicated types of processing. With the emergence of more capable clients, the idea to shift the burden of imagemap computation to the browser began to pick up steam.

The major stumbling block to implementing client-side imagemaps was to devise a standard approach to sending map data that previously resided on the server to the browser. Most developers were in agreement that the map data should be part of an HTML file, but initially there were different approaches to embedding the map data in HTML. When it issued the HTML 3.2

Part
V

Ch
25

specification, the World Wide Web Consortium introduced the use of the <MAP> and <AREA> tags as the official approach. This section discusses how to use them to create your own client-side imagemaps.

Advantages

Apart from reducing the computational load on a server, using client-side imagemaps affords your users some additional advantages, including:

- **Offline viewing of Web documents** This was one of the original driving factors behind client-side imagemaps. Previously, HTML documents being viewed from a hard drive or a CD-ROM couldn't use imagemaps at all because no server is involved. By providing map data to the browser, client-side imagemaps enable you to replicate imagemap functionality in situations in which a server isn't used.

- **Immediate processing** Rather than passing the mouse click's coordinates to the server and waiting for a reply, a browser that can handle client-side imagemaps can process the click by itself almost immediately. In fact, as you move your mouse pointer over a client-side imagemap, you typically see a hot region's associated URL displayed in the status bar at the bottom of the browser window.

- **Single, consistent approach** Now that the W3C has put forward the accepted approach to client-side imagemaps, there is one and only one way to implement them. This one way is different from server-side imagemaps, which had different map file formats and link setups, depending on which type of server you were running.

Setting Up the Imagemap in Your Document

The key to creating a client-side imagemap is transferring all the data you'd put into a map file to the browser. To do this, place the data between the <MAP> and </MAP> container tags. The <MAP> tag has the mandatory attribute NAME, which assigns a unique name to the map. The name is used in the <IMG> tag that places the imagemap graphic to refer to the appropriate set of map data.

Inside the <MAP> and </MAP> tags, you must place an <AREA> tag for each hot region you want to define. An <AREA> tag takes the attributes shown in Table 25.1.

Table 25.1 Attributes of the *<AREA>* Tag

Attribute	Function
ALT	Provides a text-based alternative to the graphical hot region
COORDS	List of coordinate pairs needed to define the hot region (all coordinates separated by commas)
HREF	Provides the URL of the document you're associating with a hot region
NOHREF	Specifies that there is no URL associated with a hot region

Attribute	Function
SHAPE	Set equal to the keyword that specifies the shape of the hot region (point is not supported)

To see how the `<MAP>` and `<AREA>` tags work together, consider the following HTML, which is the client-side equivalent of the example code presented in the server-side imagemap section:

```
<MAP NAME="circles">
<AREA SHAPE="circle" COORDS="101,75,88,62"
    HREF="http://www.circles.com/index.html" ALT="Circles Link">
</MAP>
```

The preceding code defines an imagemap with a single, circular hot region that is linked to the **circles.com** site.

If a point in an image is not defined as part of a hot region in a client-side imagemap, it is taken to behave as though a NOHREF is associated with the point. This way, by default, users will not go anywhere if they click a point that isn't linked. This is nice for you as a developer because it means you don't have to build an `<AREA SHAPE="default" NOHREF>` tag into all your client-side imagemap code.

Now that you have a way to provide the map data to a browser HTML form, all you need to do to complete the client-side imagemap is to properly set up the link. To do this, you simply use the `<IMG>` tag to place the imagemap graphic with the USEMAP attribute, which tells the browser that it's dealing with a client-side map. USEMAP is set equal to the name of the map you want to use to process the imagemap. Recall that the map is named by the NAME attribute of the `<MAP>` tag. To link to the client-side imagemap previously defined, you would use the following code:

```
<IMG SRC="circlemap.gif" USEMAP="#circles">
```

The pound sign (#) tells the browser that the map information is found in the same HTML document. You can also store map data in a separate master file and have the USEMAP attribute point to the master file. For example

```
<IMG SRC="circlemap.gif" USEMAP="mapdata.html#circles">
```

references the file **mapdata.html** to find the imagemap data for the circles map. Storing map data for imagemaps used frequently on your pages is a good idea because it makes them easier to maintain. If you have to change your imagemap, it's much simpler to make your edits in a master map file than it is to make the same change in multiple files.

An Example

As the chapter title suggests, imagemaps are frequently used to help users navigate a Web site. An imagemap on the main page of the site with consistently placed maps on subordinate pages gives users a handy way to move easily among areas on your site. To illustrate imagemaps in action, this section looks at an example main page map. The graphic for the imagemap is

Part

V

Ch

25

shown in Figure 25.2 and the hot regions, their defining coordinates, and associated URLs are given in Table 25.2.

FIG. 25.2

A sample main page imagemap graphic for use in our example.

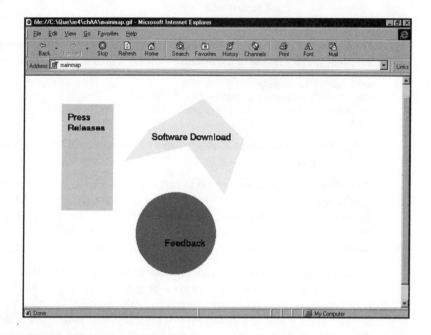

Table 25.2 Hot Regions for Example Imagemap

Shape	Coordinates	URL
Rectangle	(68,72),(176,285)	http://www.your_server.com/press.html
Circle	(305,331),(367,387)	http://www.your_server.com/feedback.html
Polygon	(199,186),(248,125),(363,60),(447,143),(407,254),(333,156)	http://www.your_server.com/download.html

To implement the preceding imagemap as a server-side map, you'd first have to find out the type of server on which the map will reside. If, for example, your Web server is running Microsoft's Internet Information Server, you must set up the map file using the NCSA format. Thus, your map file should look like this:

```
rect http://www.your_server.com/press.html 68,72 176,285
circle http://www.your_server.com/feedback.html 305,331 367,387
poly http://www.your_server.com/download.html 199,186 248,125 363,
60 447,143 407,254 33
```

If you named this preceding map file as **mainpage.map**, you would set it up with the following HTML:

```
<A HREF="mainpage.map">
<IMG SRC="mainmap.gif" ISMAP></A>
```

Conversely, to set up the map as a client-side imagemap, you would need to store the map data in `<AREA>` tags, as follows:

```
<MAP NAME="mainpage">
<AREA SHAPE="rect" COORDS="68,72,176,285"
    HREF="http://www.your_server.com/press.html">
<AREA SHAPE="circle" COORDS="305,331,367,387"
    HREF="http://www.your_server.com/feedback.html">
<AREA SHAPE="poly" COORDS="199,186,248,125,363,60,447,143,407,254,
    333,156" HREF="http://www.your_server.com/download.html">
</MAP>
```

Assuming that the preceding code is located in the same file as the code for the main page, you can set up the imagemap using the HTML:

```
<IMG SRC="mainmap.gif" USEMAP="#mainpage">
```

Or, if you're storing map data in a common file named **maps.html**, you would use:

```
<IMG SRC="mainmap.gif" USEMAP="maps.html#mainpage">
```

Imagemap Tips and Tricks

As you create imagemaps for your Web documents, you should keep some design considerations in mind to make your maps usable by the broadest audience possible. These considerations include the following:

- **Provide a text-based alternative** Users who have nongraphical browsers or who have turned image loading off will not be able to use any imagemap functionality you've built into your pages. For this reason, you should replicate the links found in an imagemap in a set of text-based links co-located with the map (see Figure 25.3). This way, all users will have access to the same set of links. When creating a client-side imagemap, you can easily create a set of alternate text-based links by making judicious use of the ALT attribute of the `<AREA>` tag.

- **Specify a default region** You should specify a default hot region whenever possible. The simplest thing to do when setting up the default region is to link it back to the same HTML page, but you can take things a step further by creating a special page that advises users that they did not click a linked region and that they should go back and try again.

- **Be careful using the point keyword** Linking a point can create difficulty for the end user. First of all, it's hard to click precisely on the single pixel that is linked. Also, if you specify a point as a hot region and also try to specify a default region, the default specification will essentially be ignored. This happens because a click on a nonlinked region is treated as a click on the closest point region whenever the point keyword is used.

FIG. 25.3
Duplicating the links in an imagemap with a set of text-based links is an important user service.

Imagemap

Text links replicate imagemap links

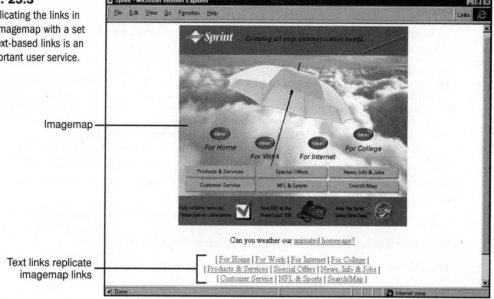

- **Don't overlap hot regions**   Allow enough space between your hot regions so that they don't overlap. If users click a point that is part of more than one hot region, they will link to the document associated with the hot region that is listed first in the map file (for server-side maps) or in the <MAP> and </MAP> container tags (for client-side maps).

- **Use comments**   Commenting your imagemap information makes it easier for others to see what's going on. If you're coding a server-side imagemap with the map file in NCSA format, you can initiate a comment by using the pound sign (#). For client-side imagemaps, you can use the standard HTML comment container tags <!-- and -->.

- **Use server-side and client-side maps together**   If you know that some members of your audience won't be using a browser that can process client-side imagemaps, you can use both approaches together so that all users can take advantage of your imagemap functionality. To set up a combination map, you would use HTML such as the following:

```
<A HREF="circles.map>
<IMG SRC="circlemap.gif" ISMAP USEMAP="#circles">
</A>
```

In the preceding code, the <IMG> tag sets up the client-side map and the <A> and </A> tags set up the server-side map. If a browser can process client-side maps, it will recognize the USEMAP attribute and do the processing itself. Otherwise, the ISMAP attribute will direct the browser to treat the imagemap as a server-side map.

Imagemap Tools

As useful as imagemaps are, site developers found them hard to set up in the early days of the Web because the developers had to determine all of the defining coordinates of the hot regions in a graphics program and then code the map file by hand. Nowadays, very handy software tools take on this burden and make imagemap preparation a snap. Two popular mapping tools are LiveImage and Mapedit.

Live Image

On the CD

LiveImage is the successor program to the very popular software tool Map This! Figure 25.4 shows the LiveImage main window opened with the graphic used in the example presented earlier in the chapter.

FIG. 25.4
The LiveImage main window is split in two: The left half lists defined hot regions, and the right half is where you trace out new hot regions.

Hot region definitions——

Shaded hot regions——

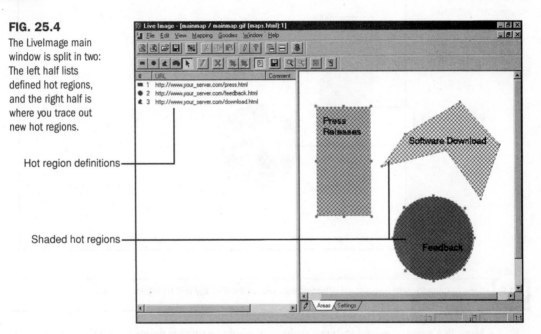

Part
V
Ch
25

LiveImage makes imagemapping easy because you simply need to trace out your hot regions using one of LiveImage's tools. Once you trace out a region, a pop-up dialog box will prompt you for the associated URL, any comments you want to make and, if you're using a framed layout, which frame you want to target. Hot regions that have been defined show up as shaded in the right side of the LiveImage window.

LiveImage also comes with a bunch of neat features including a grid that you can overlay on the graphic to help you trace more accurately and zoom in and out, a map test facility, and a "smooth polygon" tool that will take the sharp edges off your polygonal regions. One limitation from which LiveImage suffers, however, is that it can only prepare client-side imagemaps. If you're preparing a server-side map, you'll need to get a copy of Map This! (which does both types of maps) or Mapedit, the program discussed in the next section.

Mapedit

Mapedit was one of the first imagemap tools on the Web and it's still one of the best. Figure 25.5 shows the Mapedit main window open with your main page graphic inside.

When you start a new imagemap in Mapedit, you have the choice between creating a server-side (CERN or NCSA style) or a client-side map. Defining hot regions with Mapedit is simple. Just select the appropriate tool and trace out the region. When you're done, a dialog box will prompt you for the associated URL and any comments.

FIG. 25.5

The Mapedit main window is largely devoted to the image-map graphic, with small buttons for the different hot region tools.

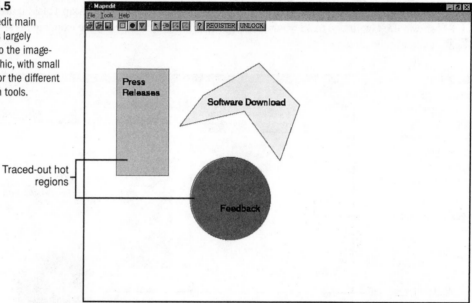

Traced-out hot regions

TIP   If you're unhappy with how a trace is turning out, just hit the ESC key and try again.

Mapedit's more advanced features enable you to add or remove points from a polygon, to move an entire hot region, and to test the map.

N O T E   Neither LiveImage nor Mapedit are freeware. You may evaluate them for 14 and 30 days, respectively, after which you must register and pay for your copy. ■

CHAPTER 26

Creating Forms and Server Scripts

As Web technology has evolved, it has also become more pervasive. Consider some of the things happening over the Web today:

Understanding the two sides of interactive Web pages

Interactivity is when information is put forward and then a response, based on that information, is returned. In the context of interactive Web pages, HTML forms are used to collect information from users and some type of script, either on the client-side or the server-side, provides the response.

Creating HTML forms

You only need to know a few tags to be able to compose HTML forms. Simply by varying the attributes of these tags, you can place just about any popular graphical user interface (GUI) control on a Web page.

What happens when the user clicks the Submit button

Form data must be bundled in a particular way before it makes its journey to the server. And once it's ready to go, you can use two different methods to send it.

Back-end processing with CGI scripts

Programs running on the server receive the form data and process it. They then compose a response page and send it back to the user's browser.

■ You can now shop online, in many cases with a "virtual shopping bag" into which you place the items you want to buy. When you're ready to check out, your purchases are totaled and you are queried for your credit card information.

■ Corporate intranets are making it possible to move to a "paperless office" concept whereby requisitioning, time recording, and other business processes are being put online. The forms you used to fill out on paper you now fill out in a browser screen.

■ Users are registering for custom start pages at many Web sites. They choose what kind of information they want to see when they hit a site and store their choices in profiles that servers can use to generate the custom pages.

None of the HTML you've read about so far can support this type of interactivity. A handful of very versatile tags begin to make these types of Web applications possible, however. These are the HTML form tags that produce the popular controls—such as text entry fields, check boxes, and option buttons—seen on Web pages. These controls guide users through the visible part of these interactive pages—the gathering of information.

The behind-the-scenes part of interactivity is the processing of the information gathered. This processing is typically done by a Common Gateway Interface (CGI) script on the Web server. CGI scripts process form data and return a response (usually an HTML page) back to the browser. The response could be a simple static page, a list of records from a database that match a query, or another form that asks for further information based on the data submitted in the original form.

N O T E Limited processing can occur on the client-side, too, thanks to scripting languages like JavaScript and VBScript. ■

This chapter introduces you to both sides of the operation. In the first part of the chapter, you'll look at the form tags and how to use them to create a sharp-looking, information-gathering interface. Then, in the second part of the chapter, you'll begin to explore CGI and how you can manipulate information submitted through an HTML form. ■

Using the Form Header to Control the Response

HTML's form support is simple and complete. A handful of HTML tags creates the most popular elements of modern graphical interfaces, including text windows, check boxes and radio buttons, pull-down menus, and push buttons.

Composing HTML forms might sound like a complex task, but you must master surprisingly few tags to do it. All form-related tags occur between the <FORM> and </FORM> container tags. If you have more than one form in an HTML document, the closing </FORM> tag is essential for distinguishing between the multiple forms.

TIP Adding a </FORM> tag immediately after creating a <FORM> tag is a good practice; then you can go back to fill in the contents. Following this procedure helps you avoid leaving off the closing tag once you've finished.

Each HTML form has three main components: the *form header*, one or more named *input fields*, and one or more *action buttons*.

The form header and the <FORM> tag are actually one and the same. The <FORM> tag takes the three attributes shown in Table 26.1. The ACTION attribute is required in every <FORM> tag.

Table 26.1 Attributes of the <FORM> Tag

Attribute	Purpose
ACTION	Specifies the URL of the processing script
ENCTYPE	Supplies the MIME type of a file used as form input
METHOD=GET ¦ POST	Tells the browser how it should send the form data to the server

Using the *ACTION* Parameter to Specify the URL of the Processing Script

The ACTION parameter is set equal to the URL of the processing script so that the browser knows where to send the form data once it is entered. Without it, the browser would have no idea where the form data should go.

The ACTION URL can also contain extra path information at the end of it. The extra path information passes on to the script so that it can correctly process the data. The extra path information is not found anywhere on the form so it is transparent to the user. Allowing for the possibility of extra path information, an ACTION URL has the following form:

```
protocol://server/path/script_file/extra_path_info
```

You can use the extra path information to pass an additional file name or directory information to a script. For example, on some servers, the imagemap facility uses extra path information to specify the name of the map file. The name of the map file follows the path to the image map script. A sample URL might be **http://www.company.com/cgi-bin/imagemap/navigation**.

The name of the script is imagemap, and navigation is the name of the map file that imagemap uses.

Using the *ENCTYPE* Parameter to Specify the MIME Type of File to Be Uploaded

Netscape introduced the ENCTYPE attribute to provide a file name to be uploaded as form input. You set ENCTYPE equal to the MIME type expected for the file being uploaded. The ENCTYPE attribute does not create the input field for the file name; rather, it just alerts the browser to the kind of file it is sending. When prompting for a file to upload, you'll need to use an <INPUT> tag with TYPE set equal to FILE.

Part

V

Ch

26

As an example of the three <FORM> tag attributes, examine the following HTML:

```
<FORM ACTION="process_it.cgi" METHOD=POST ENCTYPE="text/html">
Enter the name of the HTML file to validate:
<INPUT TYPE="FILE" NAME="html_file">
<INPUT TYPE="SUBMIT" VALUE="Validate it!">
</FORM>
```

The form header of this short form instructs the server to process the form data using the program named process_it.cgi. Form data is passed using the POST method and the expected type of file being submitted is an HTML file.

Using the *METHOD* Parameter to Specify How to Send the Information

The METHOD parameter specifies which HTTP method to use when passing the data to the script and can be set to values of GET or POST. When you're using the GET method, the browser appends the form data to the end of the URL of the processing script. The POST method sends the form data to the server in a separate HTTP transaction.

The METHOD parameter is not a mandatory attribute of the <FORM> tag. In the absence of a specified method, the browser uses the GET method.

N O T E   Some servers may have operating environment limitations that prevent them from processing an URL that exceeds a certain number of characters—typically, 1 kilobyte of data. This limitation can be a problem when you're using the GET method to pass a large amount of form data. Because the GET method tacks the data onto the end of the processing script URL, you run a greater risk of passing an URL that's too big for the server to handle. If URL size limitations are a concern on your server, you should use the POST method, which sends information over a separate HTTP connection, to pass form data. ∎

Creating Named Input Fields

The named input fields typically comprise the bulk of a form. The fields appear as standard GUI controls, such as text boxes, check boxes, radio buttons, and menus. You assign each field a unique name that eventually becomes the variable name used in the processing script.

You can use several different GUI controls to enter information into forms. The controls for named input fields appear in Table 26.2.

Table 26.2   HTML Form Named Input Fields

Field Type	Tag
Text field	`<INPUT TYPE="TEXT">`
Password field	`<INPUT TYPE="PASSWORD">`
Check box	`<INPUT TYPE="CHECKBOX">`

Field Type	Tag
Option button	`<INPUT TYPE="RADIO">`
Hidden field	`<INPUT TYPE="HIDDEN">`
Images	`<INPUT TYPE="IMAGE">`
File	`<INPUT TYPE="FILE">`
Text window	`<TEXTAREA> </TEXTAREA>`
Menu	`<SELECT> <OPTION> </SELECT>`

You'll note in Table 26.2 that the `<INPUT>` tag handles the majority of named input fields. The `<INPUT>` tag is a stand-alone tag that, thanks to the many values of its TYPE attribute, can place most of the fields you need on your forms. The `<INPUT>` tag also takes other attributes, depending on which TYPE is in use. These additional attributes are covered for each type, as appropriate, over the next several sections.

N O T E   The `<INPUT>` tag and other tags that produce named input fields just create the fields themselves. You, as the form designer, must include some descriptive text next to each field so that users know what information to enter. You may also need to use line breaks, paragraph breaks, and nonbreaking space to create the spacing you want between form fields. ▪

 T I P   Because browsers ignore white space, aligning the left edges of text input boxes on multiple lines is difficult because the text to the left of the boxes is of different lengths. In this instance, HTML tables are invaluable. By setting up the text labels and input fields as cells in the same row of an HTML table, you can produce a nicely formatted form.

Part
V

Ch
26

Creating Text and Password Fields

Text and password fields are simple data entry fields. The only difference between them is that text typed into a password field appears on-screen as asterisks (*). Figure 26.1 shows a text and password field used together to produce a login screen. The HTML source for these fields is shown in Listing 26.1. Note in the listing how the form fields are lined up by placing them in table cells.

CAUTION

Using a password field may protect users' passwords from the people looking over their shoulders, but it does not protect the password as it travels over the Internet. To protect password data as it moves from browser to server, you need to use some type of encryption like that provided by Secure Sockets Layer (SSL).

FIG. 26.1

Allaire requires beta testers to log in before accessing its special beta Web site.

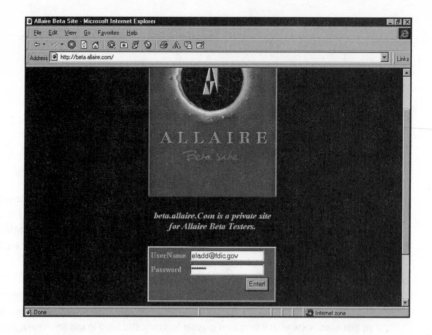

Listing 26.1 Creating Text and Password Boxes

```
<FORM ACTION="/login.cfm" METHOD="POST">
<INPUT TYPE="Hidden" NAME="username_required" VALUE="You must enter a username">
<INPUT TYPE="Hidden" NAME="password_required" VALUE="You must enter a password">

                                                    <table width=250
nowrap>
   <TR><TD><b>UserName</FONT></TD> <TD><INPUT NAME="username" TYPE="Text">
</TD></TR>
<TR><TD><b>Password</FONT></TD> <TD><INPUT NAME= "password" TYPE="Password">
</TD></TR>
<TR><TD COLSPAN="2" ALIGN="Right"><INPUT NAME="Logon" TYPE="Submit"
VALUE="Enter!"></TD></TR></TABLE>
</FORM>
```

The most general text or password field is produced by the HTML (attributes in square brackets are optional):

```
<INPUT TYPE="{TEXT¦PASSWORD}" NAME="name" [VALUE="default_text"] [SIZE="width"]
[MAXLENGTH=max_width"]>
```

The NAME attribute is mandatory because it provides a unique identifier for the data entered into the field.

The optional VALUE attribute enables you to place some default text in the field, rather than have it initially appear blank. This capability is useful if a majority of users will enter a certain text string into the field. In such cases, you can use VALUE to put the text into the field, thereby saving most users the effort of typing it.

The optional SIZE attribute gives you control over how many characters wide the field should be. The default SIZE is typically 20 characters, although this number can vary from browser to browser. The MAXLENGTH attribute is also optional and enables you to specify the maximum number of characters that users can enter into the field.

Creating Check Boxes

Check boxes are used to provide users with several choices. Users can select as many choices as they want. An <INPUT> tag to produce a check box option has the following syntax:

```
<INPUT TYPE="CHECKBOX" NAME="Name" VALUE="Value" [CHECKED]>
```

Each check box option is created by its own <INPUT> tag and must have its own unique NAME. If you give multiple check box options the same NAME, the script has no way to determine which choices the user actually made.

The VALUE attribute specifies what data is sent to the server if the corresponding check box is chosen. This information is transparent to the user. The optional CHECKED attribute preselects a commonly selected check box when the form is rendered on the browser screen. You can see how Internet Explorer renders check boxes in Figure 26.2. The corresponding HTML for the column of National Maps is shown in Listing 26.2.

FIG. 26.2

When customizing your Weather Channel start page, you can choose from a long list of maps to display.

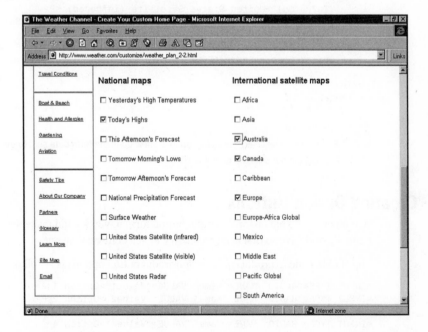

Part
V

Ch
26

Listing 26.2   Creating Check Boxes

```
<TABLE WIDTH="100%" BORDER="0" CELLPADDING="0" CELLSPACING="0">
<TR VALIGN=TOP>
<TD>
<FONT FACE="ARIAL,HELVETICA"><B>National maps</B><P></FONT></TD>
<TD COLSPAN=2>
<FONT FACE="ARIAL,HELVETICA"><B>International satellite maps</B><P></FONT>
</TD>
</TR>
<TR VALIGN="TOP">
<TD><FONT FACE="ARIAL,HELVETICA" SIZE="2">
<INPUT TYPE="checkbox" NAME="summary" VALUE="Yesterday's High
     Temperatures">Yesterday's High Temperatures<P>
<INPUT TYPE="checkbox" NAME="summary" VALUE="Today's Highs">
     Today's Highs <P>
<INPUT TYPE="checkbox" NAME="summary" VALUE="This Afternoon's Forecast">
     This Afternoon's Forecast <P>
<INPUT TYPE="checkbox" NAME="summary" VALUE="Tomorrow Morning's Lows">
     Tomorrow Morning's Lows <P>
<INPUT TYPE="checkbox" NAME="summary" VALUE="Tomorrow Afternoon's
     Forecast">Tomorrow Afternoon's Forecast <P>
<INPUT TYPE="checkbox" NAME="summary" VALUE="National Precipitation
     Forecast">National Precipitation Forecast <P>
<INPUT TYPE="checkbox" NAME="summary" VALUE="Surface Weather">
     Surface Weather <P>
<INPUT TYPE="checkbox" NAME="summary" VALUE="United States Satellite
     (infrared)">United States Satellite (infrared) <P>
<INPUT TYPE="checkbox" NAME="summary" VALUE="United States Satellite
     (visible)">United States Satellite (visible) <P>
<INPUT TYPE="checkbox" NAME="summary" VALUE="United States Radar">
     United States Radar</FONT>   </TD>
...
</TR>
</TABLE>
```

N O T E   If they are selected, check box options show up in the form data sent to the server. Options that are not selected do not appear. ■

Creating Option Buttons

When you set up options with a radio button format, you should make sure that the options are mutually exclusive so that a user won't try to select more than one.

The HTML code to produce a set of four radio button options is as follows:

```
<INPUT TYPE="RADIO" NAME="Name" VALUE="Value1">Option 1<P>
<INPUT TYPE="RADIO" NAME="Name" VALUE="Value2">Option 2<P>
<INPUT TYPE="RADIO" NAME="Name" VALUE="Value3" CHECKED>Option 3<P>
<INPUT TYPE="RADIO" NAME="Name" VALUE="Value4">Option 4
```

The VALUE and CHECKED attributes work exactly the same as they do for check boxes, although you should have only one preselected radio button option. A fundamental difference with a set of radio button options is that they all have the same NAME, which is permissible because the user can select only one option. Figure 26.3 shows a number of option buttons on Microsoft's search page. The code to produce this page is shown in Listing 26.3.

FIG. 26.3
On Microsoft's search page, you may search Microsoft's site in its entirety or you may search the Internet using one of many available search engines.

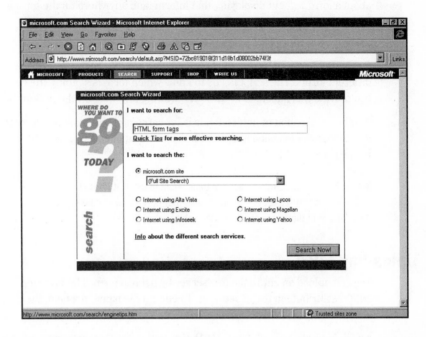

Part
V

Ch
26

Listing 26.3   Creating Option Buttons

```html
<TR>
<TD WIDTH="225" COLSPAN="1">
<FONT FACE="MS Sans Serif, Arial, Helv" SIZE="1">
<BR>
<INPUT NAME="SearchType" TYPE="RADIO" VALUE="altavista">
     Internet using Alta Vista<BR>
<INPUT NAME="SearchType" TYPE="RADIO" VALUE="excite">
     Internet using Excite<BR>
<INPUT NAME="SearchType" TYPE="RADIO" VALUE="infoseek">
     Internet using Infoseek<BR>
</FONT>
</TD>
<TD WIDTH="225" COLSPAN="1">
<FONT FACE="MS Sans Serif, Arial, Helv" SIZE="1">
<BR>
<INPUT NAME="SearchType" TYPE="RADIO" VALUE="lycos">
     Internet using Lycos<BR>
<INPUT NAME="SearchType" TYPE="RADIO" VALUE="magellan">
     Internet using Magellan<BR>
<INPUT NAME="SearchType" TYPE="RADIO" VALUE="yahoo">
     Internet using Yahoo<BR>
</FONT>
</TD>
</TR>
```

Creating Hidden Fields

Technically, hidden fields are not meant for data input. You can send information to the server about a form without displaying that information anywhere on the form itself. The general format for including hidden fields follows:

```
<INPUT TYPE="HIDDEN" NAME="name" VALUE="value">
```

One possible use of hidden fields is to allow a single general script to process data from several different forms. The script needs to know which form is sending the data, and a hidden field can provide this information without requiring anything on the part of the user.

Another application of hidden fields is for carrying input from one form to another. This capacity enables you to split a long form into several smaller forms and still keep all the user's input in one place.

N O T E Because hidden fields are transparent to users, it doesn't matter where you put them in your HTML code. Just make sure they occur between the <FORM> and </FORM> tags that define the form that contains the hidden fields. ■

Uploading Files

You can upload an entire file to a server by using a form. The first step is to include the ENCTYPE attribute in the <FORM> tag. To enter a file name in a field, the user would need the <INPUT> tag with TYPE set equal to FILE:

```
<FORM ACTION="upload.cgi" ENCTYPE="application/x-www-form-urlencoded">
What file would you like to submit: <INPUT TYPE="FILE" NAME="your_file">
...
</FORM>
```

Being able to send an entire file is useful when submitting a document produced by another program—for example, an Excel spreadsheet, a résumé in Word format, or just a plain Notepad text file.

Creating Multiple Line Text Input

Text and password boxes are used for simple, single-line input fields. You can create multiline text windows that function in much the same way by using the <TEXTAREA> and </TEXTAREA> container tags. The HTML syntax for a text window follows:

```
<TEXTAREA NAME="Name" [ROWS="rows"] [COLS="columns"]>
Default_window_text
</TEXTAREA>
```

The NAME attribute gives the text window a unique identifier just as it does with the variations on the <INPUT> tag. The optional ROWS and COLS attributes enable you to specify the dimensions of the text window as it appears on the browser screen. The default number of rows and columns varies by browser. For example, Internet Explorer uses 3 rows and 30 columns as defaults.

The text that appears between the <TEXTAREA> and <TEXTAREA> tags shows up in the input window by default. To type in something else, users must delete the default text and enter their text.

Multiline text windows are ideal for entering long pieces of text, such as feedback comments or e-mail messages (see Figure 26.4 and Listing 26.4). Corporate sites on the Web that collect information on potential employees may ask you to copy and paste your entire résumé into multiline text windows!

FIG. 26.4
Macromedia collects Webmaster feedback by using a multiline text window.

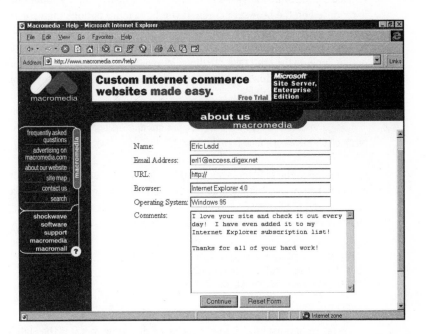

Part
V

Ch
26

Listing 26.4   Creating Multiline Text Windows

```
<tr>
<td valign=top>
Comments:
</td>
<td>
<TEXTAREA NAME="comments" ROWS=10 COLS=40 WRAP="virtual">
</TEXTAREA>
</td>
</tr>
```

Creating List Boxes

The final technique for creating a named input field is to use the <SELECT> and </SELECT> container tags to produce list boxes. The HTML code used to create a general menu follows:

```
<SELECT NAME="Name" [SIZE="size"] [MULTIPLE]>
<OPTION [SELECTED]>Option 1</OPTION>
<OPTION [SELECTED]>Option 2</OPTION>
<OPTION [SELECTED]>Option 3</OPTION>
...
<OPTION [SELECTED]>Option n</OPTION>
</SELECT>
```

In the <SELECT> tag, the NAME attribute again gives the input field a unique identifier. The optional SIZE attribute enables you to specify how many options should be displayed when the list is rendered on the browser screen. If you have more options than you have space to display them, you can access them either by using a drop-down display or by scrolling through the list with scroll bars. The default SIZE is 1. If you want to let users choose more than one list box option, include the MULTIPLE attribute. When MULTIPLE is specified, users can choose multiple options by holding down the Ctrl key and clicking the options they want.

N O T E If you specify the MULTIPLE attribute and SIZE=1, a one-line scrollable list box will display instead of a drop-down list box. This box appears because you can select only one item (not multiple items) in a drop-down list box. ■

Each option in the list box is specified inside its own <OPTION> container tag. If you want an option to be preselected, include the SELECTED attribute in the appropriate <OPTION> tag. The value passed to the server is the list box item that follows the <OPTION> tag unless you supply an alternative using the VALUE attribute. For example:

```
<SELECT NAME="STATE">
<OPTION VALUE="MA">Massachusetts</OPTION>
<OPTION VALUE="ME">Maine</OPTION>
<OPTION VALUE="MI">Mississippi</OPTION>
...
</SELECT>
```

In the preceding list box, the user clicks a state name, but it is the state's two-letter abbreviation that passes to the server.

Figure 26.5 shows the registration screen for a Personalized Search Agent on the **careerbuilder.com** site. The list boxes you see in Listing 26.5 enable multiple selections, thanks to the MULTIPLE attribute.

Listing 26.5   Creating List Boxes

```
<SELECT MULTIPLE SIZE=4 NAME="nsCT" ALIGN="TOP">
<OPTION SELECTED>(Any)
<OPTION>*Accounting & Finance
<OPTION>*Adm. Asst. & Secretarial
<OPTION>*Advertising & Public Relations
<OPTION>*Architecture
<OPTION>*Automotive
<OPTION>*Banking
<OPTION>*Construction Services
<OPTION>*Credit/Loan/Collections
```

```
<OPTION>*Customer Service
<OPTION>*Data & Info Services
<OPTION>*Education & Training
<OPTION>*Engineering, Chemical
<OPTION>*Engineering, Computer
<OPTION>*Engineering, Electrical
<OPTION>*Engineering, General
<OPTION>*Engineering, Internet
<OPTION>*Engineering, Mechanical
<OPTION>*Engineering, Network
<OPTION>*Engineering, Software
<OPTION>*Entry Level Positions, College Degree Not Required
<OPTION>*Entry Level Positions, College Degree Required
<OPTION>*Environmental & Waste Mgmt.
<OPTION>*Facilities Services
<OPTION>*Financial Services, Investments, Insurance
<OPTION>*Graphic Arts
<OPTION>*Health & Medical
<OPTION>*Human Resources
<OPTION>*Legal
...
</SELECT>
```

FIG. 26.5

You can configure your CareerBuilder search agent to search for many different types of jobs in many different cities.

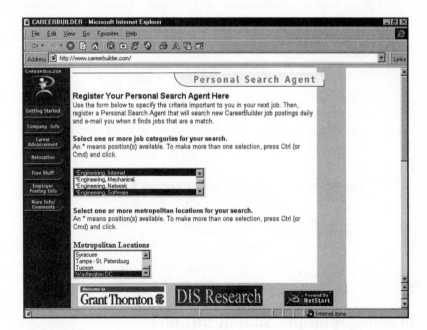

Part
V

Ch
26

Creating Action Buttons

The handy <INPUT> tag returns to provide an easy way of creating the form action buttons you see in many of the preceding figures. Buttons can be of two types: Submit and Reset. Clicking a Submit button instructs the browser to package the form data and send it to the server.

Clicking a Reset button clears out any data entered into the form and sets all the named input fields back to their default values.

Creating Submit and Reset Buttons

Any form you compose should have a Submit button so that users can submit the data they enter. The one exception to this rule is a form containing only one input field. For such a form, pressing Enter automatically submits the data. Reset buttons technically are not necessary but are usually provided as a user courtesy.

To create Submit or Reset buttons, use the following <INPUT> tags:

```
<INPUT TYPE="SUBMIT" VALUE="Submit Data">
<INPUT TYPE="RESET" VALUE="Clear Data">
```

Use the VALUE attribute to specify the text that appears on the button. You should set VALUE to a text string that concisely describes the function of the button. If VALUE is not specified, the button text reads Submit Query for Submit buttons and Reset for Reset buttons.

Creating Images That Submit the Form

You can create a custom image to be a Submit button for your forms and set up the image so that clicking it instructs the browser to submit the form data. To do this, set TYPE equal to IMAGE in your <INPUT> tag and provide the URL of the image you want to use with the SRC attribute:

```
<INPUT TYPE="IMAGE" SRC="images/submit_button.gif">
```

You can also use the ALIGN attribute in this variation of the <INPUT> tag to control how text appears next to the image (TOP, MIDDLE, or BOTTOM) or to float the image in the left or right margins (LEFT or RIGHT). Figure 26.6 shows an image used as a Submit button on the United Airlines Web site. The corresponding HTML is shown in Listing 26.6.

Listing 26.6   Using Images as Submit Buttons

```
<TR>
<TD ALIGN=center VALIGN=top COLSPAN=3><BR>
<INPUT TYPE="image" BORDER=0
     SRC="http://www.ual.com/images/retrieve_flts_button.gif">
</TD>
</TR>
```

Creating Multiple Submit Buttons

It's possible to have more than one Submit button on a form, although there is not yet consistent browser support for multiple submit buttons.

FIG. 26.6
United Airlines uses a special image, rather than the standard Submit button, for submitting a form.

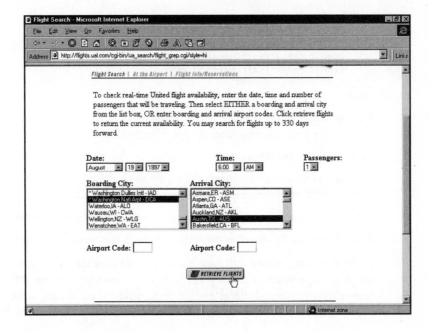

You distinguish between Submit buttons by using the NAME attribute in the <INPUT> tags used to create the buttons. For example, you might have

```
<INPUT TYPE="SUBMIT" NAME="SEARCH" VALUE="Conduct Search">
<INPUT TYPE="SUBMIT" NAME="ADD" VALUE="Add to Database">
```

to produce buttons that enable users to search the information they've entered or add the information they've entered to a database.

Because there is only tentative support for multiple Submit buttons, you may want to wait to implement them until they are standard.

Passing Form Data to the Server

Once a user enters some form data and clicks a Submit button, the browser does two things. First, it packages the form data into a single string, a process called encoding. Then it sends the encoded string to the server by either the GET or POST HTTP method. The next two sections provide details on each of these steps.

Sending Data via URL Encoding

When a user clicks the Submit button on a form, his or her browser gathers all the data and strings together in NAME=VALUE pairs, each separated by an ampersand (&) character. This process is called *encoding*. It packages the data into one string that is sent to the server.

Part
V

Ch
26

Consider the following HTML code:

```
<FORM ACTION="http://www.website.com/cgi-bin/getname.cgi" METHOD="POST">
    <INPUT TYPE="TEXT" NAME="first">
    <INPUT TYPE="TEXT" NAME="last">
    <INPUT TYPE="SUBMIT">
</FORM>
```

If a user named Mickey Mouse enters his name into the form produced by the preceding HTML code, his browser creates the following data string and sends it to the CGI script:

```
first=Mickey&last=Mouse
```

If the GET method is used instead of POST, the same string is appended to the URL of the processing script, producing the following *encoded URL*:

```
http://www.website.com/cgi-bin/getname.cgi?first=Mickey&last=Mouse
```

A question mark (?) separates the script URL from the encoded data string.

Further encoding occurs with data that is more complex than a single word. Such encoding simply replaces spaces with the plus character (+) and translates any other possibly troublesome character (control characters, the ampersand and equal sign, some punctuation, and so on) to a percent sign followed by its hexadecimal equivalent. Thus, the following string

```
Happy Birthday!
```

becomes

```
Happy+Birthday%21
```

HTTP Methods

You can read the form data submitted to a CGI script in two ways, depending on the METHOD the form used. The type of METHOD the form used—either GET or POST—is stored in an environment variable called REQUEST_METHOD, and, based on that, the data should be read in one of the following ways:

- If the data is sent by the GET method, the input stream is stored in an environment variable called QUERY_STRING. As noted previously, this input stream usually is limited to only about 1 kilobyte of data, which is why GET is losing popularity to the more flexible POST.

- If the data is submitted by the POST method, the data is fed to the standard input of the CGI program. The POST attribute accepts data of any length, up into the megabytes, although it is not very common yet for form submissions to be that large.

CGI Scripts

Now that the form data has been collected, bundled, and shipped to the server, you must provide some kind of way to handle the data. As you read earlier in the chapter, this handling is most commonly done with a CGI script. CGI scripts are computer programs that run when the

Web server requests them to do so. The server passes the form data to these external programs and waits for some kind of output from them—usually, an HTML page.

CGI scripts are not written in HTML. Rather, they are written in a scripting language, such as Bourne shell or Perl, or in a programming language, such as C, C++, Pascal, or Small Talk. Either way, you'll need to know a language in addition to HTML to be able to write your own scripts. But this extra effort is worth the trouble when you consider how using HTML forms and CGI scripts together can make your site much more dynamic.

This section explores CGI scripts as a means of processing form data. By examining a few simple scripts, you'll begin to develop an appreciation for what's possible when you use CGI. The chapter then closes by taking a quick look at some alternative ways to handle form data.

One of the best ways to learn what goes on with CGI programming is to take a look at a few scripts and see how they perform. Three simple example scripts follow, giving you a glimpse of what CGI can bring to your pages.

Hello World!

Depending on what they have to do, some CGI programs are necessarily complex. They don't all have to be made up of hundreds of lines of complicated code, however. Consider the Unix shell script in Listing 26.7.

Listing 26.7   A Simple "Hello World!" Script

```
#!/bin/sh
echo "Content-type: text/html"
echo ""
echo "<HTML>"
echo "<HEAD>"
echo "<TITLE>A Simple CGI Script</TITLE>"
echo "<BODY BGCOLOR=#FFFFFF>"
echo "<H1>Hello World!</H1>"
echo "</BODY>"
echo "</HTML>"
```

Part
V

Ch
26

Even though it's a short script, many important things are happening in it that are vital to any CGI program.

The first line of the script (**#!/bin/sh**) tells a UNIX operating system that this script is to run in the Bourne shell, one of the many available in UNIX. Bourne is the most common, however, and is the only one with which every version of UNIX ships. If this were a Windows 95 or NT batch file, you could just omit this first line altogether.

The second line tells a browser like Internet Explorer what type of data it is about to receive. The **Content-type:** is required for all CGI scripts and it must correspond to a valid MIME type. Multipurpose Internet Mail Extensions (MIME) is a method for delivering a myriad of different file types over the Internet, and browsers use MIME type information to decide how to handle arriving files. The two most common MIME types used in CGI scripts are text/html for HTML output and text/plain for an ASCII text file.

CAUTION

One common error you may make when writing CGI scripts is to have the wrong Content-type for the type of data you're returning. If your script returns HTML, but the Content-type is set to text/plain, the user's browser will interpret none of the HTML tags, leaving your response page looking like HTML code.

The third line of the script returns an empty line that separates the Content-type header from the main body of the response. All CGI scripts must include this blank line in their output.

The remaining lines produce the actual HTML code that's sent to a user's browser. These lines are passed back to the server and then on to the browser, where they are interpreted as though they'd been read from the following HTML file:

```
<HTML>
<HEAD>
<TITLE>A Simple CGI Script</TITLE>
</HEAD>
<BODY BGCOLOR=#FFFFFF>
<H1>Hello World!</H1>
</BODY>
</HTML>
```

Users see the message "Hello World!" rendered as a level 1 heading on a white background on their browser screens.

N O T E When a CGI script produces HTML output, the page is said to be dynamically generated, or created on-the-fly. ■

Using Server-Side Information

You can add a little more pizzazz to a script's output by using some of the information that a Web server provides to every CGI program. A CGI script that uses server information isn't doing anything special—it's just taking advantage of something that's already there.

When a CGI script is executed, several environment variables are set by the server, each containing information about the server software, the browser from which the request came, and the script itself. The CGI script can reference these variables and use them in producing the script's output. As an example, consider the Bourne shell script in Listing 26.8, which greets each user with the name (or IP address) of his or her machine and the name of the browser software he or she is using.

Listing 26.8   Using Environment Variables

```
#!/bin/sh
echo "Content-type: text/html"
echo ""
echo "<HTML>"
echo "<HEAD>"
```

```
echo "<TITLE>Big Brother is Watching ...</TITLE>"
echo "</HEAD>"
if [ "${REMOTE_HOST}" == ""]; then
    REMOTE_HOST =${REMOTE_ADDR}
fi
if [ "${HTTP_USER_AGENT}" == ""]; then
    HTTP_USER_AGENT="a browser I'm not familiar with"
fi
echo "<BODY BGCOLOR=#FFFFFF>"
echo "You are using ${HTTP_USER_AGENT}, on ${REMOTE_HOST}."
echo "</BODY>"
echo "</HTML>"
```

This script uses three environment variables set by the server—REMOTE_HOST, REMOTE_ADDR, and HTTP_USER_AGENT—to determine the name of the site visitor's machine (or its IP address, if the name is not available) and what kind of browser the visitor is using. The only "processing" the script does is to see whether either the REMOTE_HOST or the HTTP_USER_AGENT variables are null. If they are, the REMOTE_HOST is simply set equal to the IP address (REMOTE_ADDR) and the HTTP_USER_AGENT is set equal to some text that tells the visitor that the script is unfamiliar with his or her browser.

When you write CGI scripts, a number of environment variables are available to you. Some of the more popular variables are listed in Table 26.3. For a complete list of CGI environment variables, visit **http://hoohoo.ncsa.uiuc.edu/docs/cgi/env.html**.

Table 26.3 Popular CGI Environment Variables

Variable	Contents
REMOTE_HOST	The English-language name of the machine from which the CGI request came
REMOTE_ADDR	The IP address of the machine from which the CGI request came
SCRIPT_NAME	The name of the CGI script currenty invoked
SERVER_NAME	The English-language name of the Web server
HTTP_USER_AGENT	The browser software that made the CGI request

By using environment variables creatively, you can do all sorts of neat tricks. For example, by combining SERVER_NAME and SCRIPT_NAME, you can compose the URL of the script being run, thereby allowing it to reference itself!

A Guest Book

As a final and more complex example of a CGI script, consider the code in Listing 26.9. This script, written in Perl, is designed to record the names of people who visit your site in a guest book.

Part
V

Ch
26

Listing 26.9 CGI Script to Maintain a Guest Book

```
#!/usr/local/bin/perl
print "Content-type: text/html\n\n";
#Load the CGI library
do "cgi-lib.pl" || die "Fatal error: could not load cgi-lib.pl";
# Use library routine to read in and parse form data
&ReadParse;
#Set location of the guest book
$guestbook = "guestbook.txt";
#Get the visitor's name as submitted on the form
$name = $in{'name'};
#Add to the guestbook if they entered something
if (length($name) > 0) {          #If the name field isn't null,
    open(FILE,">>$guestbook");    #open the guest book file,
    print FILE "$name\n";         #print the name to it,
    close FILE;                   #and close the file.
}
#Show who's already signed in
#print statements send text in quotes to the output stream
print "<HTML>\n<HEAD>\n<TITLE>Site Guestbook</TITLE>\n</HEAD>\n";
print "<BODY BGCOLOR=#FFFFFF>\n<H1>Guestbook</H1>\n<HR>\n
    <H2>Current Guests:</H2>\n";
print "<UL>\n";      #Start a bulleted list
#Start printing guest names.  Open the file or say "You're the first"
#if the file is empty.
open (FILE,"<$guestbook") || print "You're the first\!\n";
while (<FILE>) {         #While not at end of file
    print "<LI>$_";   #print the next guest's name as a list item.
}
close FILE;             #Close the file when you get to the end of it.
print "</UL>";          #End the bulleted list
#Ask for new sign-ins by giving users a form to enter their information
print "<HR>\nAdditional guests sign in here:<BR>\n";
print "<FORM METHOD=\"GET\" ACTION=\"$ENV{'SCRIPT_NAME'}\">";
print "Your name: <INPUT TYPE=\"TEXT\" NAME=\"guestname\"
    SIZE=\"20\">";
print "<INPUT TYPE=\"SUBMIT\" VALUE=\"Sign in\!\">\n;
print "</FORM>\n</BODY>\n</HTML>\n";
```

N O T E The **\n** you see in the print commands is an instruction to break to a new line. ■

One important thing to note about this CGI script is that is does more than place a guest's name into the guest book file. It also displays who has signed the guest book and provides an input field so that others may sign in. That is, the script generates a form that calls itself! This trick is becoming fairly common and shows you some of the power of CGI programming.

Another thing to note if you're planning on coding scripts in Perl is that the preceding script uses the **cgi-lib.pl** library to parse the encoded form information. By using this utility, the form data is de-encoded and stored in a Perl array called **$in**. You can reference the values of each named form input field by asking **$in** for it, referencing it by its unique name. For instance, if a text input field has the NAME address, the following line of Perl code would return the value the user entered:

```
$address = $in{'address'};
```

Before you can use this handy routine, you must load the **cgi-lib.pl** library and call the routine that sets up the table (lines 4 and 6 in the listing).

Other Techniques for Handling Form Data

Though custom-written CGI scripts are the most popular way to process submitted form data, you can deal with the data in other ways as well. The chapter closes with a quick look at a few of these techniques.

Electronic Mail

If you want to process the data by hand, you can instruct a browser to e-mail you the data by using the mailto: statement in your ACTION attribute. Thus, you might use something like the following:

```
<FORM ACTION="mailto:data_collection@your_firm.com">
```

In this case, the form data is e-mailed to the **data_collection** account on your mail server.

The one thing to keep in mind about this approach is that the form data will be encoded when it shows up in your mailbox. It's up to you to decode the data, and that can be a very tedious process if done manually.

Middleware Solutions

Many companies are now releasing middleware products that serve as a go-between for the form and the back-end processing. One particularly popular program is Allaire's Cold Fusion, which serves as middleware between the HTML form and a back-end database. By directing your ACTION attribute to point to a Cold Fusion template, the server will automatically invoke the Cold Fusion engine. The template file contains the Sequential Query Language (SQL, pronounced "sequel") statement that specifies what action should be taken with the database. In the case of a query against the database, the template also contains HTML code with "holes" that the Cold Fusion engine fills with the matching record to produce the response page.

If you're using Microsoft's Internet Information Server, you already have a similar functionality built in. Microsoft's Internet Database Connector (IDC) works very similarly to Cold Fusion. To use IDC, direct your ACTION attribute to point at an .idc file, which contains the SQL code and the name of a template to use to construct the response page. The template file (which typically has the extension .htx) is again an HTML file with holes that the IDC fills with matching database records.

N O T E To learn more about Cold Fusion, visit Allaire's Web site at **http://www.allaire.com/**. You can also check out **http://www.microsoft.com/sql/inet/inetdevstrat2.htm** for more information about IDC. ▪

Style Sheets

One thing many browser users got tired of quickly was the constant barrage of text in 12 point Times Roman text (or 10 point Courier for fixed-width characters). In response to this, browser software companies began introducing functionality whereby the user could modify the default font and size as part of the browser's preferences or options. This enables users to see text-based content with the font and size of their choice and was an especially good idea for those who are visually impaired and could benefit from a larger type size.

Then the same companies began to give this control over to the content developer by extending HTML to include tags like <FONT>, which, through its various attributes, can modify the size, color, and face of the type used. But this was a dangerous precedent because HTML is intended as a markup language and should only be describing the structure and the contents of documents, not how they look.

That brings us to the notion of style sheets. Style sheets give content developers a way to store specifications about how a document should look separate from the description of the document's structure. By having a means to describe document appearance separately, HTML won't be constantly extended to accommodate new tags that control typographical attributes. It will be free to describe only the document's content, consistent with its original intent.

What are style sheets and why are they important?

Style sheets provide a way to keep layout separate from content. They take care of how a page looks, thereby allowing HTML to focus on describing what's on the page.

Approaches to implementing style sheets

Internet Explorer supports three different ways to apply style information against your documents.

Layout attributes you can control with style sheets

Style sheets enable you to modify typographical features such as font, type size, line spacing, margins, and special formatting like italics or underlining.

Developing content with style sheets

Learn tips on how to deploy style sheets on your site intelligently and find out about where style sheets are heading in the future.

The World Wide Web Consortium is already pushing the idea of style sheets. It has reserved a tag for embedding style information within an HTML document. It is also considering proposals for a general style sheet language that could be used to describe how a document should look just as HTML describes what the page contains. This chapter surveys the approaches to style sheets as they have been proposed and, in the case of Internet Explorer 4, implemented.

Before looking at the different ways to build style information into your pages, it is helpful to review some of the basics behind the concept of a style sheet. ■

What Style Sheets Are

Style sheets are collections of style information to be applied to plain text. Style information includes font attributes such as type size, special effects (bold, italic, underline), color, and alignment. It also provides broader formatting instructions by specifying values for quantities like line spacing and left and right margins.

Style sheets are not really a new concept—word processing programs like Microsoft Word have been making use of user-defined style for a number of years. Figure 27.1 shows a Word style definition in the Style dialog box. Note how the style accounts for many of the presentation attributes previously mentioned.

FIG. 27.1

Word processors such as Microsoft Word can store typographical attributes collectively as a style. Style sheets bring a similar functionality to the Web.

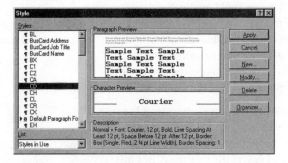

Why Style Sheets Are Valuable

Simply put, style sheets separate content and presentation. Apart from freeing HTML to develop as a content description language, it gives Web page designers precise control over how their content appears on screen. Other benefits of style sheets include the following:

■ **Central repositories of style information**   If you're using a standard set of styles on all your pages, you can store the corresponding style information in one file. This way, if you have to edit the style information, you just have to make the change in one place instead of in every file.

■ **Little to no new HTML to learn**   With style information being stored in style sheets, there should be virtually no need for the introduction of new HTML tags for the purposes of formatting. This promises to reduce the confusion that often arises out of browser-specific extensions to HTML.

- **Consistent rendering of content** Browsers vary slightly in how they render content, especially the logical text styles. By assigning specific style information to logical style tags, Web page authors can be assured that their content will look exactly the same on every browser.

Different Approaches to Style Sheets

The World Wide Web Consortium (W3C) is advocating the "Cascading Style Sheet" (CSS) proposal for implementing style sheets. Cascading refers to the fact that browsers use a certain set of rules in cascading order to determine how to use the style information. Such a set of rules is useful in the event of conflicting style information because the rules would give the browser a way to determine what style gets precedence.

Even though the style sheet specification has yet to be formally approved by the W3C, Internet Explorer 4 is already able to use the approaches proposed in the specifications. In fact, Internet Explorer 4 supports styles in each of three different ways:

- **Embedded styles** Style information is defined in the document head using the `<STYLE>` and `</STYLE>` tags.
- **Linked styles** Style information is read in from a separate file specified in the `<LINK>` tag.
- **Inline styles** Style information is placed inside an HTML tag and applies to all content between that tag and its companion closing tag. For example, you could left indent an entire paragraph one-half inch by using the `<P STYLE="margin-left: .5 in">` tag to start the paragraph.

N O T E The W3C has reserved the `<STYLE>` and `</STYLE>` container tags for use in implementing cascading style sheets, once the standard is adopted. ■

The next three major sections look at each of these approaches in greater detail.

Part
V

Ch
27

Storing Style Information in Its Own File

One important thing to realize is that you don't have to store your style sheet information inside each of your HTML documents. In fact, if you anticipate applying the same styles across several HTML pages, it is much more efficient for you to store the style information in one place and have each HTML document linked to it. This makes it *much* easier to change the formatting of all your pages by changing the style sheet instead of changing every page! Additionally, with the global style sheet stored in a browser's cache, users should notice faster page download times.

Setting Up the Style Information

To set up a linked style sheet, you first must create the file with the style information. This file takes the form of a plain-text file with style information entries. Each entry starts with an HTML tag followed by a list of presentation attributes to associate with the rendering of the effect of that tag. Some sample lines in a style sheet file might look like this:

```
BODY {font: 10 pt Courier; color: red; margin-left: 0.5in}
H1 {font 18 pt Arial; color: blue}
H2 {font 16 pt Arial; color: FF8080}
```

The first line sets the body text to 10 point Courier type rendered in red with a half-inch left margin. The second line redefines the level 1 heading to 18 point Arial type rendered in blue, and the third line sets the level 2 heading to 16 point Arial type rendered in the color represented by the hexadecimal triplet "FF8080."

 TIP When setting colors in your style sheet file, you can use one of the 16 English-language color names or an RGB hexadecimal triplet to describe the color.

Remember that the syntax for specifying a characteristic has the following form:

```
{characteristic: value}
```

Multiple characteristic/value pairs should be separated by semicolons. For example:

```
P {font: 12 pt Times; line-height: 14 pt; color: FF00FF; text-indent: .25 in}
```

CAUTION
You may be greatly tempted to use the syntax **characteristic=value** when you first start to work with style sheets. Make sure you use the syntax previously noted.

The cascading style sheet specification enables you to specify more than just fonts, typefaces, and colors. Table 27.1 lists the different style attributes you can assign to a file containing style information.

Table 27.1 Typographical Characteristics Controlled from HTML Style Sheets

Characteristic	Purpose and Possible Values
font-family	Sets the font that the browser uses to any typeface available to the browser through Windows (the default font is used if the specified font is not available)
font-size	Changes the size of text to any size in points (pt), inches (in), centimeters (cm), or pixels (px)
font-weight	Controls the use of boldface; possible values are normal or bold

Characteristic	Purpose and Possible Values
font-style	Controls the use of italics; only one possible value: italics
text-decoration	Controls the following text effects: none, underline, italics, line-through
color	Sets the font color to any RGB hexadecimal triplet or HTML 3.2 English-language color name
text-align	Aligns text according to one of the following: left, center, right
text-indent	Indents text any number of points (pt), inches (in), centimeters (cm), or pixels (px)
text-transform	Controls capitalization; possible values: capitalize, uppercase, lowercase
margin-left	Sets the left margin to any number of points (pt), inches (in), centimeters (cm), or pixels (px)
margin-right	Sets the right margin to any number of points (pt), inches (in), centimeters (cm), or pixels (px)
margin-top	Sets the top margin to any number of points (pt), inches (in), centimeters (cm), or pixels (px)
margin-bottom	Sets the bottom margin to any number of points (pt), inches (in), centimeters (cm), or pixels (px)
line-height	Sets the height of a line to any number of points (pt), inches (in), centimeters (cm), or pixels (px)
background	Controls the use of a background color or image; possible values: any image URL, RGB hexadecimal triplet, or HTML 3.2 English-language color name
word-spacing	Sets the space between words to any number of points (pt), inches (in), centimeters (cm), or pixels (px)
letter-spacing	Sets the space between letters to any number of points (pt), inches (in), centimeters (cm), or pixels (px)
vertical-align	Controls vertical alignment; possible values: baseline, sub, super, top, text-top, middle, bottom, text-bottom or a percentage of the current line-height

Part

V

Ch

27

N O T E The line-height characteristic in Table 27.1 refers to the leading or space between lines that the browser uses. ▨

You can see from the table that you have control over a large number of presentation characteristics—certainly more than you have with just HTML tags alone.

Including the Style Sheet Using the *<LINK>* Tag

Once you've created your style sheet file, save it with a .css extension and place it on your server. Then you can reference it using the <LINK> tag in the head of each of your HTML documents, as follows:

```
<HEAD>
<TITLE>A Document that Uses Style Sheets</TITLE>
<LINK REL=STYLESHEET HREF="styles/sitestyles.css">
</HEAD>
```

The REL attribute describes the relationship of the linked file to the current file—namely, that the linked file is a style sheet. HREF specifies the URL of the style sheet file.

Style sheet files are of MIME type text/css, though not all servers and browsers register this automatically. If you're setting up a site that uses style sheets, be sure to configure your server to handle the MIME type text/css.

Embedding Style Information in Your Documents

Figure 27.2 shows the entrance page to the Microsoft Style Sheets Gallery, which makes use of an embedded style sheet. The style information is stored in the document head, as shown in the following HTML source listing:

```
<STYLE  TYPE="text/css">
<!--
BODY {        background: black;
      color: red;
      font-size: 10px;
      font-family: Verdana, Arial, helvetica, sans-serif }
A:link { text-decoration: none;
      color: black;
      font-size: 18px;
      font-family: Verdana, Arial, helvetica, sans-serif }
.type {        color: black;
      weight: medium;
      font-size: 36px;
      font-family: Arial Black, Arial, helvetica, sans-serif }
.choice { color: white;
      font-weight: bold;
      font-size: 36px;
      font-family: Comic Sans MS, Verdana, Arial, helvetica, sans-serif }
.vlayer1 { color: black;
      margin-left: 10px;
      margin-top: 25px;
      margin-right: 230px;
      font-weight: bold;
      font-size: 8px;
      font-family: Verdana, Arial, helvetica, sans-serif }
.vlayer3 { color: white;
      margin-left: 130px;
      margin-right: 320px;
      font-weight: bold;
```

```
        margin-top: -182px;
        font-size: 6px;
        font-family: Verdana, Arial, helvetica, sans-serif }
.vlayer4 { color: black;
        text-indent: 30px;
        margin-left: 30px;
        margin-right: 30px;
        margin-top: 34px;
        font-size: 18px;
        font-family: Verdana, Arial, helvetica, sans-serif }
.vlayer5 { color: black;
        margin-left: 10px;
        margin-right: 230px;
        margin-top: -215px;
        font-weight: bold;
        font-size: 90px;
        font-family: Verdana, Arial, helvetica, sans-serif }
.list1 { color: white;
        margin-left: 500px;
        margin-top: -50px;
        font-size: 18px;
        font-family: Verdana, Arial, helvetica, sans-serif }
.list2 { color: white;
        margin-left: 500px;
        font-weight: bold;
        font-size: 18px;
        font-family: Verdana, Arial, helvetica, sans-serif }
.list3 { color: white;
        margin-left: 500px;
        font-style: italic;
        font-size: 18px;
        font-family: Verdana, Arial, helvetica, sans-serif }
.list4 { color: white;
        margin-left: 500px;
        font-weight: bold;
        font-size: 18px;
        font-style: italic;
        font-family: Verdana, Arial, helvetica, sans-serif }
.hl { color: white;
        background: black; }
-->
</STYLE>
```

The structure of the style information takes the same form that you saw for setting up style information in a separate file: an HTML tag name, followed by curly braces containing the style characteristics. For example, in this style sheet, Microsoft makes all hypertext links bold, not underlined, and rendered in the Verdana font. Unvisited links are painted with the color represented by #6060FF and visited links are colored with #303090.

Creating Your Own Style Using the *<STYLE>* Tag

As you can see from the listing above, embedded style information is placed between the <STYLE> and </STYLE> tags, the tags that the W3C reserved for using in implementing style sheets.

Part

V

Ch

27

FIG. 27.2
Microsoft's Style Sheet
Gallery pages are
themselves done with
style sheets.

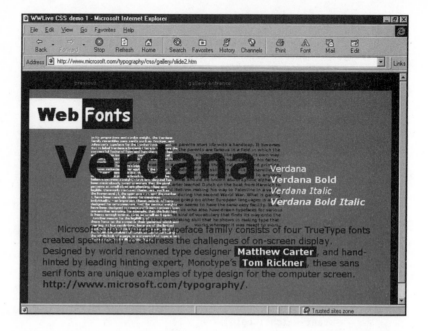

The TYPE attribute tells a browser what type of style information setup is being used. This attribute allows for some flexibility in the implementation of other style information specification schemes in the future. This attribute also makes it easier for browsers that do not support style sheets to ignore the style information between the two tags.

N O T E   Style information specified in the head of a document using the <STYLE> tag will only apply to that document. If you want to use the same styles in another document, you must embed the style information in the head of that document as well. ■

Setting Up the Style Information

Style information of the MIME type text/css is set up the same way as style information was set up in a linked style sheet file. The first entry on each line is the keyword from an HTML tag, followed by a list of characteristic/value pairs enclosed in curly braces.

One important thing to note is that the style information you saw in the listing above is enclosed in comment tags (<!-- and -->) so that browsers that do not understand style sheets will ignore the style information rather than presenting it on screen. Another way you can give style sheet-challenged browsers a heads-up is by including the TYPE="text/css" attribute in the <STYLE> tag.

Placing Style Information in HTML Tags

You can specify inline styles inside an HTML tag. The style information given applies to the document content up until the defining tag's companion closing tag is encountered. Thus, with the following HTML:

```
<P STYLE="text-align: right; color: red">
Red, right-justified text
</P>
<P>
Back to normal
</P>
```

the words "Red, right-justified text" will be centered on the page and colored red. This style applies up until the </P> tag, at which point the browser reverts back to whatever style it was using before the inline style (see Figure 27.3).

TIP Don't forget the closing tag when embedding style information in an HTML tag. Otherwise, the effects of the style may extend beyond the point in the document where you wanted them to stop.

FIG. 27.3

The inline styles you specify only apply over the effect of the tag where they're defined.

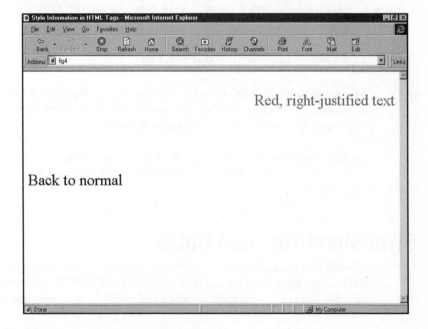

Other Tags that Take the *STYLE* Attribute

You saw in the example that the <P> tag can take the STYLE attribute to define an inline style. Many other tags can take the style attribute as well, including the following:

- `<DIV>`
- `<H1>` to `<H6>` (the heading styles)
- `<UL>` and `<OL>`
- `<LI>`
- `<BODY>`

Using The *<SPAN>* Tag to Contain a Style

For those times when you want to apply a style to part of a document that is not nicely contained between two tags, you can use the `<SPAN>` and `</SPAN>` tags to set up the part of the document to which the style will be applied. You assign style characteristics to the area set by the `<SPAN>` by using the STYLE attribute, as in the preceding example with the `<P>` tag.

As an example of how you might use the `<SPAN>` tag, consider the following HTML:

```
<H2>Style Sheet Advantages</H2>
<UL>
<SPAN STYLE="font-weight: bold; font-decoration: italics; color: teal">
<LI>Separate content and layout</LI>
<LI>Applicable across an entire site from one master file</LI>
<LI>Multiple approaches to implementation</LI>
</SPAN>
<LI>Easy to give your site a whole new look and feel</LI>
<LI>Supported by Internet Explorer</LI>
</UL>
```

The code in the example produces the screen you see in Figure 27.4. Note in the figure that the colored, bold, italics prescribed in the `<SPAN>` tag apply only to the first three items in the list because the `</SPAN>` tag occurs after the third item.

N O T E Using inline styles is fine for changes to small sections of your document. You should consider using a linked style sheet or the `<STYLE>` tag, however, if your styles are to be more global. ■

Style Sheet Tips and Tricks

Although they are in the formative stages, style sheets are already out there and being used, thanks to browsers like Internet Explorer that support them. Based on developers' experiences with style sheets so far, here are some tips you should keep in mind when developing your own styles.

Using Multiple Approaches

You aren't limited to using just one of the style sheet approaches previously described. In fact, you can use all three simultaneously, if needed! One case in which you may want to do this is on a corporate intranet site where you have the following:

FIG. 27.4
You can apply style information to a very specific portion of your document by using the <SPAN> tag.

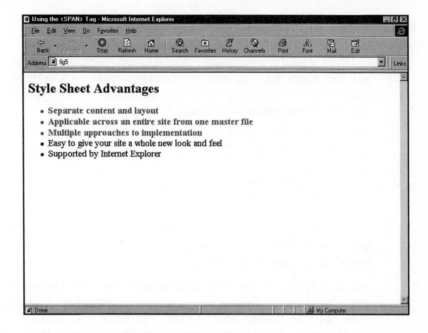

Style Sheet Advantages

- Separate content and layout
- Applicable across an entire site from one master file
- Multiple approaches to implementation
- Easy to give your site a whole new look and feel
- Supported by Internet Explorer

■ **Global styles** Certain styles that will be used on every page are best stored in a single style sheet file and linked to each page with the <LINK> tag.

■ **Subsection styles** Large corporate sites typically have many subdivisions, each with its own look and feel. You could store styles to support a subdivision's look between the <STYLE> and </STYLE> tags in the head of each document in the subdivision.

■ **Page-specific styles** If you need to make a small deviation from your chosen global or subsection styles, you can use an inline style to make the change right where you want it.

You shouldn't use all three approaches in the same document just for the sake of doing it, however. You should seek to optimize your use of style sheets by choosing the approach, or combination of approaches, that enables you to apply the styles you want where you want them without a lot of unnecessary code.

The thing you have to remember when using multiple approaches is *style precedence*. Recall that the idea behind a cascading style sheet was that browsers apply a set of rules in cascading order to determine what style information takes precedence. You must be aware of these rules so that you do not produce unintended style effects on your pages. In general, you'll be fine if you remember the following:

■ Inline styles override both linked style sheets and style information stored in the document head with the <STYLE> tag.

■ Styles defined in the document head override linked style sheets.

■ Linked style sheets override browser defaults.

Keeping these rules in mind will make troubleshooting your style sheet setup much easier.

Part
V

Ch
27

Harnessing Inheritance

Inheritance refers to the fact that HTML documents are essentially set up as hierarchies and that styles applied at one level of the hierarchy necessarily apply to all subordinate levels as well. This means that if you assign style information inside a <UL> tag, the information also applies to all of the items in the unordered list because the <LI> tags are subordinate to the <UL> tag. For example, the following HTML code:

```
<H2>Web Development Tools</H2>
<UL STYLE="font-weight: bold">
<LI>Style sheets</LI>
<LI>JavaScript</LI>
<LI>ActiveX Controls</LI>
<LI>Dynamic HTML</LI>
</UL>
```

would produce a list in which all items are in boldface. None of the list items themselves are bolded, but the style specification in the <UL> tag applies to each item in the list and causes them to be rendered in boldface.

You can make broader use of this idea by setting up as much common style information in the <BODY> tag as you can. Because every tag between <BODY> and </BODY> is subordinate to the <BODY> tag, these tags will inherit the style information you specify in the <BODY> tag, and you should be spared from having to repeat it throughout the rest of the document.

Grouping Style Information

If you want to assign the same style characteristics to a number of tags, do so all in one line rather than using a separate line for each tag. For example, if you want all paragraphs, divisions, and lists to be rendered in the same style, you could list them all individually

```
P {font-size: 12 pt; font-weight: bold; font-decoration: underline}
DIV {font-size: 12 pt; font-weight: bold; font-decoration: underline}
UL {font-size: 12 pt; font-weight: bold; font-decoration: underline}
OL {font-size: 12 pt; font-weight: bold; font-decoration: underline}
```

or you could define them all at once:

```
P DIV UL OL {font-size: 12 pt; font-weight: bold; font-decoration: underline}
```

Either set of code will make all paragraph, division, and list items text appear in 12 point type that is bold and underlined.

You can also group style information applied to just one tag. For example, if you had redefined your document body as

```
BODY {font-size: 16 pt; line-height: 18 pt; font-family: "Helvetica"; font-weight: bold}
```

you could express the same thing as

```
BODY {font: 16pt/18pt bold "Helvetica"}
```

and save yourself a bit of typing.

Creating Tag Classes

The proposed style sheet specification enables you to subdivide a tag into named classes and specify different style information for each class. For example, if you wanted three different colors of unvisited links, you could set them up as

```
A:link.red {color: red}
A:link.yellow {color: yellow}
A:link.blue {color: blue}
```

The period and color name that follow each A:link sets up a class of the A:link tag. The class name is whatever follows the period. You use the class names in the <A> tag to specify which type of unvisited link you want to create:

```
Here's a <A CLASS="red" HREF="red.html">red</A> link!
And a <A CLASS="yellow" HREF="yellow.html">yellow</A> one ...
And a <A CLASS="blue" HREF="blue.html">blue</A> one!
```

Wider Support of Style Sheets

The idea of style sheets is not exactly new, but it is a fairly new capability that content authors can use on Web pages. Even so, the first implementation of Web style sheets promises to elevate Web content presentation to impressive new heights.

Just as HTML has evolved quickly over its brief existence, you should expect to see style sheet capabilities evolve as well. This chapter concludes with a few sections that discuss some of the directions in which this evolution is likely to occur.

Probably the greatest impediment to style sheets becoming big right from the onset is that so few browsers support them. Internet Explorer 3 was the first mainstream browser that supported the cascading style sheet draft specification. This, of course, obliged Netscape to update the Netscape Navigator to be able to process style information as well and, indeed, Netscape Navigator 4.0 now supports the CSS spec plus the notion of JavaScript-enabled style sheets.

In the meantime, you can continue to use Internet Explorer 4 to view pages created with style sheets or you can try out one of the following browsers:

- Netscape Navigator 4.0
- Arena, the World Wide Web Consortium's test browser, partially supports the style sheet specification
- Emacs-w3 (also known as "GNUscape Navigator")
- Amaya, the World Wide Web Consortium's browser/editor software package

ON THE WEB

For more information on Arena and Amaya, visit the World Wide Web Consortium's site at **http://www.w3.org/**. To learn more about Emacs-w3, consult **http://www.cs.indiana.edu/elisp/w3/docs.html**.

Part
V

Ch
27

User-Defined Style Sheets and Other Standards

Users will be able to get into the act in the future and define their own style sheets. User-defined styles will override browser defaults but will probably be overridden by author-specified styles.

Currently, the World Wide Web Consortium's Cascading Style Sheet proposal (CSS level 1, or CSS1) is the only style sheet proposal that is being implemented. There is another proposal for style sheets, though. The Document Style Semantics and Specification Language (DSSSL)) has been proposed by the International Standards Organization as a means of defining style sheet languages (much the same way as SGML is used to define markup languages like HTML). Efforts are now underway to identify a subset of DSSSL that would be an appropriate basis for a common Web style sheet language. To learn more about DSSSL, consult **http://www.jclark.com/dsssl/**.

Style Sheet Resources

As you explore using cascading style sheets on your own, visit and bookmark these sites so you can stay on top of any new developments in the CSS standard and so you can see how others are using style sheets on their sites.

- **http://www.w3.org/Style/**   The World Wide Web Consortium's main style sheet page (created with a style sheet, of course!). The W3C also has a CSS Resources Page at **http://www.w3.org/Style/CSS/**.

- **http://www.htmlhelp.com/reference/css/**   A comprehensive guide to style sheets brought to you by the Web Design Group.

- **http://www.microsoft.com/truetype/css/gallery/entrance.htm**   Microsoft's popular CSS gallery page.

Enhancing Your Web Pages with Scripts

by Jim O'Donnell

With the introduction of JavaScript by Netscape, the concept of client-side scripting—small, easy-to-write programs that you can run on a Web browser—was born. With version 3 of its Internet Explorer Web browser, Microsoft introduced the Visual Basic Scripting Edition (VBScript) language, as well as JScript, its implementation of Netscape's JavaScript.

By learning how to create client-side scripts, you can add functionality and greater interactivity to your Web pages. Also, as you will see in other chapters in this book, some of the best new features of Internet Explorer 4, including Cascading Style Sheets, Dynamic HTML, and ActiveX Control and Java applet support, require scripting to really come to life. ■

Learn the essentials of client-side scripting

Find what kinds of things you can do using client-side scripting— scripts that are run on the end-user's Web browser—and what common elements there are between VBScript and JScript.

Learn details of the Web browser object model used for scripting

For them to do anything, scripting languages must have things to sense and manipulate. In this section, you can learn details of the Web Browser Object Model, which dictates the actions that you can take through scripting.

Study VBScript and JScript examples

Two detailed examples are presented showing form input validation using VBScript and Web browser window creation and manipulation using JScript.

Scripting Essentials

Scripting has been around as long as Web browsers have. In the early days, however, these scripts were server-side scripts, usually referred to as CGI scripts, that ran on the Web server in response to some user input from a Web browser. Though these scripts provided increased functionality and interaction for Web pages, the need to communicate back and forth over the Web for each interaction limited their usefulness.

With the introduction of Netscape Navigator 2, Netscape introduced the first *client-side* scripting language, which it originally named *LiveScript*. Netscape rechristened the language *JavaScript* when Sun Microsystems introduced its Java language. Client-side scripts are sent to the user with the rest of an HTML document and are executed on their Web browser.

With version 3 of its Internet Explorer Web browser, Microsoft introduced support for two client-side scripting languages: Visual Basic Script (VBScript), based on Microsoft's own Visual Basic and Visual Basic for Applications languages, and JScript, its open implementation of Netscape's JavaScript language.

Why Use a Scripting Language?

Although HTML provides a good deal of flexibility to page authors, it is static by itself; once written, HTML documents can't interact with the user other than by presenting hyperlinks. Creative use of CGI scripts (which run on Web servers) has made it possible to create more interesting and effective interactive sites, but some applications can really benefit from programs or scripts that the client executes. Even Dynamic HTML, which enables more elements of an HTML document to come to life, needs something to drive it. That something is client-side scripting, such as with VBScript or JScript.

Client-side scripts enable Web authors to write small scripts that execute on the users' browsers instead of on the server. For example, an application that collects data from a form and then posts it to the server can validate the data for completeness and correctness before sending it to the server. This process can greatly improve the performance of the browsing session because users don't have to send data to the server until it's been verified as correct.

Another important use of Web browser scripting languages comes as a result of the increased functionality being introduced for Web browsers in the form of Cascading Style Sheets, Dynamic HTML, Java applets, plug-ins, ActiveX Controls, and VRML objects and worlds. You can use each of these things to add extra functions and interactivity to a Web page. Scripting languages act as the glue that binds everything together. A Web page might use an HTML form to get user input and then set a parameter for an ActiveX Control based on that input. Usually, it is a script that will actually carry this out.

What Can Client-Side Scripts Do?

VBScript and JScript provide a fairly complete set of built-in functions and commands, enabling you to perform math calculations, manipulate strings, play sounds, open new windows and new URLs, and access and verify user input to your Web forms.

You can embed code to perform these actions in a page that will execute when the page loads. You can also write functions that contain code that's triggered by events you specify. For example, you can write a method that is called when the user clicks the Submit button of a form or one that is activated when the user clicks a hyperlink on the active page.

You can also use client-side scripts to set the attributes, or *properties*, of ActiveX Controls, Java applets, and other objects present in the browser. This way, you can change the behavior of plug-ins or other objects without having to rewrite them. For example, your code could automatically set the text of an ActiveX Label Control based on what time the page is viewed.

CAUTION

As you read this chapter, you will see that VBScript and JScript have many similarities, with similar syntax and capabilities. Because of this, some of the material presented is repeated in the VBScript and JScript sections.

VBScript and JScript are different languages, however, and you should be careful not to mix them up when you are programming.

Client-Side Scripts and Web Browsers

The most important thing you will do with your client-side scripts is interact with the content and information on your Web pages and, through it, with your user. Scripts interact with your Web browser through the browser's object model. Different aspects of the Web browser exist as different objects with properties and methods that you can access with client-side scripts. For instance, `document.write()` uses the `write` method of the `document` object. Understanding this Web browser object model is crucial to scripting effectively. Also, understanding how the Web browser processes and executes your scripts is also necessary.

When Scripts Execute   When you put client-side script code in a page, the Web browser evaluates the code as soon as it's encountered. Functions aren't executed when they're evaluated, however; they are just stored for later use. You still have to call functions explicitly to make them work. Some functions are attached to objects, like buttons or text fields on forms, and they are called when some event happens on the button or field. You might also have functions that you want to execute during page evaluation. You can do so by putting a call to the function at the appropriate place in the page.

Where to Put Your Scripts   You can put scripts anywhere within your HTML page as long as you surround them with the `<SCRIPT></SCRIPT>` tags. One good system is to put functions that will be executed more than once into the `<HEAD>` element of their pages; this element provides a convenient storage place. Because the `<HEAD>` element is at the beginning of the file, functions and other script code that you put there will be evaluated before the rest of the document is loaded. Then, you can execute the function at the appropriate point in your Web page by calling it, as in

```
<SCRIPT language="JavaScript">
<!-- Hide this script from incompatible Web browsers!
```

Part

V

Ch

28

```
myFunction();
<!-- -->
</SCRIPT>
```

Another way to execute scripts is to attach them to HTML elements that support scripts. When scripts are matched with events attached to these elements, the script is executed when the event occurs. You can be make these matches with HTML elements, such as forms, buttons, or links.

Sometimes, though, you have code that shouldn't be evaluated or executed until after all the page's HTML has been parsed and displayed. An example would be a function to print out all the URLs referenced in the page. If this function is evaluated before all the HTML on the page has been loaded, it will miss some URLs, so the call to the function should come at the page's end. You can define the function itself anywhere in the HTML document; it is only the function call that should be at the end of the page.

N O T E You must execute script code to modify the actual HTML content of a document (as opposed to merely changing the text in a form text input field, for instance) during page evaluation. ■

Using Functions, Objects, and Properties

VBScript and JScript are, in some ways, object-oriented languages. An *object* is a collection of data and functions that have been grouped together. A *function* is a piece of code that plays a sound, calculates an equation, or sends a piece of e-mail, and so on. The object's functions are called *methods* and its data are called its *properties*. The programs you write will have properties and methods and will interact with objects provided by the Web browser, its plug-ins, Java applets, ActiveX Controls, and other things.

N O T E Though the terms *function* and *method* are often used interchangeably, they are not the same. A method is a function that is part of an object. For instance, `writeln` is a method of the object `document`. ■

T I P Here's a simple guideline: An object's *properties* are the information it knows; its *methods* are how it can act on that information.

You access objects by specifying their names. For example, the active document object is named `document`. To use `document`'s properties or methods, you add a period and the name of the method or property you want. For example, `document.title` is the title property of the `document` object, and `explorer.length` calls the length member of the string object named `explorer`. Remember, literals are objects, too. By using client-side scripts to access the properties of objects—either those associated with the scripting language itself, those associated with the Web page (such as HTML forms), or objects created otherwise by things such as Java applets or ActiveX Controls—you enable the Web page to be much more dynamic and interactive.

VBScript and JScript Overview

Though VBScript and JScript are not as flexible as C++ or Visual Basic, they are quick and simple. Because you can embed them easily in your Web pages, adding interactivity or increased functionality with a script is easy—a lot easier than writing a Java applet to do the same thing (though, to be fair, you *can* do a lot more with Java applets). This section gives you a quick overview of VBScript and JScript programming.

A full language reference for VBScript and JScript, as well as Microsoft's tutorials for programming in them, is included on the CD-ROM included with this book. Because VBScript and JScript are evolving languages, you can get up-to-the-minute information on them at the Microsoft VBScript Web site at **http://www.microsoft.com/vbscript/** and the JScript Web site at **http://www.microsoft.com/jscript/**.

How Do VBScript and JScript Look in an HTML Document?

Script commands are embedded in your HTML documents. Embedded scripts are enclosed in the HTML container tag `<SCRIPT></SCRIPT>`. The `<LANGUAGE>` attribute of the `<SCRIPT>` tag specifies the scripting language to use when evaluating the script. For VBScript, the scripting language is defined as `LANGUAGE="VBSCRIPT"`. For JScript, which is Microsoft's implementation of the JavaScript language, it is `LANGUAGE="JavaScript"`.

VBScript resembles JScript/JavaScript and many other computer languages with which you may be familiar. It bears the closest resemblance, as you might imagine, to Visual Basic and Visual Basic for Applications because it is a subset of these two languages. The following lists some of the simple rules you must follow to structure VBScript and JScripts.

- VBScript is case-insensitive, so `function`, `Function`, and `FUNCTION` are all the same. JScript, on the other hand, is case-sensitive.

- A single VBScript statement can cover multiple lines if a continuation character, a single underscore, is placed at the end of each line to be continued. Also, you can put multiple short statements on a single line by separating each from the next with a colon.

  JScript is pretty flexible about statements. A single statement can cover multiple lines without a continuation character. You can put multiple short statements on a single line—just make sure to add a semicolon (;) at the end of each statement.

- Braces (the { and } characters) group JScript statements into blocks. A *block* may be the body of a function or a section of code that is executed in a loop or as part of a conditional test. VBScript's syntax allows you to use blocks of statements without special grouping characters.

N O T E If you're a Java, C, or C++ programmer, you might be puzzled when looking at JScript programs—sometimes each line ends with a semicolon, sometimes not. In JScript, unlike those other languages, the semicolon is not required at the end of each line. ■

VBScript and JScript Variables

Both VBScript and JScript variables are all loosely typed, which means that you can use them for any of the supported data types. Some of the more common types of data that you will store in these variables are integers, floating-point numbers, Boolean variables, and strings.

Expressions

An *expression* is anything that you can evaluate to get a single value. Expressions can contain string or numeric variables, operators, and other expressions, and they can range from simple to quite complex. For example, the following syntax is an expression, valid in either VBScript or JScript, that uses the assignment operator to assign the result 3.14159 to the variable pi:

```
pi = 3.14159
```

By contrast, the following syntax are more complex expressions in which the final value of flag depends on the values of the two Boolean variables quitFlag and formComplete:

```
VBScript        flag = (quitFlag = TRUE) And (formComplete = FALSE)

Jscript         flag = (quitFlag == TRUE) && (formComplete == FALSE)
```

Operators

Operators do just what their name suggests: they operate on variables or literals. The items on which an operator acts are called its *operands*. Operators come in the following two types:

- **Unary** These operators require only one operand and the operator can come before or after the operand. An example of this type is the operator that performs the logical negation of an expression—Not in VBScript, ! in JScript.

- **Binary** These operators need two operands. The four math operators (+ for addition, - for subtraction, * for multiplication, and / for division) are all binary operators, as is the = assignment operator you saw previously. The other important class of binary operators is the comparison operators, such as <, >, <=, and >=.

Testing Conditions in VBScript and JScript

Both VBScript and JScript provide statements for making decisions—the most common is the if statement. To make a decision, you supply one or more expressions that evaluate to true or false; the code that is executed depends on what your expressions evaluate.

The simplest form of the if statement has only one test and one result. If the condition is true, an action is performed; otherwise, nothing is done. For example, in the following code fragment, the message appears only if the variable x is less than pi:

```
VBScript        if (x < pi) then document.write("x is less than pi")

Jscript         if (x < pi) document.write("x is less than pi")
```

Both languages also allow other clauses to be used in the if statement and other actions to be taken, and also allow an else clause to be performed if no other condition is true.

Repeating Actions   If you want to repeat an action more than once, VBScript and JScript provide a variety of constructs for doing so. The first, called a `for` loop, executes a set of statements some number of times. You specify three expressions: an *initial* expression, which sets the values of any variables you need to use; a *final value*, which tells the loop how to see when it's done; and an *increment* expression, which modifies any variables that need it. Here's a simple example:

```
VBScript        for count = 0 to 100 step 2
                    document.write("Count is " + CStr(count) + "<BR>")
                next

Jscript         for (count=0; count <= 100; count+=2)
                    document.write("Count is " + count + "<BR>");
```

In this example, the expressions are all simple numerical values—the initial value is 0, the final value is 100, and the increment is 2. This loop executes 51 times and prints out a number each time.

A second form of loop that both VBScript and JScript have is the `while` loop. Unlike the `for` loop, which executes a set of statements a fixed number of times, the `while` loop executes statements as long as its condition is true.

Other VBScript and JScript Statements and Functions

Both VBScript and JScript have a large number of other statements and functions that you can use to create a wide variety of scripts to perform many different functions. Too many, in fact, to really get into in detail in this book. What you can see instead, in the following sections, is a quick discussion of the relative merits of VBScript and JScript, followed by example Web pages with applications using each language. The code for these pages is included on the CD-ROM that comes with this book, and the pages, along with the language resources on Microsoft's Web VBScript and JScript Web sites, will get you started if you want to start writing your own scripts.

If you want to read more about what you can do with VBScript and JScript, Que has a pair of excellent books that cover them in detail, *Special Edition Using VBScript*, and *Special Edition Using JScript*.

What Scripting Language Should You Use?

With the choice of scripting languages that are now available, the question of which to use quickly arises. JScript/JavaScript and VBScript have similar capabilities. Also, because they are both relatively new, you don't have a lot of history on which to rely for making a choice. The following are a few points to consider:

■ With what language are you more comfortable?   JScript/JavaScript is based on the Java and C++ languages; VBScript is based on Visual Basic and Visual Basic for Applications. If you are proficient at one of these parent languages, using the scripting language on which it is based might be a good idea.

Part

V

Ch

28

■ What are you trying to do? Both languages are object oriented and can interact with a compatible Web browser and other objects that it may have loaded, such as Java applets or ActiveX Controls. But, if you will be primarily working with Internet Explorer 3 using a feature of Microsoft's ActiveX technologies, using VBScript is probably a good idea because it is designed with that use in mind.

■ Who is your target audience? For "general-purpose" uses—like processing form inputs or providing simple interactivity—the biggest question to answer is who the audience for your Web pages will be. Though Microsoft Internet Explorer has a growing share of the Web browser market, Netscape Navigator has the lion's share. Unless your Web pages are targeted at a specific audience that will definitely be using Internet Explorer, you will probably want to use JScript/JavaScript. At least in the short term, using JScript/JavaScript will ensure you maximum compatibility.

Example VBScript Application

Your first task in implementing client-side scripting in your site will probably be to perform form validation. Many Web applications need to gather input from users. Traditionally, this data is entered in the browser and then transmitted to the server. The server checks the validity of the data and either stores the data on the server or sends back a message to the user requesting additional information or asking him or her to enter valid data.

Not only does this process slow down your Web sever, but it creates unnecessary Web traffic as well. With just a few lines of code, you will be able to validate much of this data on the client's machine and send it to the server only when it is complete.

To learn how this works, first you'll design an HTML document using a traditional form using standard HTML, and then you'll enhance it with client-side scripting.

The HTML Document Form

Listing 28.1 shows an excerpt from **Form.htm**, a traditional HTML page used to gather input from a user. Let's take a closer look at a few of the elements of this page.

N O T E You can find the full listings for all examples on the CD-ROM that accompanies this book. ■

Listing 28.1 Form.htm (excerpt) An HTML Document Using a Standard HTML Form

```
<FORM NAME="MyForm">
<TABLE>
<TR><TD>First Name:</TD>
    <TD> </TD>
    <TD><INPUT TYPE=TEXT NAME="FirstName" SIZE=20 Value=""></TD></TR>
<TR><TD>Last Name:</TD>
```

```
    <TD> </TD>
    <TD><INPUT TYPE=TEXT NAME="LastName"  SIZE=20 Value=""></TD></TR>
<TR><TD COLSPAN=3><HR></TD></TR>
<TR><TD>Payment Date:</TD>
    <TD> </TD>
    <TD><INPUT TYPE=TEXT NAME="PayDate"   SIZE=10 Value=""></TD></TR>
<TR><TD>Payment Amount:</TD>
    <TD><B>$</B></TD>
    <TD><INPUT TYPE=TEXT NAME="Amount"     SIZE=10 Value=""></TD></TR>
Were credit card number and expiration date left out of the source listing on
purpose? RGE
```

FIG. 28.1
This HTML document appears differently in Figure 28.2.

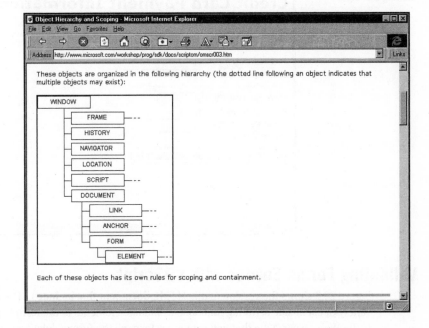

This HTML document, when you view it in Internet Explorer, appears as shown in Figure 28.2. The different elements of the HTML document, as shown in **Form.htm**, follow.

■ <FORM></FORM> tags

These container tags must surround the HTML form input elements. The NAME="MyForm" attribute is used to help identify the form from which that data came when it is being processed. You might notice that neither the METHOD nor ACTION attribute for the <FORM> tag has been sent; this is because this form is being used as an example. Normally, you would set METHOD=POST and set the ACTION to the appropriate URL of where on your Web server you want the data to be sent.

■ <INPUT TYPE=TEXT> tags

Each of these tags is used to receive one piece of information from the user. Each is named, using the NAME attribute, to allow the resulting data to be identified.

Part
V

Ch
28

■ `<INPUT TYPE=SUBMIT>` tag

This tag puts the button on the form that is used to submit the information. Like the other elements, it is named using the NAME attribute, and the VALUE attribute is used to customize the text appearing on the button.

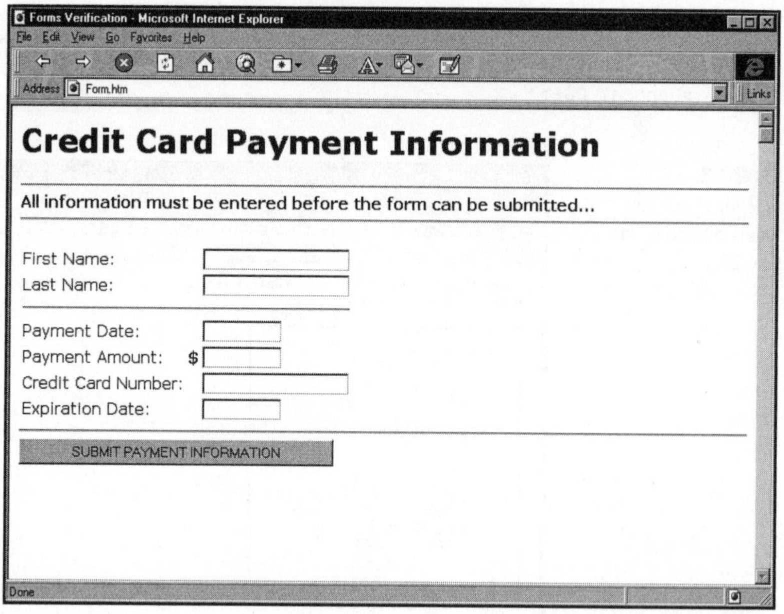

FIG. 28.2

You can use standard HTML form elements to set up a document for receiving user input.

Validating Forms Entries with VBScript

Figure 28.3 shows the version of this HTML document that includes VBScript to perform a variety of client-side scripting functions to validate elements of the form before it is submitted to the Web server. Note that you cannot perform all the form validation at the client—for instance, for this example, you would definitely need to validate the payment information at the server—but you definitely can perform some of the simpler things.

CAUTION

This example is meant to be illustrative and designed to show some of the types of user input that you can validate by using VBScript at the client. It is not meant to be a realistic example of how to implement a Web-based payment system. If you want to do that, note that there are a lot of concerns with security and validation of payment information that are not addressed here. If you are interested and depending on what Web server you are using, you can find this information in Que's *Running a Perfect Netscape Site* or *Special Edition Using Microsoft Internet Information Server 2.*

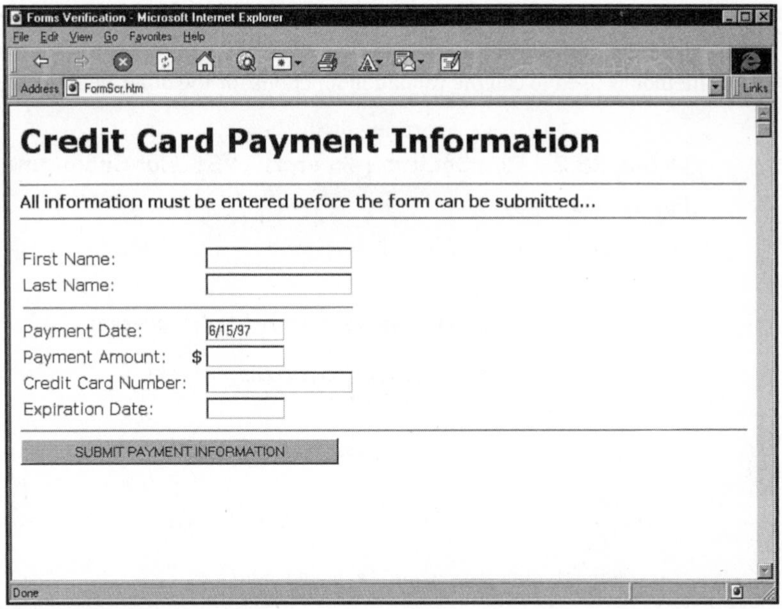

FIG. 28.3

Other than having its payment date entry prefilled, this VBScripted form doesn't look very different from the unscripted version.

Using VBScript to Prefill Entries   The only apparent change between the unscripted to scripted versions of this example in Figure 28.3 is that the payment date has been prefilled. Because an obvious default entry exists for this field—the current date—it makes sense to let VBScript fill in this date and save the user a little bit of effort. To do this, execute the VBScript statement

```
Document.MyForm.PayDate.Value = Date()
```

when the HTML document is loaded.

Note that the user can change this entry, picking a payment date that is later than the current date. You might not want to allow the user to select a payment date earlier than the current date, however—if his or her payment is late, for instance, you don't want him or her to be able to predate his or her check. You can easily prevent this manipulation with VBScript, as you will see later in this chapter.

Validating and Formatting Currency Entries   Listing 28.2 shows Check_Amount, a VBScript subroutine for validating and formatting an entry that is meant to be an amount of money. Primarily, this entry must be a numerical value, but it is a little more forgiving than that because it will remove a leading dollar sign if the user has put one in. Then, after making sure that the value is numerical, the subroutine formats it as dollars and cents and writes it back out to the form field from which it came.

To call this subroutine, attach the attribute onChange="Check_Amount(MyForm.Amount)" to the <INPUT> element for the appropriate entry. Recall from **Form.htm** previously that the form was

Part

V

Ch

28

named MyForm and the payment amount entry named Amount. The Check_Amount subroutine is then called whenever the entry is changed and the cursor is moved to another entry. (This method is used to call the validation functions for the other fields as well.)

Listing 28.2 FormScr.htm (excerpt) VBScript Subroutine to Validate and Format Currency

```
Sub Check_Amount(Obj)
   Dim Temp
   '
   ' Get object value and remove leading $, if present
   '
   Temp = Mid(Obj.VALUE,InStr(Obj.Value,"$")+1)
   If Not IsNumeric(Temp) Then
      '
      ' If not numeric (not a valid currency), blank out value
      '
      Temp = ""
   Else
      '
      ' Format current as dollars and cents
      '
      Temp = CStr(Fix(100*CDbl(Temp)))
      Temp = Left(Temp,Len(Temp)-2) & "." & Right(Temp,2)
   End If
   '
   ' Write value back into object
   '
   Obj.Value = Temp
End Sub
```

If you are not familiar with VBScript, you might be confused a little by the Check_Amount subroutine because it seems to treat the same value alternatively as a number or as a string. VBScript has only one type of data, known as Variant, which you can use to store any kind of data that VBScript recognizes. VBScript generally treats data as the subtype—such as integer, floating point, or string—appropriate to the operation. You can explicitly tell VBScript to treat the data as a specific subtype by using one of its conversion functions, such as the CStr and CDbl functions used in the Check_Amount subroutine.

As a final note, you see that, for an entry that is incorrectly formatted, Check_Amount will blank the entry. How your VBScripts respond to incorrect entries is up to you—you can remove the incorrect entry, as is done in this example, leave it but set an error flag that will prevent the user from submitting the form until he or she corrects it, bring up an Alert box, or anything else you would like to do.

Validating and Formatting Date Entries   The Check_Date subroutine, shown in Listing 28.3, is very similar to Check_Amount except that it validates a correct date entry rather than amount. Note that by explicitly calling the CDate function, even after the entry has been verified to be a valid date, Check_Date gets VBScript to "complete" the date. If the user enters just the month and day, VBScript will append the current year. If the user enters just the month and year, VBScript will add a day (the first of the month).

Listing 28.3 FormScr.htm (excerpt)   VBScript Subroutine to Validate and Format Date

```
'
' This subroutine checks to see if the value of the object that is
' passed to it is a valid date, and then formats it.
'
Sub Check_Date(Obj)
   Dim Temp
   '
   '  Get object value
   '
   Temp = Obj.Value
   If Not IsDate(Temp) Then
   '
   '    If not a valid date, blank out value
   '
      Temp = ""
   Else
   '
   '    Format date according to local settings
   '
      Temp = CDate(Temp)
   End If
   '  Write value back into object
   '
   Obj.Value = Temp
End Sub
```

Validating Numerical Entries   Even if it would be possible to do, you would probably not want to verify a credit card number on the client for reasons of account security. You can perform a little bit of validation on the numerical credit card number entry before the form data is sent along for final validation at the Web server, however. The Check_Number subroutine, shown in Listing 28.4, ensures that this entry is numerical and is the proper length for a credit card number (defined here as between 13 and 16 digits, though you can adjust this, if necessary).

Listing 28.4 FormScr.htm (excerpt)   VBScript Subroutine to Validate Numerical Entry

```
'
' This subroutine checks to see if the value of the object that is
' passed to it is a valid credit card number.
'
Sub Check_CCNumber(Obj)
   Dim Temp,minLength,maxLength
```

continues

Part
V

Ch
28

Listing 28.4   Continued

```
'
'   Specify minimum and maximum length of valid credit card numbers
'
    minLength = 13
    maxLength = 16
'
'   Get object value
'
    Temp = Obj.Value
    If Not IsNumeric(Temp) Then
'
'       If not a valid number, blank out value
'
        Temp = ""
    Else
        TempLength = Len(CStr(Temp))
        If TempLength < minLength Or TempLength > maxLength Then
'
'           If too short or too long, blank out value
'
            Temp = ""
        End If
    End If
'
'   If value has changed, write back new value to object
'
    If Temp <> Obj.Value Then
        Obj.Value = Temp
    End If
End Sub
```

Validating Complete Forms with VBScript

Once the user has entered all the information into the form and each individual entry has been validated, there are still some form-level checks that you might want to do before the form is submitted. You can perform these checks by attaching a VBScript function to the onSubmit event of the Submit button with onSubmit="Check_Form(Document.MyForm)". If the function returns True, the form is submitted; if it returns False, it is not. The Check_Form subroutine is shown in Listing 28.5.

```
'
'  This function will verify that the current form is ready to
'  be submitted before allowing it to be submitted.
'
Function Check_Form(Obj)
```

```
'   Verify that all fields have information in them
'
    If (Len(Obj.FirstName.Value) = 0) Or _
       (Len(Obj.LastName.Value)  = 0) Or _
       (Len(Obj.PayDate.Value)   = 0) Or _
       (Len(Obj.Amount.Value)    = 0) Or _
       (Len(Obj.CCNumber.Value)  = 0) Or _
       (Len(Obj.ExpDate.Value)   = 0) Then
       Alert "All fields must be filled with valid information!"
       Check_Form = False
       Exit Function
    End If
'
'   Verify that the payment date is on or after the current date
'
    If DateDiff("d",Obj.PayDate.Value,Date()) > 0 Then
       Alert "Payment date must be on or after current date!"
       Check_Form = False
       Exit Function
    End If
'
'   Verify that the payment date is on or before the card expiration date
'
    If DateDiff("d",Obj.PayDate.Value,Obj.ExpDate.Value) < 0 Then
       Alert "Payment date must be on or before card expiration date!"
       Check_Form = False
       Exit Function
    End If
'
'   Allow form to be submitted
'
    Alert "Submitting payment information..."
    Check_Form = True
End Function
```

The Check_Form subroutine does three things. First, it verifies that information has been entered into each field on the form. If any field is still blank, an Alert box is given (see Figure 28.4), and the form is not submitted.

Even if the form is completely filled out and each of the entries has the correct type of data in it, there might still be problems that you can catch at the client with VBScript. The Check_Form subroutine also checks for two types of invalid entries that can occur with either the payment or credit card expiration date. It is incorrect if the payment date is either past the expiration date of the card (see Figure 28.5) or before the current date. In either of these cases, an appropriate alert box is displayed, as shown in Figure 28.6, and the form is not submitted.

Part
V
Ch
28

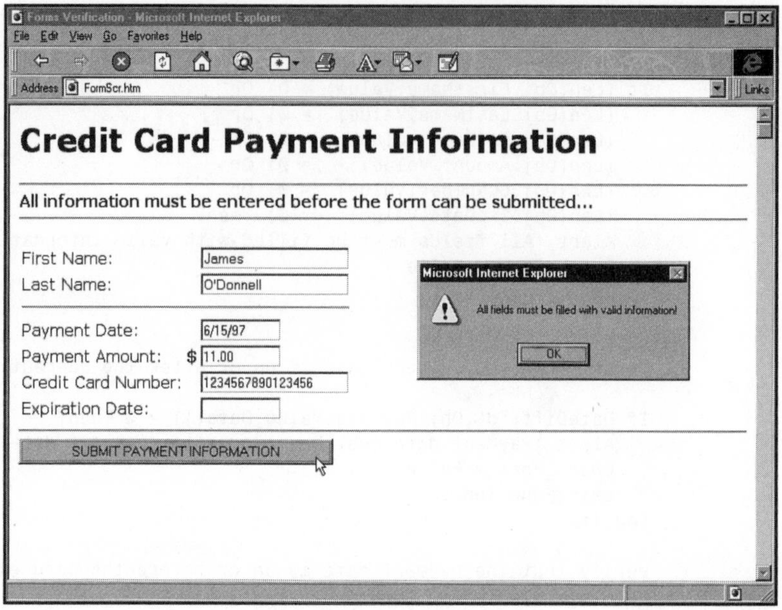

FIG. 28.4
Client-side processing is ideal for catching situations, such as this incomplete form, before submission.

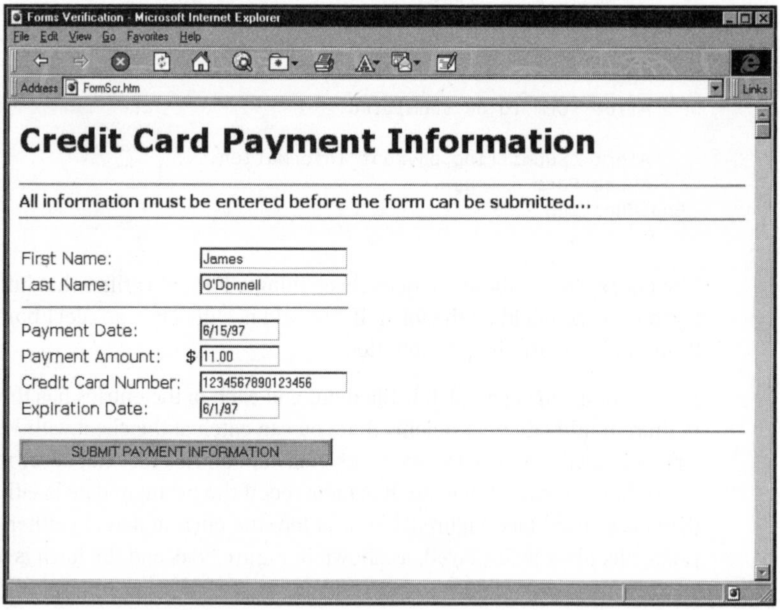

FIG. 28.5
Though this form seems to be filled out properly, note that the credit card has apparently expired.

FIG. 28.6
You can save effort on
your Web server by
using scripting to catch
simple errors, such as
this one, at the client.

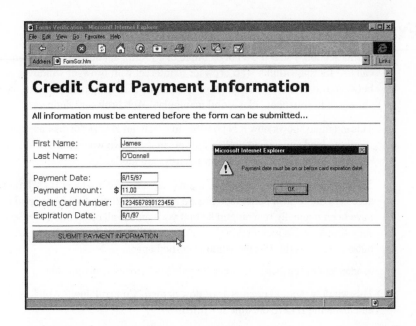

Once Check_Form has verified all the entries in the form, the form is then ready to be submitted
to the Web server for further payment information verification. You can also use VBScript to
put up an Alert box to let you know that your information is on its way (see Figure 28.7).

FIG. 28.7
Once Check_Form has
validated all the entries
at the client as much
as possible, the entries
can be submitted to
processing at the
server.

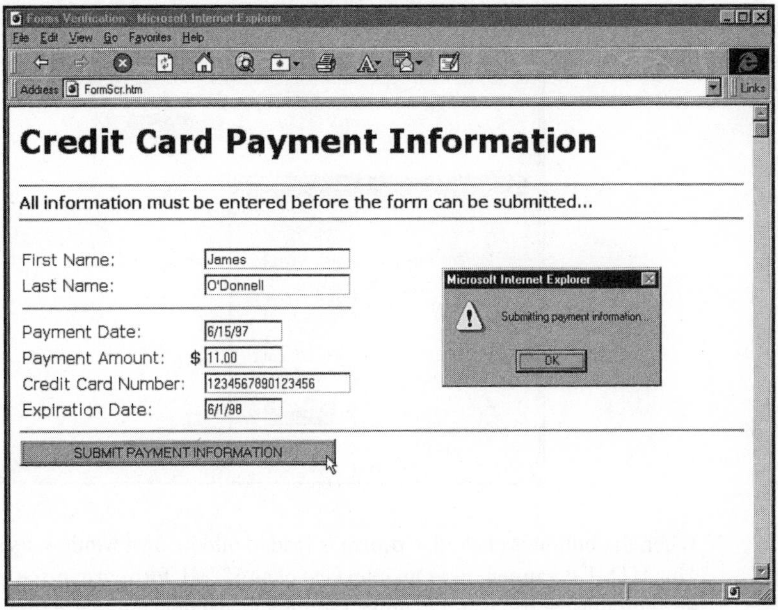

Part

V

Ch

28

Example JScript Application

In this section, you'll see an of example of a JScript application. The example will show how you can use JScript within a Web browser to interact with browser windows. As usual, the interface between the user and the JScript code remains HTML forms elements. The examples also show you how to open, close, and manipulate Web browser windows.

This example shows how it is possible to create an HTML forms-based control panel that uses JScript to load and execute other JScripts in their own windows. You do this through using the window Web browser object, its properties, and methods.

The file **CpMain.htm** shows the "main program," the top-level HTML document that gives access to the control panel (see Figure 28.8—note that in this figure and the next, the windows have been manually rearranged so that you can see all of them). The JScript in this example is very simple and is included in the onClick attribute of the form's <input> tag. Clicking the button executes the JScript window method open:

```
window.open('cp.htm','ControlPanel','width=300,height=250')
```

This window method creates a window named "ControlPanel," which is 300 by 250 pixels large and loads the HTML document **Cp.htm**.

FIG. 28.8

The Control Panel button calls a JScript and creates a new browser window.

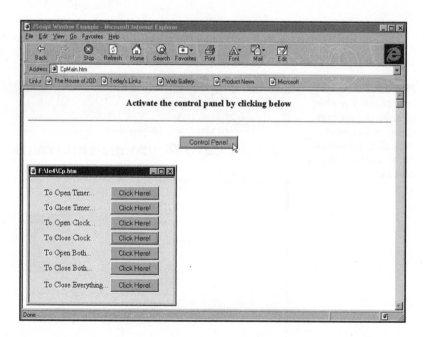

When the button is clicked, **Cp.htm** is loaded into its own window, as shown in Figure 28.8. This HTML document uses an interface of an HTML form organized in a table to give access through this control panel to other JScript applications, namely, a timer and a real-time clock. The HTML documents to implement these interfaces are in the files on the CD-ROM,

CpTimer.htm and **CpClock.htm**. Listing 28.6 shows **Cp.htm**. The JScript functions `openTimer()`, `openClock()`, `closeTimer()`, and `closeClock()` are used to open and close windows for a JScript timer and clock, respectively. These functions are attached to forms buttons that make up the control panel. Note that because the JScript variables `timerw` and `clockw` are defined outside any of the functions, you can use them anywhere in the JScript document. You use them to remember whether the timer and clock windows are open.

Listing 28.6   Cp.htm   This HTML Form Calls JScripts to Create and Destroy Windows for a Timer or a Real-time Clock

```
<HTML>
<HEAD>
<SCRIPT LANGUAGE="JavaScript">
<!-- Hide this script from incompatible Web browsers!
var timerw = null;
var clockw = null;
function openTimer() {
   if(!timerw)
      timerw = open("cptimer.htm","TimerWindow","width=300,height=100");
}
function openClock() {
   if(!clockw)
      clockw = open("cpclock.htm","ClockWindow","width=50,height=25");
}
function closeTimer() {
   if(timerw) {
      timerw.close();
      timerw = null;
   }
}
function closeClock() {
   if(clockw) {
      clockw.close();
      clockw = null;
   }
}
<!-- -->
</SCRIPT>
</HEAD>
<BODY BGCOLOR=#EEEEEE>
<FORM>
<CENTER>
<TABLE>
<TR><TD>To Open Timer...</TD>
    <TD ALIGN=CENTER>
       <INPUT TYPE="button" NAME="ControlButton" VALUE="Click Here!"
          onClick="openTimer()"></TD></TR>
<TR><TD>To Close Timer...</TD>
    <TD ALIGN=CENTER>
       <INPUT TYPE="button" NAME="ControlButton" VALUE="Click Here!"
          onClick="closeTimer()"></TD></TR>
<TR><TD>To Open Clock...</TD>
    <TD ALIGN=CENTER>
```

continues

Listing 28.6   Continued

```
                <INPUT TYPE="button" NAME="ControlButton" VALUE="Click Here!"
                    onClick="openClock()"></TD></TR>
<TR><TD>To Close Clock...</TD>
    <TD ALIGN=CENTER>
        <INPUT TYPE="button" NAME="ControlButton" VALUE="Click Here!"
            onClick="closeClock()"></TD></TR>
<TR><TD>To Open Both...</TD>
    <TD ALIGN=CENTER>
        <INPUT TYPE="button" NAME="ControlButton" VALUE="Click Here!"
            onClick="openTimer();openClock();"></TD></TR>
<TR><TD>To Close Both...</TD>
    <TD ALIGN=CENTER>
        <INPUT TYPE="button" NAME="ControlButton" VALUE="Click Here!"
            onClick="closeTimer();closeClock();"></TD></TR>
<TR><TD></TD></TR>
<TR><TD>To Close Everything...</TD>
    <TD ALIGN=CENTER>
        <INPUT TYPE="button" NAME="ControlButton" VALUE="Click Here!"
            onClick="closeTimer();closeClock();self.close();"></TD></TR>
</TABLE>
</CENTER>
</FORM>
</BODY>
</HTML>
```

The **CpTimer.htm** and **CpClock.htm** files each use the properties of the JScript Date object to access time information. Figure 28.9 shows the Web page with the control panel, timer, and real-time clock windows all open.

FIG. 28.9

JScript can create multiple browser windows, each running its own JScripts and independently performing its functions.

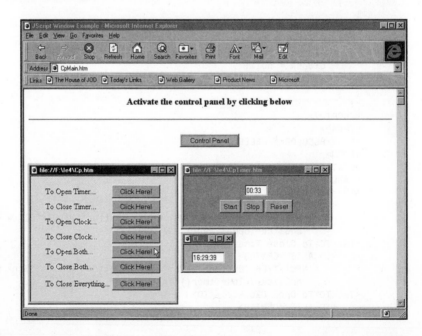

Dynamic HTML

When HTML was first developed, its mixing of text and graphics, as well as the inclusion of the hypertext link for linking information, revolutionized the way information was presented and distributed across the Internet. Since the inception of HTML, Web developers and vendors have been looking for ways to make the information that can be presented more dynamic and to create more ways to interact with the user. Animated GIFs, Web browser plug-ins and ActiveX Controls, Java applets, and scripting languages are all examples of ways to make Web pages more exciting.

HTML itself is basically a static language, though; information is sent to a client Web browser, which renders it for the viewer. Now, with Dynamic HTML, that has changed. Using Dynamic HTML, you can access, change, and interact with every HTML tag and every bit of information in your HTML documents. ▪

Learn about Microsoft's Dynamic HTML

Dynamic HTML is Microsoft's term for the new technology they have embedded in their Internet Explorer 4 Web browser. Through Dynamic HTML, you can create Web pages that can change dynamically and have a much higher degree of interaction than in the past.

The Dynamic HTML Document Object Model

The heart of Dynamic HTML is Microsoft's new Document Object Model. This model is what provides you, and scripts that you write, with the ability to interact with and change any element in an HTML document.

See what Dynamic HTML can do

This chapter will show you some examples of the kinds of things you can do with Dynamic HTML. None of the examples shown represent anything you couldn't have done in the past—now, however, it is possible to do them using HTML alone.

Where to get more information on Dynamic HTML

Dynamic HTML is a new technology still under development. People are just scratching the surface of what is possible with it. You will find some of the best places to look for examples and more information.

Internet Explorer 4 Document Object Model

The heart of Dynamic HTML is the new Document Object Model that the Internet Explorer 4 Web browser supports. You can think of every element in an HTML document as an object, including the HTML tags and information that they contain, as well as aspects of the Web browser itself and any included Java applets, ActiveX Controls, or other elements. The Document Object Model is what *exposes* these objects, making them accessible to you through scripts that you can write and include with the document.

Before Internet Explorer 4 and Dynamic HTML, the Document Object Model was very limited. It was able to expose Java applets, ActiveX Controls, and the Web browser window properties, such as window size and location. The model exposed a very limited number of HTML elements, however. The HTML tags that were supported by past object models were primarily limited to HTML forms elements. Thus, just about the only HTML elements that you could access and change within a Web page were those that were a part of HTML forms.

Microsoft's Dynamic HTML changes all that. With Dynamic HTML, every HTML tag is exposed by the Document Object Model. The contents of all HTML container tags are also exposed. So, not only can you change the styles or formats associated with a <P> tag, for instance, but you can also change its text contents. And this is all done on the client-side, without any need to interact with the Web server.

Dynamic HTML: Microsoft versus Netscape

Both Microsoft and Netscape have come out with something in the latest releases of their Web browsers called Dynamic HTML. There are a few similarities and many differences between the two. Both implementations of Dynamic HTML support style sheets, and can reformat and reposition text and other Web elements dynamically on the page. This can be done either automatically or in response to some user input.

Using Microsoft's Dynamic HTML, Web authors have access to anything on the Web page, and can manipulate any content, any HTML tag, and any attribute on the page. This is all done at the client, without having to go back to the Web server.

Netscape, on the other hand, does not support most of the Document Object Model, which is what allows Microsoft's Dynamic HTML to manipulate anything on the Web page. Therefore, Web authors can access a limited set of page elements when viewed with Netscape Navigator. Netscape uses JavaScript Accessible Style Sheets and their own proprietary dynamic font technology.

For the moment, Microsoft's brand of Dynamic HTML seems more in line with existing and proposed Internet standards. Only time will tell which approach will win out in the end.

In the rest of this section, I will discuss aspects of the Document Object Model for Internet Explorer 4. It is important to at least understand the different terms used with the object model—object, property, method, collection, and event— and what they mean. This section will give you a good basis for understanding the Dynamic HTML samples later in the chapter.

Understanding Objects and the Object Hierarchy

Figure 29.1 shows the hierarchy of objects that is part of the Internet Explorer 4 Document Object Model. In the simplest terms, an object in this model is a recognizable element of the whole. Objects can contain other objects, however; thus, all of the objects are organized into an object hierarchy.

Part
V

Ch
29

FIG. 29.1

The boxed elements of the Document Object Model represent the additions that Dynamic HTML uses.

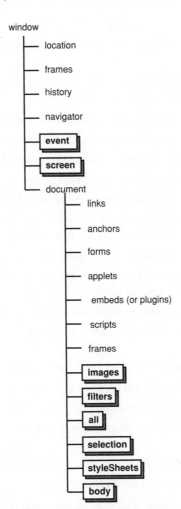

Looking at Figure 29.1, the window object, at the top of the hierarchy, includes everything you see within a given Web browser window. That object can and will, in turn, contain other objects. This object hierarchy is used when referencing these objects, with the following example notation:

```
window.document.links[0]
```

This line of code refers to the first link object contained in the current document of a given Web browser window (normally, unless you are authoring Web pages that use multiple windows, you can omit `window`).

A description of each type of object in the Internet Explorer 4 Document Object Model follows:

- **`window`** Represents an open Web browser window
- **`location`** Information for the current URL
- **`frames`** A collection of `window` objects, one for each separate frame in the current window
- **`history`** Information for the recently visited URLs
- **`navigator`** Information about the browser itself
- **`event`** Maintains the state of events occurring within the browser
- **`screen`** Statistics on the physical screen and the rendering abilities of the client
- **`document`** Contains all the information attached to the current HTML document
- **`links`** A collection of links referenced in the current document
- **`anchors`** A collection of anchors present within the current document
- **`forms`** Can contain a number of other objects corresponding to the forms elements within it; there is one `forms` object for each HTML form in the document
- **`applets`** Contains information about the Java applets present
- **`embeds`** Has information about all objects included using the `<EMBED>` tag; this object can also be referenced using the synonym `plugins`
- **`scripts`** A collection of all the script elements within the document
- **`frames`** A collection of `window` objects, one for each separate frame in the current document
- **`images`** A collection that contains one element for each image in the document
- **`filters`** Contains a collection of the `filter` objects associated with the document
- **`all`** Allows access to all of the HTML tags that are a part of the document
- **`selection`** Represents the current active selection, a user-selected block of text within the document
- **`styleSheets`** A collection of the Style Sheets attached to the current document
- **`body`** Accesses the `<BODY>` section of the document

You will note that many of these objects are collections of other objects. The `images` object, for instance, is a collection of objects associated with all the images in the current document. You can access elements in these collections either by name or by number. For instance, if the first image in an HTML document is defined by the following tag:

```
<IMG SRC="ryan.jpg" ID=Ryan>
```

you can use the `images` object to access that image in one of two ways:

```
document.images("Ryan")
document.images[0]
```

Note that arrays in the object model are zero-based, so the first element in an array is referenced using zero.

Using Properties

Every object has properties. To access a property, just use the object name followed by a period and the property name. To get the length of the `images` object, which would tell you how many images are in the current document, you can write the following:

```
document.images.length
```

If the object you're using has properties that can be modified, you can change them in the same way. For example, you can change the URL of the current window by setting the `href` property of the `location` object, as in the following line:

```
Location.href = "http://www.rpi.edu/~odonnj/"
```

If this line is executed within a script, the HTML document referenced by it (my home page) will be loaded into your Web browser window.

Listing 29.1 shows an example of a program that uses Dynamic HTML's `all` object to access all the HTML tags included within the document. In this case, when the document is loaded, a script pops up a series of alert boxes showing each HTML tag found. The script does this by using the `length` property of the `all` object to see how many tags there are and then stepping through them using the `tagName` property to display what the tags are (see Figure 29.2).

Listing 29.1   disptags.htm   The *all* Object Enables You to Access Every HTML Tag

```
<HTML>
<HEAD>
<TITLE>Dynamic HTML Example</TITLE>
</HEAD>
<BODY>
<CENTER>
<H1>Document Object Model: <EM>all</EM> Object</H1>
<HR>
<P>
The script in this example will put up a series of alert boxes
showing all of the HTML tags used in this document. The script
uses the <EM>length</EM> and <EM>tagName</EM> properties of
the <EM>all</EM> object.
</P>
<HR>
</CENTER>
<ADDRESS>
Jim O'Donnell, <A HREF="mailto:odonnj@rpi.edu">odonnj@rpi.edu</A>
</ADDRESS>
</BODY>
```

continues

Listing 29.1   Continued

```
<SCRIPT LANGUAGE="JavaScript">
for(i = 0;i < document.all.length;i++) {
    alert("Tag " + (i+1) + " of " + document.all.length +
          " = " + document.all(i).tagName);
}
</SCRIPT>
</HTML>
```

FIG. 29.2
Dynamic HTML enables
you to access all of the
information in the
current HTML document.

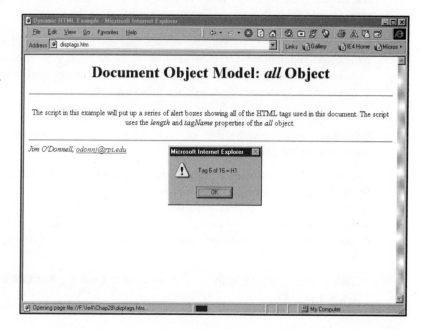

Two specific types of object properties, *methods* and *events*, deserve special mention. A method is a function attached to the object for performing a specific task. An event is something to which the object responds. You will see examples of methods and events in some of the Dynamic HTML samples following.

The rest of this chapter is devoted to giving you a feel for some of the things that you can do with Dynamic HTML. These samples will only scratch the surface of what is possible, but they should give you some ideas. At the end of the chapter, Web resources for getting more information are shown.

Using Dynamic HTML with Styles

Dynamic HTML works very well with another aspect of Internet Explorer 4 for dynamically changing the formatting of elements in an HTML document: styles and style sheets. One property associated with all HTML tags—which, as you will recall, you can access through the `all` object—is that tag's style. The style property, in turn, has properties of its own that you can access and change to immediately change the appearance of the Web page.

Listing 29.2 shows an example of dynamically changing the style of elements of an HTML document. In this example, the format is applied to two different elements in different ways—either through an embedded style sheet created with the <STYLE> tag or through the STYLE attribute. No matter which way you do it, the script changes the format in response to the onClick event. Figures 29.3 and 29.4 show the before and after screen shots of this HTML document.

Listing 29.2   style1.htm   Dynamic HTML Can Change Document Styles

```
<HTML>
<HEAD>
<TITLE>Dynamic HTML Example</TITLE>
<STYLE>
    .clicked {font-size:36pt;color:red}
</STYLE>
<SCRIPT LANGUAGE="JScript">
function changeH1Style() {
    document.all.tags("H1").item(0).className = "clicked";
    document.all.tags("P").item(0).style.fontSize = "24pt";
}
</SCRIPT>
</HEAD>
<BODY onClick="changeH1Style()">
<CENTER>
<H1>Dynamic HTML and Styles</H1>
<HR>
<P>
When you click the mouse, the script in this example will
dynamically change the style of the heading and of this
text. The script uses the <EM>className</EM> and
<EM>style.fontSize</EM> properties of the
<EM>all.tags.item</EM> object.
</P>
<HR>
</CENTER>
<ADDRESS>
Jim O'Donnell, <A HREF="mailto:odonnj@rpi.edu">odonnj@rpi.edu</A>
</ADDRESS>
</BODY>
</HTML>
```

Dynamic HTML and the Data Source Object

Another Dynamic HTML capability works hand-in-hand with Microsoft's Data Source Object to allow what is called *data binding*. The Data Source Object is an ActiveX Control that references an external file to provide data for the HTML document. Dynamic HTML enables you to use the DATASRC and DATAFLD attributes to bind this data to HTML elements. This way, the data that is displayed within a document can be kept separate from the formatting. Also, once the data is transmitted to the client Web browser, the Data Source Object can perform operations on it locally.

FIG. 29.3

You can attach formatting styles to HTML elements in a variety of ways.

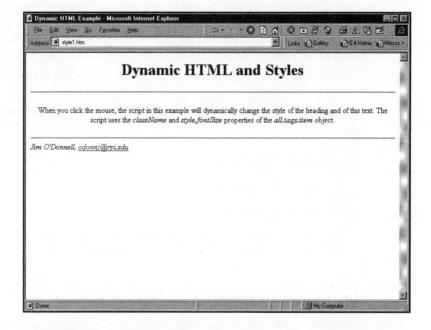

FIG. 29.4

You can change formats and immediately update the Web browser window in response to any event.

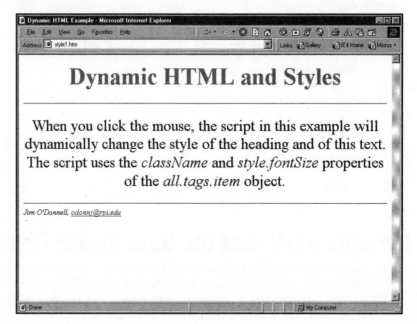

Listing 29.3 shows an example of data binding using the Data Source Object and Dynamic HTML. In this example, a data file of chapter, page count, and author information is bound to the columns of an HTML table. The Data Source Objects SortColumn() method is attached to the table headings, using the onClick event. When a column heading is clicked, the table is sorted by the contents of that column and immediately redisplayed. Figures 29.5 and 29.6 show examples of this, with the table sorted either by chapter number or chapter title.

Listing 29.3   databind.htm   Dynamic HTML and Data Binding Enable Easy Client-Side Data Manipulation

```
<HTML>
<HEAD>
<TITLE>Dynamic HTML Example</TITLE>
</HEAD>
<BODY>
<OBJECT ID="inputdata"
        CLASSID="clsid:333C7BC4-460F-11D0-BC04-0080C7055A83"
        align="baseline" border="0" width="0" height="0">
<PARAM NAME="DataURL"   VALUE="authors.txt">
<PARAM NAME="UseHeader" VALUE=TRUE>
</OBJECT>
<CENTER>
<H1>Data Binding with Dynamic HTML</H1>
<HR>
<P>
   This example shows an example of how you can use
   Dynamic HTML to bind an HTML element, in this case
   the columns of a table, to a Data Source Object.
   This allows the data to be kept separately from the
   formatting information in the HTML document. It
   also allows the data to be operated on at the client.
   In this example, if you click on the table headers
   of the table below, it will be sorted by the
   elements in that column.
</P>
<HR>
<TABLE DATASRC="#inputdata" BORDER>
<THEAD>
<TR><TH><U><DIV ID=chapNum onclick="sort1()">
        Chapter<BR>Number</DIV></U></TH>
    <TH><U><DIV ID=chapTitle onclick="sort2()">
        Chapter<BR>Title</DIV></U></TH>
    <TH><U><DIV ID=pageCount onclick="sort3()">
        Estimate<BR>Page Count</DIV></U></TH>
    <TH><U><DIV ID=authorName onclick="sort4()">
        Author</DIV></U></TH></TR>
</THEAD>
<TBODY>
<TR><TD ALIGN=RIGHT><DIV DATAFLD="ChapNum"></DIV></TD>
    <TD>            <DIV DATAFLD="ChapTitle"></DIV></TD>
    <TD ALIGN=RIGHT><DIV DATAFLD="PageCount"></DIV></TD>
    <TD>            <DIV DATAFLD="Author"></DIV></TD></TR>
```

continues

Listing 29.3 Continued

```
</TBODY>
</TABLE>

<SCRIPT LANGUAGE="JavaScript">
function sort1() {
  inputdata.SortColumn = "ChapNum";
  inputdata.Reset();
}
function sort2() {
  inputdata.SortColumn = "chapTitle";
  inputdata.Reset();
}
function sort3() {
  inputdata.SortColumn = "pageCount";
  inputdata.Reset();
}
function sort4() {
  inputdata.SortColumn = "authorName";
  inputdata.Reset();
}
</SCRIPT>
<HR>
</CENTER>
<ADDRESS>
Jim O'Donnell, <A HREF="mailto:odonnj@rpi.edu">odonnj@rpi.edu</A>
</ADDRESS>
</BODY>
</HTML>
```

FIG. 29.5

The Data Source Object enables you to include external data within an HTML document using Dynamic HTML.

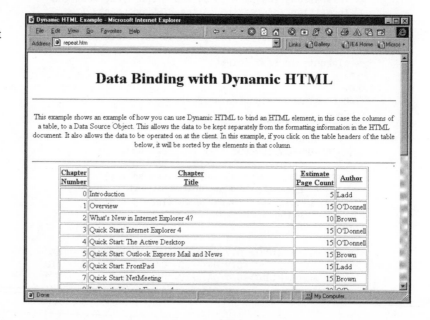

FIG. 29.6

Using Dynamic HTML, you can automatically sort or manipulate data, and then immediately redisplay it.

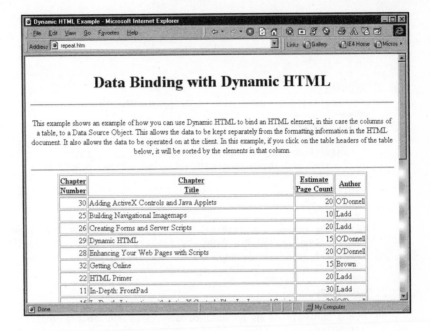

Position HTML Elements with Dynamic HTML

One exciting thing possible with Dynamic HTML is the ability to reposition HTML elements on the Web page. To do this, change the `left` and `top` properties of the element's `style` object (which, in turn, is a property of the element). This change can be done either automatically or in response to user interaction.

Listing 29.4 shows an example of a Dynamic HTML document that automatically positions an HTML element on the Web page. In this example, two nested regions are created using the HTML `<DIV>` tag. The outer region has a yellow background and contains only the inner region. The inner region holds an image. This example waits for the `onClick` event and then calls a script that moves the image across and down the outer region. The last thing that this script does before exiting is use the `window.setTimeout()` method to arrange to have itself execute again 500 milliseconds (a half a second) later. So, once the movement is enabled, it continues to move as long as the page is displayed (see Figures 29.7 and 29.8).

Listing 29.4   position.htm   With Dynamic HTML, You Can Change the Position of Any HTML Element

```
<HTML>
<HEAD>
<TITLE>Dynamic HTML Example</TITLE>
</HEAD>
<BODY onClick="moveRyan()">
```

continues

Listing 29.4 Continued

```
<HTML>


<CENTER>
<H1>Positioning Elements with Dynamic HTML</H1>
<HR>
<DIV ID=Block
 STYLE="position:relative;height:55%;width:50%;background-color:yellow">
    <DIV ID=Ryan STYLE="position:absolute;width:132">
        <IMG SRC="Ryan.jpg" WIDTH=132 HEIGHT=198 BORDER=0>
    </DIV>
</DIV>
<HR>
<P>
Click the mouse, and this example will show you how HTML elements
can be moved on the Web page, by setting the <EM>style.top</EM> and
<EM>style.left</EM> properties of the HTML element.
</P>
<HR>
</CENTER>
<ADDRESS>
Jim O'Donnell, <A HREF="mailto:odonnj@rpi.edu">odonnj@rpi.edu</A>
</ADDRESS>
</BODY>
<SCRIPT LANGUAGE="JScript">
ctr = 0;
function moveRyan() {
   ctr++;
   if (ctr > 9)
      ctr = 0;
   document.all.Ryan.style.top  =
      ctr*(document.all.Block.offsetHeight -
           document.all.Ryan.offsetHeight)/9;
   document.all.Ryan.style.left =
      ctr*(document.all.Block.offsetWidth -
           document.all.Ryan.offsetWidth)/9;
   window.setTimeout("moveRyan();",500);
}
</SCRIPT>
</HTML>2
```

Changing HTML Documents On-The-Fly

The last example shows the use of Dynamic HTML to create dynamic content: HTML elements that are changed within the Web browser on-the-fly. Listing 29.5 shows this example, which illustrates two ways in which this can be done. The digital clock (see Figure 29.9) is an HTML element, but it changes automatically each second to reflect the local time. The paragraph following it, on the other hand, is changed in response to user input—when the user clicks the Change HTML button, the contents of the text box above the button are substituted for the paragraph. As you can see in Figure 29.10, this substitution can also include any HTML elements, as shown with the <MARQUEE> and hypertext link in this example.

FIG. 29.7
You can use the HTML <DIV> container tag to group other HTML elements into one region.

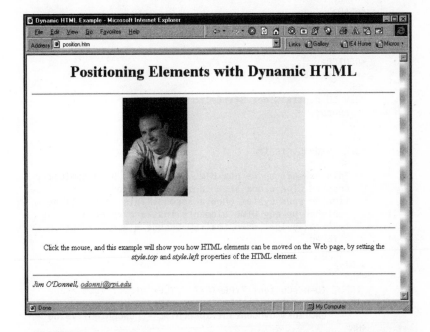

FIG. 29.8
The top and left style properties make it easy to move HTML elements around the page.

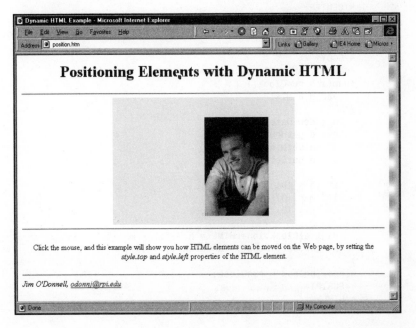

Listing 29.5 dyncon.htm Dynamic HTML Can Change HTML Documents Without Going Back to the Web Server

```
<HTML>
<HEAD>
<TITLE>Dynamic HTML Example</TITLE>
</HEAD>
<BODY>
<CENTER>
<H1>Dynamic Content</H1>
<HR>
<DIV ID=digitalClock STYLE="font-size: 60">
    
</DIV>
<HR>
<DIV ID=dynContent>
   <P>
   This example shows how HTML content can be dynamically
   changed. The clock shown above is updated with the local
   time on your system once a second. This text will be
   replaced by any HTML elements that are entered in the
   text box below, when the <EM>Change HTML</EM> button is
   clicked.
   </P>
</DIV>
<HR>
<INPUT ID=newContent TYPE=TEXT STYLE="width: 100%"><BR>
<INPUT TYPE=BUTTON VALUE="Change HTML"
       onclick="dynContent.innerHTML = newContent.value">
<HR>
</CENTER>
<ADDRESS>
Jim O'Donnell, <A HREF="mailto:odonnj@rpi.edu">odonnj@rpi.edu</A>
</ADDRESS>
</BODY>
<SCRIPT LANGUAGE="JScript">
function runClock() {
   var d,h,m,s;
//
   d = new Date();
   h = d.getHours();
   m = d.getMinutes();
   s = d.getSeconds();
//
   if (h < 10) h = "0" + h;
   if (m < 10) m = "0" + m;
   if (s < 10) s = "0" + s;
//
   digitalClock.innerHTML = h + ":" + m + ":" + s;
   window.setTimeout("runClock();",100);
}
window.onload = runClock;
</SCRIPT>
</HTML>
```

FIG. 29.9
Real-time clocks appearing in Web pages are common, but with Dynamic HTML, you can make them appear using only HTML elements.

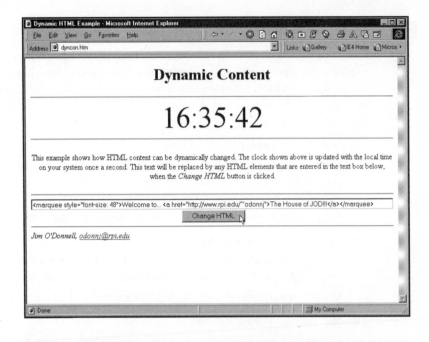

FIG. 29.10
Dynamic HTML can dynamically change the contents of a displayed HTML document, which is automatically redisplayed by Internet Explorer 4.

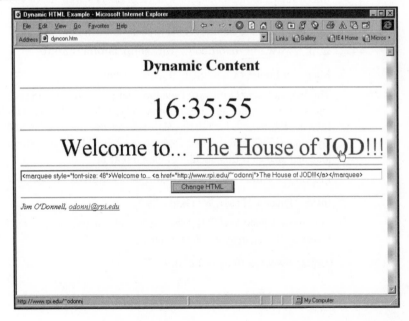

Find Out More About Dynamic HTML

It would be possible to write an entire book on Dynamic HTML, so there's no way it can be covered in the space that has been allotted here. The object of this chapter was to give you a flavor of some of what is possible using Dynamic HTML and Internet Explorer 4. If you would like to see more examples and find out more information, try some of these links on the Microsoft Web site.

- Features of Dynamic HTML in Internet Explorer 4

  The Internet Explorer 4 Web site includes introductory information on all the features of its suite of applications and technologies. The information on Dynamic HTML is located at:

  http://www.microsoft.com/ie/ie40/features/ie-dhtml.htm

- Internet Explorer 4 Demos

  In addition to information, the Internet Explorer 4 also offers a series of demos, many of which make use of the new features of Dynamic HTML. The demos are at:

  http://www.microsoft.com/ie/ie40/demos/

- Microsoft SiteBuilder Network

  Microsoft's SiteBuilder Network is the area of its Web site devoted to providing information to Web authors and developers who use Microsoft products. The SiteBuilder Network hosts a Dynamic HTML Gallery at the following URL:

  http://www.microsoft.com/workshop/author/dhtml/

- Microsoft Internet Client SDK Documentation

  The Internet Client Software Development Kit (SDK) includes the technical information and software needed to author pages and develop applications and components that use Internet Explorer 4. Part of the SDK is extensive information and documentation on Dynamic HTML and the new Document Object Model that supports it. You can download and also view this documentation online at:

  http://www.microsoft.com/msdn/sdk/inetsdk/help/

- Inside Dynamic HTML Web Site

  The Inside Dynamic HTML Web site includes a mass of information and samples of Dynamic HTML in action. It is located at:

  http://www.insidedhtml.com /

Adding ActiveX Controls and Java Applets

With Internet Explorer 4, Microsoft continues its support for both ActiveX Controls and Java applets. ActiveX Controls combine the convenience of Java applets with the permanence and functionality of Netscape Navigator plug-ins. As with Java applets, you can automatically download ActiveX Controls to your system if they are either not currently installed or if the installed version is not the most recent. Like plug-ins, ActiveX Controls remain available to your Web browser continuously once you install them.

This chapter introduces you to ActiveX Controls and shows you examples of the available controls and how they are used in Web pages. It also provides more information about programming the controls into your HTML documents both by hand and by using Microsoft's ActiveX Control Pad. This HTML Web page authoring tool offers an automated, WYSIWYG interface to ActiveX Control configuration and automatically generates the HTML code to implement the control. The Control Pad supports any locally-installed ActiveX Control and frees the programmer of the burden of knowing the class IDs and configurable parameters of each control. It also supports

Learn about Microsoft's ActiveX Controls

This chapter discusses Microsoft's ActiveX Controls and how you can use them to increase the capabilities of Internet Explorer and other compatible applications.

Find out what ActiveX Controls mean for users and programmers

Find out what ActiveX Controls mean to the users and developers of World Wide Web software, information, and products.

See what ActiveX Controls can do and how to use them in a Web page

Find out what some of the ActiveX Controls can do when you use them in a Web page. Learn how to embed and configure ActiveX Controls in HTML Web pages, including making use of the ability to automatically download and install needed controls.

Create Web pages with the ActiveX Control Pad and Microsoft's Script Wizard

Microsoft's ActiveX Control Pad gives a simple, point-and-click interface to embed ActiveX Controls and to create sophisticated scripts for HTML documents.

the Script Wizard, with which you can create interactive, scripted Web pages without having to learn a scripting language.

Additionally, details of including and configuring Java applets into your Web pages are discussed. ■

What Are Internet Explorer ActiveX Controls?

With Internet Explorer, Microsoft has extended the concept of Web browser add-ins to its ActiveX Controls. These controls, formerly known as OLE Controls or OCXs, build on Microsoft's highly successful Object Linking and Embedding (OLE) standard to provide a common framework for extending the capability of its Web browser.

But ActiveX Controls are more than just a simple Web browser plug-in or add-in—because of the nature of ActiveX Controls, they can not only be used to extend the functionality of Microsoft's Web browser, but they also can be used by any programming language or application that supports the OLE standard. For example, an ActiveX Control could be written to enable Internet Explorer to automatically search UseNet newsgroups for specific information and, at the same time, can perform a similar function through integration into Microsoft Office products such as Excel or Access. Netscape Navigator plug-ins, on the other hand, can only be used within Navigator or a compatible browser such as Internet Explorer.

As with Netscape Navigator's plug-ins, ActiveX Controls are dynamic code modules that exist as part of Microsoft's Application Programming Interface (API) for extending and integrating third-party software into any OLE-compliant environment. The creation of (and support for) ActiveX Controls by Microsoft is significant, primarily because it enables other developers to integrate their products seamlessly into the Web via Internet Explorer or any other OLE application without having to launch any external helper applications.

For Internet Explorer users, ActiveX Controls support enables you to customize Internet Explorer's interaction with third-party products and industry media standards. Microsoft's ActiveX Control API also attempts to address the concerns of programmers, providing a high degree of flexibility and cross-platform support.

What ActiveX Controls Mean for End Users

For most users, integrating ActiveX Controls is transparent because the controls open up and become active whenever Internet Explorer is opened. Furthermore, you often will not even see ActiveX Controls at work because most ActiveX Controls are not activated unless you open a Web page that initiates them. For example, after you install Macromedia's Shockwave ActiveX Control, you will notice no difference in the way Internet Explorer functions until you come across a Web page that features Shockwave.

Once an ActiveX Control is installed on your machine and initiated by a Web page, it will manifest itself in one of these three potential forms:

- Embedded
- Full-screen
- Hidden

Embedded Controls   An embedded ActiveX Control appears as a visible, rectangular window integrated into a Web page. This window may not appear to be any different from a window created by a graphic, such as an embedded GIF or JPEG picture. The main difference between the previous windows supported by Internet Explorer and those created by ActiveX Controls is that ActiveX Control windows support a much wider range of interactivity and movement, and thereby remain live instead of static.

In addition to mouse clicks, embedded ActiveX Controls also read and take note of mouse location, mouse movement, keyboard input, and input from virtually any other input device. In this way, an ActiveX Control can support the full range of user events required to produce sophisticated applications.

Full-Screen Controls   A full-screen ActiveX Control takes over the entire current Internet Explorer window to display its own content. This is necessary when a Web page is designed to display data that is not supported by HTML. An example of this type of ActiveX Control is the VRML ActiveX Control, available from Microsoft. If you view a VRML world using Internet Explorer with the VRML ActiveX Control, it loads into your Web browser like any other Web page, but it retains the look and functionality of a VRML world, with three-dimensional objects through and around which you can navigate.

Hidden Controls   A hidden ActiveX Control has no visible elements but works strictly behind the scenes to add some features to Internet Explorer that are not otherwise available. An example of a hidden control would be the Preloader Control, discussed later in this chapter. This ActiveX Control is used to preload a graphic, sound, or other element that will subsequently be viewed by the Internet Explorer user. Because the element is downloaded while the user is browsing through the current Web page, appearance response time is much greater.

Regardless of which ActiveX Controls you use and whether they are embedded, full-screen, or hidden, the rest of Internet Explorer's user interface should remain relatively constant and available. So, even if you have a VRML world displayed in Internet Explorer's main window, you'll still be able to access its menus and navigational controls.

What ActiveX Controls Mean for Programmers

For programmers, ActiveX Controls offer the possibility of creating Internet Explorer add-on products and using development ActiveX Controls to create your own Internet-based applications. Creating a custom ActiveX Control requires much more intensive background, experience, and testing than actually using one. Microsoft has released programming tools, however, such as the Visual Basic Controls Creation Edition, that make the process of creating an ActiveX Control much simpler. If you are a developer or are interested in creating an ActiveX Control, the following discussion will be useful.

The current version of the ActiveX Control Application Programming Interface (API) supports four broad areas of functionality.

ActiveX Controls can do the following:

- Draw into, receive events from, and interact with objects that are a part of the Internet Explorer object hierarchy.
- Obtain MIME data from the network via URLs.
- Generate data for consumption by Internet Explorer, by other ActiveX Controls, or by Java applets.
- Override and implement protocol handlers.

ActiveX Controls are ideally suited to take advantage of platform-independent protocols, architectures, languages, and media types such as Java, VRML, and MPEG. While ActiveX Controls should be functionally equivalent across platforms, they should also be complementary to platform-specific protocols and architectures.

When the Internet Explorer client is launched, it knows of any ActiveX Controls available through the Windows 95 Registry but does not load any of them into RAM. ActiveX Controls simply reside on disk until they are needed. By having many ActiveX Controls readily available, without taking up any RAM until just before the time they are needed, the user is able to view seamlessly a tremendous amount of varied data. An ActiveX Control is deleted from RAM as soon as the user moves to another HTML page that does not require it.

Integration of ActiveX Controls with the Internet Explorer client is quite elegant and flexible, allowing the programmer to make the most of asynchronous processes and multithreaded data. ActiveX Controls may be associated with one or more MIME types, and Internet Explorer may, in turn, create multiple instances of the same ActiveX Control.

At its most fundamental level, an ActiveX Control can access an URL and retrieve MIME data just as a standard Internet Explorer 3 client does. This data is streamed to the ActiveX Control as it arrives from the network, making it possible to implement viewers and other interfaces that can progressively display information. For instance, an ActiveX Control may draw a simple frame and introductory graphic or text for the user to look at while the bulk of the data is streaming off the network into Internet Explorer's existing cache. All the same bandwidth considerations adhered to by good HTML authors need to be accounted for in ActiveX Controls.

Of course, ActiveX Controls can also be file-based, which requires that you first download a complete amount of data before the ActiveX Control can proceed. This type of architecture is not encouraged due to its potential user delays, but it may prove necessary for some data-intensive ActiveX Controls. If an ActiveX Control needs more data than can be supplied through a single data stream, the ActiveX Control may request multiple, simultaneous data streams, so long as the user's system supports this.

While an ActiveX Control is active, if another ActiveX Control or Internet Explorer needs data, the ActiveX Control can generate data itself for these purposes. Thus, ActiveX Controls not only process data, they also generate it. For example, an ActiveX Control can be a data translator or filter.

ActiveX Controls are generally embedded within HTML code and accessed through the <OBJECT> tag.

N O T E   Though creating an ActiveX Control is much easier to do than, say, writing a spreadsheet application, it still requires the talents of an experienced programmer to develop more than just the simplest controls. Microsoft and other, third-party developers offer visual programming tools or BASIC environments that provide ActiveX Control templates, making the actual coding of ActiveX Controls much less tedious. For more in-depth information on ActiveX Control creation, consult a reference such as Que's *Web Programming with Microsoft Tools 6-IN-1*. ■

    T I P   If you are interested in learning more about creating ActiveX Controls, check out **http://www.microsoft.com/workshop/prog/default.asp**. This site is part of Microsoft's SiteBuilder Network and contains a lot of useful information.

ActiveX Control Security

ActiveX Controls are pieces of software; therefore, all of the dangers of running unknown software apply to them as much as anything you may download from the Internet. ActiveX Controls are unlike Java applets, which run in an environment designed to ensure the safety of the client and can usually only cause trouble by exploiting bugs or flaws in the Java run-time security systems. ActiveX Controls, on the other hand, can do *anything* on the client computer. Although this increases their potential to perform functions within your Web browser, and other compatible applications, it also poses an added security risk. How do you know that a downloaded ActiveX Control won't erase your hard drive?

To address this concern, Microsoft's Internet Explorer Web browser supports Authenticode code-signing technology. This technology enables vendors of ActiveX Controls and other software components to digitally *sign* these components. When they are downloaded and the digital signature is recognized, a code signature certificate, like that shown in Figure 30.1, is displayed on the screen. This certificate ensures that the software component is coming from the named source and that it hasn't been tampered with. At this point, you may choose whether you want to install the software component.

You can find out all about Authenticode and Internet Explorer's other security features in Chapter 16, "In-Depth: Security."

▶ **See** "Handling Digital Certificates" for more information on Internet Explorer 4's code-signing capabilities, **p. 302**

FIG. 30.1

Authenticode technology in Microsoft's Internet Explorer helps ensure that downloaded software components are genuine and come from a trusted source.

Including ActiveX Controls in an HTML Document

Including ActiveX Controls in HTML documents requires use of the <OBJECT> tag to embed the control within the page. Controls are configured through the attributes of the <OBJECT> tag, and configuration parameters set using the <PARAM> tag within the <OBJECT></OBJECT> container.

You can include ActiveX Controls in HTML Web pages by directly entering the code into the HTML document. There are also tools that make the use of ActiveX Controls much easier. One such tool is Microsoft's freeware program called the ActiveX Control Pad, which takes a lot of the grunt work out of using ActiveX Controls in Web pages.

Using the ActiveX Control Pad, you can place any locally installed ActiveX Control within a Web page using a WYSIWYG interface. Individual Label Controls can be displayed as they would appear, for instance, as will images and other elements. The Control Pad enables you to configure the many options of each embedded ActiveX Control—set the <OBJECT> and <PARAM> configuration values—using a simple dialog box customized for each control. When control configuration is complete, the HTML code needed to implement the control in your Web page is written into the HTML document.

In addition to its ActiveX Control Web authoring capabilities, the ActiveX Control Pad also includes support for Microsoft's Script Wizard. Using the Script Wizard, you can create interactive Web pages by using the Wizard to implement actions that occur in response to events. This is done in the Script Wizard using a simple, point-and-click interface; the Wizard automatically generates the script code to implement the action.

Inserting an ActiveX Control Using the *<OBJECT>* Tag

ActiveX Controls are embedded in HTML documents through use of the HTML <OBJECT> tag; they are configured through use of the <PARAM> tag. Listing 30.1 is an example of using the ActiveX Marquee Control embedded within an HTML Web page. The attributes of the <OBJECT> tag itself determine the ActiveX Control (or other Web object) used, as well as its size and alignment on the Web page. The <OBJECT></OBJECT> container tags also enclose the <PARAM> tags that set the control-specific parameters.

The next sections discuss each of the important attributes of the <OBJECT> tag and also discuss some of the possibilities for using the <PARAM> tags.

Listing 30.1   Marquee.htm   Example Using the ActiveX Marquee Control

```
<HTML>
<HEAD>
<TITLE>Marquee Example</TITLE>
</HEAD>
<BODY BGCOLOR=#FFFFFF>
<CENTER>
<HR>
<OBJECT
    ID="Marquee1"
     CLASSID="CLSID:1A4DA620-6217-11CF-BE62-0080C72EDD2D"
    CODEBASE="http://activex.microsoft.com/controls/
               iexplorer/marquee.ocx#Version=4,70,0,1161"
    TYPE="application/x-oleobject"
    WIDTH=100%
    HEIGHT=100
>
<PARAM NAME="szURL" VALUE="queet.gif">
<PARAM NAME="ScrollPixelsX" VALUE="2">
<PARAM NAME="ScrollPixelsY" VALUE="2">
<PARAM NAME="ScrollStyleX" VALUE="Bounce">
<PARAM NAME="ScrollStyleY" VALUE="Bounce">
</OBJECT>
<HR>
</CENTER>
</BODY>
</HTML>
```

N O T E   The CODEBASE line in Listing 30.1 has been split across two lines so that it will fit correctly on this page. In reality, however, it all needs to be on one line. ■

The *ID* Attribute

The ID attribute of the <OBJECT> tag is used to give the ActiveX Control a name that can be used within the Web browser (or other application) environment. This is the easiest way for other elements running within the Web browser (usually VBScript or JavaScript applications) to access and manipulate the parameters of the ActiveX Control. For example, in Listing 30.1, a VBScript to change the background color of the Marquee Control to red, if clicked, would look like this:

```
Sub Marquee1_OnClick()
    Marquee1.BackColor = 16711680
End Sub
```

The *CLASSID* Attribute

The CLASSID attribute is perhaps the most intimidating-looking piece of the <OBJECT> tag of an ActiveX Control. It is simply the identification code for the ActiveX Control being used, however. Internet Explorer uses this attribute to load the correct ActiveX Control code module from your computer, and its value is set for each control by the control's author. The CLASSID is unique for each ActiveX Control, though it doesn't change from one version of the control to the next. The code for the ActiveX Marquee Control, displayed in Listing 30.1, is **CLSID:1A4DA620-6217-11CF-BE62-0080C72EDD2D.**

The *CODEBASE* Attribute

Unlike with Netscape Navigator plug-ins, you can automatically download and install ActiveX Controls when Internet Explorer (or another compatible application) encounters a document that makes use of them. The key to this feature is the CODEBASE attribute. The CODEBASE attribute defines the URL from which the ActiveX Control can be downloaded and defines the version of the control used. Then, when Internet Explorer attempts to render the Web page on a client machine, the CODEBASE attribute checks whether each ActiveX Control embedded in the HTML document exists on that machine and whether it is the latest version. If a more recent version exists at the URL defined by the CODEBASE attribute, it is automatically downloaded and installed, subject to the security settings in place in the local copy of Internet Explorer being used.

The *TYPE* Attribute

The TYPE attribute defines the MIME type of the ActiveX Control. In general, this will be application/x-oleobject. For other object types embedded in an HTML document using the <OBJECT> tag, the value of this attribute will be different.

The *WIDTH* and *HEIGHT* Attributes

The WIDTH and HEIGHT attributes of the <OBJECT> tag define the size of the ActiveX Control within the Web page. For hidden controls, such as the Timer or Preloader Controls, these attributes can stay at their default values of 0. For controls such as the Marquee or Label Controls, you must size these attributes correctly for the appearance you desire.

Setting Parameters Using *<PARAM>* Tags

The <PARAM> tags are used to configure the appropriate parameters of each ActiveX Control. In general, the syntax of the <PARAM> tag is

```
<PARAM NAME="ParameterName" VALUE="ParameterValue">
```

For instance, in the Marquee Control example shown in Listing 30.1, the URL of the document being placed in the marquee is given by

```
<PARAM NAME="szURL" VALUE="queet.gif">
```

To effectively make use of ActiveX Controls, you must know the names and possible values of all of its parameters that can be set with the <PARAM> tag. One benefit of using Microsoft's ActiveX Control Pad to create Web pages that use ActiveX Controls is that the Control Pad knows what parameters are used by each control. Without the ActiveX Control Pad, you would need to get this information from the documentation provided with the control by its author. (The ActiveX Control Pad will be discussed later in this chapter, in the "ActiveX Control Pad" section.)

Part
V
Ch
30

ActiveX Marquee Control Example

The ActiveX Marquee Control example defined by Listing 30.1 is shown in Figure 30.2. The area of the marquee was defined horizontally to take up 100 percent of the width of the Web page and vertically for 100 pixels. Because ScrollPixelsX and ScrollPixelsY are both non-zero and ScrollStyleX and ScrollStyleY are set to "BOUNCE," the effect is to send the image **queet.gif** bouncing around the marquee area.

FIG. 30.2
You can use the ActiveX Marquee Control to create interesting special effects, such as this bouncing logo.

Marquee Area ⎯⎯

Bouncing Logo ⎯⎯

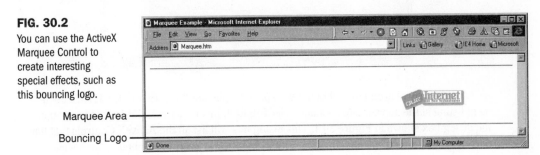

ActiveX Control Pad

Microsoft has developed and made available its ActiveX Control Pad to make it easier to use and configure ActiveX Controls within a Web page. The Control Pad does not quite have the capabilities of a program such as Microsoft FrontPage 97 for WYSIWYG Web authoring, but it does offer extensive support for creating ActiveX Controls, including a WYSIWYG interface for the controls themselves, and automatically generates the HTML code necessary to embed the control in the Web page. The ActiveX Control Pad also offers a Script Wizard to simplify the script-writing procedure.

Downloading and Installing the ActiveX Control Pad

The ActiveX Control Pad can be downloaded from Microsoft's ActiveX Control Pad Web site at **http://www.microsoft.com/msdownload/default.asp**. It comes in the form of the self-installing file **Setuppad.exe**. Simply save this file into a temporary directory on your hard drive and execute it. After the installation procedure is complete, you can execute the ActiveX Control Pad by selecting Start, Programs, Microsoft ActiveX Control Pad, Microsoft ActiveX Control Pad.

Including ActiveX Controls

When initially executed, the ActiveX Control Pad gives you a screen similar to that shown in Figure 30.3. The skeleton of an HTML file is created into which you can add HTML code, HTML Layouts, scripts, and ActiveX Controls.

FIG. 30.3

The ActiveX Control Pad enables you to edit HTML documents manually and includes tools and Wizards to add ActiveX Controls.

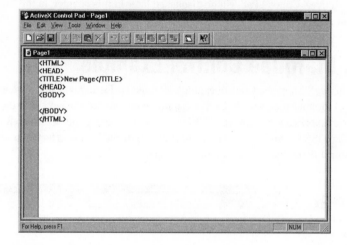

An ActiveX Control is embedded in the Web page by placing the cursor in the HTML document listing at the appropriate spot and selecting Edit, Insert ActiveX Control. This prompts the dialog box shown in Figure 30.4. This dialog box will list all the ActiveX Controls that have been installed in your system. You can select the ActiveX Control to embed from this list.

FIG. 30.4

The Insert ActiveX Control dialog box enables you to include any locally installed ActiveX Control in the HTML document.

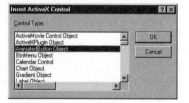

ActiveX Control Configuration

Once you have selected the ActiveX Control, two window panes are put on the screen. The first is the Edit ActiveX Control window, which gives a WYSIWYG representation of the current configuration of the ActiveX Control. This is most evident for controls such as the Label Control—for hidden controls, this window merely shows the current size for which the control is configured, which may be zero by zero.

The other window is the Properties dialog box for the specific ActiveX Control chosen. This dialog box gives you the ability to set all of the necessary parameters of the <OBJECT> and <PARAM> tags needed to configure the ActiveX Control. You don't need to know the class ID code, and you don't need to remember the specific parameter names that must be configured. The ActiveX Control Pad does all of that for you. To change a parameter in the Properties box, click the parameter in the dialog box, type in a new value (or select one from a drop-down or pop-up menu, if one appears), and click the Apply button.

Figure 30.5 shows an example configuration of the Animated Button Control. Keep the following items in mind:

- It's always a good idea to give the ActiveX Control a descriptive name in the ID field. Doing so will make it easier to figure out what each control is doing when you look at the HTML code later.

- It is difficult to determine the appropriate size for some controls, such as the Animated Button Control. This difficulty exists because the controls need to be sized to fit an animation file that the ActiveX Control Pad isn't able to show you. Some trial and error may be necessary.

- When sizing and placing the ActiveX Control in the Edit ActiveX Control window or when setting parameters in the Properties box, you may notice that position numbers slightly adjust when you set them. This most often occurs because the ActiveX Control Pads snap-to-grid option is selected. This option makes it easier to align objects but decreases a bit of your mobility. To activate or deactivate the snap-to-grid option or to access the Control Pad's other alignment tools, select Tools, Options, HTML Layout, and check or clear the Snap To Grid box.

FIG. 30.5
The Edit ActiveX Control and Properties dialog boxes allow you to set the control parameters and appearance.

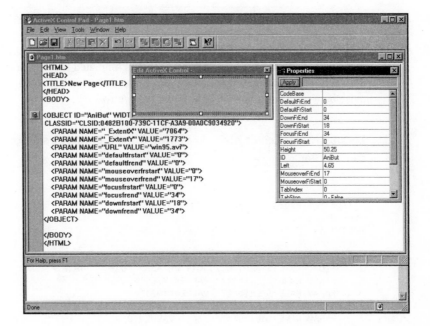

When you finish entering the parameters for the ActiveX Control pad, close the Edit ActiveX Control and Properties windows. At this point, the HTML code needed to implement the control, using the parameters you selected, is automatically generated and placed in the HTML document (see Figure 30.6). The ActiveX Control icon displayed in the left margin indicates the presence of the control—clicking that icon gives you access to the Edit ActiveX Control and Properties windows for that control again.

FIG. 30.6

When you finish editing the properties of the ActiveX Control, the necessary HTML code is inserted in your document.

ActiveX Control icon

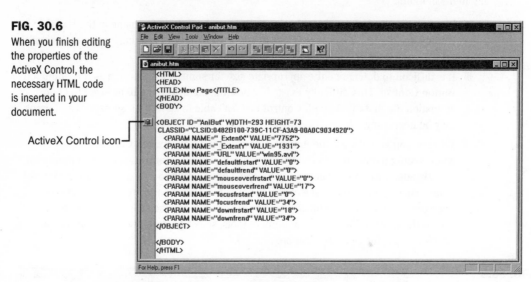

Listing 30.2 shows the completed listing for this example. The resulting Web page, including the animated button, is shown in Figure 30.7. The Animated Button Control shows different sections of an animation in response to one of four events: default, mouse over the control, left mouse button clicked and held, or focus on the control.

Listing 30.2   Anibut.htm   Animated Button Control Using the ActiveX Control Pad

```
<HTML>
<HEAD>
<TITLE>New Page</TITLE>
</HEAD>
<BODY>

<OBJECT ID="AniBut" WIDTH=293 HEIGHT=73
 CLASSID="CLSID:0482B100-739C-11CF-A3A9-00A0C9034920">
    <PARAM NAME="_ExtentX" VALUE="7752">
    <PARAM NAME="_ExtentY" VALUE="1931">
    <PARAM NAME="URL" VALUE="win95.avi">
    <PARAM NAME="defaultfrstart" VALUE="0">
    <PARAM NAME="defaultfrend" VALUE="0">
    <PARAM NAME="mouseoverfrstart" VALUE="0">
    <PARAM NAME="mouseoverfrend" VALUE="17">
```

```
           <PARAM NAME="focusfrstart" VALUE="0">
           <PARAM NAME="focusfrend" VALUE="34">
           <PARAM NAME="downfrstart" VALUE="18">
           <PARAM NAME="downfrend" VALUE="34">
        </OBJECT>

        </BODY>
        </HTML>
```

FIG. 30.7

The embedded ActiveX
Animated Button
Control behaves
according to the
parameters set in the
Properties box.

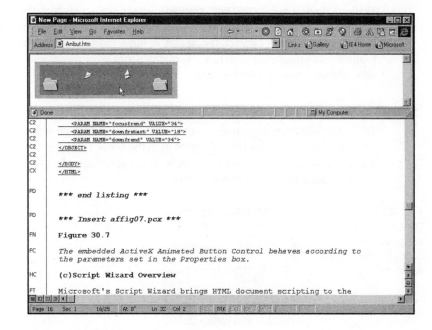

Script Wizard Overview

Microsoft's Script Wizard brings HTML document scripting to the masses. Using its simple, point-and-click interface, it is possible to create sophisticated scripts by using either VBScript or JavaScript, without knowing either of those two languages.

But the Script Wizard is not just for scripting novices. Experts can also use it to create scripts to do any of a variety of functions. The Script Wizard can display and access any of the events and other properties associated with the Web browser, HTML forms, ActiveX Controls, Java applets, or other objects that can exist within the Web browser. This frees them from needing to memorize what properties are associated with what objects, allowing them to concentrate their efforts on creating the scripts needed to manipulate these objects to do what they want them to do.

Access the Script Wizard from the ActiveX Control Pad by selecting Tools, Script Wizard, or by pressing the Script Wizard toolbar button. From the FrontPage Editor, select Insert, Script, and, at the Script dialog, press the Script Wizard button.

The primary use of the Script Wizard is to create scripts that perform a desired action in response to a particular event. The Script Wizard's point-and-click interface makes creating a script as simple as one-two-three.

1. Select an event from the list of events supported by the current HTML document.
2. Select an action or object property.
3. Enable that action or supply a value to be assigned to the object property.

That's all there is to it! In this way, you can easily create scripts that change background or foreground colors, display images, or manipulate any of the objects or properties of any HTML form element, ActiveX Control, Java applet, or other object in the document. Plus, if you want to attach more than one action to an event, the Script Wizard enables you to define global variables and your own procedures, which you can then attach to events.

Script Wizard Options

The Script Wizard in both programs enables you to select which scripting language to use. In FrontPage, you make this selection right from the Script Dialog. In the ActiveX Control Pad, you select the language by selecting Tools, Options, Script, and selecting the desired language from the dialog box shown in Figure 30.8.

FIG. 30.8

The Script Wizard can be used to create scripts in either VBScript or JavaScript.

> **CAUTION**
>
> Though it is possible to create HTML documents in which multiple scripts in both VBScript and JavaScript peacefully coexist, creating such documents is not an option currently supported by the Script Wizard. If you wish to use the Script Wizard, you must confine yourself to one language within each separate document.

Script Wizard Window

The Script Wizard window is divided into three separate panes, as shown in Figure 30.9. It is within these areas that the Script Wizard enables you to easily create scripts for your HTML documents. The three areas—the Event Pane, the Action Pane, and the Script Pane—make it a matter of a few clicks of the mouse for you to script actions that are attached to events that can occur within a Web browser or other compatible HTML viewer when viewing your HTML documents.

FIG. 30.9

The tree views of the events and actions represented in the Script Wizard window make Web scripting a point and click away.

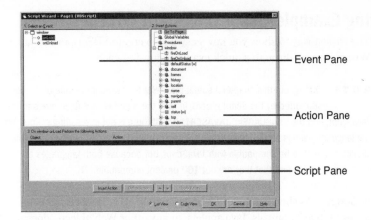

Event Pane

Action Pane

Script Pane

Part
V

Ch
30

Event Pane   The Script Wizard Event Pane shows an expandable tree view of all of the events associated with objects currently in the HTML document. These objects include those associated with the Web browser itself, HTML forms, and other objects such as ActiveX Controls and Java applets.

When the Script Wizard is opened, it analyzes the HTML document and creates the list of events shown in the Event Pane. As other elements are added to the HTML document, each time the Script Wizard is opened, the list of events shown will be automatically updated as well.

Action Pane   The Action Pane of the Script Wizard lists two things: both the methods of the current objects contained in the HTML document and the other object properties. You can use methods to create actions in and of themselves, such as loading a different Web page in a Web browser or submitting an HTML Form. You can create actions from object properties by setting them equal to a different value. In this way, you can change images (by changing their source path), alter colors, and assign a new value to any other object property.

The properties shown in the Action Pane are always those appropriate to the current event selected. If none is selected, all of the properties are shown. If an event is selected, some of them might disappear because they cannot be altered in response to that event.

Script Pane   The Script Pane is used to display the current list of actions attached to a given event. When an event has actions associated to it, indicated by a filled-in diamond beside it in the Event Pane, those actions are shown in the Script Pane when the event is selected. The actions can be shown in one of two ways, either through the List View or the Code View.

List View   By selecting the List View radio button, a text description of the actions is displayed in the Script Pane. If you always use this view, it is possible to create scripts in your HTML documents without ever actually dealing directly with, or even seeing, and script code.

Code View   The Code View radio button reveals the actual VBScript or JavaScript code used to implement an action. Also, when this view is selected, you can actually edit the code itself. This is one way to create your own procedures, as I will discuss later in this chapter. Note that if you create a procedure that the Script Wizard is not able to understand, when you switch back to the List View, a list of actions will not be displayed.

Scripting Example Using the Script Wizard

The easiest way to show you how easy it is to create VBScripts and JavaScripts with the Script Wizard is to go through a quick example showing each.

> **N O T E** Throughout this chapter, I sometimes refer to JavaScript as one of the scripting languages supported by the Script Wizard. In fact, the Script Wizard itself refers to the language as JavaScript, and the LANGUAGE="JAVASCRIPT" attribute is set in resulting scripts. Actually, though, the language used is JScript, Microsoft's open implementation of Netscape's JavaScript language. JScript is meant to be compatible with JavaScript, but because both languages are still evolving, don't be surprised if you find that they are not 100 percent compatible. ▓

VBScript   As shown in Figure 30.9, an "empty" HTML document—one without any HTML forms, ActiveX Controls, Java applets, or any other Web object—does not expose very many events to which actions can be assigned. In fact, the only events are those that occur when the HTML document is loaded or unloaded.

You will create a simple, scripted HTML document, using first VBScript and then JavaScript, that responds to the onLoad event of the HTML document to load a different HTML document. This occurs quite often on the Web when the Home Page of a Web site is moved; the old location can be used to automatically send users to the new one. (Before the advent of scripting on the Web, this was done using a technique called *client pull*.)

To script this action, following the three-step process previously shown, follow these steps.

1. Click the window, onLoad event in the Event Pane.
2. Click the Go To Page action in the Action Pane.
3. Click the Insert Action button in the Script Pane, and then type the URL of the new Web page in the resulting Go To Page dialog box (see Figure 30.10).

FIG. 30.10

The HTML document name entered indicates that it is located in the same place as the original document. You can also enter a full URL to redirect the user to another location.

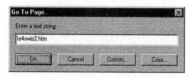

> **N O T E** The Script Wizard is smart enough to know what kind of value to which the object property can be set or what kind of event can be triggered. As a result, when you insert or modify an action, you will be given an appropriate dialog box, whether it is for a text string, number, color, font, or other type of value. ▓

Once you enter the action, it appears in the Script Pane of the Script Wizard. When the List View radio button of the Script Pane is selected, a text description of the action is shown, as shown in Figure 30.11. If the Code View button is selected, the actual scripting language code (VBScript, in this case), is shown (see Figure 30.12).

FIG. 30.11

Once the action has been inserted, the Script Pane's List View gives a text description of what the resulting script will do.

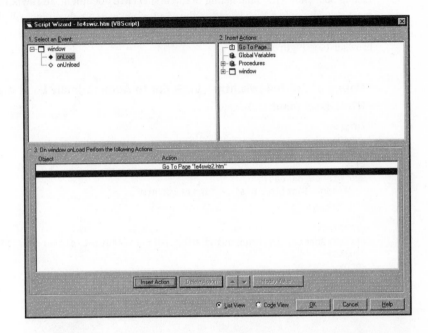

FIG. 30.12

The Code View shows the actual VBScript that will be inserted into your HTML document.

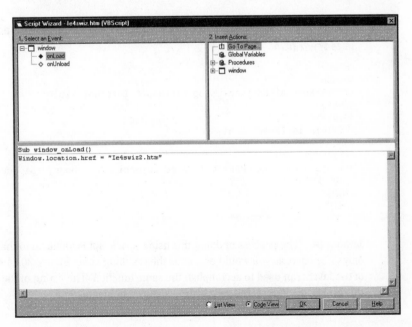

If you're a VBScript or JavaScript beginner trying to learn the language, use the Code View to see how different actions are scripted to help you pick up the basics of either language.

Listing 30.3 shows the final listing of the first HTML document, **Ie4swiz.htm**. When this document is loaded into a Web browser, the `window_onLoad()` subroutine will be called, which will automatically load the new document, **Ie4swiz2.htm**, shown in Listing 30.4, into the Web browser (see Figure 30.13).

Listing 30.3   Ie4swiz.htm   VBScript to Automatically Load Another HTML Document

```
<HTML>
<HEAD>
<SCRIPT LANGUAGE="VBScript">
<!--
Sub window_onLoad()
    Window.location.href = "Ie4swiz2.htm"
End Sub
-->
</SCRIPT>
<TITLE>Special Edition Using Microsoft Internet Explorer 4</TITLE>
</HEAD>
<BODY>
<H1>This is Ie4swiz.htm</H1>
</BODY>
</HTML>
```

Listing 30.4   Ie4swiz2.htm   Resulting HTML Document Loaded By VBScript in *Ie4swiz.htm*

```
<HTML>
<HEAD>
<TITLE>Special Edition Using Microsoft Internet Explorer 4</TITLE>
</HEAD>
<BODY>
<H1>This is Ie4swiz2.htm</H1>
<HR>
<ADDRESS>
Jim O'Donnell, <A HREF="mailto:odonnj@rpi.edu">odonnj@rpi.edu</A>
</ADDRESS>
</BODY>
</HTML>
```

JavaScript   The process of doing this using JavaScript is identical to that using VBScript. The only difference, as you would expect, is the resulting code. Figure 30.14 shows the Code View of the JavaScript used to accomplish the same function. The listing of the JavaScript version of this HTML document, **Ie4swizJ.htm**, is shown in Listing 30.5.

FIG. 30.13
As expected, loading *Ie4swiz.htm* automatically triggers the loading of *Ie4swiz2.htm*.

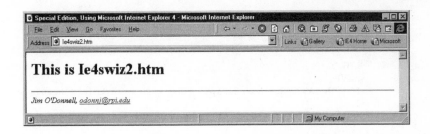

Notice that to attach an action to an *event* of an *object*, VBScript uses the following syntax:

```
<SCRIPT LANGUAGE="VBScript">
Sub object_event()
   ...
End Sub
</SCRIPT>
```

JavaScript, on the other hand, uses the FOR and EVENT attributes of the <SCRIPT> tag to designate *object* and *event*:

```
<SCRIPT LANGUAGE="JavaScript" FOR="object" EVENT="event()">
   ...
</SCRIPT>
```

FIG. 30.14
JavaScript uses different syntax to attach its scripts to object events.

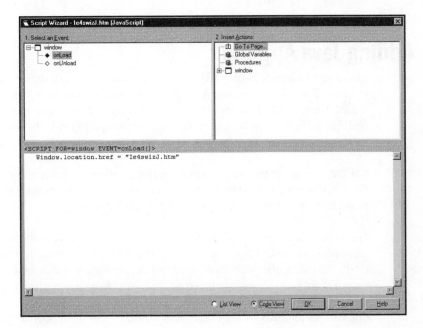

Listing 30.5   Ie4swizJ.htm   JavaScript to Automatically Load Another HTML Document

```
<HTML>
<HEAD>
<SCRIPT LANGUAGE="JavaScript" FOR="window" EVENT="onLoad()">
<!--
   Window.location.href = "Ie4swizJ.htm"
-->
</SCRIPT>
<TITLE>Special Edition Using Microsoft Internet Explorer 4</TITLE>
</HEAD>
<BODY>
<H1>This is Ie4swizJ.htm</H1>
</BODY>
</HTML>
```

N O T E   The code that comes out of the Script Wizard will execute well in Internet Explorer, but it might not be formatted the way you like. You can tweak the appearance of the final HTML document when you are finished (as I have done with the listings shown in this chapter), if you'd like. Be warned, though, if you use the Script Wizard again to further revise the code in that document, it will revert it back to its format. ■

Adding Java Applets

Including Java applets in your Web pages is, in many ways, very similar to including ActiveX Controls. Both Java applets and ActiveX Controls can be placed in a Web page using the HTML <OBJECT> tag, though Java applets can also be placed with the more specialized <APPLET> tag. And, like ActiveX Controls, Java applets may be configured using the <PARAM> tag to set the values of the parameters defined by the applet's author.

N O T E   This section tells you how to include a Java applet into a Web page that you are creating. The process of creating Java applets is beyond the scope of this book. If you are interested, be sure to check out *Special Edition Using Java*, from Que Books. ■

Listing 30.6 shows an example of the two ways to include a Java applet within a Web page, using either the <OBJECT> or <APPLET> tag. For this example, the only difference is the tag used—the values of the other attributes and the parameters set are otherwise exactly the same. Figure 30.15 shows how this example looks when viewed with Internet Explorer.

N O T E   You can download Sergy Alpin's Temptations.class Java applet class file from his Web site at **http://www.snafu.de/~alpin/**. ■

**Listing 30.6   JavaApp.htm   Java Applets Can Be Included Using *<OBJECT>*
or *<APPLET>* Tags**

```
<HTML>
<HEAD>
<TITLE>Including Java Applets</TITLE>
</HEAD>
<BODY>
<CENTER>
<H1>Including Java Applets</H1>
<HR>
<APPLET CODE="Temptation.class" WIDTH="500" HEIGHT="40">
    <PARAM NAME="Wort1"   VALUE="Temptation">
    <PARAM NAME="Wort2"   VALUE="Temptation.class by Sergy Alpin">
    <PARAM NAME="Wort3"   VALUE="Including Java applets...">
    <PARAM NAME="Wort4"   VALUE="...in your Web pages...">
    <PARAM NAME="Wort5"   VALUE="...is easy!!!">
    <PARAM NAME="Adresse" VALUE="http://www.snafu.de/~alpin/">
    <PARAM NAME="Author"  VALUE="Sergy Alpin">
</APPLET><BR>
<EM>Java Applet included using <TT>&lt;APPLET&gt;</TT> tag</EM>
<HR>
<OBJECT CODE="Temptation.class" WIDTH="500" HEIGHT="40">
    <PARAM NAME="Wort1"   VALUE="Temptation">
    <PARAM NAME="Wort2"   VALUE="Temptation.class by Sergy Alpin">
    <PARAM NAME="Wort3"   VALUE="Including Java applets...">
    <PARAM NAME="Wort4"   VALUE="...in your Web pages...">
    <PARAM NAME="Wort5"   VALUE="...is easy!!!">
    <PARAM NAME="Adresse" VALUE="http://www.snafu.de/~alpin/">
    <PARAM NAME="Author"  VALUE="Sergy Alpin">
</OBJECT><BR>
<EM>Java Applet included using <TT>&lt;OBJECT&gt;</TT> tag</EM>
<HR>
<TABLE WIDTH=400>
<TR><TD ROWSPAN=2>The Temptation.class applet was written by
        Sergy Alpin; links to his Web site and e-mail address
        are shown at right...</TD>
    <TH><A HREF="http://www.snafu.de/~alpin/">
            <IMG SRC="http://www.snafu.de/~alpin/alpin_JavaHaus.jpg"
                 BORDER=0 HEIGHT=21 WIDTH=94>
        </A></TH></TR>
<TR><TH><I><A HREF="mailto:sa@medialab.midat.de">
             alpin
         </A></I></TH></TR>
</TABLE>
</CENTER>
<HR>
<ADDRESS>
Jim O'Donnell, <A HREF="mailto:odonnj@rpi.edu">odonnj@rpi.edu</A>
</ADDRESS>
</BODY>
</HTML>
```

FIG. 30.15

Java applets can be used to add special effects to Web pages, such as these buttons whose captions change when the mouse is moved over them.

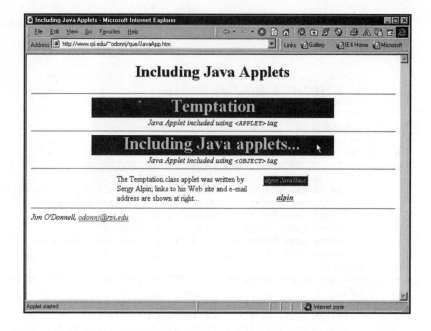

If you are looking for Java applets that you can use in creating your own Web pages, a great resource is EarthWeb's Java Directory, located at **http://www.gamelan.com**. ●

Microsoft Servers

The last several chapters have shown you how to prepare a document for publication on the Internet. But whether it's a simple, static page or a page that's dynamically generated by a CGI program, you still must have some kind of server in place to deliver the pages to the browsers that request them. Microsoft has two server products that it makes available to users free of charge:

Using the Personal Web Server

Microsoft's Personal Web Server (PWS) turns a Windows 95 machine into a full-fledged HTTP and FTP server. Learn how to set up and administer PWS on your computer.

Using the Internet Information Server

Internet Information Server (IIS) is Microsoft's Web server for the Windows NT platform. You can configure IIS to provide FTP and Gopher services as well.

Getting started with Active Server Pages

Active Server Pages (ASPs) are pages with script code embedded in them. IIS interprets and executes the script before serving the page and incorporates the script output into finished documents.

Looking ahead

The next generation of Microsoft server products promises to be even more robust than those available now. Take a look ahead at some of the features you can expect.

■ **Personal Web Server** Microsoft's Personal Web Server (PWS) provides HyperText
Transfer Protocol (HTTP) and File Transfer Protocol (FTP) services on a Windows 95
machine.

■ **Internet Information Server** Designed to run on Windows NT, Microsoft's Internet
Information Server (IIS) supports HTTP, FTP, and Gopher services that receive a high
volume of requests.

This chapter introduces you to each of these products and tells you how you can get each of
them up and running on your computer. Additionally, you'll learn about some of the special
features that IIS supports and how Microsoft intends to develop IIS's functionality even
further. ■

Personal Web Server

Microsoft's Personal Web Server (PWS) provides HTTP and FTP services on smaller machines that are running Windows 95. Though it is not robust enough to host major corporate
sites, it is well-suited for serving up smaller sites within a corporate intranet or for serving a
personal site from home. And even though it may not be optimal for a high-volume site, it is
still fully HTTP- and CGI-compliant and supports Internet Server Applications Programming
Interface (ISAPI) calls, so it can do just about everything you'd need a Web server to do.

If you don't have the PWS installed on your Windows 95 machine, it's very easy to get yourself
a copy. The two easiest ways to do so follow:

■ Download it from Microsoft's Web site at **http://www.microsoft.com/msdownload/
ieplatform/pws/pws.htm**.

■ Install PWS from the FrontPage CD-ROM if you've purchased FrontPage with the
Bonus Pack.

Once you install PWS and get it running, you'll see an icon for it on your Task Bar (see Figure
31.1). This icon is the easiest way for you to get to the PWS Properties panel because no PWS
program group or item is added to your Start Menu when you install PWS.

Double-clicking the PWS icon launches the Personal Web Server Properties dialog box, from
which you can configure most PWS settings. The specifics of this activity are discussed in the
next section.

Setting Personal Web Server Properties

The Personal Web Server Properties dialog is comprised of four different tabs, each with a
different function. The General tab, shown in Figure 31.2, is displayed by default. This tab
shows the name of your server and the name of the default home page that PWS serves. You
can click the Display Home Page button to launch Internet Explorer and look at the default
page that PWS puts in place during the installation (see Figure 31.3). If you click the More
Details button, you'll bring up a set of HTML-based documentation on the Personal Web
Server and how it works (see Figure 31.4).

FIG. 31.1
An icon on your Task Bar tells you that the Personal Web Server is up and running on your machine.

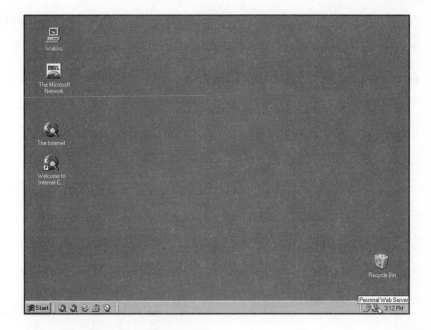

FIG. 31.2
The General tab tells you your server's name and what page it serves by default.

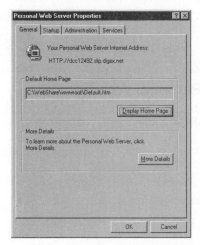

 You can customize this default page with personal information by opening it in FrontPage Express and typing over the existing text.

FIG. 31.3

When you install PWS, it places a shell of a home page in your server's root directory.

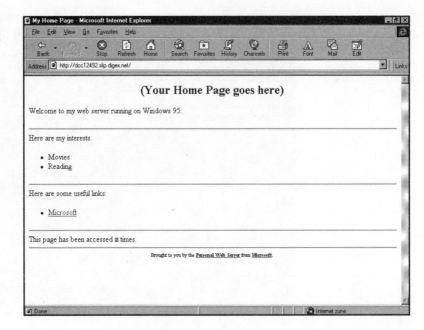

FIG. 31.4

Basic information about PWS is readily available through Internet Explorer.

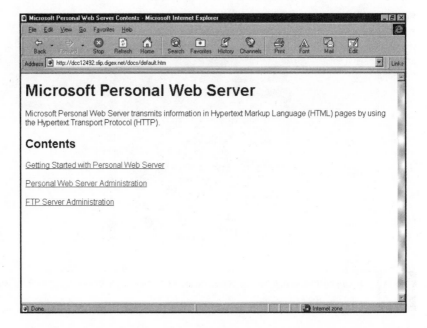

TIP   Add the PWS documentation page to your Favorites folder if you plan to reference the documentation often.

The next tab is the Startup tab, shown in Figure 31.5. From here, you can stop the server if it's running or start it if it has stopped. You can also specify that the server should start automatically when you start your computer and you can specify whether the PWS icon should appear on your Task Bar.

FIG. 31.5
You can start or stop your server or configure its start-up options from the Startup tab.

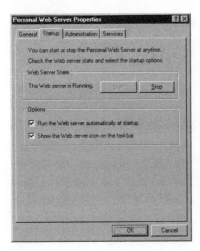

Part
V

Ch
31

NOTE   If you suppress the PWS Task Bar icon, you can still access the Personal Web Server Properties dialog box through the Control Panel. ▓

Skipping over the Administration tab for a moment, you'll find the Services tab (see Figure 31.6). From here, you can see the status (running or stopped) of the PWS FTP and HTTP services. You can also start or stop either service by selecting it and clicking the appropriate button. If you select the FTP service and click the Properties button, you'll see another dialog box with the FTP service start-up option (manual or automatic), Internet address, and root directory. You can change the root directory by clicking the Change FTP Home Root button. A similar Properties dialog for the HTTP service also includes a listing of the default home page and a button for changing it.

Finally, on the Administration tab, you'll find a single button labeled Administration. Clicking this button will launch Internet Explorer and load a browser-based interface for administering your Web and FTP services. The specifics of using this interface to administer your Internet services is the topic of the next section.

Administering Your Personal Web Server

When you fire up the PWS Administration page, you'll see the screen shown in Figure 31.7. Three main administration options are available from the browser:

■ **WWW Administration**   For changing service parameters, Web content directories, and logging options

■ **FTP Administration** For changing service parameters, server messages, content directories, and logging options

■ **Local User Administration** For setting up users and groups of users with different levels of access

FIG. 31.6
Key information about HTTP and FTP services is available through the Services tab.

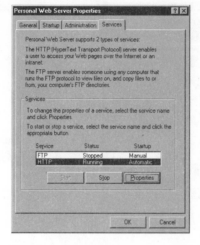

FIG. 31.7
You can control PWS's component services through Internet Explorer.

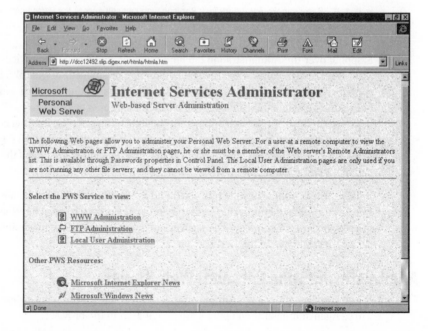

For the HTTP and FTP services, clicking their administration links will take you to a Web page that has tabs much like a dialog box. With the Services tab, you can set service parameters, such as number of simultaneous connections and how long to wait before a connection times out. On the HTTP side, you can set up password protection at anonymous, basic (unencrypted), and Windows NT Challenge/Response (encrypted) levels. The FTP service parameters also include an option for allowing anonymous and normal login connections and anonymous connections only.

> **CAUTION**
>
> If you're setting up password-protected directories, you should almost always use the NT Challenge/Response security level. Otherwise, an intruder can easily determine usernames and passwords as they travel unencrypted over your network.

The HTTP and FTP services also share the Directories tab, from which you can add directories to your server. These directories can be those in the normal sense or "virtual" directories that users reference with an alias. You can set up FTP directories as read only, write only, or read/write, and you can set up HTTP directories as read only, execute only, or read/execute. The Directories tab is also where you would establish a new home directory for either service, should you choose to do that.

The Logging tab is the other tab common to both HTTP and FTP services. From this tab, you can turn logging on or off, specify where the log file should be written, and under what conditions a new log file should be started.

The FTP Administration page has an extra tab—the Messages tab—from which you can specify server messages that are displayed to users when they first log in to the service, when they log out, and when the number of simultaneous connections has been exceeded.

N O T E A service must be running for you to be able to perform administration functions on it. ▨

With the Local User Administration page, you can create individual local users for the services. Further, you can create groups and put users into these groups to grant them certain levels of access. You should only create local users if you're not running any other file servers, in which case users should presumably have their own network usernames and passwords.

N O T E Windows NT Challenge/Response security levels won't work if you're setting up a server for local use. The Challenge/Response setting is only appropriate over a local area network with at least one NT domain. ▨

N O T E Remote users can perform service administration tasks through their browsers if they have been added to the PWS Remote Administrators list. Users can gain access to this list from the Passwords option under the Control Panel. Local user administration cannot occur remotely. ▨

Expanding the Personal Web Server's Capabilities

You read earlier that the PWS supports HTTP, CGI, and ISAPI, but you can take steps to enhance its capabilities even further. If you'll be using Microsoft FrontPage to develop and maintain your site, you'll very likely want to install the FrontPage server extensions. The extensions come with FrontPage if you bought it with the Bonus Pack option. In this case, you just need to pop your FrontPage CD-ROM into your CD-ROM drive and select the Server Extensions installation option.

If you don't have FrontPage with the Bonus Pack, you can download the server extensions from Microsoft's Web site. Additionally, Microsoft frequently makes other special FrontPage add-ons available. You can find out about the FrontPage server extensions and other special offers by visiting **http://www.microsoft.com/frontpage/**.

> **N O T E**   Though the FrontPage 97 server extensions support Active Server Pages (ASPs), you must install them on Microsoft's Internet Information Server for them to work. ASP functionality is not available through the Personal Web Server. ■

Internet Information Server 3.0

The Personal Web Server you've read about so far is good for smaller, more personal sites, as the name implies. It is not meant to be deployed in support of major sites that will receive thousands of hits per day, as many corporate Web and intranet sites do. Additionally, you may want your server to work with back-end databases or be able to provide support for secure communications between it and the client programs with which it works. The Personal Web Server can't do all of this for you, so if you want advanced server functionality, you'll have to trade up to Microsoft's Internet Information Server (IIS)—a high-end server program that runs on Windows NT Server and supports all the features you need for a high-volume Web site.

Using IIS's Internet Service Manager

IIS is actually much more than a Web server. It supports three different Internet services:

- World Wide Web publishing service (WWW)
- FTP file transfer service (FTP)
- Gopher publishing service

The three services are all controlled from the Internet Service Manager shown in Figure 31.8. Note that the Service Manager can detect servers running on other machines on your network. This useful feature enables you to administer Internet services on multiple machines from a single console.

The figure shows the Service Manager displaying its information in the Report View, though you can also look at the services by server (Servers View, see Figure 31.9) or by type of service (Services View, see Figure 31.10). You can change from one view to another by selecting your desired view from the View menu.

FIG. 31.8

The Internet Service Manager is your administrative interface to the three IIS services.

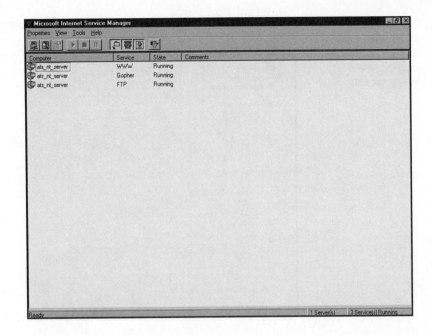

FIG. 31.9

The Servers View displays the services running on each machine that the Service Manager detects.

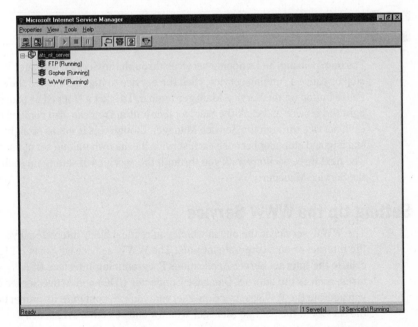

FIG. 31.10

You can key in on a specific type of service using the Service Manager as well.

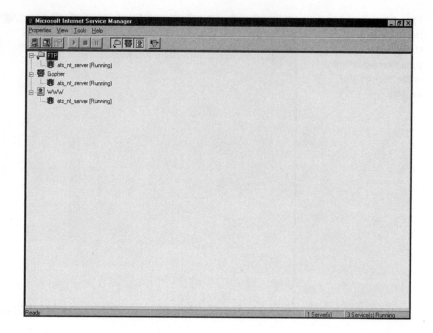

T I P Most server administrators find the Servers View the most useful.

Starting, pausing, and stopping services through the Service Manager is a simple matter. To stop or pause a running service, click the service to highlight it and then click the Stop or Pause button on the Service Manager toolbar. To start a stopped or paused service, just highlight the service and click the Start toolbar button. You can also configure the properties of each service through the Service Manager, though this is not as straightforward an activity as starting and stopping because each service has its own unique set of operating parameters. The next three sections walk you through the specifics of setting up each IIS service through the Service Manager.

Setting Up the WWW Service

The WWW service is the one in which you're most likely interested if you want to publish on the Internet or on a corporate intranet. The WWW service supports HTTP and CGI protocols, calls to the Internet Server Applications Programming Interface (ISAPI), and IIS-specific features, such as the Internet Database Connector (IDC) and Active Server Pages (ASP). Once you activate the WWW service on a server, you can configure its properties by right-clicking the service in the Service Manager window and selecting Properties from the pop-up menu that appears. You'll then see the dialog box shown in Figure 31.11.

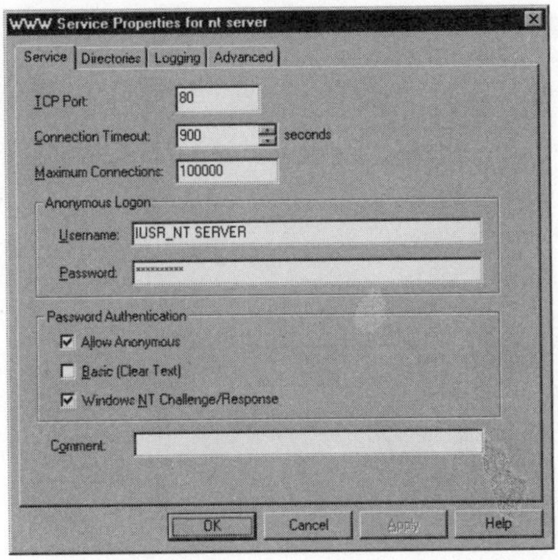

FIG. 31.11

You administer IIS's WWW service from the WWW Service Properties dialog box.

Of the four tabs in the dialog box, the Service tab is displayed initially. From here, you can change the port on which the service is running, how many connections the server should have open at once, how long before a connection time out, and password information for both anonymous and user-authenticated logons. The Anonymous, Basic, and Windows NT Challenge/Response settings mean exactly the same thing as they did when you configured the Personal Web Server.

N O T E WWW services typically run on port 80. You should determine values for Maximum Connections and Connection Timeout based on how powerful your machine is and how much bandwidth is available on your network. ■

The Directories tab, shown in Figure 31.12, enables you to specify aliases for directories on your server. Though most WWW service directories are under C:\InetPub\wwwroot (the default Home directory), you can make any directory on your machine available through your WWW service. To add a directory, click the Add button and browse to the desired directory (see Figure 31.13). Once you find the directory, you can set up an alias to it so that you can reference it more easily in your HTML documents. You can also designate the directory as the Home directory, if appropriate, and set up read and execute privileges for the directory.

The Enable Default Document option lets you specify a filename that is served automatically if it's found in a directory. Microsoft servers use the filename default.htm as their default filename, but you are welcome to change it to whatever you'd like. If checked, the Directory Browsing Allowed checkbox presents a list of all files in the directory if no file with the default filename is found.

CAUTION

Allowing users to browse the contents of a directory is considered a security risk, so you are advised to leave this option unchecked.

Part
V

Ch
31

FIG. 31.12

You can make every directory on your server available through the IIS WWW service.

FIG. 31.13

When adding a directory to your WWW server, you can give it its own alias, make it your Home directory, or set it up as a virtual server.

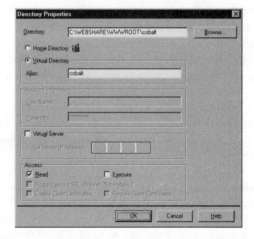

One other feature to note is the idea of a *virtual server*. You can add a directory to your WWW service and set it up as a virtual server. This is a separate server only in the logical sense—all virtual servers run as part of the same WWW service. Virtual servers are handy because they are referenced separately and each has its own root directory, which is useful if you're providing server support for multiple clients and each one wants his or her own unique domain. To set up a directory as a virtual server, click the Virtual Server checkbox after browsing to the new directory and provide the IP address by which you'd like to be able to reference the server.

N O T E Each virtual server needs to have its own unique IP address, which you specify at the time you set up the server. ▪

N O T E Your global IIS settings will apply to all virtual servers that you create. The only attributes unique to a virtual server are its IP address and its root directory. ▪

The Logging tab of the WWW Properties dialog box (see Figure 31.14) gives you control over how connections to your server are logged. You can choose to log accesses to a file that is rotated on a schedule you specify or you can log accesses directly to a specific table in a SQL or ODBC data source on your system. Which access to choose depends on what kind of log analysis you want to do. If you've purchased one of the many available log analysis tools, then logging to a file in standard log format is probably the way to go. If you want to be able to run custom reports on your site's traffic, you should consider logging to a data source and using a tool such as Access to do the reports.

FIG. 31.14

Server logs record all the transactions that the server handles. Log analysis can reveal what pages on your site are the most popular.

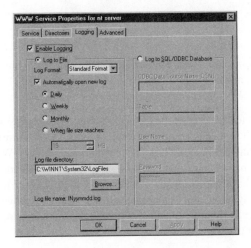

 TIP If you're really motivated, you can log your WWW service transactions to an ODBC data source and then use a tool such as the Internet Database Connector to develop a Web interface to your logs. Doing so will enable you to view and run queries against your logs right from your browser.

Figure 31.15 shows the Advanced tab of the WWW Properties dialog box, from which you can grant or deny access to your server by IP address and limit the volume of network use by WWW service. Limiting access by IP address is a useful additional security layer as long as the people to whom you want to give access have fixed IP addresses.

Setting Up the FTP Service

Even if you're not using it to make files available for public download, the IIS FTP service can be useful for other reasons. For example, content developers using your WWW service may do their development work on a separate machine, in which case they need a way to be able to transfer the content to the server when it's ready to go live. Having an FTP service running on your server enables the developers to do this quickly and easily.

FIG. 31.15

You can restrict access to your WWW service to certain machines on your network by filtering IP addresses.

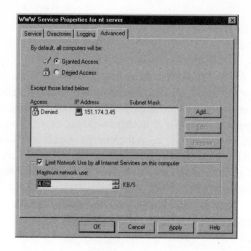

The IIS FTP service has its own set of properties you can configure. Some are similar to the WWW properties, but a number of them are unique to supporting an FTP service. This section takes you through the various tabs of the FTP Properties dialog box shown in Figure 31.16.

The Service tab very much resembles the corresponding tab in the WWW Properties dialog box. From here, you can specify port number (typically port 21), maximum number of connections, and connection time-out interval, just as you would with the WWW service. The other item on the Service tab has to do with allowing anonymous access. If you allow anonymous FTP users, they do not have to provide an NT username and password to log in. Rather, they use a username of "anonymous" and their e-mail address as their password. Once this information is passed to the server, the user is actually logged in under the name *IUSR_machinename*, a special username that IIS sets up.

N O T E   If you do not allow anonymous access, FTP users will have to provide a valid NT username and password to log in. You can restrict these users' rights in the FTP directories by setting appropriate permissions in the NT File Manager. ▪

CAUTION

Allowing anonymous FTP users increases the security risk to your server because it gives anyone a way to get to files on your server. By only allowing users with NT usernames and passwords to log in, you have more control over who has access to your files.

The Messages tab of the FTP Properties dialog box is unique to the IIS FTP service. On this tab, you specify the FTP services welcome and exit messages and how the server should respond when it reaches its maximum number of connections. Figure 31.17 shows some sample messages you might use with your server.

FIG. 31.16
IIS supports both anonymous and NT-authenticated FTP service.

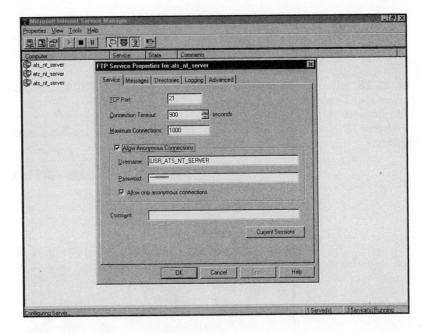

FIG. 31.17
Greeting a user or notifying users that the service has reached its maximum number of connections is unique to the FTP service.

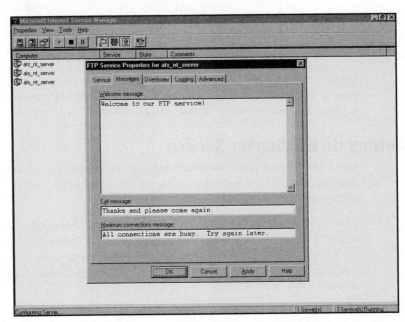

The Directories tab looks somewhat like the corresponding tab for WWW Properties. You can add new directories and set up aliases for them just as you would with the WWW service. One fundamental difference is that you can choose how the contents of FTP directories are displayed (see Figure 31.18). You can opt for UNIX mode, which uses forward slashes (/) when composing directory paths, or MS-DOS mode, which uses backslashes (\).

FIG. 31.18

Aliases that you set up on the Directories tab can reference FTP directories.

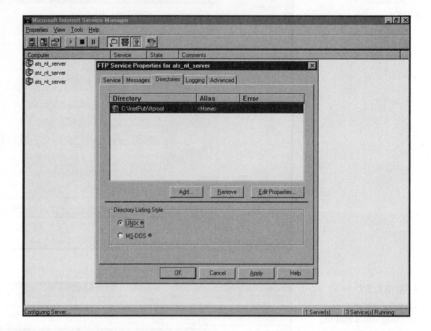

The last two tabs of the FTP Properties dialog box—Logging and Advanced—are exactly the same as they are for the WWW service. You can log your FTP transactions to a file or to a database and you can restrict access to your FTP server by IP address.

Setting Up the Gopher Service

The Gopher service is best used for text-based content that is easily navigated by a menu or folder structure. Fewer and fewer people are using Gopher these days, but it's still a useful service under the right set of conditions.

If you select a running Gopher service from the Internet Service Manager and right-click it to access its properties, you'll see the dialog box shown in Figure 31.19. The tabs for the Gopher service are virtually the same as those for the WWW service, so you can defer to the WWW service properties discussion for the details. A few things to note on the Service tab for Gopher properties:

- The typical TCP port for Gopher service is 70.
- The Gopher service makes the service administrator's name and e-mail address available.
- All Gopher access is handled anonymously via the **IUSR_machinename** user that IIS sets up.

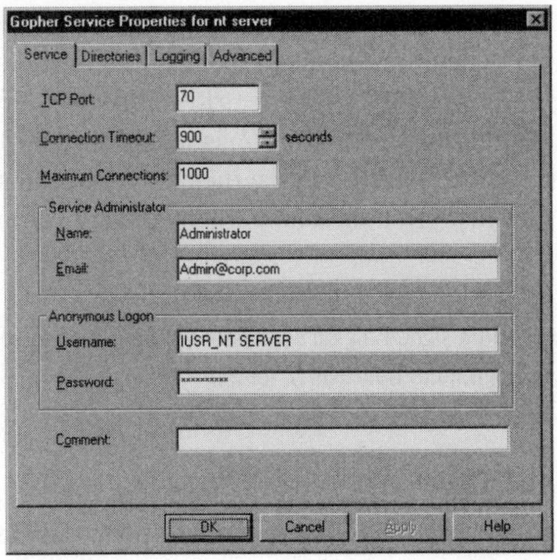

FIG. 31.19

Though rarely used, the IIS Gopher service can be used to publish large volumes of text-only content.

Gopher Service Properties for nt server

Service | Directories | Logging | Advanced

TCP Port: 70

Connection Timeout: 900 seconds

Maximum Connections: 1000

Service Administrator
Name: Administrator
Email: Admin@corp.com

Anonymous Logon
Username: IUSR_NT SERVER
Password: *********

Comment:

OK   Cancel   Apply   Help

Part
V

Ch
31

IIS Security

Security is an enormous concern to the Web community. Site administrators don't want ill-intentioned users trying to break into their servers, and users don't want ill-intentioned hackers trying to steal their credit card numbers and other personal information. In a time when people clamor for privacy of information, the protection of data as it moves over the Internet will continue to be of paramount importance.

IIS provides several security options that protect both the server and the end user. Some of these options, like using the NT File Manager to assign document-specific permission levels, have been discussed earlier in the chapter. The following list notes some of the other options.

■ **Windows NT Server Security** The NT Server is a very secure operating system that permits fine control over access to network files and resources. Because it is tightly integrated with the NT Server, IIS is able to avail itself of some of NT's functionality to provide a good basic level of security.

■ **The IUSR_machinename Account** As mentioned earlier in the chapter, IIS sets up the **IUSR_machinename** user to handle all IIS client requests. Rights to the IUSR account are only granted locally, so no one outside your system should be able to gain unauthorized access. You can instruct IIS to grant remote access to the IUSR account, in which case remote users do not need a username and password, and they have only the permissions assigned to that account.

■ **Auditing Access** Auditing refers to the tracking of who accessed what documents and when they did it. IIS uses the auditing capabilities that are already built into NT. The NT Event Log makes it easy to see each IIS transaction because they are all logged under the IUSR username.

■ **Using Secure Sockets Layer (SSL)** The Secure Sockets Layer (SSL) protocol was put forward by Netscape as a means of protecting data as it moves over the Internet. SSL accomplishes this by encrypting the data, authenticating the server, and checking message integrity. By acting as an intermediate layer between TCP/IP and HTTP, SSL initiates a "handshake" when the client and the server first make contact. During the handshake, SSL figures out what level of security to use and performs the necessary authentications. Once the connection is established, SSL encrypts the data as it leaves the server and decrypts it when it arrives at the client. You can specify that the SSL should be used for files in a given directory when adding that directory to your WWW service.

N O T E   Remember that you need a signed digital certificate before you can use SSL on your site. Visit **http://www.verisign.com/microsoft/** for more details. ■

IIS Security Tips and Tricks

In the last section, you read about some of the security features built into IIS. You can take things a step further, though, by implementing some security measures of your own. This section offers the following suggestions for ways you can enhance the level of security in place on your IIS server.

- Disable the NT Guest account and rename the Administrator account to something that is difficult to guess. These are well-known account names and hackers are frequently able to gain access through them, which is especially dangerous in the case of the Administrator account!

- Server applications should not run as system services because these applications listen to a particular TCP/IP port and a hacker could pass data to a well-known port number that could theoretically launch a program that you don't want to run. Instead, create a special account under which the server can run and configure the account only with the access privileges it needs.

- Do not allow Write permission to CGI or ISAPI directories to anyone other than a system administrator. Doing so prevents unauthorized programs from being placed on the WWW server.

- Unbind any protocols that you do not need in place on your network.

- Monitor system and IIS logs frequently for unusual activity. This is a good way to catch someone who might be casing your system in preparation for an attack later.

- Develop a security policy for NT users. Compel them to have a password of at least six characters and require the password to be changed every three months.

Using Active Server Pages

Microsoft introduced the idea of Active Server Pages (ASPs) when they rolled out IIS 3.0. An ASP is an HTML document that contains either JScript or VBScript code that the server interprets and executes before the document is served. The output of the script is built into the document as it is sent so that the receiving browser sees only an HTML file with no script code in it. This is an important feature because it means that ASPs are browser independent.

When a server serves an ASP, it's really just sending a dynamically generated HTML file, so any browser should be able to properly display an ASP.

As a simple example of an ASP, consider the following code:

```
<HTML>
<HEAD>
<TITLE>Greetings!</TITLE>
</HEAD>
<BODY BGCOLOR="WHITE">
<H1>Hello!</H1>
Welcome to our site.  You are using the
     <% = Request.ServerVariables("http_user_agent") %>
     browser, aren't you?
<P>
<HR>
<P>
<% = now %>
</BODY>
</HTML>
```

When a user requests this page, the server will parse the file and find the scripted instructions between the <% and %> characters. In this case, the file uses VBScript to find the type of browser the visitor is using (taken from the server environment variables) and at what time the page is being served. Then, as the file is being served, this information is built right into the file in place of everything between and including the <% and %> characters. Thus, what the server sends is really just an HTML document stripped of all the script code.

ASPs enable content developers to bring the power of JScript or VBScript to bear without having to rely on all users having a browser that understands these scripting languages. Also, ASPs are compiled on-the-fly, meaning that if you need to change the script code, the change will go into effect automatically just by putting the updated page on the server. The major drawback to using ASPs is that there is an extra load on the server because it has to do the work to parse and execute the script code.

 T I P Microsoft's Visual InterDev is an excellent tool for developing Active Server Pages. Allaire's HomeSite also includes a toolbar that supports ASP authoring.

N O T E ASP files have to end with an .asp extension for IIS to know to parse them.

Looking Ahead to IIS 4.0

As of this writing, Microsoft is making IIS 4.0 available to the general public in beta release. When the final release comes out, you can expect it to include the following additional features:

- **Integration with the Microsoft Transaction Server** This integration will permit the development of multiuser, Web-based applications.

- **Improved support of Active Server Pages** IIS 4.0 will feature a built-in ASP debugging facility and ASPs will be able to be transacted just like any other application.

■ **Properties Configuration**   Administrators will be able to apply properties at the server, site, directory, or file level.

■ **Enhanced Multihoming**   IIS 4.0 will provide more robust support for multiple sites by site-specific bandwidth throttling and more customizable administration.

■ **Built-in Certificate Server**   You can become your own certificate authority with IIS 4.0's certificate server. The server is closely integrated with NT security and is able to issue and manage standard X.509 digital certificates.

N O T E   For the most up-to-date information on IIS 4.0, direct Internet Explorer to **http://www.microsoft.com/iis/beta/default.asp**. ■

Getting Online

Getting a connection to the Internet can seem to be an overwhelming problem. Hundreds of Internet service providers (ISPs), many different types of connections, different levels of support, and different pricing plans are available. How are you supposed to sort through all of it so that it makes sense?

In this appendix, we tackle the major issues related to getting connected to the Internet and show you how to evaluate the various considerations. ■

Learn what kind of Internet connections there are

In this chapter, you learn what types of connections to the Internet are available, and what might best suit your needs and your budget.

Find out what kind of services are available

Learn about the different types of Internet service, what each provides to you, and get an idea of their relative cost.

Choose an Internet service provider

This chapter discusses the different factors you should take into account when choosing an Internet service provider.

Set up Windows 95 for PPP

Learn how to set up Windows 95 for an Internet connection using the Point-to-Point Protocol (PPP), the most common connection method over the telephone line.

Types of Internet Connections: Dial-Up Connections

Depending on how much money you want to spend, you can get many different levels of connection to the Internet. These connection levels primarily differ in the amount of data you can transfer over a given period of time. We refer to the rate at which data can be transferred as the *bandwidth* of the connection.

Internet connections fall into two categories: dial-up and direct connections. A *dial-up connection* uses a modem to dial another modem at an Internet service provider, perform some connection sequence, and bring up the TCP/IP network. A *direct connection* uses a dedicated, data-grade telephone circuit as the connection path to the Internet. If you have access to a direct connection, it is probably through your employer. In this appendix, we will concentrate on establishing a dial-up connection, which is the more complicated of the two.

When you sign up for a dial-up Internet account, you use a modem to dial a telephone number for an Internet service provider. After the modems connect, your computer performs some type of login sequence, and the computers start to communicate. The login sequence that your system performs depends on the requirements of your particular ISP. Many times, these login sequences are automated by using a script file. (For more information on script files, see "Setting Up Windows 95 for PPP" later in this chapter.)

 TIP   For Internet Explorer to be usable with a dial-up connection, you should have at least a 14.4 Kbps modem. A faster modem, such as a 28.8, 33.6, or 57.6 Kbps model, is recommended. Internet Explorer can be used with slower modems, but probably won't be worth your time.

The way that your computer will communicate with your Internet Service Provider through a dial-up connection is through PPP. PPP, the Point-to-Point Protocol, allows your computer to communicate over a dial-up connection. The way you start PPP varies depending on your ISP. In some cases, it starts automatically for you when you log in. In other cases, you may have to execute a command from a login shell on the ISP. Still another way is to make a selection from an interactive menu. It really depends on your ISP.

Types of Services

Now that we've got the basics out of the way, let's look at what services you can get from an ISP. Most ISPs provide dial-up and direct connect services, with a whole menu of services that you can select from.

Dial-Up IP

For most ISPs, the basic level of dial-up IP gives you PPP-based, dynamic IP addressing on a public dial-up number. This number is connected to a modem bank and rotates to the next available modem when you dial in—if a modem is available. For some ISPs, busy signals can be a common problem, especially during the prime evening and weekend hours.

APP
A

Some ISPs provide a couple of levels of service above the basic dial-up PPP account. For example, you may be able to pay an additional fee to dial into a restricted number that has a better user-to-modem ratio. For even more money, the ISP may provide you with a dedicated dial-up line—a phone line that only you can dial in on. Deciding what type of dial-up account you are going to need is important because it is one of the primary factors that affects the cost of your Internet service.

E-Mail

If you've managed to get this far and set up an Internet connection, you probably want e-mail, right? By using a dial-up PPP account, you can almost always read and send e-mail via the Post Office Protocol (POP). To do so, you get an e-mail client program, such as Outlook Express, for your PC and configure it with your e-mail account information and the IP address of your network mail server. If you have a dial-up account, your network mail server is a computer located at your ISP's offices.

N O T E E-mail is transferred between systems on the Internet using a protocol known as the *Simple Mail Transport Protocol*, or *SMTP*. POP is the protocol that a local e-mail client program uses to retrieve mail from a mail server.

Most personal dial-up accounts provide you with at least one e-mail address. Some ISPs even provide as many as five different addresses for personal or family accounts. Other ISPs make you pay an additional monthly charge for extra e-mail IDs. Business accounts usually have a fixed number as well. If you have more than one person who will be using e-mail from your system, you might want to shop around to see what the ISP policies on multiple e-mail addresses are in your area.

News

Just as with e-mail, if your Internet service provider gives you access to UseNet news, you can probably read and post news from your PC by using a newsreader that supports the *Network News Transport Protocol* (*NNTP*). To do so, you simply configure your newsreader with the names or addresses of your mail and news hosts—the computers that you exchange e-mail and news with. Most ISPs provide UseNet news as part of the basic dial-up PPP account service.

Shell Access

Another service that is often available with a dial-up account is *shell access*. This term refers to the ability to access a command-line processor on the remote ISP system.

N O T E Because most ISPs use a UNIX system to provide Internet access, and UNIX command-line processors are known as shells, the term *shell access* has become rather common.

Your ISP may or may not provide shell access as part of your basic network package. Most people can get by fine without having shell access. It is useful for accessing your account over the Internet, via Telnet or FTP from another location, as well as performing tasks such as compiling C code. But if you are just running Internet Explorer from home, you can probably survive without it.

> **CAUTION**
>
> Be aware that some ISPs sell a "shell-access-only" account as a dial-up account. Typically, you cannot run PPP from this type of account. Because Internet Explorer needs PPP to run over a dial-ip connection, you need to make sure that you get the right type of service from your ISP.

Web Servers

Another service that is provided by many ISPs is access to a Web server. Web servers allow you to put home pages on the Web so that they can be accessed by people with Web browsers such as Internet Explorer 4. Having access to a Web server means that you can write Web pages in HTML and make them available on the Web. Many ISPs provide their personal account customers the ability to create personal Web pages. Businesses usually have to pay an additional fee for the service.

> **N O T E**   Companies that have a direct connection to the Internet can simply set up their own Web server on one of their own machines. ■

If your ISP doesn't provide Web server access, don't give up hope. Many companies provide Web services alone, without providing any type of interactive access to the Internet. Basically, you pay a monthly fee to have the Web provider's site place your pages on the World Wide Web. These Web service providers also typically offer consulting and design services to help you create effective Web pages. There are also a number of groups that provide free Web pages. You can check out one of these, GeoCities, at **http://www.geocities.com**.

Virtual Domains

If you are setting up a business account, you may want to use your own domain name, instead of simply using the name of your ISP. A domain name that is actually a directory on an ISP's server is commonly called a *virtual domain.*

To set up a virtual domain, you must register your domain name with the Network Information Center (NIC). The NIC acts as the clearinghouse for all Internet domain names. You can reach the NIC by Telnet at **rs.internic.net**, on the Web at **http://rs.internic.net**, by e-mail at **question@internic.net**, or by telephone at 703-742-4777. You must fill out a domain name registration template and submit it to the NIC. The NIC charges a fee to register a domain.

As part of the registration process, you must provide information about which network name servers advertise your domain name. In short, this means that you have to find an ISP that provides virtual domains and have it enter your domain name in its name server. As with everything else, most ISPs charge an additional fee for supporting virtual domains. If you require this service, make sure that you shop around and ask questions.

Finding a National Internet Service Provider

You can divide ISPs into categories based on whether they have a national presence or they are mainly a local company. If you think about this concept, any ISP has a national presence in the sense that it is connected to the Internet and can be reached from anywhere. What we are referring to is the ability to contact the ISP via a local telephone call. Several of the larger ISPs have local dial access in many different locations, effectively making them national providers.

Using a national provider presents both pros and cons. The company is usually larger—not a basement operation—and it usually has competent technical support people working for it. Also, national providers usually have a better uptime percentage than local providers and also have a better price structure. On the other hand, because national ISPs tend to be larger, reaching a technical support person when you have a problem may be harder. You may find that their policies are less flexible than local providers and that they are less willing to make exceptions and work with you. If you are setting up a business connection, your ISP's office may be hundreds or thousands of miles away. If you are the kind of person who values working with a local company, this distance could present a problem for you.

Locating Regional and Local Providers

Local and regional providers are ISPs that serve a regional market, instead of having a national presence. Like national providers, these providers present both pros and cons here, too. You will probably find that local providers are more flexible on their services and policies. For business, you can usually meet face to face with someone in the office to discuss your Internet needs. On the down side, the service quality of local ISPs tends to be less reliable. Sometimes these companies are very small operations, with limited hardware and technical support. You may find that connecting is difficult because of busy signals during certain times of the day.

Local and regional ISPs are notorious for expanding their customer base faster than their hardware will support. When their servers get overloaded, response creeps to a crawl and uptime suffers. Phone lines are continually busy. If this problem happens to an ISP, it has to respond immediately; otherwise, its systems will become unusable. Before you pick any provider, it's a good idea to look in your local paper, computer magazines, or talk to friends to see what providers they recommend.

Using Private Information Services

Many people belong to private national information services such as CompuServe or America Online. Increasingly, such services are beginning to provide full access to the Internet, and can be an attractive option for their subscribers who want to start accessing the Internet and the World Wide Web. They are typically able to provide their users with extensive technical support in setting up their Internet connections. However, Internet access through these information services tends to be a lot more expensive than going through an ISP. Unless you have a specific need for one of the proprietary services that CompuServe, AOL, and so on provide, you are probably better off going with a dedicated Internet service provider.

Service Levels and Cost

As you have seen, you must consider several issues when selecting an ISP. The level of service you need is probably the main thing that affects the cost of your connection. Dial-up modem connections in the general public modem pool are usually cheapest. A restricted modem group is more expensive. A dedicated dial-up line costs even more. Direct connections via leased lines are among the most expensive.

In addition to service level, many ISPs offer different connection pricing plans. Some plans give you a fixed number of connect hours per month and charge you for extra hours. Other plans may give you unlimited hours during a certain time period and charge you for hours outside that window. Still other plans give you unlimited connect time for your fee.

Before you choose an ISP, take time to evaluate how you are going to use the service and what level of service you need. Check with computer users in your area to see if they can recommend a local service or a national service that works well.

Setting Up Your Internet Connection

In Chapter 3, "Quick Start: Internet Explorer 4," you saw how you could use Internet Explorer 4's Internet Connection Wizard in order to establish your first connection to the Internet. In this appendix, you will learn how to do this manually, which will show you each of the steps involved, and make you better prepared to troubleshoot your Internet connection if you should ever have problems.

▶ **See** "If You Don't Have a Connection Set Up" to see how the Internet Connection Wizard can be used to easily set up your first link to the Internet, **p. 32**

By using Internet Explorer 4 and Windows 95, you're already ahead of the game a little, because Windows 95 includes support for PPP, which is what enables Internet Explorer 4 to access the Internet. Assuming that you have an account already set up with an Internet service provider, configuring Windows 95 so that it provides you dial-up PPP support is not too difficult.

You need several bits of information to configure PPP for Windows 95 correctly. Your ISP should provide all this information when you set up your account. If you don't know some of these items, contact your ISP for help. You need to know the following:

- The username that you use to log in to your ISP
- The password for your ISP account
- The telephone number for your ISP
- The host name for your computer
- The network domain name for your ISP
- The IP address of your ISP's default gateway or router
- The IP subnet mask of your ISP's network
- The IP address of your ISP's DNS name server(s)

- Whether you have a static or dynamic IP address
- The IP address of your computer, if you have a static address

After you gather all the preceding information, you're ready to start installing PPP for Windows 95. You might not have installed all the components for PPP when you installed Windows 95, so you need to check to see what's already there and install the ones that are missing.

APP
A

What Is the Difference Between Static and Dynamic IP?

Your computer has to have an IP address to communicate on the Internet. How does it get the address? Well, in most cases, it is assigned by your ISP when you set up your account. Even if you are setting up a whole network of computers, your ISP will probably handle everything for you. For direct Internet connections, the IP address of your computer is permanently assigned to you. It never changes. These addresses are known as static IP addresses. Most Internet service providers, however, use a scheme known as dynamic IP addressing.

Because most ISPs typically have many more dial-up customers than they do modems, only a fraction of their dial-up customers can be online at any given moment. Only being able to support a limited number of users online usually isn't a problem. In short, this means that an ISP can "recycle" IP addresses by assigning them only when your system dials up to connect to the service. This way, ISPs can get by with far fewer IP addresses than if they were statically assigned.

How does this limitation affect you, the network user? First, you have to configure your networking software differently depending on whether you have a static or dynamic IP address. Second, you just can't do a few things if you have a dynamic IP address. Specifically, because your IP address is dynamic —it changes every time you log in—your host name cannot be registered in a domain name service database along with your IP address. Basically, this restriction prevents anyone out on the Internet from being able to initiate contact with your computer for anything more than your current session. You can't run an FTP server or a Web server if your computer has a dynamic IP address. Similarly, some commercial database services limit access to specific IP addresses based on subscription. Obviously, if your IP address is changing all the time, this scheme doesn't work.

While these limitations don't really affect a lot of people, they can be a real problem if you really want to run an FTP or Web server. Some ISPs charge extra for static IP addresses—sometimes a lot extra! If having a static IP address is a real issue for you, make sure that you check with your ISP before signing a service contract.

Dial-Up Networking, the Dial-Up Adapter, and TCP/IP

The dial-up networking and dial-up adapter items are necessary to set up a dial-up account to the Internet. Make sure you have your Windows 95 installation media handy throughout this process. For simplicity, let's assume that you are installing from a the Windows 95 CD-ROM. To see whether dial-up networking is installed, follow these steps:

1. Click the Start button, and choose Settings, Control Panel.
2. Double-click the Add/Remove Programs icon.
3. Select the Windows Setup tab. The section of the Add/Remove Programs dialog box that allows you to install or change various components of Windows 95 then appears.

4. Select the Communications option.

5. Click the Details button. The Communications dialog box then appears showing the current configuration of your Windows 95 communications system.

6. Make sure the Dial-Up Networking entry is selected. If it is not selected, select it and click OK.

Now that the dial-up networking package is installed, you need to check for the dial-up adapter. Basically, this program allows Windows 95 to use your telephone to make a network connection. To see whether the dial-up adapter is installed, follow these steps:

1. Click the Start button, and choose Settings, Control Panel.

2. Double-click the Network icon. The Network dialog box appears. Here, you can configure your network setup.

3. Select the Configuration tab. This portion of the Network dialog box allows you to add new network protocols and adapters to your Windows 95 environment (see Figure A.1).

FIG. A.1

The Network dialog box allows you to configure your Internet connection environment.

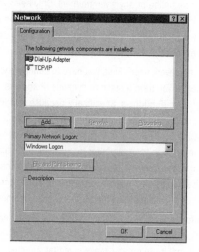

4. Look for TCP/IP and Dial-Up Adapter in the list.

Follow these steps if you don't see the Dial-Up Adapter in the Configuration tab of the Network dialog box:

1. Click the Add button. The Select Network Component Type dialog box then appears. Here, you tell Windows 95 what sort of networking item you want to add to your computer.

2. Double-click Adapter. The Select Network Adapters dialog box appears. You want to add the Dial-Up Adapter so that you can use dial-up networking.

3. Scroll the Select Network Component Type box on the left until you see the Microsoft entry.

4. Select Microsoft from the Select Network Component Type scroll box. Choose Dial-Up Adapter from the Network Adapters scroll box on the right.

5. Click OK.

Follow these steps if you don't see TCP/IP in the Network dialog box:

1. Click the Add button to add the protocol to your computer.

2. Double-click Protocol. TCP/IP is a networking protocol, and that is what you need to add. Clicking this option opens the Select Network Protocol dialog box.

3. Scroll the Manufacturers scroll box on the left until you see the Microsoft entry.

4. Select Microsoft in the left scroll box, and then choose TCP/IP in the Network Protocols scroll box on the right.

5. Click OK.

At this point, you should see both TCP/IP and the dial-up adapter in the Network dialog box. Select Dial-Up Adapter and click Properties. The Dial-Up Adapter Properties dialog box appears. Select the Bindings tab. Then verify that the TCP/IP box is selected (see Figure A.2).

FIG. A.2

Make sure that the TCP/IP protocol is bound to your dial-up adapter so that you can use Internet Explorer 4.

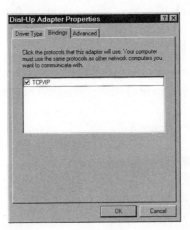

Dial-Up Scripting

Some Internet Service Providers require additional steps, beyond just logging in, to begin your PPP connection. If yours is like this, you will probably want to create a script that handles logging you in to your ISP's system. This way, you can just double-click an icon and have Windows 95 dial your ISP, log you in automatically, and start PPP. You'll come back to scripting in a bit, but first you need to verify that the Dial-Up Scripting program has been installed. To do so, follow these steps:

1. Click Start and choose Programs, Accessories.

2. Look for an entry for the Dial-Up Scripting Tool.

Follow these steps if the Dial-Up Scripting Tool isn't installed:

1. Click the Start button, and choose Settings, Control Panel.

2. Double-click the Add/Remove Programs icon.

3. Select the Windows Setup tab. Remember, on this tab you add components to your Windows 95 system. We need to install the Dial-Up Scripting Tool from your Windows 95 CD.

4. Click the Have Disk button. Clicking this button tells Windows 95 that you need to install something from the CD.

5. Enter the path to the Dial-Up Scripting program on your Windows 95 CD. For example, if your CD is drive G:, you enter **G:\admin\apptools\dscript**.

6. Click the OK button.

Entering the Address Information

At this point, you should have all the drivers and other programs installed so that you can configure TCP/IP with your network information. A couple of steps in this section depend on whether you have a static or dynamic IP address, so pay attention. To enter the address, follow these steps:

1. Click the Start button, and choose Settings, Control Panel.

2. Double-click the Network icon. The Network dialog box appears.

3. Select the TCP/IP Protocol entry and click the Properties button. The TCP/IP Properties dialog box appears.

4. Select the IP Address tab (see Figure A.3).

FIG. A.3

If you have a static IP address, enter it here. Otherwise, check the Obtain an IP Address Automatically box.

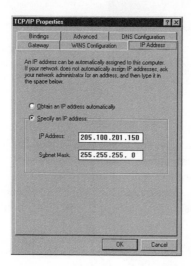

APP

A

5. If you have a static IP address, select the Specify an IP Address option, type your IP Address into the box, and enter your subnet mask into the Subnet Mask box.

6. If you have a dynamic IP address, choose the Obtain an IP Address Automatically option.

7. Choose the WINS Configuration tab and select Disable WINS Resolution.

8. Select the Gateway tab, type the IP address for your ISP's gateway or router in the New Gateway box, and then click the Add button, as shown in Figure A.4.

FIG. A.4

Add the IP address of your ISP's gateway computer here; this machine connects your computer to the Internet.

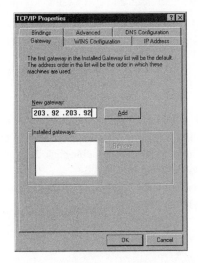

9. Select the DNS Configuration tab and choose the Enable DNS radio button (see Figure A.5).

FIG. A.5

The information in this box configures your computer to use your ISP's domain name server(s).

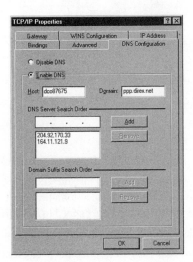

10. Type the host name of your computer in the Host box.

11. Enter the domain name of your ISP in the Domain box.

12. In the DNS Server Search Order section, enter the IP address of your ISP's DNS server. Press Add.

13. Type the domain name for your ISP in the Domain Suffix Search Order section, and then click the Add button. You can add other frequently used domain names here as well. By doing so, you can specify their addresses and URLs using host names only.

14. Double-check all your entries, and then click OK.

15. At this point, Windows 95 asks you to reboot your computer. Click Yes.

Your Windows 95 environment should have support for dial-up networking, TCP/IP, and the Dial-Up Scripting tool. Now you're ready to establish your first Internet connection.

Creating a Connection Icon

To configure a connection icon, double-click the My Computer icon on your desktop. Next, double-click the Dial-Up Networking icon, and then double-click the Make New Connection icon. A wizard box then appears, as shown in Figure A.6.

FIG. A.6

Microsoft's Internet Connection Wizard leads you through the steps of setting up and configuring a dial-up connection.

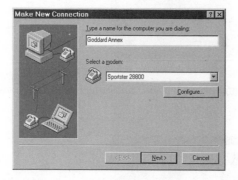

This wizard helps you set up a new connection entry. To do so, simply follow these steps:

1. Enter the connection name that you want to use into the dialog box.

2. Click the Configure button. A dialog box with the properties of the modem you selected appears.

3. Select the General tab in the Properties dialog box (see Figure A.7).

4. In the Maximum Speed box, set the port speed for your modem. In general, 115,200 is a good setting. This is because most modems will automatically set their connection speed as fast as they can go, so you want to set the port speed to be higher than this.

5. Make sure that the box marked Only Connect at This Speed is not checked.

6. Open the Connection tab so you can set the connection preferences that your ISP expects (see Figure A.8). If you don't know them for sure, set Data Bits to 8, Parity to None, and Stop Bits to 1. This is a good set to try.

FIG. A.7
The General tab allows you to configure the communications port your dial-up connection will use.

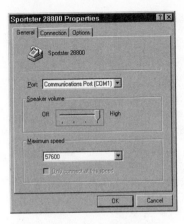

FIG. A.8
The Connection tab configures Windows 95's communications software to communicate correctly with your ISP.

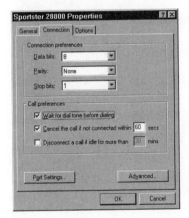

TIP If your modem doesn't dial when you attempt a connection, call waiting or some other phone system option may be keeping your modem from recognizing the dial tone. Try unchecking the Wait for Dial Tone before Dialing box to try to correct this problem.

7. If you are not going to use a script to automate your login process, select the Options tab in the Properties dialog box. From here, you can have PPP open a login window for you so that you can manually log in to your server (see Figure A.9).

8. Click OK, and then click Next in the Wizard dialog box.

9. Enter the area code and phone number of your ISP in the dialog box, and click Next.

10. Click Finish.

At this point, you should see a new connection icon, with the name that you specified, on your system. You just have a couple more steps to do before it's ready to use:

1. Right-click your connection icon. A pop-up menu for the connection icon appears.

2. Choose Properties from the pop-up menu.

3. Click the Server Type button. The Server Types dialog box appears (see Figure A.10).

FIG. A.9

The Options tab enables you to get a terminal window if you need to enter information manually during the connection process.

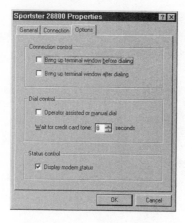

FIG. A.10

The Server Types dialog box allows you to configure the correct communications protocol.

4. Select PPP from the drop-down list box.

5. Verify that the TCP/IP box in the Allowed Network Protocols section is checked, and make sure that the Log on to Network box is not selected.

6. Click OK.

7. Click OK again.

You're done configuring your Internet connection! If you want to set your modem to redial automatically, you can do so by choosing the Settings option from the Connections menu in the Dial-Up Networking folder.

Scripting Your Dial-Up Connection

As mentioned earlier, using a script to automate your login process makes your job a lot easier. You can start your connection session and run to the fridge while Windows 95 retries your ISP dial-up line and logs you in! Also, scripting is very easy. You can think of a script as telling

Windows 95 what to look for from the ISP server. Just as you might look for a `login:` prompt to type your username, you can have your script do the same thing. The Dial-Up Scripting Tool is the way you create scripts to control your dial-up network session (see Figure A.11).

FIG. A.11

The Windows 95 Dial-Up Scripting Tool gives you an easy way to create a script to automate your PPP login process.

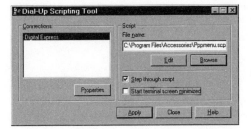

To make a script, follow these steps:

1. Click the Start button, and choose <u>P</u>rograms, Accessories.
2. Select the Dial-Up Scripting Tool. Its dialog box appears.
3. Click the <u>E</u>dit button to start editing a script.

All scripts start with the following line:

```
proc main
```

They end with the following line:

```
endproc
```

Between these two statements, you enter the commands that tell Windows 95 what to transmit and what to wait for. You need to know three basic commands to write a script: `transmit`, `waitfor`, and `delay`.

The `delay` statement causes your script to wait for a specified number of seconds. For example, the following line causes the script to pause for three seconds:

```
delay 3
```

The `waitfor` statement makes the script wait until the specified string is received. For example, the following line waits for the string `"ssword"` to be received by your system:

```
waitfor "ssword"
```

The third statement, `transmit`, transmits a string to the remote system. It does not automatically send a carriage return at the end of the string. To send a carriage return, you need to transmit the string `"^M"` to the remote system. Listing A.1 is an example of a script.

Listing A.1   Sample Dial-Up Script

```
proc main
delay 1
transmit "^M"
```

continues

Listing A.1 Continued

```
delay 1
transmit "^M"
delay 1
transmit "^M"
waitfor "name>"
transmit $USERID
transmit "^M"
waitfor "ssword>"
transmit $PASSWORD
transmit "^M"
waitfor "enu:"
transmit "3"
transmit "^M"
endproc
```

T I P Using only the last part of a string in a `waitfor` statement is usually a good idea, in case the first character or two get garbled by the network. For example, you should use `waitfor "ssword>"` instead of `waitfor "password>"`.

The preceding script waits for one second and then sends a carriage return to the remote system. It then repeats this sequence two more times. The script then waits for the string name from the remote system. It sends the contents of the special variable `$USERID`, which contains the user ID that you enter when you start the network connection program. It follows the user ID with a carriage return.

The script then waits for the `ssword>` prompt from the remote system and sends the contents of the `$PASSWORD` variable. This variable contains the password that you enter when you start the network connection program. It follows the password with a carriage return. It then waits for the string `enu:`, and sends the number 5 and a carriage return. This will select option `"5"` from the ISP's connection `"menu:"`, which, in this case, initiates a PPP connection. That's all there is to it!

Once you have written your script, save it with the .SCP extension. Then, in the Dial-Up Scripting Tool, select the network connection that you want to attach the script to and click Apply. Your script is now associated with that network connection and will be executed automatically any time you run that particular network connection.

You can also select the Step through Script checkbox to be able to step through the script one line at a time to debug it. By selecting the Start Terminal Screen Minimized checkbox, you see no terminal box displaying the progress of your script. Uncheck this box if you want to watch your script execute as it runs.

You've done it! You're ready to connect to the Internet. Just double-click your connection icon, and you get the Connect To dialog box, shown in Figure A.12. Click the Connect button, and you're on your way to the Internet.

FIG. A.12

Once you've set up your dial-up connection, just click the Connect button to initiate the Internet connection process.

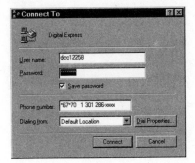

Index

Symbols

& (ampersands), HTML entities, 439

{ } (braces), JScript statements, 545

/ (forward slashes), HTML tags, 438

+ (plus signs), URL encoding, 520

 # (pound signs), imagemap links, 499

; (semicolons), JScript statements, 545

A

<A> tag, 461-462
attributes, 462
graphic anchors, 471-472
imagemaps, 497
non-Web Internet service links, 464
within document links, 463

<ABSTRACT> tag (CDF), 430

Access 97 Web integration, 338, 359-360
ActiveX Controls, 360-361
exporting databases to the Web, 359-360

accessibility options, user-defined style sheets, 121-122

action buttons, forms, 517-519
Reset, 518
Submit, 518-519
multiple Submit buttons, 518-519

ACTION parameter, form headers, 507

Active Channel Viewer, 411-413

Active Desktop, 8-9, 46-50, 128-141
background, 128-133
customizing, 131-132
setting, 130-131
channel Active Desktop components, 402-403
code listings
ActiveX Controls, 131
background framework, 132
components, 47, 133-138
adding, 47-48, 133-136
configuring, 48-49, 137-138
downloading, 47-48
Gallery, 47-48, 134-136
updating, 134-136
creating, 48-50
disabling functions, 130
HTML layer, 47, 129
icon layer, 46, 129
installing Web pages
Internet, 139
local, 140-141
Start Menu Internet features, 154
see also Explorer Web integration, Start menu, Taskbar

Active Setup Wizard, 30-31, 106-107
downloading, 30
installing
ActiveX controls, 273-275
NetMeeting, 202-205

ActiveX Control Pad, 585-589
configuring controls, 586-589
names, 587
downloading/installing, 585
inserting controls into pages, 586
Script Wizard, 589-596
accessing, 589
Action pane, 591
creating scripts, 590
Event pane, 591
JavaScript example, 594-596
JScript, 592
options, 590
Script pane, 591
VBScript example, 592-595

ActiveX controls, 272, 577-581
Access 97 databases, 360-361
Active Desktop, 131-132
code listing, 131
ActiveX Documents, viewing documents in Internet Explorer, 328-332
Animated Button control code listing, 587-589
configuring, 587-589
names, 587
Control Pad, *see* ActiveX Control Pad

C

X-Y-Z

Check out Que® Books on the World Wide Web
http://www.quecorp.com

As the biggest software release in computer history, Windows 95 continues to redefine the computer industry. Click here for the latest info on our Windows 95 books

Make computing quick and easy with these products designed exclusively for new and casual users

Examine the latest releases in word processing, spreadsheets, operating systems, and suites

The Internet, The World Wide Web, CompuServe®, America Online®, Prodigy® —it's a world of ever-changing information. Don't get left behind!

Find out about new additions to our site, new bestsellers, and hot topics

In-depth information on high-end topics: find the best reference books for databases, programming, networking, and client/server technologies

A recent addition to Que, Ziff-Davis Press publishes the highly-successful *How It Works* and *How to Use* series of books, as well as *PC Learning Labs Teaches* and *PC Magazine* series of book/disc packages

Stay on the cutting edge of Macintosh® technologies and visual communications

Find out which titles are making headlines

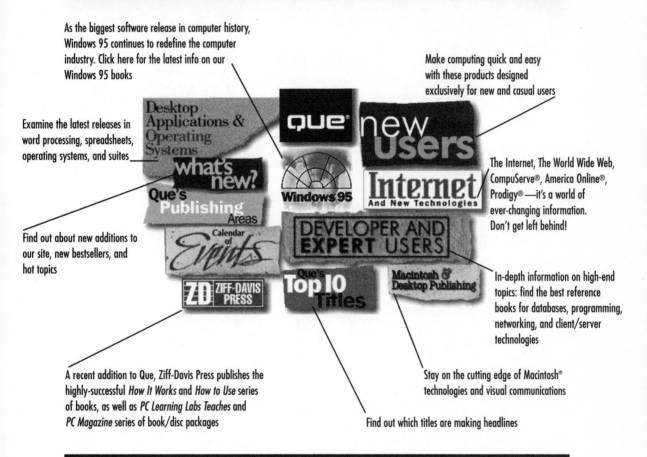

Desktop Applications & Operating Systems

que®

new users

what's new?

Que's Publishing Areas

Windows 95

Internet And New Technologies

Calendar of Events

DEVELOPER AND EXPERT USERS

Macintosh & Desktop Publishing

ZD ZIFF-DAVIS PRESS

Que's Top 10 Titles

With 6 separate publishing groups, Que develops products for many specific market segments and areas of computer technology. Explore our Web site and you'll find information on best-selling titles, newly published titles, upcoming products, authors, and much more.

- Stay informed on the latest industry trends and products available
- Visit our online bookstore for the latest information and editions
- Download software from Que's library of the best shareware and freeware

que®

Complete and Return this Card
for a *FREE* Computer Book Catalog

Thank you for purchasing this book! You have purchased a superior computer book written expressly for your needs. To continue to provide the kind of up-to-date, pertinent coverage you've come to expect from us, we need to hear from you. Please take a minute to complete and return this self-addressed, postage-paid form. In return, we'll send you a free catalog of all our computer books on topics ranging from word processing to programming and the internet.

Mr. ☐   Mrs. ☐   Ms. ☐   Dr. ☐

Name (first) ☐☐☐☐☐☐☐☐☐☐☐☐   (M.I.) ☐   (last) ☐☐☐☐☐☐☐☐☐☐☐☐☐☐☐☐☐

Address ☐☐☐☐☐☐☐☐☐☐☐☐☐☐☐☐☐☐☐☐☐☐☐☐☐☐☐☐☐☐

City ☐☐☐☐☐☐☐☐☐☐☐☐☐☐☐☐   State ☐☐   Zip ☐☐☐☐☐ ☐☐☐☐

Phone ☐☐☐ ☐☐☐ ☐☐☐☐   Fax ☐☐☐ ☐☐☐ ☐☐☐☐

Company Name ☐☐☐☐☐☐☐☐☐☐☐☐☐☐☐☐☐☐☐☐☐☐☐☐☐☐☐☐

E-mail address ☐☐☐☐☐☐☐☐☐☐☐☐☐☐☐☐☐☐☐☐☐☐☐☐☐☐

1. Please check at least (3) influencing factors for purchasing this book.

Front or back cover information on book ☐
Special approach to the content ☐
Completeness of content ☐
Author's reputation ☐
Publisher's reputation ☐
Book cover design or layout ☐
Index or table of contents of book ☐
Price of book ☐
Special effects, graphics, illustrations ☐
Other (Please specify): _____ ☐

2. How did you first learn about this book?

Saw in Macmillan Computer Publishing catalog ☐
Recommended by store personnel ☐
Saw the book on bookshelf at store ☐
Recommended by a friend ☐
Received advertisement in the mail ☐
Saw an advertisement in: _____ ☐
Read book review in: _____ ☐
Other (Please specify): _____ ☐

3. How many computer books have you purchased in the last six months?

This book only ☐   3 to 5 books ☐
2 books ☐   More than 5 ☐

4. Where did you purchase this book?

Bookstore ☐
Computer Store ☐
Consumer Electronics Store ☐
Department Store ☐
Office Club ☐
Warehouse Club ☐
Mail Order ☐
Direct from Publisher ☐
Internet site ☐
Other (Please specify): _____ ☐

5. How long have you been using a computer?

☐ Less than 6 months   ☐ 6 months to a year
☐ 1 to 3 years   ☐ More than 3 years

6. What is your level of experience with personal computers and with the subject of this book?

	With PCs	With subject of book
New	☐	☐
Casual	☐	☐
Accomplished	☐	☐
Expert	☐	☐

Source Code ISBN: 0-7897-1046-3

7. Which of the following best describes your job title?

Administrative Assistant .... ☐
Coordinator .... ☐
Manager/Supervisor .... ☐
Director .... ☐
Vice President .... ☐
President/CEO/COO .... ☐
Lawyer/Doctor/Medical Professional .... ☐
Teacher/Educator/Trainer .... ☐
Engineer/Technician .... ☐
Consultant .... ☐
Not employed/Student/Retired .... ☐
Other (Please specify): _____ ☐

8. Which of the following best describes the area of the company your job title falls under?

Accounting .... ☐
Engineering .... ☐
Manufacturing .... ☐
Operations .... ☐
Marketing .... ☐
Sales .... ☐
Other (Please specify): _____ ☐

Comments: _____
_____
_____

9. What is your age?

Under 20 .... ☐
21-29 .... ☐
30-39 .... ☐
40-49 .... ☐
50-59 .... ☐
60-over .... ☐

10. Are you:

Male .... ☐
Female .... ☐

11. Which computer publications do you read regularly? (Please list)

_____
_____
_____
_____
_____
_____
_____
_____
_____
_____
_____
_____

Fold here and scotch-tape to mail.

MACMILLAN COMPUTER PUBLISHING USA

A VIACOM COMPANY

Technical ---- Support:

If you need assistance with the information in this book or with a CD/Disk accompanying the book, please access the Knowledge Base on our Web site at **http://www.superlibrary.com/general/support**. Our most Frequently Asked Questions are answered there. If you do not find the answer to your questions on our Web site, you may contact Macmillan Technical Support **(317) 581-3833** or e-mail us at **support@mcp.com**.